Business Valuation Across the Industry Life Cycle

Adelin Trusculescu

Business Valuation Across the Industry Life Cycle

A Quantitative Study Focusing on Internet-Enabled Businesses

Springer Gabler

Adelin Trusculescu
München, Germany

ISBN 978-3-658-49125-3 ISBN 978-3-658-49126-0 (eBook)
https://doi.org/10.1007/978-3-658-49126-0

This Springer Gabler imprint is published by the registered company Springer Fachmedien Wiesbaden GmbH, part of Springer Nature.
The registered company address is: Abraham-Lincoln-Str. 46, 65189 Wiesbaden, Germany

Foreword

This thesis represents the culmination of the study conducted at the Politehnica University of Timişoara in collaboration with goetzpartners Corporate Finance GmbH in Munich, Germany, which together provided the educational and professional framework necessary to successfully research, formulate, implement, and publish my research activities.

This long and challenging journey would not have been possible without many people's encouragement, guidance, and support.

Firstly, I would like to extend my deepest gratitude to my supervisors, Professor Anca Drăghici and Professor Claudiu Tiberiu Albulescu, for believing in my research proposal and ability to deliver while providing guidance, feedback, and mentorship with the greatest commitment throughout this project.

I want to acknowledge the undisputed understanding and support of my mentors and colleagues in Germany, who provided from the first day the ecosystem, information, and knowledge, as well as perfect working conditions and access to databases required to complete this thesis. I am especially thankful to Dr. Stephan Goetz and Dr. Gernot Wunderle for supporting this endeavor from the very beginning, Christian Muthler and Philipp Widmaier for their advisership, and Professor Jan-Hendrik Röver for his always constructive suggestions.

I am also grateful for the uninterrupted care provided by the team of the Politehnica University of Timişoara, led by Professor Florin Drăgan, the Doctoral School of Engineering Studies and Faculty of Management in Production and Transport, led by Professors Marian Mocan, Matei Tămăşilă, and Ilie Mihai Tăucean who believed in me and my venture from day one.

I would also like to express my appreciation for the openness and willingness to collaborate and provide invaluable contributions of my research colleagues and friends in the finance community.

Last but not least, I owe my family a special debt of gratitude for their unconditional love, continuous encouragement, endless patience, and unwavering inspiration.

20 March 2023 Adelin-Emanuel Truşculescu

Contents

Notations, Abbreviations, Acronyms

General Notations, Abbreviations, Acronyms

5G	Fifth-generation technology for cellular networks
AI	Artificial intelligence
AOL	Application programming interface
App	Application (usually on mobile devices)
AR	Augmented reality
ARPANET	Advanced Research Projects Agency Network
Avg.	Average
AWS	Amazon Web Services
B2B	Business-to-business
B2C	Business-to-consumer
BPO	Business process outsourcing
BPS	Book-value per share
BS or B.S.	Balance Sheet
c.	Circa (Latin word for "approximately")
CAD	Computer-aided design
CAPEX	Capital expenditure
CCTV	Closed-circuit television
CERN	European Organization for Nuclear Research
CRM	Customer relationship management
CF	Cash flow
CFD	Contract for difference
Co.	Company

Corp.	Corporation
COVID-19	Coronavirus disease
CPU	Central processing unit
CSV	Comma-separated values (Filetype)
Cumul.	Cumulative
DDOS	Distributed denial of service
Div.	Dividend
DIY	Do-it-yourself
DNS	Domain name system
DRM	Digital rights management
DPS	Dividend per share
DSL	Digital subscriber line (data over telephone lines)
EBIT	Earnings before interest and taxes
EBITDA	Earnings before interest, taxes, depreciation, and amortization
EBITDARD	Earnings before interest, taxes, depreciation and amortization plus research and development expense
EBITDA-CX	Earnings before interest, taxes, depreciation, and amortization minus CAPEX
EHR	Electronic health record
EM	Emerging markets
EPS	Earnings per share
ERP	Enterprise resource planning software
EqV	Equity Value
EU	European Union (as part of company classification, also includes Israel)
EUR	Euro currency
EV	Enterprise Value
Excl. or ex.	Excluded or excluding
Expend.	Expenditure
FCF	Free cash flow
finOps	Financial operations
FTP	File Transfer Protocol
FY	Fiscal year (augmented by a value ranging from −2 to 3); FY-1 means the fiscal year before the last reported year
GPA	Grade point average
GDP	Gross domestic product
GM	Gross Margin
Gr. or Grow.	Growth
HCM	Human capital management software

HR	Human resources
HTLM	HyperText Markup Language
HTTP	Hypertext Transfer Protocol
IaaS	Infrastructure as a Service
ICT	Information and communications technology
IEEE	Institute of Electrical and Electronics Engineers
Inc.	Incorporated
IoT	Internet of Things
IP	Intellectual Property
IP	Internet Protocol, when used as a technical term
IPO	Initial public offering
IPTV	Internet Protocol television
IRC	Internet Relay Chat
ISP	Internet service provider
IT	Internet technology
KNIME	Konstanz Information Miner
KPI	Key performance indicator
LED	Light-emitting diode
Legal entities	Over 50 countries represented with various legal entities: A.S., A/S, AB, ABEE, AG, AS, ASA, Berhad, Bhd., d.d., GDR, K.K., KGaA, N.V., OY, Oyj, Plc, S.A., S.p.A., SA, SE, SpA, Tbk
LT	Long term
Ltd.	Limited
LTE	Long-Term Evolution (fourth-generation technology for cellular networks)
LTM	Last twelve months
LTV	Lifetime value
M2M	Machine-to-machine (usually communication)
Mar.	Margin
MAU	Monthly active users
MBA	Master of Business Administration
MMORPG	Massively multiplayer online role-playing game
MIT	Massachusetts Institute of Technology
Mngt.	Management
MVNE	Mobile virtual network enabler
n.a.	Not available
n.m.	Not meaningful
NA	North America

Neg.	Negative
NFT	Non-fungible token
NSFNET	National Science Foundation Network
NTM	Next twelve months
NYU	New York University
OCR	Optical character recognition
OEM	Original equipment manufacturer
Op.	Operations
Sh.	Share
SLTM	Second last twelve months (the twelve months before LTM)
SNTM	Second next twelve months (the twelve months after NTM)
PaaS	Platform as a service
PBX	Private branch exchange (business telephone system)
PC	Personal Computer
PLM	Product Lifecycle Management (also used as PLM software)
PR	Public relations
PS or P	Price per share
R&D	Research and development
Rev.	Revenue
RFID	Radio Frequency Identification
ROI	Return on investment
RoW	Rest of World
SaaS	Software as a service
Sal.	Sales or revenue
SEPA	Single Euro Payments Area
Sh. Equity	Shareholders' equity
SME	Small and mid-size enterprise
SMS	Short Message/Messaging Service
SQL	Structured Query Language (programing language)
TCP/IP	Transmission Control Protocol/Internet Protocol
TV	Television
UCLA	University of California, Los Angeles
UFCF	Unlevered free cash flow
URI	Uniform Resource Identifier
US SEC	U.S. Securities and Exchange Commission
USD	US Dollar currency
USP	Unique selling point
VAT	Value-added tax
Valuation base	Multiple of valuation expressed as price per financial unit

Valuation driver	Financial matric influencing the valuation base
VBA	Visual Basic for Applications
VoIP	Voice over Internet Protocol
VPN	Virtual Private Network
VR	Virtual reality
Wi-Fi or WiFi	Wireless network

Valuation Multiples (Bases)

EV/Sales	Enterprise value divided by sales (revenue)
EV/GM	Enterprise value divided by gross margin
EV/EBITDA	Enterprise value divided by EBITDA
EV/EBITDARD	Enterprise value divided by EBITDARD
EV/EBITDA-CX	Enterprise value divided by EBITDA-CAPEX
EV/EBIT	Enterprise value divided by EBIT
EV/FCF	Enterprise value divided by free cash flow
EV/OP CF	Enterprise value divided by operative cash flow
EV/Asset	Enterprise value divided by total assets
P/Sales	Equity value divided by sales (revenue)
P/FCF	Equity value divided by free cash flow
P/E	Share price divided by earnings per share or price to earnings
P/B	Share price divided by the book value per share or price to book
PEG	Price to earnings growth

Valuation Drivers (Financial Indicators)

Sales Gr.	Sales (revenue) growth
Gross M. Grow. GM Gr.	Gross margin growth
EBITDA Gr.	EBITDA growth
EBITDARD Gr. E..ARD Gr.	EBITDARD growth
EBITDA-CX Gr. E..A-CX Gr.	EBITDA-CAPEX growth
EBIT Gr.	EBIT growth
Op.CF Gr.	Operative cash flow growth
FCF Gr.	Free cash flow growth

Net In. Gr.	Net income growth
EPS Gr.	Earnings per share growth
CAPEX Gr.	Capital expenditure growth
R&D Gr.	Research and development expenditure growth
DPS Gr.	Dividend per share growth
Gross Mar. or GM	Gross margin
EBITDA Mar.	EBITDA margin
EBITDARD Mar. E..ARD Mar.	EBITDARD margin
EBITDA-CX M. E..A-CX M.	EBITDA-CAPEX margin
EBIT Mar.	EBIT margin
FCF/Sales	Free cash flow divided by sales (revenue)
Op. CF/Sales	Operative cash flow divided by sales (revenue)
Net Mar.	Net income margin
R&D/Sales	Research and development expenditure divided by sales (revenue)
CAPEX/Sales	CAPEX divided by sales (revenue)
Divid. Yield	Dividend yield
Asset Turno. Asset Tur.	Asset turnover
RoA	Return on assets
RoE	Return on equity
S.Gr.+EBITDA% S.Gr.+E..A%	Sales growth plus EBITDA margin

Industries

Analytics S.	Analytics Software
B2C Services	Online Business-to-Consumer Services
C. Mon. F.	Financial Content Monetization
Cont. Mon.	Content Monetization
Cust. Acq.	Customer Acquisition
Divers./ Port.	Diversifieds and Portals
Horizontal S.	Horizontal Software
O. Brokerage	Online Brokerage
Platform S.	Platform Software
Security S.	Security Software
Soc. Netw.	Social Networks
Vertical S.	Vertical Software

Countries

AE	United Arab Emirates
AU	Australia
BE	Belgium
BM	Bermuda
BR	Brazil
CA	Canada
CH	Switzerland
CL	Chile
CN	China
DE	Germany
DK	Denmark
ES	Spain
FI	Finland
FR	France
GB	United Kingdom
GR	Greece
HK	Hong Kong
HR	Croatia
ID	Indonesia
IE	Ireland
IL	Israel
IN	India
IT	Italy
JP	Japan
KR	Korea, Republic of
LK	Sri Lanka
MA	Morocco
MO	Macao
MT	Malta
MX	Mexico
MY	Malaysia
NL	Netherlands
NO	Norway
NZ	New Zealand
PH	Philippines
PL	Poland
PR	Puerto Rico

PT	Portugal
RS	Republic of Serbia
RU	Russia Federation
SE	Sweden
SG	Singapore
SI	Slovenia
TH	Thailand
TN	Tunisia
TR	Turkey
TW	Taiwan, Province of China
US or USA	United States
VG	Virgin Islands, British
VN	Vietnam
ZA	South Africa

List of Figures

List of Tables

1 Introduction and Research Objective

The internet has expanded to become the "cornerstone of our very society" (Whistler, 2022), impacting virtually every aspect of our lives. The latest report published by Hootsuite shows that the 4.95 billion internet users worldwide spend on average 6 hours and 58 minutes daily using the internet (Hootsuite Inc., 2023), implying that over 60% of the world population spends over 40% of the time awake online. Most interestingly, this adoption took place in less than 30 years, enabling unprecedented connectivity, speed, and transparency for humans and, increasingly, machines which effectively necessitated all businesses to adopt this new technology and medium of communication. The internet has enabled some existing businesses, created entirely new businesses and economic sectors as well as made some existing businesses obsolete. Following the episode of "irrational exuberance" (Greenspan, 1996) preceding the dot-com bubble, for finance professionals, the internet represents a unique natural experiment on the grounds that it gave birth and brought to adulthood an entirely new sector in times when precise tracking and quantification are possible and with a tempo in which maturity was achieved within the lifespan of a human.

Supplementary Information The online version contains supplementary material available at https://doi.org/10.1007/978-3-658-49126-0_1.

A. Trusculescu, *Business Valuation Across the Industry Life Cycle*,
https://doi.org/10.1007/978-3-658-49126-0_1

1.1 Motivation and Importance Arguments for the Research Topic

While the importance and overall reach of the internet are undisputed, researchers of related fields, such as valuation of internet-enabled businesses, are often left in the dust by the development speed. During the seven-year period in which the Ph.D. study was carried out (2016—2023), the business environment, business processes, and workflows have been dramatically reshaped. Following the launch of 5G in 2019, which enabled completely new possibilities such as IoT, AI, M2M communication in addition to very fast, low-latency wireless communication (Attaran, 2021), COVID-19 forced on one side, all employees working from a computer to work from home and on the other side forced virtually all companies to embrace digitalization. The entirety of the human economic system was effectively obliged to decentralize overnight and use a relatively new system of interaction as its backbone. COVID-19 will likely have everlasting effects on society and represents the starting point "of new digital products and services based on the principle of flexibility" (Almeida et al., 2020). Lastly, with the commercialization of Starlink, virtually every human could gain access to the internet for unprecedented connectivity.

With virtually every emerging technology relying on the internet and digitally driven ecosystems, ranging from metaverses to machine-to-machine communication and IoT, which according to Ericsson, should comprise 24 billion connected devices by 2050 (Ericsson, 2023), the relevance of understanding what drives the valuation of internet-driven companies is more important than ever. The study provides entrepreneurs, shareholders, and other stakeholders with a new framework to optimize business, financing structures, and exit points once they are not the best owners. In addition to few empirical studies in the field, even fewer address the topic of change over time while examining the entire internet sector to draw conclusions for future industries.

1.1.1 Scientific Reasons and Arguments Based on Trends and Developments in the Scientific Literature

Despite the research idea being ignited by practice-rooted questions, the research phase could not answer the questions and showed multiple gaps between what is possible from the available data and the internet as a natural experiment perspective and available research. Limitations of existing research can be grouped into three categories. Firstly, most studies are performed at one point in time and do not evaluate if such conclusion changes over time or other indicators of industry development, let alone over half of the lifespan of internet-driven business models. Secondly, all studies focus on a limited number of peers compared to all companies that are relevant to this sector. And third, most companies focus on a limited number of financial information in terms of types of variables and timeframes. All three factors are required to answer the research questions the study has commenced with.

Relevant scientific literature can be grouped into finance literature, internet development literature, and internet-based business models. While the finance literature discusses the idea of change in multiples and drivers, there is little empirical research. In addition to providing a history of the development of the internet, Internet development literature covers extensively the lessons learned from the Dot-Com bubble from all perspectives. Despite extensively covering valuation trends in the Dot-Com literature, such studies do not continue in the post-Dot-Com period, leaving a void in understanding. The study of business models is particularly important as it defines the relevance of the findings to future industries that will sprout around the Internet ecosystem. While a direct extrapolation is difficult without knowing how such future models will resemble, the conclusions from past Internet industries will likely carry on into the future Internet industries.

The study complements and extends the current Internet-focused finance literature on one side, provides conclusions on the past development of certain Internet industries that could be extrapolated, and, most importantly, proposes a framework for such studies in the future.

While the present study will not harvest all the potential the Internet as a natural experiment offers, it is the first study that tries to cover the entirety of the sector over a long period of 15 years with an extensive range of variables and tries to draw conceptual conclusions regarding the evolution of multiples and drivers of valuation across certain industry life stages.

1.1.2 Professional Reasons Based on Developments in the Field of Finance

Like technology, the art and science of business valuation have also evolved considerably over the last years. Driven by the internet's transparency across all economic sectors and, implicitly, the financial sector, finance professionals were pushed to be more transparent and precise. The urge for precision has created new metrics, such as the Rule of 40 or User-based Valuation Metrics, and forced investors to consider new factors besides the traditional discounted cash flow methods when evaluating investments. New factors range from a company's ability to act as a consolidation platform for buy-and-build activities (the acquisition of smaller market players) to the company's ability to act as an organic platform by having excellent access to human capital and the ability to deploy new employees profitably from day one. The organic platform factor is of the essence for companies in knowledge-driven industries such as internet-driven businesses.

One such factor is the evolution of the relationship between valuation multiples and drivers and industry life cycles. While the change from Sales based multiples to Profitability based multiples is often mentioned in the practice of corporate finance, there is little empirical research to document such changes. Multi-year academic research goes beyond the pragmatic approach of corporate finance professionals in practice and is the correct setting to evaluate such factors without having time pressure or implicit biases.

This study tries to close this understanding gap and hopefully spark the introduction of a new valuation dimension to the toolbox of corporate finance professionals.

1.1.3 Personal Reasons: Natural Professional and Academic Career Development

In addition to the motivation to implement an extensive study, the researcher has the background required to combine academic and professional expertise and methods for a value-adding study.

The academic background of the author comprises a Bachelor of Science in Business Administration from the School of Management of Boston University (renamed Questrom School of Business) with a dual concentration in Finance and International Management and a Minor in Economics, a Master's degree in Entrepreneurial Management in Business Administration from the Politehnica University of Timisoara and over ten relevant academic publications.

The author's professional experience comprises over 12 years of Corporate Finance experience with a focus on Mergers and Acquisitions at HSBC, Citigroup, and goetzpartners, with the latest position being Director in the Technology Mergers and Acquisitions practice. Over this period, the author has successfully closed over 30 transactions, of which over 25 were concerning companies with internet-enabled business models and related.

The author has the ideal combination of academic and professional experience to conduct such research and the required competencies to tackle this overarching and extensive study. The research also enables the author to widen his understanding of the valuation of internet-enabled business models while expanding the academic and professional knowledge base on the topic.

1.2 Summary of the Research Objective with Tangible Example

With the risk of oversimplifying the study's objective, a short explanation of the types of variables used, the relationship between the types of variables, and a short example illustrating the reason for conducting such a study will provide the background and perspectives required to understand the study.

Comparing the sale or acquisition of a company with the sale or acquisition of an apartment will put all variables into perspective. The value of an apartment is usually calculated as Euro per square meter, with factors such as location or year of construction driving the price per square meter up or down. Applying this concept to companies, one arrives at value multiples defined as Euro per Unit of Revenue or Profit, and growth or profitability as the factor defining such values. While companies are organic beings that evolve, grow, and eventually die, the metrics used to value them vary over their lifetime. Furthermore, complex organisms such as companies have significantly more factors that can be measured compared to an apartment that is a non-evolving object. Consequently, the key valuation metric or base of "price per square meter" for companies does not always have to be the same and can change over time.

Depending on many reasons, the price for companies can be based on "price per revenue" or "price per some type of profitability or cash cash-flow" and can be driven by a multitude of factors similar to "location" or "year of construction." This study tries to find the "price per square meter" and the key factors changing this price, such as location and year of construction for companies over certain stages of their life.

The importance of changes in valuation bases (and drivers) can be exemplified by simulating a hypothetical company in the vertical software industry, as shown in Table 1.1. This company had, in the year 2013, 100 units of revenue which grew at the average industry growth rate of 13% to 129 units in 2015. As observed during these years, the average EBITDA margin went from 20% in 2013 to 16% in 2015. While the reason for the decline is unknown, it is likely due to growth-focused strategies, as can be observed in the high growth rate. Based on the results of this study, if the shareholder had decided to sell the company in 2013, it would have received a multiple of 3.7× Revenues representing 371 units, while if he had waited for two years, he would have received 19× EBITDA representing 381 units. The reason for a different valuation base is that in this period, the valuation changed from being Sales based to being EBITDA based. Consequently, due to changes out of the shareholder's control, he would have received roughly the same value for the company despite two years passing and the company growing nearly 30%.

Table 1.1 Example valuation to highlight importance of valuation bases over time

	2013	2014	2015
Revenue	100	113	128
Growth		13%	13%
EBITDA	20	20	20
Margin	20%	18%	16%
Revenue multiple	3.7x		
EBITDA multiple			19.0x
Valuation	371		381

This example shows tangibly that valuation bases change which should be reflected in the strategy of the company and the timing of an exit or shareholder change to maximize value. Hundreds of examples and discussions such as this one sparked a craving to empirically understand the evolution of a "value-maximizing strategy" in internet-enabled businesses.

1.3 Research Objectives and Approach: Considerations Concerning Expected Impact of Research Results

Considering the arguments above, describing the motivation for choosing to research this topic, and the mentioned research gaps in the academic literature as well as empirical professional knowledge combined with the tangible example, the importance of investigating and answering the research question can be summarized.

From an academic standpoint, the proposed research would fulfill four separate research gaps. Firstly, the proposed study would continue the series of analyses often focused on individual industries and points in time by expanding both the coverage through the inclusions of 21 separate industries and the time period by covering 15 years of data representing half of the lifespan of the internet. Secondly, the proposed study would try to empirically demonstrate the change in bases and drivers over the industry life cycle that some scholars suggested. Thirdly, the study will try to find non-time-related variables to predict changes in bases and drivers, representing an entirely new area of research. And lastly, the framework developed together with the well-researched clusters will provide an ecosystem for future research around the natural experiment of internet-enabled business models.

From a professional point of view, the research will add new insights into three separate areas. Firstly, the study will provide a tangible analysis of the development of multiples and drivers over a long time and segmented across 21 industries helping management teams and shareholders of such industries implement value-maximizing strategies. Secondly, the research introduces a new factor (the connection between relevant multiples/ drivers and industry life-cycle) that can further improve valuations' precision. And lastly, it provides a framework that can be extrapolated to new internet-enabled industries helping the management teams and shareholders not to be surprised by fundamental changes in valuation bases and drivers.

The research approach is presented as a logical diagram together with all the research phases in Fig. 1.1. The broad research objective can be summarized by condensing the four hypotheses that will be evaluated:

1) Segmentation/ clustering based on industries and business models will increase the explanatory power of Bases and Drivers
2) Valuation Bases represented by valuation multiples change over the industry development from being sales to being profitability based
3) Valuation Drivers represented by various financial metrics evolve over time from being growth focused to being profitability focused
4) Metrics other than time can provide valuable insights into the inflection points of Bases and Drivers.

The operational objectives of each stage in the research process can be seen in Fig. 1.1, shown as goal, and can be discussed stage by stage. The first stage focuses on formulating the research questions and hypotheses based on the practice-rooted questions and the internet as a natural study. The second stage reviews the relevant literature to answer parts of the questions and derive the required building blocks for the overall study framework.

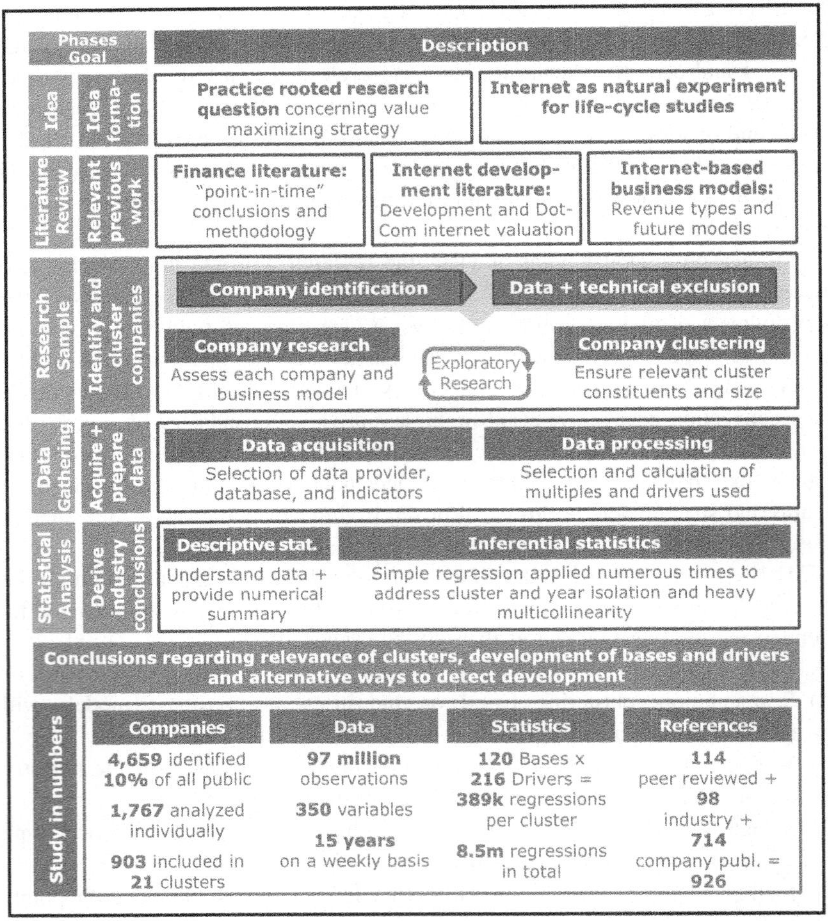

Fig. 1.1 Logical research diagram with research stages. (Own illustration)

The third stage focuses on identifying, understanding, and clustering all companies for the study. This stage will be one of the most time-consuming as the study will review and classify thousands of companies. Furthermore, the stage will be implemented as exploratory research because the review of the business models will impact the classification of each company, while the clusters in which companies are classified are in a permanent chance since they need to be precise by grouping only comparable models while being sufficiently large for the later statistical analysis.

The fourth stage focuses on acquiring and processing the required data, which given the size of the study, will be a challenge requiring data analytical skills, while the fifth stage will perform the required descriptive and inferential statistical analyses to evaluate the hypotheses.

To highlight the size of the endeavor, some tangible numbers are worth emphasizing. The study identified 4,659 companies representing over 10% of all public companies worldwide, with 1,767 requiring individual analysis to find 903 companies that ended up in the final form of the study. These companies were clustered in 21 industries and analyzed separately across 120 Valuation Bases and 216 Valuation Drivers using weekly observations totaling over 97 million observations. Inferential statistics required implementing and analyzing over 8 million regressions to derive industry-level conclusions. It can be said that almost no shortcut was taken to derive and analyze such a large dataset.

In order to achieve the research objectives, a complex research methodology has been designed that is supported by methods and tools from different scientific fields such as management, database creation and management, data analytics, statistics, econometry, business financial analysis, and business valuation. The multidisciplinary design will be described in detail in each chapter. The chapters follow the operational objectives and study stages as described above and can be summarized as follows:

Chapter 1 sets the stage by explaining the motivation and relevance of the study in addition to describing the scientific, professional, and personal reasons for the endeavor. The chapter also provides a simplistic explanation of the concept of Base and Driver of valuation and shows a tangible example of a practical situation in which the results would be useful for strategic and managerial decisions. The section also summarizes the stages of research, the research and knowledge gaps it tries to close, the research objects, and the operational objectives to implement the study. The chapter ends with a summary of the chapters.

Chapter 2 presents the research context and challenge as well as presents the internet as a natural experiment for such studies. The chapter starts with a short summary of the relevance of the internet in the context of industrial revolutions and technology adoption before diving into the history of the internet with the overarching goal of understanding the emergence of internet-enabled business models and their development. It continues with a detailed summary of the Dot-Com bubble and its valuation learnings and implications before discussing the bubble's aftermath and the emergence of sustainable business models. The next subchapter summarizes the types of business models and types of revenue before diving into future business models, their dependence on the internet, and the study's relevance for future models.

Chapter 3 continues the research context with a literature review of comparable studies, their findings, limitations, and learnings for the present study, in addition to summarizing the professor's Damodaran work around life cycles. The chapter also briefly discusses the idea of valuation and its development over time, defining the research scenario, the hypotheses, and the proposed methodology.

Chapter 4 tackles the research sample by describing the methods used to identify, understand and classify the companies. While the summary of the work on a company level is presented in the Annexes, this chapter provides the background required to perform the work. The first sub-chapter describes the sources used to identify the companies as well as the process implemented to identify and assess every company. A simplified overview of the process is also presented and discussed. The second sub-chapter discusses the importance of clustering, key factors for clustering businesses, and summarizing relevant business models and clusters. While this sub-chapter is closely tied to each company's individual analysis and classification, the order represents the exploratory nature of the study in which included companies influence the cluster, and the clusters influence the inclusion of the companies. The chapter concludes by summarizing the clusters identified and their business models.

Chapter 5 continues the research by discussing the data acquisition and processing methodology. It starts by explaining potential data providers and data sources and the process followed to find the best source. The chapter continues by explaining the technical implementation of the acquisition as well as the relevant variables and time frames. The second sub-chapter discusses the data quality and provides coverage ratios, while the third sub-chapter presents the research variables split into Valuation Multiples (Bases) and Valuation Drivers in addition to the process of defining relevant ranges. The fourth sub-chapter explains the technological implementation for processing the data and arriving at the final dataset, while the fifth sub-chapter discusses the outcome in terms of size and quality.

Chapter 6 begins the statistical analysis with descriptive statistics to understand the data and the quantitative development of key ratios. Chap. 6 describes quantitatively the pool of companies included before diving into a comparison of valuation multiples over time and across industries and discussing the data tendencies of the variables included in the study. While Chap. 7 focuses more on developing bases and drives and industry-level conclusions on a conceptual level, Chap. 6 provides the numerical summaries expected from an empirical study. The chapter concludes by summarizing the key learnings.

Chapter 7 continues the statistical analysis and dives into inferential statistics. The first sub-chapter explains the methodology, the reasoning behind choosing this certain methodology, the tested equation, and the technical implementation. The second sub-chapter is broken down into 21 further sub-chapters to discuss the results cluster-by-cluster or industry-by-industry basis. Such a detailed discussion is essential for the conclusion, as each cluster or industry represents a separate observation for testing the hypotheses. The last sub-chapter summarizes the learnings so that each hypothesis can be discussed individually. The first and second hypothesis is confirmed, while a variation of the third hypothesis is also confirmed. The study gathers sufficient evidence to neither confirm nor infirm the fourth hypothesis leaving room for future research.

Chapter 8 concludes the study by presenting the predominant conclusions, research limitations, original contributions to existing literature, and theoretical and applicative research. The study also discusses directions for future research in detail and divides these into areas that can be implemented using the current data and framework and areas that require new frameworks and/or data. The chapter ends by summarizing the praxiological implications for managers and shareholders.

The research results have also been the subject of different scientific articles published in journals and conference proceedings, as presented in ANNEX 7.

The thesis comprises 443 pages, of which 205 are the main work, 168 present the work on business models and clustering, and 64 show the references. The work also encompasses 80 tables, 49 figures and illustrations, and 7 annexes.

2 The Research Context and Challenge—the Internet as a Natural Experiment for the Study of Finance

Dividing up history in periods in a process entitled "periodization" has been well-known and applied since the beginning of the seventeenth century (Gangatharan, 2008; Green, 1992). While it has its limitations, the process is also applied in the study of finance and economics by dividing the evolution of the entire economy into periods entitled "industrial revolutions." Scholars like Peter N. Stearns dedicated much time to understanding and pinpointing these periods and, most importantly, the characteristics and drivers of these periods to draw conclusions that help understand the drivers of innovation (Stearns, 2020). While understanding these periods is useful for the study of finance, corporate valuation, econometrics, and even the study of the evolution of particular industries, these periods are, on the one side, not precise enough and, on the other side, very difficult to quantify due to the lack of data. Luckily recent history is both precise and quantifiable and allowed for the development of the Internet, which arguably became a new industry.

While scholars and economic historians such as Stearns, Horvath, and Chan disagree to some extent that certain phases are individual or just phases of a large revolution (Horvath, 2018; Stearns, 2020), they all seem to agree regarding the key drivers of each phase or revolution. The first phase (or revolution) was driven by the emergence of the usage of steam and water power for mechanical production, essentially shifting production from home into the factory (Simon Chan, 2016). The second revolution continued this trend and, with the help of electrification and the emergence of the assembly line, allowed for mass production and, most importantly, the division and specialization of labor (Ford & Crowther, 2006). It is important to mention that this revolution also pushed

A. Trusculescu, *Business Valuation Across the Industry Life Cycle*,
https://doi.org/10.1007/978-3-658-49126-0_2

the adoption of the telephone, radio, and later television, which tremendously improved communication, as seen in Fig. 2.1.

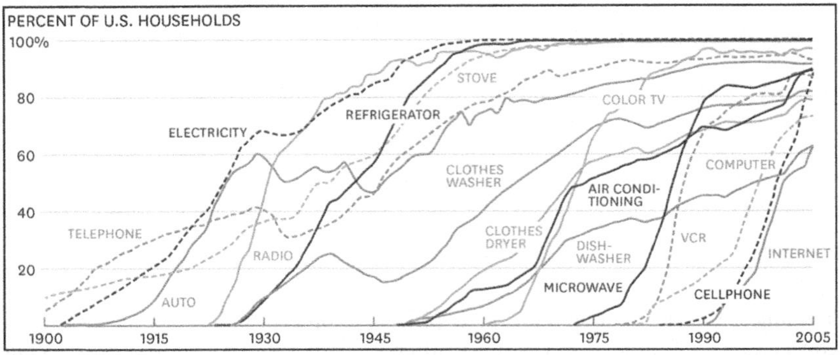

Fig. 2.1 Adoption of various technologies as percentage of U.S. households (Felton, 2008; McGrath, 2013)

The third revolution, driven by automated production and the emergence of everything "digital" (e.g., electronics, computers, Internet), came next and further pushed individual output and productivity. One of the key drivers of the third industrial revolution was the digital revolution which caused a shift from traditional mechanical and analog electronic technology to digital electronic technology (Simon Chan, 2016) and started in the middle of the 20th century with the increased adoption of the computer (Schoenherr, 2004). Arguably, compared to hardware technologies such as transistors, integrated circuits and related devices such as computers and mobile phones, and even software technologies (Schoenherr, 2004), the internet has had a significantly higher impact on the digital revolution and implicitly on the third industrial revolution as it enabled in addition to fast data processing and storage, the real-time transfer of information of all formats at large distances almost instantaneously. As an enabler, the internet has created a new distribution channel for traditional businesses (Connolly et al., 1998) and completely new business and delivery models (T. Ritter & Pedersen, 2020).

While the internet has virtually impacted all sectors, industries, and distribution channels, it has also created completely new ones. For a finance professional, the ability to observe the emergence, growth, and domination of internet-based business models creates a never previously experienced natural experiment. All sectors and industries, except for the internet and technology-based business

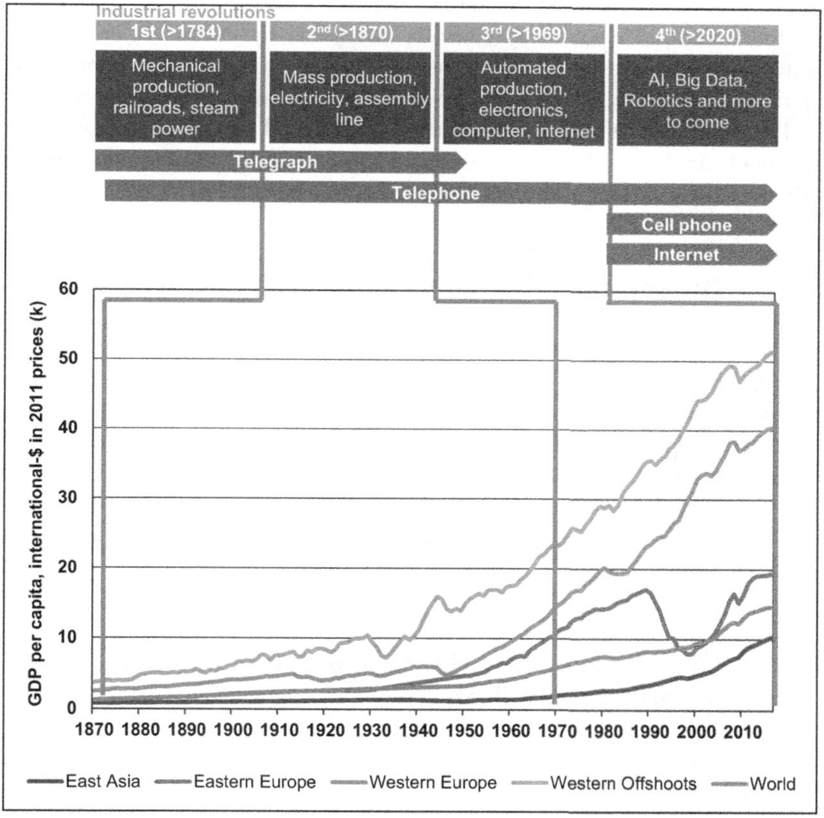

Fig. 2.2 Development of GDP per Capita in International 2011 dollars in selected regions (Roser, 2013) (University of Groningen—Groningen Growth and Development Centre, 2018) overlapped with the four industrial revolutions (Horvath, 2018) and the main fast private connectivity/ communication developments in the history (Novak, 2019)

models, had existed long before large data gathering was possible or finance as a field of science emerged. This natural experiment enables a finance professional to observe the development of various metrics, perceptions, and valuations across the development cycle of a certain sector. While until the 90s, the internet was virtually inexistent, it accounted for 10.1% of the entire GDP of the US in 2018 (Christopher Hooton, 2019). Fig. 2.2:Development of GDP per Capita in International 2011 dollars in selected regions (Roser, 2013) (University of

Groningen—Groningen Growth and Development Centre, 2018) overlapped with the four industrial revolutions (Horvath, 2018) and the main fast private connectivity/ communication developments in the history (Novak, 2019) presents an overview of the multiple industrial revlutions as discussed in this chapter.

This thesis uses the natural experiment produced by the emergence of the internet to analyze and draw some conclusions about the valuation metrics and valuation drivers during the development of a sector.

2.1 The Internet: The Emergence of Connectivity

Simon Whistler, at the start of his video on Starlink best, summarizes the importance of the internet: "in only 30 years [the internet] went from a fairly niche tool primarily reserved for businessman and enthusiasts to a cornerstone of our very society" (Whistler, 2022). As presented in the previous chapter, the internet saw an adoption rate much faster than arguably more important technologies in the past, such as electricity. According to Statista, in July 2022, the world had 5.03 billion users (Statista, 2022), which at that time of the analysis represented over 63% of the world.

2.1.1 The Internet: Early History, Successes and Path towards a Gold Rush

It all started in the 1960s when in 1965, two computers at the MIT Lincoln Lab communicated for the first-time using packet-switching technology after consulting with scientists working in the Advanced Research Projects Agency of the United States Department of Defense (Pelkey, 2022). Three years later, Beranek and Newman Inc. presented the Interface Message Processor, the packet-switching node used for the ARPANET (Living Internet, 2022; Walden, 2022). Using this technology, on October 29, 1969, computers at Stanford and UCLA connected for the first time (Craig, 2022). Another important milestone in 1960 was the operating system UNIX which later inspired Linux and FreeBSD (Ritchie, 1980).

In 1970, the Arpanet was established between Harvard, MIT, and Beranek & Newman, followed by the development of the email by Ray Tomlinson in 1971 (Craig, 2022). Also, in 1971, Project Gutenberg, the first online library, was started by Michael Hart, who typed the Declaration of Independence as the first document (Thomas, 2007). In 1973, the University College of London in the

United Kingdom and the Royal Radar Establishment in Norway connected to ARPANET by a satellite link making the first time global connection possible (Kirstein, 1999). Following this achievement, also the time "Internet" was born. Interestingly, a French research team tried to launch another computer network entitled CYCLADES in 1972, which was later shut down; however, it revolutionized the idea that hosts are responsible for delivering data, as opposed to the network itself (B.-K. Kim, 2005).

The next breakthrough came in 1974 when Vinton Cerf and Bob Kahn published "A Protocol for Packet Network Interconnection," which enabled Arpa-like networks to communicate and later became the well-known TCP/IP protocol (Abbate, 2000). Also, in 1974 Telenet, which became the first commercial and licensed public data network in the United States, was started and went into operation in 1975 (Segaller, 1998). Also in 1975, the first eMail client was developed by John Vittal, which enabled the "Reply" and "Forward" functionalities (Craig, 2022). In 1977, Dale Heatherington and Dennis Hayes created the first computer modem, the 80–103A (Oxford, 2009). Compared to the past devices that connected to the telephone lines via telephones and implicitly sound, this was the first device to connect via a special device to the telephone network. In 1978, the Bulletin Board System was developed, essentially the first internet forum (Craig, 2022). Following the Bulletin Board System, the USENET forms and discussion groups were developed in 1979 (Emerson, 1983). USENET is one of the technologies that has survived to this day, and while not being of the most adopted technologies, daily traffic continues to rise. Also in 1979, the first multiplayer game was developed: MultiUser Dungeon, or short MUD. The game was text-based, combining role-playing, fiction, and online chat (Craig, 2022).

The development of the internet continued strongly in the 1980s, with the first noteworthy development taking place in 1980 when Tim Berners-Lee from the European Organization for Nuclear Research (known as CERN) wrote a simple "hypertext" software entitled ENQUIRE that allowed the lab to keep track of "people, software, and projects using hypertext (hyperlinks)" (Craig, 2022). Tim Berners-Lee would later play an important role in the invention of the world wide web (Abbate, 2000). In 1981, the Computer Science Network (CSNET) was established to extend the benefits of the ARPANET to computer science departments that could not be connected directly to ARPANET (Comer, 1983). An important technological adoption that remains at the foundation of the internet to this day came in 1982, with the effective implementation date being the 1st of January 1983, the TCP/IP protocol. Following the adoption of the TCP/IP protocol by the US Department of Defense for all military communication, it was also decided to implement it on the ARPANET (Shacklett, 2021). While explaining the protocol is beyond the scope of this research, it is important to mention that it is based on layers built on many protocols that have developed over time. One such protocol that is part of the application layer is the Domain Name System (DNS) which was defined by Paul Mockapetris in November 1983 (Robachevsky, 2013) and first implemented by four students at Berkeley in May 1984 (Terry et al., 1984) which enables the distributing naming of computers essentially converting IP addresses such as 1.1.1.1 into https://www.cloudflare.com/ making it a lot more user friendly.

In 1985, Stewart Brand and Larry Brilliant developed one of the first online communities, entitled "The WELL," which is still in operation today (Craig, 2022). Also in 1985, the website of Symbolics Computer Corp, Symbolics.com, became the first registered domain (Wauters, 2009b). In 1986, another important event happened when the National Science Foundation Network NSFNET went online by connecting six supercomputer centers at 56,000 bits per second, essentially building a network of networks (Zimmermann & Emspak, 2022). The network of networks went through various revisions and speed increases and only six years later opened up to allow commercial internet service providers to join in (Reuter, 2019). Following these developments, the number of hosts connected to the internet grew to over 20,000 (Zimmermann & Emspak, 2022) or nearly 30,000 (Craig, 2022), depending on the source, by the year 1987. It is important to mention that reaching this stage took over 20 years since this first pocket-based communication. Compared to the billions of users today, the internet had a fairly slow and computer science expert driven evolution during the first 1/3 of its existence. The adoption of the TCP/IP standard also facilitated the growth, which enabled a much larger number of hosts (Craig, 2022).

In 1988, another application layer protocol was deployed, the Internet Relay Chat (IRC), which enabled real-time chat for the first time (Craig, 2022). In 1989 several major developments which pushed the development and adoption of the internet took place, the first commercial provider of dial-up started, World.std.com, America Online (AOL is born), and most importantly, the proposal for the World Wide Web was released by Tim Berners-Lee (Craig, 2022; Zimmermann & Emspak, 2022). The world, also known as World.std.com and World.com, was the first commercial ISP that started in 1989, and while it was first threatened to be blocked by universities and government institutions, it was eventually granted permission to sell internet on an experimental basis (Muíneacháin, 2012). Also in 1989, with Apple leaving AppleLink, the America Online project was born, which was renamed to AOL and became the most popular ISP by focusing on customers that were not internet affine (Nollinger, 1995). AOL was arguably the first company that benefitted from the explosive growth of the internet-enabled from all the companies that subsequently used the internet to gain momentum and scale. The last notable development of the 1980s was the "Information Management" proposal by Tim Berners-Lee from CERN in March 1989 and redistributed in May 1990, which was initially thought of as a document management system originally called "Mesh" (Berners-Lee, 1989) that was renamed during the code writing phase in 1990 to the "World Wide Web".

A lesser-known fact is that David Chaum also started the first digital currency in 1989, DigiCash. This was the first digital currency that also ensured anonymity based on the cryptographic protocols developed by Chaum (Pitta, 1999) two decades before the well-known Bitcoin and other cryptocurrencies emerged. Despite going bankrupt in 1998 due to competition and slow adoption (Pitta, 1999), its technology and ideas inspired many other similar projects, including the famous project Libra supported by giants like Facebook, Visa, and Mastercard with a planned launching date in 2020 (Pentland, 2019) but canceled later in 2022 due to scrutiny from financial regulators (Ou, 2019; Sharma, 2022). Fig. 2.3 presents a summary of all events until 1989.

During the first version of the World Wide Web, Berners-Lee specified the HyperText Markup Language or HTML and wrote the first browser and server to work with such pages as well as invented the Universal Resource Identifier (URI), which became the well-known Uniform Resource Locator (URL) and the Hypertext Transfer Protocol (HTTP) the application layer protocol that allows one computer to fetch a resource from another. From the beginning, these three developments were designed to be decentralized and based on "democratic principles." Berners-Lee used to send the code out for free and only request ideas in exchange for how to improve (Tobin, 2012). Using this technology, the first website went online on the 6th of August 1991 under the link: http://info.cern.ch/hypertext/ WWW/TheProject.html, which is still active today. The webpage essentially explains the World Wide Web (Dutfield & Laura Mears, 2022; Shontell, 2011). In 1990 also, the first search engine entitled "Archie" was launched as part of a school project. Unfortunately, the inventor Alan Emtage did not monetize or patent the idea that generated hundreds of billions of revenues nowadays (Grandoni, 2013). While this search engine essentially only indexed files available on FTP servers, it was the first one to allow searching (Samuel, 2017). The importance of such a service or idea for developing the internet cannot be overstated.

In addition to the first web page, in 1991, the MP3 standard had its initial release, and the first webcam was deployed by a Cambridge University computer lab aiming to monitor a coffee machine (Craig, 2022). In the year 1993, several major developments also took place, with the internet reaching 2 million users

1965	2 computers at MIT Lincoln Lab communicate using packet-switching technology
1968	Interface Message Processor, the pocket switching for the ARPANET
1969	ARPANET: computers at Stanford and UCLA connected for the first time
1970	ARPANET network between Harvard, MIT, and Beranek and Newman Inc.
1971	Development of the eMail by Ray Tomlinson
	Project Gutenberg by Michael Hart by typing Declaration of Independence
1972	French CYCLADES pioneered the idea that the host is responsible for data trans.
1973	University College of London (England) and Royal Radar Establishment (Norway) connect to ARPANET; the term internet is born
1974	A transmission protocol (which later became TCP/IP) was started to enable inter-communication of Arpa-like networks
1975	Telenet, the first commercial "ARPANET" went into operation
	First eMail client developed by John Vittal
1977	The first PC modem was developed and sold
1978	The Bulletin Board System was developed
	USENET forms focusing on news and discussion groups are started
1979	Multi User Dungeon (MUD) the first multi-player game developed
1980	Tim Berners-Lee at CERN launched ENQUIRE a hypertext program
1981	CSNET established to extend ARPANET and connect CS departments
1983	ARPANET computers switch to the TCP/IP protocol used to this day
1984	First implementation of the Domain Name System
1985	Oone of the first online community entitled "The WELL" is developed
	Symbolics.com becomes the first registered domain
1986	NSFNET connects six supercomputer hubs at 56 Kbps
1987	Number of hosts between 20,000 and 30,000 depending on source
1988	IRC was deployed, enabling real-time chat for the first time
1989	World.com becomes the first commercial ISP
	AOL, which will later become the most successful ISP is launched
	First digital currency was started by David Chaum - DigiCash
	Tim Berners-Lee wrote the proposal for the World Wide Web

Fig. 2.3 Key developments of the internet from 1965 until 1989 (Craig, 2022; Zimmermann & Emspak, 2022)

(Zimmermann & Emspak, 2022), the first graphical web browser—Mosaic—being released (Andreessen & Bina, 2022), and the White House and the United Nations launching their websites (Craig, 2022). Mosaic was a milestone in the development of the internet because it enabled the web for non-technical users while incorporating support for graphics, sound, and even videos. The browser was later sold to Spyglass Inc., and the technology was subsequently licensed to Microsoft for use in Internet Explorer and to other users (Andreessen & Bina, 2022). In 1994, the first commercial browser was launched entitled, Netscape. It was essentially a more developed version of Mosaic developed by the same Marc Andreessen (Abbate, 2000).

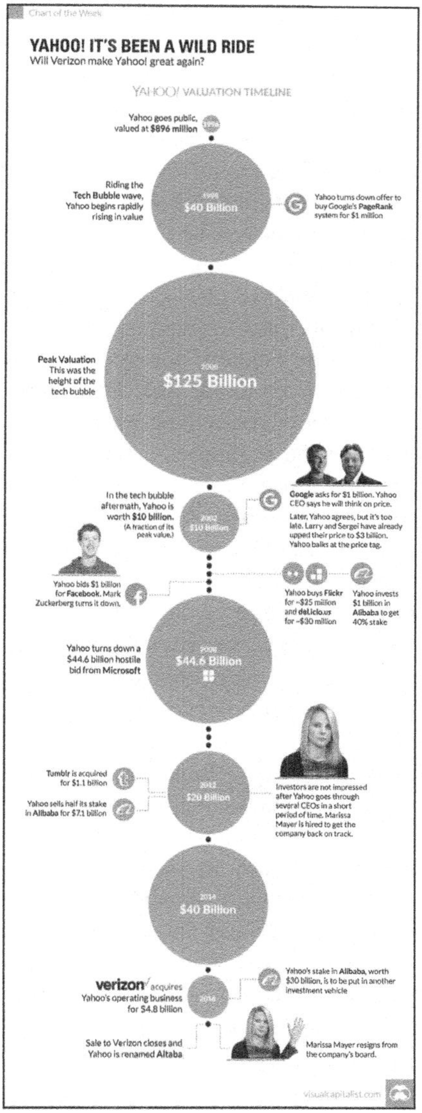

Fig. 2.4 Chart: The Rise and Fall of Yahoo (Desjardins, 2016)

Also in 1994, Yahoo! was created by Jerry Yang and David Filo under the name "Jerry's guide to the world wide web." Even though the company was incorporated only in March 1995 (Clark, 2008; Zimmermann & Emspak, 2022), it went public in 1996, increasing its share prices by over 150% on the first day of trading (Clark, 2008). While Yahoo! was the undisputed online portal when it went public in 1996, its fast-growing competition with Google and other players, as well as some wrong corporate decisions, made it become one of the most well-known fallen stars in the era of the internet with its valuation developing from USD0.9bn at its IPO to USD40bn 2 years later and USD125bn at the peak before the dot.com bubble in 2000 before coming down to only USD 10bn after the dot.com, increasing to USD 44.6bn as it turned down the bid from Microsoft and eventually selling for only USD 4.8bn to Verizon in 2016. Fig. 2.4:Chart: The Rise and Fall of Yahoo (Desjardins, 2016) presents a summary of the development of Yahoo! over time prepared by Jeff Desjardins from Visualcapitalist. The case of Yahoo! is not unique, and while many early internet companies even did not survive to tell such as story, this development highlights the importance of defining or researching what drives valuation for internet-enabled businesses. While at the beginning of the industry, the narrative, equity story, and market potential sometimes dictate valuations far from reality, as the industry matures more, tangible metrics take over. The last noteworthy development was the execution of the first secure online transaction. As Netscape included the protocol Secure Socket Layer (SSL), which enabled sending and receiving encrypted information, and some credit card processing companies started implementing it, the first transaction was possible on the 11th of August 1994 (The FulfillmentLab Inc., 2021) laying the foundation of what will become eCommerce.

1995 was a reference year for the internet, and as Craig names it, the year of the "Commercialization of the Internet." Several important businesses, which exist to this day, launched in 1995. The most well-known include Amazon (launched as an online book shop by Jeff Bezos), eBay (launched as "AuctionWeb") (The FulfillmentLab Inc., 2021), match.com (an online dating website launched by Gary Kremen, which at that time explained it as classifieds as this space covered by traditional classifieds (Krieger, 1995)), and Craigslist (started by Craig Newmark as a simple emailing list that ended up becoming the largest local classifieds player in the United States (Boulton, 2013)). As AOL was reaching the three million user mark, two other important ISPs launched in 1995, Compuserve and Prodigy, while the NSFNET backbone, as known until then, was discontinued (Zimmermann & Emspak, 2022). On the technological side, two major developments need to be noted: Microsoft launched Internet Explorer as part of the Windows 95 Microsoft Plus! pack that is sold separately (Fried, 2010), and the famous JavaScript programming language is implemented by Netscape (Peyrott, 2017).

In April 1996, Internet Explorer version 2.0 was released as a free-of-charge download, essentially launching the first internet browser war. Internet Explorer version 2.0 was also made available for all major platforms, including Windows 3.1, Windows 95, Windows NT, and even Macintosh, across as many as 24 languages (Microsoft Corp, 1996). While this browser war, as Sebenius said, "inspired important books on antitrust, legal and business-strategy issues" (Sebenius, 2002), it is an amazing story of how big tech uses dominant positions to take over entire markets, especially in those that enable winner takes it all subsegments. Had Netscape not failed to secure an exclusive deal with the leading internet service provider AOL, its market position might not have fallen to less than 25% of the market by mid-1999 (Sebenius, 2002).

Also in 1996, CNET decided to buy the TV.com domain for USD 15,000, demonstrating that companies started valuing the online visitors and the simple internet domains (Zimmermann & Emspak, 2022) and HoTMaiL (later renamed to Hotmail), the world's first browser-based email is launched. Microsoft acquired it one year later for USD 400m (Gibbs, 2016).

1997 has also brought significant developments in the internet, particularly in application and business models. Netflix was started by Reed Hastings, and Marc Randolph as a mail-order DVD service with the key differentiator of allowing its customers to hold on to the DVD for as long as needed instead of charging late fees in exchange for a fixed fee per month (Jenner, 2018; O'Brien, 2002). While Netflix became the first company to stream movies at scale, the monthly subscription was a key innovation that holds to this day. Also, in 1996, the first online social network, entitled Six Degrees, was launched by Andrew Weinreich (Craig, 2022). While the network survived only three years until 2020, due to failing to create a suitable business model, it especially contained functions typical for a modern social network, such as the user profile and friend lists (Boyd & Ellison, 2007). Also, in 1997, the first version of Wi-Fi was released, with the first products implementing the standard coming to market in 1999 (Links, 2022). Another important development in 1997 was the US Justice Department suing Microsoft for forcing computer vendors to include Internet Explorer with Windows. While the legal battle took years to complete, Microsoft extensively increased the market share of Internet Explorer (CNN Money, 2000). Microsoft faced several anti-trust inquiries also in 1995 after offering Internet Explorer for free (Richtel, 1997).

In 1998, the largest development was the start of Google, which despite having its roots in a project dating back to 1995 at Stanford, it was incorporated only in 1998 by Larry Page and Sergey Brin (Google LLC, 2022). Few know that a

1990	Tim Berners-Lee developed the HTML, HTTP, URL as well as coded the first web browser and web server
	Alan Emtage created the first search engine as a school project
1991	The first webpage http://info.cern.ch is launched
	Initial MP3 standard and the first web cam deployment
1993	Number of internet users reaches 2 million and the websites of the White House and the United Nations are launched
	The first graphical internet browser for non-techies is launched - Mosaic
1994	The first commercial internet browser is launched - Netscape Navigator
	The first secure eCommerce transaction due to SSL in Netscape
	Yahoo! launches under the name "Jerry's guide to the world wide web"
1995	"Commercialization of the Internet" takes place with Amazon, eBay, match.com, craigslist among others launching
	Compuserve and Prodigy launch while the NSFNET backbone is discontinued
	Microsoft launched Internet Explorer JavaScript is implemented by Netscape
1996	Internet Explorer version 2.0 is released as free product for all major platforms
	CNET buys the TV.com domain for USD 15,000
1997	HoTMaiL the world's first browser-based email is launched
	Netflix is started by as a mail-order DVD service
	Creation of the first social media network entitled Six Degrees
	The first wireless standard, 802.11-1997, was released
	Continuation of legal battle between US Justice Department and Microsoft
1998	Google is born
1999	Napster is launched, enabling file-sharing of audio files over the internet
	Salesforce is founded becoming the first SaaS company
2000	Dot-com buddle bursts

Fig. 2.5 Key developments of the internet from 1990 until 2000 (Craig, 2022; Zimmermann & Emspak, 2022)

third founder, Scott Hassan, wrote most of the code that went into Backrub, the first version of Google (McHugh, 2003).

1999 brought two major developments. The first was the launch of Napster, the peer-to-peer file-sharing program focusing on music. While the following copywriting lawsuits forced it to shut down only two years later (Evangelista, 2002), it inspired many additional services and eventually one operating legally and paying artists—Spotify (Pollack, 2010).

However, the most important development of 1999 was the foundation of Salesforce by Marc Benioff and his partners Parker Harris, Dave Moellenhoff, and Frank Dominguez, with initial funding from Larry Ellison, founder and CEO of Oracle. Marc Benioff was a successful executive at Oracle before 1999 that believed that software should be made available to everyone via the global infrastructure of computers as opposed to client-based instances as before (E. Kim, 2015; O'Connell, 2020). This idea was the birth of Software as a Service (SaaS) as we know it today. This development is particularly important because it made the internet a delivery channel for business software and made the delivery process significantly more efficient. In 1999 AOL bought Netscape (Zimmermann & Emspak, 2022). All developments until the Dot-Com bubble are summarized in Fig. 2.5:Key developments of the internet from 1990 until 2000 (Craig, 2022; Zimmermann & Emspak, 2022)

2.1.2 The Internet: The Dot-Com Bubble, its Aftermath and Implications for the Study

The year 2000 is the year known for the dot-com bubble burst when, as Craig puts it, "(resulted) in huge losses for legions of investors" (Craig, 2022). While many saw it coming and argued before and during the burst that "the old rules still apply" and companies will have to eventually demonstrate cash flows (Higson & Briginshaw, 2000), the story component of the valuation, together with other factors got out of hand with dramatic consequences for the companies, investors and employees of the internet companies.

A quick glimpse at the development of the NASDAQ from 1995 to 2005 shows how painful this "irrational exuberance," as Alan Greenspan, the Chairman of the Federal Reserve, put it at the end of 1996, was (Greenspan, 1996). While some of the most important events in this timeframe are highlighted by Browning and Price in Fig. 2.6, some events are worth mentioning. TheGlobe.com, essentially a social networking website that went through an IPO in 1998, saw its share prices increase from its IPO target price of USD 9 to USD 87 and USD 97 during the first day of trading, just to close at US 63.50 (Kawamoto, 2002). The company then ended up being delisted in 2001 at 16 USD cents on the share, essentially a drop of 98% from the IPO price and 99.8% from the highest price it has achieved (Browning, 2005; Price, 2011). Overall, the NASDAQ, a stock index that included most of the internet stocks, increased from slightly over 1,000 points in 1996 to over 2,000 points during 1999 to a maximum of 5,048 points in March 2000 only to drop back to 1,114 points in October 2002 (Browning, 2005; Price, 2011).

The dot-com bubble became one of history's most researched stock market bubbles. Some of these studies provide valuable insights for studies such as the present one. For example, Alexander Ljungqvist and William J. Wilhelm Jr. looked in 2003 at the effect of pre-IPO ownership structures and insider selling

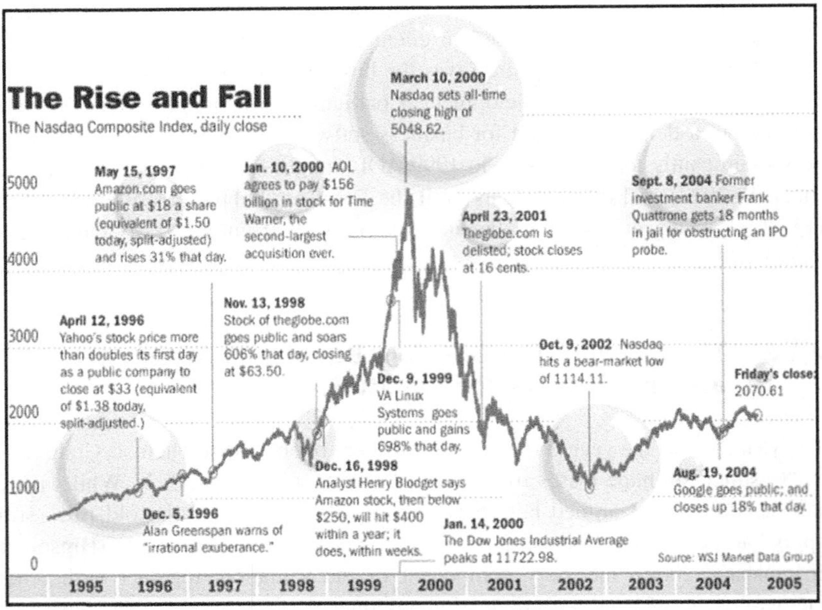

Fig. 2.6 The rise and fall of the NASDAQ index and the main events (Browning, 2005; Price, 2011)

behavior and concluded that "pricing behavior can be at least partially accounted for by marked changes in pre-IPO ownership structure and insider selling behavior over the period, which reduced key decision makers' incentives to control underpricing" (Ljungqvist & Wilhelm Jr., 2003) demonstrating that financial fundamentals or even story considerations did not drive pricings, but rather artificial factors such as wrong incentivization for insiders such as management.

Other researchers focused on what financials and metrics drove or not the valuations during the growth years. Peter Robert Wheale and Laura Heredia Amin, for example, looked at a multitude of "measures of performance" and concluded that "price–sales ratio, price–earnings ratio, book value, and free cash flow are value relevant over the period before market correction" while "all basic measures of performance included in the model, namely, return on assets, return on equity, price– sales ratio, price–earnings ratio, book value, and free cash flow are value-relevant over the post-market correction period" highlighting that financials measures all of a sudden become relevant once funding was tight and "availability of cash would determine the destiny of many Internet companies" (Wheale & Amin, 2003). Interestingly, Wheale and Amin even identified a strong negative correlation between stock prices and their free cash flows leading to the counter-intuitive relation of "larger losses translate[ing] into higher stock prices" (Wheale & Amin, 2003). In the prolonged aftermath, entire books have been written on the valuation of negative earnings, such as the one by Ana Paula Matias Gama et al. that came out in 2017. Due to data availability, no non-financial metrics were included in this study. Interestingly, Wheale and Amin used an approach similar to the one used in this study, focusing on forecasting stock price based on the dependent variables FCF, PS, ROA, PE, BV, and RoE and not with a focus on understanding relevant multiples and drivers. John Morris and Pervaiz Alam did a similar study that empirically confirms the trend reverse following the bubble in 2012. In addition to confirming the return to "traditional accounting and financial information," also has an interesting secondary finding, saying "that earnings quality may contribute to the changes in value relevance, but not the aggressiveness of analyst forecasts" (Morris & Alam, 2012). This secondary finding means that investors usually have their own forecast of expectations for the future and might, to some extent, disregard the findings of sell-side analysts. It will be very interesting to see if this finding holds up to the data set included in this study, considering that in the meantime that internet business models have matured, and businesses in this sector can be planned considerably better. From a methodological perspective, the study done by Morris adds little new information.

As mentioned, Ana Paula Matias Gama et al. have done significant research on the impact of negative earnings on the valuation of the equity in the book entitled "Equity Valuation and Negative Earnings—The Case of the dot.com Bubble" published by Springer in 2017 (Gama et al., 2016). The study of Gama et al. starts by analyzing the implications of the model developed by Ohlson (Ohlson, 1995) and later Feltham and Ohlson (Feltham & Ohlson, 1995) that concluded that costs incurred by start-ups are "costs that create an effect of conservatism accounting" leading to "undervaluation of assets," however, "this situation tends to be reversed over time, because given the principle of rationality" essentially saying accounting fails to account for the value created by early investments that need to be expensed in the year that they are incurred even though at some point this reverses to rationality (Gama et al., 2016). On the concept of the lifetime value of a customer, the way of describing the cost of getting in someone's brain (generating sufficient attention) compared to the revenues generated over the entirety of the relationship, there has been just as much research as on the Dot-Com bubble, however, this is beyond the scope of this research. To summarize, it is costly to reach people via all channels (from offline to Google and Facebook advertising) while people do not necessarily react as expected, forget, or are simply not interested, making it extremely complicated for companies to know-how much revenue they can generate. The study of Gama et al. continues by examining similar situations in the past, such as the telecommunications sector in the 1980s (Gama et al., 2016), a well thought empirical study spanning multiple chapters comparing "new economy firms" with existing firms to confirm the effect of "positive valuation of the losses" as long as a "variable equity" variable is not included. The variable equity was introduced by (Ohlson, 1995) and later Feltham and Ohlson (Feltham & Ohlson, 1995) as a "proxy for expected future abnormal results" (Gama et al., 2016). Form a theoretical and practical point of view, the question is how much of such variable equity variable is actually the story component of valuation described by Aswath Damodaran, especially since stories are impossible to quantify.

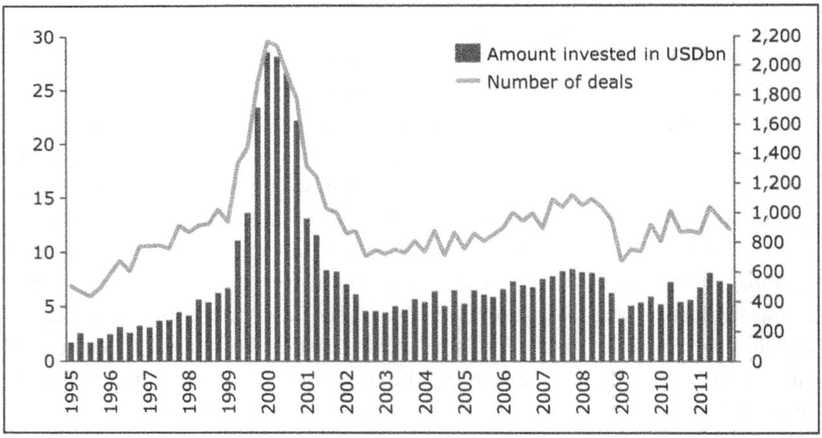

Fig. 2.7 Total venture capital investments in the U.S. by quarter compiled by the U.S. National Venture Capital Association from own data and data from PwC and Thomson Reuters (U.S. National Venture Capital Association, 2012)

To continue with the learnings from the Dot-Com aftermath, it is important also to mention the results of studies that looked at non-financial metrics. One such study that looked at web traffic as a "non-financial indicator of the market values of Business to Consumer (B2C) Internet firms" (Rajgopal et al., 2000) was published by Rajgopal et al. in February 2000 with interesting findings. The first finding was that the relevance "of traffic disappears once the exogenous determinants of traffic," such as alliances, affiliate referral programs, media visibility, marketing expenditure, and cash availability, are accounted for (Rajgopal et al., 2000). The second interesting finding is that "traffic contains no predictive information about future revenues once past revenues are accounted for" (Rajgopal et al., 2000) despite the stock market using "traffic as a measure of the web businesses' ability to create network effects" and "market values of web businesses" increasing "non-linearly with traffic" (Rajgopal et al., 2000). These findings are relevant for this study because, on the one side confirm that irrationality of investing decisions during the Dot-Com bubble, and on the other side confirms the difficulty of forecasting future performance based on internet traffic. While it would have been interesting to include such variables in the study, retrieving historical traffic information for the entire study timeframe is nearly impossible.

Lastly, some studies try to look for reasons for the "irrational exuberance" (Greenspan, 1996). Several studies show that the high availability of capital, or as Price names it, the "Democratization of Capital" (Price, 2011), significantly impacted the disconnect between fundamentals and financials and the valuations. A quick look at any statistics on the USD volume and the number of venture capital transactions during the Dot-Com bubble period confirms this fact. Fig. 2.7 shows how extreme this jump was from USD 8 bn in 1995 to USD 21bn in 1998 and USD 105bn in 2000 (U.S. National Venture Capital Association, 2012). There was simply too much capital "thrown" at these companies for the management team to keep being efficient.

Price also explains that the race to "Go Public" (Price, 2011) contributed to the exuberance and concludes that while this chapter encouraged entrepreneurship, it has led to the loss of entrepreneurial discipline and funding of a high number of unrealistic projects (Price, 2011). Min et al. add to this conclusion in their paper from 2008, also that certain key factors were ignored, starting with "hidden costs of e-tailing," implying that, after all, the cost structure of online companies is not as much different from traditional retailing, continuing with the "lack of niche marketing" explaining that physical stores also have advantages compared to online considering that have some experience tight to them (e.g. jewellery) or complex logistics (e.g. groceries) among others and finishing with the "negligence of competitive forces" describing that barriers of entry were low for online shops allowing for fast market entry (Min et al., 2008).

For the purpose of the study, the Dot-Com bubble and its aftermath represent the point where financial metrics and, ultimately, cash flows started to matter in the valuation of internet-driven companies and business models. The detailed studies represent a starting point in understanding the industry and the relevant metrics and an invaluable inspiration concerning the relevant and available methodologies and models.

2.1.3 The Internet: The Emergence of Sustainable Business Models

In February of 2000, a major denial of service attack brought down several major websites, including CNN.com, Amazon.com, eBay, and Yahoo!, highlighting the importance of security (Long, 2012). The year 2001 came with the launch of the famous online encyclopedia Wikipedia, and a federal judge ordered the takedown of Napster before copyrighted materials were taken down (Craig, 2022; Zimmermann & Emspak, 2022). While Wikipedia was not the first online encyclopedia, it was the first one to succeed due to its simplicity and content-orientated focus (Megan Garber, 2011). Wikipedia also arguably "paved the way for collective web content generation" (Craig, 2022), an important step for today's online-based collaboration. The takedown of Napster sparked a new product in the Baltics called Kazaa, which essentially offered the same service as Napster without storing the files centrally. While a long legal battle with the media industry was started that was eventually settled with the two founders, Zennström and Friis, paying USD 100m in settlements (Peters, 2007), the technology that was developed for Kazaa laid the foundation of the Peer-to-Peer (transfer) which is an addition to sparking unofficial content distribution networks also became the backbone of the Voice over IP (VoIP) service Skype (Tänavsuu, 2018).

While 2002 was fairly silent, 2003 had several important developments starting with the famous Skype. Skype was founded by Niklas Zennström and Janus Friis and created by Ahti Heinla, Priit Kasesalu, Jaan Tallinn, and Toivo Annus based on the Kazaa P2P backbone (Tänavsuu, 2018). Due to the fast success after launching in August 2003, funding was never an issue and was sold to eBay in September 2005 for USD 2.6bn and later to Microsoft for USD 8.5bn. Some of these funds went to pay for the settlement the founders still had for Kazaa (Peters, 2007; Tänavsuu, 2018). Also in 2003, the SQL Slammer worm managed to spread to over 75,000 hosts in less than 10 minutes, again highlighting the importance of security (Taylor, 2020), WordPress was launched, and the known social network company MySpace launched and became the most popular social network (Gillette, 2011; Zimmermann & Emspak, 2022). While MySpace also declined afterward fairly quickly, Gillette interestingly reports that in addition to the technical superiority and clear feature focus of companies like Facebook, one main issue with social networks that makes them, so "combustible" is that they are "particularly sensitive to public perception" (Gillette, 2011). While social networks have essentially the same revenue streams as most free B2C internet services, paid to advertise, they seem to have this particularity also observed later in past winners like Facebook.

Fig. 2.8 Facebook: quarterly number of MAU (Statista, 2022)

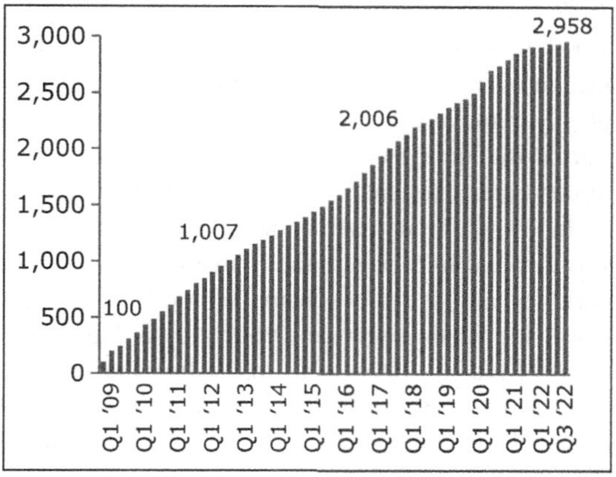

2004 brought three major developments: "The" Facebook, Digg.com, and Mozilla Firefox. Facebook launched on the 4th of February 2004 after Mark Zuckerberg identified the need for a digital "Facebook" at Harvard. Moreover, while discussing the evolution of Facebook and its advantages compared to MySpace is beyond the scope of this research, it is worth noting that after launching within Harvard, half of the student body signed up within the first two weeks, and it had over one million uses by November 2004 (McGirt, 2007) with it currently approaching three billion (Statista, 2022) as shown in Fig. 2.8:Facebook: quarterly number of MAU (Statista, 2022). Facebook grew its user base and built a successful business model with over USD 100bn in revenues in 2022 and over 20% net income margin (FactSet Research Systems, 2022). In the same year, the social news website Digg.com launched, being a front-runner for websites like Reddit and creating a way for users to vote news and weblinks (Craig, 2022). Lastly, the well-known web browser Mozilla Firefox is launched (Zimmermann & Emspak, 2022).

In 2005, the well know website Youtube launched, essentially launching online video streaming at scale. Interestingly, the company was acquired one year later by Google for USD 1.65bn (Helft & Richtel, 2006). Also in 2005, Reddit launched (Zimmermann & Emspak, 2022). One year later also, the know messaging platform Twitter launched (Craig, 2022). Also in 2006, the popular music streaming service Spotify launched and "democratized" the music industry while providing an alternative to piracy (Branchereau, 2018). 2007 brings another push towards streaming with Hulu launching as a joint venture between News Corp. and NBC Corporation, seen at that time as an alternative to Youtube (Hoffman, 2007), and Netflix launching the streaming feature with a limited catalog of c. 1,000 movies (Helft, 2007). Another important development in 2007 was the launch of the iPhone by Steve Jobs (Farber, 2014), which on the one side, completely removed the well-known buttons on the phone and, on the other side, started the app-based smartphone revolution, essentially enabling mobile access to computer-like features and changing the way we interact with the internet.

In 2008, the domain bitcoin.org was registered, and the famous whitepaper was emailed to a cryptography mailing list, essentially giving birth to the digital currency and the blockchain (Finley, 2018). Also in 2008, the known cloud-based file-hosting service Dropbox was launched as part of the TechCrunch50 event (Kincaid, 2009), and the online marketplace Airbnb was started (Aydin, 2019). 2009 brought Google Docs as the Apps exited the beta phase paving the way for browser-based office software and office software collaboration (Matthew Glotzbach, 2009) and the launch of the known social fundraising platform Kickstarter (Wauters, 2009a). Also in 2009, the messaging app Whatsapp was launched, which due to its large adoption, ended up becoming, on the one side, a big issue for telecommunication operators as they were used to charge for SMS and, on another side, paved the way for communication to take place via internet data. Facebook later acquired the company for an incredible value of USD 19bn (Olson, 2014).

The next ten years in the development of the internet were less exciting as most of the developments can be seen as "faster, more of the same", some developments are noteworthy. 2010 saw the launch of Pinterest and Instagram (Zimmermann & Emspak, 2022), with Instagram being acquired by Facebook only two years later for USD 1bn at a time when the company only had 13 employees (Business Standard, 2020; Rusli, 2012) highlighting on the one side how fast internet companies can become valuable an on the other side that large technology companies used their own equity and high valuation simply acquire competition when challenged (Business Standard, 2020).

The next important development for the internet as a whole came in 2019 when 5G launched as it was "more than just a generational step" since it enables new possibilities such as IoT, AI, M2M communication in addition to very fast, low-latency wireless communication (Attaran, 2021). The year 2020 was arguably

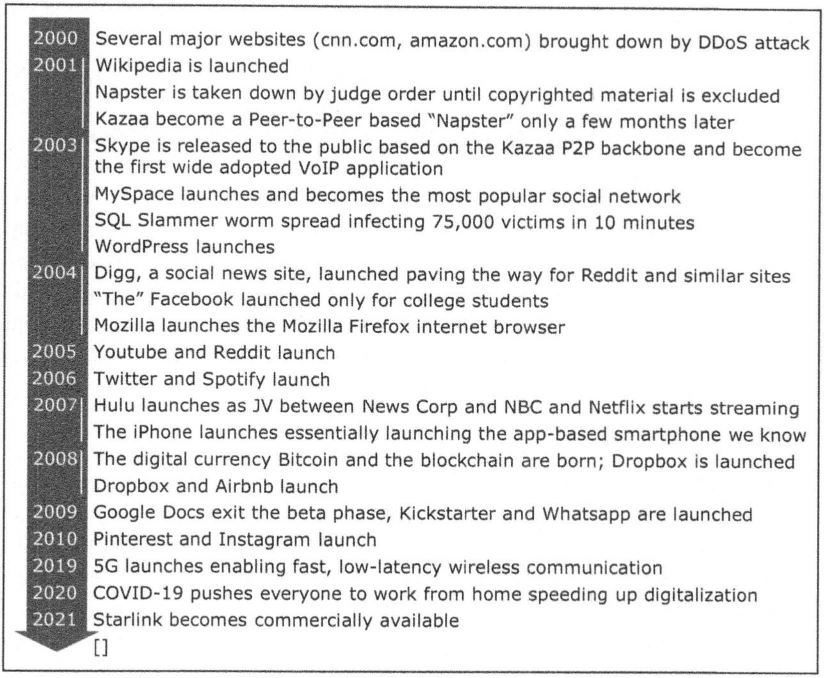

Fig. 2.9 Key developments of the internet from 2000 until 2021 (Craig, 2022; Zimmermann & Emspak, 2022)

one of the largest push towards digitalization, with COVID-19 virtually forcing all people working from a computer to work from home, not from the office. This push will have long-lasting effects on society as it adds a new dimension of flexibility and enables the "emergence of new digital products and services based on the principle of flexibility" (Almeida et al., 2020). While it is too early to assess the true impact of COVID-19 on the internet and digitalization, most researchers seem to agree that it acted as the "great accelerator" and a "catalyst" "towards embracing modern emerging technologies" (Amankwah-Amoah et al., 2021). In 2021 Starlink from SpaceX becomes a commercial reality, making pre-orders available to consumers (Shah, 2021). Starlink is important as it makes the internet even more accessible and not dependent on governments or traditional infrastructure. As summary of these events is presented in Fig. 2.9 Key developments of the internet from 2000 until 2021 (Craig, 2022; Zimmermann & Emspak, 2022)

2.2 Development of Internet-Based Business Models

Internet-based business models increased in complexity with the demands of the end-users and simultaneously with the technological capabilities and computational power. Arguably, most types of internet-based business models were conceived during the early stages of the commercialization of the internet. While these business models adapted and made use of the higher bandwidth and computational power to evolve, the revenue types they generate have not changed significantly and can be summarized in a few categories:

Sale of goods

With the launch of Amazon in 1995, the race for being relevant in online commerce started. The model is a simple replication of the traditional retail model in which a retailer buys goods in its own account, intending to resell them at a higher price. The obvious difference is that traditional retail requires a retail space and less warehouse space as they also often use wholesale distributors, while online retail relies on a virtual presence, central warehousing, and individual order distribution infrastructure.

While providing an answer with regards to what is better is impossible as consumer expectations are different depending on the product acquired (e.g., for a standardized product such as electronics obtaining the lowest price is most likely one of the key purchasing criteria, while for some other like a kitchen the ability to customize as well as experience it in person might be more important than optimizing for every Euro spent) what is clear is that online retail provides for sellers a much deeper understanding of the customers since their behavior can be tracked more precisely online. Research demonstrates that convenience is a highly important factor for online retail, however, consumers research before purchasing mostly online, with the decision to acquire either online or offline depending on many factors (Aw et al., 2021; Gligorijevic, 2011).

To the disadvantage of online retailers, price transparency is significantly higher as customers can "teleport" from one shop to another and compare prices (in the meantime, there are even price comparison websites available). Simultaneously, online marketing offers significantly more capabilities than traditional advertising, and online retailers can discriminate on pricing individually (dynamic pricing), a tool unavailable to traditional retailers.

Certain is, however, that online retail disrupted traditional retail as virtually all sizable traditional retailers joined the online retail scene at some point over the past 30 years. Today's retail is often a merger between traditional shops and online presence with interactions between the two forms such as "pick up in shop" or discounts obtained online applied on purchases offline. Very good retailers follow an "omnichannel" strategy that allows, on the one side, seamless integration for customers and, on the other side, precise profiling of the customer independent of where the customer is welcomed, in the physical shop or online with research confirming that even pricing is aligned in over 70% of cases (Cavallo, 2017).

An important innovation of online retail is the creation of digital goods. Before the internet, media especially (e.g., books, music, movies) had to be delivered via physical media. In the era of digital delivery, where a customer is happy to download the newly acquired book immediately on a digital device, production and delivery costs are virtually zero and instantaneous.

A second important innovation in the eCommerce space was the emblement of a "direct to consumer" channel in which brands or producers adopted the model of selling via their own websites directly to consumers, effectively cutting the middleman (e.g., retailers). This is a noteworthy innovation, as implementing such a strategy in times of only traditional retail would have been very difficult.

Marketplace (commission-based models)

This type of business model was initiated with the foundation of eBay, also in 1995, and at the beginning, was very closely related to eCommerce as both platforms were focused on goods, with the difference being that Amazon had the goods sold on stock (sold from own inventory) while eBay was simply selling used goods people owned and charged a commission for this service. This is a significant difference, as marketplaces usually can only recognize the commission as revenue.

While selling used goods online opened up the market for individuals to sell to a much larger audience (selling offline as an individual is not comparable), the commission-based model extended rapidly to other goods usually sold via classifieds or intermediaries as well as to services at a later point in time. Very soon, houses, cars, and jobs, among other similar products, joined the internet and essentially fully displaced traditional channels. It is to be noted that such platforms usually work on a commission basis except for jobs that usually charge per posting. Other industries, such as the marketing of insurance or financial products, were soon also "digitalized" and displaced, to some extent, banks or insurance brokers. While fees for such products are usually calculated on a "per lead" basis, they are implicitly driven by the fees that can be generated from selling such products.

Online brokers for stocks and other products also joined the development and virtually moved entirely online in a few years.

The emergence of marketplaces and commission-based models also facilitated the development of "platform business models" or "network business models" that enable via marketplaces like Airbnb and Uber "to connect previously unmatched demand-side and supply-side participants" (Täuscher & Laudien, 2018). Täuscher & Laudien identified six clusters of such products following an empirical analysis of 100 companies deploying a platform business model. These models are particular as they could only be implemented in a significantly less efficient way and at a significantly smaller scale compared to what is possible via the internet. As can be seen in Fig. 2.10, the models identified by Täuscher & Laudien, nearly all types of models have a customer-to-customer component, essentially creating an "N-to-N" relationship between the human population and hence unlocking economic value. Interestingly, other researchers that spent significant time with such platform models concluded that for such a model to be successful, they need, in addition to being aware of what the competition is doing and using a mix of innovation and imitation, to "generate interdependencies between the various elements of their business model" (Y. Zhao et al., 2020) confirming the need for playing a role in an "N-to-N" world.

Such "platform business models" facilitate a shared economy enabling the "sharing of underutilized assets in ways that improve efficiency and sustainability" (Hossain, 2020) in addition to the "gig economy," which enables an entirely flexible project-by-project type of freelancing (Roy & Shrivastava, 2020).

Advertising

Almost every service delivered as a free service to the end-consumer relies on advertising or other forms of audience monetization independently if the service provided is a search engine, a social network, a web portal, or any content monetization service. While the forms and delivery methods have changed over the years from simple online banners to complex videos and in-app advertising, the ultimate role has not changed: market/ advertise a product or service to an end-consumer and charge the advertiser a fee for that service. What has drastically changed over the timeframe since the existence of the internet is the ability to profile and ultimately target customers and the ability to match an advertising space with the best-paying advertiser in real-time. Both of these changes would have been impossible without the speed and scale the internet enables. Lastly, the ecosystem of tools and services available to professionals in the online

Business model type	Platform type	Platform participants	Value proposition	Transaction type & good	Revenue model	Example
Efficient product transactions	Web-based platform	C2C, B2B	Large product variety	Physical products	Commission fee, subscription fee; mostly supply side	*Beepi* (eBay for used cars)
Digital product community	Web-based platform	C2C	Being part of a primary non-commercial community	Digital products; physical products	Commission fee; supply side, demand side	*Sellfy* (connecting 'neighbors' to share durable goods with each other)
Product aficionados	Web-based & mobile platform	B2C, C2C	Exchanging knowledge about niche products with community of like-minded people	Physical products	Commission fee; supply side	*HobbyDB* (Knowledge database and transaction platform for collectibles)
On-demand offline services	Web-based & mobile platform	B2C	Large service variety in a novel form	Offline services	Commission fee, subscription fee; mostly supply side	*StyleSeat* (connecting beauty salons & consumers)
Online services	Web-based platform	C2C, B2C	Novel online services with social networking character	Online services	Commission fee, subscription fee; mostly supply side	*iTalki* (connecting language learners with teachers for 1-on-1 online lessons)
Peer-to-peer offline services	Web-based & mobile platform	C2C	Novel services with community feeling within & outside digital platform	Offline services	Commission fee (demand & supply side), subscription fee (third parties)	*Airbnb* (connecting people to list, discover, and book private accommodations)

Fig. 2.10 Summary of platform business models (Täuscher & Laudien, 2018)

advertising space has increased exponentially with every development as gaining the audience's attention is a transparent place, such as the internet is a race for newness.

Kingsnorth, in its book on "Digital Marketing Strategy," which has reached the 3rd edition, provides a good overview of all aspects of online marketing that need to be controlled to be successful: digital consumer, marketing strategy, search engine presence, paid search engine advertising, display advertising, programmatic advertising, social media, email marketing, affiliate, content strategy, customer journey, design, CRM, big data, analytics and measurement (Kingsnorth, 2022). While discussing each aspect is beyond this work's scope, a simple list of topics that need to be considered is sufficient to exemplify the complexity of today's online marketing ecosystem.

Furthermore, as Saura et al. demonstrate, the online advertising space is already going beyond the obvious data collection and mining processes (Saura, 2021) or simple CRM activities with the use of artificial intelligence to derive outcomes and understandings that are not necessarily obvious for humans (Saura et al., 2021) all with the goal of a better customer profiling and implicitly a better targeting in the future. The collection of customer data on such a humongous scale raises, in addition to various data processing and security concerns (Sachdev, 2020), many privacy concerns and literacy questions concerning the usage of data and digital footprint (Portes et al., 2020), especially because of the privacy paradox referring to the "discrepancy between 'consumers' expressed privacy concerns and their digital behavior" (Scarpi et al., 2022; Xu et al., 2011). Some researchers even tried to put a price the customers are willing to pay to maintain privacy and concluded that USD 5 per month is the average, however, the same consumers reported that they would be willing to provide access to their data for USD 80 (Winegar & Sunstein, 2019).

The connection between privacy and technology is for the future of online advertising of crucial importance as the majority of the technology part of the online advertising ecosystem focuses on monetizing the data collected as best as possible by selling the right people the right products at the highest possible price while permanently trying to collect more data from deriving better conclusions.

Subscriptions

Similarly, with the creation of "platform business models," the establishment of "everything as a service" was driven by the internet as it converted the sale of a product into a service by making it available over a network on a 24/7 basis. While the first large Software as a Service company documented was Salesforce, the idea of subscription has spread beyond software into media (e.g.,

Netflix, Spotify) and late into the physical world through the concept of "shared economy."

Renting or granting usage rights for software instead of selling it brings numerous benefits to software developers and users. SaaS significantly decreases the maintenance and support costs as only one version needs to be maintained, upgraded, and delivered while simplifying the infrastructure on which it runs due to it being cloud-based (Liao, 2010), all while providing the developer with a steady and easy-to-plan stream of revenue. It also saves the customer the upfront investment and reduces the operation costs while enabling a simple global distribution and the ability to implement mobile solutions (Hoseini, 2013). While the adoption of SaaS depends on "technological, organizational and environmental readiness" (Yang et al., 2015), pricing plays a huge factor in the adoption of SaaS solutions (Kinnunen, 2022) both in terms of running costs and implementation and migration costs with a very diverse pricing strategy among providers (Saltan & Smolander, 2021) which might deter companies for adopting such solutions. Customization is another factor that stops some customers, as SaaS solutions are typically less customizable than on-premise solutions (Xiao et al., 2021). Nevertheless, the software industry will keep moving towards more SaaS products as the benefits outweigh the costs, and upcoming industries seem to be pricing in SaaS from the very beginning (Chaudhary et al., 2021).

Streaming services were some of the first consumer subscription models that entered the market and displaced fairly quickly the traditional sale of media, with often a negative effect on the media creation industry (Wlömert & Papies, 2016). The internet provided the content consumer with a value proposition that can not be neglected: access to virtually all songs ever recorded from any device at almost any time in exchange for a moderate monthly fee. Movie streaming services also implemented a similar strategy. It is important to observe, however, that similarly to SaaS, where switching costs are often high and implicitly impact natural churn, streaming services used this strategy by getting to know their customer so well that the recommendation algorithm generates value for the end consumer leading to phenomenon like binge watching (Pilipets, 2019).

The "as a service" model even extended into the infrastructure part of the internet, with platforms and infrastructure being rented instead of acquired. Latest studies show that even the acceptance of "product-service-systems" in which end users rent even personal devices such as phones is gaining acceptance (Raihanian Mashhadi et al., 2019), with sustainability and lifecycle management being important decision factors (Zheng et al., 2019). It can be concluded that subscription models will likely continue to thrive and substitute other types of ownership.

The infrastructure of the internet

The backbone of the internet relays on an intricate system of computer hardware and software. This system has evolved and continues to evolve together with the internet and will only become more complex with the introduction of IoT and the Internet of Everything and the related explosion in the number of devices. While the sale of hardware can also be seen as eCommerce and the sale of software as sales of licenses and later subscriptions, it is important to acknowledge that revenues from infrastructure are on one side driven by the development of the internet, but on the other side often an investment with a different motivation then providing a product or service via a new distribution channel. Hence, they should be recognized as a separate revenue type because these revenues would not exist in any form without the internet. An example clarifies the reasoning best: while physical goods have been in demand and sold offline since the existence of humanity, there would have been no demand for routers or other internet-enabling hardware, not for security software, had the internet not existed.

Combined forces for a shared economy

Having summarized the types of internet business models, one must observe that all models find their place in the definition of the "shared economy." The concept of the shared economy presents four sub-business models: subscription, transactional, unlimited platform, and commission-based (M. Ritter & Schanz, 2019), with all four being represented as part of the revenue models. Transactional represents the eCommerce space, unlimited platforms, and commission based to represent the marketplaces and their subsequent developments, while subscription is self-explanatory. The internet has not only influenced our technology but our society as a whole because its instantaneous and transparent nature effectively changed the idea of trust (e.g., Airbnb enabled people to sleep in strangers' apartments) (Kong et al., 2020) while enabling a never expected level of sustainability (Curtis & Lehner, 2019).

2.3 Increasing Importance of Internet-driven Businesses

With the types of revenues that the internet is enabling defined, it is worth looking at the future of software and computing-based technology and assessing the importance of connectivity and, implicitly, the internet for these future technologies. This sub-chapter is important as it tries to demonstrate the future applicability of the results and methodology of this study, as today's early-stage internet industries will be tomorrow's mature industries, and the stakeholders will face the same dilemmas.

Gartner, a well-known technology research company, provides an always refreshing overview of upcoming technologies every year based on the detailed industry reports their industry experts write (Perri, 2022). Fig. 2.11 presents the latest Hype Cycle for emerging technologies, published in August 2022.

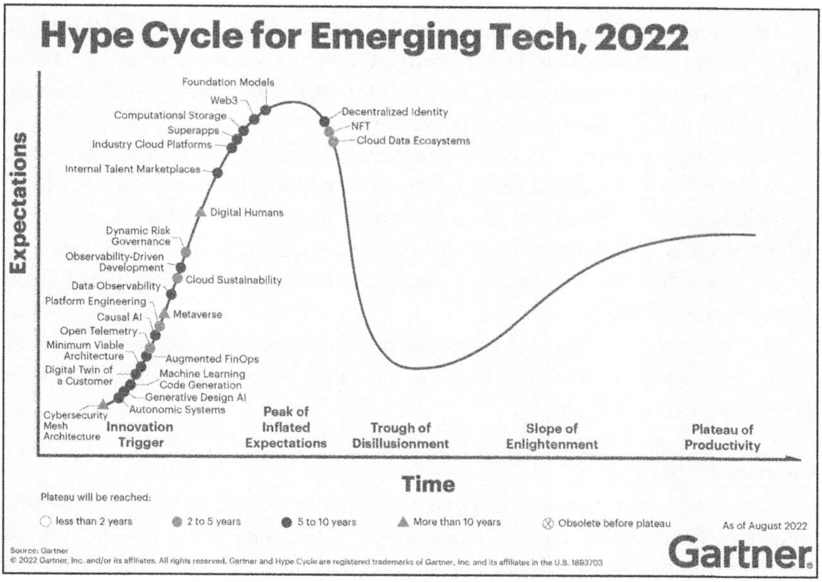

Fig. 2.11 Hype Cycle for Emerging Tech, August 2022 Gartner (Perri, 2022)

While some technologies are developments of existing technologies such as: cybersecurity mesh architecture, augmented finOps, minimum viable architecture, openTelemetry, platform engineering, data observability, cloud sustainability, observability-driven development, dynamic risk governance, internal talent marketplaces, industry cloud platforms, superapps, computational storage, and cloud data ecosystems, with most even being categorized as "optimized technologist delivery" by Gartner (Perri, 2022) other technologies have a significantly higher chance of disruption. Such technologies with potential should be discussed in detail, especially in light of the relevance of the internet as a whole and the relevance of the internet for these technologies.

Software and computing technologies with high potential for disruption:

Generative (design) artificial intelligence

Represents AI that can "generate novel content, rather than simply analyzing or acting on existing data" (Gozalo-Brizuela & Garrido-Merchan, 2023). While ChatGPT has received vast attention over the last months and even managed to become a "cultural sensation" (Thorp, 2023) because it can generate relevant output even when asked difficult questions on complex topics and conclusions for the finance industry (Dowling & Lucey, 2023) or summaries of healthcare papers (Aydın & Karaarslan, 2022), there are numerous other generative AI tools across at least eight groups as identified by Gozalo-Brizuela and Garrido-Merchan (Gozalo-Brizuela & Garrido-Merchan, 2023).

Even though generative IT must not necessarily be internet based to be useful, as the algorithm and the data required can be stored locally, the technology benefits immensely from the ability to run centrally in the cloud and deployed easily, making it fairly internet dependent for large-scale applications. Consequently, it can be concluded that this industry can be analyzed using a similar framework as the one in this study.

The "machine learning code generation" and "foundation models" segments which are addressed later by Gartner, can also be seen as sub-segments or dependencies of this segment.

Autonomic systems

As defined by Gartner are examples of "accelerated AI automation" that are self-managing (Perri, 2022). Despite representing a wide range of potential systems, autonomy implies that it should not necessarily rely on external connectivity to work. The concept is, however, established at such a high level of abstractness that it is difficult to assess if business models and devices will be internet dependent. It is important to mention that many such devices will likely also rely on M2M communication which implicitly will make them internet and connectivity dependent.

Digital twin

The concept appears in various forms, however, Chen defined it as encompassing virtually all forms. It was defined as a "computerized model of a physical device or system that represents all functional features and links with the working elements" (Chen, 2017). This concept addresses the "challenge of seamless integration between IoT and data analytics" (Fuller et al., 2020). Fuller et al. showed, based on a wide literature review, that digital twins can be used for a multitude of applications such as smart cities, manufacturing, and healthcare, while Liu et al. demonstrated that it could be used at all stages in manufacturing and across the life-cycle of the product (M. Liu et al., 2021). Jones et al. even characterized the life-cycle aspect as the 13 main characteristics of digital twins (Jones et al., 2020).

Considering the wide range of applications, it is also very difficult to assess the level of internet dependence of each potential business model using this technology. While some business models will likely be connectivity dependent, there are multiple scenarios in which a company can play a role in this segment without being dependent on the internet.

The idea of the "digital twin of a customer," as presented by Gartner, takes this application to another level by attempting to "twin" the behavior of a customer (Perri, 2022). The conclusion relating to all digital twins should apply to this unique field.

Causal AI

An AI that "identifies and utilizes cause-and-effect relationships" (Perri, 2022) to improve the quality of predictions from more simple models. Despite this type of AI differentiation from an application perspective from the generative AI, it will likely be implemented with a similar level of internet dependence and central deployment.

Metaverse

Although the idea of a metaverse being publicized by Facebook while renaming itself to "Meta" (Isaac, 2021), the idea of a "synthetic environment linked to the physical world" (Lee et al., 2021) was first devised by Stephenson as part of a sci-fi novel in 1992 (Stephenson, 1992) who depicted it as a "massive virtual environment parallel to the physical world" (Lee et al., 2021). A metaverse relies on connectivity and interactivity at its core, making it fully dependent on a platform such as the internet.

Lee et al. describe the metaverse as an "immersive Internet" and demonstrate that the metaverse depends on several enabling technologies: Extended Reality, User Interactivity, AI, Blockchain, Computer Vision, IoT and Robotics, Edge and Cloud computing, and future Mobile Networks (Lee et al., 2021) essentially making the metaverse the fabric that allows these technologies to coexist. Lee et al. even propose the concept of duality, which is the evolution of digital twins into the "co-existence of physical-virtual reality" (Lee et al., 2021), linking the concept of digital twins to the metaverse as well.

It is safe to assume that if the metaverse as technology flourishes, the involved businesses will be internet-driven independent if the metaverse turns out to be a new type of social network or a realm comprising most aspects of life as hypothesized by many.

The technology summarized under the concepts of Virtual Reality and Augmented Reality is an integral part of the metaverse, with an increasing number of experiences in existence today implying that treatment of these technologies similar to the metaverse is recommended (Han et al., 2022).

Digital humans

Despite being to some extent similar to the concept of digital twins and also the metaverse, "digital humans" focuses on the "personality, knowledge and mindset of a human" (Perri, 2022). While the concept has existed for over ten years and has been broken down into multiple parts such as body, senses, mind, communication, and embodiment (Burden & Savin-Baden, 2019) and while a multitude of companies focuses on simulating selected aspects, there is a long way to simulate a personality and mindset.

It is difficult to assess the dependency on the internet of technology as a whole, as business models can take on various forms at various stages in the individual value chains. Let us take as an example a company simulating the physical body of a human for fashion design purposes. While companies can benefit from implementing the product via the cloud, however, it is not required as the computation of complex 3D models is often done locally today. Such a business model would qualify as part of the "digital humans" technology.

Blockchain and Web 3.0

As Sherman et al. highlight in their paper "On the Origins and Variations of Blockchain Technologies," the idea of a blockchain originated from David Chaum's Ph.D. thesis "Computer Systems Established, Maintained, and Trusted by Mutually Suspicious Groups" from 1982 (Sherman et al., 2019) in which Chaum describes a system in which computers can be "trusted by groups who do not necessarily trust one another" (Chaum, 1982) despite Satoshi Nakamoto made the idea popular by Bitcoin (Vlad Costea, 2020).

The blockchain has gained traction over the last decade and managed to escape the cryptocurrency space by being regarded as a new form of trust (Hawlitschek et al., 2018) based on a distributed network of entities validating the chain while each block essentially locks the previous block from changes (Aste et al., 2017; Nofer et al., 2017).

The idea of blockchain is reliant on the internet because individual nods need to communicate in order to validate each other and the blockchain they are on, hence it is difficult to imagine a scenario in which a business model implementing this technology in its current form without the use of the internet.

Web 3.0 is a new iteration of the world wide web based on the idea of decentralized ownership and a blockchain-like structure (Chohan, 2022). Consequently, without diving deeper into these technologies, it can be concluded that the business models will be internet based. The concepts of "decentralized identity" and "NFT," later described by Gartner, imply the use of a blockchain and can consequently be treated similarly.

Internet of everything /internet of things

Similarly to AI or Metaverse, IoE, and IoT have gained popularity over the last years, driven by the explosion in the number of internet-connected devices and technologies such as 5G. The main difference between the two terms is that IoE encompasses "four components: things, processes, data, and people", all "connected intelligently" (Vaya & Hadpawat, 2020), while IoT focuses on physical objects (Sakovich, 2023).

As Langley et al. show, the objects around us show an increasing level of smartness, enabling new business models and changing existing ones (Langley et al., 2021). Such objects can be categorized by the level of smartness and capabilities, going from being reactive to being adaptive, autonomous, and ultimately collaborative, with the level of smartness also adjusting the level of interoperability and ability to create "macro-level changes" (Langley et al., 2021). In addition to objects, IoE also takes into account topics such as "security, network congestion, privacy and consumption of energy" (Vaya & Hadpawat, 2020), with Masoud et al. demonstrating that IoE is already being implemented and many of the topics discussed above have already become relevant (Masoud et al., 2019). These technologies can practically be applied to anything as they connect virtually every object and create smart cities, another topic with extensive traction in the last few years (Camero & Alba, 2019).

Due to the nature of these technologies, the connection is the backbone enabling all functionalities essentially. It is safe to assume that most business models implementing, maintaining, or using the exponential number of connected devices will be internet driven. The concept of machine-to-machine communication is a fundamental part of the IoE and IoT (Rajagopal et al., 2022) as they enable the last level of smartness defined as "collaborative" (Langley et al., 2021) and can consequently be treated similarly.

Lastly, as Reis et al. demonstrate that the concept of the "Internet of Services" is also developing strongly and comprises areas of "infrastructure, service operation, business applications, and social applications" (Reis et al., 2022) effectively also connecting the tangible idea of everything as a service to the IoE and implicitly showing the dependency of this component on the internet.

To conclude the chapter, it is worth summarizing the conclusions. Of the eight software and computation technologies with the potential to disrupt, five will defiantly rely on the internet (Generative AI, Causal AI, Metaverse, Blockchain and Web 3.0, Internet of Everything /Internet of Things), making all business models built around these technologies internet enabled while the remaining three (Autonomic Systems, Digital Twin, Digital Humans) can benefit from the internet, however not all business model will be internet dependent.

Technologies such as 6G, Quantum Computing, and Robotics were excluded as they make up the internet's infrastructure and are building the backbone of the internet-driven business model.

It can be concluded that the framework and the conclusions of this study will likely apply to a wide extent to a multitude of future technologies making the study and its conclusions highly relevant to tomorrow's entrepreneurs and stakeholders in future internet-enabled business models.

Literature Review: Research Hypotheses and Methodology

3

With the risk of stating the obvious, a thorough literature review of similar papers and studies is a good start to understanding past researchers' methodologies, hypotheses, and conclusions. While various books, studies, and papers were used during the study and cited accordingly, the following pieces of research influenced the overall approach of the study.

3.1 Relevant Scientific Literature Review: Learnings

This chapter provides an overview of the main resources that helped define the methodology, together with a summary of the goals, findings, limitations, and learnings:

Andreas Schreiner—Equity Valuation Using Multiples: An Empirical Investigation (Schreiner, 2007):
Goals: The study tries to close the gap between "the widespread usage of multiples in valuation practice and the deficiency of relevant research." The study breaks down the underlying drivers of various multiples and tries to close the gap between intrinsic and relative valuations. It also explores the idea of two-factor multiples valuations combining "book value and earnings multiples" as well as the idea of comparable companies.
Relevant findings: "1) equity value multiples outperform entity value (Enterprise Value) multiples; 2) knowledge-related multiples outperform traditional multiples in science-based industries; and 3) forward-looking multiples, particularly two-year forward-looking P/E multiple, outperform trailing multiples. The results suggest using a preferably fine industry definition for the selection of comparable firms."

A. Trusculescu, *Business Valuation Across the Industry Life Cycle*,
https://doi.org/10.1007/978-3-658-49126-0_3

Limitations: While the study provides extensive literature research in the field and uses a wide range of multiples and analyses such as EqV vs. EV multiples, trailing vs. forward multiples, and knowledge-related vs. traditional multiples, the study used a cross-sectional analysis, peer vs. industry tests to determine the reliability of multiples and fairly standard industry classifications. However, these topics are addressed in the current study with the limitation that the theoretical background will be more limited.
Learnings: The conclusions can be used to design the current study better and ensure that both equity, as well as entity value multiples are included, trailing and forward-looking multiples are included, depending on the data availability, inclusions of some knowledge-based multiples, and finally ensure that all relevant multiples are adopted. Furthermore, some of the sources used by the study can be useful for this study.

Arif Harbott—What drives Internet company valuation?—A business model approach to Internet value drivers (Harbott, 2012):
Goals: "This research aims to determine what drives market valuations for Internet companies and to discover whether value drivers vary across the different types of business models," mainly: 1) identify the value drivers; 2) create a categorization of internet business model and 3) understand if different models have different drivers
Relevant findings: The author concluded that "revenue is the dominant driver of Internet market value", however, when split into categories or clusters, "each category had unique value drivers" with a "combination of financial and non-financial." The author also mentioned that the internet seems to go through "different phases" regarding drivers.
Limitations: The study focuses, similarly to other studies, on a cross-sectional analysis instead of focusing on the evolution of bases and drivers. Additionally, only a group of 71 companies from the Nasdaq was included in the study, making it fairly limited.
Learnings: Firstly, the study provides a conclusion at a certain point in time that can be compared to the conclusions of the current study. As the study was performed in 2012, it covers a point in time that will also be part of the current study. Additionally, types of multiples and drivers are used to confirm the data that will be covered by this study with the limitation that traffic data, which despite being inquired via multiple databases, can not be obtained and used to verify the importance of this type of variables on the bases and drivers of valuations.

Jing Liu, Doron Nissim, and Jacob Thomas—Equity Valuation Using Multiples (J. Liu et al., 2002)
Goals: The overall goal of the study is to "examine the proximity to stock prices of valuations generated by multiplying a value driver (such as earnings) by the corresponding multiple, where the multiple is obtained from [...] a group of comparable firms". It essentially looks at multiples as a stock price predictor compared to peers. It also accounts for trailing and forward-looking multiples and data.
Relevant findings: The study concludes that forward earnings "explain stock prices remarkably well," with pricing differences within 15%. They also concluded that forward earnings were the best metric, with trailing earnings second, cash flow and book value metrics third, and sales last. The study also concluded that rankings were very similar across all industries analyzed.
Limitations: The study was performed before the year 2000, before the dot-com bubble, and before the internet took off. The companies included in the study will mostly reflect traditional industries since, at that time, internet companies did not have positive earnings. While the learnings are interesting, they mostly reflect mature companies and industries.
Learnings: The ranking described in the findings paragraph are highly relevant to the study. This study expects the ranking to be very different, if not almost inverse. Lastly, this is one of the only studies looking at the relevance of multiples over time covering a multi-year period.

In addition to scientific works and papers, various books have been used as references when confirmation is needed. The main books used are:

Joshua Rosenbaum, Joshua Pearl—Investment Banking: Valuation, LBOs, M&A, and IPOs 2nd and 3rd edition (Rosenbaum et al., 2013, 2020)
Rosenbaum's book on investment banking, which has been published in 3 editions already, is one of the key reference books used by professionals and aspiring professionals when it comes to simple, practical tips on how to valuations. It covers topics such as comparable company analysis, a form of valuation highly tight to this study, precedent transaction analysis, discounted cash flow valuations, leveraged buyouts, IPOs, and types of projects that investment banking practitioners must know.

Tim Koller, Marc Goedhart, David Wessels—Valuation: Measuring and Managing the Value of Companies 5ht and 7th edition, both published together with the management consulting company McKinsey (Koller et al., 2010, 2020)
Koller's book, published now in 7 editions, is another reference book that corporate finance professionals use as reference. The book is split into five sections,

covering 1) the fundamentals of valuation such as basic principals, risk cost of capital, and growth, among others; 2) core valuation techniques such as frameworks for planning, cost of capital, multiples, and valuation by parts; 3) advanced valuation techniques such as leases, taxes, pensions, and cross-border topics; 4) managing for value including topics such as strategic management, mergers and acquisitions, capital structures, investor communications, and others; and lastly 5) special situations covering emerging markets, cyclicality, valuation of banks, and the valuation of flexibility. Hopefully, the management of valuation across the industry life-cycle, which is the main topic of this study, will also become part of such a well-regarded compendia.

James R. Hitchner—Financial Valuation: Applications and models 4th edition (Hitchner, 2017)
Lastly comes Hitchner's financial valuation book, another reference book practitioners use. This book covers, in addition to standard topics already covered by the last 2, topics like databases, asset valuation, a dedicated chapter to discounts and premiums, valuation standards, the impact of various entity forms, employee stock options, business damages, various chapters on special industry valuations among others.

3.2 Relevant Scientific Findings of Aswath Damodaran

The corporate finance literature and researchers list would not be complete without Aswath Damodaran and his work. There is a reason why he has been named the "Dean of Valuation" (Harris, 2018). Mr. Damodaran is a professor of Finance at the Stern School of Business at New York University, teaching mainly corporate finance and valuation since 1986 (over 35 years) (Damodaran, 2022). In addition to having published several books such as Damodaran on Valuation, Corporate Finance: Theory and Practice, Investment Valuation, and The Dark Side of Valuation, Mr. Damodaran also maintains a very wide website entitled Damodaran Online (accessible via http://www.damodaran.com) which has been active since 1998 and publishes a wide range of resources in the area of corporate finance and valuation and a blog with over 23 million views at the time of writing accessible via https://aswathdamodaran.blogspot.com where he also publishes opinions and short articles on various related topics.

Table 3.1 Summary of Aswath Damodaran's view on the stages and important factors in the corporate life cycle (Damodaran, 2018a, 2018b) summarized and simplified by the author

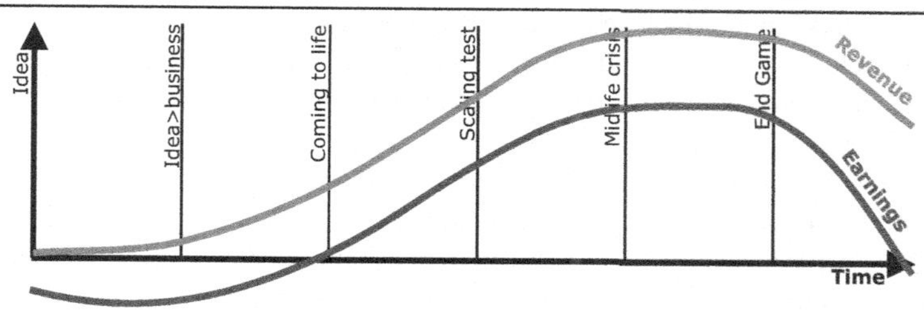

Growth stage	Stage 1 Start-up	Stage 2 Young grow.	Stage 3 High growth	Stage 4 Mature grow.	Stage 5 Mature stable	Stage 6 Decline
Description	Idea that meets unmet demand	Business converting idea into business	Building the business with a focus on scale	Growing the business with a focus on profitability	Defend business from competition	Scale down business as market shrinks
Cash flows						
FCF	Negative	Negative	Cross over to positive	Positive and growing	Positive and stable	Positive and declining
Invest. focus	Upside focused	Max. value for growth	Scaling investing	Defensive investing	Maintenance investing	Divesting
Financing	All equity (private)	All equity (public pos.)	First debt capacity	Expand. debt capacity	Benefits from debt	Pay down debt
Dividend	Need cash from eq. inv.	Cash needs multiplies	Move tow. sufficiency	Positive net cash flows	Excess free cash flows	Cash flows + sale of assets
Largest business issue, narrative and management s job						
Biggest issue	Lack of capital	Allocating capital to best project	Balance existing and new invest.	Live with less attractive investments	To much capital	What to pull first
Narrative	How big narrative?	How plausible narrative?	How profitable narrative?	How scalable is the narrative?	How sustainable is narrative?	Is there a happy ending?
Mngt s job	Tell a compelling and plausible story with potential	Stay consistent in word and actions with story	Start delivering number to back-up story	Keep narrative in sync with numbers	Adjust narrative to life cycle stage	Act the age of the company
Valuation metrics and drivers						
Pricing Metrics	EV/Market Potential, Cash Burn	EV/User, EV/User Intensity	EV/Sales	PEG	PE, EV to EBITDA	BP, EV/Invested Capital
Pricing Measure	Market size, Cash, Cash access	Number of users, intensity	User engagement, revenues	Revenue growth rate, Earnings	Earnings growth, RoC	Asset liquidity, cash flows

One area in which Mr. Damodaran has spent significant time in the last years was that of the corporate life cycle. Table 3.1 summarizes the most relevant views and inputs Mr. Damodaran has published via different relevant media for the study. It is to be noted that the valuation metrics and drivers named are also consistent with past writings of the author of this study and the assumptions of this study.

A good summary of Mr. Damodaran's work on this topic is available as a half-hour lecture that he held at the Nordic Business Forum in 2018 (Damodaran, 2018a, 2018b). The four main messages of this lecture can be summarized as such: 1) companies go through life cycles like human beings—get born, mature, and decline—and "like human beings companies do not like to age [...] and fighting it is the most dangerous thing a company can do", 2) "focus of companies needs to change as they age" with corporate value "being destroyed by companies not acting their age [...] and companies keep buying into face-lifts over and over again", 3) "valuation can never be just about the numbers [...] it has a story embedded in it, and [...] the balance between story and numbers changes as the company matures", and 4) the skills of CEOs should match that of the stage in which a company is (Damodaran, 2018b).

The two most relevant observations for this study and also one of the reasons this study was designed to look at valuation across the industry life cycle are observations 2 and 3. Observation 2 states that "companies mature," their focus needs to change (Damodaran, 2018b), implying that also the basis on which the companies should be valued changes with their development. Observation 3 states that "valuation is never only about the numbers" and the "balance between story and numbers changes as companies mature" (Damodaran, 2018b), implying on the one side that not everything can be quantified and on the other side that numbers become more important as company ages. This observation has its roots in the ever idea of a business, that of generating profits for the owners and hence compensating for the investments, and implies that to some extent a valuation should be connected to profits once it has achieved a certain level of maturity.

While Mr. Damodaran's findings are consistent with the literature available, these findings are not entirely based on empirical studies. This study tries to at least partially confirm or infirm the changes in valuation across a portion of the corporate life cycle and implicitly particular industries, all while extensively using the intuitive idea that a corporate valuation has a "story" and "numbers" component.

3.3 Brief Corporate Valuation History and the Idea of Multiples

The idea of value dates back to Aristotle, who defined value as "the ability to satisfy wants" (Younkins, 2005) and identified two types of value: "use value" governed by the "desirability of a good" and that "exchange value" representing the "use value as communicated through market demand." Aristotle also introduces money as a medium of exchange (Meikle, 1994), effectively linking the two valuation types with a monetary value.

While the idea of discounted cash flow dates back to the industrial revolution when it helped facilitate the exploration of coal reserves (Brackenborough et al., 2001), it took until the 1930s for it to popularize, mostly likely driven by the stock market crash of 1929. In 1930, Irving Fisher published the book "The Theory of Interest," introducing widely the idea of delayed gratification and investment as well as the idea of discount rates and discounted cash flows (Fisher, 1930). Fisher's work was continued and applied to corporate valuations by John Burr Williams, who published in 1938 "The Theory of Investment Value," a 613 pages book describing the idea of intrinsic value and the "dividend discount model" (Williams, 1997), a model which lays at the very foundation of modern finance.

Despite being impossible to highlight the point in time when relative valuation has started to be used, as it simply compares the value of one item again the known value of similar items in the market relative to a dimension (e.g., revenue or EBITDA), it is fair to assume that with the development of business planning and discounted cash flow methods, the path to using financials as the relative measure was very short and obvious. In the 1970s also, the idea of EBITDA and alternative measures of profitability derived by going up the income statement emerged, with John Malone being often credited with popularizing the idea of EBITDA and the idea of cash flow. The main reasons for popularizing such a measure were the exclusions of taxes and the ability to use such a measure in discussions with both equity holders and lenders (Peter Lynch, 2023).

As professor Damodaran explains it, "multiples are just standardized estimates of price" (Damodaran, 2021) as they simply take the absolute value a company has in the market (either the value of equity or the value of the firm including other liabilities minus cash) and divides the value by some financial metric. Fig. 3.1 shows an overview of what multiples are possible, as explained by professor Damodaran in his lecture on relative valuation during the 2021 valuation course at NYU. In short, multiples help calculate a simple price per unit, comparable to EUR per KG, but by using EUR value per EUR of Revenue.

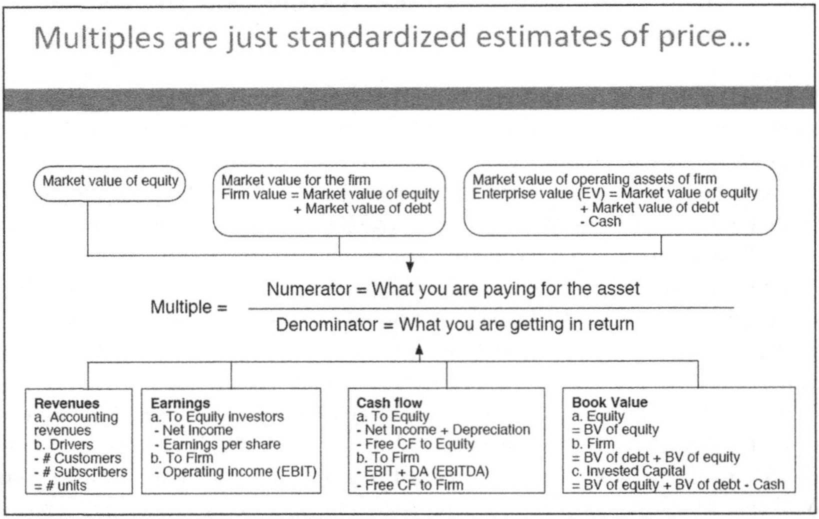

Fig. 3.1 Composition of valuation multiples (Damodaran, 2021)

3.4 The Research Scenario

Based on the research context described in Chap. 2 and the relevant literature identified in Sects. 3.1 and 3.2, this chapter formulates the hypothesis that will be tested in Chap. 7 using inferential statics and summarizes the proposed methodology for the study. The rationale behind each hypothesis will also follow the formulation of each hypothesis.

3.4.1 Formulation of the Research Hypothesis

Hypothesis 1: segmentation/ clustering of companies based on industries and business models underneath the "internet-enabled" business sector will increase the explanatory power of the multiples and drivers.

Rationale: as discussed in the previous chapter, several revenue and monetization models are part of the internet-enabled sector. These differences lead to vastly different economics, margins, financials, risk profiles, and applicable markets. Consequently, clustering the companies is expected to increase the explanatory power significantly. Based on this hypothesis, significant time has been invested in clustering the companies in over 20 clusters/ segments. The roots of this hypothesis lay at the epicenter of relative business valuation, as described in Chap. 4.

Hypothesis 2: valuation bases represented by the valuation multiples change over the development of the industry from being sales based to being profitability based.

Rationale: as companies and implicitly an industry develops, it goes from an idea and proof of case (implicitly story) to generating revenues and growing and later generating profitability, eventually reaching the declining phase where only what is left matters. This development should also be observed in the multiples that investors pay attention to the most over the development of an industry. As there is always one leading multiple, it is essential to focus on finding the best-fitting base and not on finding the best-fitting regression. It is to be noted that Damodaran proposes a similar development over the development phases of companies. While bases most likely continue to develop towards cash flow and ultimately book or liquidation value multiples, it is unlikely that any segment of the internet-enabled segment to have reached this stage, hence the hypothesis focused on the transition from sales to profitability.

Hypothesis 3: drivers of valuation represented by various financial metrics such as growth and margin also evolve over time from growth-focused to profitability and return-focused.

Rationale: Similar to valuation bases, the drivers of such bases will likely change with the life phases of the companies and the industry. It is likely that in the first phases, growth is most important, with margin becoming more important as a company and industry mature. Similarly to bases, Damodaran proposes a model similar to the hypothesis.

Hypothesis 4: while time is a good indicator for the development of an industry, additional metrics such as industry growth rates and industry margins could provide additional insights into the infliction points of Bases and Drivers.

Rationale: if most players in an industry experience decreasing growth rates or profitability ratios, likely, investor expectations will also be driven by industry-wide changes aligning the bases and drivers of individual companies with the development of the industry

3.4.2 Description of the Research Methodology

The methodology of this study can be split into five separate phases and has originated as a combination between the information and methodologies found in the existing literature and the innovative solutions required for such a broad study. The study methodology was built step by step, as presented in Fig. 3.2, and often comprised an investigative component. The exploratory nature of the research in the first phases has widened the objective drastically beyond the scope of the initial intention leading to a longer than expected timeframe and scope of work.

The study has started with a practice-rooted research question originating from discussions with founders and shareholders of internet-driven businesses. Based on hundreds of discussions, two questions have stuck with the author: "what is a value-maximizing strategy?" and "what is the optimal point for shareholder changes?". The first question sparks the arguably most crucial business strategy question of deciding between growth and profitability. Selling anything at a lower price helps sell more, in turn increasing revenues, however, to increase profitability, precisely the opposite needs to take place: higher prices. This question has even higher importance for businesses in the internet sector where fast scale is easier to achieve, and market position is more important than in traditional industries. The second question usually comes in the context of "When should I sell?" or "When should I buy?". While the discussion of market timing and economic cycles is well beyond the scope of this research, the practical observations show that once a particular industry reaches a certain level of maturity, the factors based on which investors value a business change.

While these two questions ignited the research, during the early stages of the research, it was observed that internet businesses represent an ideal natural experiment. Internet businesses have grown from early stage to maturity during the "data era" allowing precise observation and, due to the size and importance of the sector, it allows for significant clustering with each cluster representing an independent observation of industries.

The next phase intends to answer the questions by looking at the existing studies with the aim of understanding if there is a research gap between what is possible and what has already been done. The literature review has focused on three main areas: 1) finance literature looking on the one side at how such analyses can be conducted and actual case studies on internet-enabled businesses on the other side, 2) internet development literature to understand the technological evolution of the internet on the one side and the evolution of internet business models and their valuation on the other side, and lastly, 3) internet-enabled business models focusing on revenue and types and most importantly emerging future business model to assess the future relevance of such a study. A total of 114 peer-reviewed sources and 98 industry articles and publications have been found to have relevance to the current study, with the relevant conclusions and finds being related and cited in the current study.

Following the literature review, it has been recognized that no comprehensive study covering the entirety of internet-enabled businesses has previously been conducted, and the research questions do not have an obvious and already researched answer. Consequently, an exploratory research process has been initiated to understand the relevant internet-enabled industries and the main players. Following the review of several industry reports, certain directions have been identified that, while not being comprehensive, provided a good starting point for further research. Following the initial research, a detailed screening for relevant players across comprehensive databases such as Factset and Bloomberg has been conducted. Each screening usually revealed additional players that could come into question. The key challenge in this phase was to have a preliminary understanding of the business model of the included companies that could be internet-enabled without spending too much time with each company. 4,659 companies were identified, representing 10.5% of all publicly listed companies worldwide. This figure highlights the size of the study attempted.

Following the identification of companies, it was important to ensure that all companies have sufficient high-quality data available before spending significant time understanding business models and clustering businesses. Consequently, an initial download of key variables was performed to enable the filtering of the companies by some later described selected criteria. After using the filters, 2,892 companies were excluded, with 1,767 deemed fit to potentially be included in the study.

The next step in the research sample phase was to review each of the 1,767 companies individually to understand the revenue and business model and cluster such companies into segments or industries. This multi-year time investment was required to ensure that all businesses are truly internet-enabled and that peers included in each segment are sufficiently comparable. The main resources for this phase were, in addition to usual databases such as Factset, Reuters, and Bloomberg, each company's annual reports and other company materials.

The definition of the clusters took place in parallel with the review of each individual business model via exploratory research. Each company helped further define each cluster and vice versa. The main challenges in this phase were threefold. Firstly, companies often present themselves as what they want to be instead of what they are. Looking behind what is obvious requires, in addition, experience, often a detailed reading of the segment reporting, product descriptions, and indications concerning the value chain, which requires significant time. Secondly, many services companies present themselves as product/intellectual property companies. Services-focused business models have significantly different economics and often scale only with the addition of employees, while internet product models (e.g., SaaS) scale without hiring new employees. Lastly, the size of the clusters had to be managed such that they were sufficiently large to be suitable for statistical analysis while avoiding the mix of business models that are not fully comparable. This phase has excluded 864 companies leading to 903 companies that were included in the final study.

Building upon the previous steps, the study continued with downloading all required data for the analysis. Factset has been selected as the primary data provider, while the "Estimate" database was selected as the main data source, with details regarding the selection process presented in the relevant chapter. The study covers the period 2007–2021, which represents, on the one side, about half of the relevant history of the internet-based sector and, on the other side, the period since the last major financial downturn in 2007–2008, including the COVID-19 caused turmoil. The period covers one large economic cycle in addition to the movements driven by the COVID-19-induced central banks' policy which increased liquidity significantly and consequently influenced the valuation levels of all listed companies.

As part of the study, it was also decided to use ten separate timeframes (e.g., LTM, NTM, FY 0) with weekly observations for each individual metric to reflect a wide range of both past and future financials at the time of each observation. The weekly frequency represents an excellent middle ground between too much data and the granularity of observations. In total, 17 financial indicators and 3 valuation metrics were downloaded for each company on a weekly basis representing 173 individual metrics and 51 million observations.

The downloaded data was adjusted for continuity (small gaps in financials were bridged) before a complex processing endeavor combining Microsoft Excel and the data analytics platform KNIME was started. While the entire process is detailed in the respective chapter, it can be noted that it resulted in a dataset comprising 13 valuation metrics across 128 bases, 24 financial indicators across 216 drivers, and 6 industry drivers representing in total 350 variables and 97 million observations.

The next phase of the research focused on analyzing the data from descriptive and inferential perspectives. The descriptive part aims to provide, in addition to a deep understanding of the data, the quantitative data points industry professionals, management teams, and shareholders in various analyzed industries expect from such a research paper.

Setting up the inferential statistics model presented a few challenges as financial data has some particularities. Firstly, to understand the leading bases and drivers in each period, the analysis of each period had to be "ringfenced" from the other periods making time-series type analysis irrelevant. The study aims to identify the best multiples and drivers in each period and observe the development over time in bases and drives, not to find the best-fitting regression. The reason for this requirement is the binary nature of business strategy. As discussed at the beginning of this sub-chapter, growth vs. margin is the most crucial strategic business decision companies with internet-driven business models face, making optimizing strategies for many parameters impossible. Secondly, the model needs to be able to work with variables that are often highly related to each other, creating a case of multicollinearity. Beyond the evident connection between variables varying only due to different timeframes, financial indicators often move in similar directions. To exemplify, a company with growing revenues and constant margins will also show the same relative amount of growth in EBITDA and other profitability measures. Including both a revenue and a profitability measure in the same analysis is difficult without affecting the predicting power of either of the variables.

The solution to both challenges was to use the same strategy as all similar studies and focus on the simple linear regression trying to find the best fit between multiples and drivers to understand the best-fitting pricing measure and drivers of such measures. The strategy resulted in 389k individual regressions for each industry. The analysis then focused on the top-performing regressions with sufficient observations, presented the expected relationship (e.g., higher growth correlated with higher valuation), and was statistically significant. The analysis yielded, in most cases, one or two leading multiples that, combined with some drivers, explained most of the valuation. In total, 8.5 million regressions had to be carried out to find the best-fitting ones.

The implementation of both descriptive and inferential statistics models required, in addition to the traditional Microsoft Excel functions and Pivot Tables also, the smart use of the INDIRECT function in combination with the more traditional functions. The final dataset was structured as a large industry and year-sorted matrix to enable the use of simple ranges via INDIRECT functions.

The methodology and implementation have been conducted in the structured manner presented and are consistent with other relevant methodologies and professional best practices. The five phases presented allow a logical breakdown of the study's goal while keeping related topics as part of the same phase.

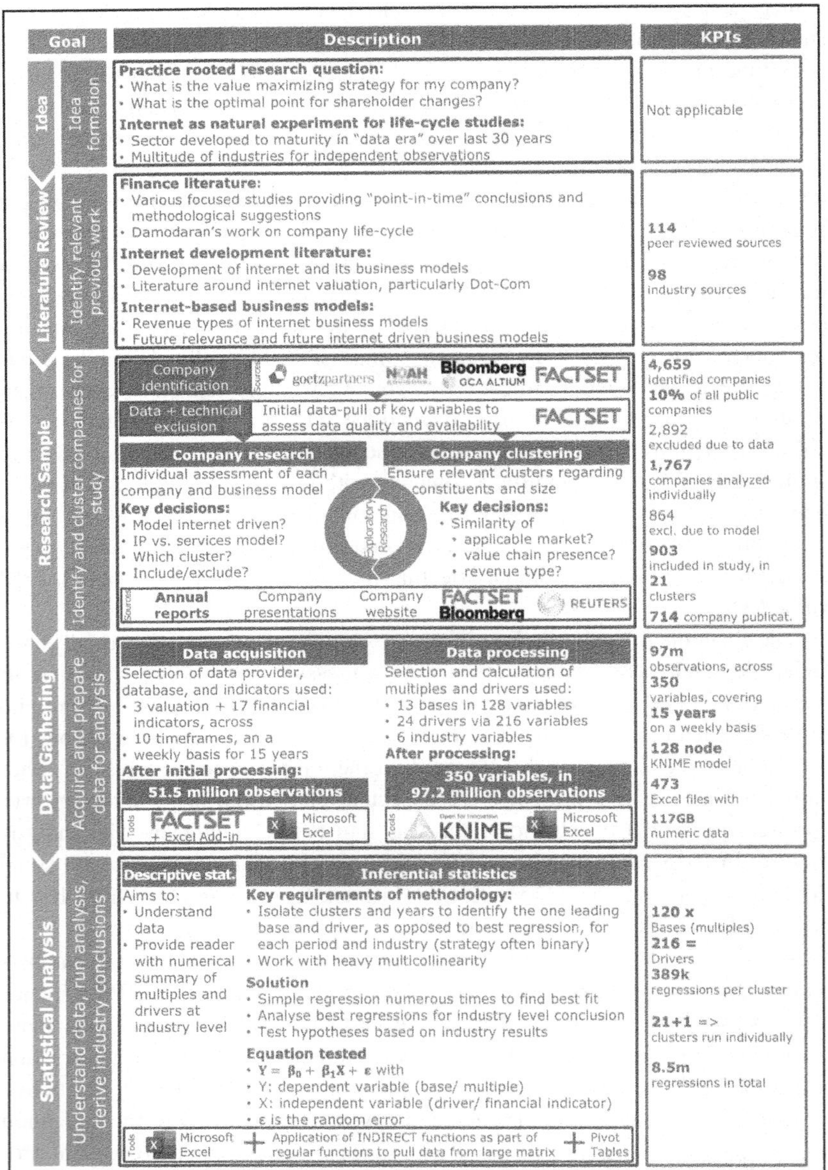

Fig. 3.2 Research methodology at a glance. (Own illustration)

Definition and Characterization of the Research Sample: The Considered Companies and Their Business Models

4

To draw a comprehensive conclusion, it is essential to ensure that all companies that can provide relevant data for the study are identified and included in the study. Furthermore, to draw conclusions on certain sub-industries, companies in the same peer group must be directly comparable in business model, market dynamics, and other characteristics described in this chapter. This chapter will use all available resources to identify and classify all relevant players in the target sector of internet-enabled businesses.

While significant time has been spent researching and understanding the best approach for such a comprehensive study and collecting and processing data, more than 50% of all time has been spent understanding the business models of each individual company. Of the total number of companies included, 4,659, 2,845 companies did not meet the necessary requirements. In comparison, the remaining 1,767 companies had to be analyzed individually by reading the relevant parts of the annual report to reach 903 companies to be included in the study. It is worth mentioning that over 10% of all listed companies worldwide have been considered in one way or another for this study, highlighting the breadth of the research.

Supplementary Information The online version contains supplementary material available at https://doi.org/10.1007/978-3-658-49126-0_4.

A. Trusculescu, *Business Valuation Across the Industry Life Cycle*,
https://doi.org/10.1007/978-3-658-49126-0_4

4.1 Companies Included in the Study—Definition of the Research Sample

This sub-chapter will explain the process of identifying relevant companies for the study and the selection process used to decide which companies should be analyzed in more detail by reading parts of annual reports, product sections on the website, or other more detailed materials.

The process started with the use of own past analyses, continued with reports published by M&A consulting companies and similar players, and lastly, by using various screenings in databases such as Factset as described below. This process was followed by a comprehensive data pull of key company information for an initial screening and assessment.

4.1.1 Sources Used to Identify Companies

Reports written as part of various projects and pitches and reports written by other industry experts have been analyzed to have a starting point and cover the most important relevant companies. This research has been complemented by detailed screenings in Factset. Reading the reports and spending time with the industry classification in Factset allowed the author to form an opinion on the possible peer groups. While finding companies for every industry segment described in the following sub-chapters would have been ideal, we must ensure that each group includes sufficient companies to be statistically significant. Main sources:

- Reports derived as part of working in the finance sector: while reports derived as part of projects and pitches are proprietary and confidential, the companies including are public, and hence the selection of players can be used as a starting point
- Reports of other M&A advisors and similar advisors, such as:
    - GCA Altium (in the meantime acquired by Houlihan Lokey) publishes sector reports focusing on Digital Media, Software, and Semiconductors. The Q3 2018 reports have been used for the study (GCA Altium, 2018a, 2018b, 2018c)
    - NOAH Advisors, similarly to GCA Altium, used to have a website providing multiples classified by vertical, which were also valuable (NOAH Advisors, 2018)

- Screenings were conducted in the Factset database using the screening function and the industry as the main criteria. Additionally, only public companies have been included. Industries used (any industry, main or additional):

  - [1352] Computer Communications
  - [1435] Recreational Products
  - [3210] Advertising/Marketing Services
  - [3300] Technology Services
  - [3310] Packaged Software
  - [3305] Data Processing Services
  - [3308] Information Technology Services
  - [3320] Internet Software/Services
  - [3445] Casinos/Gaming
  - [3550] Internet Retail
  - While some industries also include the sub-industries below, to ensure all relevant companies are included in the study, they were also included as screening criteria
  - A total of 4,497 companies were identified using this tool, with many of them being already found using the previous sources confirming that the right criteria have been used

- However, a screening like the one conducted in Factset has also been performed in Bloomberg, with no new relevant results. This fact is not surprising as all four large financial information providers: Bloomberg, Factset, Capital IQ, and Thomson, contain all publicly listed companies in developed markets and have a similar level of information

4.1.2 The Process for Selecting the Companies Included in the Study

The process of identifying companies resulted in 4,659 companies. To fully assess the potential of including these companies in the study, the next step was to download key company information from Factset. The information downloaded had to be broad enough to enable a qualified decision, however also practicable. To reach a balance, the following data items have been downloaded. It is important to mention that the process of selecting companies and the process of identifying and downloading the quantitative data for the study were two separate processes simply due to the multitude of data that can be sourced.

- **Company name**: the legal name of the company and security to ensure that the data downloaded is from the actual company and not from additional listings;
- **Website**: to enable additional research if required;
- **EV**: to ensure the company is large enough;
- **EqV**: to ensure the company is large enough and does not have low amounts of equity as part of the EV. Such companies could be distressed;
- **First trading date**: to know when the company had the IPO and consequently calculate the number of years since it has been trading;
- **Last price**: the current share needed to see how the company is currently trading compared to the 52 weeks high;
- **52 weeks high**: to assess how the company is trading vs. the high;
- **Last reported revenue in EUR**: to assess the size of the company.

Lastly, a full data download for the entire period covered by the study on a weekly basis, identical to the final data download, to get a glimpse of the amount of data points available for each individual company. The items selected were EV, EqV, Sales LTM, and EBITDA LTM, which are the most important for the study. This initial data download covered c. 769 weeks compared to the 783 weeks the final data download covered. This download will enable an educated decision on which companies are suitable for the study.

Following this data pull, a well-defined process has been set up to exclude companies with technical trading or data availability issues. The main reason for these exclusions is that spending significant time with each company (sometimes as much as one hour) is neither goal-oriented for the purpose of the study nor practicable to review nearly 5,000 companies in detail. The following filters were applied:

Technical factors:

- **Size**: companies with an EV or an EqV below EUR 10 m were excluded as such companies are either too small to be covered properly, have business models that are subject to additional risks, or are "fallen angels" that are usually restructuring cases; this factor leads to the exclusion of 608 companies;
- **Time since listing**: companies that have become public for less than three years were also excluded as such companies usually have sporadic trading prices. The reason for such sporadic behavior varies from lack of history to a less favorable than expected development during the IPO and lock-up periods in which insiders are not allowed to sell their shares. As regulations differ worldwide, three years is a good time frame for a newly listed company to normalize its trading. Lastly, a company listed only three years ago could have a maximum of 156 weeks of

data, very little compared to the 783 weeks that the study is covering; this factor led to the exclusion of 853 companies;

- **Short-term drop-in share price**: companies trading below 20% of their 52-week high were also excluded as such companies usually have problems and represent "fallen angels"; this factor led to the exclusion of 77 companies;
- Lastly, 276 companies showed a mixture of these three factors and were consequently excluded as well;
- Altogether, 1,814 companies were excluded during this stage, leading to 2,845 companies.

Data availability factors

- **Data availability:**using the Sales LTM and EBITDA LTM data pull described above, the companies were assessed if sufficient data was available. The "cut off" was 156 observations, representing three years of data. Companies with such little data on the main 2 data items will unlikely provide significant relevant observations for the study; this factor led to the exclusion of 784 companies;
- **Negative EV:** using the EV data pull, the companies were tested for negative observed EVs. Experiencing a negative EV is an anomaly as it is almost impossible for the sum of the debt a company owes and the equity to be negative; such situations are usually restructuring cases or companies before insolvency; consequently, companies with more than ten negative EVs observed were also excluded representing companies that experienced negative EV over periods longer than ten weeks; this factor led to the exclusion of 160 companies;
- Lastly, 134 companies experienced both factors and were consequently excluded as well;
- Altogether, during this stage, 1,078 companies were excluded leading to 1,767 high-quality companies that need to be assessed individually based on each individual business model.

Figure 4.1 presents an overview of the described steps and the outcome.

It is important to acknowledge that the 4,659 companies considered for the study represent 10.5% of all companies listed worldwide, and the 1,767 companies whose business model was analyzed in detail represent 4% of all companies listed worldwide.

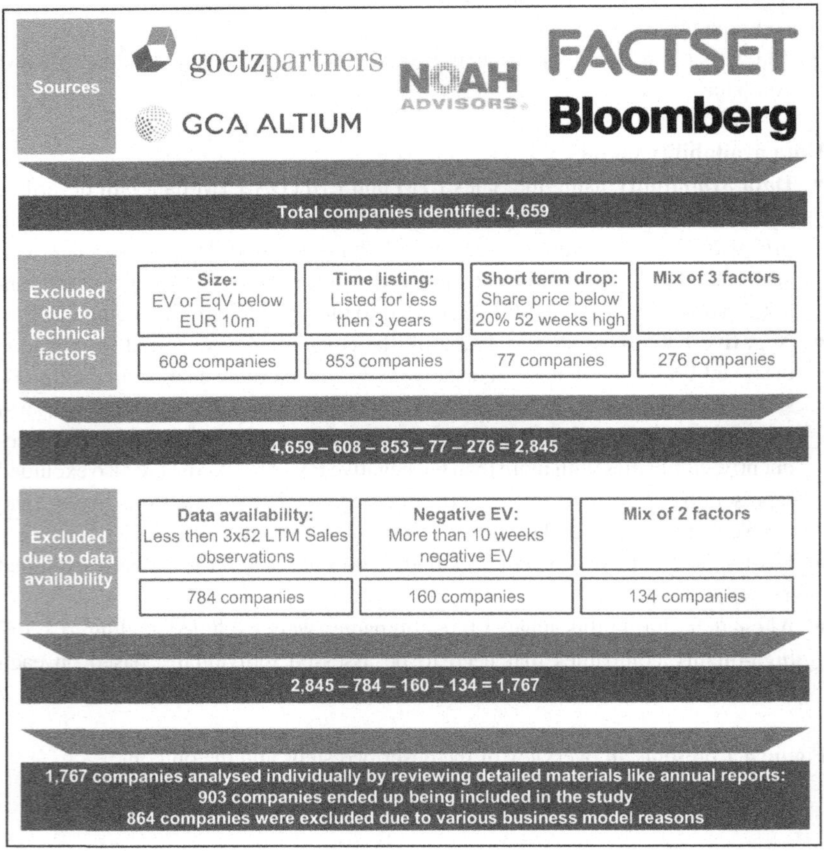

Fig. 4.1 Overview of the identifying and filtering of companies included in the study. (Own research)

4.1.3 The Process of Assessing Business Models and Categorization of Companies

The process of assessing, documenting, and summarizing the business model of each individual company required somewhere between 15 and 60 minutes per company. Various sources had to be considered, with the annual report representing the main source of information. A decision based on data available from databases such as Factset, Bloomberg, or Reuters was not possible, as the data available was not granular enough. Additionally, as companies included in the study are from over 50 countries reporting standards and annual report disclosure were often different, requiring a truly individualistic assessment.

Additionally, as the categories used were often adjusted based on the new information learned during the individual assessment of each company, multiple hundreds of companies required one or more reassessments to ensure a fit to the latest trading peer.

An interesting observation during this process was that while the end services and products delivered globally are comparable, the revenue and pricing types, industry structures, and value chains are often very different, making the task of categorizing companies very difficult. Additionally, it was observed that similar companies often deliver their products and services to different actors worldwide. A good example is China, where many companies have the government as a main customer making their product and internal processes vastly different from those in Western nations with private companies as clients.

The language was an additional challenge for companies in East Asia. Translation services such as Google Translate were used to better understand how such companies function.

The most important sources of insights used to understand the true business model of companies are as follows:

- Segment information: annual reports most often provide revenues by segment and sometimes even profitability (EBITDA or EBIT) which, on the one side, provide a description of the actual business lines and, on the other hand, provide a clear share of where the money is coming from. Segment descriptions are also very helpful when available. If one were to look at Amazon, for example, one would learn that it generates 88% of its revenues with the traditional business and 12% with Amazon Web Services, but only 40% of its operating income with the traditional business and 60% with Amazon Web Services (Amazon.com Inc., 2022). While this is an extreme example, understanding and recognizing such business model details helps classify businesses correctly. In this case, due to such large differences, it is safe to assume that the traditional business gives Amazon the reach it needs to monetize the Web Services, and it can consequently be classified as eCommerce.

- Business section in the annual report: Item 1 in US SEC-compliant annual reports is entitled "Business." Similar sections are available in most annual reports and describe the product and business model in a few pages. These explanations were very helpful in understanding the business model and the true nature of the various segments, even though this task required significant time investment.
- Product section on the website: a self-explanatory item, however the official product description, delivery models, and pricing helped in understanding the true nature of the business
- The companies' product websites: corporate and product websites are often separate, especially if consumer products are provided. Consequently, spending time on the websites dedicated to end-consumers can also help understand what the company offers
- Search engines: Lastly, searching on Google for "Company Name" + "SaaS" or "Software," or "Pricing" often yields results very helpful in understanding the company and its business model

The main question that had to be answered during the decision whether to include or not a company was: "Would this company exist if there was no internet?" and if the answer was "Yes," "Did the internet play a major role in the existence of this company?". Considering the thesis focusing on "internet-driven business models" and the natural experiment the internet presents, for the inclusion of a certain company in the study, the internet should be a driving force in its existence. While for some companies, the internet is simply a distribution channel, for others is a business model defining medium. If we take computer games or movies as an example, we can see that both existed and thrived before the internet picked up in importance, they were where just delivered via other media such as CDs and DVDs. If we look at online games or cloud-based software companies, we can quickly see that the entire value proposition is based on the existence of the internet. Consequently, to look at "internet-driven business models," one should include only the companies in the second category, one of the key research aspects of this study.

Another important aspect to consider when selecting companies is understanding the true business model compared to the presented one. The presented business model can differ from the true business model due primarily to marketing reasons. Marketing reasons range from increasing the valuation companies are valued at based on the perceived model (highly scalable software companies should be worth more than people-driven IT services companies, all things being equal) to rebranding strategies and efforts to attract different types of clients. The most often encountered difference is that of IT services companies trying to present themselves as software companies to achieve much higher valuations on the stock exchanges. Such companies had to be excluded from the study as they do not scale like software companies. Such IT services businesses can only grow by hiring more people instead of producing a highly scalable product that can be sold to numerous clients without adjusting it much. In addition to different growth and scale trajectories, IT services companies experience very different margin profiles compared to highly scalable software companies.

Following the detailed analysis, 903 companies met all the criteria and were included in the study. 864 companies were excluded based on business model criteria. The main reasons for excluding these companies were either not internet-based business models (the business would have existed and done well also without the internet) or were people-driven (businesses that scale with people are services companies that are also not necessarily internet dependent to provide their services). It is indisputable that all businesses, even the ones not included in the study, would have operated very differently had the internet not existed, however, the main question is if such businesses would have existed at all in order to be "internet driven."

4.1.4 Overview of Companies Included in the Study

The details of the analysis regarding the inclusion and classification of companies have been described in detail over 169 pages in the annex of this study, which can be found online. The annex has been structured as follows based on the logic described previously:

- ANNEX 1: Companies Included in the Study includes information on all 903 companies to be included together with the year of foundation, date of the first trade following the IPO, the country in which it is headquartered or generates the most revenue, a short description derived from the sources consulted, the classification and where relevant the main source of information used to understand and classify the business; the annex spans over 66 pages and is presented as a table
- ANNEX 2: Companies Excluded due to the Business Model includes all 864 companies analyzed in detail but excluded due to the business model together,

with the year of foundation, date of the first trade following the IPO, the country in which it is headquartered or generates the most revenue, a short description derived from the sources consulted, and where relevant the main source of information used to understand and classify the business; the annex spans over 66 pages as well

- ANNEX 3: Companies Excluded due to Technical Reasons, includes the names of the companies that were excluded due to technical reasons grouped in 4 tables, companies excluded due to size, companies excluded due to the time length of the listing, companies excluded due to an unusual drop in share price and companies excluded due to a mixture of factors
- ANNEX 4: Companies Excluded due to Data Availability, presents the companies excluded due to data topics summarized in 3 tables, companies excluded due to the limited data available, companies excluded due to negative Enterprise Values, and companies excluded due to a mixture of the two factors

While it is highly unusual to include such vital information for the study as part of the annex or to spend years preparing the annex, the true value of this study, in addition to the thorough research and data coverage, is the precise assessment and categorization (or clustering) of business models.

4.2 Business Models and Clustering of Companies in the Research Sample

Before trying to group, segment, or cluster the companies identified in 4.1, it is important to understand what sub-industries and business models researchers of the internet-enabled businesses models have previously identified and build on the previous knowledge. This chapter will try to identify all relevant types of segmentations identified by other researchers and, based on the previous segmentations and understanding of business models from Sect. 4.1, segment the companies for the purpose of this study.

4.2.1 Importance of Proper Business Model Segmentation

As Rosenbaum et al. explain in their book "Investment Banking: Valuation, Leveraged Buyouts, and Mergers and Acquisitions," "the selection of a universe of comparable companies for the target is the foundation for performing trading comps" (Rosenbaum et al., 2013, p. 15). While his explanation focuses on the peer groups used to value a particular company, it is equally important when trying to conclude on the valuation bases and drivers of certain sub-industries or the industry as a whole. Rosenbaum suggests a very structured approach based on ten dimensions, which are also relevant for the industry analysis which are summarized in Table 4.1:Business and financial profile framework (Rosenbaum et al., 2013, p. 16)

Table 4.1 Business and financial profile framework (Rosenbaum et al., 2013, p. 16)

Business Profile	Financial Profile
Sector	Size
Products and services	Profitability
Customers and end markets	Growth profile
Distribution channels	Return on investment
Geography	Credit profile

For the study, the "Business profile" dimensions will be the most important for two reasons. Firstly, the study focuses on the valuation bases and drivers across the industry life cycle, implying that adopting the industry perspective should be the focus when grouping the identified players to perform the analysis. While focusing on the business profile, the industry perspective tends also to group companies with similar economics and revenue models together since they are subject to similar dynamics. Secondly, most of the financial profile dimensions are included as part of the bases and drivers in the analysis and are consequently accounted for. Furthermore, further segmenting peer groups by financial profile dimensions will likely decrease the size of the peer groups to points where they will not be statistically significant anymore.

Sector

As defined by Rosenbaum, the sector represents the "industry or markets in which a company operates." Rosenbaum also acknowledges that dividing the sector into sub-sectors is recommended as the players in a peer group should generally have similar "drivers, risks, and opportunities" (Rosenbaum et al., 2013, p. 16). In the case of this study, the sector comprises companies that use the internet as the main enabler for their business model. As discussed, companies will have to be further classified into sub-sectors.

Products and services

Generally, companies that produce similar products or services can be compared to each other (Rosenbaum et al., 2013, p. 17). In the case of this study, the products and services of individual companies will also be important as some companies are not what they seem to be.

For example, Groupon is often regarded as a marketplace because historically, it acted as an intermediary between consumers and businesses trying to sell their services (e.g., restaurants, spas), while looking at the financial reports, a different picture can be seen. From a gross billing perspective, the company is indeed a marketplace, as "direct goods" account for only 30% of gross billing, with the rest being "Third Party"—goods and services where Groupon acts only as an intermediary. However, when looking at the same figures from a revenue perspective, the "direct goods" represent nearly 59% of revenues, making it a rather eCommerce company as opposed to a marketplace. This huge discrepancy is because Groupon can recognize the "gross billings" as revenues only when it assumes inventory risk (Barr, 2012). Before 2011, the company managed to recognize "gross sales" as revenues, however, it came under significant scrutiny from the market (De Chant, 2011) (De La Merced & Rusli, 2011). The company's website (arguably the main product of a company selling goods and services online), as shown in Fig. 4.2, clearly focuses on deals that are mainly "third party" instead of direct goods. Such situations need to be considered in detail in order for companies to be clustered based on their true business model.

Customers and end markets

Rosenbaum explains that "companies with a similar customer base tend to share similar opportunities and risks" (Rosenbaum et al., 2013, p. 17). Arguably, distribution channels should be discussed before defining a customer and a market, as the economics of B2B and B2C companies are very different (reason to be addressed below in distribution channel). Nevertheless, companies sharing the same customers or customer types will also share the same pressure from clients. However, one could argue that peers in direct competition will be relatively valued differently if one is the clear leader. These situations are very difficult to assess globally and require the researcher's judgment on a case-by-case or sub-industry by sub-industry basis.

In Rosenbaum's framework, end markets represent the industry in which products of a certain sector or sub-sector will be used. He sees this dimension as important for the B2B distribution channel as the examples given relate to industries (Rosenbaum et al., 2013, p. 17), however, in B2C, this dimension is also relevant, as not all B2C consumers are equal. Individuals from certain geographies might have higher purchasing power than other geographies, or even inside the same geographic region,

Fig. 4.2 Groupon's website (Groupon, 2018)

target customers of similar players can be different (e.g., price focused vs. quality focused).

Distribution channel

Rosenbaum defines "distribution channel" as "the avenues through which a company sells its products and services to the end user" (Rosenbaum et al., 2013, p. 17). While his formulation focuses on B2C distribution, including "wholesale, retail and direct-to-consumer," when analyzing internet-enabled businesses, it is very important to differentiate between shops selling their own inventory directly to consumers and marketplaces which are selling the merchandise of other merchants to the end customers. As the Groupon example describes, companies assuming inventory risk and marketplaces are fundamentally different. As Jack Ma, the co-founder of Alibaba (the largest marketplace in the world), put it once when discussing the difference between Alibaba and Walmart (the largest retailer in the world): "If you want 10,000 new customers, you have to build a new warehouse and this and that. For me: two servers" (Cook, 2015).

Geography

Rosenbaum's view on geography is that "companies that are based in (and sell to) different regions of the world often differ substantially in terms of fundamental business drivers and characteristics" (Rosenbaum et al., 2013, p. 18). He also tries to explain, based on various factors such as demographics and regulatory environment, why companies in the same line of business can have different valuations across different geographies. To identify trends in the valuation bases and drivers of internet-enabled businesses, controlling for geography could be important and lead to new findings, however, depending on the number of players in a sub-industry, one might not have the luxury of running separate analyses on separate geographies. Considering that Asia, in particular China, sees significantly stronger growth compared to other regions, a researcher might want to control for this, particularly. Geography can be included as an additional dimension based on the number of peers and other potential differences.

Size, profitability, growth profile, ROI, credit profile

While these dimensions are self-explanatory, they will be an important part of the bases and drives used by this analysis. Consequently, their meaning and importance will be addressed in the methodology section of the study. It is important to acknowledge that Holthausen published a very interesting paper on "pitfalls when identifying and using comparable companies" for "valuation with market multiples" purposes in the Journal of Applied Corporate Finance in 2012, in which he concluded that differences in cost of goods sold or SG&A, as well as other financial metrics, could impact the comparability of companies (Holthausen & Zmijewski, 2012). While for this study, the author will not have the luxury of segmenting companies also by margins and other financial metrics, what is possible is to calculate and attempt to use EBITDA before R&D or EBITDA minus CAPEX as these data points can be obtained via the same channels as the rest of the information.

4.2.2 Identification of Segments: Company Cluster Definitions

Before diving into the companies and their business model, it is useful to understand what kinds of segments, sub-segments, and business models exist that are internet-enabled in order to be able to understand the companies analyzed more quickly on the one side and on the other side to be able to put them in the correct cluster as efficiently and correctly as possible. While many authors have spent significant time categorizing internet business models, the best model was developed by Kenneth and Carol Traver, who, over a period of 20 years, has published sixteen editions of their "E-commerce: Business. Technology. Society." textbook, which has become a reference in the industry. For the purpose of this study, two versions will be used: the fifteenth edition, published in 2019, and the sixteenth edition, published in 2020 (Laudon & Traver, 2019, 2020). Kenneth Laudon and Carol Traver's categorization falls short from this research's perspective in two aspects: 1) a detailed model on the soft factors that define internet businesses and their characteristics and 2) a detailed categorization of internet-based software business models and applications. One must acknowledge that both shortcomings represent areas that go too far for a textbook focusing on eCommerce (a sub-segment of internet-driven business models), and consequently, the authors can not be criticized for this. Fortunately, three other authors came in and filled both gaps in research.

The first researcher is Karl Täuscher, who, in his working paper entitled "Business Models in the Digital Economy: An Empirical Study of Digital Marketplaces," spends significant time in understanding the characteristics of "digital business models" and goes as far as defining a framework with 21 attributes and multiple specifications for each attribute that are used for his study (Täuscher, 2022). Discussing the entire framework is well beyond the scope of this research, however, Täuscher's summary of the characteristics is highly relevant and useful.

To solve the second gap, significantly more research was required as multiple classifications and taxonomies are available, however, not all classifications are directly applicable to the available pool of companies. In this area particularly, the clustering was, in addition to being influenced by existing research, also significantly influenced by the author's professional experience and detailed research of the companies, essentially creating a feedback loop during the research which not only changed the classification of individual companies but rather the definition of clusters. The two best sources identified to use as inspiration for this part of the research were Höfer and Karagiannis' paper "Cloud computing services: taxonomy and comparison," which provides, in addition to an extremely detailed service tree for cloud computing, also a summary of the layers and types of software which are excellent as a starting point (Höfer & Karagiannis, 2011). Secondly, Forward and Lethbridge from the University of Ottawa provide in their paper "A taxonomy of software types to facilitate search and evidence-based software engineering" a very detailed break-down of the types of software by application which combined with the previous source and some further industry articles cemented the understanding of the types of software (Forward & Lethbridge, 2008).

Characteristics of online businesses

Starting the research with Täuscher's characteristics makes the most sense as these apply to both B2B and B2C companies. These characteristics mainly help answer the question: "Would this company exist if the internet had not existed?". The split between companies serving other companies and companies catering to end customers does not need to be documented as it is virtually explained by every researcher in this field and is also self-explanatory.

Täuscher's characteristics start with the level of connectivity, as this is the main USP of the internet; it allows systems to communicate (Täuscher, 2022). Seeing characteristics at the top of the list is not a surprise, as there are no internet-based business models that do not depend on connectivity. Asking the question if a business is dependent on connectivity is a simple way of already excluding a large number of companies whose business model is not internet dependent.

The list continues with "low geographic limitations," which, while valid, is not required for a business to be internet driven as language barriers and different supply chains in different countries can affect this aspect. It is, however, worth keeping in mind. The "low switching cost" characteristic only applies to B2C companies as B2B solutions often depend on complex infrastructures and databases, which are very difficult to migrate without disrupting operations. This is generally a key factor B2B software vendors put at the top of their priority list to maximize the LTV and customer stickiness. The following two characteristics, "high transparency of customer behavior" and "high transparency of firms," are difficult to be assessed externally as the information is internal and proprietary. However, these dimensions are simple to answer after understanding the business model.

The last three dimensions are very important and good generalizations of internet-driven business models: "low transaction costs," "opportunities for price discrimination," and "low menu costs" (Täuscher, 2022). These dimensions generally describe the ability of online businesses to deliver without significant transaction costs while being able to charge individual prices. With few exemptions, most

Characteristics of digital businesses	Description	Number of studies
High levels of connectivity between actors	Digital technologies serve as mediators and connectors between different parties leading to a higher connectivity between organizations and between firms' and users. This partly dissolves traditional firm boundaries	3 studies
Low geographic limitations	Digital technologies reduce the strength of physical boundaries; pure digital markets are global by design	6 studies
Low switching costs	Customers can switch businesses at a relatively low cost due to low search costs through accessible and comparable information	5 studies
Transparency of customer behavior	Businesses in the digital economy can capture a large amount of data and information about their consumers' behavior. More customer interaction, better data collection and analysis tools lead to high information about customers	3 studies
High transparency of firms	Customers and partners, in return, have more information on the focal firm since activities can be traced and retrieved more efficiently through digital channels. For instance, new "customers can inform themselves more easily about the experience of other customers"	4 studies
Low transaction costs	Transaction costs are lowered due to reduced coordination costs, low geographic barriers, and high information levels	2 studies
Opportunities for price discrimination	Price discrimination arises when a digital business charges different prices based on a consumer's willingness to pay. Internet enables firms to collect better information about consumer characteristics and WTP	3 studies
Low menu costs	Menu costs incur when a price is changed. Digital media allow changing prices at almost no cost. Low menu costs make it more cost effective to dynamically change prices online	1 study

Fig. 4.3 Characteristics of digital businesses and the number of relevant studies identified by Täuscher confirming the characteristics (Täuscher, 2022)

internet-driven businesses should show these characteristics. Fig. 4.3:Characteristics of digital businesses and the number of relevant studies identified by Täuscher confirming the characteristics (Täuscher, 2022) presents the eight characteristics identified by Täuscher as well as their description and the number of studies Täuscher identified confirming these dimensions.

Layers of cloud computing

Following the definition of characteristics of digital businesses, the next step is to define the software layers. The layers everyone in the research community uses originate from a paper written by Zhang et al. in 2010 entitled: "Cloud computing: state-of-the-art and research challenges" (Zhang et al., 2010) shown in Fig. 4.4. While it is not entirely sure if he was the first to propose this framework, everyone in the research community seems to be crediting this paper with this framework. Höfer and Karagiannis also use this frame in their paper on cloud computing services.

The framework has essentially four layers: hardware, infrastructure, platform, and application. Hardware represents the CPU, Memory, Storage, etc., while Infrastructure represents the combined hardware and the lowest level of software. These two layers are entitled by Zhang et al. the "Infrastructure as a service" (IaaS) layer. The next layer is the "Platform as a Service" layer which represents the databases and the software framework that run the applications. This is a particularly important layer as, on the one side, a very large application independent addressable market, and on the other side, applications can evolve to become platforms. Such an example is Salesforce which in 2010 was essentially seen as an application for CRM and has evolved in the meantime to become a platform whose implementation can be tailored to virtually any industry and company while allowing for sub-applications to be developed as part of its main platform.

The last layer is represented by the Software as a Service layer which essentially includes any application that is run centrally and distributed via the internet. This is essentially the tool that the end-user sees.

Understanding and differentiating between layers is essential for this study as layers have, on the one side, very different total addressable target markets and, on the other side, very different economics, making companies operating in different layers not comparable. A deep understanding is even more important when analyzing companies positioned between layers or evolved in a position such as Salesforce. This discussion of the total addressable market will become once more important when we try to further cluster the companies in the application layer.

B2C Business Models

This sub-chapter will dive into Laudon and Traver's 20-year work that will ultimately be used as a guiding hand for clustering any companies in the B2C segment. Luckily, Laudon and Traver also spent time clustering, describing, and providing some examples of B2C Business model enablers. While these are presented in Fig. 4.5, it is worth mentioning that some will become again relevant when looking at B2B models as any B2B provider is, one way or another, a supplier to a B2C/

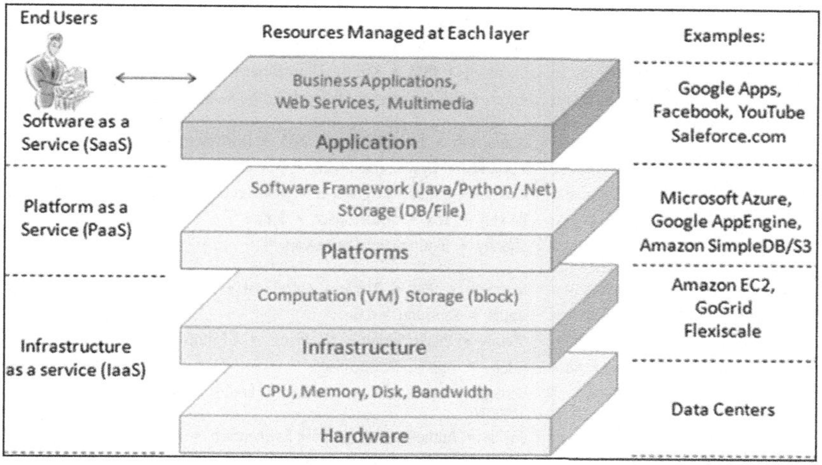

Fig. 4.4 Cloud computing architecture (Zhang et al., 2010)

end-customer company and hence an enabler. Also noteworthy is that most of the groups part of the enabler segmentation activate in the infrastructure and platform layers as defined by Zhang et al..

Laudon and Traver start clustering with web server hardware, software, and cloud providers. While hardware providers who are necessarily internet-driven will be excluded from the study (also the reason why Apple was also excluded early on), some of the web service/ cloud providers will end up being included in the infrastructure/ platform clusters of the study.

Hosting services will receive their own cluster as these businesses are the foundation of the internet. It is important to acknowledge that many players operate at the intersection between real estate and technology as they start with providing and setting up the locations of the data center all the way to proving the platform on which applications run. Domain name registration, while being an important segment, can have different characteristics as some players also provide hosting, while there are simple domain registration providers that do not sell infrastructure. Content delivery networks are to be treated similarly to site design companies. The various SME, Enterprise, and eCommerce platforms clustered separately by Laudon and Traver will definitely be included, however likely under an overarching platform cluster as there are few players for each sub-cluster. The streaming cluster will, dependent on the business model, also be treated like CDNs and domain name companies.

INFRASTRUCTURE	PLAYERS
Hardware: Web Servers	HP • Dell • Lenovo
Software: Web Server Software	Microsoft • IBM • Red Hat Linux (Apache) • Oracle
Cloud Providers	Amazon Web Services • Microsoft Azure • IBM Cloud • Google Cloud Platform
Hosting Services	Liquid Web • WebIntellects • 1&1 • HostGator • Hostway
Domain Name Registration	GoDaddy • Network Solutions • Dotster
Content Delivery Networks	Akamai • Limelight Networks • Amazon CloudFront
Site Design	Weebly • Wix • Squarespace • Jimdo
Small/Medium Enterprise E-commerce Platforms	Shopify • BigCommerce • YoKart
Enterprise E-commerce Platforms	Magento • IBM • Oracle • Salesforce • SAP • Intershop
M-commerce Hardware Platforms	Apple • Samsung • LG
M-commerce Software Platforms	Mobify • PredictSpring • Usablenet • GPShopper
Streaming, Rich Media, Online Video	Adobe • Apple • Webcollage
Security and Encryption	VeriSign • Check Point • GeoTrust • Entrust Datacard • Thawte • Intel Security
Payment Systems	PayPal • Authorize.net • Chase Paymentech • Cybersource
Web Performance Management	Compuware • SmartBear • Dynatrace
Comparison Engine Feeds/Marketplace Management	ChannelAdvisor • CommerceHub • CPC Strategy
Customer Relationship Management	Oracle • SAP • Salesforce • Microsoft Dynamics
Order Management	JDA Software • Jagged Peak • Monsoon
Fulfillment	JDA Software • Jagged Peak • CommerceHub
Social Marketing	Buffer • HootSuite • SocialFlow
Search Engine Marketing	iProspect • ChannelAdvisor • Merkle
E-mail Marketing	Constant Contact • Cheetah Digital • Bronto Software • MailChimp
Affiliate Marketing	CJ Affiliate • Rakuten LinkShare
Customer Reviews and Forums	Bazaarvoice • PowerReviews • BizRate
Live Chat/Click-to-Call	LivePerson • Bold360 • Oracle
Web Analytics	Google Analytics • Adobe Analytics • IBM Digital Analytics • Webtrends

Fig. 4.5 eCommerce enablers (Laudon & Traver, 2019)

The security and encryption cluster is a very important layer often dominated by dedicated hardware providers like Cisco. This cluster will be used in the study, and hardware providers will also be included as hardware, in this case, is just the way the service can be provided. Similarly, payment systems are an essential part of the internet with a very different and transaction-based business model and will consequently also be included and addressed separately.

The next clusters: web performance, marketplace technology, CRM, order management, and fulfillment, while different in functionality, are often provided by the same players. Depending on the number of players available, the study might either segment them separately or include them in an overarching segment comprising horizontal software or business software.

The next group of clusters: search engine marketing, e-mail marketing, and affiliate marketing, while being different segments, the overlap in providers will also exist very often combined with agency business that implements the tools and the content. As the border between such businesses is nearly impossible to be drawn, they will likely end up in separate clusters focusing on online marketing. Lastly, the three remaining segments: customer reviews, live chat, and web analytics, while being important, will likely be excluded due to the limited number of players in these segments.

Laudon & Traver continue their clustering by segmenting actual B2C business models, as presented in Fig. 4.6. The summary presents the seven overarching business models the authors have identified together with "variations," examples, descriptions, and revenue models. The simplicity of the framework should be acknowledged as it virtually clusters all B2C internet companies in only seven clusters while not giving the feeling of leaving anything significant out. The clusters are self-explanatory and will be ported into the structure of this study, with only a few required clarifications.

Inventory risk is the difference between an e-tailer (traditional eCommerce) and a market creator. eCommerce companies assume the risk of not selling an item, having acquired it already from the producer, while marketplaces do not own the item. "Market creator," as defined by Laudon and Traver, includes both the eCommerce-like players (e.g., eBay and Etsy) and true platform-like players like Uber and Airbnb. While not wrong, this combination presents a challenge as the business and monetization models are very different.

For the purpose of this study, travel companies will likely earn their own segment as they are different from the eBays of this world. Additionally, general and vertical portals often have different ways to monetize content, so a closer look will be required before putting all companies in the same cluster. Lastly, two segments that are missing from this structure are classifieds and customer acquisition. While these two segments seem to operate similarly, they are different and, if possible, will be analyzed separately.

B2B Business Models

For a full perspective on the B2B business models, a thorough analysis of Zhang et al.'s layers, the detailed interpretations provided by Höfer and Karagiannis based on Zhang et al.'s framework, Laudon and Traver's enablers, and Forward and Lethbridge's Taxonomy is required. While Zhang et al. layers and Laudon and

BUSINESS MODEL	VARIATIONS	EXAMPLES	DESCRIPTION	REVENUE MODELS
E-tailer	Virtual Merchant	Amazon Blue Nile Bluefly	Online version of retail store, where customers can shop at any hour of the day or night without leaving their home or office	Sales of goods
	Bricks-and-Clicks	Walmart Target	Online distribution channel for a company that also has physical stores	Sales of goods
	Catalog Merchant	L.L.Bean LillianVernon	Online version of direct mail catalog	Sales of goods
	Manufacturer-Direct	Dell Mattel Nike	Manufacturer uses online channel to sell direct to customer	Sales of goods
Community Provider		Facebook LinkedIn Twitter Pinterest	Sites where individuals with particular interests, hobbies, common experiences, or social networks can come together and "meet" online	Advertising, subscription, affiliate referral fees
Content Provider		Wall Street Journal Netflix Apple Music	Offers customers newspapers, magazines, books, film, television, music, games, and other forms of online content	Advertising, subscription fees, sales of digital goods
Portal	Horizontal/ General	Yahoo AOL MSN Facebook	Offers an integrated package of content, search, and social network services: news, e-mail, chat, music downloads, video streaming, calendars, etc. Seeks to be a user's home base	Advertising, subscription fees, transaction fees
	Vertical/ Specialized (Vortal)	Sailnet	Focuses on a particular subject matter or market segment	Advertising, subscription fees, transaction fees
	Search	Google Bing	Focuses primarily on offering search services	Advertising, affiliate referral
Transaction Broker		E*Trade Expedia Monster Travelocity Orbitz	Processors of online transactions, such as stockbrokers and travel agents, that increase customers' productivity by helping them get things done faster and more cheaply	Transaction fees
Market Creator		eBay Etsy Uber Airbnb	Businesses that use Internet technology to create markets that bring buyers and sellers together	Transaction fees
Service Provider		Envoy Wave RocketLawyer	Companies that make money by selling users a service, rather than a product	Sales of services

Fig. 4.6 B2C business models (Laudon & Traver, 2020)

Traver's enablers have been discussed, the additions of Höfer and Karagianni and the Taxonomy of Forward and Lethbridge need to be discussed in more detail.

Höfer and Karagiannis build on Zhang et al.'s framework: IaaS-PaaS-SaaS, by describing the layers in detail and adding a few dimensions to consider B2B business models. An overview of the dimensions proposed by Höfer and Karagiannis can be seen in Fig. 4.7.

Höfer and Karagiannis introduced very early in the technology tree the aspect of "open source" compared to proprietary software, which despite being less relevant for Höfer and Karagiannis at the time of writing, it has increased in relevance over the past years. Open source is important in the context of this study as companies that rely on own- or third-party open-source software to provide their services usually have vastly different business models compared to proprietary software providers and are more geared towards services than other pure software providers. An example of such a company is Suse. The next level (user group) has been discussed to separate B2C and B2B.

The next two levels are also particularly interesting for this study: payment system and agreements. The payment system layer acknowledges that even in an everything-as-a-service world, there might be different monetization methods, which need to be considered when analyzing and clustering business models. The agreement level is also important for this study as it questions what customers pay for: just the software, software and services, just service (e.g., open source).

The next layers are less important as they are technical. The same can be concluded for the IaaS and the PaaS levels. The SaaS levels are again relevant as they touch upon the application type provided. Forward and Lethbridge's taxonomy must be accounted for to fully define this framework.

ANNEX 5 presents the entire taxonomy as prepared by Forward and Lethbridge (Forward & Lethbridge, 2008). While it is beyond the scope of this research to discuss all items, it can be observed that the layers infrastructure and platform are separated similarly to the other frameworks but, in this case, under "Systems software" as independent sub-groups. "Strategic and operations analysis" under "Business-oriented software" build up the various business functions and processes that all businesses, independently of the sector in which they operate, require, confirming the assumption that these sub-groups are comparable and, if not sufficiently differentiated players exist, they can be grouped under an umbrella entitled "horizontal software." Also important is to observe that sector-specific tools have been grouped under "Corporate management," confirming that such tools can also be grouped under "vertical software" if not sufficiently separated players for various verticals exist.

The entire taxonomy needs to be used as a reference while reviewing the business models to ensure that companies clustered together are as comparable as possible while ensuring that sufficient players are included in each cluster.

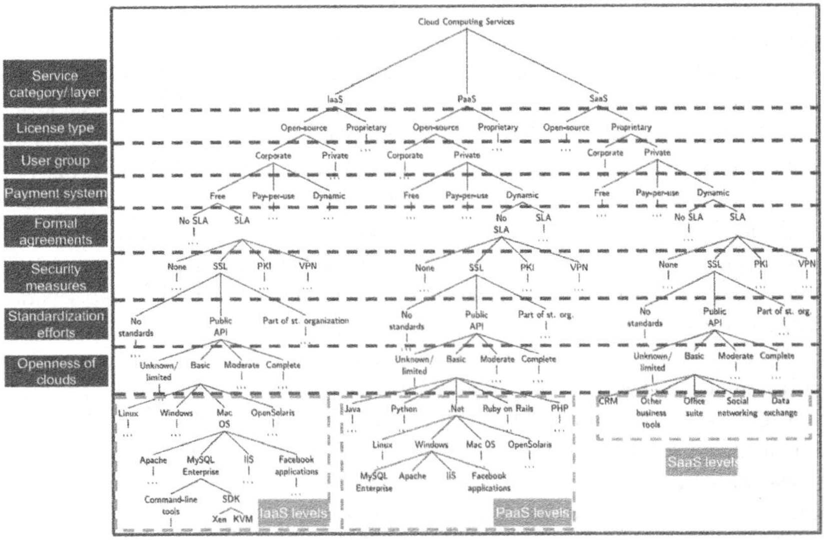

Fig. 4.7 Cloud computing services tree and taxonomy levels (Höfer & Karagiannis, 2011)

4.3 Conclusions on the Identified Clusters of Companies

Applying the frameworks from 4.2 but also considering that clusters should be statistically relevant, the following groups of companies (peer groups) have been defined:

- **Analytics Software** (22 companies): peer group focusing on companies providing software for data analytics and visualization, most often for business analytics purposes; while the segment could also be seen as horizontal software as it applies to virtually every sector, the number of peers allowed the separate clustering of such companies.
- **Classifieds** (34 companies): cluster focused on online classifies ranging from jobs to cars and real estate, among others; this segment helps end customers (individuals) find what they need; most of the time, companies generate revenues based on the inserts they promote, which is the key factor that differentiates these companies from the ones in the customer acquisition cluster; some automotive classifieds companies have been included in the marketplace

cluster as they sell new cars and usually generate a percentage of the sold vehicles as opposed to listing fees.

- **Content Monetization** (22 companies): peer group focused on the monetization of the content on their websites/ platforms generated or acquired either through users or through proprietary methods; businesses range from recipe sharing to real estate data, education, and news; companies in this cluster generate money either through advertising or through usage fees, and they differ significantly from companies in the financial content monetization because financial content companies need to source the data they sell to their users from very different sources such as stock exchanges and sell-side broker reports.
- **Content Monetization Financial** (14 companies): companies in this segment generate revenues by acquiring data from other sources, centralizing and analyzing it, and selling it very often to companies in the financial sector; due to these particularities, they are separated from the other content monetization companies.
- **Customer Acquisition** (26 companies): peer group of companies focusing on acquiring end customers (individuals) for various sectors such as insurance, financial, and even restaurants (home delivery); it differentiates from the classifieds cluster by usually providing a service comparison capability as opposed to comparing objects and selling these leads to the best offering service provider or sometimes to multiple service providers as opposed to charging per listing.
- **Data Center** (35 companies): a group of companies focusing on the provision of data center services starting with real estate and ending with the application layer; companies in this sector usually generate revenues by either renting the location, space in the location, or function servers running in applications; as there are only 35 companies in this segment it is difficult to further cluster it without looking the statistical significance.
- **Diversifieds and Portals** (19 companies): online portals such as Google that offer various service to the end consumers and monetizes these via advertising.
- **eCommerce** (76 companies): online retail companies that assume inventory risk independent of the product focus as several players are very diversified; it is essential to differentiate between eCommerce and Marketplace type companies as the latter usually generates revenues through commission as opposed to a mark-up on the products that are being sold.
- **Gambling** (23 companies): peer group containing on the one side betting companies (sports betting, casinos, etc.) and on the other side companies providing technology for the first group; as the monetization is very often based on the playing activity of the end user, independently if with or without a front

end (several companies provide both) all companies are grouped into a single cluster.

- **Gaming** (60 companies): online gaming companies that focus on the multi-player aspect of online games; it is worth noting that while several gambling companies try to present themselves as "gaming" companies, they are excluded from this group; furthermore, companies that publish and sell games that were successful before the existence of the internet or that could be successful without the internet (e.g., single player games) were also excluded.
- **Horizontal Software** (114 companies): technology companies that license their software most often as a SaaS offering to other businesses independent of the sector in which these other companies operate; for inclusion in this segment, it was essential that the software solution has applicability in more than one sector; most companies offer an ERP-like solution for various business functions.
- **Marketing** (88 companies): online marketing companies comprising both technology providers and services companies focusing on content; as the differentiation between these two sub-segments is often very blurry, it was not possible to further segment them; however, as both types of companies usually generate fees based on the volume of advertising that is being processed they are sufficiently comparable.
- **Marketplace** (34 companies): the segment includes commerce companies that do not assume inventory risk and most often generate commissions once an item is sold; this segment differs from the eCommerce segment by not assuming inventory risk, and while some companies could also be seen as classifieds they operate more like marketplaces generating commissions as opposed to listing fees
- **Online B2C Services** (18 companies): peer group comprising various end consumer services ranging from online streaming services to messaging services; while the monetization types can be different, the cluster does not include sufficient companies to enable a more precise clustering
- **Online Brokerage** (8 companies): a group of companies selling various financial securities and services to individuals and companies; these companies generate commissions based on the monetary volume of securities they process, and while the group only includes eight companies, they are not comparable to any other clusters in order to be segmented together
- **Payment** (38 companies): cluster comprising companies active in the digital payment space either as a payment processor or as a payment technology provider; such companies usually generate revenues as commission from the monetary volume processed

- **Platform Software** (30 companies): a group of companies providing software solutions that act as sector-agnostic horizontal software while also acting as a platform enabling independent software/ add-on development by external developers; such companies are to be seen separately from simple horizontal software provides as they have a significantly higher total addressable market; by combining the platform with the add-ons, the number of useful applications of such platforms increases exponentially
- **Security Software** (73 companies): a peer group that is wider than the name implies as it also includes IT infrastructure software companies; as the term infrastructure software can be misleading, a more overarching term "security software" has been used; the combination of two sub-segments took place as several players could fit into both; the software such companies provide is active in the infrastructure layer of the software stack with all other software types essentially depending on this type of software
- **Social Networks** (15 companies): a peers group including, as the name implies, social networks; as previously discussed, social networks can have particularities and be subject to popular opinions; hence, they were isolated into one segment; usually, the main revenue driver of companies in this segment is traditional online advertising on the platforms
- **Travel** (21 companies): peer group comprising all types of travel companies ranging from online agencies to global distribution systems like Amadeus; while a further segmentation might have been helpful, the number of companies does not allow it, however, all companies are players helping the booking to take place and not providing travel services themselves; the types of services booked range from flights, to hotels and buses among other related services
- **Vertical Software** (133 companies): a group of software companies that offer dedicated software for individual sectors such as PR, streaming, medical, and insurance, among multiple others; vertical software providers differ from horizontal software providers by making their solutions only applicable to one sector; the depth of the solution is implicitly higher and serves the individual needs of this type of companies as opposed to a broader need applicable to all companies

Overall, 21 clusters of companies have been formed, enabling, on the one side, direct comparison of valuations and metrics inside of individual clusters and, on the other side, a high enough number of clusters to enable the comparison of the results between clusters in order to conclude the entire internet-enabled businesses sector.

5 Acquisition and Processing of the Data for The Study

Following the identification and classification of relevant companies, the next most important step before performing the statistical analysis is sourcing, cleaning, and processing the data. The following subchapters will explain the sources of data considered, the reasons for choosing one database over another as well as data points collected, the reasons for collecting these data points, and the timeframes and time points of the data points collected. **While databases used in the previous chapters repeat (for identifying companies), the process of sourcing the data is completely separate because choosing between one of the four large data provides is a matter of finding the database providing the highest amount of accurate data across the variables and timeframes used for the study.**

A. Trusculescu, *Business Valuation Across the Industry Life Cycle*,
https://doi.org/10.1007/978-3-658-49126-0_5

5.1 Data Sources and Data Acquisition Method

Historical financial information is readily available as part of the required financial reports of public companies; however, historical information is only part of the information investors consider when making an investment decision. In addition to other publicly available resources such as news and press releases, professional investors also use sell-side broker reports. The sell-side broker reports are reports from investment banks for their clients to help with investment decisions (Chang, 2020). Additionally, as concluded by Merkley et al. in 2017, sell-side analyst reports have a positive impact on the functioning of financial markets (Merkley et al., 2017) and are usually better in countries with stronger investor protection (Arand et al., 2015). These studies confirm the benefit of such reports and the analysts' business plans. On average, all broker reports represent a consensus and implicitly are seen by market participants as the figures against which the performance of a publicly listed company is benchmarked. The present study, in addition to historical figures, will also use such consensus figures.

5.1.1 Relevant Data Providers

Considering the complexity and depth of the study, only four data providers come into question. While theoretically, all four data providers source the information from the same primary sources, in practice, there are differences in the data items that can be downloaded, as well as the time of the data and the timeframes. Luckily, due to working in the financial sector, the author had access to all four databases and could compare the type of information, time period, and timeframe available in each of the four data providers:

1. Thomson Reuters Eikon: is a database offered by Refinitiv, which is part of the London Stock Exchange Group and focuses on providing information about companies
2. Bloomberg Terminal: is the reference database offered by the known provider Bloomberg which contains most of the data the provider manages and also includes the company information the study requires
3. Capital IQ: a database provided by S&P Global, which focuses on company information and has a long-standing reputation of being the go-to platform for investment bankers

4. Factset "terminal": the desktop version of the main database provided by FactSet Research Systems, which also has a long-standing reputation for providing good company information and is fairly popular among investment professionals and, increasingly, investment bankers

Combining databases is a challenge with minimal benefits, hence, the best of the four must be selected. In this case, the choice was made by randomly selecting 100 companies, performing data pulls and observing 1) what data items, 2) what time frames, and 3) what time periods are available. Based on this preliminary data pull, Factset was chosen as the source of information as it had the best coverage from the four data providers. While there are various reasons why there are differences between the databases, discussing these is beyond the scope of the research.

5.1.2 Relevant Sub-Database and Download Method

Factset provides an outstanding Microsoft Excel plugin that will enable the download of all the relevant data, however, before proceeding, the best data items to be downloaded need to be selected. Factset uses nearly 30 data sources, meaning that when looking for a simple item such as "EBITDA," over 60 variations of this indicator are available. Following multiple discussions with the data provider, it has been decided to use the "Estimate" database that can be accessed in Excel using the "FE_ESTIMATE" function as it provides on the one had a reliable source combining lagging and forward-looking financial information and on the other hand, the historical financials are based on the financials provided by research analysts in their reports meaning that every figure that ends up in this database has been analyzed by at least one finance professional as opposed to it being simply pulled from the primary sources. An additional benefit of this approach is that financials are usually adjusted for acquisitions and other events, reflecting the financials a professional would use to derive an investment decision, a highly relevant factor in assessing the best multiples and drivers at any given point in time.

Following the selection of the data provider and the relevant database and sub-database, the next step was selecting the items to be downloaded to calculate the relevant multiples and relevant drivers. The literature review provided a good overview of the data items required. As the estimate sub-database provides over 500 data items, the most relevant ones with the highest coverage were selected. Overall, three valuation indicators: Equity Value, Enterprise Value, and Share Price and 17 financial indicators: Revenue, Gross Margin, EBITDA, EBIT, Net Income, EPS, FCF, UFCF, R&D Expend., CF from Op., Assets, Debt, Sh. Equity, BPS, BPS Tangible, CAPEX, and DPS were downloaded. The next chapter explains the financial indicators downloaded, the period covered by the study, and the timeframes included in the study.

Figure 5.1 shows an example of one of the 173 Microsoft Excel tables used to pull all the data required for the study. It can be observed that the table was structured as a matrix with the companies on the horizontal and the time of each observation on the vertical. One table could pull all the information for all the companies included in the study for one data item and one timeframe. In this case, LTM Assets are being pulled. In order to pull all the information across 17 financial indicators multiplied by 10 timeframes plus the 3 valuation indicators, 173 such matrixes had to be prepared manually and downloaded.

Due to the size of the table and the amount of data to be pulled, the indicators have been split into two Excel files, and a VBA script was needed to stop the Factset Add-on from downloading more than 100 companies at a time. If downloading more than 100 companies was attempted, the plugin would become exponentially slow and unresponsive.

As building such a large data set was essentially pioneering work based on a trial and error approach, several weeks were required just to set up the Excel Files and the VBA scripts and over 10 attempts were made to download the data, with each attempt requiring between three and four days in order to arrive at the final data set. Over 100 versions of the data pull files have been used during the time of the study.

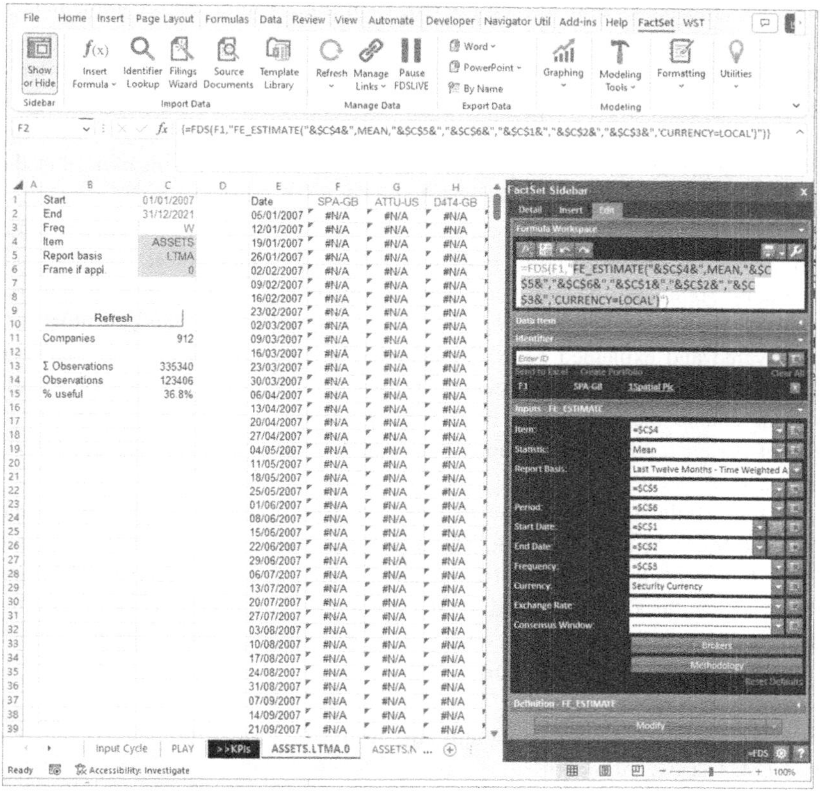

Fig. 5.1 Screenshot from Microsoft Excel presenting an example of the matrix used to download data

5.1.3 Relevant Indicators, Period Covered by the Study, and Relevant Timeframes

Table 5.1 presents an overview of all indicators downloaded from Factset and a short description of what these indicators represent. The period covered by the study is 01/01/2007 to 31/12/2021. This period was selected such that it covers the financial crises that happened during 2007 and 2008 and the lows achieved in valuation during that period, the high growth period driven by low-interest rates that followed, as well as the COVID-19 crisis and the monetary easing response of the central banks until the end of 2021. In 2022 central banks implemented monetary tightening strategies to counteract inflation, making the year the end of the cycle for the stock market. Consequently, the study covers a full economic cycle independently if seen until COVID-19 or after the monetary tightening in 2022.

The frequency of the data pull has been defined as weekly, meaning that the indicators are downloaded as of the end of each week for the entire 15 years covered by the study. This frequency has been chosen as daily observations would have made the analysis significantly more difficult (5 times more data) without providing significant benefits, and only 12 observations per year (monthly frequency) would have been too little. The timeframes of each of the indicators will be covered and explained below. Independently if the analysis is performed on the weekly data or a more aggerated form such as yearly data, weekly observations enable the calculation of average multiples and drivers as opposed to end-of-period (end-of-year) figures that would be downloaded using the yearly time period.

It is essential to differentiate between the period covered by the study and the time frame of each indicator. The period represents 15 years, while the time frame represents the time period an indicator covers. For example, the LTM timeframe means "last twelve months," and consequently, LTM Revenue represents the revenue a company has generated in the last twelve months. Overall, ten such timeframes were used in the study:

- SLTM: second last twelve months (the twelve months before LTM)
- LTM: last twelve months
- NTM: next twelve months
- SNTM: second next twelve months (the twelve months after NTM)
- Six separate timeframes based on the fiscal year: −2, −1, 0, 1, 2, 3, with 0 being the last reported fiscal year, −1 being the previous fiscal year, 2 being the fiscal year after the next one, and so on

Table 5.1 List of all financial and valuation indicators downloaded from Factset and their description and explanation

Indicator	Description
Valuation indicators	
EV	Enterprise Value or Firm Value shows the value the market ascribes to the company independent of the stakeholder. It includes the value of equity, total debt, and other items with financing character, such as preferred stock and accumulated minority interest, and excludes cash. Such a measure of valuation is capital structure independent. Mathematically explained: EV = EqV + Debt + Preferred Stock + Accumulated Minority Interest—Cash
EqV	Equity Value is derived by the multiplication of share price with the total number of shares a company has to derive the total market value of the equity in the business. As the indicator focuses on the equity holders, the capital structure might indirectly affect it
PS	Price per share or share price is simply the price at which a share in the company trades at, at the time of observation. While share price and equity value essentially represent the same data point, both items were downloaded to enable the use of "per share" financial metrics such as earnings per share "EPS"
Financial indicators	
Revenue	The starting point of every profit and loss statement; it reflects the 3rd party sales a company generates net of VAT
Gross Margin	By deducting the costs of goods sold from the revenues, one arrives at the gross margin, a financial indicator that shows the profitability before platform costs
EBITDA	Earnings before interest, taxes, depreciation and amortization is a known profitability measure that is derived by subtracting all other operating expenses from the gross margin; "D&A" are excluded in order to look at a measure that excludes non-cash expenses, providing a measure of profitability after platform costs such as personnel, markets, and S,G&A
EBIT	Earnings before interest and taxes, similar to EBITDA, however, it is derived by also deducting depreciation and amortization, reflecting the annual cost of the long-term investments
Net Income	The net income is the last number in every profit and loss statement and shows the profit after all expenses, essentially showing what equity holders receive as profit, assuming no additional cash flow effects

(continued)

Table 5.1 (continued)

Indicator	Description
EPS	Earnings per share, essentially representing the same figure as the net income, however, divided by the number of shares. It has been included as the coverage ratio is slightly better than the net income, and some valuation metrics can be calculated using this indicator
FCF	Free cash flow, as the name says, represents the cash flow following all operational outflows, such as working capital investments and CAPEX and other investment and financial inflows and outflows
UFCF	Unlevered free cash flow is the cash flow before adding/ subtracting the effect of the financial cash flow. "Unlevered" refers to being before the debt effect
R&D Expend.	Research and development expenditure; the indicator will be used to calculate the EBITDA before R&D expenditure, a new indicator that might provide some additional insights
CF from Op.	Cash flow from operations presents the cash flow following the operative effects such as investments in working capital, however, before CAPEX and financing activities
Assets	Total assets as recognized on the balance sheet
Debt	Total debt as recognized on the balance sheet
Sh. Equity	Total shareholder equity represents the book value of the equity
BPS	Book value per share represents the book value of the business divided by the number of shares
BPS Tangible	Tangible book value per share, similar to BPS, however, only includes the tangible assets
CAPEX	Capital expenditures represent the cash outflows for investments that a company has and can usually be seen as part of the investment cash flow; the indicator can be used by deducting it from the EBITDA to arrive at a CAPEX-adjusted EBITDA, a multiple used by some investors
DPS	Dividends per share represent the amount of dividends a company pays for each individual share

Figure 5.2 presents an overview of all the timeframes used in the study relative to a hypothetical date of 29/10/2021, assuming that the fiscal year ending is the 31st of December. While the fiscal year timeframe is simple to understand as it overlaps the fiscal year, the rolling timeframes: SLTM, LTM, NTM, and SNTM need explanation. LTM Revenues would represent, in this example, the revenues generated in the 12 months prior to 29/10/2021. If the analysis was performed on 15/12/2021, it would represent the 12 months prior to the new date rolling together with the date. These timeframes are only relevant for the financial

indicators as the valuation indicators are as of the day of the observation and do not cover timeframes.

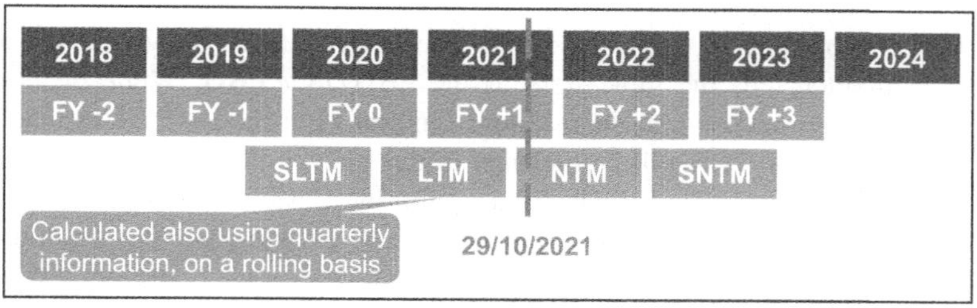

Fig. 5.2 Overview of the timeframes used in the study based on a hypothetical date of 29/10/2021

5.2 Data Availability and Coverage Ratios

Before spending significant time analyzing all the data pulled from databases, it is useful to exclude the variables that are not "covered" well enough and for which there is not sufficient data to draw statistically significant conclusions. To assess the coverage, the author first needed to look at what is possible for each company, as companies will only have data after the IPO. While some financials might be available before the starting of trading on stock exchanges (for example, on IPO fillings or public debt reportings), the actual valuation of companies can only be derived after trading has commenced. Consequently, only data points following an IPO are observed as being feasible.

One adjustment that can be performed without thinking too much is using older financial information to fill gaps in data. Just because data providers have some periods (weeks) with no data while providing data before and after these periods, it does not mean that professional investors would not use the last available information to decide. To exemplify, if week 25 of a particular company shows LTM revenues of 100 m and week 27 shows almost the same figure while week 26 is "not available," it can be easily assumed that an investor would use the data from week 25 in week 26. Consequently, up to 2 quarters of data gaps can be filled with the last available information, a measure implemented immediately after downloading the data.

From Table 5.2, it can easily be observed that 3 variables have very little coverage along all 10 timeframes considered in the study and will consequently be excluded:

1. UFCF—coverage of only 3.3%: while the unlevered cash flow is a relevant KPI, it often tells the same story as the EBITDA / EBIT. While there are some differences between the mentioned indicators, the value the UFCF adds, considering that FCF will be included in the study, is limited. Consequently, the UFCF can be excluded without a significant impact on the results
2. Debt—coverage of only 17.0%: the KPI can be excluded without much consideration as the difference between EV and EqV is the "net debt," which comprises debt minus cash plus some debt-like items, an indicator significantly more important than debt in itself. Consequently, if the indicator is required, it can be derived by subtracting the EqV from the EV
3. BPS Tangible—Coverage of 17.9%: The KPI is unimportant, considering that internet-driven models (with some exceptions, such as inventory-driven eCommerce) usually have very few tangible assets. Additionally, regular book value per share (BPS) has good coverage of over 60% and will be included

In conclusion, excluding the three variables will have little to no impact on the study, and further consideration to improve the coverage does not need to be taken into.

Table 5.3 shows the total number of observations per valuation/ financial indicator and the timeframe that has been collected. 1,459,065 valuation indicator observations and 45,527,503 financial indicator observations totaling nearly 47 million observations, have been collected, highlighting the size of the data cube. An additional 4.5 m observations could be calculated based on the pulled information.

Table 5.4 shows the coverage of the data per valuation/ financial indicator and timeframe. The one indicator that shows particularly low coverage is the R&D indicator showing only 30.3%, which influences the EBITDA-R&D indicator as well, with 29.6% coverage. While no suggestion exists to exclude the variable, results should be used with care.

Table 5.2 Data coverage of variables pulled from Factset as a percentage based on a preliminary peer group of 911 companies

	EV	EqV	PS								
Valuation	96.7	97.9	97.9								
	LTM	**NTM**	**STM**	**SLTM**	**AN-2**	**AN-1**	**AN0**	**AN +1**	**AN +2**	**AN +3**	**Avg.**
Revenue	87.6	81.7	80.4	82.3	74.7	81.3	87.3	81.8	80.7	73.5	**81.1**
Gross Margin	61.3	62.3	61.6	54.2	46.9	53.2	59.9	62.4	61.8	54.5	**57.8**
EBITDA	73.2	73.7	72.9	67.4	60.8	66.5	72.1	73.7	73.1	66.4	**70.0**
EBIT	82.4	80.3	79.0	75.9	68.0	74.9	81.6	80.2	79.2	71.9	**77.3**
Net Income	86.5	80.6	79.2	80.9	73.2	79.8	86.0	80.4	79.4	72.0	**79.8**
EPS	87.3	82.0	80.5	81.6	73.6	80.3	86.6	81.6	80.7	73.7	**80.8**
FCF	62.7	64.2	63.5	55.3	48.1	54.3	60.6	64.1	63.7	57.2	**59.4**
UFCF	3.5	4.1	4.1	2.5	1.9	2.4	2.9	4.1	4.1	3.1	**3.3**
R&D Expend.	30.1	30.8	30.5	26.2	22.2	25.7	29.2	30.8	30.7	27.5	**28.4**
CF from Op.	66.7	67.9	67.1	59.0	51.2	57.9	64.9	67.8	67.3	60.7	**63.0**
Assets	63.9	65.0	64.1	56.1	48.6	55.1	62.1	65.0	64.3	58.0	**60.2**
Debt	18.9	19.5	19.0	15.3	11.4	14.3	17.3	19.5	19.1	15.8	**17.0**
Sh. Equity	68.0	68.8	67.7	60.2	52.3	59.1	66.4	68.8	67.8	61.3	**64.0**
BPS	63.6	64.8	62.2	57.4	52.2	56.8	62.0	64.8	62.7	55.8	**60.2**
BPS Tangible	19.2	19.9	19.3	17.1	14.6	16.7	18.5	19.8	19.4	14.3	**17.9**
CAPEX	66.8	67.8	67.0	59.0	51.0	57.7	64.8	67.8	67.2	60.7	**63.0**
DPS	34.4	34.1	33.6	31.7	26.9	29.3	31.9	32.5	32.8	31.0	**31.8**
Average	**57.4**	**56.9**	**56.0**	**51.9**	**45.7**	**50.9**	**56.1**	**56.8**	**56.1**	**50.4**	

Table 5.3 Number of observations broken down by timeframe and variable (own research)

Valuation data (numer of observations)

	EV	EqV	Sh. Price	Total
Valuation	482,787	488,097	488,181	1,459,065

Financial data (numer of observations)

	SLTM	LTM	NTM	STM	AN -2	AN -1	AN 0	AN + 1	AN + 2	AN + 3	Total
Sales	409,719	436,729	407,722	400,845	372,025	404,801	434,857	407,972	402,590	367,283	4,044,543
Gross Margin	270,105	306,112	311,109	307,552	233,923	265,442	298,754	311,327	308,766	272,883	2,885,973
EBITDA	336,558	365,414	368,224	364,051	303,838	332,359	360,405	368,406	365,565	331,935	34,96,755
EBIT	378,391	411,198	400,687	394,314	338,895	373,381	407,086	400,763	396,066	359,385	3,860,166
Net Income	403,101	431,533	402,026	395,311	364,777	398,171	429,314	401,749	396,972	360,009	3,982,963
Earnings per sh.	407,083	435,562	409,459	402,629	368,274	401,932	433,294	409,219	404,350	369,489	4,041,291
Free Cash-Flow	276,097	313,176	320,971	317,700	240,138	271,307	303,217	320,902	318,666	286,329	2,968,503
R&D Expendit.	135,910	1,56,549	160,518	159,430	115,488	133,265	151,919	160,559	160,018	144,103	1,477,759
Operating CF	294,424	333,217	338,884	335,187	255,788	289,358	324,608	338,980	336,202	303,411	3,150,059
Assets	279,752	319,309	324,511	320,234	242,671	274,955	309,917	324,584	321,105	289,940	3,006,978
Sh. Equity	300,348	339,487	343,842	338,179	260,913	295,123	331,705	343,942	339,067	306,615	3,199,221
BPS	287,578	318,735	324,530	311,962	261,539	284,209	310,172	324,989	314,406	279,695	3,017,815
CAPEX	296,245	336,804	343,326	339,866	256,988	290,948	327,856	343,463	340,956	308,619	3,185,071
DPS	308,027	347,870	341,347	326,900	274,846	303,504	337,459	341,705	329,286	299,462	3,210,406
Total	4,383,338	4,851,695	4,797,156	4,714,160	3,890,103	4,318,755	4,760,563	4,798,560	4,734,015	4,279,158	45,527,503
5.											
EBITDA—R&D	132,473	153,153	157,239	156,045	112,788	129,977	148,034	157,285	156,645	139,570	1,443,209
EBITDA—CAPEX	283,543	323,038	329,347	325,738	246,009	278,488	313,931	329,485	326,852	291,382	3,047,813
Total	416,016	476,191	486,586	481,783	358,797	408,465	461,965	486,770	483,497	430,952	4,491,022

Table 5.4 Data coverage by variable and timeframe from the maximum possible represented by the share price observations (own research)

Valuation data (numer of observations)											
	EV	**EqV**	**Sh. Price**	**Avg.**							
Valuation	98.9%	100.0%	100.0%	99.6%							
Financial data (numer of observations)											
	SLTM	**LTM**	**NTM**	**STM**	**AN -2**	**AN -1**	**AN 0**	**AN + 1**	**AN + 2**	**AN + 3**	**Average**
Sales	83.9%	89.5%	83.5%	82.1%	76.2%	82.9%	89.1%	83.6%	82.5%	75.2%	82.8%
Gross Margin	55.3%	62.7%	63.7%	63.0%	47.9%	54.4%	61.2%	63.8%	63.2%	55.9%	59.1%
EBITDA	68.9%	74.9%	75.4%	74.6%	62.2%	68.1%	73.8%	75.5%	74.9%	68.0%	71.6%
EBIT	77.5%	84.2%	82.1%	80.8%	69.4%	76.5%	83.4%	82.1%	81.1%	73.6%	79.1%
Net Income	82.6%	88.4%	82.4%	81.0%	74.7%	81.6%	87.9%	82.3%	81.3%	73.7%	81.6%
Earnings per sh.	83.4%	89.2%	83.9%	82.5%	75.4%	82.3%	88.8%	83.8%	82.8%	75.7%	82.8%
Free Cash-Flow	56.6%	64.2%	65.7%	65.1%	49.2%	55.6%	62.1%	65.7%	65.3%	58.7%	60.8%
R&D Expendit.	27.8%	32.1%	32.9%	32.7%	23.7%	27.3%	31.1%	32.9%	32.8%	29.5%	30.3%
Operating CF	60.3%	68.3%	69.4%	68.7%	52.4%	59.3%	66.5%	69.4%	68.9%	62.2%	64.5%
Assets	57.3%	65.4%	66.5%	65.6%	49.7%	56.3%	63.5%	66.5%	65.8%	59.4%	61.6%
Sh. Equity	61.5%	69.5%	70.4%	69.3%	53.4%	60.5%	67.9%	70.5%	69.5%	62.8%	65.5%
BPS	58.9%	65.3%	66.5%	63.9%	53.6%	58.2%	63.5%	66.6%	64.4%	57.3%	61.8%
CAPEX	60.7%	69.0%	70.3%	69.6%	52.6%	59.6%	67.2%	70.4%	69.8%	63.2%	65.2%
DPS	63.1%	71.3%	69.9%	67.0%	56.3%	62.2%	69.1%	70.0%	67.5%	61.3%	65.8%
Average	64.1%	71.0%	70.2%	69.0%	56.9%	63.2%	69.7%	70.2%	69.3%	62.6%	
Derived financial data (numer of observations)											
EBITDA—R&D	27.1%	31.4%	32.2%	32.0%	23.1%	26.6%	30.3%	32.2%	32.1%	28.6%	29.6%
EBITDA—CAPEX	58.1%	66.2%	67.5%	66.7%	50.4%	57.0%	64.3%	67.5%	67.0%	59.7%	62.4%
Average	42.6%	48.8%	49.8%	49.3%	36.7%	41.8%	47.3%	49.9%	49.5%	44.1%	

5.3 Research Variables

The data downloaded enables not only the typical multiples and financial drivers but also some less-used multiples and drivers. This sub-chapter explains the multiples and the drivers used in the study as well as the methodology used to calculate them from a theoretical and practical perspective.

Also connected with the multiples and drives, an additional important criterion is the definition of the value ranges in which multiples and drivers are relevant for a valuation. Going back to Damodaran's conclusion that a valuation has a financial and a story component, defining the range in which multiples and drivers are in the financials component range is essential for a good analysis as otherwise, such research would try to explain valuation levels with financials while the actual driver is the story. The following sub-chapters will also explain the reasoning behind choosing the ranges, as there is little research on what is a story and what is a financials-driven valuation.

5.3.1 Relevant Multiples

Table 5.5 presents an overview of all multiples used in the study, classified into Enterprise Value multiples, Equity Value multiples, and Book Value multiples, as well as the respective timeframes and resulting number of variables relevant to the study and, lastly, the ranges deemed as appropriate to represent a financial multiple driven valuation as opposed to a story-driven valuation. For the EV/ Revenue multiple, for example, 10 separate timeframes were included: SLTM, LTM, NTM, SNTM, FY-2, FY-1, FY 0, FY +1, FY +2, and FY +3 representing EV/ SLTM Revenue, EV/ LTM Revenue, EV/ FY-2 Revenue, etc. and implicitly deriving 10 separate EV/ Revenue multiples which will be considered.

During the setup of the multiples, the valuation indicator (EV, EqV, or Share Price) had to be matched with an indicator that represents the particular stakeholder implied by the valuation indicator. For example, the Enterprise Value represents the market value that both shareholders and debt holders have in the business and consequently cannot be paired with an indicator such as earnings (net profits) calculated after servicing the debt providers and consequently owned only by the shareholders.

In addition to the traditional EV multiples such as EV/Revenue, EV/EBITDA, and EV/EBIT also, less used multiplies such as EV/Gross Margin and EV/ Operative Cash Flow were included in addition to some fairly new and unused multiples adjusting the EBITDA for Research and Development expenses and

Table 5.5 Multiples used in the study, the respective timeframes, implicit number of variables resulting, and ranges deemed as appropriate for a financials-based valuation

Multiples	Timeframes	# Var.	Range excluded
Enterprise Value multiples			
EV/Revenue	SLTM, LTM, NTM, SNTM, FY-2 to FY3	10	<0 and >20
EV/GM	SLTM, LTM, NTM, SNTM, FY-2 to FY3	10	<0 and >30
EV/EBITDA	SLTM, LTM, NTM, SNTM, FY-2 to FY3	10	<0 and >40
EV/(EBITDA-R&D)	SLTM, LTM, NTM, SNTM, FY-2 to FY3	10	<0 and >40
EV/(EBITDA-CAPEX)	SLTM, LTM, NTM, SNTM, FY-2 to FY3	10	<0 and >40
EV/EBIT	SLTM, LTM, NTM, SNTM, FY-2 to FY3	10	<0 and >45
EV/FCF	SLTM, LTM, NTM, SNTM, FY-2 to FY3	10	<0 and >45
EV/Op. CF	SLTM, LTM, NTM, SNTM, FY-2 to FY3	10	<0 and >40
Equity Value multiples			
P/Revenue	SLTM, LTM, NTM, SNTM, FY-2 to FY3	10	<0 and >20
P/FCF	SLTM, LTM, NTM, SNTM, FY-2 to FY3	10	<0 and >45
P/E	SLTM, LTM, NTM, SNTM, FY-2 to FY3	10	<0 and >60
PEG	LTM, NTM, SNTM, FY-1 to FY3	8	<0 and >20
Book Value multiples			
EV/Total Assets	SLTM, LTM, NTM, SNTM, FY-2 to FY3	10	<0 and >50
P/B	SLTM, LTM, NTM, SNTM, FY-2 to FY3	10	<0 and >100
FY-2 to FY3 = FY-2, FY-1, FY0, FY1, FY2, FY3			

one adjusting the EBITDA for CAPEX. The EBITDA-R&D indicator is used to calculate the respective multiple, and later, the respective driver essentially adds back the R&D expense to calculate the profitability before these costs. This multiple can help companies with high one-off R&D expenses normalize their profitability compared to companies that have steady or no R&D. The EBITDA-CAPEX variable is essentially a variable similar to EBIT that, while excluding the Depreciation and Amortization during the calculation of the EBITDA, includes (or deducts) the Capital Expenditures. The advantage of such a variable used both for calculating a respective multiple, and a respective driver is that it considers the most up-to-date expansion costs (CAPEX is the current investment, while D&A is a portion of the historical expansion costs). It is unclear if the investors consider such multiples in making an investment decision, however, the study will include them together with the rest of the multiples.

Regarding the Equity Value or Share Price multiple, in addition to the traditional P/E and PEG multiple, two less-used multiples were also included: P/Revenue and P/FCF. Both multiples are correct and can be used as the FCF indicates cash flow after servicing the debt providers. Lastly, two book value multiples were also included, the traditional P/B multiple, and a less frequently used EV/Total Assets multiple, which is correct as both indicators relate to sizes owned by all stakeholders.

The assessment of the ranges that are deemed to be appropriate was based on a simulated discounted cash flow valuation of an ideal internet-based company, as presented in Table 5.6. The hypothetical business model presents the absolute limit concerning visibility a highly outperforming internet business can experience. It starts with a revenue of 100 units (to be noted that it could be any currency or unit) and assumes a 50% growth rate for the entire planning period. 50% growth essentially means that the company grows by a factor of 5 over the planning period. While 50% is a high number, it can arguably still be defended with financials if it is based on similar strong history. It should be noted that such a high growth rate is extremely unusual, especially over a period of 5 years, and exemplifies an unusually well-performing business.

To continue with the margins, a 75% gross margin was assumed, which with a few exceptions, is a very good gross margin for an online business. The EBITDA and EBIT margins were assumed to be 55% and 50%, respectively, implying outstandingly good margins. Taxes of 30% were assumed to arrive at a net income margin of c. 35%. Two additional implicit assumptions are present in this hypothetical model: 1) the company does not require any working capital investment, the reason for exclusion was to present the best possible scenario, and 2) the investment in CAPEX is equal to the depreciation and amortization position implying that there is little expansion CAPEX required. Both assumptions are unlikely with such a high growth rate and represent the absolute best possible scenario.

An exit multiple of 20× was used to represent the price that can be justified for a strong and growing but mature internet business.

Table 5.6 Hypothetical financials of an ideal internet company and calculation of NPV based on a DCF

	Year 1	Year 2	Year 3	Year 4	Year 5
Revenue	100	150	225	338	506
Revenue growth		*50%*	*50%*	*50%*	*50%*
Gross Margin	75	113	169	253	380
Gross Margin	*75%*	*75%*	*75%*	*75%*	*75%*
EBITDA	55	83	124	186	278
EBITDA Margin	*55%*	*55%*	*55%*	*55%*	*55%*
EBIT	50	75	113	169	253
EBIT Margin	*50%*	*50%*	*50%*	*50%*	*50%*
Taxes	(15)	(23)	(34)	(51)	(76)
Tax rate	*30%*	*30%*	*30%*	*30%*	*30%*
Net income	35	53	79	118	177
Net margin	*35%*	*35%*	*35%*	*35%*	*35%*
Exit multiple (EV/EBITDA)					20.0x
EV at exit					5,569
Total cash flows	35	53	79	118	5,746
NPV Calculation					
Discount Rate	25%				
NPV	2,033				
Implied multiple					
Revenue	20x				
Gross margin	27x				
EBITDA	37x				
EBIT	41x				
Net income	58x				

Lastly, a discount rate of 25% was used to calculate the net present value of the future cash flows (NPV), which is in line with Damodaran's finding in his paper on the valuation of young companies (Damodaran, 2009) and KPMG's study done by Aggarwal and Bahl which summarizes four separate sources for discount rates across the various evolution phases of companies (Aggarwal & Bahl, 2021). This simulation leads to a valuation for the simulated firm of over 2,000 units representing a revenue multiple of 20x, a gross margin revenue of 27x, an EBITDA multiple of 37x, an EBIT multiple of 41x, and a net income multiple of 58x. Based on this analysis, the limits for a multiple to still be based on financials were set in this study at 20× for revenues, 30× for gross margin, 40× for EBITDA and EBITDA-like items, 45× for EBIT and EBIT-like variables, and 60× for earnings multiples. The EV/Total Assets and Price to Book limits were based on the observations in the study and aimed only to exclude extreme values, with 20× being a high threshold for any business.

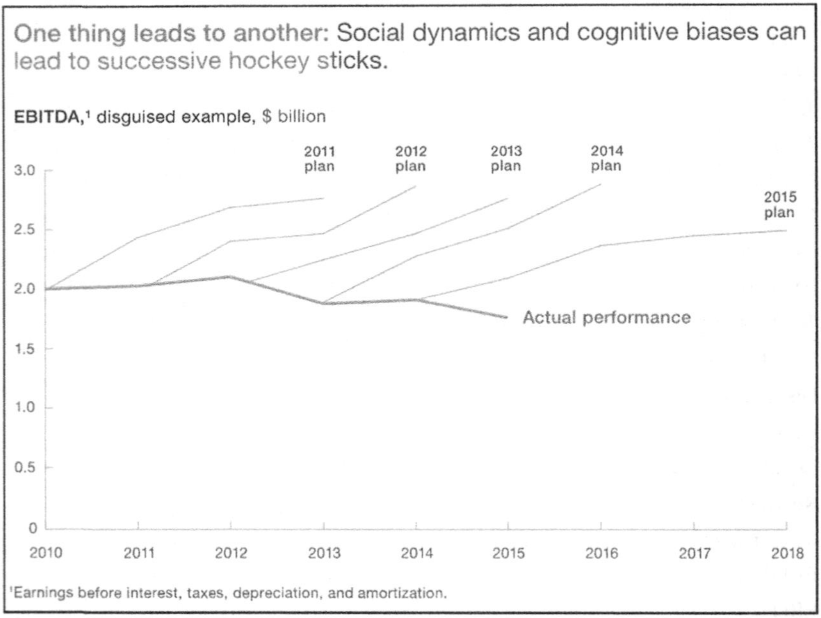

Fig. 5.3 An example of a business plan where every year the plan shows growth while the reality shows stagnation (Bradley et al., 2018)

The 5-year planning period was selected based on an assumption concerning the visibility of the management teams concerning the business. As shown by Bradley et al. in the article "Strategy to beat the odds," published by McKinsey, management teams usually have a problem planning the next year, let alone five years in advance. The idea of a hockey stick is that business plans often look like a hockey stick by having a period of investment (loss-making) followed by a prolonged period of growth, making it look like a "J-Stick" or "hockey stick." Figure 5.3 shows such an example published by McKinsey in which the management team plans growth every year despite it not happening in the actual figures (Bradley et al., 2018). This leads to the phenomenon of saying that "this year is different" when in reality, it is more of the same. Assuming 5-year visibility at a 50% growth rate is consequently more than an ideal case, ultimately ensuring that the cut-off points for the extreme values in the variables are not too low while still reflecting the relevance of financials in valuations. The used cut-off points are higher than typically practiced in valuations performed as part of professional financial services, ensuring an inclusive study.

5.3.2 Relevant Drivers

This sub-chapter, similarly to the previous sub-chapter, explains the drivers used and the assumptions and logic behind the chosen ranges.

Table 5.7: Drivers used in the study, the respective timeframes, implicit number of variables resulting, and ranges deemed as appropriate for financial drivers Table 5.7 presents an overview of all drivers included in the study, the timeframes used, the resulting number of variables, and the range in which the observations are deemed relevant for a financials driven valuation. The timeframes used for calculating the drivers are the same timeframes as the ones used for calculating the multiples: SLTM, LTM, NTM, SNTM, FY-2, FY-1, FY 0, FY +1, FY +2, and FY +3, except for the growth drivers which exclude the SLTM and the FY − 2 timeframe. The reason for exclusion is that for the calculation of a growth rate, the data point before the observation is required, and since the rolling timeframes start with SLTM and the fiscal year timeframes start with FY −2, there is no way of calculating growth for the SLTM and the FY -2 timeframes.

The ranges were set up at large for all drivers and only tried to exclude values that would obviously be wrong or too high to base a valuation on. All margin drivers were calculated by dividing the respective indicator by the revenue for the respective timeframe.

Table 5.7 Drivers used in the study, the respective timeframes, implicit number of variables resulting, and ranges deemed as appropriate for financial drivers

Multiples	Timeframes	# Var.	Range excluded
Divident as driver			
Divident yield	SLTM, LTM, NTM, SNTM, FY-2 to FY3	10	None
Margin Drivers			
GM Margin	SLTM, LTM, NTM, SNTM, FY-2 to FY3	10	<0% and >100%
EBITDA Margin	SLTM, LTM, NTM, SNTM, FY-2 to FY3	10	<−50% and >100%
EBITDA-R&D Margin	SLTM, LTM, NTM, SNTM, FY-2 to FY3	10	<−50% and >100%
EBITDA-CAPEX M.	SLTM, LTM, NTM, SNTM, FY-2 to FY3	10	<−50% and >100%
EBIT Margin	SLTM, LTM, NTM, SNTM, FY-2 to FY3	10	<−50% and >100%
FCF Margin	SLTM, LTM, NTM, SNTM, FY-2 to FY3	10	<−50% and >100%
Op. CF Margin	SLTM, LTM, NTM, SNTM, FY-2 to FY3	10	<−50% and >100%
Net Margin	SLTM, LTM, NTM, SNTM, FY-2 to FY3	10	<−50% and >100%
R&D % Revenue	SLTM, LTM, NTM, SNTM, FY-2 to FY3	10	<0% and >50%
CAPEX % Revenue	SLTM, LTM, NTM, SNTM, FY-2 to FY3	10	<0% and >100%
Growth Drivers			
Revenue	LTM, NTM, SNTM, FY-1 to FY3	8	<−20% and >100%
GM	LTM, NTM, SNTM, FY-1 to FY3	8	<−50% and >200%
EBITDA	LTM, NTM, SNTM, FY-1 to FY3	8	<−100% and >2000%
(EBITDA-R&D)	LTM, NTM, SNTM, FY-1 to FY3	8	<−100% and >2000%

(continued)

Table 5.7 (continued)

Multiples	Timeframes	# Var.	Range excluded
(EBITDA-CAPEX)	LTM, NTM, SNTM, FY-1 to FY3	8	<−100% and >2000%
EBIT	LTM, NTM, SNTM, FY-1 to FY3	8	<−100% and >2000%
FCF	LTM, NTM, SNTM, FY-1 to FY3	8	<−100% and >2000%
Op. CF	LTM, NTM, SNTM, FY-1 to FY3	8	<−100% and >2000%
Net Income	LTM, NTM, SNTM, FY-1 to FY3	8	<−100% and >2000%
EPS Growth	LTM, NTM, SNTM, FY-1 to FY3	8	<−100% and >2000%
R&D Growth	LTM, NTM, SNTM, FY-1 to FY3	8	<−100% and >2000%
CAPEX Growth	LTM, NTM, SNTM, FY-1 to FY3	8	<−100% and >2000%
DPS Growth	LTM, NTM, SNTM, FY-1 to FY3	8	<−100% and >2000%
Other Drivers			
Return on Assets	LTM, NTM, SNTM, FY-1 to FY3	10	None
Return on Equity	LTM, NTM, SNTM, FY-1 to FY3	10	None
Asset Turnover	LTM, NTM, SNTM, FY-1 to FY3	10	None
Rev. Gro. + EBITDA M.	LTM, NTM, SNTM, FY-1 to FY3	8	<−100% and >2500%

FY-2 to FY3 = FY-2, FY-1, FY0, FY1, FY2, FY3

Negative margins and margins above 100% were excluded from the GM margin. The reason for excluding negative margins is that a business should at least earn some margin on selling a service or a product. A business that sells only at a price below the acquisition price is not sustainable by any means. Furthermore, it would be unnatural for a business to earn a Gross Margin higher than the revenues, and the variable is hence capped at 100%. A gross margin of 100% implies acquisition costs of zero. Having negative acquisition costs and a margin of over 100% is not feasible.

The remaining margins: EBITDA margin, EBITDA-R&D margin, EBITDA-CAPEX margin, EBIT margin, FCF margin, operative cash flow margin, and net margin range from −50% on the lower end, with a 100% cap on the higher end. While the reasoning for excluding values above 100% is the same as for the gross margin, the reason for using a lower range of −50% was chosen based on the assumption that a company having costs observed at any level in the profit and loss statement, that are more than 1.5 times higher than the revenues must have and still has a positive valuation, must have as an implicit driver of such a valuation the story component as opposed to the financial component.

The ranges used to deem an observation as being realistic and relevant for a financials-driven valuation for the growth variables were derived similarly. For revenue growth, a range of between −20% and 100% was used as businesses decreasing more than 20% in one year usually have a deeper problem, while companies more than doubling every year are seen as defiantly having a large story component in the valuation. A range between −50% and over 200% was used for the gross margin growth with a similar argumentation. For the remaining growth variables: EBITDA growth, EBITDA-R&D growth, EBITDA-CAPEX growth, EBIT growth, FCF growth, operating cash flow growth, free cash flow growth, net income growth, EPS growth, and DPS growth, a lower range of −100% was used as these multiples should not be able to decrease by more than their last year absolute value and a higher range of 2000% (20× last year) as a growth higher is definitely above what is normal for any business and most likely driven by a mathematical or one-off type reason. Growth by a factor of 20× is highly unusual, however, an inclusive study should not use values that are too low.

The ranges for RoA, RoE, and asset turnover variables were derived similarly. The return on assets is calculated by dividing the net income by the total assets, while the return on equity is calculated by dividing the net income by the equity. The asset turnover was calculated by dividing total revenue by the total assets. The RoE and RoA variables are similar to the margin variables from an importance and meaning perspective while relating the profits to other sizes, the total assets, and the total equity of the business, consequently showing the efficiency of the deployed assets and equity. For the RoA, a range between −20% and 50% was deemed appropriate based on the observations included in the study and the assumption that a business losing at net income level more than 20% of its assets or gaining more than 50% of it assets in profit is highly unusual and likely is not the key driver. Similarly, a range for RoE of between −50% and 100% was deemed appropriate based on observations and business logic. The asset turnover ratio shows how efficiently a company generates revenues with its assets. The range of 0% to 500% was derived from the observations in the study, and plausibility was checked based on business logic. There is no reason for revenues or total assets to be negative; hence the variables should not be below zero under normal circumstances, and generating yearly revenues of over 5× the total assets of a company is, based on the observations in the study, also highly unusual even for internet businesses and will be excluded.

Lastly, the dividend yield was calculated by dividing the dividend per share by the share price to determine how much dividends a shareholder receives from investing 1 EUR into a particular company. As the variables did not show any extreme values, it did not require a range of inclusion.

The last variable that needs to be discussed is the revenue growth + EBITDA margin driver or the Rule of 40 driver. While the ranges are simple to be explained as they are essentially a rounded up/ down version of the sum of ranges for the revenue growth and EBITDA margin variables (−100% to 2500%), the reason for inclusion and significance is much deeper.

In 2015, Brad Feld published a blog post in which he cited the board meeting of an unnamed company where it has been detailed that a successful software company, including SaaS companies, should have their growth rate plus their profit defined as EBITDA equal to at least 40% (Feld, 2015). To exemplify, a company with 15% profitability should have 25% growth and vice versa. This rule also applies to loss-making companies, hence a company growing 50% can lose 10% of its revenues. This idea is highly interesting as it addresses both sides of the main internet business model dilemma: growth vs. profitability. While the principle is simple, as Roche and Tandon detail in their article "SaaS and the Rule of 40: Keys to the critical value creation metric" published by McKinsey, only some companies manage to achieve this, and the ones achieving it show consistently higher valuations than those that do not (Roche & Tandon, 2021). Consequently, this variable was also included in the study to test these relatively new ideas and ways of looking at and measuring internet companies.

5.4 Data Processing for the Final Data Set

Calculating the variables to be used for the study from raw financial data as well as implementing the described range limits required in addition to Microsoft Excel, a dedicated data analytics software (in this case Knime), and the implementation of a complex model combined with a well thought "divide and concur strategy." This subchapter will describe the process, and the KNIME model developed and used to calculate the variables for the study.

Transforming the Excel output into a large matrix

Following the process described in the sub-chapter 5.1.2, the data cube for the study comprised two large Excel files containing 173 matrices of 911 companies × 783 observations = 173 matrices (3 valuation indicators plus 17 financial indicators with 10 timeframes) containing each 713,313 cells with formulas. The first step in consolidating the data was to convert all matrices to "value only" cells, breaking the link to the data providers and disposing of all Excel formulas to enable simpler processing. Following the conversion, the step described in 5.1 of filling small gaps could be performed as matrices could be processed in batches of c. 10 per step. Following this initial processing, the next step was to consolidate the data into one giant matrix comprising all companies and observations on the vertical and the indicators on the horizontal.

Luckily, Microsoft Excel supports up to 1,048,576 rows, so reformatting each matrix into one column with 713,313 + 1 rows was possible. Consolidating all columns into one matrix created a large 713314 rows × 180 columns matrix (173 indicators and 7 metadata columns). During this process, the exclusion of the three indicators that did not have sufficient observations: UFCF, Debt, and BPS Tangible was also possible. Furthermore, calculating the EBITDA-R&D and EBITDA-CAPEX indicators was possible, leading to a 713,314 rows × 170 columns matrix. Lastly, during the final review of the companies included in the study, further 7 companies were excluded for various reasons. These seven companies are included in the "excluded" Annexes. The exclusion of these 7 companies lead to the deletion of 7×783 = 5,481 rows, leaving the study with a matrix of 707832 + 1 rows × 170 columns (163 with data + 7 with metadata).

Introduction to KNIME

As calculating the variables to be included in the study and implementing the ranges is well beyond what is possible in Excel, the file was imported into Knime for further processing via a divide-and-conquer strategy to calculate the final variables. KNIME (short for The Konstanz Information Miner) is a free and open-source data analytics software developed by KNIME AG based in Zurich, Switzerland. The team describes the software as a "modular environment, which enables easy visual assembly and interactive execution of a data pipeline" (Berthold et al., 2008). It is a modular environment enabling the processing of data step by step via "nodes." At the time of writing, the environment contains over 4,000 nodes, 1,285 components, and 222 extensions that have been developed over the nearly 20 years since the software exists.

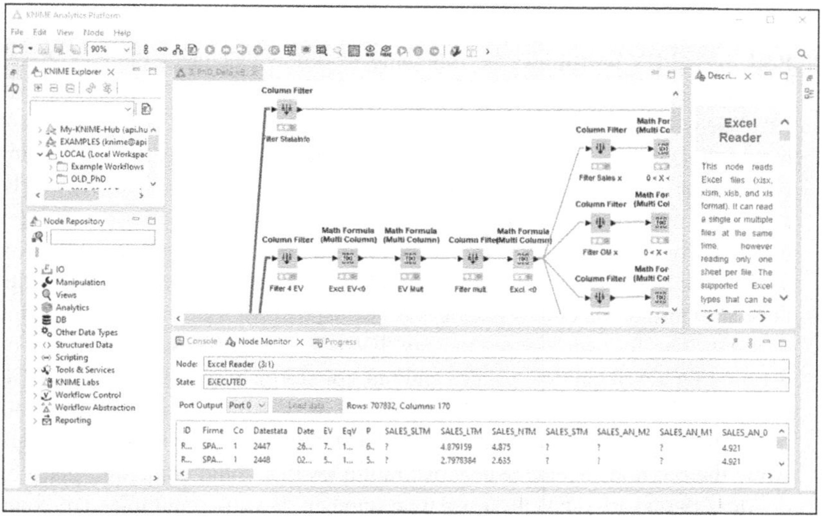

Fig. 5.4 Screenshot of the KNIME platform

Figure 5.4 shows a screenshot of the KNIME platform together with the main menus: KNIME Explorer (a workflow manager), the Node Repository (all nodes: processing steps available), the main workflow editing window, the Node Monitor (showing the output) and the Description window (explaining the functionality of the selected node).

Calculating the multiples

Data processing has been divided into 14 individual workflows comprising 128 nodes. The first group of workflows displayed in Fig. 5.5 focuses on calculating the multiples. The Input shown as the "Excel Reader" node is the starting point for all of these many variable-focused workflows and links to the Excel-based matrix. The workflows used:

1. **Metadata:** the first workflow just passes the main metadata, such as company names, company number, date, industry, and IPO date, to the output. The workflow can be seen in Fig. 5.5, noted with "1".
2. **P&L-based EV multiples:** the following workflow calculates the P&L-based EV multiples. It can be observed in Fig. 5.5 as part of the box annotated with "2". The workflow starts with a "Column Filter" node that filters from the large matrix the columns needed to calculate these multiples. The reason for filtering columns is to limit the resources required for processing this workflow. The next node removes the negative EVs using a simple "IF" function as having a negative company valuation poses on the one side mathematical challenges (e.g., combining with a negative EBITDA leads to a false positive multiple), and on the other side, it should never happen for a normally functioning business. The following node, named "EV Mult." calculates the multiples by dividing the EV by all Sales, GM, and multiple forms of EBITDA, EBIT, FCF, and Op. CF and creates new columns for all the calculated multiples. The 4th node filters original columns and leaves only the columns with the multiples, while the 5th node excludes negative multiples that could come into place by dividing the positive EV by a negative number. Negative multiples are counterintuitive as they combine a positive company valuation with a loss-making business model, essentially regarding an increasingly loss-making company.

   The workflow continues by breaking into four separate sub-workflows based on the group of ranges that were defined in the previous chapter: EV/Sales, EV/GM, EV/ EBIT, and the remaining EV/EBITDA in all forms, including the CF multiples. The sub-workflows include only two nodes, with the first one filtering the columns required for the calculation and the second one doing the calculation using two layered "IF" functions. The remaining nodes in this workflow merge the finalized multiples and connect them into a "Final Aggregator."
3. **Total Assets-based EV multiple:** this workflow calculates the EV/Total Assets multiple similarly to the previous workflow. It can be observed in Fig. 5.5 as part of the box annotated with "3".

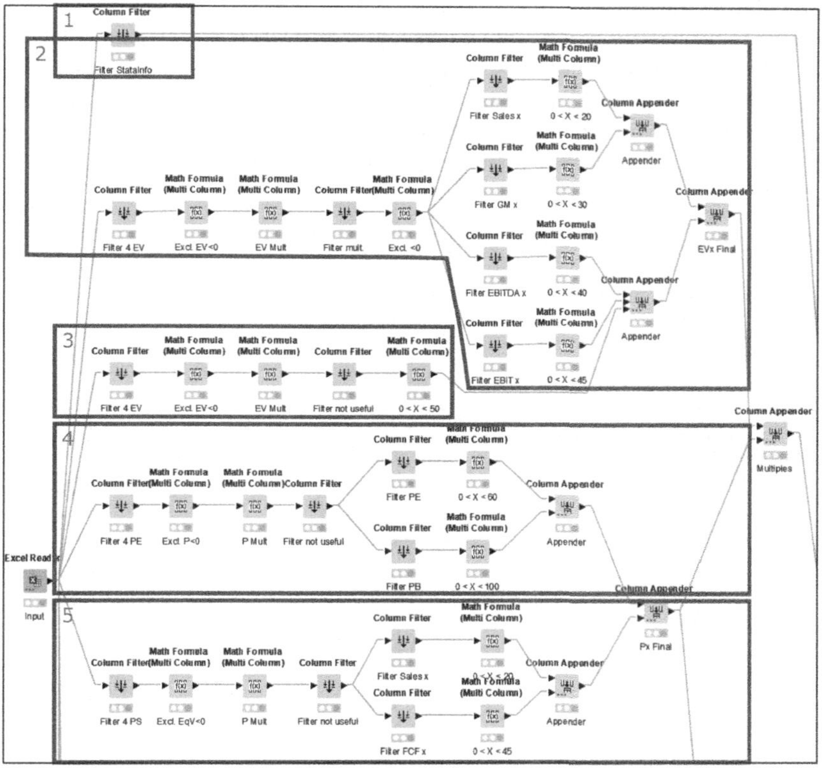

Fig. 5.5 Multiples part of the KNIME model used for the study

4. **Price to Earnings and Price to Book value multiples:** the 4th workflow calculates the named P/E and P/B multiples using a similar strategy and implementing the previously described different ranges. It can be observed in Fig. 5.5: Multiples part of the KNIME model used for the study as part of the box annotated with "4".
5. **Price to Sales and Price to FCF multiples:** similarly, the last multiples, P/Sales, and P/FCF, were calculated as shown in Fig. 5.5 as part of the lower part of the box annotated with "5". The reason for having two separate streams for the price multiples is that where "per share" values were available, these were used, while for the sales and FCF multiples, the Equity Value was used.

Calculating the drivers

As the implementation of a rolling division in KNIME (e.g., dividing column 1 by column 11 and column 2 by column 12) is very difficult, some drivers, particularly the simple margin and growth drivers, as well as asset turnover and RoE and RoE ratios, were calculated in Microsoft Excel with only the implementation of ranges and merger with the remaining variables performed in KNIME.

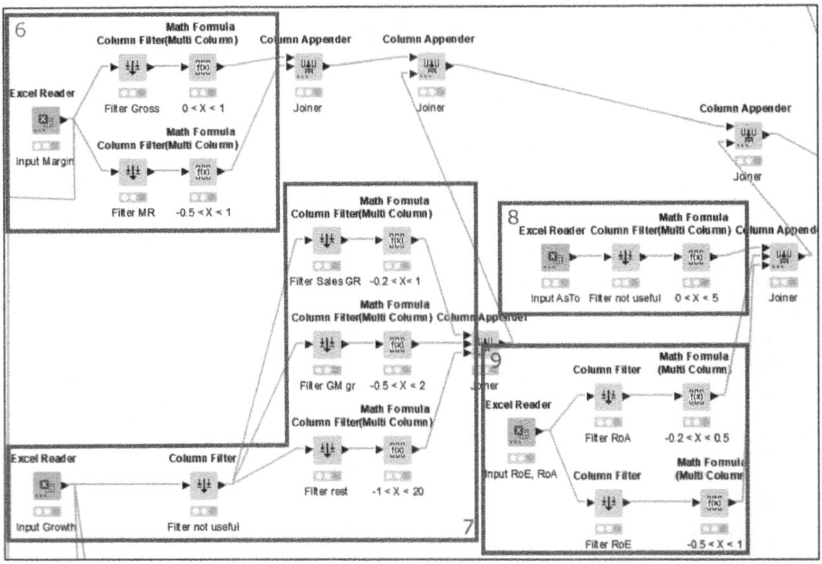

Fig. 5.6 Simple drivers part of the KNIME model used for the study

6. **Margin drivers:** workflow 6 illustrated in Fig. 5.6 box "6" calculates the final margin drivers. While the actual calculation was performed in Excel, implementing the ranges was done in KNIME as it was faster and would integrate the data into the large data cube. GM margin was calculated separately from the rest of the margin drivers (EBITDA, EBIT, Net income, FCF, Op. Cash Flow, EBITDA-R&D, and EBITDA-CAPEX) which grouped together in the node "Filter MR" as the same relevant ranges were used.
7. **Growth drivers:** this workflow is shown in Fig. 5.6 box "7," which calculates the final growth drivers. Similarly, with the margin drivers, sales and gross margin growth are calculated separately from the rest as these variables

have different relevant ranges. Also, similarly to the margin driver, the actual calculation was done in Excel, and only the filtering using the range was performed in KNIME.

8. **Asset turnover driver:** a very simple workflow illustrated in Fig. 5.6 box "8" imports the driver calculated in Excel and implements the filters described previously.
9. **Return on assets and equity drivers:** similarly to workflow 8, this workflow imports the data calculated in a separate file in Excel and implements the range filters as shown in Fig. 5.6 as part of box "9".

   Calculating more difficult to calculate drivers

   The drivers calculated in this section (PEG, Revenue growth + EBITDA margin, and Dividend Yield) are not more difficult to describe, however, they require input from various already calculated variables.
10. **PEG ratio / multiple:** the price to earnings growth ratio is calculated by taking the previously calculated P/E ratio and dividing it by the earnings growth rate. Box "10" in Fig. 5.7 shows the workflow. In addition to importing and filtering the required columns, one node per timeframe had to be used due to the challenging implementation of a rolling division, as described in the simple driver section. The nodes were structured in two sub-workflows with five sequential nodes to speed up the processing time.
11. **Revenue growth + EBITDA margin driver:** workflow 11, as presented in the box "11" in Fig. 5.7, shows the flow used to calculate this new driver based on the previously calculated growth rate and EBITDA margin using a similar 5×2 node structure as in workflow 10.
12. **Dividend yield:** the last workflow in Fig. 5.7, highlighted with the box "12," shows the dividend yield workflow, which takes the dividend per share and divides the share price at the date of the calculation, with the only range limitation being that share price cannot be negative.
13. **Time since IPO indicator:** this workflow shown in Fig. 5.8 box "13" calculates the time since each individual company has had its IPO. While this variable is not a financial variable, it could be useful in testing some of the timing hypotheses.
14. **By cluster aggregated data:** also to gain some insights relating to the timing of changes in the drivers and bases, the workflow shown as part of Fig. 5.8 in the box "14" imports data from a separate Excel file in which the aggregated LTM and NTM growth rates, as well as EBITDA margins for each cluster, were calculated in addition to the corona dummy to help sort time-wise between "pre" and "post" corona observations. The aggregated data was calculated using two methodologies: simple average between peers to give

every individual company an equal weight and size adjusted based on the absolute values converted in Euro to calculate the industry as a whole.

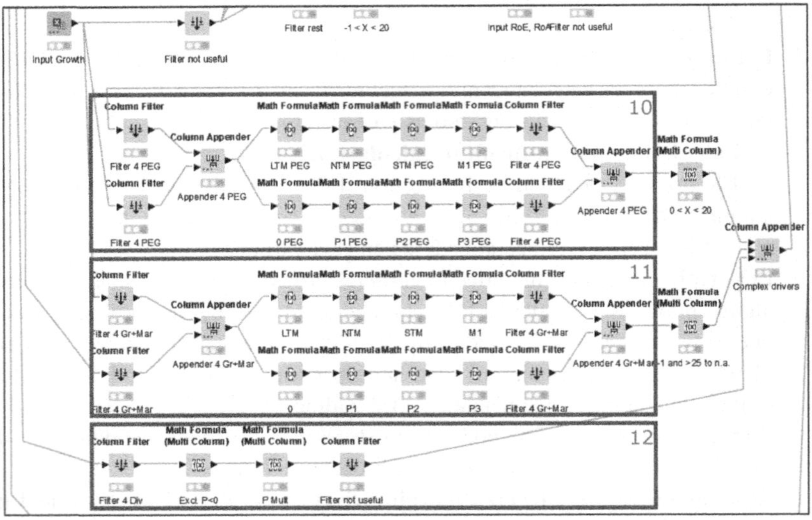

Fig. 5.7 Complex to calculate drivers part of KNIME model used for the study

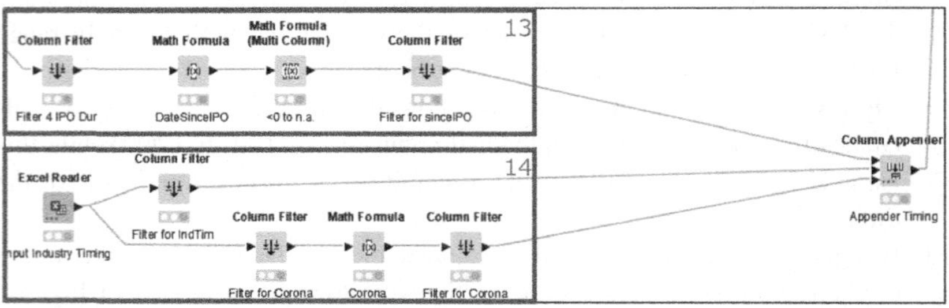

Fig. 5.8 IPO time and industry aggregations part of KNIME model

The last workflow shown in Fig. 5.9 aggregates all workflows into one large matrix of 707,832 rows × 405 columns. The final workflow also excludes one last company due to very limited and "patchy" data availability to reach the 903 companies included in the study. While meeting the criteria described before, this company had by far the worst coverage compared to all others. The Excel import is required to rename the companies, while the "Resort" node is used to resort the order of the columns.

Furthermore, as part of the final Excel input, one additional column was added to help further cluster the companies by region: "EU" for Europe and Israel, "NA" for North America, and "RoW" for the Rest of the World to enable later analyses by geography if the study requires it.

Lastly, the last two red nodes, "CSV Writer" and "Excel Writer," output the final matrix of 707,049 rows × 406 columns to Excel and CSV. Both outputs are required to enable data analysis independent of the statistical software used: Stata or Microsoft Excel.

The study will continue with the analysis in Excel as implementing such a large number of separate regressions (methodology to be explained in a later chapter) is simpler in Excel than in Stata. Furthermore, as the study's overall goal is to find the best-fitting multiple and driver at each point in time, a time-series analysis, which is possible only in dedicated software such as Stata, is not required.

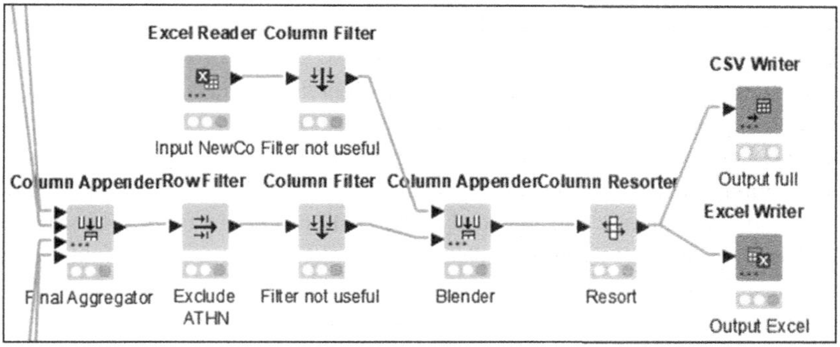

Fig. 5.9 Final aggregation and sorting of variables for output in the KNIME model

5.5 Extent of Variables Included in the Study

Based on the previous sub-chapters and processes, a total of 350 variables were derived for the study comprising 13 multiples across 10 timeframes (except PEG) totaling 128 variables and c. 31.4 million observations, as well as 24 financial indicators to be used as drivers across 10 timeframes for margin drivers and 8 for growth drivers in addition to the 6 industry cumulative financial indicators (altogether 222 variables) to be used to test timing hypotheses together totaling c. 65.9 million observations.

Across multiples and drivers, a total of over 97 million observations will be used in the study. Fig. 5.10 presents an overview of all variables independently if multiples or drivers, as well as the number of observations for each relevant variable across each relevant timeframe.

While the study size seems exaggerated, this amount of data will enable a more precise aggregation at later states. While it is very difficult to draw conclusions from 15 years of data on a weekly basis comprising 783 separate observations for each company, having collected this data will enable the researcher to look at average values each year or each month as opposed to just end of period values if the data would have been collected only o a yearly basis. End-of-period data would reflect only the analysis and sentiment of investors in a particular company at that particular point in time as opposed to an average of analyses and sentiments that would be reflected in a yearly value that is calculated based on the average of weekly observations.

In addition to looking at the number of observations, it is also important to look at the coverage of each variable across each timeframe in order to identify variables that will be unreliable. It is important to mention that the number of observations and the coverage ratios calculated in Fig. 5.11: Overview of the coverage ratios for all variables included in the study (except industry aggregations) are based on the final number of observations after applying the relevant ranges for a financials-based valuation.

Analyzing the coverage ratios, it can be observed that while some variables have relatively low ratios, such as the ones depending on R&D (e.g., EV/EBITDARD, EBITDARD Margin), the lowest coverage ratio is achieved by the PEG multiple. While this multiple could have added value to the study, it must be excluded due to the extremely low number of observations and implicitly coverage.

	SLTM	LTM	NTM	STM	FY-2	FY-1	FY0	FY+1	FY+2	FY+3	Total
EV/Sales	377,223	413,010	391,542	387,016	326,002	365,154	404,109	388,078	387,324	355,157	3,794,615
EV/GM	244,673	286,701	296,905	296,189	199,194	234,942	274,542	293,870	295,847	263,016	2,685,879
EV/EBITDA	233,773	268,193	295,777	312,657	192,631	220,999	251,795	277,442	301,361	291,588	2,646,216
EV/OP CF	184,408	228,159	263,156	283,321	140,835	170,585	206,468	241,451	270,361	262,384	2,251,128
EV/EBITDARD	101,550	123,973	136,377	142,256	78,178	95,229	114,691	130,037	138,312	128,852	1,189,455
EV/EBITDA-CX	165,331	203,091	237,995	260,007	130,377	155,811	185,105	215,794	245,486	238,903	2,037,900
EV/EBIT	224,300	260,652	291,741	316,591	186,823	213,473	243,350	266,720	299,822	299,116	2,602,588
EV/Asset	264,053	306,650	313,408	309,734	217,998	254,324	295,328	312,872	310,185	280,220	2,864,772
P/E	238,824	273,335	299,391	324,713	205,192	229,327	256,877	273,553	307,893	309,883	2,718,988
P/B	251,241	286,682	295,796	286,937	216,965	241,821	273,681	293,714	287,128	257,931	2,691,896
P/Sales	379,924	415,979	395,143	390,974	327,535	367,265	407,053	391,299	391,012	359,126	3,825,310
P/FCF	143,063	177,685	223,187	249,415	112,616	133,689	159,740	193,473	234,436	232,920	1,860,224
PEG	n.a.	16,856	26,278	24,974	n.a.	20,820	22,520	24,942	30,660	27,114	194,164
Gross Margin	263,655	298,724	302,200	298,707	228,911	259,170	291,080	302,594	299,832	264,201	2,809,074
EBITDA Margin	327,091	356,508	363,446	362,366	294,801	322,108	348,844	360,271	362,036	330,652	3,428,123
EBIT Margin	365,130	398,464	394,685	391,666	327,121	359,618	390,864	389,856	391,433	357,530	3,766,367
Net Margin	382,481	413,798	394,842	392,002	345,329	376,431	405,532	389,152	391,261	357,678	3,848,506
FCF/Sales	266,480	303,092	316,391	315,711	231,681	261,234	290,939	311,619	315,078	284,437	2,896,662
Op. CF/Sales	286,389	325,581	335,075	333,880	248,373	280,556	314,372	331,409	333,231	302,515	3,091,381
EBITDARD Mar.	131,022	151,722	156,531	155,725	111,280	128,209	145,920	155,911	155,990	139,432	1,431,742
EBITDA-CX M.	273,663	313,059	324,110	324,059	237,193	267,943	301,581	320,115	323,067	290,331	2,975,121
Sales Growth	n.a.	378,211	390,995	397,490	n.a.	334,792	361,875	374,755	394,449	361,564	2,994,131
GM Growth	n.a.	251,534	295,794	306,252	n.a.	215,350	244,018	283,883	305,348	271,220	2,173,399
EBITDA Growth	n.a.	278,015	314,373	332,752	n.a.	248,153	268,849	299,058	321,807	308,481	2,371,488
EBIT Growth	n.a.	282,593	313,784	338,188	n.a.	251,550	272,298	296,052	321,239	316,565	2,392,269
Net In. Growth	n.a.	273,605	297,560	326,961	n.a.	240,792	258,419	276,712	307,740	307,439	2,289,228
EPS Growth	n.a.	294,259	317,225	341,802	n.a.	263,172	281,895	299,612	325,017	323,448	2,446,430
FCF Growth	n.a.	189,853	235,544	272,402	n.a.	158,948	177,303	209,601	250,575	251,383	1,745,609
Op. CF Growth	n.a.	234,689	283,089	308,159	n.a.	198,421	222,484	260,506	293,898	283,301	2,084,547
DPS Growth	n.a.	152,191	162,861	164,689	n.a.	128,061	140,048	150,123	157,827	151,822	1,207,622
EBITDA-R&D Gr.	n.a.	119,935	143,275	151,107	n.a.	100,933	115,900	136,105	148,906	136,337	1,052,498
EBITDA-CX Gr.	n.a.	211,376	257,533	281,952	n.a.	178,607	200,146	235,500	267,498	257,062	1,889,674
Asset Turno.	278,857	318,404	322,979	318,099	241,835	274,075	309,086	323,521	319,375	287,794	2,994,025
RoA	257,681	297,447	310,321	311,456	222,432	251,603	284,255	305,030	309,104	283,020	2,832,349
RoE	278,296	317,279	326,865	325,645	241,345	272,084	305,740	323,352	324,033	296,895	3,011,534
Dividend Yield	301,803	342,680	336,502	322,124	267,542	297,117	332,275	336,850	324,482	295,248	3,156,623
S.Gr+EBITDAMa	n.a.	334,859	363,294	363,556	n.a.	299,525	327,136	358,217	364,616	331,272	2,742,475
Ind. S.Gr.Cumu	n.a.	707,049	n.a.	n.a.	n.a.	n.a.	n.a.	n.a.	n.a.	n.a.	707,049
Ind.E.Mar.Cumu	n.a.	707,049	707,049	n.a.	n.a.	n.a.	n.a.	n.a.	n.a.	n.a.	1,414,098
Ind. S.Gr.Avg	n.a.	704,354	n.a.	n.a.	n.a.	n.a.	n.a.	n.a.	n.a.	n.a.	704,354
Ind.E.Mar.Avg	n.a.	706,979	704,424	n.a.	n.a.	n.a.	n.a.	n.a.	n.a.	n.a.	1,411,403
Total	6,220,911	12,924,275	12,137,443	11,021,534	5,332,189	8,671,891	9,686,118	10,333,049	10,807,669	10,095,837	97,230,916

Fig. 5.10 Overview of the variables and the number of observations that will be included in the study

	SLTM	LTM	NTM	STM	FY-2	FY-1	FY0	FY+1	FY+2	FY+3	Total
EV/Sales	77%	85%	80%	79%	67%	75%	83%	79%	79%	73%	78%
EV/GM	50%	59%	61%	61%	41%	48%	56%	60%	61%	54%	55%
EV/EBITDA	48%	55%	61%	64%	39%	45%	52%	57%	62%	60%	54%
EV/OP CF	38%	47%	54%	58%	29%	35%	42%	49%	55%	54%	46%
EV/EBITDARD	21%	25%	28%	29%	16%	20%	23%	27%	28%	26%	24%
EV/EBITDA-CX	34%	42%	49%	53%	27%	32%	38%	44%	50%	49%	42%
EV/EBIT	46%	53%	60%	65%	38%	44%	50%	55%	61%	61%	53%
EV/Asset	54%	63%	64%	63%	45%	52%	60%	64%	64%	57%	59%
P/E	49%	56%	61%	67%	42%	47%	53%	56%	63%	63%	56%
P/B	51%	59%	61%	59%	44%	50%	56%	60%	59%	53%	55%
P/Sales	78%	85%	81%	80%	67%	75%	83%	80%	80%	74%	78%
P/FCF	29%	36%	46%	51%	23%	27%	33%	40%	48%	48%	38%
PEG	n.a.	3%	5%	5%	n.a.	4%	5%	5%	6%	6%	5%
Gross Margin	54%	61%	62%	61%	47%	53%	60%	62%	61%	54%	58%
EBITDA Margin	67%	73%	74%	74%	60%	66%	71%	74%	74%	68%	70%
EBIT Margin	75%	82%	81%	80%	67%	74%	80%	80%	80%	73%	77%
Net Margin	78%	85%	81%	80%	71%	77%	83%	80%	80%	73%	79%
FCF/Sales	55%	62%	65%	65%	47%	54%	60%	64%	65%	58%	59%
Op. CF/Sales	59%	67%	69%	68%	51%	57%	64%	68%	68%	62%	63%
EBITDARD Mar.	27%	31%	32%	32%	23%	26%	30%	32%	32%	29%	29%
EBITDA-CX M.	56%	64%	66%	66%	49%	55%	62%	66%	66%	59%	61%
Sales Growth	n.a.	77%	80%	81%	n.a.	69%	74%	77%	81%	74%	77%
GM Growth	n.a.	52%	61%	63%	n.a.	44%	50%	58%	63%	56%	56%
EBITDA Growth	n.a.	57%	64%	68%	n.a.	51%	55%	61%	66%	63%	61%
EBIT Growth	n.a.	58%	64%	69%	n.a.	52%	56%	61%	66%	65%	61%
Net In. Growth	n.a.	56%	61%	67%	n.a.	49%	53%	57%	63%	63%	59%
EPS Growth	n.a.	60%	65%	70%	n.a.	54%	58%	61%	67%	66%	63%
FCF Growth	n.a.	39%	48%	56%	n.a.	33%	36%	43%	51%	51%	45%
Op. CF Growth	n.a.	48%	58%	63%	n.a.	41%	46%	53%	60%	58%	53%
DPS Growth	n.a.	31%	33%	34%	n.a.	26%	29%	31%	32%	31%	31%
EBITDA-R&D Gr.	n.a.	25%	29%	31%	n.a.	21%	24%	28%	31%	28%	27%
EBITDA-CX Gr.	n.a.	43%	53%	58%	n.a.	37%	41%	48%	55%	53%	48%
Asset Turno.	57%	65%	66%	65%	50%	56%	63%	66%	65%	59%	61%
RoA	53%	61%	64%	64%	46%	52%	58%	62%	63%	58%	58%
RoE	57%	65%	67%	67%	49%	56%	63%	66%	66%	61%	62%
Dividend Yield	62%	70%	69%	66%	55%	61%	68%	69%	66%	60%	65%
S.Gr+EBITDAMa	n.a.	69%	74%	74%	n.a.	61%	67%	73%	75%	68%	70%
Total	53%	56%	59%	61%	46%	48%	54%	57%	60%	56%	

Fig. 5.11 Overview of the coverage ratios for all variables included in the study (except industry aggregations)

6 Descriptive Statistics

While descriptive statistics, defined as the characterization of basic features of the data in this study, uses informational coefficients meant to portray a given data set (input data for the analysis), this chapter tries, in addition to describing the data, to also provide some reference values with regards to typical multiples and financial KPIs overall and for selected industries to the reader. The inferential statistics chapter performs all analyses using empirical research, however, the conclusions will rather be at a high conceptual level describing the types of bases and drivers most relevant at various points in time.

This chapter will also close a gap often found in traditional financial and industry publications by comparing, in addition to multiple industries as part of the same analysis, also the same industry over a longer period of time (15 years) to enable the observation of long-term multiples and financial KPIs.

Statistics presented will either relate to the entire sample of companies (studied population) or to a cluster or segment of the entire sample. The presentation will also focus on selected variables and timeframes where the entire dataset is not feasible.

6.1 Methodological Aspects

The descriptive statistics will be based on yearly values calculated as average from the weekly observations as presenting 783 weekly observations is, on the one hand, challenging and, on the other hand, too detailed to conclude.

The research approach will focus on the following:

A. Trusculescu, *Business Valuation Across the Industry Life Cycle*,
https://doi.org/10.1007/978-3-658-49126-0_6

- Measuring the central tendency by using the average, median and
- Determining data variability or spread based on the calculation of the standard deviation, first and third quartile, kurtosis, and skewness, with the overarching goals of:
- Data understanding in preparation for the inferential statistical analysis, and
- Determine industry-level tendencies and comparisons useful for corporate finance professionals as well as management teams and shareholders

The main analysis tool will be Microsoft Excel, which contains all functions required to perform the calculations and think-cell in combination with Microsoft PowerPoint for the visualizations.

The yearly data is structured in a large matrix of 13,545 lines × 403 columns, and the weekly data is structured in a matrix of 707,049 lines × 403 columns sorted by year and industry, the INDIRECT function will be used to generate the ranges required for each calculation. As the inferential statistical analysis will use the same approach and the inferential part is more complex, an example of an Excel Sheet, an explanation of the input fields, and an example of such a formula will all be provided in the respective methodology sub-chapter.

6.2 Research Results with Deliberations and Interpretations

6.2.1 Understanding of the Companies Included in The Study: Count, Size, and Break-Down by Industry

The first piece of analysis shows that the number of companies included in the study is broken down by industry. The analysis is based on the number of LTM observations, as this is one of the variables with the best coverage ratios. Figure 6.1 presents the overview.

While some industries show many companies, such as eCommerce, Marketplace, and most Software segments, some industries are significantly less covered, such as Online Brokerage, Financial Content Monetization, Social Networks, and Travel, to name a few. Such industries will have to be observed closely during the next phases of the study as such a low number of companies can generate misleading conclusions. Unfortunately, all less well-covered industries have individual business models that cannot be compared to any other clusters to facilitate a "merger."

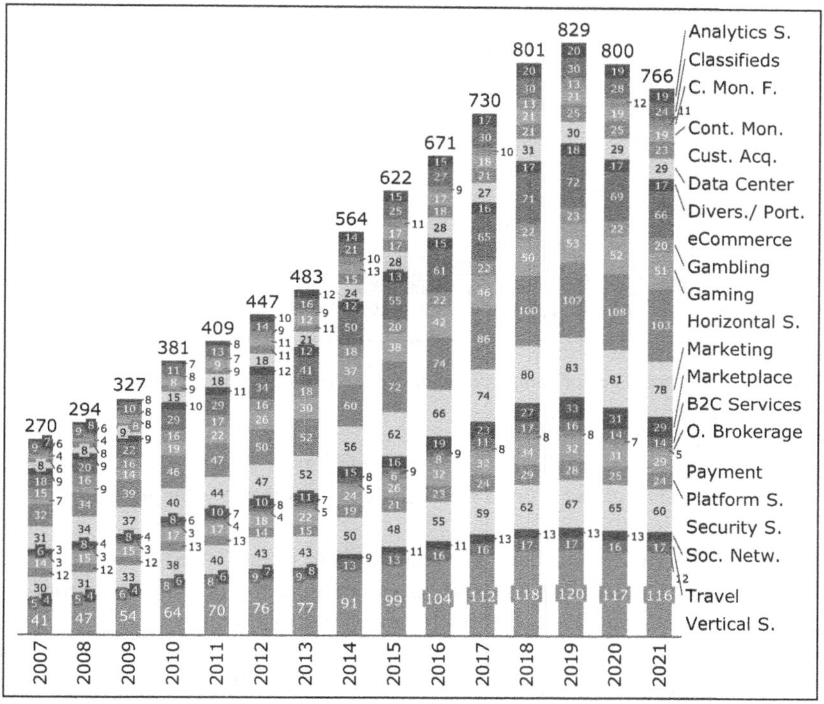

Fig. 6.1 Number of companies included in the study broken down by industry

The next piece of analysis looks at the Enterprise Value of the companies included in the study at the end of each year. It should be noted the number of companies increased by a factor of 2.8x, and the Enterprise Value of the companies represented increased by 11.7× resulting in the average EV increasing from EUR 3.4bn in 2007 to EUR 14bn in 2021 as seen in Fig. 6.2: Enterprise Value of companies included in the study by year (EURbn). This development shows how the growth in company valuation that investors ascribe to internet-driven businesses and increasing importance in the economy.

Breaking down the Enterprise Value by the industry as shown in Fig. 6.3, some interesting developments can be observed:

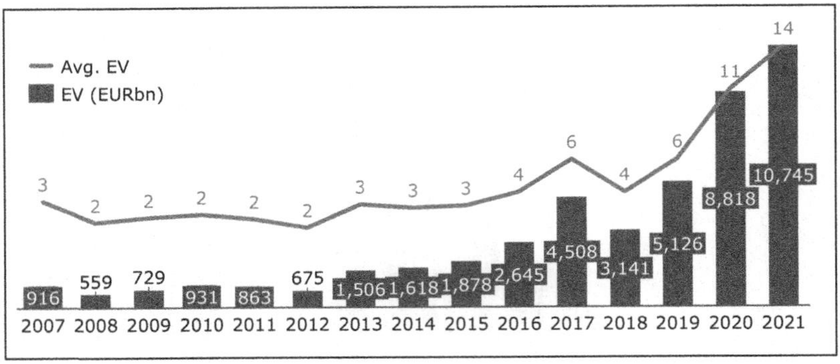

Fig. 6.2 Enterprise Value of companies included in the study by year (EURbn)

- Platform software, which in 2021 represented more than ¼ of the total Enterprise Value, has grown from 20% of the total enterprise value in 2007 to 28% in 2021
- Diversifieds and Portals have lost relative share from 27% to 22%
- eCommerce and Marketplace have also seen extreme growth in share from 5% to 17% for eCommerce and from 1% to 6% for marketplaces
- Security software has decreased significantly from 21% to 3%, however, this can only be attributed to the lower number of IPOs compared to other industries, as can be observed in Fig. 6.1

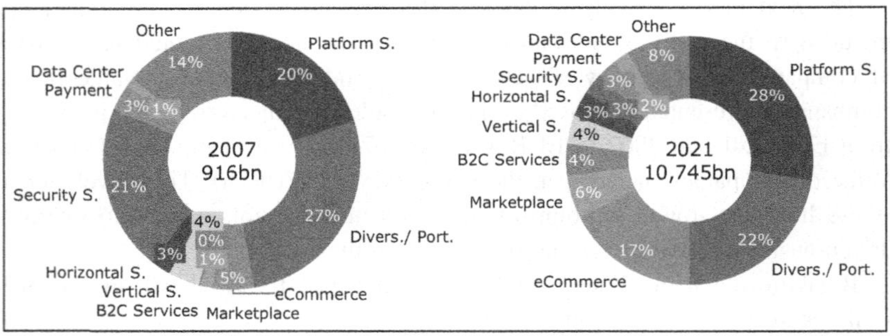

Fig. 6.3 Breakdown of the Enterprise Value by industry (top 10 industries in 2023)

Figure 6.4 presents a similar analysis, however, based on revenues. It can be seen that while the growth is not as extreme, revenues have also grown from EUR 288bn in 2007 to EUR 2,356bn in 2021, representing a factor of 8.2x. The average revenue per company also increased from EUR 1.1bn to 3.1bn representing an increase of 2.9x. The overproportioned growth in Enterprise Value implies that the valuation multiples must have also increased, as observed in the line's development. While the average valuation was 3.2× Sales in 2007, dropping to 1.7× in 2008 and 1.3× in 2012, it has increased to 4.6× in 2021.

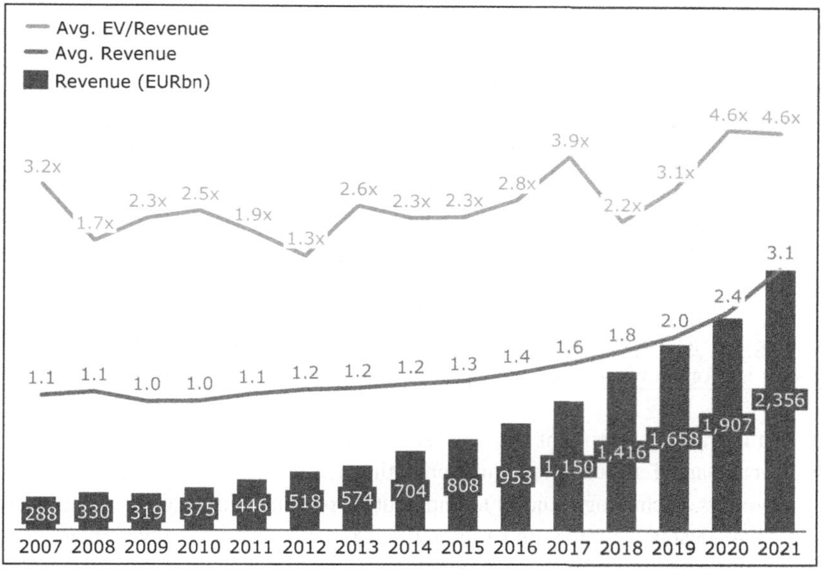

Fig. 6.4 Revenue of companies included in the study and relevant multiple

A last piece of analysis regarding all companies will focus on the top 20 companies included in the study, as shown in Table 6.1. The most obvious finding is that the largest companies, both in terms of EV and LTM Revenue, have grown roughly by a factor of 10 from 2007 to 2021. This finding is consistent with previous findings.

Diving into the details of the components of the top 20 analysis, it can be seen that while some companies kept their presence, multiple companies have disappeared, losing implicitly relative size in terms of valuation and revenue, with new companies joining the top 20 leagues. Some notable companies that made the cut in 2007 but not in 2021 are:

- VMware: the virtualization and cloud computing company, which despite developing well, has not kept the pace
- RELX: the information and analytics company which had a similar story
- Z Holding: the company owning Yahoo! Japan
- TD Ameritrade: was acquired
- Paychex: despite the good development, it could not keep up with the other fast-growing internet companies
- Expedia: the travel segment was one of the most hit during the COVID-19 pandemic making it natural that it disappeared from the list
- eBay: despite the history and strong presence, the company has not only lost in importance but also had years with negative growth; the main reasons are most likely competition and some inadequate management decisions
- NortonLifeLock: despite being an important name in the Cybersecurity space, the company has split since 2007 into two separate entities, with one being sold; the space has not only become increasingly competitive but also came under pressure with Microsoft launching its own solutions

The period has also made room for some new companies that managed to go public and/or grow sufficiently to join the list, with the most notable being:

- Netflix: a very important success story in the B2C streaming services
- Alibaba and Tencent: despite implementing very separate strategies (B2B commerce vs. technology and entertainment) represent two success stories from China; despite coming under pressure from the Chinese government, they managed to keep their relative position
- Shopify: an incredible story around software for the eCommerce space that profited from the rebirth of eCommerce during the COVID-19 pandemic that made eCommerce as a business model accessible to everyone
- Meituan and JD.com: represent another 2 success stories from China
- Facebook: went public and consequently joined the top 20

Table 6.1 Top 20 companies with internet-enabled business models in 2021 and 2007

Top 20 companies at the end of 2021 vs. at the end of 2007

	End 2021				End 2007			
	by EV in bn EUR		by Revenue in bn EUR		by EV in bn EUR		by Revenue in bn EUR	
No	Company	EV	Company	Rev.	Company	EV	Company	Rev.
1	Microsoft	2,424	Amazon.com	449	Alphabet	200	Microsoft	53
2	Alphabet	1,792	Alphabet	243	Cisco	149	Cisco	35
3	Amazon.com	1,723	Microsoft	174	Oracle	113	Oracle	19
4	Tencent	548	JD.com	143	Amazon.com	38	Amazon.com	14
5	Oracle	279	Alibaba	125	Microsoft	37	Alphabet	11
6	Netflix	279	Facebook	112	VMware	29	SAP	10
7	Alibaba	261	Tencent	85	RELX	23	Auto. Da. P.	8
8	Shopify	167	Cisco	49	Adobe	23	CoreLogic	8
9	Meituan	153	Oracle	40	Auto. Da. P.	22	First Data	7
10	ServiceNow	127	Netflix	28	Z Holding	21	eBay	7
11	Booking	95	SAP SE	28	Thomson R.	16	IAC/InterActive	6
12	Fiserv	87	Meituan	27	TD Ameritrade	13	RELX	6
13	Equinix	85	salesforce.com	25	Paychex	13	NortonLifeLock	5
14	Fidelity N.I.S.	83	PayPal	24	Tencent	12	Thomson R.	5
15	Recruit	79	Recruit	19	Fidelity N.I.S.	12	Fidelity N.I.S.	5
16	Snap	72	Baidu Inc	19	Expedia	10	Fiserv	4

(continued)

Table 6.1 (continued)

Top 20 companies at the end of 2021 vs. at the end of 2007								
17	Digital Realty T.	64	Vipshop	18	Fiserv	10	Adobe	3
18	Fortinet	56	Square	17	Int. Game T.	8	Juniper Netw.	3
19	IHS Markit	56	Adobe	15	NAVER Corp.	8	Int. Game T.	3
20	Thomson R.	56	Auto. Da. P.	15	salesforce.com	7	Expedia	3

Some other notable developments are:

- Microsoft: which completely transformed over this period growing from EUR 53bn revenues to 174bn to become the most valuable company in the study also due to its incredibly high profitability
- Amazon: a company that grew in terms of revenue by over 30× and in terms of valuation by over 45x
- Google (Alphabet): increased in both revenue and valuation by over 20x
- Oracle: despite its market arguably having a slower growth than the large internet players managed to roughly keep its position and grow by over 2× in both revenue and valuation
- SAP: a similar development even if the company is not in the top 20 by valuation
- Cisco: despite not making the cut to be included in the top 20 valuations in 2021, managed to stay in the top 10 by revenue despite sliding from position 2 in 2007

The number of changes shows on the one side how dynamic the internet-enabled space is and on the other side the shifts in importance and relative size.

6.2.2 Comparison of Multiples and Drivers Between Industries

The study will continue by providing a comparative analysis of valuations between the industries included in the study. The following six pages will present the EV/Revenue multiple, the EV/EBITDA multiple, the Price to Earnings Ratio as well as the Revenue Growth and EBITDA margin on the LTM and NTM timeframes at three different points in time 2021, 2019, and 2009 for each industry included in the study. The time points were selected to represent the latest available valuation level, the highest valuation observed on average before the COVID-19 pandemic, and the lowest valuation observed following the 2007–2008 financial crisis.

The goal of this sub-chapter is on the one side to discuss differences in valuations across internet-enabled industries and provide the readers with some tangible points as to what is the average valuation, average growth, and average EBITDA margin for each industry are. The following six pages contain the six figures: Fig. 6.5, Fig. 6.6, Fig. 6.7, Fig. 6.8, Fig. 6.9, and Fig. 6.10, with each figure containing five bar charts presenting the discussed valuation and financial metrics. The industries' order has been adjusted to show software companies close together (always the last five bars).

The first interesting finding relates to the overall valuation level of all industries. While the Revenue based multiples are fairly volatile, EBITDA multiples are fairly close to each other in 2021 and 2019. In particular, in 2021, EV/ LTM EBITDA multiples are, with a few exceptions, all in the 20× range. Travel is one understandable exception that shows a much higher multiple due to low profitability. On the lower side of the exceptions, Online Brokerage companies and Social Network companies have the lowest valuation, with 13× and 12x, respectively. Gaming, Gambling, and Marketing also show lower valuation levels at 15× LTM EBITDA. It is remarkable how close the valuation are to one another, particularly software valuations.

Evaluating the same factors in 2019, a similar picture can be observed, however, traveling is joining the group of low-valuation industries at 12× LTM EBITDA. Gambling and Gaming companies were also trading significantly lower at 10× and 12× LTM EBITDA, respectively. Another interesting development between 2019 and 2021 is the Financial Content Monetization companies which were trading in 2019 at an average multiple of 18× LTM EBITDA and at an average multiple of 27× LTM EBITDA in 2021. This shift can be explained by the increased attention financial investments have received over the COVID-19 period from retail investors.

Assessing 2009, two main observations can be made. Firstly, the multiples are significantly lower, ranging from 5× to a maximum of 14× LTM EBITDA, with most industries trading around the 10–12× mark. Secondly, the range is higher from a minimum of 5× to a maximum of 14× LTM EBITDA. Surprisingly, while most industries were trading lower, the Gaming industry had roughly the same multiple compared to other industries.

Observing the results of the NTM tables: Fig. 6.8, Fig. 6.9, and Fig. 6.10, the same conclusions can be repeated, with the overall valuation level being, in each case, lower than the growth investors expect from such companies. The only outlier that should be highlighted is the Analytics Software industry which shows a higher multiple in the NTM analysis compared to LTM in 2019. Motivations for this unusual divergence can vary, and a detailed analysis would be required to understand the reasons.

The variation in revenue multiples across all six analyses is natural, as revenue models and margins vary considerably across industries. It should be, however, not concluded that Revenue multiples are not relevant since an industry-level analysis as well as the integration of drivers, is required to explain the variance and relevance of multiples as bases.

Earnings multiples show, however, across all time periods and timeframes (LTM and NTM), lower variance than Revenue multiples but considerably higher variance than EBITDA multiples. The conclusions drawn using EBITDA multiples can also be observed in the Earnings multiples with the mentioned higher variance.

Continuing the evaluation of the results with the average growth rates and average EBITDA Margins, the first interesting finding is that average Growth Rates in internet-enabled businesses have not changed significantly over time. The growth rates of all companies included in the study show that the average LTM Growth Rate in 2009 was 13%, while it was 16% in 2019 and 15% in 2021. Comparing these figures to the NTM results of 22%, 19%, and 19%, it can be said that brokers seem optimistic and always plan with higher growth rates than last year.

Some industries show outstandingly higher growth, with Online B2C Service being the most interesting one. On an LTM basis, the industry grew at 14% in 2009, a rate which jumped to 27% in 2019 and stayed at 27% in 2021. End consumers' adoption of online services such as Netflix can explain the high growth rate. The NTM growth rates for this industry show similar levels of growth.

The second interesting cluster is the Marketplace industry, which went from 15% growth in 2009 to 19% in 2019 and 27% in 2021. These growth rates should be compared to eCommerce, which showed 12%, 14%, and 16%. These figures highlight two interesting trends. The first trend is that the marketplace is growing faster than eCommerce, which is unsurprising given the multiple advantages business models have over traditional eCommerce. Secondly, it can be observed that growth rates have accelerated in the last year. The 2021 growth rates can be explained by a general COVID-19 effect in which consumers ordered considerably more online since the shops were closed. Another industry affected by

COVID-19 was the travel industry. It is not surprising that LTM growth in 2021 is flat (1% growth) since the largest impact on travel happened in 2020, and this growth rate compares 2021 with 2020. On the opposite spectrum is NTM growth for travel in 2021 which essentially estimates the expected growth for the year 2022 following the post-COVID-19 recovery.

Continuing the analysis with a discussion of the EBITDA margins, two industries stand out. The first industry is the online brokerage industry, which enjoys outstandingly high margins in every single piece of analysis. On an LTM basis, the Online Brokerage industry shows margins of 51% in 2009, 40% in 2019, and 48% in 2021 compared to the overall average of 20%, 17%, and 18%. The NTM-based schedules do not change the conclusion despite the slightly different figures.

The second interesting industry is the data center industry which also presents above-average LTM margins of 26% in 2009, 34% in 2019, and 37% in 2021. These margins are, however, not usual since data center companies are usually CAPEX intensive, so EBITDA is not the best figure to capture the true profitability of this industry. If we look at the Price to Earnings ratios of this industry, we will observe that historically these were not extraordinarily high compared to other internet-enabled industries suggesting that EBITDA margins are in this care misleading.

The travel industry is also worth mentioning again. It is surprising that it only shows a −4% EBITDA margin for LTM 2021, however, 2021 was better than 2020, and companies had the chance to adjust their costs. 2021 NTM shows an 11% margin, representing a good recovery despite being below historical figures.

Surprisingly, all margins decreased on average over time from 20% in 2009 to 17% in 2019 and 18% in 2021. Three observations are, however, not sufficient to conclude the development of margins over time.

The analysis and discussion should provide a good indication to management teams and shareholders regarding the valuation levels of individual industries in the internet-enabled sector.

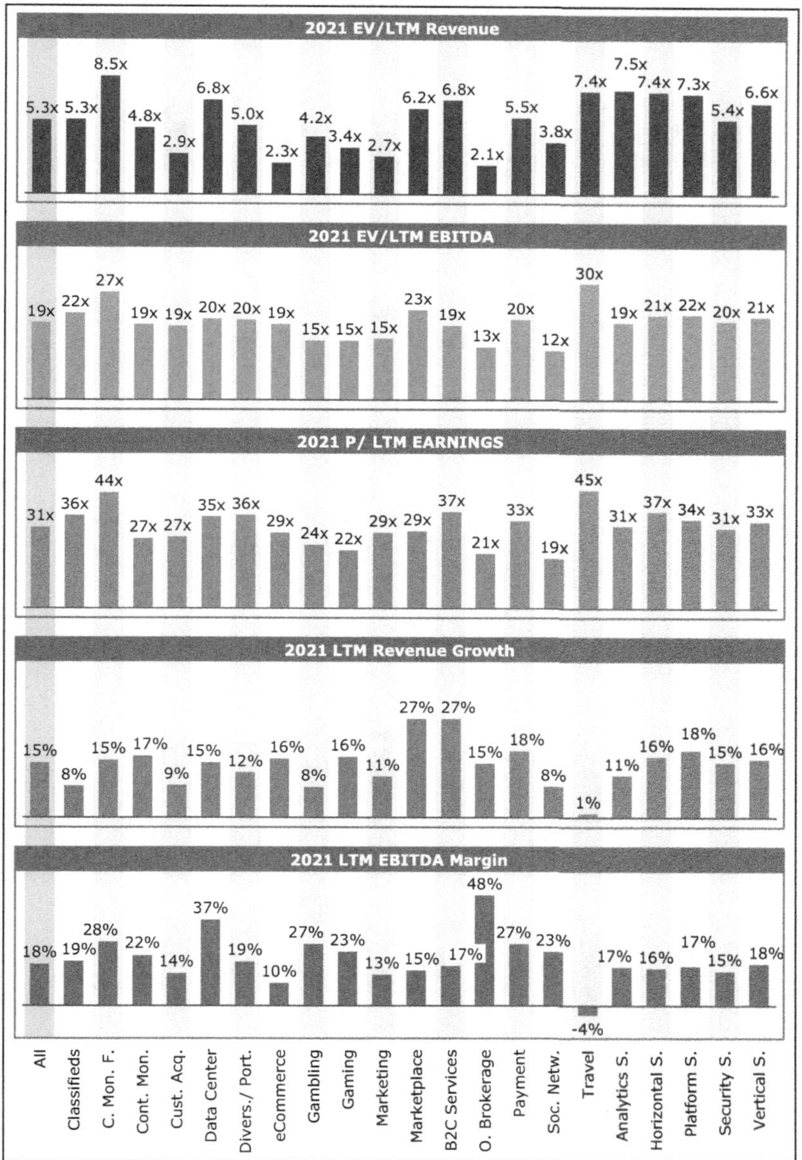

Fig. 6.5 Comparison of valuation and financial metrics between industries—2021 LTM

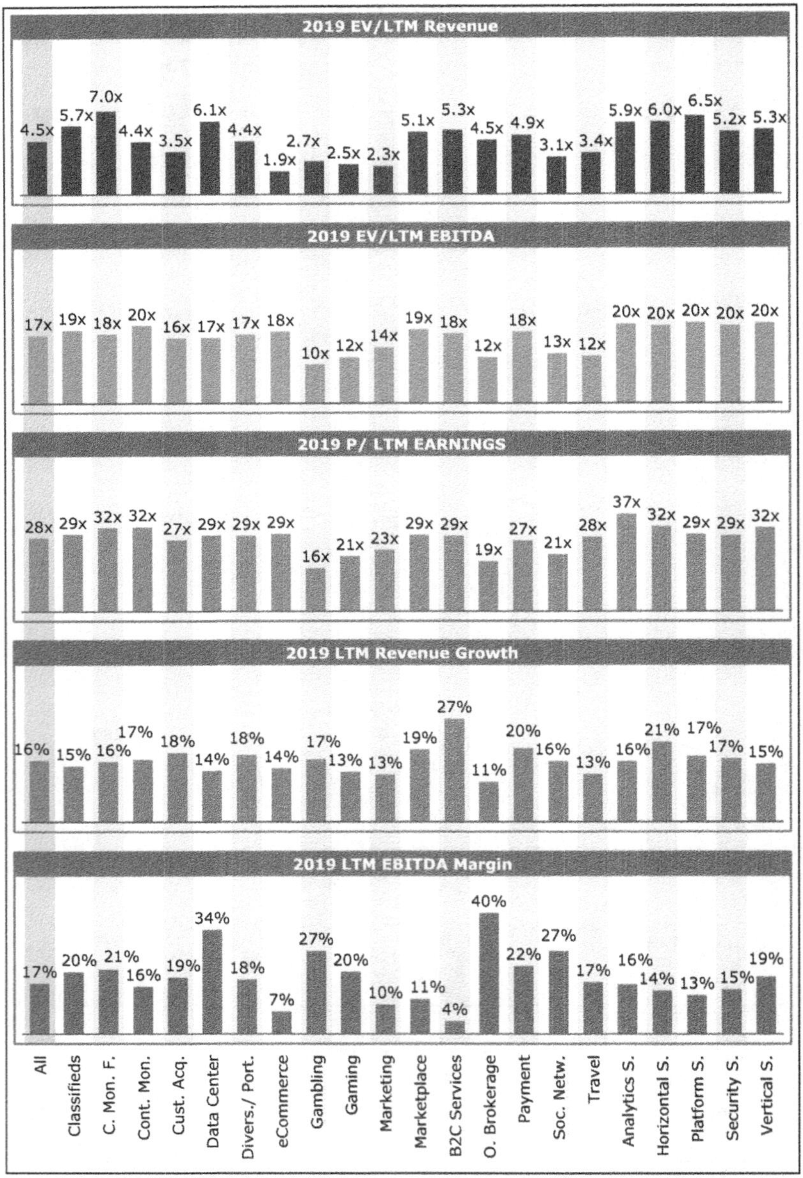

Fig. 6.6 Comparison of valuation and financial metrics between industries—2019 LTM

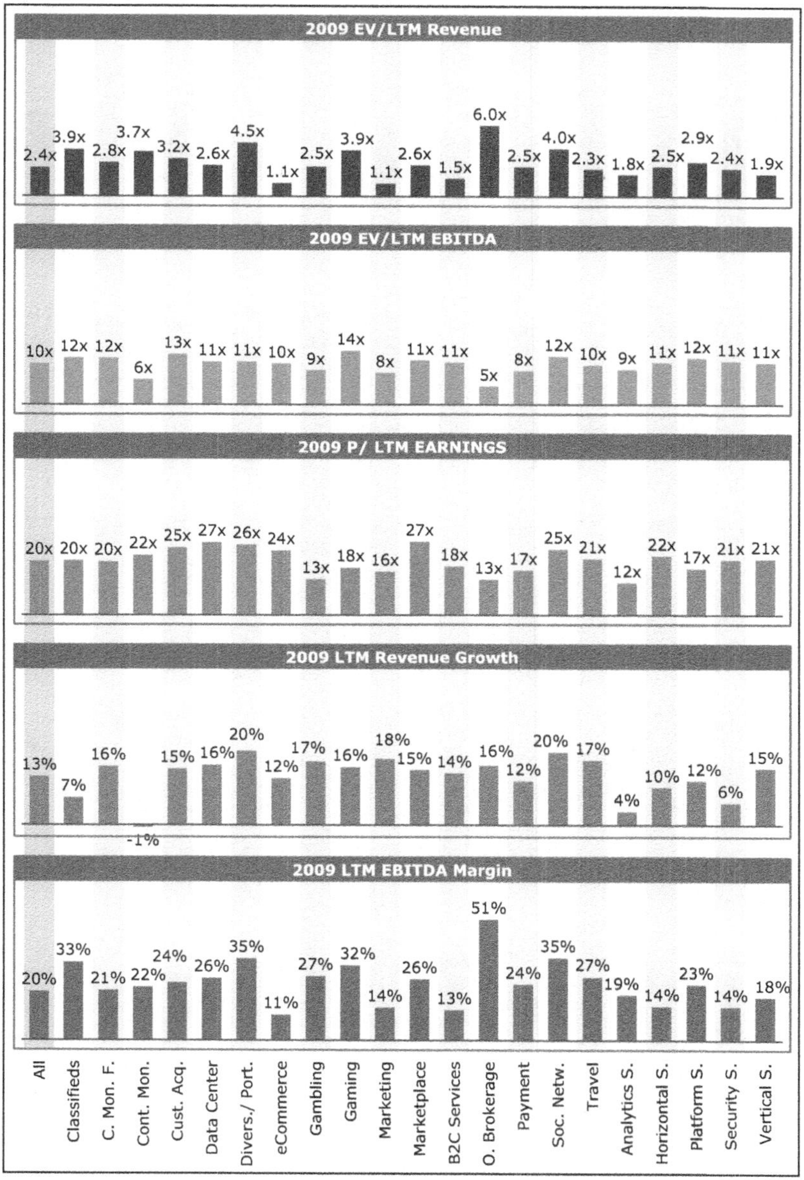

Fig. 6.7 Comparison of valuation and financial metrics between industries—2009 LTM

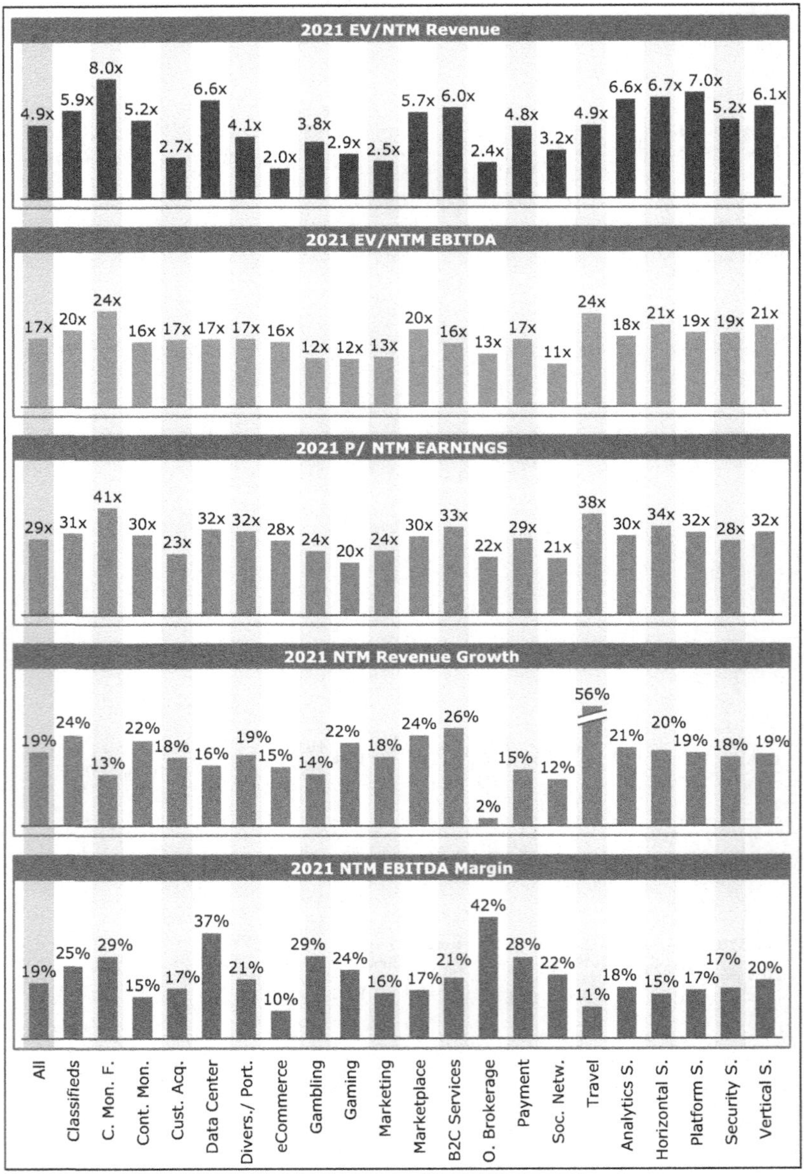

Fig. 6.8 Comparison of valuation and financial metrics between industries—2021 NTM

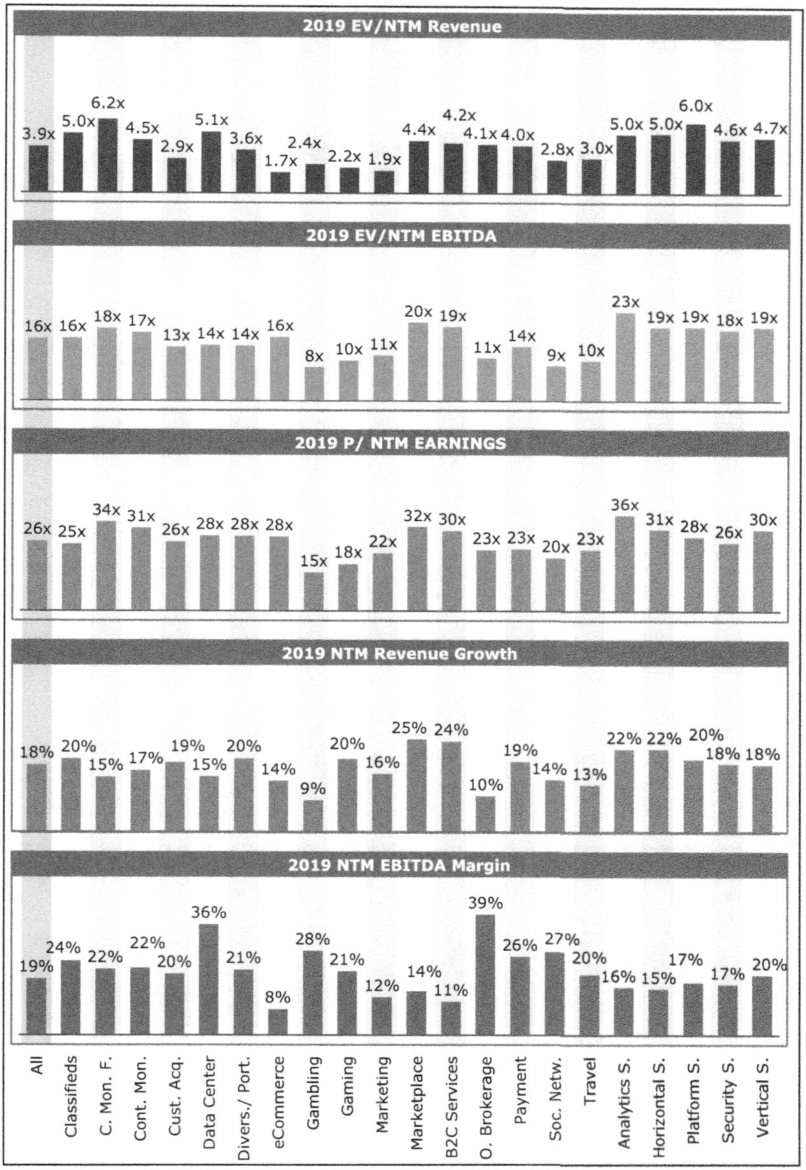

Fig. 6.9 Comparison of valuation and financial metrics between industries—2019 NTM

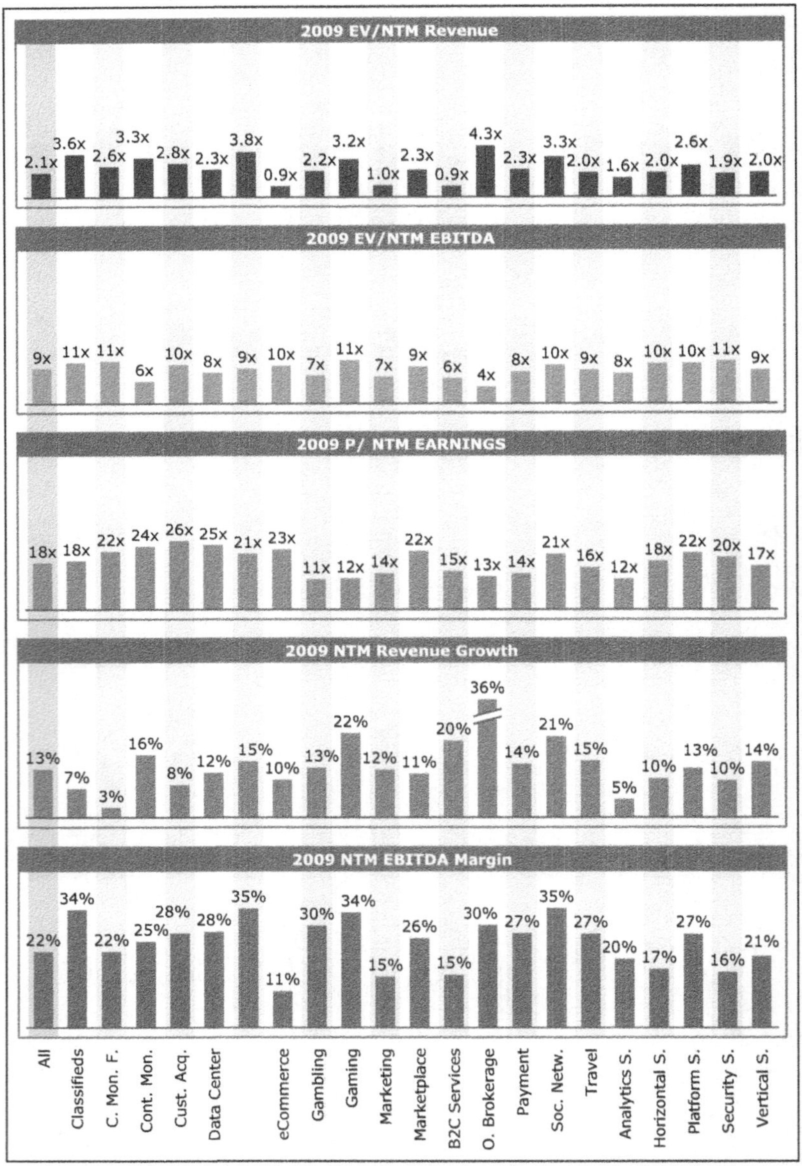

Fig. 6.10 Comparison of valuation and financial metrics between industries—2009 NTM

6.2.3 Development of Industry Multiples and Drivers Over Time

This subchapter and the next one will focus on LTM multiples and drivers, as LTM is based on actual performance and usually tells a similar story to other timeframes. Discussing every timeframe would take 10× the space without presenting new trends. Additionally, the EV/ LTM Revenue and EV/ LTM EBITDA multiples were chosen in addition to Growth and EBITDA Margin as these are the most watched multiples and drivers from all included in the study.

Figure 6.11 presents an overview of the average EV/ LTM Revenue and EV/ LTM EBITDA multiples over time and by industry, while Fig. 6.12 shows LTM Revenue Growth and EBITDA Margin over time and by industry. Due to the number of industries included in the study, the data has been split into 4 separate charts in order for it to be readable. The lines were combined into one chart so that software companies, B2B, and B2C companies were grouped. Each chart also presents the overall average in a thick black line.

As expected, the trends show an average decline first due to the financial crisis of 2007–2008, and recovery and development to reach new highs in 2021 with a small decrease in 2020 caused by the COVID-19 pandemic. It can be observed that almost all industries trade independently of the multiple at a value higher than the ones observed during the 15 years period. Some industries/ groups of industries are worth discussing individually:

- **All companies**: both Revenue and EBITDA multiple trends follow the expected development. It is interesting to see that growth has decreased on average from over 20% to c. 15% while the margin has also come slightly under pressure, however, it remains fairly constant at c. 20%.
- **Classifieds**: while the revenue multiple shows an uneven development, the EV/ EBITDA multiple has constantly developed upwards to reach over 20× in 2021. Both growth and margin have decreased significantly. Growth decreased from upwards of 40% to c. 10% while margin decreased from over 30% to c. 20%. Relative to the internet-enabled sector as a whole, the growth is subpar, while the margin is slightly above.
- **Customer acquisition**: the industry shows a similar trend to classifieds with decreasing EV/ Revenue multiples, constant (even in the last years below overall average) EV/ EBITDA multiples, strongly decreasing growth from 40% to c. 10%, and decreasing margins from 30% to a below average 14% margin. The trend is typical for a maturing company, even though rather negative.

- **eCommerce:** shows some interesting development with fairly constant revenue multiples that, despite dropping to almost 1× in 2009, recovered fairly quickly to 2× afterward. However, EBITDA multiples showed a similar trend, landing in 2021 above 2007. Growth was in line with averages and also fairly constant between 10% and 20%, with the EBITDA margin also fairly constant at around 10%.
- **Marketplace:** was expected to show a similar trend as eCommerce, however, there are some important differences. Both revenue multiples and EBITDA multiples have increased over the period. While revenue multiples are naturally higher than in eCommerce, EBITDA multiples have developed very similarly, except for the last two years. The growth rate also developed differently compared to eCommerce, with a growth of over 20% at the beginning and the end of the period covered. However, the EBITDA margin has dropped significantly to near the eCommerce level of 10% in 2020 despite increasing post-2009 to over 30%.
- **Travel:** is an industry that needs to be discussed by excluding the last COVID-19-affected three years, which pushed both margins and growth rates into the negative (even though on an average and yearly basis, this is not to be observed in the growth rates) and multiples to not meaningful values. The period beforehand showed fairly constant revenue and multiples of 4 to 5× Revenue and 10 to 14× EBITDA. Growth rates decreased to the overall sector average even before COVID-19, while margins also came under pressure from well over 20% to c. 20%.
- **Payment:** is an industry that, from the perspective of the multiples, is average developing similar to the overall average with the EV/ EBITDA surpassing, however, the average in the final years to move above 20x. The growth profile is also "average," while the margin is usually above average, with a slight decrease in 2017. The final years show an above-average margin of 27%.
- **Content monetization:** shows from an EV/Revenue multiple perspectives an unusual "bump" in the middle of the covered period, however, EV/EBITDA developed in line with the overall average. Growth has increased over the observed period from below 10% to above 15%, while the margin also showed an unusual jump from 20% to 30% before dropping again to 20%.
- **Gaming:** from a multiples perspective, tracked the overall average for a period of time before dropping both in terms of revenue and EBITDA below average. Growth was in line with the sector average, and with some years above and some below, however, the margin has increased post-2007 from 17% to nearly 40%, only to drop again to slightly above 20%.

- **Diversifieds/ Portals:** EV/Revenue multiples decreased over the observed period significantly from c. 9× to c. 5x, while EBITDA multiples, despite declining sharply after 2007 from 20× to c. 10× recovered over the period to surpass again 20× in 2021. Both Growth Rates and EBITDA margin have dropped significantly from over 40% to 12% and from 35% to 19%.
- **B2C Services:** represents an industry that includes services such as Netflix, which showed an interesting development. Both Revenue multiples and EBITDA multiples have increased significantly over the period to reach nearly 7× Revenues and nearly 20× EBITDA. At the same time, despite spiking to as high as 50%, growth seems to have stabilized at c. 25%, which is high even from internet-enabled business models. At the same time, despite declining to values as low as 5%, the margin has recovered and even increased to surpass 17% in 2021. The industry seems to be developing strongly in terms of both growth and margin.
- **Social Networks:** the last industry to be discussed in the second group of charts is one of the worst-performing over the observed period. Revenue multiples dropped significantly from over 10× to c. 3–4x, while EBITDA multiples also dropped from over 30× to 12x. At the same time, growth has decreased from c. 20% average with spikes as high as 40% to below 10%. Margin also had an uneven development with ups and downs. While the last observation shows a margin of well over 20%, the general trend is to decrease.

- **Financial content monetization**: represents an industry that usually delivers its services to other businesses. Nevertheless, the development was very good, with both revenue and EBITDA multiples increasing significantly from 5× to nearly 9× and from 15× to nearly 30x, respectively. The growth rate, despite declining, has stabilized around the 15% mark while the margin has hovered around the 25% mark, with a slight increase on both ends of the period covered. It should be noted that a certain spike has been observed in the last 2 years.
- **Datacenter:** presented a development with EV/Revenue multiples declining after 2008 but recovering over the period, with the EV/EBITDA multiples showing a similar trend. Growth rates, despite declining, seem to have stabilized around the 15% mark, with margins increasing from 25% to 37% in 2021.
- **Gambling:** shows the usual trends, however, it should be noted that valuation multiples in the last years were below average both in terms of EV/Revenue and EV/EBITDA. This is not surprising as the industry is excluded

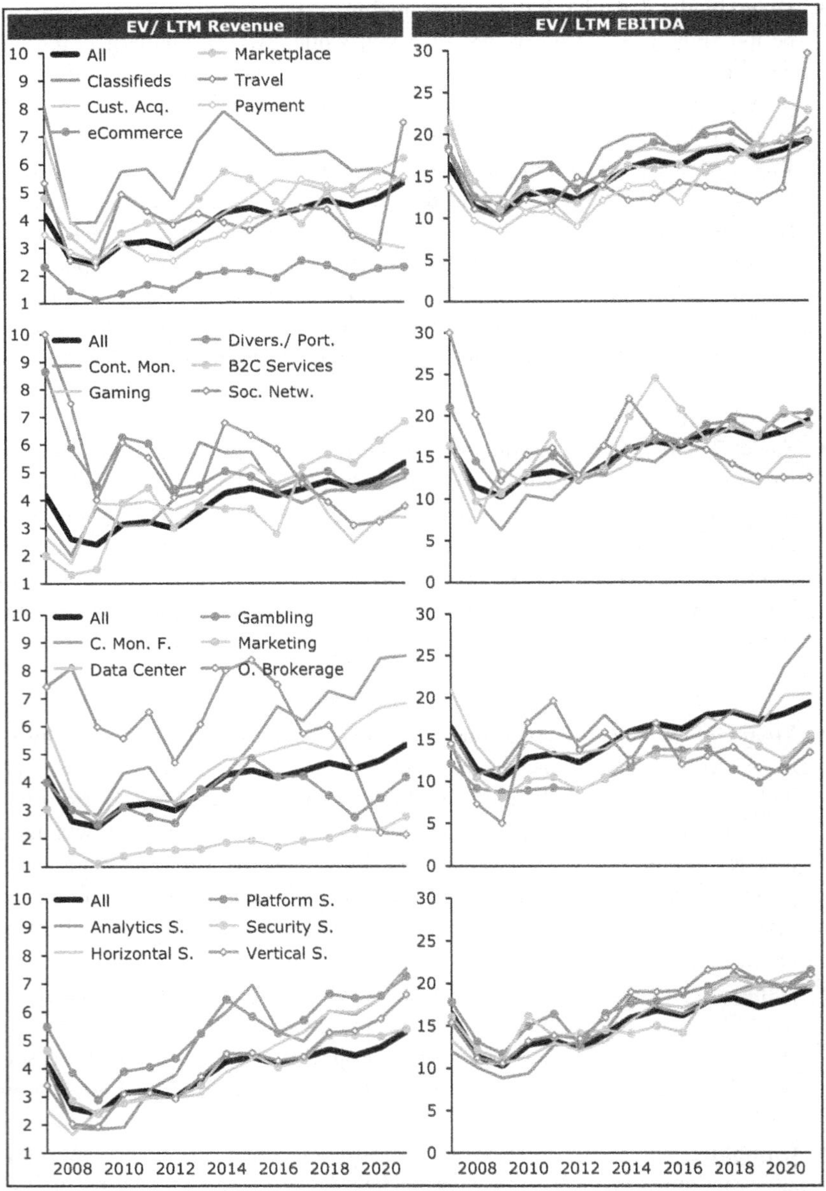

Fig. 6.11 Evolution of Revenue and EBITDA multiples over time

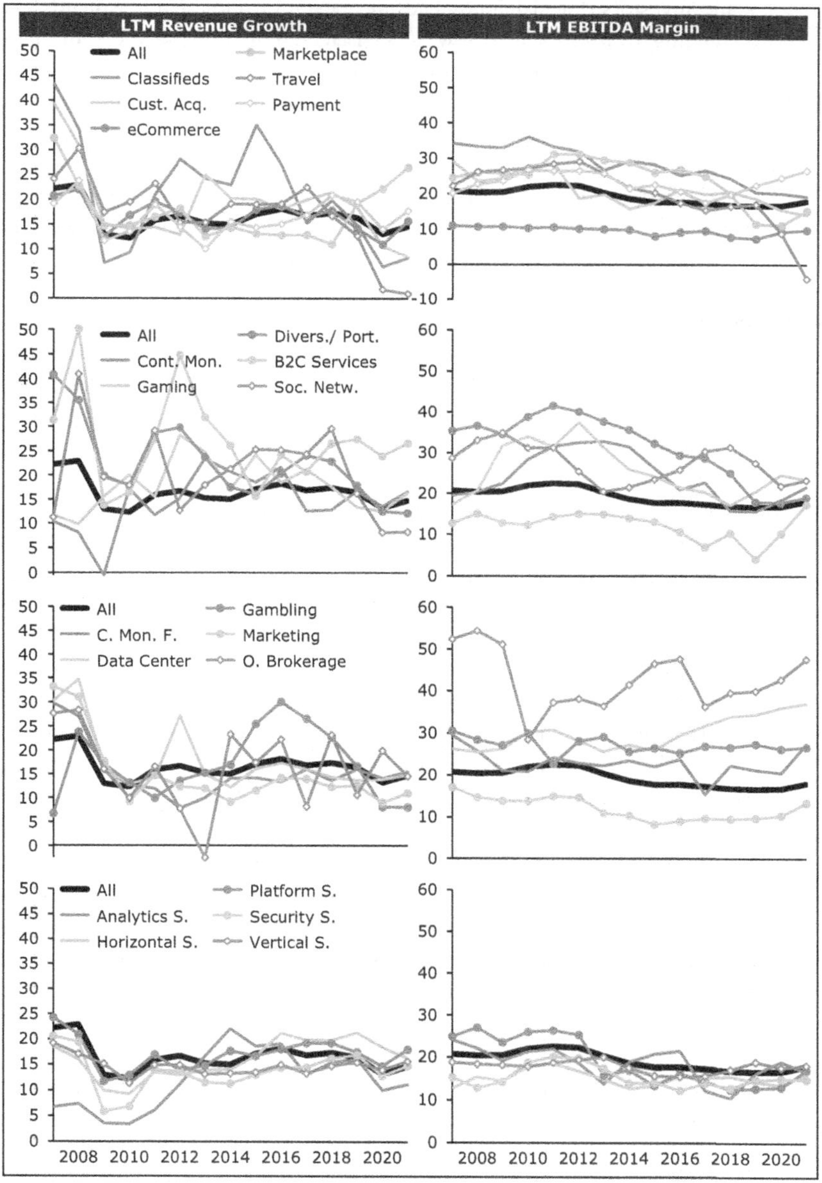

Fig. 6.12 Evolution of Revenue Growth and EBITDA Margin over time

for some investors. Growth rates had an uneven development, with ups and down ranging from 30% to below 10%. EBITDA margins at the same time remain constant around the 25–30% range, with a slight decline over time.

- **Marketing:** shows in all metrics a below-average development and absolute position. This finding is unsurprising as the marketing industry has come under significant pressure from large players. However, both EV/Revenue and EV/EBITDA multiples evolved with the general trend, with a widening gap from the average. The growth rate was also subpar, hovering around 10%, with the EBITDA margin coming slightly under pressure from 15% towards 10%, with a slight recovery in the last few years.
- **Online brokerage:** shows the most volatile development from all industries with decreasing EV/Revenue multiples but constant EV/EBITDA multiples. At the same time, Growth and EBITDA margins have moved in all directions. What can be said, though, is that the industry showed the entire time very healthy margins of almost always above 30%, with most of the time above 40%.
- **Software:** The last charts in Fig. 6.11 and Fig. 6.12 present the development of the Software industries included in the study. These will be discussed together as the development is surprisingly similar despite having very different target markets and total addressable markets. Starting with the EV/Revenue multiple, it can be observed that despite following the same general trend, all multiples ended up higher at the end of the period covered. A similar development can be observed in the EV/EBITDA multiples. It should be noted that all software industries show a valuation of above average most of the time. Shifting to Growth rates, it can be observed that with the exception of Analytics software which followed its own path, all industries followed the same path with a slight decrease in growth rates. It should be noted that all industries experience growth north of 10% most of the time. Considering the B2B nature of the business, this is very interesting. Most of the time, margins are below the average margin in internet-enabled business models and decreasing slightly. Two exceptions are Security Software and Horizontal Software, which started with lower margins despite merging with the rest of the industries at the end of the period.

The industry-level presentation, comparison, and discussion should be useful for all management teams and shareholders of companies in these respective industries. While the next sub-chapter discusses the same variables from a statistical perspective, it does not provide a visual summary and development-focused discussion.

6.2.4 Data Tendencies for Variables in the Study

This subchapter will discuss statistical aspects for the same variables as the last chapter: EV/ LTM Revenue, EV/ LTM EBITDA, Revenue Growth, and EBITDA margin, however from a statistical perspective covering topics such as Skewness, Kurtosis, Median, Standard Deviation, and 1st and 3rd Quartile as well as the difference of each industry to the overall average.

Table 6.2 shows a summary of the share of data sets for each industry and cumulative for all years that have a skewness below −2, above +2, below −3, above +3, as well as kurtosis of −7, above +7, below −9, above +9. The first ranges were chosen as these are the normally used cutoff points for normality tests. While in other models, such a high share could present challenges, which are difficult to overcome because the sets with high skewness or kurtosis are not grouped but rather dispersed, making it difficult to leave out variables or time-frames, or adjust the data, in the present model used for the inferential statistics analysis these topics are not a problem. The simple linear regression model does not assume normality concerning the input variables. It must be noted that the skewness and kurtosis are not unusual for financial data, which is usually more one-tailed with individual extreme values. While the ranges described in the past chapters partially address this topic beyond the story vs. financials component, if models assuming normality were to be used on this or similar databases, this topic would need to be addressed in detail.

Table 6.3 presents the described statistical measures for the EV/LTM Revenue variables. While averages have been described in detail, it can be noted that median multiples are most of the time lower by 1 to 2 points showing the positive skewness. At the same time, it can be observed that standard deviations are high for this multiple, however, the use of Drivers is the reason why Multiples/Bases are paired with Drivers in the analysis. Quantifying the differences between individual industries and ht overall average makes the differences more obvious and easy to interpret. As far as the EV/Revenue multiple is concerned, eCommerce, Marketing, Gambling (partially), Gaming (partially), and B2C Services (partially) traded below average. Other industries also show negative differences, however, not consistently.

Table 6.2 Skewness and Kurtosis of variables

	Skewness				Kurtosis			
	Share of sets with skewness				Share of sets with kurtosis			
	<−2	>+2	<−3	>+3	<−7	>+7	<−9	>+9
Analytics S.	1%	12%	0%	3%	0%	6%	0%	3%
Classifieds	0%	13%	0%	5%	0%	9%	0%	6%
C. Mon. F.	0%	6%	0%	0%	0%	1%	0%	0%
Cont. Mon.	0%	12%	0%	2%	0%	6%	0%	3%
Cust. Acq.	0%	11%	0%	2%	0%	6%	0%	3%
Data Center	0%	14%	0%	5%	0%	8%	0%	6%
Divers./ Port.	0%	8%	0%	2%	0%	4%	0%	3%
eCommerce	0%	21%	0%	10%	0%	16%	0%	12%
Gambling	1%	18%	0%	6%	0%	12%	0%	8%
Gaming	0%	17%	0%	7%	0%	12%	0%	9%
Horizontal S.	0%	23%	0%	12%	0%	18%	0%	15%
Marketing	0%	24%	0%	11%	0%	18%	0%	14%
Marketplace	0%	15%	0%	5%	0%	8%	0%	5%
B2C Services	0%	8%	0%	1%	0%	3%	0%	1%
O. Brokerage	1%	7%	0%	0%	0%	0%	0%	0%
Payment	1%	20%	0%	8%	0%	13%	0%	10%
Platform S.	1%	15%	0%	5%	0%	10%	0%	6%
Security S.	0%	22%	0%	11%	0%	17%	0%	13%
Soc. Netw.	0%	6%	0%	1%	0%	2%	0%	1%
Travel	1%	14%	0%	3%	0%	6%	0%	3%
Vertical S.	0%	25%	0%	16%	0%	22%	0%	19%

Evaluating the 1st and 3rd quartile, it can be noted that the ranges are fairly high, a finding which is not surprising given the high standard deviation. These high ranges can either mean that EV/Revenue is not the correct measure for valuation as it will be analyzed later or that Drivers have a high importance in defining the value.

Table 6.3 Data tendencies for EV/LTM Revenue

Average

	07	08	09	10	11	12	13	14	15	16	17	18	19	20	21
All	4.2	2.6	2.4	3.1	3.2	3.0	3.6	4.2	4.4	4.1	4.4	4.7	4.5	4.7	5.3
Classifieds	8.1	3.9	3.9	5.7	5.8	4.7	6.8	7.9	7.1	6.3	6.3	6.4	5.7	5.8	5.3
C. Mon. F.	4.8	3.0	2.8	4.3	4.5	3.2	3.5	4.3	5.3	6.7	6.2	7.2	7.0	8.4	8.5
Cont. Mon.	3.2	2.0	3.7	3.1	3.1	4.0	6.1	5.7	5.7	4.3	3.9	4.3	4.4	4.4	4.8
Cust. Acq.	7.0	3.9	3.2	5.0	4.3	3.1	3.7	4.2	4.8	5.4	5.3	5.0	3.5	3.1	2.9
Data Center	6.1	3.7	2.6	3.7	3.4	3.3	4.2	4.8	4.9	5.2	5.4	5.2	6.1	6.6	6.8
Divers./ Port.	8.6	5.9	4.5	6.3	6.0	4.4	4.5	5.0	4.8	4.4	4.8	5.0	4.4	4.5	5.0
eCommerce	2.3	1.4	1.1	1.3	1.7	1.5	2.0	2.1	2.1	1.9	2.5	2.3	1.9	2.2	2.3
Gambling	4.0	3.0	2.5	3.1	2.7	2.5	3.7	3.8	4.8	4.2	4.2	3.5	2.7	3.4	4.2
Gaming	2.7	1.7	3.9	3.8	3.9	3.6	4.0	4.7	5.2	4.6	5.0	3.5	2.5	3.4	3.4
Marketing	3.0	1.6	1.1	1.4	1.6	1.6	1.6	1.8	1.9	1.7	1.9	2.0	2.3	2.3	2.7
Marketplace	4.8	3.4	2.6	3.5	3.9	3.9	4.8	5.7	5.4	4.6	3.8	5.0	5.1	5.7	6.2
B2C Services	2.0	1.3	1.5	3.9	4.4	3.0	3.8	3.7	3.7	2.8	5.2	5.6	5.3	6.1	6.8
O. Brokerage	7.4	8.1	6.0	5.6	6.5	4.7	6.1	8.0	8.3	7.5	5.7	6.0	4.5	2.2	2.1
Payment	3.5	2.9	2.5	3.1	2.6	2.5	3.1	3.4	4.0	4.2	5.4	5.2	4.9	5.1	5.5
Soc. Netw.	12.4	7.5	4.0	6.1	5.5	4.1	4.3	6.8	6.3	5.8	4.6	3.9	3.1	3.2	3.8
Travel	5.3	2.5	2.3	4.9	4.3	3.8	4.2	3.9	3.6	4.2	4.4	4.3	3.4	3.0	7.4
Analytics S.	4.1	1.9	1.8	1.9	3.3	3.8	5.3	6.0	7.0	5.3	5.0	6.0	5.9	6.5	7.5
Horizontal S.	2.5	1.7	2.5	2.8	3.0	3.0	3.1	3.9	4.3	4.9	5.3	6.0	6.0	6.5	7.4
Platform S.	5.5	3.9	2.9	3.9	4.0	4.4	5.2	6.4	5.8	5.2	5.7	6.6	6.5	6.6	7.3
Security S.	4.6	2.9	2.4	2.8	3.1	2.9	3.4	4.5	4.5	4.0	4.3	5.2	5.2	5.1	5.4
Vertical S.	3.4	2.0	1.9	3.1	3.1	2.9	3.7	4.5	4.5	4.3	4.4	5.3	5.3	5.8	6.6

Median

	07	08	09	10	11	12	13	14	15	16	17	18	19	20	21
All	3.0	1.9	1.6	2.1	2.3	2.2	2.6	3.1	3.1	2.9	3.2	3.5	3.1	3.3	3.8
Classifieds	6.9	2.7	3.3	5.9	6.2	4.3	6.1	7.5	6.2	6.2	5.8	5.7	4.3	3.2	3.7
C. Mon. F.	4.5	2.7	2.8	3.3	3.3	2.6	2.9	3.7	4.0	4.9	6.1	6.7	6.2	6.7	8.6
Cont. Mon.	3.0	1.9	1.7	1.2	2.6	3.3	3.8	4.2	3.5	2.6	2.7	3.0	2.6	1.7	2.6
Cust. Acq.	7.4	3.6	2.3	3.0	3.0	2.2	2.7	2.2	2.8	3.6	5.0	3.5	2.8	3.1	2.2
Data Center	3.7	1.9	1.2	1.9	2.7	2.1	2.8	4.6	3.2	3.1	3.9	4.5	4.5	4.8	4.8
Divers./ Port.	11	5.1	2.9	5.0	4.7	3.4	4.1	4.9	5.1	4.3	4.2	3.7	3.4	4.5	3.4
eCommerce	1.4	1.1	0.6	1.0	1.0	0.8	1.1	1.0	1.1	1.0	1.3	1.1	0.9	1.0	1.2
Gambling	2.8	3.0	1.9	2.4	2.4	2.3	2.8	3.1	4.0	3.4	3.4	2.8	1.7	2.0	2.2
Gaming	3.0	1.6	2.3	3.1	3.4	2.6	3.3	3.7	4.0	2.5	3.8	2.6	1.7	1.9	2.8
Marketing	2.1	1.0	0.8	1.0	0.9	0.9	1.2	1.2	1.2	1.1	1.3	1.3	1.2	1.0	1.8
Marketplace	5.1	2.8	1.8	2.6	1.9	2.7	4.3	4.2	4.2	3.0	2.4	4.0	4.9	4.9	4.7
B2C Services	1.5	1.2	1.5	2.1	1.5	1.3	1.8	3.1	3.0	2.0	2.8	5.5	3.7	3.8	5.0
O. Brokerage	5.6	4.4	2.6	4.4	5.0	4.1	5.1	5.4	6.2	4.5	4.0	5.0	3.3	2.6	2.5
Payment	2.8	2.4	2.2	2.7	2.5	2.5	2.9	3.2	3.8	3.9	4.6	4.6	4.3	4.3	5.3
Soc. Netw.	12	7.1	3.5	5.0	3.4	2.7	2.5	4.8	3.3	3.4	4.1	2.8	1.9	1.5	2.3
Travel	3.6	2.6	2.4	3.6	3.0	3.3	3.7	2.0	2.4	3.8	3.6	3.6	2.3	2.2	7.0
Analytics S.	3.4	2.0	1.8	2.0	2.5	2.8	3.3	3.4	4.8	4.2	4.6	4.8	5.3	5.5	5.4
Horizontal S.	1.7	1.1	1.5	1.8	2.1	2.1	2.4	2.8	3.2	3.4	4.3	4.7	4.5	4.8	6.1
Platform S.	5.5	3.6	2.9	3.7	3.6	3.7	4.3	4.4	4.3	4.2	4.4	5.0	5.2	5.4	6.0
Security S.	3.6	1.6	1.7	2.5	2.0	2.0	2.9	3.0	3.0	3.2	3.5	3.9	3.7	3.6	4.4
Vertical S.	2.4	1.6	1.3	1.9	2.3	2.2	2.7	3.3	3.6	3.2	3.5	3.9	3.9	3.7	4.7

(continued)

Table 6.3 (continued)

Difference between industry and average of all companies

	07	08	09	10	11	12	13	14	15	16	17	18	19	20	21
All															
Classifieds	4	1	2	3	3	2	3	4	3	2	2	2	1	1	0
C. Mon. F.	1	0	0	1	1	0	0	0	1	3	2	3	2	4	3
Cont. Mon.	-1	-1	1	0	0	1	2	1	1	0	-1	0	0	0	-1
Cust. Acq.	3	1	1	2	1	0	0	0	0	1	1	0	-1	-2	-2
Data Center	2	1	0	1	0	0	1	1	0	1	1	0	2	2	2
Divers./ Port.	4	3	2	3	3	1	1	1	0	0	0	0	0	0	0
eCommerce	-2	-1	-1	-2	-2	-1	-2	-2	-2	-2	-2	-2	-3	-3	-3
Gambling	0	0	0	0	0	0	0	0	0	0	0	-1	-2	-1	-1
Gaming	-2	-1	1	1	1	1	0	0	1	0	1	-1	-2	-1	-2
Marketing	-1	-1	-1	-2	-2	-1	-2	-2	-3	-2	-2	-3	-2	-2	-3
Marketplace	1	1	0	0	1	1	1	1	1	0	-1	0	1	1	1
B2C Services	-2	-1	-1	1	1	0	0	-1	-1	-1	1	1	1	1	1
O. Brokerage	3	6	4	2	3	2	2	4	4	3	1	1	0	-3	-3
Payment	-1	0	0	0	-1	0	0	-1	0	0	1	1	0	0	0
Soc. Netw.	8	5	2	3	2	1	1	3	2	2	0	-1	-1	-2	-2
Travel	1	0	0	2	1	1	1	0	-1	0	0	0	-1	-2	2
Analytics S.	0	-1	-1	-1	0	1	2	2	3	1	1	1	1	2	2
Horizontal S.	-2	-1	0	0	0	0	0	0	0	1	1	1	2	2	2
Platform S.	1	1	0	1	1	1	2	2	1	1	1	2	2	2	2
Security S.	0	0	0	0	0	0	0	0	0	0	0	1	1	0	0
Vertical S.	-1	-1	0	0	0	0	0	0	0	0	0	1	1	1	1

Standard deviation

	07	08	09	10	11	12	13	14	15	16	17	18	19	20	21
All	3.8	2.6	2.7	3.4	3.1	2.7	3.5	4.0	4.0	3.9	3.7	4.0	4.2	4.5	4.7
Classifieds	5.2	2.9	3.1	3.6	3.8	4.0	5.4	5.5	4.8	4.6	4.2	4.8	5.6	5.8	4.8
C. Mon. F.	1.9	1.8	2.3	3.4	3.2	1.8	2.2	3.5	4.7	5.8	3.6	3.4	3.8	4.8	3.8
Cont. Mon.	2.8	1.7	6.2	4.3	2.5	3.2	5.2	4.7	5.8	4.5	3.8	3.9	4.3	4.8	5.3
Cust. Acq.	2.8	3.3	2.7	5.8	3.8	2.0	3.3	3.9	4.3	4.0	3.4	3.5	2.6	2.2	2.5
Data Center	4.8	3.5	2.8	3.9	2.9	3.0	3.9	4.0	4.0	4.7	4.4	4.0	4.9	5.0	5.3
Divers./ Port.	6.9	5.2	4.7	6.1	5.2	3.6	3.3	3.5	3.1	2.8	3.3	4.0	3.8	3.3	3.5
eCommerce	3.3	1.4	1.0	1.2	1.9	1.8	2.5	3.0	2.8	2.4	3.4	3.4	2.8	3.0	2.8
Gambling	3.8	2.8	2.3	2.7	1.9	1.5	3.4	2.7	3.5	3.2	2.9	2.6	2.4	3.5	4.5
Gaming	0.9	0.6	3.1	2.6	3.0	2.8	3.7	4.1	4.7	4.7	4.0	2.5	1.9	3.1	2.7
Marketing	2.3	1.3	1.0	1.2	1.5	1.7	1.3	1.6	2.0	1.6	1.7	1.9	3.3	2.9	2.7
Marketplace	1.8	3.1	2.3	3.7	3.9	3.8	4.0	4.5	4.5	4.1	3.5	4.0	4.1	5.0	4.9
B2C Services	1.3	0.4	0.9	5.5	5.5	3.7	4.6	3.2	2.9	1.9	5.2	3.7	4.1	4.7	5.6
O. Brokerage	3.3	7.2	6.2	2.9	3.9	2.0	3.5	5.8	5.2	6.4	5.3	5.3	5.5	1.2	1.1
Payment	2.3	2.2	1.6	1.6	1.4	1.2	2.2	2.0	2.3	2.7	4.1	3.8	3.3	3.4	3.6
Soc. Netw.	3.5	1.9	1.3	6.2	4.9	3.5	4.2	6.0	5.6	5.2	3.7	3.1	2.6	2.8	3.5
Travel	4.4	0.7	0.5	5.1	3.8	2.4	3.2	3.6	2.4	2.8	3.1	3.9	3.3	2.2	4.2
Analytics S.	3.2	0.7	0.9	0.7	2.7	3.1	5.2	5.1	5.0	4.2	3.2	4.3	4.3	4.9	5.0
Horizontal S.	1.9	1.4	3.6	3.1	3.2	3.4	3.5	3.7	4.0	4.3	4.0	4.2	4.5	4.9	5.3
Platform S.	2.4	2.1	1.2	2.1	2.1	2.2	3.4	4.6	4.0	3.4	4.5	4.8	4.9	5.0	5.3
Security S.	4.3	2.9	2.4	2.2	2.8	2.5	2.6	4.0	4.0	3.6	3.5	4.0	4.4	4.3	3.9
Vertical S.	3.4	1.9	2.0	3.8	3.1	2.6	3.3	3.9	3.7	3.6	3.3	4.2	4.5	5.2	5.4

(continued)

Table 6.3 (continued)

1st quartile

	07	08	09	10	11	12	13	14	15	16	17	18	19	20	21
All	1.7	0.9	0.7	0.9	1.0	0.9	1.1	1.3	1.4	1.4	1.6	1.6	1.4	1.4	1.7
Classifieds	4.0	1.5	1.3	2.9	2.5	1.7	2.4	2.3	3.5	2.0	2.9	2.4	1.9	1.5	1.4
C. Mon. F.	3.8	1.7	0.8	2.6	2.7	2.2	2.0	2.4	2.9	3.3	3.7	5.0	5.1	5.1	5.8
Cont. Mon.	1.0	0.5	0.8	1.0	1.4	1.7	2.0	2.3	1.5	1.9	1.7	1.5	1.2	1.2	0.9
Cust. Acq.	5.5	1.6	1.7	1.4	1.1	1.8	1.8	1.7	1.1	2.2	2.4	2.6	1.8	1.6	1.6
Data Center	2.2	1.2	0.9	0.8	0.9	0.8	1.1	1.1	2.0	1.7	1.7	2.2	2.3	3.1	2.6
Divers./ Port.	2.4	0.9	0.5	1.5	2.1	1.7	1.5	1.8	2.1	2.0	2.4	2.1	1.5	1.4	2.2
eCommerce	0.6	0.4	0.3	0.3	0.2	0.3	0.5	0.6	0.6	0.7	0.7	0.6	0.5	0.6	0.6
Gambling	2.0	1.2	0.8	1.3	1.3	1.1	2.1	1.7	2.2	2.1	2.0	1.9	1.1	1.2	1.9
Gaming	1.9	1.6	1.8	1.4	1.2	1.6	1.5	1.8	1.9	1.2	2.2	1.6	1.0	1.2	1.1
Marketing	1.5	0.6	0.4	0.5	0.5	0.4	0.5	0.6	0.7	0.6	0.8	0.6	0.6	0.6	1.0
Marketplace	3.5	1.9	1.4	1.3	1.6	1.3	1.4	1.4	1.9	0.7	1.0	1.8	1.4	1.5	2.4
B2C Services	1.3	1.1	1.1	0.7	1.0	1.0	0.8	1.1	1.2	1.5	1.9	3.3	3.0	3.1	2.9
O. Brokerage	5.5	4.0	2.4	3.9	4.3	3.7	3.9	5.4	5.2	3.2	2.4	3.2	1.6	1.5	1.9
Payment	1.9	1.3	1.5	2.0	1.5	1.4	1.2	2.0	2.2	2.2	3.1	2.6	2.7	2.2	2.4
Soc. Netw.	9.9	6.3	3.4	2.7	2.6	1.4	1.3	2.0	1.8	2.4	1.9	1.5	1.1	1.1	0.9
Travel	2.6	2.1	1.9	2.2	1.9	1.6	1.8	1.7	1.8	1.7	2.2	1.6	1.4	1.4	4.4
Analytics S.	2.3	1.9	1.6	1.6	2.1	2.0	2.5	2.1	3.1	2.5	2.7	2.7	2.8	3.0	3.1
Horizontal S.	1.2	0.6	0.6	0.7	0.7	0.7	1.0	1.2	1.5	2.0	2.3	2.6	2.3	2.7	3.3
Platform S.	3.4	2.4	2.2	2.6	2.7	3.0	3.0	3.7	3.5	2.9	2.3	3.0	2.2	1.8	2.8
Security S.	1.7	0.8	0.6	0.9	1.0	1.0	1.5	2.0	1.4	1.9	2.0	2.2	2.1	2.2	2.2
Vertical S.	1.6	0.9	0.6	0.8	0.9	0.9	1.3	1.5	1.5	1.4	1.7	2.0	1.8	1.6	2.5

3rd quartile

	07	08	09	10	11	12	13	14	15	16	17	18	19	20	21
All	6	3	3	4	4	4	5	6	6	6	6	7	6	7	7
Classifieds	14	7	6	9	7	6	11	13	11	9	8	9	6	9	7
C. Mon. F.	6	4	4	4	5	4	5	5	6	6	9	10	7	9	10
Cont. Mon.	5	3	3	3	4	6	10	7	6	5	4	5	6	6	7
Cust. Acq.	9	5	4	6	6	5	4	5	9	9	8	9	5	4	4
Data Center	10	7	4	6	5	5	6	7	7	9	9	8	10	11	11
Divers./ Port.	14	9	6	7	9	6	7	7	6	6	7	6	5	6	7
eCommerce	2	2	1	2	2	2	2	3	2	2	3	2	2	2	2
Gambling	4	3	3	3	4	4	4	4	5	5	5	4	3	4	4
Gaming	3	2	6	6	6	5	4	6	6	6	6	5	4	5	5
Marketing	4	2	1	2	2	2	3	3	3	2	2	3	2	2	3
Marketplace	6	4	3	3	4	4	7	9	8	8	6	8	7	8	10
B2C Services	2	1	2	3	6	4	5	5	5	4	7	8	9	9	9
O. Brokerage	8	10	8	7	7	5	5	6	11	9	6	7	4	3	3
Payment	5	4	3	4	3	3	4	4	5	5	6	7	7	8	8
Soc. Netw.	14	8	4	6	9	6	7	9	10	9	7	6	4	6	6
Travel	6	3	3	4	5	6	5	5	5	6	6	6	4	4	10
Analytics S.	5	2	2	2	3	4	5	9	11	6	7	8	8	9	11
Horizontal S.	4	2	2	4	4	4	3	5	6	7	7	8	9	9	10
Platform S.	8	5	4	5	5	5	7	8	8	8	8	9	9	10	12
Security S.	5	3	3	3	4	5	5	6	7	5	5	7	7	7	7
Vertical S.	4	3	2	3	4	4	5	6	7	6	7	7	7	8	9

Table 6.4 continues the data tendencies analysis with the EV/EBITDA multiples presented along the same statistical measures. The median is for the EV/LTM EBITDA indicator lower than the average (in most cases). The trends are, however, similar to the averages discussed previously. Observing the standard deviation and the 1st and 3rd quartile analysis, it can be seen that the ranges for this variable are significantly tighter, which should help with the later inferential analysis. The difference to the overall average multiples highlights interestingly new industries. eCommerce is no longer below average, while Marketing, Gambling, and Gaming remain below average. Payment and travel interestingly join the group below average for most years.

Table 6.5 continues the data tendency analysis with the LTM Sales Growth variable. Observing the median, it can be seen that the median is generally lower than the average, implying a positive skewness. The range for the variable is also high with standard deviation as well as 1st and 3rd quartal analysis showing this. This finding is not particularly surprising as companies in the internet-enabled space usually have a wide range of dynamics. Analyzing the average tendency by industry compared to the overall average, it can be observed that Marketing and some of the Software industries show a negative difference implying a lower growth than the overall average.

Lastly, Table 6.6 presents the data tendencies of the LTM EBITDA Margin variable. The median, interestingly, does not show a tendency in either relative to the average. While individual sets and years show differences, these differences are not always in the same direction. Standard deviations vary significantly by industry and year of observation, while the 1st and 3rd quarter analyses show more relevant ranges. Regarding the tendency of individual industries compared to the overall average, it can be said that some industries show a clear negative tendency over all periods. These industries are eCommerce, Marketing, B2C Services, and generally Software, however not always. The most interesting finding is the Software, however, this was discussed in the last sub-chapter.

Beyond providing a glimpse at the data used for the study, the statistical analysis can also be used by management teams and shareholders to calculate relevant ranges for multiples, growth, and margins. The selection of variables discussed represents the most important variables and timeframes. It should be noted that discussing all 350 variables over 15 years of data would have been impossible.

Table 6.4 Data tendencies for EV/LTM EBITDA

Average

	07	08	09	10	11	12	13	14	15	16	17	18	19	20	21
All	16	11	10	13	13	12	14	16	17	16	18	18	17	18	19
Classifieds	22	12	12	17	17	13	18	20	20	18	21	21	19	19	22
C. Mon. F.	16	11	12	16	16	15	18	15	16	15	16	18	18	24	27
Cont. Mon.	18	10	6	10	10	13	17	15	14	17	17	20	20	18	19
Cust. Acq.	22	13	13	11	12	9	14	18	18	18	18	19	16	17	19
Data Center	21	14	11	15	13	13	14	16	16	15	18	16	17	20	20
Divers./ Port.	21	14	11	13	15	12	13	16	17	17	19	19	17	20	20
eCommerce	18	13	10	15	16	14	15	17	19	18	20	20	18	19	19
Gambling	12	9	9	9	9	9	10	12	14	14	14	11	10	12	15
Gaming	14	7	14	12	12	13	13	14	18	15	16	13	12	15	15
Marketing	14	10	8	10	10	9	10	13	13	13	15	16	14	13	15
Marketplace	21	14	11	14	12	12	14	16	16	16	15	17	19	24	23
B2C Services	16	10	11	13	18	12	14	20	25	21	17	19	18	21	19
O. Brokerage	14	7	5	17	20	14	16	12	17	12	13	14	12	11	13
Payment	14	10	8	11	11	9	12	14	14	12	16	17	18	19	20
Soc. Netw.	36	20	12	15	16	13	16	22	18	17	16	14	13	12	12
Travel	18	11	10	12	11	15	14	12	12	14	14	13	12	13	30
Analytics S.	12	10	9	9	13	13	14	18	17	16	18	19	20	19	19
Horizontal S.	13	11	11	11	13	12	13	16	18	17	18	19	20	21	21
Platform S.	18	13	12	15	16	13	16	18	18	19	20	21	20	20	22
Security S.	16	12	11	16	14	14	14	14	15	14	19	21	20	20	20
Vertical S.	15	11	11	13	14	13	16	19	19	19	22	22	20	19	21

Median

	07	08	09	10	11	12	13	14	15	16	17	18	19	20	21
All	14	10	9	11	11	10	12	13	15	14	16	16	15	16	18
Classifieds	23	12	11	17	14	14	17	20	20	18	20	21	18	21	24
C. Mon. F.	15	11	10	15	15	14	16	12	14	16	17	19	20	22	26
Cont. Mon.	17	9	6	8	9	8	9	11	11	14	16	17	14	15	17
Cust. Acq.	18	10	11	9	9	12	13	14	18	16	14	17	14	15	16
Data Center	21	13	10	16	12	13	13	13	14	16	17	16	17	22	20
Divers./ Port.	23	13	8	12	10	10	12	13	15	15	17	17	17	19	17
eCommerce	14	10	9	13	14	12	13	15	18	17	17	18	16	18	17
Gambling	13	10	8	9	7	8	10	11	12	11	11	11	8	8	13
Gaming	13	5	11	13	9	10	13	10	15	14	14	11	11	13	15
Marketing	13	9	7	8	8	7	8	11	10	11	13	13	10	11	14
Marketplace	19	12	9	10	11	11	12	13	15	14	13	16	17	26	24
B2C Services	20	10	11	13	18	10	12	19	29	17	16	16	17	19	16
O. Brokerage	10	7	5	8	18	12	10	10	13	9	9	11	8	6	5
Payment	12	10	8	9	10	9	11	12	13	13	16	16	16	18	19
Soc. Netw.	35	20	12	15	10	8	17	26	17	16	16	12	9	14	9
Travel	18	10	9	11	10	12	13	9	12	13	13	13	13	14	30
Analytics S.	13	7	8	9	10	10	11	13	14	14	14	16	18	19	18
Horizontal S.	13	8	8	10	11	9	12	14	15	16	17	18	17	19	21
Platform S.	13	10	9	11	11	11	12	12	13	13	19	17	18	17	18
Security S.	15	12	9	13	13	10	13	12	12	13	16	18	18	16	18
Vertical S.	14	10	9	12	13	12	14	17	17	15	20	21	18	18	20

(continued)

Table 6.4 (continued)

Difference between industry and average of all companies

	07	08	09	10	11	12	13	14	15	16	17	18	19	20	21
All															
Classifieds	5	1	1	4	3	1	4	4	3	1	3	3	1	1	3
C. Mon. F.	0	-1	1	3	3	3	4	-1	-1	-1	-2	0	0	6	8
Cont. Mon.	1	-1	-4	-2	-3	1	3	-1	-2	1	-1	2	2	0	0
Cust. Acq.	6	1	2	-2	-1	-3	0	2	1	1	0	0	-1	-1	-1
Data Center	5	3	0	2	0	1	0	0	-1	-1	0	-2	-1	2	1
Divers./ Port.	4	3	0	0	2	0	-1	0	0	0	1	1	0	2	1
eCommerce	2	1	0	2	3	1	1	2	2	2	2	2	1	1	0
Gambling	-4	-2	-2	-4	-4	-3	-4	-4	-3	-3	-4	-7	-7	-6	-4
Gaming	-2	-4	3	-1	-1	1	-1	-2	1	-1	-2	-6	-6	-3	-4
Marketing	-2	-1	-2	-3	-3	-3	-4	-3	-4	-3	-3	-3	-3	-6	-4
Marketplace	4	3	1	1	-1	0	0	0	-1	0	-2	-1	1	6	3
B2C Services	0	-2	0	0	4	0	0	4	8	4	-1	0	0	3	-1
O. Brokerage	-2	-4	-6	4	6	2	2	-4	0	-4	-5	-4	-6	-7	-6
Payment	-3	-2	-2	-2	-2	-3	-2	-2	-3	-4	-2	-1	1	1	1
Soc. Netw.	19	9	2	2	3	1	2	6	1	1	-2	-4	-5	-6	-7
Travel	2	0	0	-1	-2	3	0	-4	-5	-2	-4	-5	-5	-5	10
Analytics S.	-5	-1	-1	-3	-1	1	0	2	0	0	0	1	3	1	0
Horizontal S.	-3	-1	0	-1	0	0	-1	0	1	1	0	1	2	3	2
Platform S.	1	2	1	2	3	0	2	2	1	3	2	3	3	2	2
Security S.	0	1	1	3	0	2	0	-2	-2	-2	1	2	2	2	0
Vertical S.	-1	0	0	0	1	1	2	3	2	3	4	4	3	1	2

Standard deviation

	07	08	09	10	11	12	13	14	15	16	17	18	19	20	21
All	8	7	6	7	8	8	8	9	9	9	9	9	10	10	9
Classifieds	10	7	7	8	7	7	9	9	9	10	10	8	7	10	11
C. Mon. F.	6	4	9	4	5	7	7	8	6	6	8	4	8	6	7
Cont. Mon.	11	5	3	8	6	8	12	9	10	10	8	10	11	10	8
Cust. Acq.	10	10	7	6	9	5	6	9	7	8	8	9	8	10	10
Data Center	6	9	7	8	6	5	6	7	9	7	7	6	6	7	8
Divers./ Port.	9	8	8	7	9	6	6	7	7	7	7	8	7	8	9
eCommerce	10	7	5	8	10	9	9	9	9	8	10	10	10	10	10
Gambling	5	4	4	4	6	4	4	5	7	8	8	5	7	9	9
Gaming	9	6	8	7	7	10	7	8	10	10	10	7	7	8	7
Marketing	6	6	5	7	7	6	8	7	9	8	9	9	11	8	9
Marketplace	8	6	7	9	8	8	9	9	8	8	9	8	10	11	9
B2C Services	8	6	1	6	10	8	10	14	15	13	14	13	11	10	10
O. Brokerage	8	1	1	16	13	8	9	5	13	9	13	12	12	14	17
Payment	4	3	3	5	5	3	7	6	4	5	8	8	9	9	9
Soc. Netw.	2	4	5	7	14	11	12	10	13	9	10	9	9	6	9
Travel	6	4	3	4	5	10	6	7	6	7	7	5	4	4	5
Analytics S.	2	10	4	2	6	6	7	11	10	10	10	8	8	9	7
Horizontal S.	7	7	8	7	8	8	8	8	9	9	9	8	10	10	9
Platform S.	10	7	7	9	11	9	12	12	11	10	11	10	10	9	8
Security S.	6	6	6	9	9	10	7	7	8	7	9	9	10	10	10
Vertical S.	7	7	6	8	7	7	8	10	9	10	10	11	11	10	10

(continued)

Table 6.4 (continued)

1st quartile

	07	08	09	10	11	12	13	14	15	16	17	18	19	20	21
All	11	7	6	8	7	7	8	9	10	10	11	11	9	11	12
Classifieds	13	6	6	13	13	8	14	14	15	10	16	18	15	11	9
C. Mon. F.	12	10	8	12	14	12	14	11	12	13	13	17	14	21	24
Cont. Mon.	12	7	5	5	7	7	8	10	8	10	11	13	11	11	12
Cust. Acq.	16	6	8	7	5	6	9	11	12	13	11	12	9	11	13
Data Center	18	7	5	8	9	10	11	12	10	9	12	11	11	15	16
Divers./ Port.	16	10	7	10	9	7	8	11	13	12	14	14	13	13	15
eCommerce	12	7	7	9	9	6	8	10	11	12	13	13	10	11	11
Gambling	9	7	6	6	6	6	7	8	8	8	8	8	6	7	8
Gaming	10	4	7	7	6	5	6	8	10	7	8	7	6	7	11
Marketing	9	5	4	5	5	5	6	7	7	7	9	8	7	7	9
Marketplace	16	10	7	9	9	7	9	12	11	10	12	12	10	13	16
B2C Services	14	7	10	11	10	8	8	8	15	12	8	12	13	13	15
O. Brokerage	10	7	4	8	9	7	9	10	10	8	7	8	7	5	4
Payment	11	8	7	8	8	7	7	11	12	11	12	12	13	13	14
Soc. Netw.	35	17	8	10	9	5	6	19	7	9	8	9	8	8	7
Travel	14	9	8	10	8	9	10	7	8	8	8	9	8	11	27
Analytics S.	11	7	7	8	9	9	11	12	12	10	11	13	13	13	13
Horizontal S.	9	6	7	8	7	7	8	10	12	11	13	13	12	13	16
Platform S.	13	9	8	10	9	8	9	10	10	9	11	14	14	13	15
Security S.	12	7	7	9	6	8	9	9	11	9	11	12	12	12	12
Vertical S.	10	7	7	8	8	8	9	11	12	12	13	12	13	11	13

3rd quartile

	07	08	09	10	11	12	13	14	15	16	17	18	19	20	21
All	20	15	12	16	17	15	17	21	22	21	24	25	23	25	27
Classifieds	29	14	17	19	19	14	24	25	24	24	24	24	22	23	31
C. Mon. F.	19	12	10	19	15	15	21	15	18	18	18	20	22	24	31
Cont. Mon.	23	12	8	14	12	18	27	18	19	22	22	29	28	21	23
Cust. Acq.	28	17	16	13	17	12	19	22	25	20	24	26	26	21	23
Data Center	26	17	13	17	16	14	15	18	18	19	21	20	20	25	26
Divers./ Port.	25	17	12	13	20	18	17	17	20	20	24	26	21	27	24
eCommerce	26	16	14	19	25	16	21	25	27	23	25	31	25	26	27
Gambling	15	10	10	11	11	11	11	13	17	15	15	13	10	14	20
Gaming	17	9	20	14	19	19	16	20	25	20	26	17	15	21	19
Marketing	17	15	10	13	17	11	12	18	16	16	18	23	18	16	19
Marketplace	24	17	12	12	12	14	15	22	20	19	18	19	26	33	28
B2C Services	21	13	11	18	24	16	18	31	36	33	26	26	19	30	22
O. Brokerage	17	8	5	22	29	19	23	13	18	11	10	13	9	8	14
Payment	15	11	9	13	12	11	13	17	16	15	17	20	20	24	25
Soc. Netw.	36	24	15	20	17	18	27	26	30	23	24	17	15	16	16
Travel	22	11	12	13	12	16	16	13	15	18	16	16	14	17	33
Analytics S.	14	8	10	11	15	14	14	25	18	18	25	23	29	24	27
Horizontal S.	17	12	11	13	18	15	16	19	25	21	24	25	29	31	27
Platform S.	20	16	10	17	22	13	15	24	22	29	29	31	28	22	26
Security S.	18	15	13	24	19	19	19	17	18	17	25	28	27	28	28
Vertical S.	19	13	14	17	17	17	19	26	25	27	30	32	31	27	28

Table 6.5 Data tendencies for LTM Sales Growth

Average

	07	08	09	10	11	12	13	14	15	16	17	18	19	20	21
All	22	23	13	12	16	17	15	15	17	18	17	17	16	13	15
Classifieds	43	34	7	9	21	28	24	23	35	27	15	20	15	7	8
C. Mon. F.	30	27	16	13	12	8	10	14	14	13	16	14	16	14	15
Cont. Mon.	10	8	-1	17	12	15	23	21	18	22	12	13	17	13	17
Cust. Acq.	39	31	15	14	14	13	25	20	20	18	20	22	18	11	9
Data Center	30	35	16	13	14	27	15	12	16	17	16	14	14	14	15
Divers./ Port.	41	36	20	18	29	30	24	17	16	20	24	23	18	12	12
eCommerce	21	22	12	17	20	17	14	14	18	19	17	18	14	11	16
Gambling	7	24	17	13	10	14	15	17	25	30	27	23	17	8	8
Gaming	12	10	16	20	15	28	25	17	24	18	21	18	13	12	16
Marketing	33	31	18	9	15	12	12	9	11	14	14	12	13	9	11
Marketplace	32	23	15	15	16	18	13	14	13	13	13	11	19	22	27
B2C Services	31	50	14	16	27	45	32	26	16	24	21	26	27	24	27
O. Brokerage	28	28	16	10	17	8	-3	23	17	22	8	23	11	20	15
Payment	19	24	12	14	19	14	10	16	14	15	17	21	20	14	18
Soc. Netw.	11	41	20	18	29	13	18	21	25	25	24	30	16	8	8
Travel	24	30	17	19	23	15	15	19	19	19	23	17	13	2	1
Analytics S.	7	7	4	3	6	11	17	22	19	19	13	15	16	10	11
Horizontal S.	18	16	10	9	13	13	14	14	17	21	20	20	21	18	16
Platform S.	24	21	12	13	17	14	15	18	17	18	19	19	17	15	18
Security S.	21	19	6	7	14	14	12	11	13	14	14	16	17	13	15
Vertical S.	19	17	15	11	15	15	13	13	13	15	13	15	15	14	16

Median

	07	08	09	10	11	12	13	14	15	16	17	18	19	20	21
All	21	18	8	8	13	13	11	11	12	14	13	14	12	9	10
Classifieds	45	35	8	8	22	22	18	19	26	19	13	17	13	0	2
C. Mon. F.	30	26	7	7	11	5	8	7	10	11	13	14	15	8	7
Cont. Mon.	11	17	3	7	9	21	26	22	16	17	7	7	10	9	11
Cust. Acq.	39	36	11	16	11	12	15	17	19	11	12	16	13	5	9
Data Center	32	37	14	12	9	19	14	10	12	14	16	15	9	11	10
Divers./ Port.	42	40	10	11	27	31	23	14	18	19	20	21	19	10	10
eCommerce	17	14	8	13	14	13	13	12	13	17	12	14	12	9	12
Gambling	5	15	13	8	6	14	9	12	14	30	21	16	8	4	3
Gaming	13	8	18	14	10	28	23	16	12	12	9	15	11	7	12
Marketing	35	33	10	3	12	6	8	3	7	8	9	9	6	4	5
Marketplace	33	22	9	14	13	13	15	13	13	12	12	10	11	10	16
B2C Services	31	48	10	10	22	61	26	19	12	20	20	22	29	24	23
O. Brokerage	28	28	16	10	9	1	-1	10	7	16	8	23	14	14	9
Payment	14	15	9	11	17	10	9	12	9	8	14	14	15	10	15
Soc. Netw.	11	47	22	17	19	17	19	15	17	23	26	39	18	8	6
Travel	16	29	22	25	19	10	17	20	16	14	16	13	5	-1	-1
Analytics S.	1	-1	1	5	1	7	8	17	11	11	12	8	14	6	6
Horizontal S.	19	13	5	4	11	12	9	9	9	13	17	15	16	17	13
Platform S.	23	19	5	14	17	13	10	10	16	17	16	16	13	9	17
Security S.	21	14	7	7	12	9	9	10	9	9	11	10	14	7	8
Vertical S.	19	18	10	6	12	12	9	9	12	13	12	13	10	9	9

(continued)

Table 6.5 (continued)

Difference between industry and average of all companies

	07	08	09	10	11	12	13	14	15	16	17	18	19	20	21
All															
Classifieds	21	11	-6	-3	5	11	9	8	18	9	-2	3	-2	-7	-6
C. Mon. F.	8	4	3	0	-4	-9	-5	-1	-3	-5	-1	-4	0	1	1
Cont. Mon.	-12	-15	-14	5	-4	-2	8	6	1	3	-4	-5	0	0	2
Cust. Acq.	17	8	2	2	-1	-4	10	5	3	0	3	4	2	-3	-6
Data Center	8	12	3	1	-2	10	0	-3	-1	-1	-1	-3	-3	1	0
Divers./ Port.	19	13	7	6	13	13	8	2	-1	2	7	5	1	-1	-3
eCommerce	-2	-1	0	5	4	1	-1	-1	1	1	0	1	-2	-2	1
Gambling	-16	1	4	1	-6	-3	0	2	8	12	10	5	0	-5	-7
Gaming	-11	-13	3	8	0	12	9	2	7	0	4	0	-3	-1	2
Marketing	11	8	5	-3	-1	-4	-3	-6	-6	-4	-3	-5	-4	-4	-4
Marketplace	10	0	2	3	1	2	-3	-1	-4	-5	-4	-6	3	9	12
B2C Services	9	27	1	4	11	28	17	11	-2	6	4	9	11	11	12
O. Brokerage	5	5	3	-2	1	-9	-18	8	0	4	-9	6	-6	7	0
Payment	-3	1	-1	1	3	-2	-5	1	-3	-3	0	4	3	1	3
Soc. Netw.	-11	18	7	6	13	-4	3	6	8	7	8	12	0	-5	-7
Travel	2	7	5	7	7	-1	0	4	2	1	6	-1	-4	-11	-14
Analytics S.	-15	-16	-9	-9	-10	-6	1	7	2	1	-4	-2	0	-3	-4
Horizontal S.	-4	-7	-3	-3	-2	-4	-1	-1	0	3	3	2	5	5	2
Platform S.	2	-2	-1	1	1	-3	0	3	0	0	2	2	1	1	3
Security S.	-2	-3	-7	-5	-2	-3	-4	-4	-4	-4	-2	-1	1	0	0
Vertical S.	-3	-6	2	-1	-1	-2	-2	-2	-4	-3	-4	-3	-1	1	1

Standard deviation

	07	08	09	10	11	12	13	14	15	16	17	18	19	20	21
All	20	22	18	18	17	19	17	18	20	20	19	19	19	18	19
Classifieds	27	9	11	11	9	22	20	19	28	21	16	14	15	15	19
C. Mon. F.	30	21	21	19	14	10	15	14	11	11	19	22	23	21	25
Cont. Mon.	14	15	9	28	19	13	19	21	23	26	17	24	24	19	21
Cust. Acq.	20	14	14	18	16	16	24	14	17	19	25	23	23	20	15
Data Center	16	20	13	14	15	29	14	13	19	15	11	14	15	13	18
Divers./ Port.	22	32	28	23	24	21	13	12	15	14	21	15	11	12	14
eCommerce	25	24	18	16	17	16	15	13	18	19	18	19	15	13	17
Gambling	17	30	20	25	14	13	15	21	28	22	23	22	18	20	21
Gaming	11	14	17	26	19	23	19	19	28	25	30	22	21	22	19
Marketing	21	25	28	21	20	19	20	19	17	20	22	17	21	18	20
Marketplace	15	8	14	12	9	13	8	11	15	16	14	15	26	27	27
B2C Services	1	41	17	28	25	39	31	36	11	27	13	22	22	15	19
O. Brokerage	4	13	25	8	15	20	5	34	22	22	12	18	17	22	23
Payment	16	23	13	13	16	20	10	18	19	20	18	23	18	17	18
Soc. Netw.	2	30	22	18	29	14	14	33	31	27	20	24	16	12	10
Travel	21	17	11	13	16	13	9	10	24	21	21	18	22	11	12
Analytics S.	17	16	9	6	9	16	21	22	22	21	15	16	16	14	15
Horizontal S.	17	20	16	16	19	14	19	19	19	21	19	18	20	19	16
Platform S.	16	11	21	10	9	12	16	20	16	19	19	17	17	20	18
Security S.	15	21	12	11	14	16	14	12	16	17	15	19	19	17	16
Vertical S.	18	13	17	16	17	15	14	15	15	16	14	16	18	18	22

(continued)

Table 6.5 (continued)

1st quartile

	07	08	09	10	11	12	13	14	15	16	17	18	19	20	21
All	9	8	0	0	3	4	4	3	3	4	4	4	3	0	1
Classifieds	23	30	-1	2	18	18	13	14	15	13	8	10	6	-3	0
C. Mon. F.	22	21	1	2	0	0	1	6	8	4	1	-2	4	5	4
Cont. Mon.	0	4	-2	2	7	4	11	0	0	6	1	2	0	-2	1
Cust. Acq.	32	25	8	5	3	1	8	12	9	4	6	6	-1	1	-2
Data Center	26	31	11	0	0	6	5	3	3	9	7	2	4	7	1
Divers./ Port.	26	14	4	5	18	17	13	12	13	11	13	15	9	3	2
eCommerce	6	5	0	2	5	3	3	6	7	6	5	5	3	2	4
Gambling	-6	3	1	1	0	5	5	8	8	11	9	6	4	-2	-6
Gaming	2	0	6	0	5	11	10	0	3	-2	0	3	0	-2	1
Marketing	17	9	-3	-5	1	-2	-3	-3	-1	1	0	0	-1	-1	-1
Marketplace	27	21	3	4	10	9	8	8	1	6	6	4	2	2	4
B2C Services	31	16	1	2	10	14	15	0	9	14	16	10	11	13	19
O. Brokerage	26	22	7	7	8	-2	-4	-3	0	6	0	9	-7	8	-3
Payment	12	11	3	5	8	5	5	4	3	5	4	7	8	0	7
Soc. Netw.	10	24	5	3	15	7	10	-1	5	5	3	8	6	-1	1
Travel	14	16	8	7	12	7	7	11	4	8	7	5	2	-3	-7
Analytics S.	-3	-4	0	2	0	1	4	5	1	3	4	5	8	0	3
Horizontal S.	5	4	0	0	0	2	1	2	3	6	5	5	7	5	4
Platform S.	17	14	1	5	10	6	2	3	7	5	7	5	5	0	5
Security S.	12	7	-1	-1	4	2	5	4	3	1	6	4	4	3	4
Vertical S.	9	8	3	1	2	4	3	4	1	3	3	3	2	3	1

3rd quartile

	07	08	09	10	11	12	13	14	15	16	17	18	19	20	21
All	31	33	21	21	23	25	24	23	26	30	26	27	26	20	22
Classifieds	68	39	18	17	25	34	34	31	51	39	28	29	21	10	14
C. Mon. F.	35	33	29	24	21	11	13	22	22	17	25	21	18	19	15
Cont. Mon.	21	17	4	21	16	24	30	27	32	42	25	16	19	20	32
Cust. Acq.	46	41	24	17	27	17	46	27	31	29	40	39	34	15	15
Data Center	40	44	18	22	27	29	18	19	21	24	23	21	17	14	18
Divers./ Port.	57	47	21	16	30	43	28	18	25	30	35	28	21	14	21
eCommerce	20	34	20	28	39	31	25	21	27	29	26	25	22	18	26
Gambling	19	27	33	17	18	21	21	25	32	47	42	33	31	12	19
Gaming	21	21	31	32	24	44	40	27	44	36	39	27	19	17	26
Marketing	42	48	28	19	22	21	22	15	23	28	19	22	22	13	17
Marketplace	39	29	23	18	17	28	16	17	22	20	16	14	30	42	45
B2C Services	32	82	22	23	36	71	50	42	22	25	25	39	41	33	34
O. Brokerage	30	35	25	13	21	11	1	34	39	31	16	35	23	30	23
Payment	31	28	19	22	22	19	14	22	18	19	21	28	26	23	25
Soc. Netw.	12	64	24	25	51	18	27	24	52	37	40	45	28	15	13
Travel	27	42	24	25	36	25	23	27	26	25	32	26	12	1	10
Analytics S.	18	13	13	8	10	16	11	40	39	40	17	26	22	17	16
Horizontal S.	29	24	19	16	18	18	17	23	26	37	32	34	32	27	25
Platform S.	27	26	12	21	22	21	23	27	25	24	26	28	28	22	25
Security S.	28	24	13	14	19	21	16	16	18	25	23	23	26	20	22
Vertical S.	26	27	22	22	21	20	19	22	22	23	20	23	22	20	21

Table 6.6 Data tendencies for LTM EBITDA Margin

Average

	07	08	09	10	11	12	13	14	15	16	17	18	19	20	21
All	21	20	20	22	23	22	20	19	18	18	17	17	17	17	18
Classifieds	34	33	33	36	33	32	27	29	28	25	27	24	20	20	19
C. Mon. F.	29	26	21	21	24	23	22	23	22	24	15	22	21	20	28
Cont. Mon.	20	20	22	28	32	32	33	31	26	21	23	16	16	18	22
Cust. Acq.	29	24	24	28	28	19	20	16	17	21	20	20	19	15	14
Data Center	26	25	26	30	31	28	26	27	26	29	32	34	34	36	37
Divers./ Port.	35	37	35	39	42	40	38	36	32	29	29	25	18	18	19
eCommerce	11	11	11	10	11	10	10	10	8	9	10	8	7	9	10
Gambling	31	28	27	30	23	28	29	26	26	25	27	27	27	26	27
Gaming	17	21	32	34	31	37	31	26	24	21	20	17	20	25	23
Marketing	17	15	14	14	15	15	11	10	8	9	10	9	10	10	13
Marketplace	24	26	26	25	31	31	30	29	26	27	25	20	11	11	15
B2C Services	13	15	13	12	14	15	15	14	13	10	7	10	4	10	17
O. Brokerage	52	54	51	28	37	38	36	41	46	48	36	40	40	43	48
Payment	20	23	24	27	26	27	26	21	23	21	17	20	22	24	27
Soc. Netw.	29	33	35	31	31	25	20	21	23	26	30	31	27	22	23
Travel	22	26	27	27	28	29	26	22	20	17	15	16	17	9	-4
Analytics S.	24	22	19	21	22	19	14	19	21	21	12	11	16	19	17
Horizontal S.	13	15	14	18	18	17	15	13	13	16	15	15	14	13	16
Platform S.	25	27	23	26	26	25	16	17	13	16	14	13	13	13	17
Security S.	15	13	14	19	20	20	17	14	14	12	14	13	15	15	15
Vertical S.	19	18	18	18	19	19	20	17	16	16	16	17	19	18	18

Median

	07	08	09	10	11	12	13	14	15	16	17	18	19	20	21
All	20	20	19	20	21	21	20	19	18	17	18	17	17	16	18
Classifieds	34	28	28	37	36	38	31	30	27	21	21	23	24	22	21
C. Mon. F.	30	26	17	15	26	24	18	21	19	24	18	20	21	24	30
Cont. Mon.	13	14	14	20	24	26	31	32	26	23	26	23	20	18	18
Cust. Acq.	31	22	24	24	26	23	18	16	18	17	17	19	16	16	13
Data Center	15	17	18	25	30	33	34	35	25	26	29	34	35	36	36
Divers./ Port.	42	44	42	40	43	45	39	37	32	31	30	26	20	19	22
eCommerce	11	10	9	9	8	9	7	7	6	6	6	5	5	7	8
Gambling	29	30	31	29	28	28	27	24	27	26	26	25	26	21	23
Gaming	21	24	28	26	27	37	27	24	26	23	24	21	18	23	23
Marketing	14	13	12	11	12	12	11	11	10	9	10	8	9	9	10
Marketplace	22	26	28	29	33	30	24	23	22	21	22	20	9	8	13
B2C Services	14	13	15	13	10	10	9	10	9	7	8	8	5	9	18
O. Brokerage	54	54	51	46	37	37	43	47	47	47	45	44	50	50	53
Payment	21	23	23	26	24	24	26	22	26	25	24	23	24	25	25
Soc. Netw.	25	37	35	27	27	22	21	21	23	22	29	31	26	21	21
Travel	25	27	28	29	31	31	27	23	24	24	22	22	23	11	-2
Analytics S.	28	25	22	23	26	25	12	19	22	23	22	10	15	17	18
Horizontal S.	17	15	14	18	18	15	16	15	15	17	16	15	15	14	14
Platform S.	29	27	26	27	27	29	28	25	17	17	18	17	18	16	21
Security S.	17	12	15	19	21	19	17	18	19	13	14	12	14	17	16
Vertical S.	19	18	18	19	21	21	20	18	17	17	17	17	18	18	19

(continued)

Table 6.6 (continued)

Difference between industry and average of all companies

	07	08	09	10	11	12	13	14	15	16	17	18	19	20	21
All															
Classifieds	14	13	13	14	11	10	6	11	11	8	9	8	4	3	1
C. Mon. F.	9	5	1	-1	2	1	2	5	4	6	-2	6	5	4	10
Cont. Mon.	-1	0	2	6	9	10	12	13	9	3	5	-1	-1	2	4
Cust. Acq.	8	3	4	6	6	-4	0	-3	0	4	3	4	2	-1	-4
Data Center	6	5	6	8	8	6	5	9	8	12	14	17	18	19	19
Divers./ Port.	15	16	14	17	19	18	17	17	15	12	11	8	1	1	1
eCommerce	-10	-10	-10	-12	-12	-12	-10	-9	-10	-9	-8	-9	-9	-7	-8
Gambling	10	8	7	8	0	6	9	7	9	8	10	10	11	10	9
Gaming	-4	0	11	12	9	15	11	7	7	4	3	0	4	8	5
Marketing	-4	-6	-7	-8	-8	-8	-9	-8	-9	-9	-8	-7	-7	-6	-5
Marketplace	4	6	5	3	9	9	9	10	8	9	8	3	-5	-6	-3
B2C Services	-8	-5	-8	-10	-8	-7	-6	-5	-5	-7	-10	-7	-13	-7	-1
O. Brokerage	32	34	31	6	15	16	16	23	29	30	19	23	23	26	30
Payment	-1	2	3	5	4	4	5	3	5	3	0	3	6	8	9
Soc. Netw.	8	13	14	9	9	3	0	3	6	8	13	15	11	5	5
Travel	1	6	6	5	6	7	5	3	3	0	-2	0	0	-8	-22
Analytics S.	3	2	-1	-1	-1	-4	-6	0	3	4	-5	-6	0	2	-1
Horizontal S.	-8	-5	-6	-4	-4	-6	-5	-6	-4	-2	-2	-1	-2	-3	-2
Platform S.	4	7	3	4	4	3	-5	-2	-4	-2	-3	-4	-4	-4	-1
Security S.	-6	-8	-6	-3	-2	-3	-3	-5	-4	-5	-3	-4	-2	-2	-3
Vertical S.	-2	-2	-2	-4	-4	-3	0	-1	-2	-2	-2	0	2	1	0

Standard deviation

	07	08	09	10	11	12	13	14	15	16	17	18	19	20	21
All	17	17	16	16	16	16	18	18	19	19	19	19	19	19	18
Classifieds	13	14	16	15	18	25	29	24	23	23	22	28	29	29	29
C. Mon. F.	6	9	12	13	13	10	9	13	12	12	20	15	15	13	10
Cont. Mon.	19	18	16	19	18	21	14	12	11	25	22	25	25	23	19
Cust. Acq.	12	17	17	16	14	23	17	17	15	16	17	16	17	15	17
Data Center	18	18	19	17	15	20	28	24	23	21	18	16	17	16	18
Divers./ Port.	21	20	20	18	15	15	15	13	14	13	13	13	20	18	16
eCommerce	7	7	7	7	8	9	10	10	14	11	12	13	11	10	10
Gambling	15	21	20	15	22	12	10	14	18	17	12	11	12	12	16
Gaming	33	31	19	19	17	15	14	14	16	15	16	22	18	15	15
Marketing	13	10	9	10	10	11	16	15	16	13	14	15	15	15	14
Marketplace	13	12	11	11	18	18	17	20	21	21	21	22	26	26	18
B2C Services	5	6	11	5	16	17	18	11	11	11	19	15	21	16	16
O. Brokerage	5	1	1	37	14	12	14	18	10	12	19	21	23	20	22
Payment	19	16	15	15	13	13	15	20	18	19	25	18	18	18	18
Soc. Netw.	11	11	8	11	13	20	21	20	18	15	13	13	15	16	12
Travel	9	8	9	11	10	11	14	14	15	20	22	20	18	17	18
Analytics S.	13	14	8	8	9	12	14	10	8	9	21	16	11	9	17
Horizontal S.	18	15	15	13	13	15	18	20	21	22	20	18	21	21	17
Platform S.	17	14	17	12	13	17	28	23	22	18	22	21	21	21	20
Security S.	18	19	21	16	15	15	15	21	22	22	21	22	20	20	20
Vertical S.	17	16	12	15	15	13	12	15	17	16	16	15	14	16	17

(continued)

Table 6.6 (continued)

1st quartile

	07	08	09	10	11	12	13	14	15	16	17	18	19	20	21
All	11	10	10	11	12	11	9	8	6	6	6	5	5	6	7
Classifieds	22	23	24	26	19	18	17	15	14	13	13	13	8	2	6
C. Mon. F.	26	19	11	12	19	17	16	16	13	17	9	11	7	7	23
Cont. Mon.	9	8	12	14	21	22	27	22	17	16	17	1	2	5	5
Cust. Acq.	18	19	15	20	20	12	13	9	9	8	10	11	11	8	6
Data Center	14	14	12	17	19	18	13	11	14	15	19	22	23	25	24
Divers./ Port.	14	21	16	30	36	33	30	28	22	17	17	14	9	9	14
eCommerce	6	5	5	5	5	5	4	3	2	3	4	2	2	3	3
Gambling	23	22	20	22	16	18	22	23	22	22	21	18	18	17	18
Gaming	7	8	23	19	18	26	22	17	8	8	13	7	10	14	17
Marketing	9	7	8	7	8	8	4	4	3	2	3	3	3	2	6
Marketplace	15	15	15	13	17	22	21	14	9	7	8	3	-7	-7	2
B2C Services	11	11	9	11	6	5	6	8	4	3	-2	-2	-5	0	7
O. Brokerage	51	54	51	16	29	31	22	32	39	39	33	35	31	44	51
Payment	13	13	14	19	20	20	17	13	12	10	10	8	16	18	20
Soc. Netw.	20	28	32	24	22	11	6	7	9	18	25	24	19	13	16
Travel	13	20	21	22	24	20	19	15	11	5	5	8	9	3	-14
Analytics S.	16	11	14	19	15	10	3	9	15	14	6	2	9	13	12
Horizontal S.	7	8	7	9	11	9	7	7	3	8	5	6	5	5	6
Platform S.	20	18	16	14	15	16	0	-3	-4	2	4	4	4	5	7
Security S.	6	2	2	8	9	8	9	7	6	2	3	-2	1	4	3
Vertical S.	13	12	11	11	12	12	14	9	5	5	7	7	10	9	9

3rd quartile

	07	08	09	10	11	12	13	14	15	16	17	18	19	20	21
All	30	29	29	30	31	32	31	30	30	30	30	29	28	29	30
Classifieds	42	44	47	43	42	44	44	47	43	39	38	37	35	35	30
C. Mon. F.	32	32	31	29	29	28	28	31	29	31	29	34	31	27	32
Cont. Mon.	23	27	26	44	44	52	41	36	35	33	30	30	32	35	36
Cust. Acq.	38	33	35	44	39	33	28	21	24	29	29	27	23	22	23
Data Center	38	40	44	44	40	40	44	44	44	45	46	46	48	50	51
Divers./ Port.	51	51	49	53	54	51	48	45	45	37	37	32	31	29	29
eCommerce	16	16	16	17	16	14	14	13	13	11	12	13	14	13	13
Gambling	35	36	34	34	34	37	37	34	36	37	38	35	36	35	36
Gaming	33	34	42	51	46	49	43	35	38	33	30	29	33	35	33
Marketing	24	21	17	19	22	22	20	20	19	17	18	15	16	17	23
Marketplace	34	36	36	35	35	35	34	41	37	45	39	36	32	31	29
B2C Services	15	17	18	16	14	17	14	18	21	13	14	23	21	26	33
O. Brokerage	55	55	51	50	46	45	43	52	48	49	48	51	53	52	57
Payment	26	31	29	35	32	34	34	32	32	32	32	34	33	35	37
Soc. Netw.	37	39	37	34	36	38	31	31	30	31	33	39	38	31	30
Travel	27	31	33	35	33	36	38	30	31	31	30	28	27	20	7
Analytics S.	31	28	25	26	28	28	26	28	26	29	23	23	25	24	26
Horizontal S.	24	25	22	25	25	25	24	25	25	27	26	26	27	26	26
Platform S.	35	37	33	32	33	36	35	33	33	33	31	28	26	25	27
Security S.	29	26	29	30	30	31	26	26	26	28	27	27	27	26	25
Vertical S.	23	25	25	26	27	26	26	27	27	28	27	27	27	28	29

6.3 Conclusions of the Descriptive Statistics

The descriptive statistics chapter serves multiple goals. On the one side, it helps the reader understand the breakdown of companies included in the study, while on the other side, it evaluates the most important statistical tendencies and provides the development of averages for the most relevant variables on a year-by-year and an industry-by-industry basis. The last role should be particularly interesting for management teams, founders, and shareholders to understand numerical tendencies.

While the first sub-chapter describes the methodological aspects, the second sub-chapter dives into the number and breakdown of companies and their cumulative valuation. The interesting finding is that on a cumulative basis, the value of publicly listed internet-enabled business models increased by more than 10x (partially driven by the number of public companies) while the average EV also increased from EUR 2bn to EUR 14bn over the period covered by the study. Revenue on a cumulative basis presents about the same trend. Valuations have also increased from 3.2× Revenue in 2007 and c. 2.0× Revenue over the period 2008–2011 to over 4.5× Revenue in the last two years in the study.

The chapter continues by discussing the top 20 companies by EV and revenue in 2007 and 2021 before comparing valuation multiples and financial metrics between industries at three points in time. The most remarkable finding in this sub-chapter is that EV/EBITDA multiples are comparable from a numeric value between industries, with many being around the 20× EBITDA mark.

The next sub-chapter discusses the multiples and financial metrics development over time on an industry-by-industry basis and relative to the internet-enabled businesses overall. Valuation multiples decreased after the 2007–2008 financial crisis and recovered over the period following to reach new heights in 2021. Growth rates have decreased on average significantly from over 20% to c. 15%, while margins remained constant around the 20% mark.

The final sub-chapter discusses general statistical tendencies and recognizes the high ranges and statistical deviations. EV/EBITDA seems to have the least variation among the four chosen variables.

While the discussed variables, timeframes, and perspectives cover only 1% of all variables and data included in the study, they provide a good sense of developments and tendencies.

Testing the Hypothesis and the Model (Inferential Statistics)

7

This chapter connects the company segmentation, data download, and processing with the statistical methodology to test the hypotheses defined at the beginning of the study. **It is important to note that the goal of the study is not to find the best-fitting regressions by combining multiple variables or inter-period statistical methods but rather to treat every time period independently across each industry and observe which combination of base (multiple) and driver (financial indicator) explains most of the variance.** It is also worth noting that with a few exceptions caused by the limited number of peers in selected industries, **each individual regression or statistical analysis is based on a peer group of at least 10 individual companies with relevant data for the individual combination base/driver/year/industry**.

7.1 Methodological Aspects

Considering the overarching goal of the study is to identify the best-fitting multiples and financial drivers for each period and industry to understand the evolution of the bases and drivers over the industry life-cycle and not to find the best-fitting regression by using multivariate regressions or time-series-like methodologies where one period affects the following period a simple linear regression applied for every cluster/ company segment and potential combination of multiples and drivers across each timeframe and over the entirety of the study period is the best approach.

A. Trusculescu, *Business Valuation Across the Industry Life Cycle*,
https://doi.org/10.1007/978-3-658-49126-0_7

Selecting the simple regression also has managerial and strategic implications as it enables one to identify the one financial metric on which the valuation is based and the one financial metric that drives it. As the study includes all major multiples and drivers used by investors in their investment decision as well as covering the most important financial indicators of a company, it is less likely that some indicators that are not included to have a higher impact. **Considering the exhaustive nature of the study, in order to facilitate managerial and strategic decisions, it is essential to identify the one best multiple and driver for which the management and the shareholders should optimize at each particular point in time in order to maximize shareholder valuation and to map these multiples and drivers across the life-cycle of the industry to potentially apply the conclusions for future internet-enabled industries.**

Management and shareholder can not optimize a company for all financial measures. To exemplify, an online retailer can fairly easily increase its sales by decreasing the sales prices and giving up its profit margins, trading consequently margin for growth. If the result of a multivariate scenario is that both growth and margin are almost equally important, the conclusion would have no practical application and would not help maximize valuation as strategy and business can not be maximized for both. Consequently, these need to be applicable to provide practical conclusions that can potentially be used in the future to maximize the value of emerging technologies.

Currently, management teams identify the best strategy based on feeling and experience while finance professionals conduct selected analyses at certain points in time to make recommendations, however, often based on limited peer groups and only selected financial indicators due to practicability in the day-to-day consulting business. This study attempts to help decision makers make decisions based on past quantitative observations, bring some data into a space often driven by feelings, and link valuation concepts to the life-cycle of companies and industries quantitively.

Beyond the managerial and strategic argumentation for using simple linear regression, it should be considered that many variables likely experience a high level of multicollinearity, making it impossible to be included as part of the same regression. Two examples can best explain the reason for multicollinearity.

1. Variables differentiated only by timeframe (FY 0, FY 1, etc.) are likely to be highly correlated. Revenues in FY 0 will likely be similar to revenues in FY 1,

and consequently, multiples and financial indicators dependent on these values will likely be highly correlated. Including 10 timeframes helps when trying to find the best indicator, however, it does not allow for inclusion simultaneously.
2. Variables closely related, such as EBITDA and EBIT, also usually have a high level of correlation. For some companies, depreciation and amortization are so low that EBITDA is almost equal to EBIT. Running separate regression to find the best indicator is useful, however, inclusion in the same regression is not possible.

The proposed methodology is consistent with the methodology used by other researchers in the field, as discussed in Chaps. 2 and 3, as well as with the professional best practices in the field of corporate finance and natural business acumen.

7.1.1 Methodology: Equation Tested and Breadth of Study

The study implements the simple linear regressions across 22 clusters (21 segments/ clusters defined in Sect. 4.3 + a cluster comprising all companies included in the study in order to test hypothesis 1) over 15 independent years, 120 multiples (drivers), and 216 drivers (financial indicators) for a total of 388,800 regressions for each industry. Due to the sheer size of the study, it has been decided to focus on yearly values derived as average from the weekly observations, as calculating weekly regressions would mean calculating nearly 500 million individual regressions. This would not only be unpracticable but would also make the results impossible to interpret.

Consequently, the study conducts 8.5 million regressions to find the best-fitting base (multiple) and driver (financial indicator) for each year and industry and test the various hypotheses defined in Sect. 3.4.1.

Equation tested:

$$Y = \beta_0 + \beta_1 X + \varepsilon, \text{ where}$$

1. Y is the dependent variable, in this case also base or multiple
2. X is the independent variable, in this case, also driver or financial indicator
3. $\boldsymbol{\varepsilon}$ is the random error
4. $\boldsymbol{\beta}_0$ is the y-intercept of the line $y = \beta_0 + \beta_1 x$
5. $\boldsymbol{\beta}_1$ is the slope of the line $y = \beta_0 + \beta_1 x$

7.1.2 Methodology: Technical Implementation

While implementing a simple regression is straightforward, in any software, including Microsoft Excel, implementing and analyzing the results of over 9 million regressions was challenging. Following two weeks of trial and error, it has been decided to perform the analysis in Microsoft Excel as the combination of the multiple regression functions (RSQ, INTERCEPT, SLOPE, CORREL) required and the INDIRECT function is possible and yields the required results. Furthermore, while the INDIRECT function outputs the number "zero" for an empty cell when required to generate an output in a cell, as part of other functions, the empty cell carries on implicitly also dealing with situations in which only one of the observations is available for a data point inside of a regression.

Figure 7.1 shows a small part of such a table used in the calculation, which in reality is much longer and is applied once for each industry:

1. The area highlighted with "A" is used as input to select the industry that the particular Excel Sheet is calculating, the input for the cut-off p-value deemed as statistically significant (in this case 0.05), and the input for the cut-off number of observations per regression (in this case 10).
2. The area highlighted with "B" shows the years and the vertical location of the data for the particular industry. Considering that the input matrix contains 13,546 lines and 403 columns, the indirect functions described before help locate the correct data for the required analysis. The input data is structured such that each column represents a variable while each row contains an observation with all data sorted by industry and year. If we take the first column for the year 2007, the excel shows that the required data is located between lines 772 and 904. These values will be used as input for the indirect functions.
3. The area highlighted with "C" serves as input for which multiple should be tested again which driver. The final Excel included 120 multiples × 216 drivers = 25,920 rows for each such table.

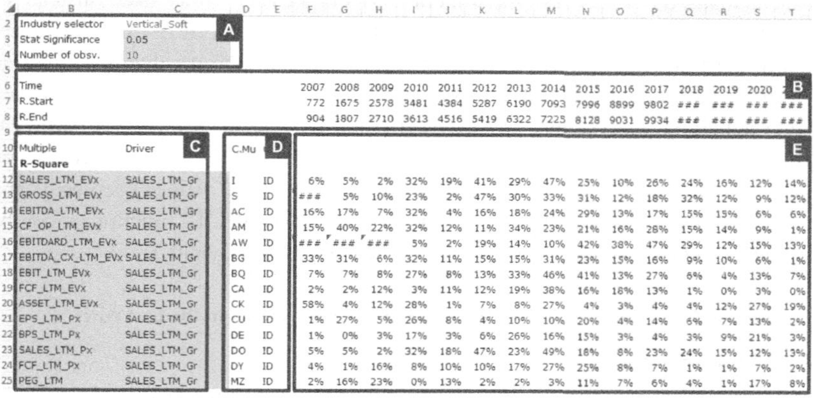

	B	C	D	E	F	G	H	I	J	K	L	M	N	O	P	Q	R	S	T
2	Industry selector	Vertical_Soft																	
3	Stat Significance	0.05																	
4	Number of obsv.	10																	
5																			
6	Time				2007	2008	2009	2010	2011	2012	2013	2014	2015	2016	2017	2018	2019	2020	[illegible]
7	R.Start				772	1675	2578	3481	4384	5287	6190	7093	7996	8899	9802	###	###	###	###
8	R.End				904	1807	2710	3613	4516	5419	6322	7225	8128	9031	9934	###	###	###	###
9																			
10	Multiple	Driver	C.Mu																
11	**R-Square**																		
12	SALES_LTM_EVx	SALES_LTM_Gr	I	ID	6%	5%	2%	32%	19%	41%	29%	47%	25%	10%	26%	24%	16%	12%	14%
13	GROSS_LTM_EVx	SALES_LTM_Gr	S	ID	###	5%	10%	23%	2%	47%	30%	33%	31%	12%	18%	32%	12%	9%	12%
14	EBITDA_LTM_EVx	SALES_LTM_Gr	AC	ID	16%	17%	7%	32%	4%	16%	18%	24%	29%	13%	17%	15%	15%	6%	6%
15	CF_OP_LTM_EVx	SALES_LTM_Gr	AM	ID	15%	40%	22%	32%	12%	11%	34%	23%	21%	16%	28%	15%	14%	9%	1%
16	EBITDARD_LTM_EVx	SALES_LTM_Gr	AW	ID	###	###	###	5%	2%	19%	14%	10%	42%	38%	47%	29%	12%	15%	13%
17	EBITDA_CX_LTM_EVx	SALES_LTM_Gr	BG	ID	33%	31%	6%	32%	11%	15%	15%	31%	23%	15%	16%	9%	10%	6%	1%
18	EBIT_LTM_EVx	SALES_LTM_Gr	BQ	ID	7%	7%	8%	27%	8%	13%	33%	46%	41%	13%	27%	6%	4%	13%	7%
19	FCF_LTM_EVx	SALES_LTM_Gr	CA	ID	2%	2%	12%	3%	11%	12%	19%	38%	16%	18%	13%	1%	0%	3%	0%
20	ASSET_LTM_EVx	SALES_LTM_Gr	CK	ID	58%	4%	12%	28%	1%	7%	8%	27%	4%	3%	4%	4%	12%	27%	19%
21	EPS_LTM_Px	SALES_LTM_Gr	CU	ID	1%	27%	5%	26%	8%	4%	10%	10%	20%	4%	14%	6%	7%	13%	2%
22	BPS_LTM_Px	SALES_LTM_Gr	DE	ID	1%	0%	3%	17%	3%	6%	26%	16%	15%	3%	4%	3%	9%	21%	3%
23	SALES_LTM_Px	SALES_LTM_Gr	DO	ID	5%	5%	2%	32%	18%	47%	23%	49%	18%	8%	23%	24%	15%	12%	13%
24	FCF_LTM_Px	SALES_LTM_Gr	DY	ID	4%	1%	16%	8%	10%	10%	17%	27%	25%	8%	7%	1%	1%	7%	2%
25	PEG_LTM	SALES_LTM_Gr	MZ	ID	2%	16%	23%	0%	13%	2%	2%	3%	11%	7%	6%	4%	1%	17%	8%

Fig. 7.1 Example Excel table used for testing the hypothesis

4. The area highlighted with "D" identifies in which column the data for the variables selected in the area "C" can be found. If we take the first row, Sales_LTM_EVx vs. Sales_LTM_Gr (meaning EV/LTM Sales vs. LTM Sales Growth), it can be seen that the EV/LTM Sales data can be found in column "I" while the LTM Sales Growth data can be found in column "ID." Combining the information from area "B," it can be concluded that the data for the year 2007 for this particular regression (EV/LTM Sales vs. LTM Sales Growth) is to be found in I772:I904 and ID772:ID904.
5. The area highlighted with "E" calculates the particular regression out in this particular care, the R-Squared. Similarly, the Slope, the Intercept, the number of usable observations, and the Correlation were also calculated to have all the required information to calculate the p-value for each regression.

The calculations were performed using the mentioned INDIRECT function combined with the relevant statistical function with an example for the first row and year 2007 shown below (same example as discussed on the previous page):

The function used to calculate the R-Squared for 2007 first row:

= RSQ(INDIRECT("Data!"&$D12&F$7&":"&$D12&F$8),

INDIRECT("Data!"&$E12&F$7&":"&$E12&F$8))

To calculate the Intercept, the function "INTERCEPT" was used instead of "RSQ," while for calculating the Slope, the function "SLOPE" and for correlation, the function "CORREL" was used. To calculate the p-value, the function "T.DIST.2 T" was used. The calculation of the number of observations required some ingenuity as the function "ISNUMBER," used to determine if a particular value is empty or a number, has as output the value "TRUE" or "FALES." When applying, however, a "minus minus" function, the "TRUE" values become 1, and "FALSE" values become 0. Lastly, using a "SUMPRODUCT" function, it can be calculated which observations as only multiplying 1 by 1 yield 1.

The function used to calculate the number of observations in the first row:

= SUMPRODUCT(

--ISNUMBER(INDIRECT("Data!"&$D29&F$7&":"&$D29&F$8)),

--ISNUMBER(INDIRECT("Data!"&$E29&F$7&":"&$E29&F$8)))

In order to calculate the p-value, first, the T-Score needs to be calculated using the standard formula:

$$\textbf{Formula to calculate the T} - \textbf{Score}:$$

$$t = {}^{r\sqrt{n-2}}\Big/\sqrt{1-r^2}, \ where$$

1. t is the T-Score
2. r is the correlation coefficient calculated using the "CORREL" function
3. n is the sample size calculated using the observations formula above

Lastly, using the T-Score, the p-value can be calculated using the "T.DIST.2 T" function, the T-Score, and the number of observations above minus 2.

7.1.3 Methodology: Ensuring Rational Correlations and Statistical Significance

Having calculated all results required to analyze the regressions, the next step is to ensure that the depicted relationships are logical and rational while the sample of each of the regressions is sufficiently large to be statistically significant. Lastly, regressions should be statistically significant with a p-value (the probability of a null hypothesis being correct) below 0.05.

Testing for a positive correlation (slope) between multiples and drivers is important as it is abnormal and counterintuitive for a financial indicator developing in a positive direction to negatively impact the valuation. To exemplify, such a situation would imply that a company growing faster would be punished with an ever-decreasing valuation. As highlighted in the dot com portion of the literature review, such scenarios are rare and irrational and should be excluded from the analysis.

These tests were implemented by using a simple IF function for each of the three criteria. If any of the regressions showed less than 10 observations, a negative correlation explained via a negative slope or a p-value of over 0.05 was disregarded. For some industries, the number of companies included was too low to pass the number of observations result, with the threshold being lowered to 7, however, this will be noted in the discussion of the results.

7.2 Research Results with Deliberations and Interpretations

This sub-chapter will discuss the results for each of the 21 industries analyzed and draw some conclusions for each of the industries to enable testing the hypotheses. The results will focus on the regressions with the highest R-Squared for each industry. The first 20 regressions for each year will be discussed in order to draw conclusions, as extending the analysis with further regressions does not strengthen the conclusion. Depending on the variance in outcomes, either the top 10 or the top 20 regressions will be shown to preserve space and enable a clearer view of the results, however, the analysis will always be based on the top 20 regressions with the occurrence of each driver, or multiple types showed at the bottom.

The discussion of results on an industry-by-industry basis is important as the businesses in each cluster have similar business models and represent an industry together. Considering that each variable includes 10 or 8 timeframes, each variable is given the best possible scenario to come out on top and explain as much of the variance as possible independent of the timeframe covered by the individual multiple or driver.

Table 7.1 presents a summary of the industries that were analyzed as well as the number of companies that are included in each cluster/segment, the p-value used to decide if a regression is statistically significant (column "Thold Stat. Sign." meaning threshold statistical significance; all analyses used a p-value of 0.05), the number of minimum observations used to decide if a regression is deemed as useful and significant (for the initial analysis, 10 was used a benchmark) as well as the number of regressions that satisfy these criteria. "Suff. Obs." meaning "sufficient observations," shows the number of regressions that has sufficient observations to be included, "Positive Correl." shows the number of regressions from the ones with sufficient observations that experienced a positive correlation between base and driver, while "Stat. Signif." shows the number of regressions from the ones with sufficient observations that were statistically significant based on the previously defined p-value. The column "Usab. Regr." shows the number of usable regressions that satisfy all criteria, while the "Usab. Regr. as %" shows this number as a percentage from a total possible number of regressions of 388,800. The total potential number of 388,800 does not account for companies not being public and other technical reasons hence should not be used as an indicator for coverage. The fact that the column statistical significance and usable regressions are equal shows only that statistically significant regressions have the expected slope/ relationship and sufficient observations, however, there could have been situations where the regression is statistically significant, but the relationship is counterintuitive.

Some industries might show a high relevance of book value multiples and drivers. While such findings would be unexpected since internet-enabled businesses usually have "light" balance sheets, such situations would require an additional analysis excluding balance sheet metrics to provide managerial and strategic recommendations. Balance sheets reflect the status quo of a longer period of activity, and while some strategic decisions can change balance sheet values in the long term, it is difficult to influence such values in the short or medium term. Hence, deriving value-maximizing recommendations from such multiples and drivers is difficult.

The results for some of the industries are surprising and worth discussing individually before diving into the details of each of the industries/ clusters:

1. **Analytics software**: despite the peer group having 22 companies, only about 1.5% of the regressions were statistically significant and passed all required filters. There could be various reasons, however, since the field is relatively new, business models might not be entirely developed or even comparable. It will be interesting to look at the detailed results as the number of regressions enables some level of analysis.
2. **Financial content monetization** shows low usable regressions due to the number of observations. The segment only has 14 publicly listed companies, and since some have become public recently, going back in time is difficult as the number of observations decreases. However, this segment differs from all others and can consequently not be merged with others. Despite dropping the minimum number of observations to 7, the analysis only yields 3,707 statistically significant regressions. Running the analysis with the 10-observation requirement yields only c. 500 regressions. Depending on the consistency of the outcomes, the industry might be excluded from the detailed analysis as trying to interpret varying outcomes based on little data will not lead to value-adding conclusions.
3. **Content monetization** shows a similar issue, with only 2.6% of regressions ending up being useful for the study, with statistical significance being the filter reducing the number of regressions the most. The number is, however, high enough to enable the analysis. It will be interesting to see which bases and drivers pass all filters and provide some insights into the metrics important for investors in this industry.

Table 7.1 Summary of usable regressions for all industries

Industry	# companies	TholdStat. Sign.	# min. obs.	Suff.Obs.	Posit. Correl.	Stat. Signif.	Usab. Regr.	Usab. Regr. as %
All	903	0.05	10	367,390	260,655	150,636	150,636	38.7%
Analytics Soft.	22	0.05	10	68,778	39,823	5,807	5,807	1.5%
Classifieds	34	0.05	10	186,309	124,536	34,803	34,803	9.0%
Content Mone. Fin.	22	0.05	10	10,462	5,097	521	521	0.1%
Content Mone.	22	0.05	10	60,445	42,882	10,083	10,083	2.6%
Customer Acq.	26	0.05	10	129,675	81,309	19,451	19,451	5.0%
Data Center	35	0.05	10	161,057	95,239	22,209	22,209	5.7%
Diversifieds/ Portals	19	0.05	10	134,581	88,542	22,931	22,931	5.9%
eCommerce	76	0.05	10	316,790	222,500	79,272	79,272	20.4%
Gambling	23	0.05	10	296,397	207,793	52,840	52,840	13.6%
Gaming	60	0.05	10	261,978	158,177	36,407	36,407	9.4%
Horizontal Soft.	114	0.05	10	343,412	205,894	57,174	57,174	14.7%
Marketing	88	0.05	10	331,807	219,702	64,445	64,445	16.6%
Marketplace	34	0.05	10	146,630	93,516	19,222	19,222	4.9%
Online B2C Serv.	18	0.05	10	26,079	11,788	1,147	1,147	0.3%
Online Brokerage	8	0.05	10	0	0	0	0	0.0%
Payment	38	0.05	10	246,862	134,445	32,578	32,578	8.4%
Platform Soft.	30	0.05	10	232,404	122,733	32,925	32,925	8.5%
Security Soft.	73	0.05	10	350,222	196,146	56,277	56,277	14.5%
Social Networks	15	0.05	10	54,374	36,861	5,084	5,084	1.3%

(continued)

Table 7.1 (continued)

Industry	# companies	TholdStat. Sign.	# min. obs.	Suff.Obs.	Posit. Correl.	Stat. Signif.	Usab. Regr.	Usab. Regr. as %
Travel	21	0.05	10	124,706	81,991	19,406	19,406	5.0%
Vertical Soft.	133	0.05	10	355,753	243,412	86,572	86,572	22.3%

4. **Online B2C services** is the next problematic segment which, despite dropping the required number of observations per regression from 10 to 7, only showed 0.7% of useful regressions. The analysis using 10 observations as a requirement only yield 1,100 useful regressions corresponding to a percentage of 0.3%. This result is surprising as there are sufficient observations, and the peer group is sufficiently large and mature to expect a different outcome. It will be interesting to see the detailed results and if there are any continuous conclusions to be drawn for this industry.
5. **Online brokerage** is an industry with almost no useful regressions, primarily due to the low number of observations, however, considering that only 8 companies were identified, this result is not surprising. This industry will also be excluded from the detailed analysis as the number of useful regressions does not enable any type of useful analysis. Even decreasing the number of observations required from 10 to 7 only yields 82 useful regressions.
6. **Social networks:** similarly to other industries, the results show a surprisingly low number of usable regressions primarily due to the statistical significance. The number of 5,084 useful regression is sufficient for the analysis.

The remaining industries demonstrated sufficient useful regressions and did not require any special discussion before the detailed results. It is surprising to see that, by far, the factor that ended up excluding a large share of regressions is the statistical significance factor. While the expectation was that many bases and drivers would not yield statistically significant results, it was not expected that only 1/4 of all regressions with sufficient observations would yield statistically significant results. Positive correlation does not seem to be a significant problem, with more than 50% of all regressions with sufficient observations showing a natural relationship.

7.2.1 Results for All Companies Included in the Study Analyzed Simultaneously

Before diving into the results of each industry, it is worth spending some time with the results of all companies included in the study. Table 7.2 presents an overview of the R-Squared values of the top 10 usable regressions for all companies in the study analyzed simultaneously. It is to be observed that R-Squared values decrease significantly over time, from c. 70% in 2007 to c. 30% in 2021. There can be several reasons for this, such as investors starting to differentiate between types of businesses in the internet-enabled sector or certain industries starting to be valued based on different multiples and drivers as opposed to the one size fits all top line and growth-focused approach typical for the growth phase of companies and industries. It is also worth noting that R-Squared values of individual industries will likely end up being significantly higher than the overall peer group analyzed as a whole due to the focus and comparability of business models.

Table 7.2 R^2 of top 20 regressions for all companies

#	'07	'08	'09	'10	'11	'12	'13	'14	'15	'16	'17	'18	'19	'20	'21
1	80	62	89	66	58	57	61	53	45	52	45	40	41	34	29
2	69	60	85	65	57	52	58	53	44	51	45	40	39	32	29
3	65	60	78	64	55	52	54	52	42	49	43	39	37	31	28
4	65	60	78	62	55	51	54	49	41	47	42	38	37	30	27
5	64	60	78	61	55	50	52	49	40	47	42	37	36	29	27
6	64	59	78	60	55	49	51	48	40	46	41	36	36	29	27
7	64	59	76	60	54	48	50	47	39	46	40	36	33	29	27
8	63	58	76	58	54	47	50	47	39	45	40	35	33	29	26
9	62	58	76	57	53	47	50	46	39	44	40	34	33	28	26
10	62	58	76	55	52	46	49	46	39	44	39	33	33	28	26
11	62	58	76	55	51	46	49	45	38	43	39	33	32	28	25
12	62	58	75	54	51	45	48	45	38	42	38	33	30	28	25
13	62	57	75	54	50	45	48	44	38	42	37	31	30	28	24
14	62	57	75	54	50	44	47	44	38	42	37	30	30	28	24

(continued)

Table 7.2 (continued)

#	'07	'08	'09	'10	'11	'12	'13	'14	'15	'16	'17	'18	'19	'20	'21
15	61	57	75	54	50	44	47	43	37	42	37	30	30	28	23
16	61	57	75	54	49	44	47	43	37	42	37	30	29	27	23
17	61	57	75	54	49	44	46	43	37	41	37	30	29	27	23
18	61	57	74	53	49	44	45	42	37	41	37	29	28	27	23
19	61	56	74	53	49	43	45	42	37	41	37	29	28	27	23
20	61	56	74	53	48	42	44	41	37	41	37	29	28	27	23

Table 7.3 presents the results of the top 10 regressions for the entire group of companies included in the study and the results of the top 3 bases and drivers based on the top 20 regressions.

From a multiples (driver) perspective, the results match expectations. Sales multiples dominated most of the years until 2012, followed by the EV/EBITDARD coming into focus starting in 2012 and leading until 2021 when a shift back to Sales multiples happened. This transition is consistent with Damodaran's suggestions. What is interesting is the relatively high relevance of EV to Asset multiples in 2007. This year was driven by the financial crisis when more traditional valuation methods became relevant and most likely explain this phenomenon.

Additionally, the shift back to EV/Sales and P/Sales multiples in 2021 is surprising and most likely driven by the post-COVID-19 measures the central banks implemented. The availability of liquidity in the markets drove valuations high, making sales multiples more relevant for this year. While the study ends in 2021, it should be expected for this to reverse in 2022 when valuations came down together with the shift in policy toward monetary tightening.

Table 7.3 Results of top best-fitting regressions for all companies analyzed simultaneously

		2007	2008	2009	2010	2011	2012	2013	2014	2015	2016	2017	2018	2019	2020	2021
Multiples of top 10 regressions	1	EV/Asset FY+3	EV/GM FY+3	EV/E.ARD LTM	EV/GM FY-2	P/Sales SLTM	EV/E.ARD FY-2	EV/E.ARD FY-2	EV/E.ARD FY-2	EV/E.ARD SLTM	EV/E.ARD SLTM	P/Sales SLTM	EV/E.ARD LTM	EV/E.ARD LTM	EV/E.ARD LTM	EV/Sales LTM
	2	EV/Asset FY+3	P/B FY-2	EV/E.ARD LTM	EV/GM FY-2	EV/Sales FY-2	EV/Sales SLTM	EV/E.ARD FY-2	EV/E.ARD FY-1	EV/E.ARD SLTM	EV/E.ARD FY0	EV/Sales SLTM	EV/E.ARD FY0	EV/E.ARD LTM	EV/E.ARD LTM	P/Sales LTM
	3	P/Sales FY0	P/Sales FY+3	EV/Sales STM	EV/GM FY-2	P/Sales FY-2	EV/E.ARD FY-2	EV/E.ARD FY-2	EV/E.ARD FY-2	EV/EBITDA FY-1	EV/E.ARD FY-2	EV/E.ARD FY0	EV/E.ARD SLTM	EV/E.ARD FY+1	EV/E.ARD FY0	EV/Sales FY+1
	4	P/Sales LTM	P/Sales FY+3	EV/Sales STM	EV/E.ARD LTM	EV/Sales FY-1	P/Sales SLTM	EV/E.ARD FY-2	EV/E.ARD FY-1	EV/E.ARD FY0	EV/E.ARD SLTM	EV/Sales FY-1	EV/E.ARD FY-1	EV/E.ARD LTM	EV/E.ARD LTM	P/Sales FY+1
	5	EV/Asset STM	P/Sales SLTM	EV/Sales FY+3	EV/E.ARD FY0	P/Sales FY-1	EV/Sales FY-1	EV/Sales FY-1	EV/E.ARD FY-1	EV/E.ARD SLTM	EV/E.ARD FY-2	EV/E.ARD SLTM	EV/E.ARD FY-1	EV/E.ARD LTM	EV/Asset FY-2	EV/Sales LTM
	6	P/Sales FY+1	P/B FY-2	EV/Sales STM	EV/GM FY-2	EV/E.ARD FY0	EV/E.ARD FY-2	EV/E.ARD FY-2	EV/Sales FY-1	EV/E.ARD FY-2	EV/E.ARD FY+1	EV/E.ARD LTM	EV/E.ARD FY+1	EV/E.ARD FY0	EV/Sales FY0	EV/Sales FY0
	7	EV/Sales FY0	P/Sales FY+3	EV/EBIT LTM	EV/GM FY-2	EV/Sales FY-2	EV/E.ARD FY-2	EV/E.ARD FY-2	EV/Sales FY-2	EV/E.ARD SLTM	EV/E.ARD LTM	P/Sales LTM	EV/E.ARD LTM	EV/E.ARD FY0	P/Sales FY0	P/Sales LTM
	8	EV/OP CF LTM	P/Sales STM	EV/Sales FY+2	EV/GM FY-2	EV/Sales SLTM	P/Sales FY-1	EV/E.ARD FY-2	EV/Sales SLTM	EV/GM FY-2	EV/E.ARD SLTM	P/Sales FY-1	EV/E.ARD SLTM	EV/E.ARD FY0	EV/E.ARD FY0	EV/Sales FY+1
	9	P/Sales SLTM	P/Sales STM	EV/E.ARD FY+1	EV/GM FY-2	P/Sales FY-2	P/Sales FY-2	EV/Sales SLTM	EV/E.ARD SLTM	EV/E.ARD FY-2	EV/E.ARD SLTM	EV/E.ARD FY0	EV/E.ARD LTM	EV/E.ARD FY0	EV/Sales SLTM	P/Sales FY0
	10	EV/Asset STM	EV/Sales SLTM	EV/E.ARD FY+2	EV/GM FY-2	P/Sales FY0	EV/E.ARD FY-2	P/Sales SLTM	EV/E.ARD FY-2	EV/E.ARD SLTM	EV/E.ARD SLTM	EV/E.ARD SLTM	P/Sales FY-2	EV/E.ARD FY+1	EV/GM FY-2	EV/Sales FY0
	Σ 20	P/Sales EV/Asset EV/Sales	P/Sales EV/Sales EV/GM	EV/Sales EV/E.ARD	EV/GM P/Sales EV/Asset	P/Sales EV/Sales EV/E.ARD	EV/E.ARD EV/Sales P/Sales	EV/E.ARD EV/Sales P/Sales	EV/E.ARD EV/Sales P/Sales	EV/E.ARD EV/GM	EV/E.ARD	EV/E.ARD EV/Sales P/Sales	EV/E.ARD P/Sales	EV/E.ARD	EV/E.ARD P/Sales EV/Sales	EV/Sales P/Sales EV/E.ARD
		9-8-2	9-4-3	10-8-0	10-3-3	10-8-2	11-5-4	10-6-4	14-4-2	15-2-0	20-0-0	9-6-5	17-2-0	20-0-0	8-4-4	9-7-2
Drivers of top 10 regressions	1	RoA LTM	E.A-CX M. FY-2	EPS Gr. STM	E.ARD Gr. NTM	S.Gr.+E.A% FY+3	Sales Gr. NTM	Sales Gr. NTM	Sales Gr. STM	Sales Gr. NTM	Sales Gr. STM	S.Gr.+E.A% STM	Sales Gr. STM	Sales Gr. STM	Sales Gr. FY+3	S.Gr.+E.A% FY+3
	2	RoA FY0	RoA SLTM	EPS Gr. FY0	GM Gr. NTM	S.Gr.+E.A% STM	S.Gr.+E.A% FY+2	Sales Gr. FY+2	Sales Gr. STM	Sales Gr. FY+1	Sales Gr. STM	S.Gr.+E.A% STM	Sales Gr. STM	GM Gr. FY+2	Sales Gr. STM	S.Gr.+E.A% FY+3
	3	S.Gr.+E.A% STM	Op.CF/Sal. FY+2	E.ARD Mar. FY+1	E.ARD Gr. FY+1	S.Gr.+E.A% STM	GM Gr. NTM	Sales Gr. FY+1	Sales Gr. FY+2	E.ARD Gr. LTM	Sales Gr. FY0	Sales Gr. STM	Sales Gr. STM	Sales Gr. STM	Sales Gr. NTM	S.Gr.+E.A% FY+3
	4	S.Gr.+E.A% STM	Op.CF/Sal. STM	E.ARD Mar. NTM	GM Gr. FY-1	S.Gr.+E.A% FY+3	S.Gr.+E.A% FY+2	Sales Gr. STM	GM Gr. STM	Sales Gr. NTM	Sales Gr. FY+2	S.Gr.+E.A% STM	Sales Gr. STM	Sales Gr. FY+3	E.ARD Gr. FY+3	S.Gr.+E.A% FY+3
	5	RoA FY0	S.Gr.+E.A% STM	E.ARD Mar. FY+2	GM Gr. FY-1	S.Gr.+E.A% FY+3	S.Gr.+E.A% FY+2	S.Gr.+E.A% STM	GM Gr. FY+2	Sales Gr. LTM	Sales Gr. LTM	Sales Gr. STM	GM Gr. STM	Sales Gr. FY+2	Sales Gr. LTM	S.Gr.+E.A% STM
	6	S.Gr.+E.A% STM	RoA FY-1	E.ARD Mar. FY+2	Sales Gr. STM	Sales Gr. STM	GM Gr. FY+2	GM Gr. FY+2	S.Gr.+E.A% STM	Sales Gr. FY+1	Sales Gr. STM	Sales Gr. STM	Sales Gr. STM	GM Gr. FY+2	S.Gr.+E.A% STM	S.Gr.+E.A% FY+3
	7	S.Gr.+E.A% STM	Op.CF/Sal. NTM	E.ARD Gr. NTM	GM Gr. STM	S.Gr.+E.A% FY+3	Sales Gr. FY+2	Sales Gr. LTM	S.Gr.+E.A% STM	Sales Gr. FY+2	Sales Gr. STM	S.Gr.+E.A% STM	E.ARD Gr. STM	Sales Gr. FY+2	S.Gr.+E.A% STM	S.Gr.+E.A% STM
	8	EBITDA Gr. FY+1	Op.CF/Sal. FY+2	E.ARD Mar. FY+1	Sales Gr. LTM	S.Gr.+E.A% FY+3	S.Gr.+E.A% FY+2	GM Gr. FY+1	S.Gr.+E.A% STM	S.Gr.+E.A% STM	GM Gr. FY+2	S.Gr.+E.A% STM	GM Gr. STM	Sales Gr. STM	Sales Gr. LTM	S.Gr.+E.A% STM
	9	S.Gr.+E.A% NTM	Op.CF/Sal. STM	EPS Gr. STM	GM Gr. FY+2	S.Gr.+E.A% FY+3	S.Gr.+E.A% FY+2	S.Gr.+E.A% STM	Sales Gr. STM	Sales Gr. NTM	GM Gr. STM	GM Gr. STM	Sales Gr. FY+3	GM Gr. NTM	S.Gr.+E.A% STM	S.Gr.+E.A% FY+3
	10	RoA LTM	S.Gr.+E.A% STM	EPS Gr. STM	E.ARD Gr. FY+2	S.Gr.+E.A% FY+3	Sales Gr. LTM	S.Gr.+E.A% STM	GM Gr. FY+2	Sales Gr. STM	Sales Gr. NTM	GM Gr. STM	S.Gr.+E.A% STM	Sales Gr. FY+3	Sales Gr. LTM	S.Gr.+E.A% STM
	Σ 20	RoA S.Gr.+E.A% Op.CF/Sal.	Op.CF/Sal. S.Gr.+E.A%	E.ARD Mar. EPS Gr.	S.Gr.+E.A% GM Gr.	S.Gr.+E.A% Sales Gr.	S.Gr.+E.A% Sales Gr.	S.Gr.+E.A% Sales Gr.	Sales Gr. GM Gr. S.Gr.+E.A%	Sales Gr. S.Gr.+E.A%	Sales Gr. GM Gr.	S.Gr.+E.A% Sales Gr.	Sales Gr. S.Gr.+E.A%	Sales Gr. GM Gr.	Sales Gr. S.Gr.+E.A%	S.Gr.+E.A% Sales Gr.
		8-7-2	8-7-0	10-6-0	7-5-0	18-1-0	9-8-0	10-7-0	9-6-5	16-2-0	12-7-0	11-5-0	14-3-0	14-6-0	9-8-0	17-3-0

In terms of drivers, there is some movement over the observation period, however, the movement is also in line with expectations. The rule of 40 indicator and sales growth are the most often encountered drivers. In 2007 Return on Asset seems to have been the most relevant driver, which is surprising, however, it is probably to be expected given the financial crisis. In 2008 we see operative cash flow margin together with the rule of 40 variable taking over, while 2009 shows a shift towards EBITDARD margin. In the following years, the rule of 40 and sales growth are the most relevant drives which depending on the year, one or the other comes out on top.

Drivers show that while valuation bases have shifted towards profitability, drivers still have a focus on growth while rewarding companies that can show both growth and probability simultaneously.

It is to be noted that together with the shift towards Sales multiples in 2021 following COVID-19, the rule of 40 became by far the most important driver. This demonstrates that while the additional liquidity caused a shift in which multiple is the most important, profitability still played a role as it was considered together with growth as a driver. What can also be noted from the overview is that the relevance of future financials (particularly FY + 3), especially as a driver is very high, demonstrating that investors tried to look beyond COVID-19 toward normalization in the future. This also implies that valuations were highly driven by future expectations regarding both growth and profitability.

It would be highly interesting to see the results for 2022 and onwards and if the internet-enabled businesses, as an overarching cluster, see a shift toward profitability as a driver. With so many new technologies, however, also coming into existence, the shift in the entire group might get postponed for a few years until a certain level of maturity is achieved for all businesses in this sector.

7.2.2 Results for Analytics Software Companies

The first industry to be discussed in detail is the analytics software industry. Despite yielding very high R-Squared figures discussed, it had a fairly low share of usable regressions due to not being statistically significant. Additionally, due to the number of public companies in the early years of the study, only sufficient data is available starting in 2013; hence the output is adjusted accordingly.

Table 7.4 presents the R-Squared of the top 20 regressions for the analytics software industry with respectable figures of above 70%, implying that the explanatory power is high.

Table 7.4 R^2 of top 20 regressions for analytics software companies

#	'13	'14	'15	'16	'17	'18	'19	'20	'21
1	89	98	96	90	97	87	85	80	80
2	88	94	95	89	96	85	81	80	75
3	87	94	93	89	96	85	80	79	71
4	87	93	93	88	94	85	80	78	70
5	86	92	93	88	94	83	79	77	70
6	84	91	92	88	93	81	78	74	70
7	83	90	92	87	93	80	76	74	70
8	83	90	91	86	93	80	74	74	69
9	83	89	91	86	92	80	73	73	69
10	82	89	90	85	92	79	73	73	68
11	82	89	88	85	90	78	73	73	67
12	82	88	88	85	88	78	72	73	67
13	81	86	88	84	87	78	72	73	66
14	81	84	88	84	87	77	72	72	65
15	80	83	87	82	86	77	72	72	65
16	80	83	87	82	86	77	71	71	65
17	79	81	86	82	85	77	70	71	65
18	78	81	86	82	85	76	70	70	63
19	78	81	86	82	85	76	70	70	63
20	77	81	86	81	84	76	70	69	62

Table 7.5 presents the analysis results, which, as expected based on the number of regressions, are somehow inconsistent in development. What can be observed is that valuation bases are changing from Sales multiples in the first years (2013, 2014) towards profitability multiples in 2015, 2016, and 2017 with various forms of profitability being relevant and back to sales in the years to come. It is, however, to be noted that these changes are not so clear since the number of relevant regressions for each type of multiple evolves together.

Table 7.5 Results of top best-fitting regressions for analytics software companies

		2013	2014	2015	2016	2017	2018	2019	2020	2021
Multiples of top 20 regressions	1	P/Sales FY+1	P/Sales FY-1	EV/Sales FY-1	P/Sales FY-2	EV/GM FY-1	EV/GM FY-2	P/FCF FY+3	EV/GM LTM	EV/E..A-CX FY+3
	2	P/B LTM	P/Sales SLTM	P/Sales FY-1	EV/GM FY0	EV/GM SLTM	P/Sales SLTM	EV/GM SLTM	EV/GM FY0	EV/E..A-CX FY+3
	3	P/Sales FY+1	P/Sales FY0	EV/Sales FY-1	EV/EBIT LTM	EV/GM LTM	P/Sales FY-2	P/Sales SLTM	EV/GM FY-1	P/E FY+3
	4	EV/Sales LTM	P/Sales SLTM	EV/EBIT NTM	P/Sales STM	EV/GM FY+1	P/Sales FY-1	P/Sales FY+3	EV/GM SLTM	P/Sales SLTM
	5	P/Sales LTM	P/Sales FY0	P/Sales FY-1	P/Sales FY+3	P/Sales FY-2	P/Sales FY+3	EV/GM FY-2	EV/GM FY+1	P/Sales STM
	6	P/B FY+2	EV/Sales SLTM	EV/OP CF STM	EV/Sales FY-2	P/Sales FY-1	EV/GM SLTM	P/Sales FY0	EV/Sales FY0	EV/Sales FY+2
	7	EV/Sales FY0	EV/Sales FY0	EV/OP CF NTM	EV/EBIT FY+1	EV/GM FY0	P/Sales FY-2	EV/Asset FY-1	P/Sales LTM	P/Sales FY+3
	8	EV/Sales LTM	EV/Sales SLTM	P/E NTM	EV/EBIT NTM	P/Sales SLTM	P/Sales FY-2	EV/GM FY-2	P/Sales FY0	EV/Sales STM
	9	P/Sales FY+1	EV/Sales SLTM	EV/EBITDA FY+1	EV/EBIT FY+1	EV/GM NTM	EV/GM FY-2	P/Sales LTM	EV/GM NTM	EV/EBIT FY+3
	10	P/Sales LTM	EV/Sales FY0	EV/Sales FY-1	EV/EBITDA FY+2	EV/E..A-CX FY+2	P/Sales FY+3	EV/GM FY-2	EV/Sales LTM	EV/E..A-CX FY+3
	11	EV/Sales FY0	EV/Sales LTM	EV/EBIT FY+2	EV/Sales STM	EV/GM FY+2	P/FCF FY+2	EV/GM FY0	P/Sales FY+1	EV/Sales NTM
	12	P/Sales LTM	P/Sales LTM	EV/OP CF FY+2	EV/EBIT FY+2	EV/GM SLTM	EV/GM FY-1	EV/GM SLTM	P/Sales FY-1	EV/Sales FY+3
	13	P/B NTM	P/Sales SLTM	P/E FY+1	EV/Sales FY+3	EV/GM FY-1	P/Sales FY-2	EV/E..ARD NTM	EV/Sales FY+1	P/Sales SLTM
	14	EV/Sales LTM	P/Sales LTM	EV/OP CF FY+2	EV/EBIT LTM	EV/GM SLTM	P/FCF FY+2	EV/E..ARD FY+2	EV/Sales SLTM	P/Sales FY+2
	15	P/B FY+3	EV/Sales LTM	P/Sales FY+3	EV/GM SLTM	EV/Sales FY-2	P/FCF FY+2	P/Sales FY-2	P/Sales SLTM	EV/E..A-CX FY+3
	16	P/B LTM	EV/Sales FY+1	P/E FY+1	EV/EBIT FY+2	EV/GM FY-1	P/FCF FY+2	P/FCF NTM	EV/Sales SLTM	P/Sales SLTM
	17	EV/Sales LTM	EV/Sales FY+1	EV/EBITDA NTM	EV/EBIT NTM	EV/GM STM	P/FCF FY+2	EV/Asset FY-1	P/Sales SLTM	EV/Sales FY+1
	18	P/B STM	P/Sales FY+1	EV/EBITDA FY+2	EV/GM FY0	EV/E..A-CX FY+2	P/Sales SLTM	P/Sales STM	EV/GM FY+2	EV/E..A-CX FY+3
	19	EV/Sales LTM	EV/GM FY0	EV/E..A-CX FY+2	EV/EBIT LTM	EV/GM SLTM	P/Sales FY-1	P/FCF NTM	EV/Sales NTM	P/E FY+3
	20	P/B FY+1	P/Sales FY-1	P/E FY+1	EV/GM SLTM	EV/GM FY-1	EV/Sales FY-2	EV/GM FY-1	P/Sales FY0	EV/GM FY-1
	Σ 20	P/B EV/Sales P/Sales	P/Sales EV/Sales	P/E EV/OP CF P/Sales	EV/EBIT	EV/GM	P/Sales	EV/GM P/Sales P/FCF	P/Sales EV/GM EV/Sales	P/Sales EV/Sales EV/E..A-CX
		7-7-6	10-9-0	4-4-3	9-0-0	14-0-0	10-0-0	7-6-3	7-7-6	6-5-5
Drivers of top 20 regressions	1	EBIT Gr. FY+3	Sales Gr. STM	EPS Gr. STM	Sales Gr. STM	S.Gr.+E..A% LTM	GM Gr. FY0	GM Gr. FY0	S.Gr.+E..A% FY-1	EBITDA Gr. FY+3
	2	EBIT Gr. STM	GM Gr. STM	EPS Gr. STM	S.Gr.+E..A% NTM	S.Gr.+E..A% LTM	GM Gr. STM	S.Gr.+E..A% FY0	S.Gr.+E..A% FY-1	E..A-CX Gr. FY+3
	3	EPS Gr. STM	GM Gr. STM	EBIT Gr. STM	Sales Gr. NTM	S.Gr.+E..A% LTM	GM Gr. STM	GM Gr. FY0	S.Gr.+E..A% FY-1	FCF Gr. FY+3
	4	EBIT Gr. STM	Sales Gr. STM	S.Gr.+E..A% FY+2	GM Gr. NTM	S.Gr.+E..A% LTM	GM Gr. STM	S.Gr.+E..A% LTM	S.Gr.+E..A% FY-1	Sales Gr. STM
	5	EPS Gr. STM	Sales Gr. STM	EBITDA Gr. STM	GM Gr. NTM	GM Gr. STM	S.Gr.+E..A% FY+3	S.Gr.+E..A% STM	S.Gr.+E..A% FY-1	EPS Gr. FY-1
	6	EBIT Gr. STM	Sales Gr. STM	Sales Gr. STM	Sales Gr. STM	GM Gr. STM	GM Gr. LTM	GM Gr. FY0	S.Gr.+E..A% FY-1	EPS Gr. FY-1
	7	EBIT Gr. STM	GM Gr. STM	Sales Gr. STM	Sales Gr. NTM	S.Gr.+E..A% LTM	Sales Gr. FY0	GM Gr. FY0	S.Gr.+E..A% FY-1	EPS Gr. FY-1
	8	EPS Gr. STM	Sales Gr. FY+3	S.Gr.+E..A% FY+2	Sales Gr. FY+2	GM Gr. STM	Sales Gr. STM	S.Gr.+E..A% FY+2	S.Gr.+E..A% FY-1	EPS Gr. FY-1
	9	EBIT Gr. FY+2	GM Gr. STM	S.Gr.+E..A% FY+2	Sales Gr. FY+2	S.Gr.+E..A% LTM	S.Gr.+E..A% STM	GM Gr. FY0	S.Gr.+E..A% FY-1	E..A-CX Gr. FY+3
	10	EBIT Gr. FY+3	Sales Gr. STM	EBITDA Gr. STM	Sales Gr. STM	E..A-CX Gr. STM	S.Gr.+E..A% STM	S.Gr.+E..A% LTM	S.Gr.+E..A% FY-1	EPS Gr. FY+3
	11	EBITDA Gr. STM	Sales Gr. STM	Op.CF Gr. STM	GM Gr. NTM	S.Gr.+E..A% LTM	Gross Mar. STM	S.Gr.+E..A% LTM	S.Gr.+E..A% FY-1	EPS Gr. FY-1
	12	EBIT Gr. FY+2	Sales Gr. STM	EBIT Gr. STM	Sales Gr. NTM	S.Gr.+E..A% FY+2	GM Gr. LTM	S.Gr.+E..A% LTM	GM Gr. FY-1	EPS Gr. FY-1
	13	EBIT Gr. STM	Sales Gr. FY+3	EPS Gr. STM	GM Gr. NTM	S.Gr.+E..A% FY+1	GM Gr. FY+2	GM Gr. FY0	S.Gr.+E..A% FY-1	E..ARD Gr. FY+2
	14	EBITDA Gr. STM	GM Gr. STM	Sales Gr. STM	Sales Gr. STM	S.Gr.+E..A% FY+1	Gross Mar. FY+1	GM Gr. FY0	S.Gr.+E..A% FY-1	EPS Gr. FY-1
	15	Sales Gr. FY+3	GM Gr. STM	FCF Gr. FY+2	S.Gr.+E..A% NTM	GM Gr. STM	Gross Mar. NTM	Sales Gr. STM	GM Gr. FY-1	EBIT Gr. FY+3
	16	EBITDA Gr. STM	Sales Gr. STM	Sales Gr. FY+2	Sales Gr. FY+2	S.Gr.+E..A% FY+2	Gross Mar. FY+2	Gross Mar. FY+1	GM Gr. FY-1	E..ARD Gr. STM
	17	EBIT Gr. FY+3	GM Gr. STM	S.Gr.+E..A% FY+2	Sales Gr. NTM	S.Gr.+E..A% LTM	Gross Mar. LTM	Sales Gr. FY0	S.Gr.+E..A% FY-1	EPS Gr. FY-1
	18	Sales Gr. FY+3	GM Gr. STM	Op.CF Gr. STM	S.Gr.+E..A% FY+2	EBITDA Gr. STM	GM Gr. FY+2	S.Gr.+E..A% LTM	S.Gr.+E..A% FY-1	E..A-CX Gr. STM
	19	EBIT Gr. FY+2	GM Gr. STM	Op.CF Gr. STM	Sales Gr. FY+2	GM Gr. FY+1	GM Gr. FY+2	Gross Mar. NTM	S.Gr.+E..A% FY-1	Gross Mar. LTM
	20	EBIT Gr. STM	Sales Gr. FY+2	S.Gr.+E..A% FY+2	S.Gr.+E..A% FY+1	GM Gr. FY+1	GM Gr. STM	S.Gr.+E..A% FY0	GM Gr. FY-1	EBITDA Gr. FY+2
	Σ 20	EBIT Gr.	Sales Gr. GM Gr.	S.Gr.+E..A% Sales Gr.	Sales Gr.	S.Gr.+E..A%	GM Gr.	S.Gr.+E..A% GM Gr.	S.Gr.+E..A%	EPS Gr.
		12-0-0	11-9-0	5-4-0	12-0-0	12-0-0	10-0-0	9-7-0	16-0-0	9-0-0

Analyzing the drivers, the one common theme is "growth," with different forms of growth expressed via different indicators. While the rule of 40 indicator is very present in the analysis, some other forms of growth also appear. 2013 shows EBIT growth as being the key driver, while in 2014, sales growth and gross margin growth become more important. Starting in 2015, sales growth and the rule of 40 indicator become the main drivers depending on the year, with some years even showing gross margin growth as the most important driver. In the last year, EPS growth has become the most important.

Results for the analytics software segment should be interpreted with a grain of salt as only a small share of regressions were statistically significant to enable deriving conclusions, and the multiples and drivers do not show a clearly identifiable trend towards profitability-based and driven vallation as expected.

Based on the findings, it is difficult to make managerial recommendations, however, what can be concluded is that valuation in this sector is often top-line based, with the rule of 40 showing the most relevance. Consequently, management teams should focus on top-line growth, and once growth slows down, ensure that the company is profitable for a value-maximizing strategy.

7.2.3 Results for Classifieds Companies

As included in the study, the classifieds industry has a healthy number of 34 companies, enabling an analysis starting in 2010 and showing strong R-Squared values of sometimes in the 90s. As can be seen in Table 7.6, the R-Squared values are fairly consistent over the study period and hovering in the 70s and 80s.

Table 7.6 R^2 of top 20 regressions for classifieds companies

#	'10	'11	'12	'13	'14	'15	'16	'17	'18	'19	'20	'21
1	89	96	93	90	77	82	87	81	92	90	89	83
2	87	96	92	89	76	80	85	80	84	89	88	83
3	87	90	90	89	76	76	83	79	81	88	88	83
4	86	90	90	89	75	76	83	78	80	88	87	83
5	86	88	90	89	75	76	83	77	76	87	87	83
6	86	88	90	89	75	74	82	75	76	87	86	82
7	85	87	90	89	75	73	82	75	75	86	86	82

(continued)

Table 7.6 (continued)

#	'10	'11	'12	'13	'14	'15	'16	'17	'18	'19	'20	'21
8	85	87	89	89	73	72	80	75	74	85	85	82
9	85	87	89	88	73	72	79	74	74	85	83	82
10	85	86	89	88	72	71	79	74	74	85	83	82
11	85	86	89	86	72	71	78	73	73	85	82	82
12	85	86	89	85	71	71	78	73	73	84	82	81
13	83	86	89	85	71	71	77	73	73	84	80	81
14	83	84	89	83	71	71	77	73	73	83	80	80
15	83	84	89	83	71	70	77	73	73	83	79	80
16	83	84	88	83	70	68	76	73	73	83	79	80
17	83	84	88	83	70	68	76	73	72	83	79	80
18	83	83	88	82	70	68	75	73	72	83	79	80
19	83	83	88	82	70	68	75	73	72	83	79	80
20	83	83	88	82	70	68	75	72	72	82	78	80

Analyzing the results presented in Table 7.7, it can be seen that the valuation bases are fairly volatile over the entire period of the study. Results started with EV/Sales in 2010 and evolved into Price to Earnings the next year, only to change again into Price to Book the next year and back to EV/Sales in 2013. In the next 3 years, some constancy can be observed with various profitability-driven multiples taking the lead, however, Sales multiples and even Price to Book remain relevant. The last 5 years of the analysis luckily show a certain level of consistency, with Sales multiples being the dominant base. Interestingly, both EV and Price Sales multiples are relevant. This could, in addition to the focus of the investors on price instead of EV, be caused by the low leverage ratios in the industry.

Table 7.7 Results of top best-fitting regressions for classifieds companies

		2010	2011	2012	2013	2014	2015	2016	2017	2018	2019	2020	2021
Multiples of top 10 regressions	1	P/B NTM	P/E FY+3	P/B FY+1	EV/Sales FY+3	EV/EBIT FY+2	P/E FY-2	EV/EBITDA FY-2	EV/Sales FY+3	EV/E..A-CX FY-2	P/Sales FY0	P/Sales FY0	P/Sales FY+1
	2	P/B NTM	P/E STM	P/B FY+1	EV/Sales STM	EV/EBIT FY+2	EV/E..A-CX SLTM	P/B FY-2	EV/Sales STM	EV/EBITDA FY-1	P/Sales SLTM	P/Sales SLTM	P/Sales FY+3
	3	P/B NTM	P/E STM	P/B NTM	EV/E..A-CX FY+1	EV/EBIT NTM	EV/EBIT SLTM	P/B FY-2	EV/OP CF FY-2	EV/E..A-CX FY-1	EV/GM FY-2	EV/Sales FY0	P/Sales STM
	4	EV/Sales FY+3	P/E FY+3	P/B FY+2	EV/Sales FY0	EV/EBITDA NTM	P/E FY-2	P/B FY-2	EV/Sales FY+2	EV/EBIT SLTM	P/Sales FY0	EV/Sales SLTM	P/Sales SLTM
	5	EV/Sales FY+3	P/E STM	P/B FY0	EV/Sales FY+2	EV/EBITDA FY+2	P/B FY-1	EV/EBITDA FY-2	EV/Sales NTM	P/B FY-1	P/Sales SLTM	P/Sales FY0	P/Sales FY+2
	6	EV/Sales FY+3	P/E STM	P/B NTM	EV/Sales SLTM	EV/EBIT STM	EV/E..A-CX SLTM	EV/E..A-CX FY-2	P/Sales FY+3	P/B FY-1	EV/GM FY-2	P/Sales SLTM	P/Sales NTM
	7	EV/Sales STM	P/E FY+3	P/B FY+1	EV/Sales LTM	EV/EBITDA FY+2	EV/EBITDA FY-1	P/B FY+3	P/Sales FY+3	EV/Sales FY+3	P/Sales FY-1	EV/Sales FY0	P/Sales LTM
	8	EV/Sales FY+2	P/E STM	P/B FY+2	EV/Sales FY+1	EV/E..A-CX FY+1	EV/EBITDA FY-1	EV/EBITDA FY-2	EV/Sales FY+3	P/B FY-2	EV/GM FY-2	EV/Sales SLTM	P/Sales FY-1
	9	EV/Sales STM	P/E FY+3	P/B FY+1	EV/Sales NTM	EV/EBIT FY+1	EV/EBITDA FY-1	P/B FY-2	EV/Sales FY+1	EV/Sales STM	P/Sales FY-1	EV/GM LTM	P/Sales FY-1
	10	EV/Sales FY+2	P/E STM	P/B FY+1	EV/Sales FY-1	EV/E..A-CX FY0	EV/E..A-CX SLTM	EV/E..A-CX FY-2	P/Sales STM	P/B FY-2	EV/Sales FY-1	EV/GM FY-2	P/Sales SLTM
	Σ 20	EV/Sales	P/E	P/B	EV/Sales	EV/EBIT EV/EBITDA EV/E..A-CX	EV/E..A-CX EV/Sales P/E	P/B EV/EBITDA EV/E..A-CX	EV/Sales	P/B EV/Sales	P/Sales EV/GM EV/Sales	EV/Sales P/Sales EV/GM	P/Sales EV/Sales
		16-0-0	15-0-0	19-0-0	12-0-0	9-5-4	5-4-3	8-3-3	15-0-0	9-5-0	9-7-4	8-7-5	18-2-0
Drivers of top 10 regressions	1	Net Mar. LTM	FCF Gr. FY+1	RoE FY+3	EBIT Mar. FY-2	DPS Gr. STM	S.Gr.+E..A% FY+1	S.Gr.+E..A% FY0	FCF/Sales LTM	EBITDA Gr. FY0	E..A-CX M. FY-1	EBITDA Mar. FY-2	FCF/Sales FY0
	2	Net Mar. FY+1	FCF Gr. FY+1	Asset Tur. FY+1	EBIT Mar. FY-2	E..A-CX Gr. FY+3	S.Gr.+E..A% NTM	RoA FY+3	FCF/Sales LTM	EBITDA Gr. FY0	E..A-CX M. FY-1	EBITDA Mar. FY-2	FCF/Sales FY0
	3	EBIT Mar. LTM	E..A-CX Gr. NTM	Asset Tur. FY+1	EBITDA Gr. STM	DPS Gr. STM	DPS Gr. NTM	RoA FY-2	EBIT Gr. FY0	EBITDA Gr. FY0	Op.CF/Sal. FY-1	EBITDA Mar. FY-2	FCF/Sales FY0
	4	Net Mar. STM	E..A-CX Gr. NTM	Asset Tur. FY+1	EBIT Mar. FY-2	DPS Gr. STM	S.Gr.+E..A% LTM	RoA STM	FCF/Sales LTM	DPS Gr. FY+2	EBITDA Mar. FY-1	EBITDA Mar. FY-2	FCF/Sales FY0
	5	Net Mar. FY+3	E..A-CX Gr. FY+3	RoE FY0	EBIT Mar. FY-2	Sales Gr. STM	RoA FY-1	S.Gr.+E..A% LTM	FCF/Sales LTM	E..A-CX M. LTM	EBITDA Mar. FY-1	E..A-CX M. FY-2	FCF/Sales FY0
	6	Net Mar. FY+2	E..A-CX Gr. STM	RoE FY+3	EBIT Mar. FY-2	E..A-CX Gr. FY+3	S.Gr.+E..A% FY+2	S.Gr.+E..A% FY0	FCF/Sales FY+1	RoA FY+3	Op.CF/Sal. SLTM	E..A-CX M. FY-2	FCF/Sales FY0
	7	Net Mar. STM	E..A-CX Gr. FY+3	Asset Tur. FY+2	EBIT Mar. FY-2	DPS Gr. STM	S.Gr.+E..A% NTM	DPS Gr. LTM	FCF/Sales LTM	E..A-CX M. LTM	E..A-CX M. FY-1	E..A-CX M. FY-2	FCF/Sales FY0
	8	Net Mar. STM	EBITDA Gr. FY+2	RoE FY+3	EBIT Mar. FY-2	E..A-CX Gr. FY+3	S.Gr.+E..A% FY+1	S.Gr.+E..A% FY+1	FCF/Sales FY+1	E..A-CX M. LTM	EBITDA Mar. FY-1	E..A-CX M. FY-2	FCF/Sales FY0
	9	Net Mar. FY+3	E..A-CX Gr. STM	Asset Tur. FY+3	EBIT Mar. FY-2	E..A-CX Gr. FY+3	S.Gr.+E..A% LTM	RoE FY+3	FCF/Sales LTM	E..A-CX M. LTM	EBITDA Mar. FY-1	EBITDA Mar. FY-2	FCF/Sales LTM
	10	Net Mar. FY+3	EBITDA Gr. STM	Asset Tur. LTM	EBIT Mar. FY-2	E..A-CX Gr. NTM	S.Gr.+E..A% FY+1	S.Gr.+E..A% LTM	FCF/Sales LTM	RoA FY+3	EBITDA Mar. FY-1	EBITDA Mar. FY-2	FCF/Sales LTM
	Σ 20	Net Mar. EBIT Mar.	E..A-CX Gr. EBITDA Gr.	Asset Tur. RoE	EBIT Mar. EBITDA Gr.	DPS Gr. E..A-CX Gr.	S.Gr.+E..A% EPS Gr.	S.Gr.+E..A% RoA	FCF/Sales EBITDA Mar.	E..A-CX M. EBITDA Gr.	EBITDA Mar. E..A-CX M.	EBITDA Mar. E..A-CX M.	FCF/Sales S.Gr.+E..A%
		16-4-0	6-6-0	14-5-0	9-5-0	8-7-0	8-3-0	9-5-0	12-5-0	9-4-0	9-8-0	11-9-0	12-5-0

Analyzing the drivers, however, a certain level of variability can be observed, with some trends forming. The analysis shows Net Margin as the key driver in 2010, which switches to EBITDA-CAPEX and EBITDA growth (similar drivers) in 2011, changed to Asset Turnover in 2012, and again to EBIT margin and EBITDA-CAPEX in 2013. Starting with 2014, some consistency can be observed, with the rule of 40 indicator being the lead driver in 2015 and 2015 and various profitability measures becoming the leading drivers in the following five years. From a conceptual perspective, FCF/Sales, EBITDA-CAPEX margin, and EBITDA margin are similar drivers as they represent profitability at various levels.

Overall, despite the classifieds industry showing multiple changes over the period covered by the study, it can be said that the industry is valued on a Sales multiple as far the bases are concerned, which in turn is driven by profitability. Growth seems to be less important at this point in the development phase. This conclusion is not particularly surprising as the classifieds market is fairly mature, with each marketing already defining the leading player or players. Some companies might have some emerging market exposure which depending on the region, might have experienced growth a few years later or are still in a growth phase.

7.2.4 Results for Financial Content Monetization Companies

As included in the study, the financial content monetization industry showed relatively few regressions with sufficient observations and even less statistically significant regressions. Altogether the analysis needs to base the conclusions on only 3,707 regressions despite running the analysis with only 7 observations as the minimum requirement for each regression. As previously discussed, the results should be interpreted with a grain of salt. Nevertheless, the results enable the analysis of the results starting in 2014. While there is some data for the three previous years, there are very few regressions to allow for any conclusions.

Table 7.8 shows the R-Squared values of the top 20 regressions for this industry ranging from 70 to well into the 90 s, meaning that we should expect a high explanation power of the variance in valuation.

Table 7.8 R^2 of top 20 regressions for financial content monetization companies

#	'14	'15	'16	'17	'18	'19	'20	'21
1	92	88	85	92	92	92	83	95
2	89	87	84	88	92	90	82	93
3	89	86	84	87	92	89	79	92
4	87	86	84	85	91	87	78	91
5	87	85	82	84	91	87	77	91
6	86	84	81	83	91	86	76	90
7	86	82	81	82	90	86	74	89
8	83	81	80	81	89	85	73	88
9	83	81	79	81	89	85	73	87
10	82	81	78	81	89	85	72	87
11	82	81	78	80	88	83	72	87
12	82	81	76	79	87	82	70	86
13	81	80	76	79	86	82	70	85
14	80	80	75	79	86	82	70	85
15	80	80	73	78	86	82	69	84
16	80	79	73	78	86	80	69	84
17	80	79	72	77	86	80	69	82
18	79	79	72	77	85	80	69	82
19	79	79	72	77	84	78	69	82
20	79	79	71	77	84	78	68	82

Table 7.9 shows the analysis results, which show some variance, however, some valuable conclusions can be drawn. 2014 and 2015 show Price to Earnings as the main valuation base, which is unusual for the beginning of the industry, however, considering how mature the companies in this segment are, it is not entirely surprising. Starting with 2016, Sales multiples become the main base as both EV/Sales and Price to Sales. One exception is the year 2018 which shows EV/Asset and P/B as the main multiples. It is difficult to explain such an outlier.

Table 7.9 Results of top best-fitting regressions for financial content monetization companies

Multiples of top 20 regressions

	2014	2015	2016	2017	2018	2019	2020	2021
1	P/E LTM	EV/EBITDA FY0	EV/Sales FY+3	EV/EBIT NTM	EV/Asset STM	P/Sales FY-2	EV/GM FY-2	P/Sales FY+3
2	P/E LTM	EV/OP CF FY+2	EV/EBITDA FY+2	EV/EBIT FY+3	P/B LTM	EV/Sales SLTM	EV/Asset FY-2	P/Sales STM
3	P/E LTM	EV/EBIT LTM	EV/EBITDA STM	EV/EBITDA NTM	P/Sales FY-1	EV/Sales FY0	P/Sales FY-2	EV/Sales FY+3
4	P/E FY+1	EV/EBITDA STM	P/Sales FY-2	EV/EBITDA FY+2	EV/Asset FY+3	P/Sales FY0	P/E FY0	EV/OP CF NTM
5	P/E FY+1	EV/Sales FY-1	EV/Sales FY-1	P/Sales FY+1	P/Sales SLTM	P/Sales SLTM	EV/Asset FY-2	EV/Sales STM
6	P/E FY+1	P/E LTM	EV/Sales STM	EV/EBIT FY+2	EV/GM SLTM	P/Sales FY-1	P/E FY0	P/Sales FY+3
7	EV/EBITDA FY+1	P/E FY+1	EV/EBIT FY+3	P/Sales FY0	EV/Asset FY+2	EV/Asset FY-1	EV/Sales FY-2	EV/Sales FY+2
8	P/E FY+1	EV/OP CF STM	P/Sales FY+3	EV/GM LTM	EV/Asset FY+3	P/Sales FY-2	P/Sales SLTM	P/Sales STM
9	P/Sales FY-1	P/E SLTM	EV/Sales FY-2	P/Sales LTM	EV/Asset FY+3	EV/Asset FY-1	EV/Asset FY-2	P/Sales FY+2
10	EV/Sales FY-1	P/B FY-1	P/Sales FY-1	EV/GM SLTM	P/B NTM	EV/Sales FY-1	EV/Sales FY-2	EV/Sales FY+3
11	EV/EBITDA LTM	P/E STM	EV/Sales FY-2	EV/GM LTM	EV/Asset FY+3	EV/Sales FY-1	P/Sales FY-2	EV/Sales FY+3
12	EV/EBIT FY+1	P/E LTM	P/Sales FY-2	EV/GM FY0	EV/Sales FY-1	EV/EBITDA FY-1	EV/Asset FY-2	EV/Sales NTM
13	EV/EBITDA NTM	EV/Sales FY-1	P/Sales STM	P/Sales NTM	EV/Asset NTM	EV/Sales FY-2	P/Sales FY0	EV/Sales STM
14	P/E FY+2	EV/EBIT LTM	EV/GM LTM	P/E NTM	P/E FY+1	EV/Asset FY-1	EV/Sales SLTM	EV/Sales STM
15	EV/EBIT NTM	EV/Sales FY-1	EV/GM LTM	P/Sales SLTM	EV/Sales SLTM	P/Sales LTM	EV/Sales FY-1	P/Sales NTM
16	P/E LTM	P/E LTM	EV/Sales FY+2	EV/GM SLTM	P/B FY+1	P/Sales FY-1	P/B FY+2	EV/Sales FY+3
17	P/E LTM	EV/Sales FY+1	EV/Sales FY0	EV/EBIT FY+2	P/B FY+2	P/Sales FY+1	P/B FY+3	EV/Sales STM
18	P/E FY+1	P/Sales FY+2	EV/Sales NTM	EV/EBIT NTM	P/E FY+3	EV/Sales LTM	P/B STM	P/Sales FY+3
19	P/E FY+1	EV/Sales FY+2	EV/Sales FY-2	P/Sales SLTM	EV/GM FY-1	EV/Asset FY-1	P/Sales FY-1	EV/OP CF NTM
20	EV/EBITDA LTM	P/Sales FY+1	P/Sales FY-2	EV/GM FY0	EV/GM FY-1	EV/Sales FY+1	P/B NTM	EV/Sales FY+2
Σ 20	P/E	P/E EV/Sales	EV/Sales P/Sales	P/Sales EV/GM EV/EBIT	EV/Asset P/B	P/Sales EV/Sales	P/Sales P/B EV/Sales	EV/Sales P/Sales
	12-0-0	6-5-0	9-6-0	6-6-5	7-4-0	8-7-0	5-4-4	11-7-0

Multiples of top 20 drivers

	2014	2015	2016	2017	2018	2019	2020	2021
1	E..A-CX M. FY+3	Sales Gr. LTM	Net Mar. NTM	E..A-CX M. FY+3	Asset Tur. FY+1	E..A-CX Gr. STM	FCF Gr. FY+2	Op.CF/Sal. FY-1
2	Sales Gr. FY-1	Op.CF Gr. LTM	GM Gr. LTM	EBITDA Gr. FY-1	Asset Tur. FY+1	EPS Gr. FY+2	Sales Gr. LTM	Op.CF/Sal. FY-1
3	Sales Gr. FY0	Sales Gr. LTM	GM Gr. LTM	E..A-CX M. FY+3	E..A-CX Gr. FY-1	EPS Gr. FY+2	EBITDA Gr. NTM	Op.CF/Sal. FY-1
4	E..ARD Gr. FY+3	Op.CF Gr. LTM	GM Gr. LTM	E..A-CX M. FY+3	Asset Tur. FY+1	EPS Gr. FY+2	Op.CF Gr. FY-1	Op.CF Gr. FY+1
5	Sales Gr. FY+1	S.Gr.+E..A% LTM	GM Gr. LTM	GM Gr. FY0	E..A-CX Gr. FY-1	EPS Gr. FY+2	Sales Gr. FY0	Op.CF/Sal. FY-1
6	Net In. Gr. FY+1	EBITDA Gr. FY0	Net Mar. NTM	Sales Gr. FY-1	Net Mar. NTM	EBITDA Gr. STM	EPS Gr. STM	FCF/Sales FY+3
7	Sales Gr. LTM	E..A-CX M. FY+2	GM Gr. LTM	GM Gr. FY0	Asset Tur. FY+1	GM Gr. FY-1	EBITDA Gr. NTM	Op.CF/Sal. FY-1
8	EBIT Gr. FY0	Op.CF Gr. LTM	Net Mar. NTM	Net Mar. NTM	Asset Tur. FY0	EBITDA Gr. STM	EBITDA Gr. STM	FCF/Sales FY+3
9	Sales Gr. LTM	EBITDA Gr. FY+3	GM Gr. LTM	GM Gr. FY0	Asset Tur. LTM	E..A-CX M. FY+3	EBITDA Gr. NTM	Op.CF/Sal. FY-1
10	Sales Gr. LTM	Sales Gr. LTM	GM Gr. LTM	Net Mar. NTM	Asset Tur. FY+1	E..A-CX Gr. STM	FCF Gr. FY+2	FCF/Sales FY+3
11	Sales Gr. LTM	Op.CF Gr. LTM	GM Gr. FY0	Net Mar. STM	Asset Tur. SLTM	EBITDA Gr. STM	E..A-CX Gr. NTM	Op.CF/Sal. LTM
12	Sales Gr. LTM	Sales Gr. FY0	GM Gr. FY0	Net Mar. NTM	E..A-CX Gr. FY-1	Sales Gr. FY+2	E..A-CX M. FY+3	Op.CF/Sal. FY-1
13	Sales Gr. LTM	S.Gr.+E..A% FY0	Net Mar. NTM	GM Gr. FY0	Asset Tur. FY+1	E..A-CX M. FY+2	EBITDA Gr. STM	Op.CF/Sal. LTM
14	Sales Gr. LTM	Net In. Gr. LTM	Net Mar. STM	E..A-CX M. FY+3	FCF Gr. FY0	E..A-CX M. FY+2	EBITDA Gr. STM	FCF/Sales FY+3
15	Sales Gr. LTM	S.Gr.+E..A% FY-1	Net Mar. FY-2	S.Gr.+E..A% FY+3	E..A-CX Gr. FY-1	EPS Gr. FY+2	EPS Gr. FY0	Op.CF/Sal. FY-1
16	Sales Gr. LTM	Op.CF Gr. LTM	Net Mar. NTM	EBIT Mar. NTM	Asset Tur. FY+1	E..A-CX Gr. STM	FCF Gr. FY+2	Op.CF/Sal. FY+1
17	EBIT Gr. LTM	Op.CF Gr. LTM	GM Gr. LTM	E..A-CX M. FY+3	Asset Tur. FY+1	EPS Gr. FY+2	FCF Gr. FY+2	Op.CF/Sal. FY+1
18	EBITDA Gr. FY0	Op.CF Gr. LTM	Net Mar. STM	Sales Gr. FY-1	E..A-CX Gr. FY0	EPS Gr. FY+2	FCF Gr. FY+2	Op.CF/Sal. FY+1
19	E..A-CX Gr. FY0	Op.CF Gr. LTM	S.Gr.+E..A% STM	E..A-CX M. FY+3	Net Mar. LTM	Sales Gr. STM	EBITDA Gr. NTM	EBITDA Gr. NTM
20	Sales Gr. FY-1	Op.CF Gr. LTM	Gross Mar. LTM	Net Mar. STM	Net Mar. NTM	EPS Gr. FY+2	FCF Gr. FY+2	Op.CF/Sal. LTM
Σ 20	Sales Gr.	Op.CF Gr. Sales Gr.	GM Gr. Net Mar.	E..A-CX M. Net Mar.	Asset Tur. Net Mar.	EPS Gr. EBITDA Gr.	EBITDA Gr. FCF Gr.	Op.CF/Sal. FCF/Sales
	13-0-0	9-4-0	10-8-0	6-5-0	11-3-0	8-3-0	7-6-0	14-4-0

Analyzing the drivers can be seen some more variability. The first 3 years show growth in various forms as the main driver: 2014 shows sales growth, 2015 shows operative cash flow growth and sales growth, while the year 2016 has gross margin growth as the main driver. Considering, however, how close the R-Squared values are, this variation can be attributed to minor statistical differences. In 2017 a shift towards EBITDA-CAPEX margin and net margin can be observed. 2018 is similar to the multiples analysis, an outlier with asset turnover becoming the main driver. Deriving a conclusion would likely require a detailed analysis that will likely not provide any differentiating conclusion.

2019 and 2020 show profitability growth as being the main driver, while 2021 shows cash flow margins as the main driver. While different, these two drivers essentially show that the main driver of a sales-based multiple is profitability.

Despite the low number of regressions, the analysis allows for some managerial and strategic conclusions. Companies in the financial content monetization industry are valued based on sales, with the margin being the main driver of the multiple.

7.2.5 Results for Content Monetization Companies

Despite having 22 listed companies at the time of the analysis, the content monetization segment only had sufficient observations starting in 2012. Furthermore, despite having over 60 k regressions with sufficient observations, only c. 42 k has the expected correlation, and only 10,083 were statistically significant.

Furthermore, although content monetization companies have fairly "light" balance sheets, the first analysis yield results heavily dependent on book value and other balance sheet-based variables, requiring a second analysis excluding such variables to derive managerial conclusions.

Table 7.11 and Table 7.10 show the R-Squared values of the analysis, including all variables and the analysis excluding balance sheet variables, respectively. Both tables show respectable values ranging from the 50s to the 90s. Despite the R-Squared values of the analysis excluding balance sheet variables being lower, the values are still north of 55.

Table 7.10 R^2 of top 20 regressions for content monetization companies (excl. BS variables)

#	'12	'13	'14	'15	'16	'17	'18	'19	'20	'21
1	82	70	81	87	91	90	74	73	68	78
2	72	69	80	86	90	89	73	72	67	76
3	70	67	77	86	90	89	71	71	65	72
4	68	67	77	86	89	89	70	71	65	70
5	65	67	76	85	89	89	70	71	64	69
6	64	65	76	85	89	88	70	70	64	69
7	62	64	75	85	89	88	70	70	63	69
8	61	63	74	84	88	88	69	69	63	68
9	61	63	74	84	88	88	69	69	63	67
10	60	61	73	83	88	87	68	68	63	67
11	60	61	73	83	88	86	68	68	63	66
12	60	61	73	83	87	86	67	68	62	66
13	60	60	73	83	87	86	67	67	62	66
14	59	60	73	83	87	86	67	66	62	65
15	58	60	73	82	86	86	66	66	62	65
16	57	60	72	82	86	86	66	66	62	65
17	57	59	72	82	85	86	66	66	61	65
18	57	59	72	81	85	86	66	66	61	65
19	57	59	72	81	85	86	65	66	61	65
20	56	58	72	81	85	86	65	65	61	64

Table 7.11 R^2 of top 20 regressions for content monetization companies

#	'12	'13	'14	'15	'16	'17	'18	'19	'20	'21
1	82	70	81	93	98	90	83	84	76	87
2	72	69	80	92	97	90	80	80	76	86
3	70	67	78	90	96	89	79	78	74	79
4	68	67	77	90	93	89	77	76	74	78
5	65	67	77	90	93	89	76	74	73	78
6	64	65	77	89	91	89	76	73	72	78
7	62	64	77	88	91	89	76	73	72	76
8	61	63	76	88	90	88	75	73	70	76
9	61	63	76	87	90	88	74	73	68	75
10	60	61	76	87	89	88	73	72	68	74
11	60	61	76	87	89	88	73	72	68	74
12	60	61	75	87	89	87	73	71	67	74
13	60	60	75	86	89	86	73	71	67	73
14	59	60	74	86	88	86	72	71	67	73
15	58	60	74	86	88	86	72	71	67	73
16	57	60	74	86	88	86	72	71	66	72
17	57	59	74	86	88	86	71	70	66	72
18	57	59	73	86	88	86	71	70	66	72
19	57	59	73	86	88	86	71	69	66	72
20	56	58	73	85	87	86	71	69	66	71

The results for the multiples part of the analysis show Sales multiples as the main base for valuation in the first two years of the analysis (2012 and 2013). The coming years show surprisingly mostly EV/Asset and P/B multiples as being the best valuation base. Checking these analyses individually, the results are confirmed, with one example showing P/B LTM vs. EPS Growth NTM for content monetization companies year 2015 in Fig. 7.2.

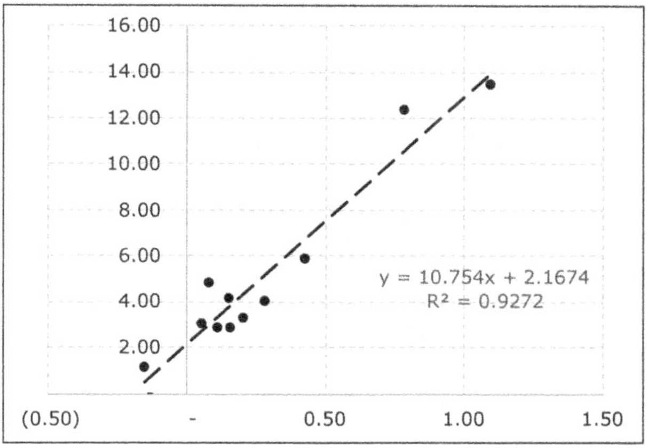

Fig. 7.2 P/B LTM vs. EPS Growth NTM for content monetization companies year 2015

While Table 7.12 shows results including all variables, while Table 7.13 shows results excluding balance sheet variables. By excluding the balance sheet multiples, the evolution of the main valuation bases become smoother and easier to understand. For the first seven years, valuation was Sales based, with either EV/Sales or P/Sales being the leading multiple, while starting with 2019, EV/Gross Margin takes over. However, one exception is the year 2015, where EV/Gross Margin can also be seen as a main multiple. This evolution is natural and follows expectations. This change confirms the maturing nature of the industry, which is not surprising given that these business models have existed for a while.

Looking at the drivers, it can be observed that nearly every year is driven by growth in different forms, with sales growth being the most common driver. Some years also show margins as drivers, with the gross margin being relevant in 2013 and net income margin being second most important in 2012, but also several years, in particular, 2014, 2015, and 2016 showing the rule of 40 drivers representing the sum of sales growth and EBITDA margin as the key driver. Operative cash and free cash flow growth are the second most important drivers in the last 3 years. These findings suggest that profitable growth for the content monetization industry was the key driver of valuation over the entire period, independent of the type of multiple.

Table 7.12 Results of top best-fitting regressions for content monetization companies

Multiples of top 20 regressions

	2012	2013	2014	2015	2016	2017	2018	2019	2020	2021
1	EV/GM LTM	EV/Sales FY0	P/Sales SLTM	P/B LTM	P/B FY0	EV/Sales FY+3	EV/Asset FY0	P/B FY0	EV/Asset FY+3	EV/Asset FY+3
2	EV/EBIT STM	EV/Sales LTM	P/Sales FY-1	EV/Asset STM	P/B LTM	P/B FY-1	EV/Asset NTM	P/B LTM	EV/Asset STM	EV/Asset FY+3
3	EV/Sales FY0	EV/Sales FY+2	EV/Asset FY+2	P/B FY0	P/B SLTM	EV/Sales STM	EV/Asset FY+1	P/B FY0	EV/Asset FY-2	EV/Asset FY-1
4	EV/Sales FY+1	EV/Sales FY+1	P/Sales FY0	P/B FY0	EV/Asset SLTM	P/B FY0	EV/Asset FY+2	P/B FY+3	EV/Asset STM	EV/Asset FY-1
5	P/E FY+3	EV/Sales NTM	EV/Asset FY+3	P/B FY0	EV/Asset FY-1	EV/Sales FY+2	EV/Asset FY+3	P/B LTM	EV/Asset FY-2	EV/OP CF SLTM
6	EV/Sales LTM	P/Sales LTM	EV/Asset FY+1	EV/Asset LTM	P/B FY+1	EV/Sales NTM	P/B FY0	EV/Asset FY+1	EV/Asset FY+2	EV/Asset SLTM
7	EV/Sales NTM	P/Sales FY0	EV/Sales FY+1	EV/Asset FY0	EV/GM LTM	EV/Sales FY+3	EV/Asset STM	P/E FY0	EV/Asset FY+3	EV/Asset FY0
8	P/E FY+3	EV/Sales LTM	EV/Sales FY+2	EV/Asset NTM	EV/GM FY+1	EV/Sales STM	P/B LTM	EV/Asset FY+3	EV/Asset FY+2	EV/OP CF SLTM
9	EV/EBIT STM	EV/Sales FY0	P/Sales FY+2	EV/Asset FY+2	EV/GM NTM	EV/Sales FY+2	EV/Sales SLTM	EV/Asset SLTM	EV/Asset NTM	EV/Asset LTM
10	P/E FY+3	EV/Sales FY+2	EV/Asset NTM	EV/EBITDA LTM	EV/Sales FY+1	EV/Sales NTM	EV/Asset LTM	EV/GM FY+3	EV/Sales FY+3	EV/Asset SLTM
11	EV/EBIT STM	EV/Sales STM	EV/Asset FY+2	P/B FY+1	P/Sales NTM	EV/Sales FY+1	P/B FY0	EV/Asset FY-1	EV/Asset SLTM	EV/Asset FY+3
12	EV/EBIT STM	EV/Sales NTM	EV/Asset STM	P/B LTM	EV/GM FY+2	EV/Sales FY+1	EV/Sales FY-1	EV/Asset FY+1	EV/Asset SLTM	EV/Asset FY0
13	EV/EBIT STM	EV/Sales FY+1	EV/GM FY0	P/B NTM	EV/Sales NTM	EV/Sales FY+3	EV/Asset FY+1	EV/GM FY-1	EV/Sales STM	EV/Asset FY0
14	P/E FY+3	EV/GM LTM	P/Sales FY+1	EV/Sales FY+3	P/B LTM	EV/Sales LTM	EV/Asset STM	P/Sales FY-2	EV/Asset FY0	EV/Asset LTM
15	P/E FY+3	EV/Sales FY0	EV/Asset FY+1	P/B FY+1	P/Sales STM	EV/Sales FY+2	EV/Asset NTM	EV/Sales FY-2	EV/Asset FY0	EV/Asset LTM
16	EV/GM FY+1	P/Sales FY+1	EV/Asset FY+3	EV/Asset FY+1	P/Sales FY+2	P/Sales FY+3	P/B FY+1	EV/Asset NTM	EV/Asset LTM	EV/OP CF SLTM
17	EV/EBIT STM	EV/Sales FY+3	P/Sales NTM	EV/Asset FY+1	EV/Asset FY0	EV/Sales NTM	EV/Asset FY+3	EV/Sales FY-2	EV/Asset FY-1	EV/Asset FY0
18	EV/Sales NTM	P/Sales NTM	EV/EBITDA FY+2	EV/GM NTM	EV/Sales FY+2	P/Sales STM	P/B FY-1	EV/Sales FY+3	EV/Asset FY+1	EV/Asset FY0
19	EV/Sales FY+1	EV/Sales FY+1	EV/Sales LTM	EV/GM STM	P/Sales FY+3	P/Sales FY+2	EV/Sales FY-2	EV/Asset STM	EV/Asset NTM	EV/Asset FY0
20	EV/Sales LTM	P/Sales LTM	EV/EBITDA NTM	EV/GM FY+1	EV/Sales STM	EV/Sales STM	EV/Asset FY+2	EV/Asset FY+3	EV/Asset FY+1	EV/Asset SLTM
Σ 20	EV/Sales EV/EBIT P/E	EV/Sales P/Sales	EV/Asset P/Sales	P/B EV/Asset	P/B P/Sales EV/Sales	EV/Sales	EV/Asset P/B	EV/Asset P/B	EV/Asset	EV/Asset
	7-6-5	14-5-0	8-6-0	8-7-0	5-4-4	15-0-0	12-5-0	8-5-0	18-0-0	17-0-0

Multiples of top 20 drivers

	2012	2013	2014	2015	2016	2017	2018	2019	2020	2021
1	Sales Gr. NTM	Gross Mar. LTM	Sales Gr. FY+1	EPS Gr. NTM	S.Gr.+E..A% FY0	FCF/Sales STM	Sales Gr. NTM	GM Gr. FY+1	Sales Gr. FY+3	FCF Gr. STM
2	Net In. Gr. STM	Gross Mar. LTM	Sales Gr. FY+1	GM Gr. FY+2	S.Gr.+E..A% FY0	S.Gr.+E..A% FY-1	Sales Gr. FY+3	Sales Gr. FY+1	Sales Gr. FY+3	EBIT Gr. FY+3
3	Sales Gr. NTM	Gross Mar. LTM	Op.CF Gr. FY+3	GM Gr. FY+2	S.Gr.+E..A% FY0	FCF/Sales STM	Sales Gr. FY+3	Sales Gr. FY+1	Sales Gr. FY+1	Sales Gr. STM
4	Sales Gr. NTM	Gross Mar. LTM	Sales Gr. FY+1	S.Gr.+E..A% FY+2	S.Gr.+E..A% FY0	S.Gr.+E..A% FY-1	Sales Gr. FY+3	Op.CF Gr. NTM	Sales Gr. STM	Sales Gr. FY+3
5	Net In. Gr. STM	Gross Mar. LTM	S.Gr.+E..A% STM	S.Gr.+E..A% NTM	S.Gr.+E..A% FY0	FCF/Sales STM	Sales Gr. FY+3	Sales Gr. NTM	Sales Gr. LTM	S.Gr.+E..A% LTM
6	Sales Gr. NTM	Gross Mar. LTM	Op.CF Gr. FY+3	GM Gr. FY+2	EPS Gr. FY0	FCF/Sales STM	Sales Gr. NTM	Sales Gr. STM	Sales Gr. STM	Sales Gr. STM
7	Sales Gr. NTM	Gross Mar. LTM	S.Gr.+E..A% STM	GM Gr. FY+2	S.Gr.+E..A% FY0	FCF/Sales FY+3	Sales Gr. FY+3	EBITDA Gr. STM	Sales Gr. STM	Sales Gr. STM
8	EPS Gr. STM	Gross Mar. FY+3	S.Gr.+E..A% STM	GM Gr. FY+2	S.Gr.+E..A% FY0	FCF/Sales FY+3	Sales Gr. NTM	Sales Gr. STM	Sales Gr. FY+3	S.Gr.+E..A% NTM
9	Net In. Gr. FY+3	Gross Mar. FY+3	S.Gr.+E..A% STM	GM Gr. FY+2	S.Gr.+E..A% FY0	FCF/Sales FY+3	S.Gr.+E..A% NTM	Sales Gr. NTM	Sales Gr. STM	Sales Gr. STM
10	EPS Gr. FY+3	Gross Mar. FY+3	Op.CF Gr. STM	EBIT Gr. NTM	S.Gr.+E..A% FY0	FCF/Sales FY+3	Sales Gr. FY+2	Op.CF/Sal. FY+1	S.Gr.+E..A% FY+3	Sales Gr. FY+3
11	EBIT Gr. FY+3	Gross Mar. LTM	Op.CF Gr. STM	S.Gr.+E..A% FY+2	S.Gr.+E..A% FY0	FCF/Sales STM	Sales Gr. FY+1	Sales Gr. NTM	Sales Gr. STM	Sales Gr. STM
12	EPS Gr. FY+3	Gross Mar. FY+3	Op.CF Gr. STM	S.Gr.+E..A% NTM	S.Gr.+E..A% FY0	FCF/Sales FY+3	S.Gr.+E..A% FY+1	Sales Gr. FY+3	Sales Gr. FY+3	Net Mar. FY-1
13	EBIT Gr. STM	Gross Mar. FY+3	Sales Gr. FY+1	S.Gr.+E..A% FY+2	S.Gr.+E..A% FY0	Op.CF/Sal. STM	Sales Gr. STM	Sales Gr. LTM	S.Gr.+E..A% FY+3	Op.CF/Sal. FY0
14	Net In. Gr. FY+3	Sales Gr. FY+1	S.Gr.+E..A% STM	S.Gr.+E..A% FY+2	S.Gr.+E..A% LTM	FCF/Sales STM	Asset Tur. FY+3	Sales Gr. FY+1	Sales Gr. STM	FCF/Sales FY+2
15	EBIT Gr. STM	Gross Mar. FY+1	Op.CF Gr. STM	S.Gr.+E..A% NTM	S.Gr.+E..A% FY0	Op.CF/Sal. STM	Sales Gr. STM	S.Gr.+E..A% LTM	Sales Gr. FY+3	FCF/Sales STM
16	Sales Gr. FY+2	Gross Mar. LTM	Op.CF Gr. STM	GM Gr. FY+2	S.Gr.+E..A% FY0	FCF/Sales STM	Sales Gr. NTM	Sales Gr. STM	Sales Gr. FY+3	S.Gr.+E..A% FY+1
17	EPS Gr. STM	Gross Mar. LTM	S.Gr.+E..A% STM	S.Gr.+E..A% NTM	S.Gr.+E..A% FY0	Op.CF/Sal. STM	Asset Tur. FY+3	Sales Gr. FY+1	GM Gr. FY+1	Sales Gr. FY+3
18	Gross Mar. LTM	Gross Mar. LTM	Sales Gr. STM	S.Gr.+E..A% FY+1	S.Gr.+E..A% FY0	FCF/Sales STM	Net Mar. FY+3	Op.CF/Sal. FY+1	Sales Gr. STM	FCF/Sales FY+2
19	Sales Gr. FY+2	Sales Gr. FY+1	S.Gr.+E..A% STM	S.Gr.+E..A% FY+1	Op.CF Gr. FY0	FCF/Sales STM	S.Gr.+E..A% NTM	Sales Gr. STM	Sales Gr. FY+3	FCF/Sales STM
20	Gross Mar. LTM	Gross Mar. FY+3	EBITDA Gr. STM	S.Gr.+E..A% FY+2	S.Gr.+E..A% FY0	Op.CF/Sal. STM	Asset Tur. FY+3	Sales Gr. FY+3	Sales Gr. FY+3	Net Mar. FY-1
Σ 20	Sales Gr. Net In. Gr. EPS Gr.	Gross Mar.	S.Gr.+E..A% Op.CF Gr. Sales Gr.	S.Gr.+E..A%	S.Gr.+E..A%	FCF/Sales	Sales Gr.	Sales Gr.	Sales Gr.	Sales Gr.
	7-4-4	18-0-0	7-7-5	11-0-0	18-0-0	14-0-0	13-0-0	14-0-0	17-0-0	8-0-0

Table 7.13 Results of top best-fitting regressions for content monetization companies (excl. BS)

Multiples of top 20 regressions

	2012	2013	2014	2015	2016	2017	2018	2019	2020	2021
1	EV/GM LTM	EV/Sales FY0	P/Sales SLTM	EV/EBITDA LTM	EV/GM LTM	EV/Sales FY+3	EV/Sales SLTM	P/E FY0	EV/Sales FY+3	EV/OP CF SLTM
2	EV/EBIT STM	EV/Sales LTM	P/Sales FY-1	EV/Sales FY+3	EV/GM FY+1	EV/Sales STM	EV/Sales FY-1	EV/GM FY+3	EV/Sales STM	EV/OP CF SLTM
3	EV/Sales FY0	EV/Sales FY+2	P/Sales FY0	EV/GM NTM	EV/GM NTM	EV/Sales FY+2	EV/Sales FY-2	EV/GM FY-1	EV/GM STM	EV/OP CF SLTM
4	EV/Sales FY+1	EV/Sales FY+1	EV/Sales FY+1	EV/GM STM	EV/Sales FY+1	EV/Sales NTM	EV/Sales FY-1	P/Sales FY-2	EV/GM STM	EV/OP CF SLTM
5	P/E FY+3	EV/Sales NTM	EV/Sales FY+2	EV/GM FY+1	P/Sales NTM	EV/Sales FY+3	EV/EBIT FY+2	EV/Sales FY-2	P/Sales FY+3	EV/GM FY+1
6	EV/Sales LTM	P/Sales LTM	P/Sales FY+2	EV/Sales STM	EV/GM FY+2	EV/Sales STM	P/Sales SLTM	EV/Sales FY-2	P/Sales STM	EV/OP CF FY+1
7	EV/Sales NTM	P/Sales FY0	EV/GM FY0	EV/GM NTM	EV/Sales NTM	EV/Sales FY+2	EV/EBIT FY+1	EV/Sales FY+3	EV/GM NTM	P/E LTM
8	P/E FY+3	EV/Sales LTM	P/Sales FY+1	EV/OP CF FY+1	P/Sales STM	EV/Sales NTM	EV/GM FY-1	P/E LTM	EV/GM NTM	EV/OP CF LTM
9	EV/EBIT STM	EV/Sales FY0	P/Sales NTM	EV/GM FY+1	P/Sales FY+2	EV/Sales FY+1	P/Sales FY-2	EV/OP CF LTM	EV/Sales FY+2	EV/GM SLTM
10	P/E FY+3	EV/Sales FY+2	EV/EBITDA FY+2	EV/GM FY+2	EV/Sales FY+2	EV/Sales FY+1	EV/EBIT NTM	EV/GM FY+3	EV/GM FY+2	EV/GM FY0
11	EV/EBIT STM	EV/Sales STM	EV/Sales LTM	EV/GM FY+1	P/Sales FY+3	EV/Sales FY+3	P/Sales FY-1	EV/Sales STM	EV/GM STM	EV/Sales LTM
12	EV/EBIT STM	EV/Sales NTM	EV/EBITDA NTM	P/Sales FY+3	EV/Sales STM	EV/Sales LTM	EV/GM FY-1	EV/GM SLTM	EV/GM FY+2	EV/GM LTM
13	EV/EBIT STM	EV/Sales FY+1	EV/EBITDA FY+2	EV/Sales FY+3	P/Sales FY+1	EV/Sales FY+2	EV/Sales FY-1	EV/Sales FY-2	EV/GM FY+1	EV/GM FY+1
14	P/E FY+3	EV/GM LTM	EV/GM LTM	EV/GM STM	P/Sales FY+3	P/Sales FY+3	EV/EBIT STM	P/Sales FY-2	EV/GM FY+1	EV/GM NTM
15	P/E FY+3	EV/Sales FY0	EV/Sales NTM	EV/GM FY+2	EV/Sales FY+3	EV/Sales NTM	EV/Sales SLTM	EV/GM FY-1	P/E LTM	EV/Sales LTM
16	EV/GM FY+1	P/Sales FY+1	P/Sales FY+3	EV/GM FY+1	P/Sales FY+3	P/Sales STM	P/Sales SLTM	EV/Sales FY-2	EV/GM FY+1	P/Sales FY-1
17	EV/EBIT STM	EV/Sales FY+3	EV/Sales FY0	P/Sales STM	EV/Sales LTM	P/Sales FY+2	P/Sales FY+3	EV/GM FY+3	EV/GM STM	EV/Sales FY0
18	EV/Sales NTM	P/Sales NTM	P/Sales LTM	EV/GM NTM	EV/Sales FY+3	EV/Sales STM	P/Sales STM	EV/GM FY-1	EV/Sales NTM	EV/GM STM
19	EV/Sales FY+1	EV/Sales FY+1	EV/EBITDA STM	EV/Sales STM	EV/Sales FY+3	P/Sales NTM	EV/Sales FY-2	EV/GM FY+3	EV/GM STM	EV/GM FY+2
20	EV/Sales LTM	P/Sales LTM	EV/Sales FY+3	EV/GM NTM	EV/Sales FY+3	EV/Sales LTM	EV/Sales FY+3	P/Sales FY-2	EV/GM STM	EV/GM FY-1
Σ 20	EV/Sales EV/EBIT P/E	EV/Sales P/Sales	P/Sales EV/Sales	EV/GM EV/Sales	EV/Sales P/Sales EV/GM	EV/Sales	EV/Sales P/Sales	EV/GM EV/Sales	EV/GM EV/Sales	EV/GM EV/OP CF
	7-6-5	14-5-0	8-6-0	12-4-0	9-7-4	16-0-0	8-6-0	8-6-0	13-4-0	9-6-0

Multiples of top 20 drivers

	2012	2013	2014	2015	2016	2017	2018	2019	2020	2021
1	Sales Gr. NTM	Gross Mar. LTM	Sales Gr. FY+1	EBIT Gr. NTM	S.Gr.+E..A% FY0	FCF/Sales STM	S.Gr.+E..A% NTM	EBITDA Gr. STM	S.Gr.+E..A% FY+3	S.Gr.+E..A% LTM
2	Net In. Gr. STM	Gross Mar. LTM	Sales Gr. FY+1	S.Gr.+E..A% FY+2	S.Gr.+E..A% FY0	FCF/Sales STM	S.Gr.+E..A% FY+1	Op.CF/Sal. FY+1	S.Gr.+E..A% FY+3	S.Gr.+E..A% NTM
3	Sales Gr. NTM	Gross Mar. LTM	Sales Gr. FY+1	S.Gr.+E..A% FY+1	S.Gr.+E..A% FY0	FCF/Sales STM	S.Gr.+E..A% NTM	Sales Gr. LTM	Net Mar. SLTM	S.Gr.+E..A% FY+1
4	Sales Gr. NTM	Gross Mar. LTM	S.Gr.+E..A% STM	S.Gr.+E..A% FY+1	S.Gr.+E..A% FY0	FCF/Sales STM	S.Gr.+E..A% NTM	Sales Gr. FY+1	Net Mar. FY0	S.Gr.+E..A% FY+2
5	Net In. Gr. STM	Gross Mar. LTM	S.Gr.+E..A% STM	S.Gr.+E..A% FY+2	S.Gr.+E..A% FY0	FCF/Sales FY+3	EBIT Gr. STM	S.Gr.+E..A% LTM	S.Gr.+E..A% FY+3	S.Gr.+E..A% FY+3
6	Sales Gr. NTM	Gross Mar. LTM	S.Gr.+E..A% STM	S.Gr.+E..A% FY+2	S.Gr.+E..A% FY0	FCF/Sales FY+3	S.Gr.+E..A% NTM	Sales Gr. FY+1	S.Gr.+E..A% FY+3	Sales Gr. FY-1
7	Sales Gr. NTM	Gross Mar. LTM	Sales Gr. FY+1	S.Gr.+E..A% FY+2	S.Gr.+E..A% FY0	FCF/Sales FY+3	EBIT Gr. STM	Op.CF/Sal. FY+1	Net Mar. SLTM	Sales Gr. FY-1
8	EPS Gr. STM	Gross Mar. FY+3	S.Gr.+E..A% STM	EBIT Gr. NTM	S.Gr.+E..A% FY0	FCF/Sales FY+3	Sales Gr. FY+1	Sales Gr. FY+3	Net Mar. FY0	Sales Gr. FY-1
9	Net In. Gr. FY+3	Gross Mar. FY+3	S.Gr.+E..A% STM	S.Gr.+E..A% FY+1	S.Gr.+E..A% FY0	FCF/Sales STM	S.Gr.+E..A% NTM	Sales Gr. FY+3	S.Gr.+E..A% FY+3	S.Gr.+E..A% STM
10	EPS Gr. FY+3	Gross Mar. FY+3	Sales Gr. STM	S.Gr.+E..A% FY+2	S.Gr.+E..A% FY0	FCF/Sales FY+3	EBIT Gr. STM	Net Mar. FY0	Net Mar. SLTM	S.Gr.+E..A% STM
11	EBIT Gr. FY+3	Gross Mar. LTM	S.Gr.+E..A% STM	S.Gr.+E..A% NTM	Op.CF Gr. FY0	Op.CF/Sal. STM	S.Gr.+E..A% NTM	Op.CF/Sal. FY+1	Net Mar. FY-1	FCF/Sales STM
12	EPS Gr. FY+3	Gross Mar. FY+3	EBITDA Gr. STM	S.Gr.+E..A% FY+2	S.Gr.+E..A% FY0	FCF/Sales STM	Sales Gr. NTM	Sales Gr. FY+1	Net Mar. FY0	S.Gr.+E..A% STM
13	EBIT Gr. STM	Gross Mar. FY+3	EBITDA Gr. STM	S.Gr.+E..A% NTM	S.Gr.+E..A% FY0	Op.CF/Sal. STM	S.Gr.+E..A% LTM	S.Gr.+E..A% FY+1	Net Mar. FY0	S.Gr.+E..A% STM
14	Net In. Gr. FY+3	Sales Gr. FY+1	Sales Gr. FY+1	S.Gr.+E..A% FY+2	EBITDA Gr. LTM	FCF/Sales STM	EBIT Gr. STM	S.Gr.+E..A% FY+1	Net Mar. SLTM	S.Gr.+E..A% FY+3
15	EBIT Gr. STM	Gross Mar. FY+1	S.Gr.+E..A% STM	S.Gr.+E..A% FY+1	EBITDA Gr. LTM	Op.CF/Sal. STM	S.Gr.+E..A% FY+2	Sales Gr. FY0	EBITDA Gr. STM	FCF/Sales FY+2
16	Sales Gr. FY+2	Gross Mar. LTM	S.Gr.+E..A% STM	GM Gr. FY+2	S.Gr.+E..A% FY0	FCF/Sales STM	S.Gr.+E..A% FY+2	Sales Gr. LTM	S.Gr.+E..A% STM	Sales Gr. FY+2
17	EPS Gr. STM	Gross Mar. LTM	S.Gr.+E..A% STM	S.Gr.+E..A% FY+2	S.Gr.+E..A% FY0	FCF/Sales STM	S.Gr.+E..A% FY+3	Op.CF/Sal. FY+3	Op.CF/Sal. STM	FCF/Sales STM
18	Gross Mar. LTM	Gross Mar. LTM	S.Gr.+E..A% STM	GM Gr. FY+2	Op.CF/Sal. FY+3	Op.CF/Sal. STM	S.Gr.+E..A% FY+3	Sales Gr. FY+1	S.Gr.+E..A% FY+3	S.Gr.+E..A% FY+3
19	Sales Gr. FY+2	Sales Gr. FY+1	EBITDA Gr. STM	S.Gr.+E..A% NTM	S.Gr.+E..A% FY0	FCF/Sales STM	S.Gr.+E..A% FY+1	Op.CF/Sal. NTM	Op.CF/Sal. FY0	S.Gr.+E..A% FY+3
20	Gross Mar. LTM	Gross Mar. FY+3	S.Gr.+E..A% STM	S.Gr.+E..A% NTM	Op.CF Gr. FY0	FCF/Sales FY+3	S.Gr.+E..A% FY+3	S.Gr.+E..A% LTM	S.Gr.+E..A% STM	S.Gr.+E..A% STM
Σ 20	Sales Gr. Net In. Gr. EPS Gr.	Gross Mar.	S.Gr.+E..A% Sales Gr. EBITDA Gr.	S.Gr.+E..A%	S.Gr.+E..A%	FCF/Sales Op.CF/Sal.	S.Gr.+E..A% EBIT Gr.	Sales Gr. Op.CF/Sal.	Net Mar. S.Gr.+E..A%	S.Gr.+E..A% Sales Gr.
	7-4-4	18-0-0	11-6-3	16-0-0	15-0-0	16-4-0	14-4-0	9-5-0	9-8-0	13-4-0

If the same analysis is performed with the exclusions of balance sheet multiples and drivers, the most relevant drivers do not change significantly, however, the last few years show a little variability than the analysis, including all variables. While in the first analysis, sales growth was the absolute dominant driver, in the second analysis excluding balance sheet drivers, 2018 is driven by the rule of 40, while 2019 sales growth is most relevant, with 2020 showing net margin becoming most relevant and 2021 presenting a comeback of the rule of 40 indicator. Taking a step back, the most relevant driver in this second analysis was, with few exceptions, the rule of 40.

Overall, it can be said that companies in this industry should expect a gross margin-based valuation, with the rule of 40 as a driver. A strategy maximizing gross profit while ensuring either growth or EBITDA margin is delivered would maximize the value of companies in this segment.

7.2.6 Results for Customer Acquisition Companies

The customer acquisition industry showed over 129 k regressions with sufficient observations, and from these, over 80 k regressions had a positive correlation, however, only 19,451 of these regressions were statistically significant and satisfied all criteria. The variety of the regressions is high enough to allow a good analysis. The period with sufficient publicly listed companies was from 2013 to 2021.

Despite the high R-Squared results, the industry shows less natural evolution patterns, which will be discussed in detail. Table 7.14 shows the R-Squared values of the analysis, including all variables, while Table 7.15 shows the analysis itself. The R-Squared values are very good, with values in the 70s and 80s, excluding the last year, which also shows values in the 60s.

In terms of multiples, the analysis shows both EV/EBITDA and P/Sales being relevant in 2013, which changes to EV/Gross Margin and EV/Sales in 2014, only to evolve into a strong EV/Gross Margin in 2015. 2016 shows a combination of P/Sales and EV/EBIT again, while the coming years show a clear move towards profitability multiples with various forms of EV/EBIT and EV/EBITDA. The last two years show a comeback of the EV/Sales and EV/Gross margin and the emergence of the Price to Book multiple. The development of the multiples is very bumpy and difficult to draw conclusions upon.

Table 7.14 R^2 of top 20 regressions for customer acquisition companies

#	'13	'14	'15	'16	'17	'18	'19	'20	'21
1	83	88	96	91	91	88	91	87	82
2	83	87	96	89	91	88	91	86	81
3	83	87	96	88	91	86	89	84	73
4	82	87	96	88	89	86	88	83	72
5	82	87	95	87	87	86	88	82	71
6	81	87	95	87	86	85	84	82	69
7	81	85	94	87	86	85	84	81	69
8	81	85	94	86	85	85	83	79	69
9	81	84	94	86	84	85	83	79	68
10	81	84	94	86	84	84	83	79	67
11	81	83	94	85	84	84	83	78	67
12	80	83	93	85	83	83	82	78	67
13	79	83	93	85	83	82	82	77	67
14	79	83	93	85	83	82	82	77	67
15	78	83	92	85	82	81	82	77	66
16	78	83	92	84	82	81	82	76	65
17	78	83	92	84	82	81	82	76	65
18	78	83	92	84	81	80	81	76	64
19	77	83	92	84	81	80	81	76	64
20	77	83	92	84	81	80	80	75	63

Fortunately, this industry's drivers are more consistent, with the Rule of 40 driver and the Sales Growth driver being the most prominent ones across the entire period. While two years show FCF/Sales as the main driver (2015 and 2016), they each show the next best driver as being the rule of 40 or the sales growth and the rule of 40.

It is difficult to make any clear managerial and strategic suggestions based on this analysis, however, what can be said is that independent from the multiple used, the rule of 40 is the main driver for a valuation.

Table 7.15 Results of top best-fitting regressions for customer acquisition companies

Multiples of top 20 regressions	2013	2014	2015	2016	2017	2018	2019	2020	2021
1	EV/EBITDA NTM	EV/GM NTM	EV/GM STM	P/Sales LTM	EV/EBIT FY-1	EV/EBITDA FY0	EV/E..A-CX FY0	EV/Sales SLTM	P/B FY+3
2	EV/EBITDA FY+2	EV/GM FY+1	EV/GM STM	EV/EBIT SLTM	EV/EBIT FY0	EV/EBITDA FY0	EV/EBITDA FY-1	EV/Sales SLTM	P/B NTM
3	EV/EBIT FY+2	EV/GM STM	EV/GM FY+3	EV/EBIT SLTM	EV/EBIT FY-1	EV/E..A-CX SLTM	EV/E..A-CX FY-1	EV/Sales FY-1	P/FCF FY+3
4	P/Sales LTM	EV/GM FY+3	EV/GM FY+3	EV/EBIT SLTM	EV/OP CF FY-1	EV/GM FY-2	EV/EBITDA SLTM	EV/GM FY-1	EV/GM FY-1
5	P/Sales LTM	EV/GM FY+2	EV/GM FY-1	P/Sales FY-2	P/FCF FY+2	EV/EBIT FY0	EV/EBITDA FY-2	EV/GM FY-1	P/B STM
6	EV/EBITDA FY+2	EV/GM LTM	EV/GM FY+2	P/Sales FY-2	EV/EBIT FY-1	EV/EBITDA SLTM	EV/Sales FY-1	P/B FY+2	EV/E..A-CX FY-2
7	EV/EBIT FY+2	EV/GM FY+3	EV/GM FY+2	EV/EBIT SLTM	EV/EBIT SLTM	EV/E..A-CX FY0	EV/EBIT FY-2	EV/GM FY-2	EV/EBITDA FY+2
8	EV/EBITDA FY+2	EV/Sales FY+3	EV/GM FY+3	P/Sales FY-2	EV/E..A-CX FY0	EV/E..A-CX FY0	EV/OP CF FY-1	EV/Sales FY0	EV/GM FY-1
9	EV/EBITDA NTM	EV/GM STM	EV/GM FY+3	P/Sales LTM	EV/EBIT FY0	EV/E..A-CX SLTM	EV/EBITDA FY-2	P/B FY+2	EV/GM FY-1
10	P/Sales FY0	EV/Sales NTM	EV/GM STM	P/Sales LTM	EV/EBIT FY0	EV/Sales FY-2	EV/EBITDA FY-1	EV/Sales SLTM	P/B SLTM
11	EV/EBITDA NTM	EV/Sales FY+2	EV/GM NTM	P/Sales LTM	EV/EBIT FY-1	EV/E..ARD FY+1	EV/EBIT FY-2	EV/EBIT FY-1	EV/EBITDA LTM
12	EV/EBITDA FY+2	EV/Sales FY+1	EV/GM NTM	P/Sales LTM	P/Sales FY-2	EV/Sales FY-2	EV/EBITDA FY-2	EV/OP CF SLTM	EV/EBITDA STM
13	P/Sales FY+1	EV/GM NTM	EV/GM FY-1	P/B FY-1	P/FCF STM	EV/OP CF LTM	EV/EBITDA SLTM	EV/OP CF FY-1	P/B NTM
14	EV/EBITDA NTM	EV/EBITDA FY+1	EV/GM FY-1	EV/EBIT SLTM	EV/EBIT FY0	EV/Sales FY-1	EV/Sales FY-2	EV/GM FY-1	EV/EBIT STM
15	EV/EBITDA FY+2	EV/GM FY+1	EV/GM STM	EV/EBITDA FY-1	EV/EBITDA FY-1	EV/E..ARD FY+1	EV/E..A-CX FY0	P/B STM	EV/OP CF STM
16	P/Sales NTM	EV/Sales STM	EV/GM FY+3	P/B FY-1	P/Sales FY-2	EV/GM FY-2	EV/OP CF FY-1	EV/E..A-CX FY-2	EV/OP CF FY+3
17	P/Sales FY+3	EV/Sales LTM	EV/GM STM	EV/EBIT FY+2	EV/EBIT FY0	EV/E..ARD FY+1	EV/E..A-CX FY-1	P/B STM	P/FCF FY+3
18	EV/EBIT FY+2	P/Sales FY+2	EV/GM FY-1	P/B FY-1	P/FCF STM	EV/EBIT FY-1	EV/OP CF FY-2	P/B FY+3	EV/GM FY-1
19	EV/EBITDA NTM	P/Sales STM	EV/GM FY+2	P/B FY-1	EV/EBIT FY0	EV/E..A-CX FY0	EV/Sales FY-2	EV/GM FY-2	EV/OP CF FY+3
20	P/Sales FY0	EV/GM FY+2	EV/GM LTM	P/B FY-1	EV/EBIT LTM	EV/EBITDA SLTM	EV/GM FY-2	EV/Sales FY-1	EV/Sales SLTM
Σ 20	EV/EBITDA P/Sales	EV/GM EV/Sales	EV/GM	P/Sales EV/EBIT	EV/EBIT P/FCF	EV/E..A-CX EV/EBITDA	EV/EBITDA EV/E..A-CX	EV/Sales P/B EV/GM	P/B EV/GM EV/OP CF
	10-7-0	11-6-0	20-0-0	8-6-0	12-3-0	5-4-0	7-4-0	6-5-5	5-4-3

Multiples of top 20 drivers	2013	2014	2015	2016	2017	2018	2019	2020	2021
1	EPS Gr. FY+3	S.Gr.+E..A% NTM	FCF/Sales STM	S.Gr.+E..A% FY+2	Sales Gr. FY+2	Sales Gr. FY+2	Sales Gr. FY+1	GM Gr. LTM	RoA FY-2
2	EPS Gr. FY+3	S.Gr.+E..A% NTM	FCF/Sales FY+3	Sales Gr. NTM	Sales Gr. FY+3	Sales Gr. FY+3	Sales Gr. FY+1	S.Gr.+E..A% LTM	RoA FY-2
3	Net In. Gr. STM	S.Gr.+E..A% NTM	FCF/Sales STM	Sales Gr. STM	Sales Gr. NTM	Sales Gr. FY+2	Sales Gr. FY+1	GM Gr. LTM	GM Gr. NTM
4	S.Gr.+E..A% FY+2	S.Gr.+E..A% FY+1	FCF/Sales FY+3	Sales Gr. FY+3	Sales Gr. FY+2	S.Gr.+E..A% FY0	Sales Gr. FY+1	GM Gr. LTM	S.Gr.+E..A% LTM
5	S.Gr.+E..A% NTM	S.Gr.+E..A% NTM	S.Gr.+E..A% FY+2	S.Gr.+E..A% FY+2	GM Gr. STM	Sales Gr. FY+3	Sales Gr. FY+1	S.Gr.+E..A% LTM	RoA FY-2
6	EPS Gr. STM	S.Gr.+E..A% NTM	FCF/Sales STM	S.Gr.+E..A% STM	Sales Gr. FY+1	Sales Gr. FY+2	S.Gr.+E..A% FY+1	Asset Tur. SLTM	Sales Gr. FY-1
7	EPS Gr. STM	S.Gr.+E..A% NTM	FCF/Sales FY+3	Sales Gr. FY+1	EBITDA Gr. STM	Sales Gr. FY+2	Sales Gr. STM	GM Gr. LTM	EBIT Gr. LTM
8	Net In. Gr. STM	S.Gr.+E..A% FY+1	FCF/Sales FY+2	S.Gr.+E..A% NTM	EBITDA Gr. NTM	Sales Gr. FY+3	Sales Gr. FY+1	GM Gr. LTM	S.Gr.+E..A% FY0
9	EPS Gr. STM	S.Gr.+E..A% FY+1	FCF/Sales NTM	FCF/Sales FY+2	Sales Gr. FY0	Sales Gr. STM	Sales Gr. NTM	Asset Tur. FY-1	S.Gr.+E..A% FY+1
10	S.Gr.+E..A% NTM	S.Gr.+E..A% NTM	FCF/Sales FY+2	S.Gr.+E..A% NTM	EBITDA Gr. FY+3	S.Gr.+E..A% LTM	Sales Gr. NTM	S.Gr.+E..A% FY+1	RoA FY-2
11	Net In. Gr. STM	S.Gr.+E..A% NTM	FCF/Sales STM	FCF/Sales STM	Sales Gr. LTM	Sales Gr. FY+3	Sales Gr. FY+3	EBIT Gr. NTM	EBIT Gr. FY+3
12	RoE FY+2	S.Gr.+E..A% NTM	FCF/Sales FY+3	FCF/Sales FY+3	S.Gr.+E..A% FY0	S.Gr.+E..A% FY+1	Sales Gr. FY+2	Sales Gr. FY0	EBIT Gr. LTM
13	S.Gr.+E..A% FY+2	S.Gr.+E..A% FY+2	S.Gr.+E..A% NTM	Net Mar. STM	Sales Gr. STM	Sales Gr. FY+3	Sales Gr. NTM	Sales Gr. FY0	Asset Tur. FY-2
14	Net In. Gr. FY+3	EPS Gr. FY+1	E..A-CX M. STM	Sales Gr. FY+2	GM Gr. NTM	Sales Gr. LTM	S.Gr.+E..A% FY+1	S.Gr.+E..A% FY+1	EPS Gr. STM
15	Net In. Gr. FY+3	S.Gr.+E..A% FY+2	FCF/Sales NTM	EBITDA Gr. FY+1	Sales Gr. STM	Sales Gr. STM	Sales Gr. NTM	RoA FY-1	S.Gr.+E..A% FY-1
16	S.Gr.+E..A% FY+2	S.Gr.+E..A% NTM	E..A-CX M. STM	FCF/Sales NTM	Sales Gr. FY0	S.Gr.+E..A% LTM	GM Gr. FY+2	Sales Gr. FY0	Sales Gr. STM
17	EBIT Mar. FY+2	S.Gr.+E..A% NTM	E..A-CX M. STM	EBIT Gr. FY+3	GM Gr. FY+2	Sales Gr. FY+2	Sales Gr. NTM	Asset Tur. SLTM	GM Gr. FY+2
18	EPS Gr. FY+3	S.Gr.+E..A% NTM	S.Gr.+E..A% STM	FCF/Sales FY+1	Sales Gr. FY+3	Sales Gr. FY+2	GM Gr. FY+2	RoA FY-1	Sales Gr. FY0
19	RoE FY+2	S.Gr.+E..A% NTM	FCF/Sales FY+2	Net Mar. FY+2	EBITDA Gr. STM	Sales Gr. STM	S.Gr.+E..A% LTM	S.Gr.+E..A% LTM	S.Gr.+E..A% FY-1
20	S.Gr.+E..A% FY+2	S.Gr.+E..A% FY+1	S.Gr.+E..A% LTM	FCF/Sales FY+2	EBITDA Gr. STM	Sales Gr. NTM	GM Gr. FY+2	S.Gr.+E..A% LTM	GM Gr. LTM
Σ 20	S.Gr.+E..A% EPS Gr. Net In. Gr.	S.Gr.+E..A%	FCF/Sales S.Gr.+E..A%	FCF/Sales Sales Gr. S.Gr.+E..A%	Sales Gr. EBITDA Gr.	Sales Gr. S.Gr.+E..A%	Sales Gr. S.Gr.+E..A%	S.Gr.+E..A% GM Gr. Sales Gr.	S.Gr.+E..A% RoA Sales Gr.
	6-6-5	19-0-0	13-4-0	6-5-5	11-5-0	16-4-0	14-3-0	6-5-3	5-4-3

7.2.7 Results for the Data Center Companies

As included in this study, the data center industry showed relatable results. Table 7.16 shows the R-Squared values of the top 20 regressions, while Table 7.17 shows all results. The R-Squared values are all north of 75, meaning that the regressions and drivers explain a fairly high share of variation. The number of companies and results enable an analysis starting in 2010.

Table 7.16 R^2 of top 20 regressions for data center companies

#	'10	'11	'12	'13	'14	'15	'16	'17	'18	'19	'20	'21
1	80	89	95	94	94	90	87	87	85	83	86	85
2	79	89	93	94	94	88	87	87	85	83	85	85
3	79	86	92	94	94	87	87	87	85	83	83	84
4	79	85	91	93	93	87	85	86	84	82	82	84
5	79	83	91	93	93	86	84	85	83	81	82	83
6	78	83	91	93	93	86	84	84	82	81	82	83
7	78	82	91	92	93	86	83	83	82	81	81	83
8	78	82	90	91	91	85	80	83	81	80	81	82
9	78	82	90	91	91	85	79	81	81	80	81	82
10	78	81	90	90	91	85	79	81	81	80	81	82
11	78	80	89	90	90	85	79	81	81	79	81	82
12	78	80	89	90	90	84	79	80	80	79	81	81
13	77	79	89	90	90	84	77	80	80	79	81	81
14	77	79	88	89	90	84	77	80	80	79	81	81
15	77	78	88	89	88	83	77	80	80	79	81	81
16	77	78	88	89	86	83	77	79	80	79	81	81
17	77	78	88	89	86	83	77	79	79	79	81	80
18	77	78	87	89	86	83	77	78	79	78	80	80
19	77	78	87	89	86	83	77	77	78	78	80	80
20	77	78	87	89	86	82	77	77	78	78	80	80

Looking at the multiples, it can be observed that EV/Sales is by far the most often seen multiple, except for three years. 2011 shows EV/EBIT as being more relevant, however, the result shows a close second EV/Sales as multiple, and the top 10 regressions are dominated by the P/Sales multiples. 2016 also shows the emergence of EV/Gross Margin as a leading multiple, however, again EV/Sales is a close second. The top 10 regressions also show EV/Asset as a multiple, which explains much of the variance. The last year that shows EV/Gross Margin as a relevant multiple is 2016. This year shows, however, also EV/Sales as a close second-best multiple. It can be concluded that companies in the data center space are valued based on a revenue multiple. Considering that this industry has continued to grow over the past years due to the increasing demand for cloud resources, this conclusion is not surprising and rather confirms the growing nature of the segment.

Drivers in this segment are also consistent with a clear development. Most years show the Rule of 40 and the EBITDA margin as the key driver. 2010 shows the EBIT margin driver as being the most relevant, however, starting in 2011, the rule of 40 takes over as the most relevant driver. 2012 and 2013 show the EBITDA margin as being most relevant, however, the rule of 40 driver is a close second. Starting in 2014, the rule of 40 becomes the most relevant driver for 5 years until 2019, when the EBITDA margin again became the most relevant driver. It should be observed that 2019 and 2020 show the rule of 40 was the second-best driver, which disappeared in 2021, leaving the EBITDA margin as the key driver. Similarly to the multiples, the data center shows a high level of consistency in the leading drivers.

Drawing managerial and strategic conclusions for the data center industry is fairly simple as it is clear that companies in this segment are valued based on EV/Sales multiples driven by the EBITDA margin a company achieves. This combination suggests a certain level of maturity, however, scale expressed as revenue seems to be the most relevant size.

Table 7.17 Results of top best-fitting regressions for data center companies

		2010	2011	2012	2013	2014	2015	2016	2017	2018	2019	2020	2021
Multiples of top 10 regressions	1	EV/Sales FY0	P/Sales NTM	P/Sales FY+1	EV/Sales NTM	P/Sales FY0	EV/Sales FY-2	EV/Asset SLTM	EV/Sales FY0	EV/GM FY-1	EV/E..A-CX FY+1	EV/GM FY-2	EV/Sales LTM
	2	EV/Sales FY+3	EV/EBIT FY+2	EV/EBITDA SLTM	EV/Sales FY+2	EV/Sales SLTM	P/B SLTM	EV/Asset SLTM	P/B LTM	EV/GM FY-1	EV/Asset FY+1	EV/GM FY-2	EV/Sales LTM
	3	EV/Sales FY0	P/Sales NTM	EV/EBITDA NTM	EV/Sales FY+1	EV/Sales FY+2	P/Sales SLTM	EV/Asset SLTM	EV/Sales LTM	EV/GM SLTM	EV/Asset FY+1	EV/GM FY-2	EV/Sales LTM
	4	EV/Sales STM	EV/EBIT STM	P/Sales FY+1	EV/Sales STM	EV/Sales STM	EV/EBITDA STM	EV/OP CF FY-1	P/B LTM	EV/GM SLTM	EV/GM FY-2	EV/Sales SLTM	EV/Sales LTM
	5	EV/Sales FY0	P/Sales NTM	EV/EBITDA FY0	EV/Sales LTM	EV/Sales NTM	P/Sales FY-1	EV/Sales FY-2	EV/Sales FY0	EV/GM FY-1	P/Sales FY+1	EV/Sales FY0	EV/Sales LTM
	6	EV/Sales FY+3	P/Sales FY+2	EV/EBITDA NTM	EV/Sales FY+3	P/Sales SLTM	EV/EBITDA FY-2	EV/Sales FY-2	EV/Sales LTM	EV/GM SLTM	P/Sales FY+1	EV/Sales LTM	EV/Sales LTM
	7	EV/Sales FY+3	EV/EBIT FY+2	EV/Asset FY-1	P/Sales LTM	EV/Sales FY+3	EV/EBITDA FY+3	P/Sales FY-2	P/Sales FY-1	EV/Sales FY-1	EV/Asset LTM	EV/Sales SLTM	EV/Sales LTM
	8	EV/Sales FY+3	P/Sales NTM	P/Sales NTM	P/Sales LTM	EV/Sales FY+1	EV/Sales FY-2	EV/Sales FY-2	EV/Sales FY-1	EV/GM FY0	EV/Sales LTM	EV/Sales FY0	EV/Sales FY0
	9	EV/Sales FY+2	EV/EBIT FY+2	P/B FY+1	EV/EBITDA SLTM	EV/Sales SLTM	P/Sales FY+3	P/Sales FY-2	EV/Sales FY-2	EV/Asset FY+1	EV/Asset LTM	EV/Sales SLTM	EV/Sales LTM
	10	EV/Sales NTM	P/Sales NTM	EV/EBITDA SLTM	EV/Sales FY0	P/Sales SLTM	P/Sales STM	EV/EBITDA NTM	P/Sales FY-1	EV/Sales FY-2	EV/Sales FY+3	EV/Sales FY0	P/B FY0
	Σ 20	EV/Sales	EV/EBIT P/Sales	P/Sales EV/EBITDA EV/Sales	EV/Sales P/Sales	EV/Sales P/Sales	EV/Sales P/Sales	EV/GM EV/Sales	EV/Sales P/Sales	EV/GM EV/Sales	EV/Sales EV/Asset P/Sales	EV/Sales	EV/Sales
		20-0-0	9-8-0	8-6-3	14-4-0	11-7-0	9-6-0	6-5-0	13-4-0	10-7-0	10-6-2	17-0-0	16-0-0
Multiples of top 10 drivers	1	EBIT Mar. STM	S.Gr.+E..A% FY+3	S.Gr.+E..A% FY+3	EBITDA Mar. SLTM	S.Gr.+E..A% FY+1	S.Gr.+E..A% FY+3	S.Gr.+E..A% NTM	S.Gr.+E..A% STM	S.Gr.+E..A% FY+2	GM Gr. FY+3	S.Gr.+E..A% STM	EBITDA Mar. FY+3
	2	EBIT Mar. FY+2	Op.CF Gr. FY+2	S.Gr.+E..A% LTM	EBITDA Mar. SLTM	S.Gr.+E..A% LTM	EBIT Gr. LTM	S.Gr.+E..A% FY+1	RoE FY+3	S.Gr.+E..A% STM	Op.CF Gr. FY+3	S.Gr.+E..A% FY+3	EBITDA Mar. STM
	3	EBIT Mar. FY+3	S.Gr.+E..A% STM	Op.CF Gr. FY+3	EBITDA Mar. SLTM	EBITDA Mar. FY-2	S.Gr.+E..A% FY-1	S.Gr.+E..A% LTM	S.Gr.+E..A% STM	S.Gr.+E..A% FY+2	EBITDA Gr. FY+3	S.Gr.+E..A% FY+2	EBITDA Mar. NTM
	4	EBIT Mar. FY+2	Op.CF Gr. FY+2	S.Gr.+E..A% STM	EBITDA Mar. SLTM	EBITDA Mar. FY-2	EPS Gr. FY+1	S.Gr.+E..A% NTM	RoE STM	S.Gr.+E..A% STM	S.Gr.+E..A% STM	EBITDA Mar. STM	EBITDA Mar. LTM
	5	EBIT Mar. FY+2	S.Gr.+E..A% NTM	S.Gr.+E..A% LTM	EBITDA Mar. SLTM	EBITDA Mar. FY-2	S.Gr.+E..A% FY-1	S.Gr.+E..A% LTM	S.Gr.+E..A% FY+3	S.Gr.+E..A% FY+3	S.Gr.+E..A% STM	EBITDA Mar. STM	EBITDA Mar. FY+1
	6	EBIT Mar. NTM	S.Gr.+E..A% FY+3	Op.CF Gr. STM	EBITDA Mar. SLTM	S.Gr.+E..A% FY0	GM Gr. FY+2	S.Gr.+E..A% NTM	S.Gr.+E..A% FY+3	S.Gr.+E..A% FY+3	S.Gr.+E..A% FY+3	EBITDA Mar. STM	EBITDA Mar. FY+2
	7	EBIT Mar. LTM	EPS Gr. FY+2	Sales Gr. NTM	S.Gr.+E..A% LTM	EBITDA Mar. FY-2	EPS Gr. FY+1	S.Gr.+E..A% LTM	S.Gr.+E..A% STM	S.Gr.+E..A% NTM	RoE NTM	EBITDA Mar. FY+3	EBITDA Mar. SLTM
	8	EBIT Mar. FY+1	S.Gr.+E..A% FY+2	S.Gr.+E..A% FY+3	S.Gr.+E..A% NTM	EBITDA Mar. FY-2	S.Gr.+E..A% NTM	S.Gr.+E..A% FY+1	S.Gr.+E..A% STM	S.Gr.+E..A% FY+2	EBITDA Mar. STM	EBITDA Mar. FY+3	EBITDA Mar. STM
	9	EBIT Mar. STM	EPS Gr. STM	RoE STM	EBITDA Gr. FY+1	S.Gr.+E..A% FY+1	Op.CF/Sal. FY-2	S.Gr.+E..A% NTM	S.Gr.+E..A% STM	EBITDA Gr. FY+3	EBITDA Gr. FY+3	EBITDA Mar. FY+2	EBITDA Mar. FY0
	10	EBIT Mar. STM	EBITDA Gr. STM	S.Gr.+E..A% FY+1	EBITDA Mar. SLTM	S.Gr.+E..A% LTM	Op.CF/Sal. FY-2	Sales Gr. FY+2	S.Gr.+E..A% FY+3	S.Gr.+E..A% FY+2	EBITDA Mar. FY+1	EBITDA Mar. FY+2	RoE FY+2
	Σ 20	EBIT Mar.	S.Gr.+E..A% Op.CF Gr.	EBITDA Mar. S.Gr.+E..A%	EBITDA Mar. S.Gr.+E..A%	S.Gr.+E..A% EBITDA Mar.	S.Gr.+E..A% EBITDA Mar.	S.Gr.+E..A% Div. Yield	S.Gr.+E..A%	S.Gr.+E..A%	EBITDA Mar. S.Gr.+E..A%	EBITDA Mar. S.Gr.+E..A%	EBITDA Mar.
		20-0-0	6-4-0	8-6-0	13-5-0	10-8-0	7-5-0	11-6-0	17-0-0	17-0-0	7-6-0	14-6-0	15-0-0

7.2.8 Results for Diversifieds and Portal Companies

Results for the diversifieds and portal segment are shown in Table 7.18 (R-Squared values) and Table 7.19 (full results). The industry enabled an analysis starting in 2011 and showed over 134 k regressions with sufficient observations, while over 88 k of these regressions had the correct slope. Nearly 23 k regressions were also statistically significant to allow for a detailed analysis.

Analyzing the bases, a certain level of consistency can be seen, but also with the emergence of the EV/Asset multiple in the last 4 years implies that in order to derive managerial conclusions, the analysis should be repeated, excluding balance sheet variables. This analysis is presented in Table 7.20. While not presented, the R-Squared values of the analysis, excluding the balance sheet variables, were also high, with values of over 70.

Table 7.18 R^2 of top 20 regressions for diversifieds and portal companies

#	’11	’12	’13	’14	’15	’16	’17	’18	’19	’20	’21
1	95	88	93	92	91	94	87	88	93	93	85
2	94	88	92	90	90	94	86	88	93	93	84
3	93	87	91	88	90	93	86	88	93	93	84
4	93	87	90	88	87	93	86	88	93	93	83
5	92	87	90	88	87	92	86	87	92	92	83
6	92	87	90	88	87	92	86	87	92	92	82
7	92	87	90	88	86	92	85	87	92	92	82
8	92	87	90	87	86	91	84	87	90	92	82
9	92	87	90	87	86	90	84	87	90	91	82
10	92	87	90	87	86	90	84	87	90	91	81
11	92	86	90	87	86	90	84	87	90	91	81
12	92	86	90	86	86	90	84	87	90	91	80
13	91	86	89	86	85	90	84	86	90	91	80
14	91	86	89	86	84	90	84	86	90	91	79
15	91	86	89	86	84	90	84	86	90	91	78
16	91	86	89	86	84	90	84	86	89	91	78
17	91	86	89	86	84	90	84	86	89	91	78
18	90	86	89	86	83	90	84	86	89	91	78
19	90	86	89	86	83	89	83	86	89	91	77
20	90	86	89	86	83	89	83	86	89	91	77

Table 7.19 Results of top best-fitting regressions for diversifieds and portal companies

		2011	2012	2013	2014	2015	2016	2017	2018	2019	2020	2021
Multiples of top 10 regressions	1	P/E LTM	P/FCF SLTM	EV/EBIT LTM	P/E FY-1	EV/E..A-CX LTM	EV/Sales STM	EV/Sales STM	EV/Asset FY+3	EV/Asset FY+1	EV/Asset NTM	EV/Asset FY+3
	2	P/E LTM	EV/Sales FY+3	EV/EBIT LTM	P/E FY-1	EV/Sales FY+3	EV/Sales FY+3	P/Sales STM	EV/Asset FY+3	EV/Asset FY+2	EV/Asset FY+2	EV/Asset NTM
	3	P/FCF LTM	EV/Sales STM	EV/EBIT FY+1	EV/Sales FY+1	EV/Sales STM	EV/Sales FY+2	EV/Sales FY+3	EV/Asset FY+2	EV/Asset FY+3	EV/Asset FY+1	EV/Asset STM
	4	P/E FY+1	P/Sales NTM	EV/Sales FY+3	EV/Sales FY+1	EV/E..A-CX NTM	EV/Sales NTM	P/Sales NTM	EV/Sales FY+1	EV/Asset NTM	EV/Asset NTM	EV/Asset FY+1
	5	P/E FY+1	P/Sales STM	EV/Sales FY+3	EV/Sales FY-2	EV/Sales FY0	EV/Sales FY+3	P/Sales FY+2	EV/Asset FY+2	EV/Asset FY0	EV/Asset FY+2	EV/Asset FY+2
	6	P/E FY+1	EV/EBIT LTM	EV/Sales FY+3	P/E SLTM	EV/Sales FY+2	EV/Sales FY+3	P/Sales FY+3	EV/Sales FY+1	EV/Asset LTM	EV/Asset FY+1	EV/Asset STM
	7	P/Sales FY+3	EV/Sales FY+3	EV/Sales FY+3	EV/Sales LTM	EV/Sales FY+3	EV/Sales STM	P/Sales STM	EV/Sales FY+1	EV/Asset STM	EV/Asset LTM	P/B STM
	8	P/E LTM	P/Sales STM	EV/EBIT FY+1	EV/Sales LTM	EV/Sales FY+3	EV/Sales STM	P/Sales STM	EV/Sales LTM	EV/Asset NTM	EV/Asset NTM	EV/Asset NTM
	9	P/E NTM	EV/EBIT FY+1	EV/Sales STM	P/Sales FY-2	EV/Sales STM	P/Sales STM	P/Sales STM	P/Sales FY+3	EV/Asset FY+1	EV/Asset NTM	EV/Asset FY+3
	10	P/E NTM	P/Sales STM	EV/EBIT LTM	P/E FY0	EV/Sales NTM	EV/Sales FY+2	EV/Sales FY+3	P/Sales LTM	P/Sales STM	EV/Asset FY-1	EV/Asset FY+1
	Σ 20	P/E	P/Sales	EV/Sales EV/EBIT	EV/Sales	EV/Sales	EV/Sales	P/Sales EV/Sales	EV/Sales EV/Asset P/Sales	EV/Asset P/Sales	EV/Asset	EV/Asset P/B P/FCF
		15-0-0	12-0-0	10-9-0	14-0-0	16-0-0	16-0-0	14-6-0	8-8-4	16-4-0	20-0-0	12-3-1
Multiples of top 10 drivers	1	EPS Gr. FY+2	FCF Gr. STM	Sales Gr. FY+2	RoE FY+3	EBITDA Gr. FY+3	S.Gr.+E..A% FY+2	Op.CF/Sal. FY-1	FCF Gr. FY+3	GM Gr. FY+2	FCF Gr. FY+3	S.Gr.+E..A% FY-1
	2	EBIT Gr. FY+2	Op.CF/Sal. FY+1	Sales Gr. STM	RoE STM	S.Gr.+E..A% FY+2	S.Gr.+E..A% FY+2	E..A-CX M. FY+1	GM Gr. FY+2	GM Gr. FY+2	FCF Gr. FY+3	S.Gr.+E..A% FY-1
	3	FCF Gr. STM	Op.CF/Sal. FY+1	Sales Gr. FY+2	Sales Gr. STM	S.Gr.+E..A% FY+2	S.Gr.+E..A% FY+2	Op.CF/Sal. FY-1	GM Gr. FY+2	GM Gr. FY+2	FCF Gr. FY+3	S.Gr.+E..A% FY-1
	4	EBITDA Gr. FY+2	FCF/Sales FY+3	Net Mar. NTM	Sales Gr. FY+3	E..A-CX Gr. FY+3	S.Gr.+E..A% FY+2	E..A-CX M. FY+1	EBIT Mar. FY+1	GM Gr. FY+2	EPS Gr. FY+3	S.Gr.+E..A% FY-1
	5	EBIT Gr. FY+2	FCF/Sales STM	Net Mar. FY+1	Sales Gr. STM	GM Gr. STM	S.Gr.+E..A% STM	E..A-CX M. FY+1	FCF Gr. FY+3	GM Gr. FY+2	EPS Gr. FY+3	S.Gr.+E..A% FY-1
	6	EPS Gr. FY+2	Sales Gr. STM	Net Mar. FY+2	RoE FY+3	S.Gr.+E..A% FY+2	S.Gr.+E..A% FY+3	E..A-CX M. FY+1	EBIT Mar. NTM	GM Gr. FY+2	EPS Gr. FY+3	EBITDA Gr. STM
	7	FCF/Sales FY+3	Op.CF/Sal. LTM	Op.CF/Sal. LTM	Sales Gr. STM	S.Gr.+E..A% STM	S.Gr.+E..A% STM	E..A-CX M. NTM	EBIT Mar. FY+2	GM Gr. FY+2	FCF Gr. FY+3	EBITDA Gr. STM
	8	EBITDA Gr. NTM	FCF/Sales FY+2	Sales Gr. STM	Sales Gr. FY+3	S.Gr.+E..A% NTM	S.Gr.+E..A% FY+3	E..A-CX M. STM	EBIT Mar. FY+1	S.Gr.+E..A% FY+1	Net In. Gr. FY+3	EBITDA Gr. STM
	9	EBITDA Gr. NTM	Sales Gr. STM	Op.CF/Sal. LTM	GM Gr. STM	S.Gr.+E..A% STM	S.Gr.+E..A% FY+2	E..A-CX M. FY+2	EBIT Mar. STM	S.Gr.+E..A% FY+1	EBITDA Gr. STM	EBITDA Gr. STM
	10	EPS Gr. FY+2	FCF/Sales NTM	Sales Gr. FY+3	RoE FY+3	S.Gr.+E..A% FY+2	S.Gr.+E..A% STM	EBIT Mar. STM	EBIT Mar. FY+1	EBIT Mar. FY+3	S.Gr.+E..A% FY0	EBITDA Gr. STM
	Σ 20	EBITDA Gr. EPS Gr.	FCF/Sales Op.CF/Sal.	Sales Gr. Net Mar.	Sales Gr. RoE	S.Gr.+E..A% GM Gr.	S.Gr.+E..A% Op.CF/Sal.	E..A-CX M. Op.CF/Sal.	EBIT Mar. GM Gr.	GM Gr. S.Gr.+E..A%	S.Gr.+E..A% FCF Gr.	EBITDA Gr. S.Gr.+E..A%
		6-4-0	12-4-0	10-8-0	11-4-0	12-4-0	18-2-0	14-3-0	10-5-0	10-5-0	6-5-0	9-7-0

Table 7.20 Results of top best-fitting regressions for diversifieds and portal companies (excl. BS variables)

		2011	2012	2013	2014	2015	2016	2017	2018	2019	2020	2021
Multiples of top 10 regressions	1	P/E LTM	P/FCF SLTM	EV/EBIT LTM	EV/Sales FY+1	EV/E..A-CX LTM	EV/Sales STM	EV/Sales STM	EV/Sales FY+1	P/Sales STM	EV/Sales FY0	EV/OP CF LTM
	2	P/E LTM	EV/Sales FY+3	EV/EBIT LTM	EV/Sales FY+1	EV/Sales FY+3	EV/Sales FY+3	P/Sales STM	EV/Sales FY+1	P/Sales NTM	EV/Sales FY+1	EV/E..A-CX STM
	3	P/FCF LTM	EV/Sales STM	EV/EBIT FY+1	EV/Sales FY-2	EV/Sales STM	EV/Sales FY+2	EV/Sales FY+3	EV/Sales FY+1	P/Sales STM	EV/Sales FY+2	EV/GM FY-1
	4	P/E FY+1	P/Sales NTM	EV/Sales FY+3	EV/Sales LTM	EV/E..A-CX NTM	EV/Sales NTM	P/Sales NTM	EV/Sales LTM	P/Sales STM	EV/Sales NTM	P/FCF NTM
	5	P/E FY+1	P/Sales STM	EV/Sales FY+3	EV/Sales LTM	EV/Sales FY0	EV/Sales FY+3	P/Sales FY+2	P/Sales FY+3	P/Sales FY+2	EV/Sales LTM	EV/EBITDA FY+3
	6	P/E FY+1	EV/EBIT LTM	EV/Sales FY+3	P/Sales FY-2	EV/Sales FY+2	EV/Sales FY+3	P/Sales FY+3	P/Sales LTM	P/Sales STM	EV/Sales FY+3	P/FCF FY+2
	7	P/Sales FY+3	EV/Sales FY+3	EV/Sales FY+3	P/Sales FY-2	EV/Sales FY+3	EV/Sales STM	P/Sales STM	EV/Sales FY+3	P/Sales NTM	EV/Sales SLTM	EV/OP CF FY+1
	8	P/E LTM	P/Sales STM	EV/EBIT FY+1	EV/Sales FY0	EV/Sales FY+3	EV/Sales STM	P/Sales STM	EV/Sales LTM	P/Sales FY+1	EV/Sales FY-2	EV/GM FY-2
	9	P/E NTM	EV/EBIT FY+1	EV/Sales STM	EV/Sales SLTM	EV/Sales STM	P/Sales STM	P/Sales STM	P/Sales FY+3	P/Sales FY+2	EV/Sales STM	EV/E..A-CX NTM
	10	P/E NTM	P/Sales STM	EV/EBIT LTM	EV/Sales SLTM	EV/Sales NTM	EV/Sales FY+2	EV/Sales FY+3	P/Sales FY0	P/Sales NTM	P/Sales FY-2	EV/E..A-CX STM
	Σ 20	P/E	P/Sales	EV/Sales EV/EBIT	EV/Sales	EV/Sales	EV/Sales	P/Sales EV/Sales	EV/Sales P/Sales	P/Sales EV/Sales	EV/Sales P/Sales	P/Sales EV/E..A-CX
		15-0-0	12-0-0	10-9-0	18-0-0	16-0-0	16-0-0	14-6-0	12-8-0	18-2-0	13-4-0	8-4-0
Multiples of top 10 drivers	1	EPS Gr. FY+2	FCF Gr. STM	Sales Gr. FY+2	Sales Gr. STM	EBITDA Gr. FY+3	S.Gr.+E..A% FY+2	Op.CF/Sal. FY-1	EBIT Mar. FY+1	EBIT Mar. FY+3	S.Gr.+E..A% FY+1	GM Gr. FY-1
	2	EBIT Gr. FY+2	Op.CF/Sal. FY+1	Sales Gr. STM	Sales Gr. FY+3	S.Gr.+E..A% FY+2	S.Gr.+E..A% FY+2	E..A-CX M. FY+1	EBIT Mar. NTM	EBIT Mar. FY+3	S.Gr.+E..A% FY+1	Sales Gr. NTM
	3	FCF Gr. STM	Op.CF/Sal. FY+1	Sales Gr. FY+2	Sales Gr. STM	S.Gr.+E..A% FY+2	S.Gr.+E..A% FY+2	Op.CF/Sal. FY-1	EBIT Mar. FY+2	E..A-CX M. FY+3	S.Gr.+E..A% FY+1	S.Gr.+E..A% FY0
	4	EBITDA Gr. FY+2	FCF/Sales FY+3	Net Mar. NTM	Sales Gr. STM	E..A-CX Gr. FY+3	S.Gr.+E..A% FY+2	E..A-CX M. FY+1	EBIT Mar. FY+1	E..A-CX M. STM	S.Gr.+E..A% FY+1	GM Gr. FY-1
	5	EBIT Gr. FY+2	FCF/Sales STM	Net Mar. FY+1	Sales Gr. FY+3	GM Gr. STM	S.Gr.+E..A% STM	E..A-CX M. FY+1	EBIT Mar. STM	EBIT Mar. FY+3	S.Gr.+E..A% FY+1	EPS Gr. LTM
	6	EPS Gr. FY+2	Sales Gr. STM	Net Mar. FY+2	GM Gr. STM	S.Gr.+E..A% FY+2	S.Gr.+E..A% FY+3	E..A-CX M. FY+1	EBIT Mar. FY+1	EBIT Mar. STM	S.Gr.+E..A% FY+1	GM Gr. FY-1
	7	FCF/Sales FY+3	Op.CF/Sal. LTM	Op.CF/Sal. LTM	Sales Gr. STM	S.Gr.+E..A% STM	S.Gr.+E..A% STM	E..A-CX M. NTM	E..A-CX M. LTM	EBIT Mar. STM	S.Gr.+E..A% FY+1	GM Gr. FY-1
	8	EBITDA Gr. NTM	FCF/Sales FY+2	Sales Gr. STM	Sales Gr. STM	S.Gr.+E..A% NTM	S.Gr.+E..A% FY+3	E..A-CX M. STM	EBIT Mar. NTM	EBIT Mar. FY+3	S.Gr.+E..A% FY+1	S.Gr.+E..A% FY0
	9	EBITDA Gr. NTM	Sales Gr. STM	Op.CF/Sal. LTM	Sales Gr. STM	S.Gr.+E..A% STM	S.Gr.+E..A% FY+2	E..A-CX M. FY+2	E..A-CX M. STM	EBIT Mar. STM	S.Gr.+E..A% FY+1	EPS Gr. LTM
	10	EPS Gr. FY+2	FCF/Sales NTM	Sales Gr. FY+3	Sales Gr. FY+3	S.Gr.+E..A% FY+2	S.Gr.+E..A% STM	EBIT Mar. STM	EBIT Mar. FY+1	E..A-CX M. FY+3	S.Gr.+E..A% FY+1	GM Gr. FY+2
	Σ 20	EBITDA Gr. EPS Gr.	FCF/Sales Op.CF/Sal.	Sales Gr. Net Mar.	Sales Gr. GM Gr.	S.Gr.+E..A% GM Gr.	S.Gr.+E..A% Op.CF/Sal.	E..A-CX M. Op.CF/Sal.	EBIT Mar. E..A-CX M.	EBIT Mar. E..A-CX M.	S.Gr.+E..A%	Op.CF/Sal. GM Gr.
		6-4-0	12-4-0	10-8-0	14-4-0	12-4-0	18-2-0	14-3-0	17-3-0	9-9-0	16-0-0	7-5-0

The results for the multiples analysis show a clear trend, with Sales multiples being the most relevant bases for almost all years. As mentioned, the last 3 years show the emergence of the EV/Asset as a key driver. Excluding balance sheet drivers shows Sales multiples again as the main base, with the year 2021 also showing EV/EBITDA-CAPEX becoming relevant.

Valuation drivers are less straightforward to interpret, however, they are from a conceptual perspective consistent. Two types of multiples are often seen: the rule of 40 and various forms of absolute margin growth. Considering that almost every year shows a different combination of these multiples coming on top, discussing every year in detail does not bring significant added value. However, the picture is from a high level clear enough to conclude that a margin is the key driver of the Sales multiples.

Based on the discussion, some managerial and strategic conclusions can be drawn. Valuation in the diversifieds and portal segments are still revenue based, however, driven by the margin development in both growth and margin terms. Consequently, size matters in this segment but not at any cost.

7.2.9 Results for eCommerce Companies

The eCommerce segment is a mature industry that enables a thorough analysis. It includes 76 companies, with 25 being from the European space, 19 from the North American space, and 32 from the rest of the world. The geographic split is important as previous research focusing on western companies concluded that bases have changed from being Sales centered to being EBITDA or similar profitability focused. Including all companies worldwide might change this result and simultaneously demonstrate that a geography-based clustering might be required for the best recommendations in addition to a segment-based clustering. The analysis included over 316 k regressions with sufficient observations, out of which over 222 k had the required correlation and over 79 k regressions were statistically significant, allowing for a very good analysis.

Table 7.21 R^2 of top 20 regressions for eCommerce companies

#	'07	'08	'09	'10	'11	'12	'13	'14	'15	'16	'17	'18	'19	'20	'21
1	87	93	92	88	88	87	92	87	84	85	85	83	86	83	82
2	86	92	91	87	85	83	91	87	82	85	82	82	84	77	75
3	86	91	89	85	85	83	87	87	81	84	80	82	82	75	75
4	86	91	89	85	85	82	86	86	81	84	80	82	82	72	73
5	86	89	87	85	84	82	86	86	80	83	80	81	81	71	72
6	86	89	85	84	83	81	86	86	80	83	79	81	80	70	72
7	86	89	84	84	83	81	86	86	79	83	79	80	79	70	72
8	85	89	84	84	83	81	85	85	79	82	79	80	79	69	71
9	85	88	84	83	82	81	85	85	79	82	78	80	79	69	71
10	85	88	84	83	82	80	85	85	79	82	78	79	78	69	71
11	85	88	84	83	82	80	85	85	78	81	78	79	78	68	71
12	85	88	84	83	81	80	84	84	78	81	78	79	78	67	71
13	85	88	83	82	81	80	84	84	78	80	77	79	78	67	70
14	84	87	83	82	81	80	84	84	77	80	77	79	77	67	69
15	84	87	83	82	81	80	84	84	77	80	77	79	76	67	69
16	84	87	83	82	81	80	84	84	77	80	77	79	76	67	69
17	84	87	82	82	81	80	84	84	77	80	77	79	75	67	68
18	84	87	82	82	81	79	83	83	76	80	77	78	75	67	68
19	83	86	82	82	81	79	83	83	76	80	77	78	75	66	68
20	83	86	82	82	81	79	83	83	76	80	77	78	75	66	68

Table 7.21 shows the R-Squared values of the analysis, presenting healthy values in the 70s and 80s depending on the year, and Table 7.22 presents the detailed analysis results.

Table 7.22 Results of top best-fitting regressions for eCommerce companies

		2007	2008	2009	2010	2011	2012	2013	2014	2015	2016	2017	2018	2019	2020	2021
Multiples of top 10 regressions	1	P/Sales FY-2	EV/Sales FY-2	P/FCF FY-1	P/Sales FY-1	EV/E..A-CX FY-2	P/E FY+2	P/Sales FY-1	P/Sales SLTM	EV/Sales FY-2	EV/EBITDA FY+1	EV/E..ARD FY-2	EV/EBITDA FY+3	P/Sales FY-2	EV/Sales FY+3	EV/E..ARD FY-1
	2	EV/Sales FY-2	EV/Asset FY+3	P/Sales FY-2	P/Sales FY-2	P/Sales FY0	P/E STM	EV/Sales FY-1	P/Sales FY-2	EV/Asset FY-2	P/Sales FY-2	EV/E..ARD FY-1	EV/Sales SLTM	EV/E..ARD FY-2	P/Sales FY+3	P/Sales LTM
	3	P/Sales SLTM	EV/Asset FY+2	EV/Sales FY-2	EV/EBITDA SLTM	P/Sales SLTM	P/Sales FY-2	P/Sales STM	P/Sales FY-2	P/Sales FY-2	EV/EBITDA LTM	EV/E..ARD FY-1	EV/Sales FY+3	P/Sales SLTM	EV/Sales STM	P/Sales FY+1
	4	EV/Sales SLTM	EV/Asset FY+2	P/E FY-2	EV/EBITDA FY-2	P/Sales FY-2	P/E NTM	EV/Sales FY-2	EV/Sales FY-2	P/Sales STM	EV/Sales FY-2	EV/Sales FY+3	EV/Sales FY+3	P/Sales FY-1	P/FCF FY-1	EV/Sales FY+3
	5	P/Sales FY0	EV/Asset FY0	P/Sales FY-2	EV/EBITDA SLTM	P/Sales FY-1	P/Sales FY-1	P/Sales FY+3	P/Sales FY-1	EV/Sales FY-2	EV/EBITDA FY+1	EV/E..ARD FY-2	EV/Sales FY-1	P/Sales FY0	P/Sales FY+1	EV/Sales LTM
	6	P/Sales FY-1	EV/Asset STM	P/B FY-2	P/Sales FY-1	EV/Asset FY-2	P/Sales SLTM	P/Sales FY-2	EV/Sales SLTM	P/Sales STM	P/Sales FY+3	EV/Sales FY-2	EV/Sales STM	P/Sales LTM	EV/E..A-CX LTM	EV/Sales FY+3
	7	P/Sales FY0	P/Sales FY-1	P/Sales FY-2	P/Sales FY-2	EV/E..A-CX SLTM	P/Sales SLTM	EV/Sales STM	P/Sales FY-1	P/Sales FY+2	P/Sales FY+1	P/Sales FY+3	EV/Sales STM	EV/E..ARD FY-2	EV/Sales FY+3	EV/Sales FY+3
	8	EV/Sales FY-1	P/Sales FY-2	P/Sales FY-2	EV/Sales FY-1	P/Sales LTM	EV/EBITDA SLTM	EV/Sales FY+3	EV/Sales FY-2	P/Sales FY-2	P/Sales NTM	EV/E..ARD FY-1	EV/EBITDA FY+3	P/Sales NTM	EV/Sales FY+3	EV/Sales FY+1
	9	EV/Sales FY0	P/Sales FY-2	P/FCF FY-1	EV/E..A-CX SLTM	P/FCF SLTM	P/Sales FY+3	P/Sales FY+2	EV/EBITDA FY+1	EV/GM FY-2	P/Sales FY+2	P/Sales FY-2	EV/Sales FY-2	P/Sales FY+1	EV/Sales FY0	EV/Sales FY+3
	10	P/Sales LTM	EV/Asset FY0	EV/Sales FY-2	P/FCF LTM	P/Sales FY-2	P/Sales FY-1	P/Sales STM	EV/Sales FY0	P/Sales FY+2	P/Sales FY+3	EV/E..ARD FY-1	EV/Sales SLTM	P/Sales STM	P/Sales NTM	EV/Sales FY0
	Σ 20	P/Sales EV/Sales	EV/Asset P/Sales	P/Sales EV/Sales	P/Sales EV/EBITDA	P/Sales P/FCF	P/Sales P/E	P/Sales EV/Sales	P/Sales EV/Sales	P/Sales EV/Sales	P/Sales EV/Sales	EV/E..ARD EV/Sales	EV/Sales EV/EBITDA	P/Sales EV/E..ARD	P/Sales EV/Sales	EV/Sales P/Sales
		12-7-0	9-4-0	8-3-0	7-5-0	15-2-0	14-3-0	13-7-0	9-8-0	9-8-0	10-7-0	11-6-0	17-2-0	16-2-0	10-6-0	10-7-0
Multiples of top 10 drivers	1	Sales Gr. FY0	S.Gr.+E..A% FY+1	Net In. Gr. LTM	S.Gr.+E..A% LTM	S.Gr.+E..A% LTM	DPS Gr. NTM	S.Gr.+E..A% FY+2	S.Gr.+E..A% FY+3	DPS Gr. LTM	E..ARD Gr. FY+2	GM Gr. FY+1	E..ARD Gr. STM	S.Gr.+E..A% STM	E..ARD Mar. FY-2	Sales Gr. FY0
	2	Sales Gr. FY0	EBITDA Gr. FY+1	S.Gr.+E..A% FY0	S.Gr.+E..A% FY0	S.Gr.+E..A% FY+2	DPS Gr. NTM	S.Gr.+E..A% FY+2	S.Gr.+E..A% FY+2	DPS Gr. LTM	S.Gr.+E..A% STM	S.Gr.+E..A% NTM	E..ARD Mar. LTM	Sales Gr. FY+2	E..ARD Mar. FY-2	S.Gr.+E..A% STM
	3	EBIT Gr. FY-1	EBIT Gr. LTM	S.Gr.+E..A% FY0	Sales Gr. LTM	S.Gr.+E..A% FY+2	S.Gr.+E..A% FY+3	EBIT Mar. STM	S.Gr.+E..A% FY+3	S.Gr.+E..A% STM	E..ARD Gr. FY+2	S.Gr.+E..A% FY+2	E..ARD Mar. SLTM	S.Gr.+E..A% STM	E..ARD Mar. FY-2	S.Gr.+E..A% STM
	4	EBIT Gr. FY-1	EBITDA Gr. FY+1	EBITDA Gr. FY+2	GM Gr. FY0	S.Gr.+E..A% FY+2	DPS Gr. NTM	S.Gr.+E..A% FY+2	S.Gr.+E..A% FY+2	Net Mar. NTM	S.Gr.+E..A% STM	E..ARD Mar. LTM	E..ARD Mar. FY-1	S.Gr.+E..A% STM	DPS Gr. FY-1	E..ARD Mar. FY+3
	5	Sales Gr. FY0	RoA STM	S.Gr.+E..A% LTM	Sales Gr. FY+1	S.Gr.+E..A% FY+2	S.Gr.+E..A% FY+3	EBIT Mar. STM	S.Gr.+E..A% NTM	S.Gr.+E..A% STM	E..ARD Gr. STM	E..ARD Gr. FY+1	E..ARD Mar. LTM	S.Gr.+E..A% STM	S.Gr.+E..A% STM	S.Gr.+E..A% STM
	6	EBIT Gr. FY-1	EBIT Gr. LTM	S.Gr.+E..A% FY0	S.Gr.+E..A% FY+3	GM Gr. FY0	S.Gr.+E..A% FY+3	S.Gr.+E..A% FY+2	S.Gr.+E..A% FY+3	Net Mar. FY+1	Net Mar. FY+2	S.Gr.+E..A% FY+1	E..ARD Mar. FY-1	S.Gr.+E..A% STM	E..ARD Gr. NTM	E..ARD Mar. STM
	7	EBIT Gr. FY-1	S.Gr.+E..A% FY+1	S.Gr.+E..A% NTM	S.Gr.+E..A% LTM	GM Gr. LTM	S.Gr.+E..A% STM	EBIT Mar. STM	S.Gr.+E..A% FY+2	Net Mar. NTM	Net Mar. FY+2	EBITDA Mar. SLTM	E..ARD Mar. SLTM	Sales Gr. NTM	E..ARD Mar. FY-1	E..ARD Mar. FY+2
	8	EBIT Gr. FY-1	S.Gr.+E..A% FY+1	S.Gr.+E..A% FY+1	S.Gr.+E..A% LTM	S.Gr.+E..A% FY+2	Sales Gr. FY+2	EBIT Mar. STM	S.Gr.+E..A% NTM	S.Gr.+E..A% FY+2	Net Mar. FY+2	E..ARD Gr. FY+1	E..ARD Gr. NTM	S.Gr.+E..A% STM	E..A-CX M. SLTM	S.Gr.+E..A% STM
	9	EBIT Gr. FY-1	S.Gr.+E..A% FY-1	Net In. Gr. FY+1	Sales Gr. LTM	GM Gr. STM	E..A-CX M. STM	EBIT Mar. STM	E..ARD Gr. STM	DPS Gr. LTM	Net Mar. FY+2	S.Gr.+E..A% NTM	E..ARD Mar. LTM	S.Gr.+E..A% STM	E..ARD Mar. FY-2	E..ARD Mar. NTM
	10	EBIT Gr. FY-1	RoA FY+3	S.Gr.+E..A% LTM	GM Gr. LTM	S.Gr.+E..A% FY+3	S.Gr.+E..A% STM	EBIT Mar. FY+2	S.Gr.+E..A% FY+3	Net Mar. FY+1	Net Mar. NTM	S.Gr.+E..A% FY+1	E..ARD Mar. STM	S.Gr.+E..A% STM	S.Gr.+E..A% STM	S.Gr.+E..A% STM
	Σ 20	EBIT Gr. Sales Gr.	S.Gr.+E..A% EBITDA Gr.	S.Gr.+E..A% Sales Gr.	S.Gr.+E..A% Sales Gr.	S.Gr.+E..A% GM Gr.	S.Gr.+E..A% E..A-CX M.	EBIT Mar. S.Gr.+E..A%	S.Gr.+E..A% E..ARD Gr.	Net Mar. S.Gr.+E..A%	Net Mar. S.Gr.+E..A%	S.Gr.+E..A% E..ARD Mar.	E..ARD Mar. E..ARD Gr.	S.Gr.+E..A% EBIT Mar.	S.Gr.+E..A% E..ARD Mar.	E..ARD Mar. S.Gr.+E..A%
		11-8-0	8-5-0	13-4-0	9-6-0	12-4-0	10-4-0	13-6-0	16-4-0	11-4-0	10-5-0	7-5-0	17-2-0	10-4-0	9-6-0	9-8-0

The interpretation of the main bases is easy as most years show Sales based multiples as the leading base. Some years show P/Sales coming at the top, while others show EV/Sales as the key base. 2018 shows EV/EBITDARD being the most relevant base, while in 2018 and 2019, EV/EBITDA and EBITDARD are the second-best multiple. While these conclusions contradict results from past research, it is not entirely surprising since this study includes companies from the entire world instead of just western companies. Despite the eCommerce existence for many years, the adoption in different parts of the world was very different. A more precise analysis focusing on the results for various regions could be helpful and might be performed if the study allows.

Drivers also show a consistent development, with the main driver being the rule of 40 for most of the years. Some years also show net margin as being relevant (2015 and 2016), as well as EBITDARD margin in 2021 and EBIT margin in 2013. Some years also show Sales Growth as a secondary driver as well as Gross Margin growth and EBITDARD Growth. The emergence of EBITDARD is a bit surprizing as the industry generally does not have significant R&D. The findings do not contradict past findings from other studies, however, it should be noted that this is the first time the rule of 40 is considered for eCommerce.

It can be concluded that Sales are still the base for the valuation of global eCommerce companies, with the rule of 40 being the best driver.

7.2.10 Results for Gambling Companies

Online-driven gambling was also an industry with good results. The segment has 23 companies, with most being listed for long enough to enable an analysis since 2007. The results showed over 296 k of regression with sufficient observations, out of which nearly 208 k had the correct correlation, and nearly 53 k were statistically significant.

Table 7.23 presents the R-Squared values of the analysis containing all regressions, while Table 7.24 shows the full results of the analysis containing all variables, and Table 7.25 shows the results of the analysis containing only regressions with non-balance sheet variables. As it will be discussed, the first analysis showed in several years book value multiples as being most relevant, and while for a valuation exercise, this might be useful, for managerial and strategic implications, P&L and cash flow based conclusions are easier to evaluate, and implement. The R-Squared of the first analysis is shown above with healthy values, with most being above 77, while the R-Squared of the second analysis showed values north of 70%.

Table 7.23 R^2 of top 20 regressions for gambling companies

#	'07	'08	'09	'10	'11	'12	'13	'14	'15	'16	'17	'18	'19	'20	'21
1	95	98	98	94	92	94	98	89	85	84	82	89	77	82	80
2	95	97	98	93	91	94	93	87	83	83	81	83	77	82	79
3	94	96	97	93	91	94	92	84	83	83	81	79	76	81	79
4	94	96	97	93	90	94	91	84	79	82	81	77	76	81	79
5	94	95	97	93	90	93	91	84	79	82	80	76	75	80	79
6	93	95	97	93	89	93	91	83	79	82	80	76	75	80	78
7	93	95	97	93	88	92	90	83	78	80	80	75	75	79	78
8	93	95	97	93	88	92	90	83	78	80	79	75	75	79	78
9	93	95	96	92	88	91	89	83	78	80	78	75	75	79	78
10	93	94	96	91	87	91	89	83	77	79	78	75	75	78	78
11	93	94	96	91	87	91	88	82	77	79	77	75	74	78	78
12	93	94	95	91	87	90	88	82	77	78	77	75	74	78	78
13	93	94	95	91	87	90	88	82	77	78	76	74	73	78	78
14	93	94	95	91	86	90	87	82	77	77	76	74	73	78	77
15	92	94	95	91	86	90	87	81	76	77	76	74	73	78	77
16	92	94	95	91	86	90	87	81	76	77	75	73	73	78	77
17	92	94	94	91	86	89	86	81	75	77	75	73	73	78	77
18	92	94	94	90	85	89	86	81	75	77	75	73	72	77	77
19	92	93	94	90	85	89	85	81	74	77	75	73	72	77	77
20	92	93	94	90	85	89	85	81	74	76	75	72	72	77	77

Table 7.24 Results of top best-fitting regressions for gambling companies

		2007	2008	2009	2010	2011	2012	2013	2014	2015	2016	2017	2018	2019	2020	2021
Multiples of top 10 regressions	1	P/Sales LTM	P/Sales SLTM	P/Sales FY-2	EV/GM FY0	EV/GM FY0	EV/GM FY-1	P/Sales FY+1	P/Sales FY-2	EV/GM FY-1	P/FCF STM	P/B STM	EV/Asset FY-2	EV/GM FY-2	EV/GM FY+3	EV/Sales LTM
	2	P/Sales FY0	P/Sales SLTM	P/Sales FY-2	P/Sales FY+3	EV/GM FY-1	EV/GM SLTM	P/Sales FY-1	P/Sales FY-2	EV/EBIT LTM	P/FCF FY+1	P/B FY+3	EV/EBITDA FY-1	EV/Asset FY+3	EV/GM STM	EV/Sales NTM
	3	P/Sales FY+1	P/Sales SLTM	P/Sales FY+3	P/Sales FY+3	EV/GM SLTM	EV/GM FY-1	P/Sales FY+1	EV/Sales FY-2	EV/EBITDA LTM	P/B FY+1	P/B FY+2	EV/E..A-CX FY-2	EV/Asset STM	EV/GM FY+3	EV/Sales FY+1
	4	P/Sales NTM	P/Sales SLTM	P/Sales FY-2	P/Sales STM	EV/GM SLTM	EV/GM SLTM	P/Sales FY-2	P/Sales FY-2	EV/GM FY-1	P/FCF FY+1	P/B STM	P/B FY+3	EV/GM FY-1	EV/GM STM	EV/Sales FY+2
	5	P/Sales FY+2	P/Sales FY0	P/Sales FY+3	P/Sales STM	EV/GM FY-1	EV/Asset FY-1	EV/Sales FY+1	EV/Sales FY+3	EV/E..A-CX LTM	P/B LTM	P/B NTM	P/B FY+3	EV/GM SLTM	EV/GM FY+2	EV/Sales STM
	6	P/Sales FY0	P/Sales SLTM	P/Sales FY+3	P/Sales STM	P/B FY0	P/Sales SLTM	P/Sales NTM	P/FCF FY0	EV/Asset FY+1	P/FCF FY+2	P/B FY+2	EV/EBITDA FY-1	EV/Asset FY+3	EV/GM FY+2	EV/Sales FY+3
	7	P/Sales STM	P/Sales FY-1	P/Sales FY-2	P/Sales FY+3	P/B FY0	EV/Asset FY-1	EV/Sales LTM	P/Sales FY-2	EV/OP CF FY0	P/FCF SLTM	P/B FY+3	P/B FY+3	EV/EBITDA FY0	EV/GM NTM	P/Sales FY+3
	8	P/Sales FY0	P/Sales FY+1	P/Sales STM	EV/GM FY0	EV/GM FY-1	P/Sales SLTM	EV/Asset SLTM	EV/Sales STM	EV/EBITDA LTM	P/B NTM	P/B NTM	EV/EBITDA FY-1	EV/EBITDA SLTM	EV/GM NTM	EV/Sales LTM
	9	P/Sales SLTM	P/Sales FY0	P/Sales STM	P/Sales FY+2	EV/Sales FY0	P/B FY-1	EV/Asset SLTM	P/Sales FY-2	P/Sales FY-2	P/FCF FY+3	EV/Asset NTM	EV/EBITDA SLTM	EV/GM SLTM	EV/GM FY+1	EV/Sales FY+3
	10	P/Sales LTM	P/Sales LTM	P/Sales FY+3	P/Sales FY+2	P/B SLTM	EV/Asset FY-1	P/Sales FY+1	EV/Sales FY-2	EV/EBIT SLTM	P/B FY+2	EV/Asset FY+1	P/B FY+3	EV/Asset STM	P/B FY+3	P/Sales STM
	Σ 20	P/Sales	P/Sales	P/Sales	P/Sales	EV/GM P/B EV/Sales	EV/GM EV/Asset P/Sales	P/Sales EV/Asset EV/Sales	EV/Sales P/Sales	EV/EBIT P/Sales	P/FCF P/B	P/B EV/Asset	P/B EV/EBITDA	EV/Asset EV/GM	P/B EV/GM	EV/Sales P/Sales
		19-0-0	17-0-0	20-0-0	17-0-0	10-4-4	6-4-3	8-5-4	10-7-0	5-4-0	12-6-0	12-6-0	8-6-0	7-5-0	10-10-0	15-4-0
Multiples of top 10 drivers	1	FCF/Sales STM	FCF/Sales NTM	FCF/Sales NTM	S.Gr.+E..A% FY+2	S.Gr.+E..A% FY+1	S.Gr.+E..A% NTM	GM Gr. FY+3	Op.CF/Sal. NTM	Sales Gr. FY+1	RoA SLTM	RoE FY+3	GM Gr. FY-1	S.Gr.+E..A% FY+1	S.Gr.+E..A% STM	S.Gr.+E..A% FY+3
	2	FCF/Sales STM	FCF/Sales FY+2	FCF/Sales FY+2	FCF/Sales FY+3	FCF Gr. FY+2	S.Gr.+E..A% NTM	GM Gr. FY+3	Op.CF/Sal. FY+1	Sales Gr. FY+3	RoA FY0	RoE FY+3	EPS Gr. LTM	RoA NTM	S.Gr.+E..A% STM	S.Gr.+E..A% FY+3
	3	FCF/Sales STM	FCF/Sales LTM	FCF/Sales FY+2	FCF/Sales STM	S.Gr.+E..A% FY+1	S.Gr.+E..A% FY+2	GM Gr. STM	Op.CF/Sal. NTM	Sales Gr. FY+3	RoE FY+3	RoE FY+3	EBITDA Gr. LTM	RoA NTM	S.Gr.+E..A% FY+3	S.Gr.+E..A% FY+3
	4	FCF/Sales STM	FCF/Sales FY+1	FCF/Sales STM	FCF/Sales FY+3	FCF Gr. FY+2	S.Gr.+E..A% FY+2	GM Gr. FY+3	Op.CF/Sal. FY+2	Sales Gr. LTM	RoA LTM	RoE STM	RoE FY+2	S.Gr.+E..A% FY+1	S.Gr.+E..A% FY+3	S.Gr.+E..A% FY+3
	5	FCF/Sales STM	FCF/Sales LTM	FCF/Sales NTM	FCF/Sales STM	S.Gr.+E..A% FY+1	RoA FY+2	GM Gr. FY+3	EBITDA Mar. FY+1	Sales Gr. FY+3	RoE FY+3	RoE FY+3	RoE STM	S.Gr.+E..A% LTM	S.Gr.+E..A% FY+3	S.Gr.+E..A% FY+3
	6	FCF/Sales FY+2	FCF/Sales STM	FCF/Sales STM	Net Mar. FY+3	RoE NTM	S.Gr.+E..A% NTM	GM Gr. FY+3	E..A-CX Gr. NTM	RoA FY+1	RoA SLTM	RoE STM	E..A-CX Gr. LTM	RoA FY+2	S.Gr.+E..A% STM	S.Gr.+E..A% FY+3
	7	FCF/Sales STM	FCF/Sales NTM	FCF/Sales FY+1	Net Mar. FY+3	RoE FY+2	RoA STM	GM Gr. FY+3	Op.CF/Sal. STM	S.Gr.+E..A% FY+1	E..A-CX Gr. NTM	RoE STM	RoE FY+3	FCF Gr. FY-1	S.Gr.+E..A% STM	Net Mar. FY+3
	8	FCF/Sales NTM	FCF/Sales LTM	FCF/Sales FY+2	S.Gr.+E..A% NTM	FCF Gr. FY+3	S.Gr.+E..A% FY+2	Sales Gr. NTM	EBITDA Mar. FY+1	Sales Gr. STM	RoE FY+3	RoE STM	GM Gr. NTM	FCF Gr. FY-1	S.Gr.+E..A% FY+3	S.Gr.+E..A% STM
	9	E..A-CX Gr. FY+2	FCF/Sales FY+1	FCF/Sales STM	Net Mar. FY+3	S.Gr.+E..A% NTM	RoE FY+1	E..A-CX Gr. FY+2	Op.CF/Sal. FY+3	Op.CF/Sal. FY+1	RoA SLTM	RoA FY+3	GM Gr. NTM	S.Gr.+E..A% FY+1	S.Gr.+E..A% STM	EBIT Mar. FY+3
	10	FCF/Sales FY+2	FCF/Sales LTM	FCF/Sales FY+1	FCF/Sales FY+3	RoE NTM	RoA NTM	S.Gr.+E..A% FY+1	Op.CF/Sal. FY+1	Sales Gr. FY+1	RoE FY+3	RoA FY+3	RoE NTM	RoA FY+2	RoA FY+3	Net Mar. FY+3
	Σ 20	FCF/Sales E..A-CX Gr.	FCF/Sales	FCF/Sales	Net Mar. FCF/Sales	S.Gr.+E..A% FCF Gr.	S.Gr.+E..A% RoA	GM Gr.	Op.CF/Sal.	Sales Gr.	RoA RoE	RoE RoA	RoE E..A-CX Gr.	RoA FCF Gr.	S.Gr.+E..A% RoA	S.Gr.+E..A% Net Mar.
		18-2-0	20-0-0	18-0-0	9-8-0	6-6-0	9-4-0	12-0-0	11-0-0	13-0-0	12-6-0	12-6-0	8-5-0	6-6-0	10-10-0	9-4-0

Table 7.25 Results of top best-fitting regressions for gambling companies (excl. BS variables)

		2007	2008	2009	2010	2011	2012	2013	2014	2015	2016	2017	2018	2019	2020	2021
Multiples of top 10 regressions	1	P/Sales LTM	P/Sales SLTM	P/Sales FY-2	EV/GM FY0	EV/GM FY0	EV/GM FY-1	P/Sales FY+1	P/Sales FY-2	EV/GM FY-1	P/FCF SLTM	EV/EBITDA FY0	EV/EBITDA FY-1	EV/GM FY-2	EV/GM FY+3	EV/Sales LTM
	2	P/Sales FY0	P/Sales SLTM	P/Sales FY-2	P/Sales FY+3	EV/GM FY-1	EV/GM SLTM	P/Sales FY-1	P/Sales FY-2	EV/EBIT LTM	EV/EBITDA SLTM	P/E SLTM	EV/E..A-CX FY-2	EV/GM FY-1	EV/GM STM	EV/Sales NTM
	3	P/Sales FY+1	P/Sales SLTM	P/Sales FY+3	P/Sales FY+3	EV/GM SLTM	EV/GM FY-1	P/Sales FY+1	EV/Sales FY-2	EV/EBITDA LTM	EV/EBITDA SLTM	EV/EBITDA LTM	EV/EBITDA FY-1	EV/GM SLTM	EV/GM FY+3	EV/Sales FY+1
	4	P/Sales NTM	P/Sales SLTM	P/Sales FY-2	P/Sales STM	EV/GM SLTM	EV/GM SLTM	P/Sales FY-2	P/Sales FY-2	EV/GM FY-1	P/FCF SLTM	EV/EBITDA LTM	EV/EBITDA FY-1	EV/EBITDA FY0	EV/GM STM	EV/Sales FY+2
	5	P/Sales FY+2	P/Sales FY0	P/Sales FY+3	P/Sales STM	EV/GM FY-1	P/Sales SLTM	EV/Sales FY+1	EV/Sales FY+3	EV/E..A-CX LTM	EV/Sales SLTM	P/Sales SLTM	EV/EBITDA SLTM	EV/EBITDA SLTM	EV/GM FY+2	EV/Sales STM
	6	P/Sales FY0	P/Sales SLTM	P/Sales FY+3	P/Sales STM	EV/GM FY-1	P/Sales SLTM	P/Sales NTM	P/FCF FY0	EV/OP CF FY0	EV/Sales SLTM	EV/EBITDA FY+1	P/Sales FY-1	EV/GM SLTM	EV/GM FY+2	EV/Sales FY+3
	7	P/Sales STM	P/Sales FY-1	P/Sales FY-2	P/Sales FY+3	EV/Sales FY0	EV/GM SLTM	EV/Sales LTM	P/Sales FY-2	EV/EBITDA LTM	EV/GM SLTM	EV/Sales FY-1	EV/EBITDA FY0	EV/Sales SLTM	EV/GM NTM	P/Sales FY+3
	8	P/Sales FY0	P/Sales FY+1	P/Sales STM	EV/GM FY0	EV/GM SLTM	EV/GM FY-1	P/Sales FY+1	EV/Sales STM	P/Sales FY-2	EV/Sales FY-1	EV/Sales SLTM	EV/EBITDA SLTM	EV/GM FY-2	EV/GM NTM	EV/Sales LTM
	9	P/Sales SLTM	P/Sales FY0	P/Sales STM	P/Sales FY+2	EV/GM FY0	EV/Sales SLTM	EV/Sales FY-2	P/Sales FY-2	EV/EBIT SLTM	EV/GM SLTM	EV/EBITDA FY-1	P/E LTM	EV/Sales FY-1	EV/GM FY+1	EV/Sales FY+3
	10	P/Sales LTM	P/Sales LTM	P/Sales FY+3	P/Sales FY+2	EV/Sales FY-1	P/Sales SLTM	P/Sales FY+1	EV/Sales FY-2	P/Sales FY-2	EV/Sales SLTM	EV/Sales FY-1	EV/Sales FY-1	EV/Sales FY0	EV/GM FY+1	P/Sales STM
	Σ 20	P/Sales	P/Sales	P/Sales	P/Sales	EV/GM EV/Sales EV/EBITDA	P/Sales EV/GM EV/Sales	P/Sales EV/Sales EV/GM	EV/Sales P/Sales	P/Sales EV/EBIT	EV/Sales P/Sales	EV/EBITDA EV/Sales	EV/EBITDA P/E	EV/GM P/E	EV/GM P/Sales	EV/Sales P/Sales
		19-0-0	17-0-0	20-0-0	17-0-0	11-5-2	9-6-3	9-7-4	11-7-0	5-5-0	8-4-0	10-5-0	13-2-0	7-3-0	15-3-0	15-5-0
Multiples of top 10 drivers	1	FCF/Sales STM	FCF/Sales NTM	FCF/Sales NTM	S.Gr.+E..A% FY+2	S.Gr.+E..A% FY+1	S.Gr.+E..A% NTM	GM Gr. FY+3	Op.CF/Sal. NTM	Sales Gr. FY+1	E..A-CX Gr. NTM	GM Gr. STM	EPS Gr. LTM	S.Gr.+E..A% FY+1	S.Gr.+E..A% STM	S.Gr.+E..A% FY+3
	2	FCF/Sales STM	FCF/Sales FY+2	FCF/Sales FY+2	FCF/Sales FY+3	FCF Gr. FY+2	S.Gr.+E..A% NTM	GM Gr. FY+3	Op.CF/Sal. FY+1	Sales Gr. FY+3	Sales Gr. STM	Sales Gr. FY+3	EBITDA Gr. LTM	S.Gr.+E..A% FY+1	S.Gr.+E..A% STM	S.Gr.+E..A% FY+3
	3	FCF/Sales STM	FCF/Sales LTM	FCF/Sales FY+2	FCF/Sales STM	S.Gr.+E..A% FY+1	S.Gr.+E..A% FY+2	GM Gr. STM	Op.CF/Sal. NTM	Sales Gr. FY+3	Sales Gr. FY+3	GM Gr. FY+3	E..A-CX Gr. LTM	S.Gr.+E..A% LTM	S.Gr.+E..A% FY+3	S.Gr.+E..A% FY+3
	4	FCF/Sales STM	FCF/Sales FY+1	FCF/Sales STM	FCF/Sales FY+3	FCF Gr. FY+2	S.Gr.+E..A% FY+2	GM Gr. FY+3	Op.CF/Sal. FY+2	Sales Gr. LTM	EBITDA Gr. NTM	GM Gr. STM	GM Gr. NTM	FCF Gr. FY-1	S.Gr.+E..A% FY+3	S.Gr.+E..A% FY+3
	5	FCF/Sales STM	FCF/Sales LTM	FCF/Sales NTM	FCF/Sales STM	S.Gr.+E..A% FY+1	S.Gr.+E..A% NTM	GM Gr. FY+3	EBITDA Mar. FY+1	Sales Gr. FY+3	S.Gr.+E..A% STM	GM Gr. FY+3	GM Gr. NTM	FCF Gr. FY-1	S.Gr.+E..A% FY+3	S.Gr.+E..A% FY+3
	6	FCF/Sales FY+2	FCF/Sales STM	FCF/Sales STM	Net Mar. FY+3	FCF Gr. FY+3	S.Gr.+E..A% FY+2	GM Gr. FY+3	E..A-CX Gr. NTM	S.Gr.+E..A% FY+1	S.Gr.+E..A% FY+3	GM Gr. FY+3	E..A-CX Gr. FY0	S.Gr.+E..A% FY+1	S.Gr.+E..A% STM	S.Gr.+E..A% FY+3
	7	FCF/Sales STM	FCF/Sales NTM	FCF/Sales FY+1	Net Mar. FY+3	S.Gr.+E..A% NTM	S.Gr.+E..A% FY+1	GM Gr. FY+3	Op.CF/Sal. STM	Sales Gr. STM	S.Gr.+E..A% FY+3	E..A-CX Gr. FY+1	GM Gr. NTM	FCF Gr. FY-1	S.Gr.+E..A% STM	Net Mar. FY+3
	8	FCF/Sales NTM	FCF/Sales LTM	FCF/Sales FY+2	S.Gr.+E..A% NTM	FCF Gr. FY+3	S.Gr.+E..A% FY+1	S.Gr.+E..A% FY+1	EBITDA Mar. FY+1	Op.CF/Sal. FY+1	S.Gr.+E..A% FY+3	GM Gr. FY+3	E..A-CX Gr. LTM	S.Gr.+E..A% LTM	S.Gr.+E..A% FY+3	S.Gr.+E..A% STM
	9	E..A-CX Gr. FY+2	FCF/Sales FY+1	FCF/Sales STM	Net Mar. FY+3	FCF Gr. FY+2	Sales Gr. NTM	GM Gr. FY+3	Op.CF/Sal. FY+3	Sales Gr. FY+1	S.Gr.+E..A% STM	GM Gr. FY+3	E..A-CX Gr. NTM	FCF Gr. FY-1	S.Gr.+E..A% STM	EBIT Mar. FY+3
	10	FCF/Sales FY+2	FCF/Sales LTM	FCF/Sales FY+1	FCF/Sales FY+3	S.Gr.+E..A% FY+2	S.Gr.+E..A% FY+1	Sales Gr. FY+3	Op.CF/Sal. FY+1	Op.CF/Sal. LTM	Sales Gr. STM	GM Gr. FY+3	E..A-CX Gr. FY0	FCF Gr. FY-1	S.Gr.+E..A% FY+3	Net Mar. FY+3
	Σ 20	FCF/Sales E..A-CX Gr.	FCF/Sales	FCF/Sales	Net Mar. FCF/Sales	S.Gr.+E..A% FCF Gr.	S.Gr.+E..A% Sales Gr.	GM Gr.	Op.CF/Sal.	Sales Gr.	Sales Gr. S.Gr.+E..A%	GM Gr. Sales Gr.	E..A-CX Gr. GM Gr.	S.Gr.+E..A% FCF Gr.	S.Gr.+E..A%	S.Gr.+E..A% Net Mar.
		18-2-0	20-0-0	18-0-0	9-8-0	7-6-0	11-4-0	14-0-0	11-0-0	16-0-0	7-6-0	9-6-0	9-4-0	7-7-0	15-0-0	9-4-0

The analysis containing all variables shows Price to Sales as being most important in the first years (2007 to 2010), with EV to Gross Margin taking over in the years 2011 and 2012. Sales-based multiples returned in 2013 and 2014, while the next two years also showed profitability-based multiples (EBIT and FCF, conceptionally not so far from one another), with the next four years being dominated by book value multiples. While the evolution is mostly natural, the online gambling industry is far from declining; hence, these book value multiples should be read with a grain of salt. The last year shows Sales multiples again as being the most relevant. Reviewing the results excluding the balance sheet variables, it can be observed that EV/EBITDA and EV/Gross Margin take over as the best multiples, a more realistic development for this industry.

Analyzing the drivers, it can be observed that the first four years showing Sales multiples had FCF/Sales as the main driver, followed by the rule of 40 for 2 years, Gross Margin growth, and Operative Cash Flow over sales. Most years with a P/B or EV/Assets multiple as a base had either the RoE or the RoE as the main driver. Lastly, 2020 and 2021 showed a return of the rule of 40 as the main driver. In the analysis excluding balance sheet drivers, the years with previous book value multiples saw a shift in drivers toward Gross Margin growth and the rule of 40 drivers.

To conclude the results for the Gambling industry, it can be said that the leading base (as of the end of 2021) is EV/Sales, and the leading driver the rule of 40. This can also be used as a value-maximizing strategy for the management teams and shareholders.

7.2.11 Results for Gaming Companies

The gaming segment included in the study has all the prerequisites for a good analysis. The cluster has 60 companies with sufficient companies listed long enough to allow for an analysis starting in 2009. The number of regressions with sufficient observations was nearly 262 k, with over 158 k thereof showing a positive correlation and ultimately over 36 k being statistically significant. While the number of statistically significant regressions seems low, it aligns with the rest of the clusters.

Table 7.26 shows the R-Squared values of the top 20 regressions, including all variables with healthy values of over 65. The same analysis was also performed, excluding book value variables as some importance of book value variables was recognized, yielding R-Squared values of over 55. Table 7.27 shows the analysis including all variables, while Table 7.28 shows the analysis excluding book value variables. For the gaming industry, book value might have some expected significance as compared to other online business models, it can recognize the value of games on their balance sheet. Depending on the jurisdiction, the recognition method will defer, however, these businesses have an obvious reason for the book value to have a saying in the valuation.

Table 7.26 R^2 of top 20 regressions for gaming companies

#	'09	'10	'11	'12	'13	'14	'15	'16	'17	'18	'19	'20	'21
1	92	95	84	82	84	83	88	92	89	81	86	76	73
2	89	95	83	81	84	82	88	91	86	77	85	76	73
3	87	93	83	80	84	80	87	91	85	77	84	76	72
4	87	92	82	79	80	78	87	91	75	76	84	75	71
5	86	91	81	78	79	76	87	83	75	76	84	74	71
6	86	91	81	78	78	75	86	81	74	75	82	73	70
7	86	90	81	76	78	73	83	77	74	74	80	72	70
8	86	90	81	76	77	73	82	76	72	74	77	72	70
9	85	90	81	76	77	72	81	76	70	73	74	71	70
10	85	90	80	76	77	71	80	76	69	72	74	71	70
11	85	90	80	75	77	69	79	75	69	72	73	71	69
12	84	90	79	75	76	69	78	75	68	72	72	70	69
13	83	88	79	75	76	68	78	74	67	71	72	70	69
14	83	88	79	75	75	68	76	74	66	69	72	69	69
15	83	87	79	75	75	67	76	74	66	69	72	69	68
16	83	87	79	74	75	67	75	73	64	69	72	69	68
17	83	86	79	73	74	66	75	73	64	68	71	68	68
18	83	86	78	73	72	66	74	71	64	68	71	68	68
19	82	85	78	73	72	66	74	71	64	67	70	67	68
20	82	85	78	73	70	66	74	71	64	67	70	67	68

Table 7.27 Results of top best-fitting regressions for gaming companies

		2009	2010	2011	2012	2013	2014	2015	2016	2017	2018	2019	2020	2021
Multiples of top 10 regressions	1	EV/Sales FY0	EV/Asset FY-1	EV/E..A-CX FY0	EV/EBITDA SLTM	EV/E..A-CX FY0	P/Sales FY+2	EV/Sales STM	EV/E..ARD FY+2	EV/EBITDA SLTM	EV/E..A-CX FY+2	EV/GM FY+2	P/B LTM	EV/Asset NTM
	2	P/E FY0	P/E FY-1	EV/Asset FY-1	EV/EBIT SLTM	EV/Sales FY-2	P/Sales NTM	EV/Sales STM	EV/E..ARD NTM	EV/E..A-CX SLTM	P/B FY+1	EV/GM NTM	P/B FY+1	EV/Asset FY+2
	3	EV/Asset FY+1	EV/Asset FY-1	EV/Sales FY+1	P/Sales SLTM	EV/E..A-CX FY0	P/Sales STM	EV/Sales FY+2	EV/E..ARD FY+2	EV/E..ARD FY+1	EV/E..A-CX NTM	EV/GM FY+3	EV/Asset LTM	EV/Asset LTM
	4	EV/Sales FY+2	EV/Asset SLTM	EV/Asset SLTM	EV/GM FY-1	EV/Asset FY+1	P/Sales FY+1	EV/Sales FY+2	EV/E..ARD NTM	EV/GM FY-1	P/B NTM	EV/GM STM	EV/Asset FY+1	EV/Asset FY+3
	5	EV/Asset NTM	EV/Asset LTM	EV/Asset FY0	P/E SLTM	EV/Asset STM	P/Sales FY+2	EV/Sales NTM	P/B FY-1	EV/E..ARD NTM	P/B FY+1	EV/Asset FY-1	P/B NTM	EV/Asset STM
	6	EV/Sales LTM	EV/Asset FY0	EV/E..A-CX STM	EV/EBIT SLTM	EV/Asset LTM	P/Sales NTM	EV/Sales NTM	EV/OP CF FY0	EV/GM SLTM	P/B FY+2	EV/Asset FY-2	EV/Asset NTM	EV/Asset FY+1
	7	P/E LTM	P/E FY-1	EV/Asset FY-1	EV/EBITDA SLTM	EV/Asset FY+2	P/Sales FY+1	EV/Sales FY+1	P/B FY+2	EV/E..ARD FY+2	EV/E..A-CX FY-1	EV/Asset FY-1	P/B FY+2	P/B FY0
	8	EV/Sales STM	EV/Asset FY+3	P/FCF STM	EV/E..A-CX LTM	EV/Asset NTM	P/Sales STM	EV/Sales FY+1	EV/Sales FY-2	EV/GM LTM	P/B NTM	P/B FY0	EV/Asset FY+2	EV/Asset NTM
	9	P/B FY0	EV/Asset SLTM	EV/Asset LTM	EV/E..A-CX LTM	P/B FY+2	P/Sales LTM	EV/Sales LTM	P/Sales FY-1	EV/Sales FY-2	EV/Asset SLTM	EV/Asset FY-2	P/B LTM	EV/Asset FY+2
	10	EV/Sales NTM	EV/Asset FY0	EV/Asset STM	EV/EBITDA SLTM	EV/E..A-CX FY0	EV/E..A-CX FY-1	EV/Sales LTM	P/B NTM	EV/OP CF FY0	P/B FY+2	EV/Asset FY-2	EV/Asset FY0	EV/Asset FY+1
	Σ 20	EV/Sales P/E	EV/Asset P/B	EV/Asset	EV/EBITDA EV/E..A-CX	EV/Asset P/B EV/E..A-CX	P/Sales	EV/Sales P/Sales	P/B EV/E..ARD	EV/GM EV/E..ARD EV/Sales	P/B EV/Asset EV/E..A-CX	EV/Asset EV/GM	P/B EV/Asset	EV/Asset
		7-5-0	13-4-0	12-0-0	6-6-0	6-4-4	16-0-0	13-6-0	8-6-0	4-4-3	7-5-4	9-8-0	10-9-0	18-0-0
Multiples of top 10 drivers	1	S.Gr.+E..A% FY+1	S.Gr.+E..A% LTM	EBIT Gr. NTM	E..A-CX Gr. STM	EBITDA Gr. FY+2	E..ARD Mar. FY+1	E..ARD Mar. FY+2	EBIT Gr. FY+1	FCF Gr. LTM	FCF Gr. LTM	FCF Gr. LTM	RoE FY+3	RoE FY+3
	2	GM Gr. FY+1	EPS Gr. LTM	GM Gr. LTM	E..A-CX Gr. STM	Sales Gr. FY+3	E..ARD Mar. FY+1	E..ARD Mar. NTM	EBIT Gr. FY+1	FCF Gr. LTM	RoE FY+3	FCF Gr. LTM	RoE FY+3	RoE FY+3
	3	S.Gr.+E..A% FY+1	S.Gr.+E..A% FY0	Net In. Gr. FY-1	GM Gr. STM	EBIT Gr. FY+2	E..ARD Mar. FY+1	E..ARD Mar. FY+2	Net In. Gr. STM	E..ARD Gr. NTM	FCF Gr. LTM	FCF Gr. LTM	RoE FY+3	RoA FY+3
	4	S.Gr.+E..A% FY+1	S.Gr.+E..A% FY0	EBIT Gr. FY-1	GM Gr. STM	S.Gr.+E..A% FY+1	E..ARD Mar. FY+1	E..ARD Mar. NTM	Net In. Gr. STM	GM Gr. FY+1	RoE FY+3	FCF Gr. LTM	RoE FY+3	RoE FY+3
	5	S.Gr.+E..A% FY+1	S.Gr.+E..A% FY0	EBIT Gr. FY-1	EBITDA Gr. NTM	S.Gr.+E..A% FY+1	E..ARD Mar. NTM	E..ARD Mar. FY+2	S.Gr.+E..A% LTM	E..ARD Gr. NTM	RoE STM	FCF Gr. FY+1	RoE FY+3	RoE FY+3
	6	S.Gr.+E..A% FY+1	S.Gr.+E..A% FY0	FCF Gr. FY+2	GM Gr. FY+2	S.Gr.+E..A% FY+1	E..ARD Mar. NTM	E..ARD Mar. NTM	DPS Gr. FY+1	FCF Gr. FY+1	RoE FY+3	S.Gr.+E..A% FY0	RoE FY+3	RoA FY+3
	7	EBIT Gr. FY+1	Net In. Gr. LTM	EBIT Gr. FY-1	E..A-CX Gr. FY+2	S.Gr.+E..A% FY+1	E..ARD Mar. NTM	E..ARD Mar. FY+2	DPS Gr. FY+1	E..ARD Gr. NTM	DPS Gr. FY+2	S.Gr.+E..A% FY0	RoE FY+3	RoE FY+3
	8	S.Gr.+E..A% FY+1	S.Gr.+E..A% FY0	E..A-CX Gr. NTM	E..A-CX Gr. FY+2	S.Gr.+E..A% FY+1	E..ARD Mar. NTM	E..ARD Mar. NTM	S.Gr.+E..A% LTM	FCF Gr. FY+1	RoE STM	RoE STM	RoE FY+3	RoE STM
	9	RoE LTM	S.Gr.+E..A% LTM	EBIT Gr. FY-1	E..A-CX Gr. STM	S.Gr.+E..A% FY+1	E..ARD Mar. FY+1	E..ARD Mar. FY+2	S.Gr.+E..A% LTM	DPS Gr. FY+2	EBITDA Gr. FY0	S.Gr.+E..A% LTM	RoE STM	RoE STM
	10	S.Gr.+E..A% FY+1	S.Gr.+E..A% LTM	Net In. Gr. FY0	GM Gr. FY+2	Net In. Gr. FY+2	GM Gr. NTM	E..ARD Mar. NTM	DPS Gr. FY+1	FCF Gr. NTM	RoE STM	FCF Gr. FY+1	RoE FY+3	RoE FY+3
	Σ 20	S.Gr.+E..A%	S.Gr.+E..A%	EBIT Gr. Net In. Gr.	E..A-CX Gr. GM Gr.	S.Gr.+E..A% Sales Gr.	E..ARD Mar.	E..ARD Mar.	DPS Gr. S.Gr.+E..A%	FCF Gr.	RoE DPS Gr.	FCF Gr. DPS Gr.	RoE	RoE RoA
		13-0-0	13-0-0	8-6-0	10-8-0	9-3-0	15-0-0	19-0-0	7-6-0	11-0-0	10-6-0	9-6-0	16-0-0	13-7-0

Table 7.28 Results of top best-fitting regressions for gaming companies (excl. BS variables)

		2009	2010	2011	2012	2013	2014	2015	2016	2017	2018	2019	2020	2021
Multiples of top 10 regressions	1	EV/Sales FY0	P/E FY-1	EV/E..A-CX FY0	EV/EBITDA SLTM	EV/E..A-CX FY0	P/Sales FY+2	EV/Sales STM	EV/E..ARD FY+2	EV/EBITDA SLTM	EV/E..A-CX FY+2	EV/GM FY+2	EV/OP CF FY-2	P/Sales FY0
	2	P/E FY0	P/E FY-1	EV/Sales FY+1	EV/EBIT SLTM	EV/Sales FY-2	P/Sales NTM	EV/Sales STM	EV/E..ARD NTM	EV/E..A-CX SLTM	EV/E..A-CX NTM	EV/GM NTM	EV/E..A-CX FY-2	EV/Sales FY0
	3	EV/Sales FY+2	P/E FY-1	EV/E..A-CX STM	P/Sales SLTM	EV/E..A-CX FY0	P/Sales STM	EV/Sales FY+2	EV/E..ARD FY+2	EV/E..ARD FY+1	EV/E..A-CX FY-1	EV/GM FY+3	P/Sales FY+3	EV/Sales LTM
	4	EV/Sales LTM	EV/Sales FY-1	P/FCF STM	EV/GM FY-1	EV/E..A-CX FY0	P/Sales FY+1	EV/Sales FY+2	EV/E..ARD NTM	EV/GM FY-1	EV/E..A-CX SLTM	EV/GM STM	P/Sales STM	P/Sales FY-1
	5	P/E LTM	P/E FY-1	EV/Sales NTM	P/E SLTM	EV/Sales FY-2	P/Sales FY+2	EV/Sales NTM	EV/OP CF FY0	EV/E..ARD NTM	EV/EBITDA FY-2	EV/GM FY+3	EV/E..A-CX FY-2	P/Sales SLTM
	6	EV/Sales STM	EV/Sales FY0	P/E FY0	EV/EBIT SLTM	EV/Sales SLTM	P/Sales NTM	EV/Sales NTM	EV/Sales FY-2	EV/GM SLTM	EV/GM LTM	EV/GM FY+2	P/Sales NTM	P/Sales FY-1
	7	EV/Sales NTM	EV/Sales SLTM	EV/OP CF SLTM	EV/EBITDA SLTM	EV/E..A-CX FY0	P/Sales FY+1	EV/Sales FY+1	P/Sales FY-1	EV/E..ARD FY+2	EV/EBITDA SLTM	EV/GM NTM	P/Sales FY+3	P/Sales LTM
	8	P/E FY+1	EV/Sales FY-1	EV/Sales FY+2	EV/E..A-CX LTM	EV/GM FY-2	P/Sales STM	EV/Sales FY+1	EV/OP CF LTM	EV/GM LTM	EV/GM STM	EV/GM STM	P/Sales NTM	P/Sales FY0
	9	P/E NTM	EV/EBITDA FY+3	EV/Sales LTM	EV/E..A-CX LTM	EV/GM FY-2	P/Sales LTM	EV/Sales LTM	EV/E..ARD FY+1	EV/Sales FY-2	EV/GM NTM	EV/Sales FY-1	P/Sales FY+2	EV/Sales FY-2
	10	EV/Sales FY+1	EV/Sales SLTM	EV/Sales STM	EV/EBITDA SLTM	EV/EBITDA FY-1	EV/E..A-CX FY-1	EV/Sales LTM	P/Sales FY-2	EV/OP CF FY0	EV/GM FY+2	EV/EBIT SLTM	P/Sales FY+2	P/Sales SLTM
	Σ 20	EV/Sales P/E	EV/Sales P/E	EV/Sales EV/EBIT EV/E..A-CX	EV/EBITDA EV/E..A-CX	EV/E..A-CX EV/Sales EV/GM	P/Sales	EV/Sales P/Sales	EV/E..ARD	EV/GM EV/E..ARD	EV/GM EV/E..A-CX	EV/GM EV/E..A-CX	P/Sales EV/Sales	P/Sales EV/Sales
		12-7-0	8-5-0	9-3-3	6-6-0	7-4-4	17-0-0	13-6-0	11-0-0	4-4-0	8-6-0	8-4-0	12-4-0	14-5-0
Multiples of top 10 drivers	1	S.Gr.+E..A% FY+1	EPS Gr. LTM	EBIT Gr. NTM	E..A-CX Gr. STM	EBITDA Gr. FY+2	E..ARD Mar. FY+1	E..ARD Mar. FY+2	EBIT Gr. FY+1	FCF Gr. LTM	FCF Gr. LTM	FCF Gr. LTM	E..ARD Gr. FY+3	S.Gr.+E..A% FY+3
	2	GM Gr. FY+1	Net In. Gr. LTM	Net In. Gr. FY-1	E..A-CX Gr. STM	Sales Gr. FY+3	E..ARD Mar. FY+1	E..ARD Mar. NTM	EBIT Gr. FY+1	FCF Gr. LTM	FCF Gr. LTM	FCF Gr. LTM	Op.CF Gr. FY0	S.Gr.+E..A% FY+3
	3	S.Gr.+E..A% FY+1	EBITDA Gr. FY0	FCF Gr. FY+2	GM Gr. STM	EBIT Gr. FY+2	E..ARD Mar. FY+1	E..ARD Mar. FY+2	Net In. Gr. STM	E..ARD Gr. NTM	DPS Gr. FY+2	FCF Gr. LTM	EBIT Mar. FY-2	S.Gr.+E..A% FY+3
	4	S.Gr.+E..A% FY+1	S.Gr.+E..A% LTM	E..A-CX Gr. NTM	GM Gr. STM	Net In. Gr. FY+2	E..ARD Mar. FY+1	E..ARD Mar. NTM	Net In. Gr. STM	GM Gr. FY+1	DPS Gr. FY+2	FCF Gr. LTM	EBIT Mar. FY-2	Op.CF/Sal. FY+1
	5	EBIT Gr. FY+1	EBIT Gr. LTM	Net In. Gr. FY-1	EBITDA Gr. NTM	Sales Gr. STM	E..ARD Mar. NTM	E..ARD Mar. FY+2	DPS Gr. FY+1	E..ARD Gr. NTM	DPS Gr. FY+2	DPS Gr. FY0	Sales Gr. FY+3	Op.CF/Sal. FY+1
	6	S.Gr.+E..A% FY+1	S.Gr.+E..A% LTM	E..A-CX Gr. NTM	GM Gr. FY+2	FCF Gr. FY+3	E..ARD Mar. NTM	E..ARD Mar. NTM	S.Gr.+E..A% LTM	FCF Gr. FY+1	DPS Gr. FY+1	DPS Gr. FY0	EBIT Mar. FY-2	Op.CF/Sal. LTM
	7	S.Gr.+E..A% FY+1	S.Gr.+E..A% LTM	Net In. Gr. FY0	E..A-CX Gr. FY+2	EBIT Gr. NTM	E..ARD Mar. NTM	E..ARD Mar. FY+2	S.Gr.+E..A% LTM	E..ARD Gr. NTM	DPS Gr. FY+2	DPS Gr. FY0	FCF/Sales FY+3	S.Gr.+E..A% FY+3
	8	EBIT Gr. FY+1	S.Gr.+E..A% FY0	Net In. Gr. FY-1	E..A-CX Gr. FY+2	GM Gr. FY+1	E..ARD Mar. NTM	E..ARD Mar. NTM	DPS Gr. FY+1	FCF Gr. FY+1	DPS Gr. FY+1	DPS Gr. FY0	FCF/Sales FY+3	Op.CF/Sal. FY+1
	9	EBIT Gr. FY+1	GM Gr. FY+3	Net In. Gr. FY-1	E..A-CX Gr. STM	Sales Gr. STM	E..ARD Mar. FY+1	E..ARD Mar. FY+2	EBITDA Gr. NTM	DPS Gr. FY+2	DPS Gr. FY+1	FCF Gr. LTM	EBIT Mar. FY-2	S.Gr.+E..A% FY0
	10	S.Gr.+E..A% FY+1	S.Gr.+E..A% FY0	Net In. Gr. FY-1	GM Gr. FY+2	Op.CF Gr. LTM	GM Gr. NTM	E..ARD Mar. NTM	S.Gr.+E..A% LTM	FCF Gr. NTM	DPS Gr. FY+1	EBITDA Gr. LTM	FCF/Sales FY+3	EBITDA Mar. FY-1
	Σ 20	EBIT Gr. S.Gr.+E..A%	S.Gr.+E..A% EBIT Gr.	Net In. Gr. EBIT Gr.	E..A-CX Gr. GM Gr.	Sales Gr. GM Gr.	E..ARD Mar. GM Gr.	E..ARD Mar.	S.Gr.+E..A% EBIT Gr.	FCF Gr. E..ARD Gr.	DPS Gr. FCF Gr.	FCF Gr. DPS Gr.	FCF/Sales EBIT Mar.	S.Gr.+E..A% Op.CF/Sal.
		8-7-0	7-4-0	7-3-0	10-8-0	5-4-0	16-2-0	19-0-0	5-5-0	11-4-0	10-4-0	9-5-0	7-5-0	8-8-0

Evaluating the multiples, unfortunately, no clear trend can be observed with Sales multiples, profitability multiples, and Book Value multiples switching very often without a clearly observable development. In the analysis excluding balance sheet multiples, it seems that Book Value multiples are getting replaced by Sales and Gross Margin multiples, however, without a clear consistency.

Drivers show a similar unclear trend, often ranging from the rule of 40 to various margin growth drivers and back to the rule of 40, EBITDARD margin, FCF growth, and sometimes RoE or RoA drivers. The analysis excluding balance sheet variables shows a similar evolution. The only common denominator seems to be the implication of profitability as a driver. While the form is unclear, all drivers have a margin component.

Some conclusions can be drawn. Valuation bases are Sales or, at most, Gross Margin based, with some importance to be ascribed to book value multiples. Drivers are various forms of margin and margin growth, which should be sufficient for defining the strategy despite being difficult to pinpoint.

7.2.12 Results for Horizontal Software Companies

The horizontal software segment has all the prerequisites for a good analysis, and the results will also show relatable outcomes. The segment has 114 companies worldwide, which is a more detailed study that might be worth breaking down into geographies. The analysis shows over 343 k regression with sufficient data, which is astonishingly 88% of what is possible. Out of these regressions, nearly 206 k regressions show the expected positive correlation, and over 57 k of all regressions are statistically significant. Looking at the R-Squared, we see that most of the time, the values are north of 60%, with only the last four years experiencing less than that. However, even in 2021, which shows the lowest overall values, the highest values are in the 60s. The R-Squared values are presented in Table 7.29, while the results are presented in Table 7.30.

Table 7.29 R^2 of top 20 regressions for horizontal software companies

#	'07	'08	'09	'10	'11	'12	'13	'14	'15	'16	'17	'18	'19	'20	'21
1	81	91	95	89	90	82	85	85	70	75	79	71	59	61	68
2	81	88	93	89	89	81	83	80	70	75	74	64	57	55	66
3	81	88	93	88	88	80	81	80	68	71	72	63	56	55	57
4	80	88	88	88	87	80	81	79	68	71	71	63	55	54	55
5	79	88	87	85	86	77	81	79	68	70	69	62	55	54	53
6	79	87	87	83	86	76	80	78	67	70	69	62	55	52	52
7	79	87	87	82	85	75	80	78	66	69	68	58	54	52	51
8	78	87	87	82	85	74	80	78	65	69	66	57	54	49	50
9	78	87	87	82	84	73	77	77	65	68	66	57	53	49	50
10	77	87	87	82	84	73	77	77	64	68	66	56	53	49	49
11	77	86	87	82	84	73	77	77	64	67	65	55	51	48	49
12	75	86	87	81	84	73	77	77	63	65	65	55	51	48	49
13	74	86	87	80	83	73	76	76	63	64	65	54	51	48	48
14	73	86	87	80	83	72	76	76	63	64	64	54	51	48	48
15	72	86	86	80	83	72	76	76	62	64	63	54	51	48	46
16	71	86	86	80	82	72	76	75	62	64	63	53	51	47	45
17	71	86	86	79	82	71	76	75	62	64	63	52	50	47	45
18	70	86	86	79	82	71	76	75	61	62	63	52	50	46	44
19	70	86	85	79	80	71	75	75	61	62	63	52	50	46	44
20	69	86	84	79	80	71	75	75	60	61	63	52	50	45	44

Evaluating the bases, it can be seen that these clearly develop from Sales multiples in the years 2007, 2008, and 2009 towards Gross Margin multiples in 2010 and 2012 and EBITDA-CAPEX in 2011 and EBITDARD in the period 2015 to 2020. In 2021 EBITDA-CAPEX comes at the top, however, EBITDARD is the second-best multiple. This evolution clearly demonstrates the expected changes over the evolution of a particular industry. It will be interesting to overlay the conclusions with the industry's growth rates later in the chapter.

Table 7.30 Results of top best-fitting regressions for horizontal software companies

Group		2007	2008	2009	2010	2011	2012	2013	2014	2015	2016	2017	2018	2019	2020	2021
Multiples of top 10 regressions	1	P/Sales FY+3	EV/EBITDA SLTM	EV/E..A-CX FY0	EV/GM FY-1	EV/EBIT LTM	EV/GM FY-2	EV/E..ARD FY+1	P/B FY+3	EV/E..ARD FY+1	EV/E..ARD FY0	EV/E..ARD LTM	EV/E..ARD LTM	EV/E..ARD FY+1	EV/E..ARD STM	EV/E..A-CX SLTM
	2	EV/Sales FY+2	P/Sales STM	EV/EBITDA LTM	EV/GM SLTM	EV/Sales SLTM	EV/GM FY-1	EV/E..ARD NTM	EV/E..ARD FY+1	EV/E..ARD FY+2	EV/E..ARD SLTM	EV/E..ARD LTM	EV/E..ARD FY0	EV/E..ARD LTM	EV/E..ARD FY0	EV/E..A-CX FY-1
	3	P/Sales FY+2	P/Sales FY+2	EV/EBITDA FY0	EV/GM FY-1	P/FCF SLTM	EV/E..ARD FY-2	EV/E..ARD STM	EV/Asset FY+3	EV/E..ARD FY+1	EV/E..ARD LTM	EV/E..ARD LTM	EV/E..A-CX SLTM	EV/E..ARD LTM	EV/E..ARD LTM	EV/E..A-CX FY-1
	4	P/Sales STM	P/Sales FY+3	P/Sales FY+2	EV/GM SLTM	EV/E..A-CX FY+1	EV/GM FY-2	EV/E..ARD FY+2	P/B STM	EV/E..ARD NTM	EV/E..ARD NTM	EV/E..ARD LTM	EV/Asset FY-2	EV/E..ARD SLTM	EV/E..ARD FY+3	EV/EBIT FY-2
	5	EV/Sales NTM	P/Sales NTM	EV/Sales FY+2	EV/GM SLTM	EV/E..ARD FY0	EV/GM FY-1	EV/E..ARD STM	EV/E..ARD FY+3	P/Sales SLTM	EV/E..ARD FY+1	EV/E..ARD LTM	EV/E..ARD LTM	EV/E..ARD FY+1	EV/E..A-CX FY-2	EV/E..A-CX FY-2
	6	P/Sales NTM	P/Sales FY+3	P/Sales NTM	EV/GM FY-1	EV/EBIT FY0	EV/Sales FY-1	EV/E..ARD FY+1	EV/Asset FY+3	EV/E..ARD FY+1	EV/E..ARD FY+1	EV/E..ARD LTM	EV/E..ARD FY+1	EV/E..ARD LTM	EV/E..ARD FY+2	EV/E..A-CX FY-1
	7	EV/Sales FY+3	EV/GM FY+2	P/Sales LTM	EV/GM SLTM	EV/E..A-CX NTM	EV/E..ARD FY-2	EV/E..ARD NTM	P/B FY+3	EV/E..ARD NTM	EV/E..ARD NTM	EV/E..ARD FY+1	EV/E..ARD FY0	EV/E..ARD FY+1	EV/E..ARD FY-1	EV/EBITDA FY-2
	8	EV/Sales STM	EV/GM FY+2	EV/Sales NTM	EV/GM FY-1	EV/E..ARD FY0	EV/GM FY-2	EV/E..ARD FY+2	P/B FY+2	EV/E..ARD NTM	EV/E..ARD FY+1	EV/E..ARD FY+1	EV/E..ARD NTM	EV/E..ARD FY+1	EV/E..ARD SLTM	EV/EBIT FY-2
	9	EV/Sales FY+1	P/B FY+3	P/Sales STM	EV/GM FY-1	EV/EBITDA FY0	EV/GM FY-1	EV/Asset FY+2	EV/Asset SLTM	EV/E..ARD FY+2	EV/E..ARD FY+2	EV/E..ARD LTM	EV/E..ARD SLTM	EV/E..ARD STM	EV/E..ARD SLTM	EV/OP CF LTM
	10	P/Sales FY+1	P/Sales FY+1	P/Sales FY0	EV/E..ARD FY0	EV/E..A-CX FY+2	EV/E..ARD FY+3	EV/Asset SLTM	P/B FY-1	EV/E..ARD FY+3	EV/E..ARD FY+1	EV/E..ARD FY0	P/FCF SLTM	EV/E..ARD STM	EV/E..ARD NTM	EV/E..ARD FY-1
	Σ 20	EV/Sales P/Sales	P/Sales EV/GM	P/Sales EV/Sales	EV/GM	EV/E..A-CX EV/Sales EV/EBITDA	EV/GM EV/Sales	EV/E..ARD EV/Asset	P/B EV/Asset EV/E..ARD	EV/E..ARD P/Sales	EV/E..ARD	EV/E..ARD	EV/E..ARD	EV/E..ARD	EV/E..ARD	EV/E..A-CX EV/E..ARD
		8-7-0	9-6-0	8-6-0	13-0-0	6-3-3	10-4-0	12-6-0	7-7-5	15-3-0	19-0-0	19-0-0	17-0-0	20-0-0	16-0-0	8-4-0
Multiples of top 10 drivers	1	FCF/Sales FY0	FCF Gr. FY+1	E..A-CX Gr. FY+1	E..ARD Gr. STM	DPS Gr. FY+3	E..ARD Gr. FY0	E..ARD Gr. FY-1	E..ARD Gr. NTM	EBIT Gr. LTM	Net In. Gr. LTM	Sales Gr. FY-1	E..ARD Gr. STM	Sales Gr. STM	GM Gr. STM	E..ARD Gr. FY+2
	2	FCF/Sales FY0	E..A-CX M. FY+3	EBIT Gr. FY0	E..ARD Gr. STM	GM Gr. STM	S.Gr.+E..A% FY+2	E..ARD Gr. FY-1	E..A-CX Gr. STM	E..ARD Gr. FY+3	Net In. Gr. LTM	E..ARD Gr. STM	E..ARD Gr. STM	Sales Gr. STM	E..ARD Gr. FY+3	E..ARD Gr. FY+2
	3	FCF/Sales FY0	E..A-CX M. FY+3	EBIT Gr. FY0	S.Gr.+E..A% NTM	E..ARD Gr. NTM	EBITDA Gr. FY-1	E..ARD Gr. FY-1	E..ARD Gr. STM	EBITDA Gr. FY0	Net In. Gr. LTM	GM Gr. FY0	E..ARD Gr. FY+2	E..A-CX Gr. FY+3	E..ARD Gr. STM	Sales Gr. FY+3
	4	FCF/Sales FY0	E..A-CX M. FY+3	E..A-CX M. SLTM	S.Gr.+E..A% NTM	DPS Gr. FY+3	S.Gr.+E..A% FY+2	E..ARD Gr. FY-1	E..ARD Gr. NTM	EBIT Gr. LTM	E..ARD Gr. STM	E..ARD Gr. FY+3	DPS Gr. FY+2	E..ARD Gr. STM	GM Gr. STM	GM Gr. LTM
	5	FCF/Sales FY0	E..A-CX M. FY+3	E..A-CX M. SLTM	S.Gr.+E..A% STM	GM Gr. STM	S.Gr.+E..A% NTM	E..ARD Gr. FY+1	E..A-CX Gr. STM	Sales Gr. STM	Net In. Gr. LTM	Sales Gr. STM	E..A-CX Gr. FY+3	E..ARD Gr. STM	E..ARD Gr. FY0	GM Gr. LTM
	6	FCF/Sales FY0	Op.CF/Sal. FY+2	E..A-CX M. SLTM	S.Gr.+E..A% STM	DPS Gr. FY+3	S.Gr.+E..A% FY+2	E..ARD Gr. FY+1	E..ARD Gr. FY+3	EPS Gr. NTM	Sales Gr. STM	GM Gr. FY-1	E..A-CX Gr. FY+3	E..ARD Gr. STM	GM Gr. STM	E..ARD Gr. NTM
	7	FCF/Sales FY0	EBITDA Mar. FY+2	E..A-CX M. SLTM	S.Gr.+E..A% FY+2	DPS Gr. FY+3	GM Gr. NTM	E..ARD Gr. FY+1	E..ARD Gr. LTM	EBITDA Gr. FY0	E..ARD Gr. FY+3	GM Gr. FY0	Sales Gr. FY+3	Sales Gr. FY+3	E..ARD Gr. STM	GM Gr. LTM
	8	FCF/Sales FY0	EBITDA Mar. NTM	E..A-CX M. SLTM	S.Gr.+E..A% FY+2	Sales Gr. STM	S.Gr.+E..A% NTM	Sales Gr. FY+2	E..ARD Gr. NTM	EPS Gr. NTM	Sales Gr. FY0	Sales Gr. FY-1	E..A-CX Gr. FY+3	E..A-CX Gr. FY+3	E..ARD Gr. STM	GM Gr. FY0
	9	FCF/Sales FY0	RoE FY+3	E..A-CX M. SLTM	EBITDA Gr. STM	DPS Gr. FY+3	S.Gr.+E..A% STM	E..ARD Gr. STM	GM Gr. STM	GM Gr. STM	EBITDA Gr. STM	Sales Gr. FY+3	E..ARD Gr. STM	DPS Gr. FY0	E..ARD Gr. FY+3	E..ARD Gr. FY0
	10	FCF/Sales FY0	E..A-CX M. FY+3	E..A-CX M. SLTM	Sales Gr. FY0	DPS Gr. FY+3	Op.CF/Sal. FY-2	GM Gr. LTM	RoA FY+3	Op.CF Gr. STM	Sales Gr. FY+3	Sales Gr. STM	E..ARD Gr. STM	Sales Gr. STM	GM Gr. STM	GM Gr. FY+3
	Σ 20	FCF/Sales	Op.CF/Sal. EBITDA Mar.	E..A-CX M.	S.Gr.+E..A% E..ARD Gr. Sales Gr.	DPS Gr.	S.Gr.+E..A%	E..ARD Gr. Sales Gr.	E..ARD Gr.	Sales Gr. E..ARD Gr.	Sales Gr. Net In. Gr.	Sales Gr. GM Gr.	E..ARD Gr. Sales Gr.	Sales Gr. E..ARD Gr.	E..ARD Gr. GM Gr.	GM Gr. E..ARD Gr.
		16-0-0	7-5-5	15-0-0	7-5-4	9-0-0	11-0-0	13-6-0	12-0-0	4-4-0	7-7-0	7-5-0	5-4-0	8-7-0	10-4-0	9-5-0

The valuation drivers do not show such a clear evolution, however, they are mostly growth-focused. While the first three years show rather margin drivers such as FCF/Sales or Operative Cash Flow / Sales and EBITDA margin, it needs to be noted that these drivers are paired with Sales multiples which already compensate for growth. In 2010 and 2012, the rule of 40 appears, while in 2021, dividends seem to come into focus. In the years to come, growth defined as Sales growth, Gross Margin growth, or EBITDA growth usually switch to become the best driver, however, end the analysis on a clear profitability growth trend as in 2021, Gross Margin growth and EBITDARD growth are the best drivers.

It can be concluded that in this segment, valuations are EBITDARD based and driven by the Gross Margin and EBITDARD growth, demonstrating the maturity level of the industry and the expectations that companies are not only profitable but increasingly profitable with profitability growth being recompensated.

7.2.13 Results for Marketing Companies

The marketing companies segment is also a cluster with sufficient data for a thorough analysis. The cluster comprises 88 companies with sufficiently listed for a long enough period to enable an analysis starting in 2007. The industry also showed sufficient regressions with observations totaling nearly 332 k regressions with sufficient data, of which nearly 220 k have a positive correlation and over 64 k are statistically significant. Table 7.31 shows the healthy R-Squared values for this cluster which range from 55 up to 88. Table 7.32 presents all results and conclusions on the relevant bases and drivers.

Table 7.31 R^2 of top 20 regressions for marketing companies

#	'07	'08	'09	'10	'11	'12	'13	'14	'15	'16	'17	'18	'19	'20	'21
1	81	90	90	92	88	82	88	94	83	82	80	79	76	83	73
2	79	89	87	89	87	81	86	87	81	79	80	73	74	77	72
3	78	88	86	89	85	81	82	87	79	79	76	71	73	72	72
4	77	85	85	87	84	81	81	86	79	79	74	71	71	72	70
5	76	84	84	84	84	80	80	86	78	79	72	70	68	68	68
6	76	83	84	84	83	80	80	86	78	79	71	70	68	67	67

(continued)

Table 7.31 (continued)

#	'07	'08	'09	'10	'11	'12	'13	'14	'15	'16	'17	'18	'19	'20	'21
7	76	83	83	83	83	80	80	85	78	78	70	70	66	67	65
8	74	83	83	82	82	79	80	84	75	77	70	69	64	65	64
9	72	82	82	81	82	79	79	84	74	77	70	69	64	64	63
10	72	81	81	79	82	78	79	84	73	77	70	69	63	64	61
11	72	80	81	79	82	78	79	83	73	76	70	69	63	64	60
12	71	80	81	79	81	77	79	83	73	76	69	68	62	63	59
13	70	80	80	79	81	75	78	83	73	76	69	68	62	63	57
14	69	80	79	79	80	75	78	82	72	75	69	68	62	62	56
15	69	79	78	78	80	74	78	82	72	75	69	68	61	62	56
16	69	79	77	78	80	74	78	82	72	74	68	68	61	60	56
17	69	79	77	78	80	74	78	81	71	74	68	67	61	60	56
18	68	79	77	78	80	73	77	81	71	74	66	67	61	60	55
19	68	78	77	77	79	72	77	80	71	74	66	64	61	60	55
20	68	78	77	77	79	72	76	80	70	74	66	63	60	60	55

Evaluating the results concerning the bases, one can see that there is a specific trend towards EBITDARD multiples, with the trend not being entirely clear in the first years. Leaving aside the multiples based on balance sheet variables which show a reasonably high occurrence, one can see that in 2007 EBITDA-CAPEX was the second-best multiple which became a Sales multiple in 2008 and 2009 and transformed into a Gross Margin multiple in 2010 and 2011. Starting in 2012, EV/EBITDARD has been on almost every year, the primary multiple, except for 2015 when Sales was the first and EBITDARD was second, and 2018 when EV/ Asset was the first and EV/EBITDARD was second. Bases develop naturally, going from Sales multiples towards Gross Margin Multiples and EBITDARD multiples as expected.

Table 7.32 Results of top best-fitting regressions for marketing companies

		2007	2008	2009	2010	2011	2012	2013	2014	2015	2016	2017	2018	2019	2020	2021
Multiples of top 10 regressions	1	EV/EBIT FY-1	EV/Sales FY+3	EV/EBITDA FY-2	EV/GM FY-1	EV/GM FY-2	EV/GM FY+3	P/B LTM	EV/E..ARD FY-2	EV/GM FY-2	EV/Asset NTM	EV/E..ARD FY-1	EV/E..ARD FY-2	P/B SLTM	EV/E..ARD LTM	EV/E..ARD FY-1
	2	P/Sales FY-2	EV/OP CF FY0	EV/Asset FY-1	EV/Asset FY-2	P/B STM	P/B STM	P/B LTM	EV/Sales FY-2	EV/E..ARD FY-1	EV/E..ARD FY-2	EV/E..A-CX FY+1	EV/E..ARD FY-2	P/B FY0	EV/E..ARD LTM	EV/E..ARD FY-1
	3	EV/EBITDA SLTM	EV/Sales STM	EV/Asset FY-1	EV/GM FY-1	P/B STM	EV/E..ARD NTM	EV/E..ARD FY-1	P/Sales FY-2	P/B FY-1	EV/Asset NTM	EV/E..ARD SLTM	EV/Asset STM	P/B FY0	EV/E..ARD LTM	EV/E..ARD FY-1
	4	EV/Sales SLTM	EV/Sales FY+3	P/B FY-2	EV/Asset FY-2	EV/Asset FY-1	P/B STM	EV/E..ARD SLTM	EV/E..ARD FY-2	EV/Sales FY-2	P/Sales LTM	EV/E..ARD SLTM	EV/Asset STM	P/B SLTM	EV/E..ARD FY+1	EV/E..ARD SLTM
	5	P/FCF LTM	EV/Sales STM	EV/Sales FY0	EV/E..A-CX FY-2	EV/Asset SLTM	EV/GM STM	P/B LTM	P/Sales FY-2	EV/E..ARD FY-1	EV/E..ARD SLTM	EV/E..ARD NTM	EV/Asset NTM	P/E FY+1	EV/E..ARD FY+1	EV/E..ARD FY-1
	6	EV/Asset NTM	EV/Sales FY+2	EV/Asset SLTM	EV/Sales FY-1	P/B STM	EV/E..ARD NTM	P/Sales SLTM	EV/E..ARD FY-2	EV/Sales FY-2	EV/Asset FY0	EV/E..ARD FY0	EV/E..ARD FY-2	P/E FY+1	EV/E..ARD LTM	EV/E..ARD FY-1
	7	EV/Asset FY+1	EV/Sales FY-2	P/Sales FY0	EV/E..A-CX FY0	P/B STM	EV/EBITDA NTM	EV/EBITDA SLTM	EV/E..ARD FY-1	P/Sales FY-2	EV/Asset FY0	EV/E..ARD FY+2	EV/Asset NTM	P/B FY-1	EV/E..ARD LTM	EV/E..ARD FY-1
	8	P/Sales SLTM	EV/Asset FY0	EV/Asset FY0	EV/Asset FY0	P/B FY+2	EV/GM FY+2	P/B STM	EV/Sales FY-2	EV/Asset FY+3	EV/Sales FY+1	EV/E..ARD FY+1	EV/Asset FY-1	EV/E..ARD FY+1	EV/E..ARD FY0	EV/E..ARD FY-1
	9	EV/Sales FY-1	P/B FY+1	EV/Sales FY-1	EV/E..A-CX FY0	P/B FY+2	EV/E..ARD NTM	EV/Asset LTM	EV/E..ARD FY-2	EV/E..ARD SLTM	EV/E..ARD FY-2	EV/E..ARD FY0	EV/Asset FY+2	EV/E..ARD LTM	EV/EBIT FY+2	EV/E..ARD FY0
	10	EV/Asset NTM	P/B NTM	EV/Asset FY-1	P/Sales FY-1	EV/GM FY-2	EV/E..ARD NTM	EV/E..ARD SLTM	EV/E..ARD FY-1	EV/Sales FY-2	EV/Sales FY+1	EV/E..ARD SLTM	EV/E..ARD FY-2	EV/E..ARD FY+3	EV/E..ARD FY+1	EV/E..ARD FY-1
	Σ 20	EV/Asset EV/E..A-CX	EV/Sales	EV/Asset P/Sales EV/Sales	EV/GM EV/Asset	P/B EV/GM	EV/E..ARD EV/GM	EV/E..ARD P/B	EV/E..ARD P/Sales	EV/Sales EV/E..ARD	EV/E..ARD EV/Asset	EV/E..ARD	EV/Asset EV/E..ARD	EV/E..ARD P/B	EV/E..ARD	EV/E..ARD
		6-4-0	14-0-0	10-4-4	7-5-0	12-4-0	8-5-0	8-6-0	9-4-0	5-5-0	9-4-0	12-0-0	15-5-0	8-7-0	17-0-0	18-0-0
Multiples of top 10 drivers	1	Sales Gr. NTM	E..A-CX M. FY+3	DPS Gr. NTM	S.Gr.+E..A% STM	S.Gr.+E..A% FY0	DPS Gr. FY+2	RoA FY+3	Sales Gr. NTM	E..ARD Gr. NTM	S.Gr.+E..A% FY+3	E..ARD Gr. FY+1	GM Gr. FY+1	E..ARD Gr. FY+2	Sales Gr. STM	GM Gr. LTM
	2	Sales Gr. LTM	FCF Gr. LTM	S.Gr.+E..A% FY+1	S.Gr.+E..A% FY+2	GM Gr. FY+1	S.Gr.+E..A% FY+3	Sales Gr. STM	Sales Gr. LTM	EPS Gr. FY0	S.Gr.+E..A% STM	E..ARD Gr. STM	Sales Gr. LTM	E..ARD Gr. FY+2	GM Gr. STM	E..ARD Gr. FY0
	3	EBITDA Gr. STM	E..A-CX M. FY+3	S.Gr.+E..A% LTM	S.Gr.+E..A% NTM	Sales Gr. FY+1	EBIT Gr. FY+3	Sales Gr. STM	Sales Gr. LTM	DPS Gr. FY-1	S.Gr.+E..A% FY+2	EBITDA Gr. FY0	S.Gr.+E..A% FY+2	E..ARD Gr. NTM	E..ARD Gr. STM	GM Gr. FY0
	4	S.Gr.+E..A% NTM	E..A-CX M. STM	RoA FY+3	E..A-CX Gr. FY0	EBITDA Gr. LTM	GM Gr. FY+3	E..ARD Gr. STM	S.Gr.+E..A% STM	S.Gr.+E..A% STM	S.Gr.+E..A% FY+3	E..ARD Gr. FY+1	S.Gr.+E..A% NTM	E..ARD Gr. NTM	Sales Gr. STM	GM Gr. LTM
	5	E..A-CX Gr. NTM	E..A-CX M. STM	S.Gr.+E..A% STM	DPS Gr. NTM	EBITDA Gr. LTM	DPS Gr. FY+2	S.Gr.+E..A% STM	Sales Gr. FY+1	EPS Gr. LTM	Sales Gr. FY0	E..ARD Gr. NTM	S.Gr.+E..A% FY+2	E..ARD Gr. FY+2	GM Gr. STM	E..ARD Gr. LTM
	6	Net Mar. STM	E..A-CX M. FY+3	Net Mar. FY+3	S.Gr.+E..A% STM	EBITDA Gr. LTM	EBIT Gr. STM	S.Gr.+E..A% STM	S.Gr.+E..A% FY+2	E..ARD Gr. NTM	GM Gr. FY+3	RoA FY-2	RoE LTM	E..ARD Gr. NTM	Sales Gr. FY+3	Sales Gr. FY+3
	7	Net Mar. STM	S.Gr.+E..A% NTM	S.Gr.+E..A% STM	DPS Gr. FY+2	E..A-CX Gr. LTM	E..ARD Gr. FY+3	E..ARD Gr. STM	S.Gr.+E..A% FY+2	E..ARD Gr. NTM	S.Gr.+E..A% FY+3	RoA FY-2	S.Gr.+E..A% NTM	E..ARD Gr. FY+2	GM Gr. FY+3	Sales Gr. STM
	8	S.Gr.+E..A% NTM	FCF Gr. FY+1	Net Mar. FY+3	E..A-CX Gr. STM	GM Gr. FY+1	DPS Gr. FY+2	DPS Gr. LTM	Sales Gr. FY+1	E..ARD Mar. LTM	FCF/Sales STM	RoA FY-2	E..ARD Gr. STM	Sales Gr. STM	Sales Gr. FY+2	Sales Gr. FY+1
	9	S.Gr.+E..A% NTM	FCF Gr. FY0	S.Gr.+E..A% FY+2	DPS Gr. LTM	GM Gr. FY-1	E..ARD Gr. FY+3	RoA FY+3	Sales Gr. LTM	EPS Gr. LTM	EBITDA Mar. STM	E..ARD Gr. FY+1	S.Gr.+E..A% FY+2	Sales Gr. STM	E..ARD Gr. NTM	GM Gr. LTM
	10	Net Mar. FY+2	FCF Gr. FY0	Sales Gr. FY+1	S.Gr.+E..A% STM	GM Gr. FY0	EBITDA Gr. STM	Sales Gr. STM	Sales Gr. NTM	S.Gr.+E..A% FY+2	S.Gr.+E..A% STM	RoA FY-2	Sales Gr. FY+1	E..ARD Gr. FY+2	E..ARD Gr. STM	GM Gr. FY+1
	Σ 20	Net Mar. Sales Gr.	E..A-CX M. FCF Gr. EBITDA	S.Gr.+E..A%	S.Gr.+E..A%	EBITDA Gr. GM Gr. S.Gr.+E..A%	E..ARD Gr. DPS Gr.	S.Gr.+E..A% Sales Gr.	Sales Gr. S.Gr.+E..A%	E..ARD Gr. S.Gr.+E..A%	S.Gr.+E..A%	E..ARD Gr. RoA	S.Gr.+E..A%	E..ARD Gr. Sales Gr.	Sales Gr. E..ARD Gr.	GM Gr. Sales Gr.
		6-5-0	9-4-4	11-0-0	8-0-0	6-5-4	6-6-0	6-5-0	11-8-0	6-5-0	7-0-0	8-6-0	14-0-0	15-5-0	7-7-0	10-6-0

Analyzing the drivers, it can be observed that depending on the year, the main drivers are the rule of 40 and the various profitability growth measures. While the first two years show Net Margin and EBITDA-CAPEX Margin as being the most relevant, 2009 makes a switch towards the rule of 40 which can be observed in 2010 and several years following. Also, EBITDARD growth is an important driver as it essentially switches places with the rule of 40 driver several times. The last two years show, in addition to the EBITDARD growth driver, the emergence of Sales growth and Gross Margin growth as drivers. Despite the bumpy development, it is clear that growth in various forms, and mostly profitable growth, is the most important driver.

It can be concluded that the main multiples for the marketing segment are EV/EBITDARD, and growth in various forms is the main driver of this multiple. Management teams and stakeholders should optimize for profitable growth to maximize value.

7.2.14 Results for Marketplace Companies

The marketplace cluster also shows healthy characteristics for a well-thought analysis. It has 34 companies, with some listed sufficiently long to allow for analysis starting in 2012. Altogether, over 146k regressions have sufficient observations; out of these regressions, over 93k have the expected correlation direction. From the 93k, 19,222 are statistically significant and can be used for the analysis. While the ratio of statistically significant regressions to regressions with a positive correlation is lower than in other industries, the difference between the marketplace industry and other industries is not significant. The R-Squared values, as shown in Table 7.33, are also healthy ranging from the mid-60s to 90. Table 7.34 presents the full results of the analysis.

The bases' evolution is simple to interpret as the first 4 years show the dominance of the Sales multiples, while the following years are profitability (mostly EBITDA or EBITDARD) based. 2014 seems to be a year in which investors also started to pay attention to EBITDA as a driver, as EBITDA-CAPEX became the second most important base. Starting in 2016, almost every year was a year where profitability multiples were the most relevant based, with EV/EBITDA being first in 2016 and 2017, P/E in 2018, and EV/EBITDARD in 2020 and 2021. 2019 was an exceptional year as EV/Assets was the main driver, with EV/FCF being a faraway second driver. The evolution clearly shows the change from sales bases to profitability bases over the period of the study.

Table 7.33 R^2 of top 20 regressions for marketplace companies

#	'12	'13	'14	'15	'16	'17	'18	'19	'20	'21
1	80	88	90	77	83	92	86	77	91	79
2	79	88	89	75	82	89	83	76	91	78
3	79	88	88	75	81	84	80	76	90	78
4	79	88	88	75	81	84	79	75	90	75
5	77	87	86	75	81	82	77	75	88	75
6	77	87	86	74	80	81	75	74	87	75
7	77	87	85	74	80	81	75	74	85	75
8	76	87	85	73	79	81	75	74	84	74
9	76	87	85	73	79	81	74	73	84	74
10	76	87	85	73	79	81	74	73	84	73
11	75	87	83	73	79	81	73	73	82	73
12	75	87	83	73	79	80	73	73	81	72
13	75	86	83	72	78	80	73	73	77	70
14	74	86	83	72	77	80	73	72	76	70
15	74	86	82	72	77	80	73	72	76	69
16	74	86	82	72	77	80	73	72	75	68
17	73	85	82	71	76	80	71	71	73	67
18	73	85	81	71	76	80	71	70	73	67
19	73	85	81	71	76	79	70	70	73	66
20	73	85	81	71	75	79	70	70	72	66

The drivers of the multiples also show an evolution, starting with the Operative Cash Flow margin in 2012 and 2013 and moving towards the rule of 40 for 2014 and 2015. Except for 2017, all following years had a form of growth as a driver, with Sales growth being at the top in 2016, the rule of 40 in 2017, EBITDA growth in 2018, EPS growth in 2019, and Sales growth in the last 2 years.

Based on the discussion, it can be concluded that companies in the marketplace segment have valuations based on EV/EBITDARD that are driven by the company's top-line growth. The conclusion can also be used to optimize the value by management and stakeholders.

Table 7.34 Results of top best-fitting regressions for marketplace companies

Multiples of top 20 regressions	2012	2013	2014	2015	2016	2017	2018	2019	2020	2021
1	P/Sales FY+3	P/Sales FY+3	EV/E..A-CX NTM	EV/EBIT FY+3	EV/E..A-CX FY-1	EV/EBITDA SLTM	EV/E..A-CX NTM	EV/EBITDA FY+2	EV/E..ARD FY+3	EV/E..ARD STM
2	EV/Sales FY+3	P/Sales STM	EV/E..A-CX FY+1	EV/Sales FY+3	P/E FY+3	EV/EBITDA FY-1	P/E FY0	EV/Asset FY+3	EV/E..ARD FY+3	EV/E..ARD FY+3
3	EV/Sales STM	P/Sales FY+3	EV/E..A-CX NTM	EV/Sales FY-2	P/E STM	P/E FY-1	P/FCF FY-1	EV/Asset STM	EV/E..ARD FY+2	EV/E..ARD STM
4	P/Sales STM	P/Sales STM	EV/E..A-CX FY+2	P/FCF NTM	EV/EBITDA FY+3	EV/Asset FY-2	EV/EBITDA NTM	EV/Asset FY0	EV/E..ARD FY+3	EV/E..ARD STM
5	P/Sales FY+3	EV/Sales FY+3	EV/E..A-CX FY+1	P/Sales FY+3	P/E FY+3	EV/EBITDA FY-1	P/E FY0	EV/Asset SLTM	EV/E..ARD FY+3	EV/E..ARD STM
6	EV/Sales FY+3	EV/Sales STM	EV/E..A-CX NTM	EV/Sales FY+3	P/E FY+3	EV/Sales FY+2	P/E FY0	EV/Asset FY+2	EV/E..ARD FY+2	EV/E..ARD FY+3
7	EV/Sales FY+2	EV/Sales NTM	EV/Sales FY+3	EV/Sales STM	EV/EBITDA STM	EV/EBITDA SLTM	EV/EBITDA FY+1	EV/Asset FY-1	EV/E..ARD FY+2	EV/E..ARD STM
8	EV/Sales STM	P/Sales FY+2	EV/E..A-CX FY+1	P/B LTM	EV/EBITDA STM	EV/EBITDA FY-1	P/E FY0	EV/Asset NTM	EV/E..ARD STM	EV/GM FY-2
9	P/Sales STM	EV/Sales FY+2	EV/Sales STM	P/Sales STM	EV/EBITDA FY+3	EV/Sales NTM	EV/E..A-CX LTM	EV/Asset LTM	EV/E..ARD STM	EV/E..ARD FY+3
10	EV/Sales NTM	EV/Sales STM	EV/E..A-CX FY+2	P/FCF FY+3	EV/EBITDA SLTM	EV/Sales FY+3	EV/EBITDA LTM	EV/Asset FY+1	EV/E..ARD FY+2	EV/E..ARD STM
11	P/Sales FY+2	P/Sales NTM	EV/EBITDA FY+3	EV/Sales FY-2	EV/EBIT FY+3	P/E FY-1	P/E LTM	P/FCF FY+2	EV/E..ARD STM	EV/E..ARD FY+3
12	EV/Sales FY+3	EV/Sales FY+1	EV/Sales FY+2	P/Sales FY+3	EV/E..A-CX FY-1	P/E LTM	P/E LTM	EV/Asset NTM	EV/E..ARD FY+3	EV/E..ARD FY+3
13	EV/Sales FY+3	EV/Sales LTM	EV/Sales NTM	P/E SLTM	EV/E..A-CX FY-1	EV/EBITDA FY-1	EV/EBITDA FY0	EV/Asset FY+1	EV/E..ARD FY+3	EV/E..ARD FY+3
14	EV/Sales FY+3	EV/Sales FY+3	EV/Sales FY+3	EV/Sales STM	EV/Asset FY-2	EV/Sales FY+3	EV/E..A-CX FY0	EV/Asset FY+2	EV/E..ARD FY+2	EV/E..ARD FY+3
15	P/Sales NTM	EV/Sales FY+2	EV/Sales STM	P/B FY0	P/E FY+3	EV/EBITDA FY-1	EV/E..A-CX FY+1	EV/E..A-CX FY+1	EV/E..ARD STM	EV/E..ARD STM
16	EV/Sales STM	EV/Sales FY0	EV/Sales SLTM	P/E SLTM	EV/EBITDA FY-1	EV/EBITDA FY-2	P/FCF FY0	P/B FY-2	EV/E..ARD FY+3	EV/E..ARD FY+3
17	EV/Sales STM	EV/Sales NTM	P/FCF NTM	P/Sales STM	P/Sales FY+3	P/E FY-2	EV/EBITDA SLTM	P/FCF NTM	P/FCF FY-1	EV/E..ARD STM
18	EV/Sales FY+2	P/Sales FY+1	EV/Sales LTM	P/Sales FY+2	EV/EBIT STM	P/E SLTM	P/B FY+1	EV/Asset STM	EV/E..ARD FY+3	EV/E..ARD FY+3
19	EV/Sales STM	P/Sales FY+2	EV/Sales FY+1	EV/GM STM	EV/OP CF SLTM	EV/Sales FY+1	EV/EBIT SLTM	P/Sales FY+3	EV/Sales FY+1	EV/E..ARD STM
20	EV/Sales FY+1	EV/Sales FY+1	EV/Sales SLTM	P/FCF LTM	EV/Sales FY+3	P/Sales NTM	P/FCF FY-1	P/FCF NTM	EV/E..ARD FY+3	EV/E..ARD STM
Σ 20	EV/Sales P/Sales	EV/Sales P/Sales	EV/Sales EV/E..A-CX	EV/Sales P/Sales P/FCF	EV/EBITDA P/E	EV/EBITDA P/E	P/E EV/EBITDA	EV/Asset P/FCF	EV/E..ARD	EV/E..ARD
	14-6-0	12-8-0	10-8-0	6-5-3	6-5-0	8-5-0	6-5-0	13-3-0	18-0-0	19-0-0

Multiples of top 20 drivers	2012	2013	2014	2015	2016	2017	2018	2019	2020	2021
1	Op.CF/Sal. FY+3	Op.CF/Sal. LTM	GM Gr. FY+2	FCF Gr. FY+2	Sales Gr. NTM	EPS Gr. NTM	GM Gr. NTM	GM Gr. LTM	GM Gr. FY+3	Sales Gr. STM
2	Op.CF/Sal. FY+3	Op.CF/Sal. FY0	GM Gr. FY+2	S.Gr.+E..A% FY+2	Net In. Gr. NTM	GM Gr. NTM	EBITDA Gr. NTM	EPS Gr. LTM	Sales Gr. FY+3	Sales Gr. STM
3	Op.CF/Sal. FY+3	Op.CF/Sal. FY0	Sales Gr. FY+2	S.Gr.+E..A% STM	EPS Gr. FY+2	EBITDA Gr. FY+2	EBITDA Gr. FY+1	EPS Gr. LTM	GM Gr. FY+3	GM Gr. FY+3
4	Op.CF/Sal. FY+3	Op.CF/Sal. LTM	Sales Gr. FY+2	E..A-CX Gr. LTM	Net In. Gr. FY+2	GM Gr. FY+2	GM Gr. NTM	E..A-CX Gr. LTM	Sales Gr. STM	GM Gr. STM
5	Op.CF/Sal. STM	Op.CF/Sal. LTM	Sales Gr. FY+2	S.Gr.+E..A% FY+2	EPS Gr. FY+2	Sales Gr. STM	EBITDA Gr. FY+2	E..A-CX Gr. LTM	GM Gr. STM	Sales Gr. FY+3
6	Op.CF/Sal. STM	Op.CF/Sal. LTM	Sales Gr. STM	S.Gr.+E..A% STM	FCF Gr. NTM	S.Gr.+E..A% LTM	EBITDA Gr. FY+1	EPS Gr. LTM	Sales Gr. FY+3	GM Gr. FY+3
7	Op.CF/Sal. FY+3	Op.CF/Sal. FY0	S.Gr.+E..A% LTM	S.Gr.+E..A% FY+2	Net In. Gr. FY+2	Net In. Gr. NTM	GM Gr. NTM	E..A-CX Gr. LTM	Sales Gr. STM	E..ARD Gr. STM
8	Op.CF/Sal. STM	Op.CF/Sal. FY0	Sales Gr. STM	E..A-CX Gr. LTM	Op.CF Gr. LTM	Sales Gr. FY+3	Op.CF Gr. FY-1	EPS Gr. LTM	Sales Gr. FY+3	EBIT Gr. STM
9	Op.CF/Sal. STM	Op.CF/Sal. FY0	S.Gr.+E..A% LTM	S.Gr.+E..A% FY+2	Op.CF Gr. LTM	S.Gr.+E..A% LTM	EBITDA Gr. NTM	E..A-CX Gr. LTM	Sales Gr. STM	Sales Gr. FY+3
10	Op.CF/Sal. FY+3	Op.CF/Sal. FY0	GM Gr. FY+2	EBIT Gr. LTM	Sales Gr. STM	S.Gr.+E..A% FY0	GM Gr. NTM	E..A-CX Gr. LTM	GM Gr. STM	Sales Gr. FY-1
11	Op.CF/Sal. FY+3	Op.CF/Sal. FY0	E..A-CX Gr. NTM	S.Gr.+E..A% FY+2	EPS Gr. FY+2	GM Gr. NTM	EPS Gr. FY-1	E..A-CX Gr. FY+1	GM Gr. FY+3	GM Gr. STM
12	EBIT Mar. NTM	Op.CF/Sal. FY0	S.Gr.+E..A% LTM	S.Gr.+E..A% STM	Sales Gr. STM	EBITDA Gr. FY+2	Net In. Gr. FY-1	E..A-CX Gr. LTM	Sales Gr. NTM	Sales Gr. FY-1
13	EBIT Mar. FY+2	Op.CF/Sal. FY0	S.Gr.+E..A% LTM	EBITDA Gr. LTM	Sales Gr. FY+2	GM Gr. LTM	EBITDA Gr. NTM	EPS Gr. LTM	Sales Gr. FY+2	E..ARD Gr. STM
14	EBIT Mar. FY+1	Op.CF/Sal. FY0	S.Gr.+E..A% FY0	S.Gr.+E..A% STM	Sales Gr. STM	S.Gr.+E..A% LTM	EBITDA Gr. NTM	E..A-CX Gr. LTM	Sales Gr. FY0	Sales Gr. FY0
15	Op.CF/Sal. FY+3	Op.CF/Sal. LTM	S.Gr.+E..A% FY0	E..A-CX Gr. LTM	EBIT Gr. LTM	Sales Gr. FY+1	GM Gr. NTM	FCF Gr. STM	GM Gr. STM	Sales Gr. FY+2
16	EBIT Mar. NTM	Op.CF/Sal. FY0	S.Gr.+E..A% FY+3	EPS Gr. LTM	Sales Gr. LTM	GM Gr. FY0	Net In. Gr. LTM	GM Gr. LTM	Sales Gr. FY+1	Sales Gr. FY+2
17	EBIT Mar. FY+2	Op.CF/Sal. LTM	E..A-CX Gr. NTM	S.Gr.+E..A% STM	S.Gr.+E..A% STM	EPS Gr. FY-1	EBITDA Gr. NTM	EBITDA Gr. FY+1	EBITDA Gr. NTM	Sales Gr. FY0
18	Op.CF/Sal. STM	Op.CF/Sal. FY0	S.Gr.+E..A% LTM	S.Gr.+E..A% FY+2	EPS Gr. FY+2	EBITDA Gr. FY+2	FCF Gr. FY0	E..A-CX Gr. LTM	GM Gr. NTM	Sales Gr. LTM
19	EBIT Mar. FY+1	Op.CF/Sal. LTM	S.Gr.+E..A% LTM	S.Gr.+E..A% FY+2	Sales Gr. NTM	S.Gr.+E..A% LTM	Net In. Gr. FY+1	Net In. Gr. FY+1	S.Gr.+E..A% FY+3	Sales Gr. LTM
20	Op.CF/Sal. FY+3	Op.CF/Sal. FY+3	S.Gr.+E..A% STM	E..A-CX Gr. FY+[illegible]	S.Gr.+E..A% STM	S.Gr.+E..A% LTM	EBITDA Gr. NTM	E..A-CX Gr. FY+1	GM Gr. FY+2	GM Gr. FY0
Σ 20	Op.CF/Sal. EBIT Mar.	Op.CF/Sal.	S.Gr.+E..A%	S.Gr.+E..A%	Sales Gr. EPS Gr. Net In. Gr.	S.Gr.+E..A% GM Gr.	EBITDA Gr. GM Gr.	EPS Gr. GM Gr.	Sales Gr. GM Gr.	Sales Gr. GM Gr.
	14-6-0	20-0-0	10-0-0	12-0-[illegible]	7-4-3	6-5-0	9-5-0	5-2-0	10-8-0	12-5-0

7.2.15 Results for Online B2C Services Companies

As previously discussed, the Online B2C Services cluster is not well covered from the perspective of the observations. The cluster has 18 companies that enabled an analysis starting in 2012 that provided only 69 k regressions with sufficient observation despite setting the threshold at seven observations. From these regressions, 33 k have the expected correlation, however, only less than 10% are statistically significant. Consequently, only less than 1% of the potential regressions are useful for the analysis. The results should be taken with a grain of salt. Table 7.35 shows the R-Squared values of the leading regressions with respectable values of above 50 and, for the last 8 years covered of above 70. Table 7.36 presents all results concerning bases and drivers.

Table 7.35 R^2 of top 20 regressions for online B2C services companies

#	'12	'13	'14	'15	'16	'17	'18	'19	'20	'21
1	80	76	94	93	92	89	88	89	85	91
2	79	75	92	87	92	85	86	88	85	91
3	72	75	91	84	89	84	83	88	80	91
4	71	75	91	83	88	84	81	88	79	90
5	69	73	90	83	88	83	79	87	79	90
6	61	73	90	82	85	83	79	86	79	87
7	60	73	89	82	84	82	78	84	79	85
8	59	73	87	81	83	81	78	82	79	85
9	59	73	87	80	81	81	76	81	78	84
10	58	72	87	80	81	80	74	80	78	84
11	56	67	86	80	81	79	74	80	77	83
12	55	63	86	80	80	79	73	80	77	83
13	55	62	86	80	80	79	72	79	76	83
14	55	62	86	79	80	78	72	77	76	82
15	54	60	85	79	80	77	72	77	76	82
16	53	60	84	79	79	77	72	77	75	81
17	53	60	84	79	79	77	71	77	75	81
18	53	60	83	78	78	77	71	76	74	81
19	52	60	83	78	78	75	71	75	74	81
20	52	59	83	78	77	75	71	73	74	80

Table 7.36 Results of top best-fitting regressions for online B2C services companies

Multiples of top 20 regressions	2012	2013	2014	2015	2016	2017	2018	2019	2020	2021
1	EV/EBIT STM	EV/Sales FY+3	P/Sales FY0	EV/EBITDA NTM	P/Sales FY-1	P/Sales LTM	EV/EBIT NTM	P/B FY-2	EV/Sales FY-2	EV/Asset SLTM
2	P/E STM	EV/Sales FY+2	EV/Sales FY0	EV/EBIT STM	EV/Sales FY-1	P/Sales LTM	EV/EBIT FY+1	EV/Asset FY+2	P/Sales FY-2	EV/Asset FY+1
3	P/B FY0	P/Sales FY+3	P/Sales LTM	P/Sales SLTM	EV/Sales SLTM	EV/Sales FY+1	EV/EBIT NTM	EV/Asset NTM	P/Sales FY-1	EV/Asset NTM
4	P/B FY0	P/Sales FY+2	EV/GM LTM	EV/Sales SLTM	P/Sales SLTM	EV/Sales LTM	EV/EBIT FY+1	EV/Asset STM	EV/Asset STM	EV/Asset FY+2
5	EV/EBIT STM	EV/Sales NTM	EV/Sales LTM	EV/Sales FY0	EV/Sales FY0	EV/Sales FY+1	EV/EBIT NTM	EV/Asset FY+3	EV/Asset FY+2	EV/Asset LTM
6	P/Sales LTM	P/Sales NTM	EV/EBIT STM	P/Sales FY0	P/Sales FY0	P/Sales LTM	P/E FY+1	EV/Asset FY+1	EV/Asset NTM	EV/Asset SLTM
7	P/Sales FY+1	EV/Sales STM	EV/GM FY+1	P/Sales FY0	EV/Asset FY-1	P/Sales LTM	EV/EBIT NTM	P/E NTM	EV/Asset FY+3	EV/Asset STM
8	P/Sales NTM	P/Sales STM	EV/Sales FY0	EV/Sales FY0	EV/EBITDA FY+2	P/Sales LTM	EV/EBIT NTM	EV/Asset LTM	EV/Asset FY+2	EV/Asset FY-1
9	P/Sales FY+2	P/Sales FY+1	P/Sales FY0	EV/EBITDA FY+2	EV/Asset SLTM	P/Sales LTM	EV/EBIT NTM	EV/GM FY+1	EV/Asset NTM	EV/Asset FY+3
10	EV/Sales LTM	EV/Sales FY+1	P/Sales FY+1	P/B NTM	P/B FY+3	P/Sales LTM	P/B FY0	P/E STM	EV/Sales FY-1	EV/Asset FY0
11	P/Sales FY+1	P/B FY+1	EV/GM NTM	EV/Asset FY0	P/Sales FY-1	EV/Sales LTM	EV/EBIT NTM	EV/GM LTM	EV/Asset STM	EV/Asset FY+1
12	P/Sales STM	EV/EBIT STM	EV/Sales FY+1	EV/Sales SLTM	EV/Sales FY-1	P/Sales LTM	P/B FY0	EV/GM FY+2	EV/Asset SLTM	EV/Asset SLTM
13	EV/Sales LTM	P/Sales FY+1	P/Sales LTM	P/B FY+3	EV/Asset FY0	P/Sales FY+1	P/B FY0	EV/Asset FY-1	EV/Asset FY+3	EV/Asset LTM
14	P/Sales NTM	EV/Sales FY+1	P/Sales FY0	P/B STM	EV/Sales FY-1	P/Sales FY+1	EV/E..A-CX FY+1	P/E FY+2	EV/Asset LTM	EV/Asset NTM
15	P/Sales FY+2	P/Sales NTM	EV/GM FY+2	P/B FY+2	EV/E..A-CX STM	P/Sales FY+1	P/B FY0	EV/GM FY0	EV/Asset FY+1	EV/Asset SLTM
16	P/Sales FY0	P/Sales FY+2	EV/Sales FY0	P/Sales SLTM	EV/Sales FY-1	EV/GM NTM	EV/Asset STM	EV/Asset FY-1	EV/Asset FY+1	EV/EBITDA SLTM
17	EV/Sales FY+1	EV/Sales NTM	EV/Sales NTM	P/B FY+1	P/B STM	EV/Sales FY+1	EV/Asset FY+2	EV/EBITDA NTM	EV/Asset LTM	EV/GM FY+3
18	P/Sales LTM	EV/Sales FY+3	P/Sales FY0	EV/Sales FY0	EV/Asset LTM	EV/Sales FY0	EV/Asset FY+2	EV/EBITDA NTM	EV/Asset SLTM	EV/Asset FY+2
19	EV/Sales NTM	EV/Sales FY+2	P/Sales LTM	EV/Asset LTM	EV/Asset FY+1	P/Sales LTM	EV/EBIT NTM	EV/GM NTM	P/Sales FY-1	EV/EBITDA SLTM
20	P/Sales STM	P/Sales FY+3	EV/GM NTM	EV/Asset STM	P/Sales FY-1	P/Sales FY+1	P/B FY0	P/E NTM	P/Sales SLTM	EV/GM FY+3
Σ 20	P/Sales EV/Sales	P/Sales EV/Sales	P/Sales EV/Sales EV/GM	P/B EV/Sales P/Sales	EV/Sales P/Sales EV/Asset	P/Sales EV/Sales	EV/EBIT P/B	EV/Asset EV/GM P/E	EV/Asset P/Sales	EV/Asset
	11-4-0	9-9-0	8-6-5	5-5-4	6-5-5	13-6-0	10-5-0	8-5-4	14-4-0	16-0-0

Multiples of top 20 drivers	2012	2013	2014	2015	2016	2017	2018	2019	2020	2021
1	EPS Gr. LTM	Sales Gr. LTM	GM Gr. FY-1	GM Gr. LTM	Sales Gr. LTM	Sales Gr. LTM	E..A-CX Gr. FY0	S.Gr.+E..A% FY+1	EPS Gr. NTM	E..ARD Gr. FY-1
2	EPS Gr. LTM	Sales Gr. LTM	GM Gr. FY-1	GM Gr. LTM	Sales Gr. LTM	E..A-CX Gr. LTM	E..A-CX M. FY+3	FCF Gr. FY+1	EPS Gr. NTM	E..ARD Gr. FY-1
3	EPS Gr. LTM	Sales Gr. LTM	GM Gr. FY-1	S.Gr.+E..A% STM	Sales Gr. LTM	GM Gr. FY+1	EBITDA Gr. LTM	FCF Gr. FY+1	EPS Gr. NTM	E..ARD Gr. FY-1
4	Sales Gr. LTM	Sales Gr. LTM	GM Gr. FY-1	S.Gr.+E..A% STM	Sales Gr. LTM	Sales Gr. FY+1	Sales Gr. FY-1	FCF Gr. FY+1	FCF Gr. FY0	E..ARD Gr. FY-1
5	Sales Gr. LTM	Sales Gr. LTM	GM Gr. FY-1	RoE FY+1	Sales Gr. LTM	Sales Gr. FY+1	Net In. Gr. LTM	FCF Gr. FY+1	FCF Gr. FY0	E..ARD Gr. FY-1
6	EBIT Mar. FY-2	Sales Gr. LTM	GM Gr. FY-1	S.Gr.+E..A% STM	Sales Gr. LTM	GM Gr. FY0	Net In. Gr. LTM	FCF Gr. FY+1	FCF Gr. FY0	DPS Gr. FY+3
7	Sales Gr. LTM	Sales Gr. LTM	GM Gr. FY-1	RoE FY+1	Sales Gr. LTM	EPS Gr. LTM	EBITDA Gr. FY+1	Net In. Gr. FY+1	FCF Gr. FY0	E..ARD Gr. FY-1
8	Sales Gr. LTM	Sales Gr. LTM	S.Gr.+E..A% FY-1	S.Gr.+E..A% STM	GM Gr. NTM	EBITDA Gr. LTM	EBITDA Gr. FY0	FCF Gr. FY+1	Op.CF Gr. FY+1	E..ARD Gr. FY-1
9	Sales Gr. LTM	Sales Gr. LTM	S.Gr.+E..A% FY+3	GM Gr. LTM	Sales Gr. LTM	Sales Gr. FY+1	Sales Gr. FY+1	Net In. Gr. LTM	Op.CF Gr. FY+1	E..ARD Gr. FY-1
10	EBIT Mar. FY-2	Sales Gr. LTM	GM Gr. FY-1	Op.CF Gr. FY-1	Sales Gr. LTM	Sales Gr. FY0	Net In. Gr. FY+1	Net In. Gr. FY+1	EPS Gr. NTM	E..ARD Gr. FY-1
11	Sales Gr. FY0	Sales Gr. LTM	GM Gr. FY-1	S.Gr.+E..A% STM	Sales Gr. FY+1	Sales Gr. LTM	E..A-CX Gr. LTM	Net In. Gr. LTM	Op.CF Gr. FY+1	DPS Gr. FY+2
12	Sales Gr. LTM	Sales Gr. LTM	GM Gr. FY-1	RoE FY+2	Sales Gr. FY+1	S.Gr.+E..A% FY+3	E..A-CX Gr. FY+1	FCF Gr. LTM	FCF Gr. FY0	Sales Gr. LTM
13	EBITDA Mar. FY+3	Sales Gr. FY0	S.Gr.+E..A% FY+3	Op.CF Gr. FY-1	Sales Gr. LTM	E..A-CX Gr. LTM	E..A-CX Gr. LTM	EPS Gr. STM	Op.CF Gr. FY+1	DPS Gr. FY+2
14	Sales Gr. FY0	Sales Gr. FY0	E..A-CX M. FY+3	Op.CF Gr. FY-1	E..A-CX M. FY+2	GM Gr. FY0	Sales Gr. FY-1	Net In. Gr. FY+1	FCF Gr. FY0	DPS Gr. FY+2
15	Sales Gr. FY0	Sales Gr. FY0	GM Gr. FY-1	Op.CF Gr. FY-1	GM Gr. NTM	Sales Gr. LTM	EPS Gr. FY+1	Net In. Gr. LTM	FCF Gr. FY0	DPS Gr. FY+2
16	EBIT Mar. FY-2	Sales Gr. FY0	E..A-CX M. FY+3	RoE FY+2	Sales Gr. STM	GM Gr. FY+1	EBITDA Gr. LTM	Sales Gr. FY+2	Op.CF Gr. FY+1	Gross Mar. FY-2
17	Sales Gr. LTM	Sales Gr. FY0	GM Gr. FY-1	Op.CF Gr. FY-1	Sales Gr. LTM	Sales Gr. LTM	EBITDA Gr. LTM	Net In. Gr. LTM	Op.CF Gr. FY+1	Div. Yield FY+2
18	EBITDA Mar. FY+3	Sales Gr. FY0	S.Gr.+E..A% FY-1	RoE FY+2	Sales Gr. LTM	EPS Gr. FY+1	E..A-CX Gr. FY+1	EPS Gr. LTM	Op.CF Gr. FY+1	DPS Gr. FY+2
19	Sales Gr. LTM	Sales Gr. FY0	E..A-CX M. FY+3	S.Gr.+E..A% STM	Sales Gr. LTM	E..A-CX M. FY+3	E..A-CX Gr. FY+1	Net In. Gr. LTM	EPS Gr. STM	Gross Mar. FY-1
20	EBIT Mar. FY-2	Sales Gr. FY0	S.Gr.+E..A% FY-1	S.Gr.+E..A% STM	E..A-CX M. FY+2	EPS Gr. LTM	EBITDA Gr. LTM	Net In. Gr. LTM	EPS Gr. NTM	Div. Yield FY+3
Σ 20	Sales Gr. EBIT Mar. EPS Gr.	Sales Gr.	GM Gr. S.Gr.+E..A%	S.Gr.+E..A% RoE Op.CF Gr.	Sales Gr. GM Gr.	Sales Gr. GM Gr.	E..A-CX Gr. EBITDA Gr.	Net In. Gr. FCF Gr.	Op.CF Gr. FCF Gr. EPS Gr.	E..ARD Gr. DPS Gr.
	11-4-3	20-0-0	12-5-0	7-5-5	16-2-0	8-4-0	6-6-0	9-7-0	7-7-6	9-6-0

Analyzing the bases, one can observe that Sales multiples are the key bases for most of the time, however, the last years also show EV/Assets as being important. Considering that the cluster also contains some companies that generate revenues with content that is usually accounted for as an asset, the results are not particularly surprising. In 2018 also the EV/EBIT multiple can be seen as being highly relevant, however, this only lasted for one year.

Evaluating the drivers, we see growth drivers as always being in the lead. During the first 2 years, as well as 2016 and 2017, Sales growth was the most important driver, while in 2014, Gross Margin growth was important, and in 2015, the rule of 40 came out at the top. In the last 4 years of the analysis, we see various profitability growth ratios as being the most important.

To summarize the results, it can be said that the outcomes are not particularly surprising considering the competition in the segment and the content-focused nature of the business models of the B2C Services companies. In addition to Asset Value, Revenues are most important from a multiples perspective, and from a driver perspective, Margin growth is most important. Management teams and stakeholders can also use these results to implement value-maximizing strategies.

7.2.16 Results for Payment Companies

The payment cluster showed all prerequisites for a thorough analysis. It included 38 companies, of which sufficient companies were listed since the beginning of the study period in 2007. Furthermore, nearly 267 k regressions had sufficient observations at a threshold of 10 observations, and from these observations, 134 k had the required positive correlation. Lastly, from the remaining regressions, c. ¼ were statistically significant, with nearly 33 k observations fulfilling all conditions. Table 7.37 presents the R-Squared values of the top regression with good values of over 65. While Table 7.38 and Table 7.39 present the analysis results, including all variables and excluding balance sheet variables. Similarly to other industries, the strong presence of book value multiples in the main analysis is not entirely justified as the payment industry has shown over the last years a strong growth on the one side, and it usually does not hold any assets on the other side. Consequently, a secondary analysis was performed, excluding balance sheet variables.

Table 7.37 R^2 of top 20 regressions for payment companies

#	'07	'08	'09	'10	'11	'12	'13	'14	'15	'16	'17	'18	'19	'20	'21
1	85	91	92	94	91	94	90	92	93	89	86	88	77	80	88
2	84	90	92	94	91	92	88	89	90	86	84	87	77	76	81
3	84	90	92	93	91	92	87	87	90	82	82	87	77	74	80
4	83	90	91	93	91	91	85	87	90	78	80	86	76	74	80
5	83	90	91	93	91	91	84	86	88	77	78	86	75	73	79
6	83	89	91	92	90	90	84	85	88	71	77	86	74	73	78
7	83	89	90	92	90	90	83	84	88	70	77	85	74	72	77
8	82	89	90	92	90	90	82	84	87	70	77	85	73	72	77
9	82	89	90	92	90	90	81	84	87	70	75	84	72	70	77
10	81	89	90	91	90	89	81	83	87	68	74	83	72	70	76
11	81	89	90	91	88	89	81	83	86	68	74	83	71	70	76
12	81	89	89	91	88	89	81	83	86	67	72	83	70	70	76
13	81	89	89	91	88	88	81	83	86	67	72	83	70	69	74
14	81	88	89	91	88	88	80	82	85	66	72	83	70	69	73
15	80	88	89	90	88	88	79	81	85	66	72	82	69	68	73
16	80	88	89	90	87	88	79	81	84	66	71	81	68	68	73
17	80	88	88	90	87	88	79	81	84	66	71	81	68	68	72
18	80	88	88	90	87	88	79	80	84	65	70	80	68	67	72
19	79	88	88	90	87	88	79	80	83	65	70	80	68	67	72
20	79	88	88	90	87	87	79	80	83	64	70	80	68	66	72

Evaluating the multiples that explain most of the variance, it can be said that Price to Book, in combination with EV/Asset and Sales multiples, dominate the results. The switch between these multiple also does not seem to follow a particular pattern or match the expectations. Looking at the analysis excluding the balance sheet variables, it can be observed that Sales Multiples dominate the results, with some years showing profitability-based multiples as being the best. Except for 2010 and 2021 also, the years that presented profitability multiples at the top showed sales multiples as the second best. 2021 shows a difference, as the second-best multiple is the Free Cash Flow multiple, implying a certain level of maturity for the industry. As growth in the industry decreases and there are various pressures on fees from the competition and regulatory bodies, this change is not surprising but rather confirms the expectations.

Table 7.38 Results of top best-fitting regressions for payment companies

		2007	2008	2009	2010	2011	2012	2013	2014	2015	2016	2017	2018	2019	2020	2021
Multiples of top 10 regressions	1	EV/Sales FY+2	EV/Sales LTM	P/E FY0	EV/Asset FY0	EV/Sales FY+3	EV/Asset NTM	EV/Asset FY-2	P/B STM	EV/Asset FY-1	EV/Asset FY-2	P/B FY+3	P/B FY+2	P/Sales FY-2	P/B FY+3	EV/Asset FY-2
	2	EV/Sales NTM	EV/EBITDA NTM	EV/EBITDA FY+1	EV/Asset LTM	EV/Sales FY+3	EV/Asset FY+1	P/B FY0	P/B FY+2	P/B FY-1	EV/Asset FY-2	P/B STM	P/B NTM	EV/Asset FY-1	P/B FY+3	EV/Asset SLTM
	3	EV/Sales FY+1	EV/Sales LTM	EV/Asset FY+1	EV/E..A-CX FY+1	EV/Sales FY+3	EV/Asset LTM	EV/EBITDA FY0	P/B NTM	EV/Asset SLTM	EV/GM FY-2	EV/Asset FY+3	P/B FY+3	P/B SLTM	P/B SLTM	EV/Asset FY+1
	4	EV/Sales LTM	EV/Sales LTM	EV/Asset NTM	P/FCF NTM	EV/Sales FY+2	EV/Asset FY+1	P/B LTM	P/B FY0	EV/Sales FY0	EV/Asset FY-1	EV/EBITDA NTM	P/B STM	EV/Asset FY-2	P/B STM	EV/Asset LTM
	5	P/B SLTM	EV/Sales NTM	EV/Asset FY+1	EV/E..A-CX FY0	EV/Sales FY+1	EV/GM LTM	P/B FY0	P/B FY0	EV/Sales LTM	P/Sales FY-2	EV/Asset FY+3	EV/Asset FY0	P/B SLTM	P/B FY+3	EV/Asset LTM
	6	EV/Sales FY+2	EV/Sales FY0	EV/Asset FY+2	P/FCF FY+2	EV/Sales NTM	EV/GM LTM	P/B FY+1	P/B LTM	EV/Sales SLTM	EV/GM FY-1	P/B FY+2	EV/Asset SLTM	EV/Asset FY0	P/B FY+3	EV/Asset SLTM
	7	P/B SLTM	EV/Sales FY+2	P/B FY-2	EV/E..A-CX FY0	EV/Sales STM	EV/GM FY0	P/FCF FY+3	EV/E..A-CX SLTM	EV/Asset FY-1	EV/GM SLTM	EV/EBITDA NTM	EV/Asset FY-1	P/B LTM	P/B FY-2	EV/Asset FY+1
	8	EV/Sales NTM	EV/Sales NTM	EV/Asset STM	P/FCF NTM	EV/Sales FY+3	EV/GM FY0	EV/Asset FY+2	P/B LTM	EV/Sales FY+1	P/B FY-2	EV/Asset FY+3	EV/Asset FY-2	EV/Asset SLTM	P/B NTM	EV/E..A-CX FY-1
	9	P/B SLTM	EV/Sales FY+2	P/E SLTM	EV/Asset FY+1	EV/Sales FY+3	EV/Asset NTM	P/B STM	P/E LTM	EV/Sales FY+3	P/Sales FY-2	P/B FY-1	P/B FY+1	P/B LTM	P/B LTM	EV/Asset NTM
	10	P/B SLTM	EV/Sales LTM	P/B FY-2	EV/Asset FY+3	EV/Sales FY+3	EV/Asset FY+2	P/B FY+3	EV/Sales FY-1	EV/Asset SLTM	P/E LTM	P/B NTM	P/B FY+2	P/B LTM	P/B FY+3	EV/Asset SLTM
	Σ 20	EV/Sales P/B P/Sales	EV/Sales	EV/Asset P/E P/B	EV/Asset P/FCF EV/E..A-CX	EV/Sales EV/Asset	EV/Asset EV/GM P/B	P/B	P/B	EV/Sales EV/Asset P/Sales	EV/GM P/B P/Sales	P/B EV/Asset EV/EBITDA	P/B EV/Asset	P/B EV/Asset	P/B EV/Sales	EV/Asset P/FCF
		11-5-4	19-0-0	8-3-3	10-5-4	14-6-0	10-6-3	9-0-0	11-0-0	8-5-4	5-4-3	7-7-5	11-8-0	11-7-0	16-3-0	15-4-0
Multiples of top 10 drivers	1	EBIT Mar. FY+3	EBITDA Mar. STM	EPS Gr. LTM	RoA FY+3	FCF/Sales NTM	RoE FY+3	Sales Gr. FY+2	GM Gr. FY0	GM Gr. FY0	GM Gr. FY-1	E..A-CX Gr. LTM	E..A-CX Gr. FY0	DPS Gr. STM	EBITDA Gr. FY-1	DPS Gr. FY+3
	2	EBIT Mar. FY+3	Net In. Gr. STM	EBITDA Gr. NTM	RoA FY+3	E..A-CX M. STM	RoE FY+3	RoE FY+3	GM Gr. FY0	FCF/Sales LTM	GM Gr. FY0	E..A-CX Gr. LTM	E..A-CX Gr. FY0	E..A-CX Gr. LTM	E..A-CX Gr. FY-1	E..ARD Gr. LTM
	3	EBIT Mar. FY+3	EBITDA Mar. FY+3	RoA STM	GM Gr. FY+2	FCF/Sales FY+2	RoE FY+3	GM Gr. NTM	GM Gr. FY0	GM Gr. LTM	GM Gr. LTM	Op.CF Gr. STM	E..A-CX Gr. FY0	E..A-CX Gr. LTM	E..A-CX Gr. FY-1	E..ARD Gr. LTM
	4	EBIT Mar. FY+3	EBITDA Mar. FY+2	RoA STM	EPS Gr. LTM	E..A-CX M. FY+3	RoA STM	RoE FY+3	RoE FY+3	FCF/Sales FY-2	Op.CF Gr. LTM	E..A-CX Gr. LTM	E..A-CX Gr. FY0	E..A-CX Gr. LTM	E..A-CX Gr. FY-1	E..ARD Gr. LTM
	5	Div. Yield FY+3	EBITDA Mar. STM	RoA FY+2	EBITDA Gr. NTM	E..A-CX M. FY+3	S.Gr.+E..A% NTM	RoE STM	FCF Gr. FY0	FCF/Sales FY-2	GM Gr. FY0	EPS Gr. STM	GM Gr. STM	EBIT Gr. LTM	GM Gr. STM	E..ARD Gr. FY+1
	6	EBITDA Mar. STM	EBITDA Mar. STM	RoA STM	EPS Gr. LTM	E..A-CX M. FY+3	S.Gr.+E..A% FY+1	RoE FY+3	RoE FY+3	FCF/Sales FY-2	GM Gr. LTM	E..A-CX Gr. LTM	GM Gr. STM	DPS Gr. STM	Net In. Gr. FY-1	E..ARD Gr. FY+1
	7	Div. Yield STM	EBITDA Mar. STM	Div. Yield FY+3	EBITDA Gr. FY+1	E..A-CX M. FY+3	S.Gr.+E..A% FY+1	Net In. Gr. STM	Net In. Gr. STM	GM Gr. LTM	GM Gr. LTM	EBITDA Gr. LTM	GM Gr. STM	EBIT Gr. STM	E..A-CX Gr. FY-1	E..ARD Gr. FY+1
	8	EBITDA Mar. STM	EBITDA Mar. FY+3	RoA STM	FCF Gr. FY+3	E..A-CX M. LTM	S.Gr.+E..A% NTM	Div. Yield FY-2	FCF Gr. FY0	FCF/Sales FY-2	Op.CF/Sal. SLTM	GM Gr. NTM	E..A-CX Gr. FY0	EPS Gr. LTM	E..A-CX Gr. FY-1	FCF Gr. LTM
	9	Div. Yield FY+2	EBITDA Mar. FY+3	EPS Gr. LTM	RoA FY+3	E..A-CX M. FY+3	RoA STM	GM Gr. FY+1	DPS Gr. STM	FCF/Sales FY-2	GM Gr. FY-1	GM Gr. FY+3	E..A-CX Gr. FY0	EBIT Gr. FY+3	E..A-CX Gr. FY-1	E..ARD Gr. FY+1
	10	Div. Yield NTM	EBITDA Mar. NTM	Div. Yield STM	Div. Yield FY+2	FCF/Sales FY+1	RoA STM	Op.CF Gr. FY+2	S.Gr.+E..A% NTM	GM Gr. FY0	EBIT Gr. FY+2	E..A-CX Gr. LTM	Net In. Gr. LTM	E..A-CX Gr. FY-1	Sales Gr. STM	E..ARD Gr. NTM
	Σ 20	EBIT Mar. EBITDA Mar.	EBITDA Mar. Net In. Gr.	RoA EPS Gr. Div. Yield	RoA EPS Gr. GM Gr.	E..A-CX M. RoA FCF/Sales	RoE S.Gr.+E..A% RoA	RoE GM Gr. Net In. Gr.	RoE GM Gr. S.Gr.+E..A%	FCF/Sales GM Gr.	GM Gr.	GM Gr. E..A-CX Gr.	E..A-CX Gr. Net In. Gr.	E..A-CX Gr. DPS Gr.	E..A-CX Gr. Sales Gr.	E..ARD Gr. Sales Gr.
		8-6-5	19-1-0	8-4-3	7-3-2	11-6-3	7-6-6	7-3-2	6-4-3	13-7-0	11-0-0	7-6-0	9-4-0	8-5-0	7-3-0	12-4-0

Table 7.39 Results of top best-fitting regressions for payment companies (excl. BS variables)

		2007	2008	2009	2010	2011	2012	2013	2014	2015	2016	2017	2018	2019	2020	2021
Multiples of top 10 regressions	1	EV/Sales FY+2	EV/Sales LTM	P/E FY0	EV/E..A-CX FY+1	EV/Sales FY+3	EV/GM LTM	EV/EBITDA FY0	EV/E..A-CX SLTM	EV/Sales FY0	EV/GM FY-2	EV/EBITDA NTM	P/Sales FY+3	P/Sales FY-2	P/Sales FY+3	EV/E..A-CX FY-1
	2	EV/Sales NTM	EV/EBITDA NTM	EV/EBITDA FY+1	P/FCF NTM	EV/Sales FY+3	EV/GM LTM	P/FCF FY+3	P/E LTM	EV/Sales LTM	P/Sales FY-2	EV/EBITDA NTM	P/Sales FY+3	EV/Sales FY-2	EV/Sales FY-1	P/FCF LTM
	3	EV/Sales FY+1	EV/Sales LTM	P/E SLTM	EV/E..A-CX FY0	EV/Sales FY+3	EV/GM FY0	P/FCF STM	EV/Sales FY-1	EV/Sales SLTM	EV/GM FY-1	EV/EBITDA NTM	P/FCF FY+2	EV/EBITDA FY+2	EV/Sales FY-2	P/FCF SLTM
	4	EV/Sales LTM	EV/Sales LTM	P/Sales STM	P/FCF FY+2	EV/Sales FY+2	EV/GM FY0	EV/EBITDA FY-1	EV/EBITDA FY-1	EV/Sales FY+1	EV/GM SLTM	EV/EBITDA FY+2	P/Sales FY+3	P/Sales FY-2	EV/Sales FY+3	P/FCF FY0
	5	EV/Sales FY+2	EV/Sales NTM	P/E SLTM	EV/E..A-CX FY0	EV/Sales FY+1	EV/Sales FY+3	EV/EBIT FY-1	EV/Sales SLTM	EV/Sales FY+3	P/Sales FY-2	P/Sales FY0	EV/EBITDA STM	EV/EBITDA LTM	P/FCF FY-2	P/FCF SLTM
	6	EV/Sales NTM	EV/Sales FY0	EV/EBITDA FY+1	P/FCF NTM	EV/Sales NTM	EV/GM FY0	EV/EBITDA FY+1	EV/E..A-CX FY+1	EV/Sales NTM	P/E LTM	EV/EBITDA LTM	P/FCF STM	EV/E..A-CX FY-1	P/FCF FY-2	EV/E..ARD NTM
	7	EV/Sales FY-1	EV/Sales FY+2	P/Sales FY+2	P/FCF FY+2	EV/Sales STM	EV/GM SLTM	EV/OP CF STM	EV/EBITDA FY+2	P/Sales SLTM	P/E LTM	P/Sales FY+1	P/Sales SLTM	EV/Sales SLTM	P/Sales FY-1	EV/E..ARD LTM
	8	P/Sales FY+2	EV/Sales NTM	P/FCF FY+2	EV/EBITDA FY-1	EV/Sales FY+3	EV/GM SLTM	EV/Sales FY+1	EV/Sales NTM	EV/Sales FY+2	EV/GM SLTM	EV/EBITDA FY+3	EV/E..A-CX FY+3	EV/EBITDA STM	EV/Sales SLTM	EV/E..ARD FY+1
	9	EV/Sales LTM	EV/Sales FY+2	P/FCF NTM	P/FCF STM	EV/Sales FY+3	EV/GM SLTM	EV/Sales NTM	P/E FY+3	EV/Sales STM	EV/EBITDA FY-2	P/Sales SLTM	EV/OP CF FY+3	EV/Sales FY0	P/FCF FY-2	P/FCF LTM
	10	EV/Sales FY+2	EV/Sales LTM	P/E FY0	EV/E..A-CX LTM	EV/Sales FY+3	EV/Sales FY-2	EV/Sales LTM	EV/Sales FY+2	P/Sales FY-1	EV/Sales FY-2	EV/OP CF FY+3	P/E STM	EV/Sales LTM	P/FCF FY-2	EV/E..ARD FY+1
	Σ 20	EV/Sales P/Sales	EV/Sales	P/Sales P/FCF P/E	P/FCF EV/E..A-CX EV/EBITDA	EV/Sales EV/EBITDA	EV/Sales EV/GM	EV/Sales EV/EBITDA	EV/Sales EV/E..A-CX	P/Sales EV/Sales	EV/GM P/E P/Sales	EV/EBITDA P/Sales EV/Sales	P/Sales P/FCF	EV/Sales P/Sales	P/Sales EV/Sales	EV/E..ARD P/FCF
		16-4-0	19-0-0	5-5-5	9-8-3	19-1-0	11-9-0	8-5-0	8-6-0	10-10-0	7-6-3	9-7-2	6-3-0	8-4-0	7-6-0	10-7-0
Multiples of top 10 drivers	1	EBIT Mar. FY+3	EBITDA Mar. STM	EPS Gr. LTM	GM Gr. FY+2	FCF/Sales NTM	S.Gr.+E..A% NTM	GM Gr. NTM	Net In. Gr. STM	FCF/Sales FY-2	GM Gr. LTM	E..A-CX Gr. LTM	E..A-CX Gr. NTM	DPS Gr. STM	Op.CF/Sal. FY0	FCF Gr. LTM
	2	EBIT Mar. FY+3	Net In. Gr. STM	EBITDA Gr. NTM	EPS Gr. LTM	E..A-CX M. STM	S.Gr.+E..A% FY+1	Net In. Gr. STM	DPS Gr. STM	FCF/Sales FY-2	GM Gr. FY0	EBITDA Gr. LTM	EBITDA Gr. FY+2	DPS Gr. STM	Sales Gr. LTM	Sales Gr. FY+2
	3	EBIT Mar. FY+3	EBITDA Mar. FY+3	EPS Gr. LTM	EBITDA Gr. NTM	FCF/Sales FY+2	S.Gr.+E..A% FY+1	Net In. Gr. STM	S.Gr.+E..A% NTM	FCF/Sales FY-2	GM Gr. LTM	Op.CF Gr. LTM	DPS Gr. FY+1	E..A-CX Gr. FY-1	Sales Gr. LTM	Sales Gr. FY+2
	4	EBIT Mar. FY+3	EBITDA Mar. FY+2	FCF/Sales FY+1	EPS Gr. LTM	E..A-CX M. FY+3	S.Gr.+E..A% NTM	EBITDA Gr. LTM	GM Gr. NTM	FCF/Sales FY-2	GM Gr. LTM	E..A-CX Gr. LTM	EBITDA Gr. NTM	DPS Gr. FY+3	Op.CF/Sal. FY0	Sales Gr. FY+2
	5	EBITDA Mar. STM	EBITDA Mar. STM	Net In. Gr. LTM	EBITDA Gr. FY+1	E..A-CX M. FY+3	E..A-CX M. FY0	E..A-CX Gr. LTM	S.Gr.+E..A% NTM	FCF/Sales FY-2	GM Gr. FY-1	GM Gr. NTM	Net In. Gr. LTM	DPS Gr. STM	S.Gr.+E..A% FY0	Sales Gr. NTM
	6	EBITDA Mar. STM	EBITDA Mar. STM	E..A-CX Gr. STM	FCF Gr. FY+3	E..A-CX M. FY+3	S.Gr.+E..A% FY-1	GM Gr. STM	FCF Gr. STM	FCF/Sales FY-2	EBIT Gr. FY+2	Sales Gr. NTM	DPS Gr. FY+1	EBIT Gr. FY0	EBIT Gr. FY-1	Op.CF Gr. STM
	7	S.Gr.+E..A% LTM	EBITDA Mar. STM	FCF/Sales FY+1	FCF Gr. FY+3	E..A-CX M. FY+3	S.Gr.+E..A% NTM	EPS Gr. LTM	Op.CF Gr. NTM	FCF/Sales FY-2	E..A-CX Gr. FY+3	GM Gr. NTM	EBITDA Gr. FY+1	E..A-CX Gr. FY0	Sales Gr. LTM	Sales Gr. NTM
	8	EBIT Mar. FY+3	EBITDA Mar. FY+3	EPS Gr. NTM	Net In. Gr. FY+1	E..A-CX M. LTM	S.Gr.+E..A% FY+1	S.Gr.+E..A% STM	S.Gr.+E..A% STM	FCF/Sales FY-2	GM Gr. FY+1	E..A-CX Gr. LTM	Net In. Gr. LTM	E..A-CX Gr. FY-1	Sales Gr. LTM	Op.CF Gr. STM
	9	EBITDA Mar. STM	EBITDA Mar. FY+3	EPS Gr. NTM	EPS Gr. LTM	E..A-CX M. FY+3	S.Gr.+E..A% FY-1	S.Gr.+E..A% STM	EPS Gr. STM	FCF/Sales FY-2	GM Gr. FY0	GM Gr. NTM	DPS Gr. FY+1	E..A-CX Gr. FY0	EBIT Mar. FY0	Sales Gr. NTM
	10	EBITDA Mar. FY+2	EBITDA Mar. NTM	Net In. Gr. LTM	GM Gr. FY+2	FCF/Sales FY+1	FCF/Sales LTM	S.Gr.+E..A% STM	S.Gr.+E..A% STM	GM Gr. FY0	GM Gr. FY0	EBITDA Gr. LTM	EPS Gr. LTM	E..A-CX Gr. FY0	EBIT Mar. SLTM	Sales Gr. NTM
	Σ 20	EBIT Mar. EBITDA Mar.	EBITDA Mar.	EPS Gr. FCF/Sales Net In. Gr.	FCF Gr. EBITDA Gr. GM Gr.	E..A-CX M. FCF/Sales	S.Gr.+E..A% E..A-CX M.	S.Gr.+E..A% GM Gr.	S.Gr.+E..A%	FCF/Sales	GM Gr. EBIT Gr.	EBITDA Gr. E..A-CX Gr.	EBITDA Gr. DPS Gr.	E..A-CX Gr. DPS Gr.	Sales Gr. Op.CF/Sal.	Sales Gr. Op.CF Gr.
		12-7-0	19-0-0	7-5-2	5-5-4	11-6-0	9-7-0	7-4-0	7-0-0	18-0-0	10-3-0	7-5-0	5-5-0	9-5-0	10-5-0	10-5-0

From the drivers' perspective, the complete analysis shows margin drivers in the first years, with RoA and RoE drivers quickly taking over. The last four years' growth drivers are shown as being the most relevant. In the analysis excluding balance sheet variables, the RoE and RoA drivers are replaced by the rule of 40 and various profitability growth rates. The last 2 years present Sales growth as being the best-fitting driver.

Based on the results, it can be concluded that the payment industry has shown some changes in the last year, with profitability multiples being the most relevant, however, such multiples are still driven by top-line growth. These conclusions can also be used for value-maximizing strategies.

7.2.17 Results for Platform Software Companies

The platform software cluster had a good starting point with 30 companies included, which enabled an analysis starting in 2007. 232 k regressions representing 60% of the total potential regressions, had sufficient observations, while nearly 123 k regressions showed the expected positive correlation. Nearly 33 k regressions were also statistically significant and will be included in the analysis. Table 7.40 presents the R-Squared values of the platform software companies' top 20 regressions yearly. The values are high and range between 70 and high 90s. Table 7.41 presents the results of the analysis.

Evaluating the analysis results, it can be observed that the most often encountered multiple is EV/EBITDA or variations thereof. This result is not surprising as the players in the platform software cluster are mature and have been conducting business for sometimes decades. It can also be observed that for some years, the EV/Asset multiple lands on the top position. This insight is surprising as companies in this segment usually do not have significant assets on their balance sheet. However, each year that shows the EV/Asset multiple as most relevant, the second or third relevant multiple is a profitability multiple. The last year is extremely EBITDA-focused, with EV/EBITDARD being the top multiple, P/FCF (a more conservative metric), and EV/EBITDA-CAPEX being the top 3 multiples. The year beforehand shows a similar conclusion.

Table 7.40 R^2 of top 20 regressions for platform software companies

#	'07	'08	'09	'10	'11	'12	'13	'14	'15	'16	'17	'18	'19	'20	'21
1	89	91	87	96	99	98	95	96	93	90	92	95	93	91	83
2	84	91	82	94	98	97	94	93	92	87	92	93	92	86	77
3	81	90	82	93	97	96	94	93	91	87	90	91	91	85	76
4	81	89	82	92	97	96	94	93	91	86	90	91	91	84	76
5	81	89	82	92	97	95	94	91	90	85	90	90	89	84	75
6	80	89	81	91	97	95	94	91	90	85	90	90	88	83	75
7	79	88	80	91	97	95	94	91	90	85	89	89	88	83	74
8	79	88	79	90	97	95	94	90	89	84	89	89	88	82	73
9	79	86	79	89	97	95	93	90	89	84	89	89	87	82	73
10	79	86	78	89	97	95	93	90	89	84	88	89	86	82	73
11	78	85	78	88	97	95	93	90	89	84	88	89	85	81	73
12	78	85	78	88	97	95	93	90	88	84	88	88	85	81	73
13	77	85	78	88	97	95	93	89	88	83	88	88	85	81	72
14	76	85	78	88	97	95	93	89	88	83	88	88	85	80	72
15	76	84	77	87	97	94	93	88	87	83	88	88	85	79	72
16	76	84	77	87	96	94	93	88	87	82	88	88	84	78	72
17	76	84	77	87	96	94	93	88	87	82	88	88	83	77	72
18	75	83	77	87	96	93	93	88	87	82	87	88	83	77	71
19	75	83	77	87	96	93	93	88	87	82	87	88	83	77	71
20	75	83	76	87	96	93	93	88	87	82	87	88	83	76	71

Diving into the results concerning the drivers of valuation in the platform software segment shows a profitability growth driver unanimously. The growth measure changes from being Sales growth during the first years of the analysis to various forms of profitability growth in the second half of the analysis period. Despite some years in the middle, switching between Sales growth and profitability growth, the last 5 years clearly show profitability growth drivers as the most important. The last year progresses from EBITDARD to Net Income growth, presenting an even more conservative driver.

It can be concluded that companies in the platform software segment trade on profitability multiples in particular (EV/EBITDARD) which are driven by growth in profitability expressed as Net Income growth or EBITDARD growth.

Table 7.41 Results of top best-fitting regressions for platform software companies

		2007	2008	2009	2010	2011	2012	2013	2014	2015	2016	2017	2018	2019	2020	2021
Multiples of top 10 regressions	1	EV/Sales FY-1	P/E NTM	EV/EBIT FY+1	EV/EBIT LTM	EV/EBIT FY+2	EV/Asset FY-2	EV/GM FY-2	EV/Asset FY-1	EV/Asset FY0	P/FCF FY+1	EV/EBIT FY-1	EV/EBIT LTM	EV/E..A-CX LTM	P/E FY-1	EV/E..ARD FY-1
	2	EV/Sales SLTM	EV/Sales FY-1	EV/EBIT NTM	EV/Asset FY0	EV/EBITDA FY+2	EV/Asset FY-2	EV/Sales STM	EV/Asset NTM	EV/EBITDA LTM	EV/EBIT LTM	EV/E..ARD NTM	EV/EBIT LTM	EV/EBIT LTM	P/E FY-1	EV/E..ARD NTM
	3	P/Sales FY-1	EV/EBITDA FY+1	EV/EBITDA FY+1	EV/EBITDA FY0	EV/E..A-CX FY+2	EV/Asset SLTM	EV/Sales NTM	EV/Asset FY+2	EV/Asset SLTM	EV/Asset SLTM	EV/E..ARD FY+2	EV/E..ARD FY-2	EV/EBIT LTM	EV/EBIT FY0	EV/E..ARD SLTM
	4	EV/Sales SLTM	P/Sales FY-1	EV/EBIT STM	EV/EBIT FY+1	EV/E..A-CX STM	EV/Asset FY-2	EV/Sales FY+2	EV/Asset FY+1	EV/Asset FY+1	P/FCF LTM	EV/EBIT FY-1	EV/EBIT FY+1	EV/EBITDA LTM	EV/E..ARD FY-2	EV/E..ARD FY+2
	5	EV/Sales SLTM	EV/OP CF LTM	EV/Sales FY-1	EV/OP CF SLTM	EV/EBITDA NTM	P/Sales FY+2	EV/Sales FY+2	EV/Asset SLTM	EV/Asset SLTM	EV/Asset FY-2	EV/EBITDA FY+1	EV/E..ARD NTM	EV/EBIT FY+1	EV/EBIT FY0	EV/E..A-CX STM
	6	EV/Sales FY-1	P/E FY+2	EV/Sales FY-2	EV/EBITDA FY0	EV/EBITDA FY0	P/Sales NTM	EV/Sales NTM	EV/E..ARD NTM	EV/Asset LTM	EV/E..ARD FY-2	EV/Asset FY-1	EV/E..ARD FY+1	EV/EBIT FY+1	P/E FY-1	P/B FY-2
	7	EV/Sales FY-1	EV/EBITDA STM	P/E NTM	EV/EBIT FY+1	P/E FY+2	EV/GM FY+2	EV/Sales FY-2	EV/Asset NTM	EV/EBITDA LTM	EV/EBIT FY+1	EV/EBITDA FY0	EV/EBIT FY+2	EV/EBIT FY+1	P/E SLTM	EV/E..ARD STM
	8	P/Sales SLTM	P/E STM	EV/EBIT NTM	EV/EBITDA FY0	P/E NTM	EV/GM FY+2	EV/Asset NTM	EV/E..ARD FY+2	EV/Asset FY0	EV/Asset FY+1	EV/E..ARD FY-2	EV/E..ARD FY+1	EV/EBIT SLTM	EV/EBITDA SLTM	EV/E..A-CX FY+2
	9	P/Sales FY-1	EV/EBIT LTM	EV/Sales FY-2	EV/OP CF FY0	EV/E..A-CX FY+3	EV/GM FY+2	EV/Asset FY+2	EV/GM LTM	EV/Asset SLTM	EV/Asset FY0	EV/E..ARD NTM	EV/E..ARD NTM	EV/E..ARD SLTM	P/E FY0	EV/E..A-CX NTM
	10	EV/Sales FY0	EV/EBITDA FY+2	P/Sales FY+3	EV/Asset SLTM	P/E NTM	EV/GM FY-2	EV/Asset STM	EV/Asset FY+1	EV/Asset FY0	EV/Asset FY-1	EV/EBIT SLTM	EV/E..ARD FY0	EV/Asset FY-2	EV/EBITDA SLTM	P/FCF FY0
	Σ 20	EV/Sales P/Sales	EV/EBITDA P/E P/Sales	EV/EBIT P/E P/Sales	EV/EBIT EV/Asset P/E	EV/EBIT P/E EV/EBITDA	EV/Asset P/Sales EV/GM	EV/Asset EV/Sales EV/GM	EV/Asset EV/GM EV/E..ARD	EV/Asset EV/EBITDA	EV/Asset EV/OP CF	EV/EBITDA EV/E..ARD EV/EBIT	EV/E..ARD EV/EBIT	EV/E..ARD EV/EBIT	P/E EV/E..ARD EV/EBITDA	EV/E..ARD P/FCF EV/E..A-CX
		13-7-0	7-5-3	7-4-3	5-5-3	7-5-5	6-5-5	8-7-5	11-4-3	17-3-0	11-3-0	6-6-4	16-4-0	9-8-0	7-6-3	8-6-3
Multiples of top 10 drivers	1	Sales Gr. FY0	EPS Gr. FY+2	Net In. Gr. STM	Net In. Gr. STM	Net In. Gr. FY+2	EPS Gr. FY+2	E..A-CX Gr. STM	Op.CF Gr. FY+1	E..A-CX Gr. FY+2	GM Gr. LTM	EBIT Gr. STM	E..ARD Gr. FY+3	E..ARD Gr. NTM	E..ARD Gr. LTM	E..A-CX Gr. FY+1
	2	Sales Gr. FY0	Sales Gr. FY-1	Net In. Gr. STM	GM Gr. STM	Net In. Gr. FY+2	EBIT Gr. FY+2	Op.CF Gr. FY+3	Net In. Gr. FY+3	Sales Gr. FY+3	FCF Gr. STM	GM Gr. FY0	E..ARD Gr. NTM	E..ARD Gr. FY0	E..ARD Gr. FY+1	Net In. Gr. FY-1
	3	Sales Gr. FY0	EBIT Gr. FY+2	Net In. Gr. STM	Net In. Gr. STM	Net In. Gr. FY+2	EBIT Gr. STM	Op.CF Gr. STM	Net In. Gr. FY+3	E..A-CX Gr. FY+2	EPS Gr. FY0	GM Gr. FY0	Sales Gr. LTM	E..ARD Gr. NTM	E..ARD Gr. LTM	E..A-CX Gr. FY+1
	4	Sales Gr. STM	Sales Gr. FY-1	Sales Gr. FY+2	Net In. Gr. STM	Net In. Gr. FY+2	EBIT Gr. NTM	Op.CF Gr. FY+3	Net In. Gr. FY+3	E..A-CX Gr. FY+2	Sales Gr. LTM	Op.CF Gr. LTM	E..ARD Gr. NTM	E..ARD Gr. NTM	Sales Gr. FY0	Net In. Gr. FY-1
	5	Sales Gr. FY+3	Sales Gr. FY+2	Sales Gr. FY0	GM Gr. STM	Net In. Gr. FY+2	E..A-CX Gr. FY+3	Op.CF Gr. STM	Op.CF Gr. FY+1	Sales Gr. STM	Sales Gr. STM	E..ARD Gr. FY0	Sales Gr. FY0	E..ARD Gr. NTM	E..ARD Gr. FY0	E..ARD Gr. FY+1
	6	Sales Gr. STM	EPS Gr. FY+2	Sales Gr. LTM	Sales Gr. FY+3	Net In. Gr. STM	E..A-CX Gr. FY+3	Op.CF Gr. FY+3	GM Gr. FY+3	E..A-CX Gr. FY+2	EBIT Gr. STM	EPS Gr. FY-1	GM Gr. LTM	E..ARD Gr. FY0	E..ARD Gr. FY0	S.Gr.+E..A% NTM
	7	Sales Gr. FY+3	Sales Gr. FY+1	Sales Gr. STM	Sales Gr. FY+3	Net In. Gr. FY+2	E..ARD Gr. STM	E..A-CX Gr. STM	E..A-CX Gr. FY+3	GM Gr. FY+3	E..ARD Gr. FY+1	GM Gr. FY0	E..ARD Gr. NTM	GM Gr. FY-1	E..ARD Gr. LTM	Net In. Gr. FY-1
	8	Sales Gr. FY+3	EPS Gr. FY+2	Sales Gr. FY+2	GM Gr. STM	Net In. Gr. FY+2	E..ARD Gr. FY+2	GM Gr. FY+2	GM Gr. FY+3	Net In. Gr. FY+2	Sales Gr. FY+1	EBIT Gr. FY+1	GM Gr. FY+1	GM Gr. FY0	E..ARD Gr. FY0	E..ARD Gr. FY+1
	9	Sales Gr. FY+3	Net In. Gr. FY+2	Sales Gr. FY0	GM Gr. STM	Net In. Gr. FY+2	E..ARD Gr. FY+3	GM Gr. FY+2	E..ARD Gr. NTM	Sales Gr. FY+3	Sales Gr. FY+1	Sales Gr. LTM	E..ARD Gr. LTM	GM Gr. LTM	E..ARD Gr. FY0	E..ARD Gr. FY+1
	10	Sales Gr. FY0	Sales Gr. FY+1	S.Gr.+E..A% FY+2	GM Gr. STM	EPS Gr. STM	Op.CF Gr. STM	GM Gr. FY+2	E..A-CX Gr. FY+3	EPS Gr. FY+2	EPS Gr. FY0	GM Gr. FY0	GM Gr. FY+1	Net In. Gr. FY0	E..ARD Gr. LTM	GM Gr. FY+1
	Σ 20	Sales Gr.	Sales Gr. EPS Gr.	Sales Gr. Net In. Gr. S.Gr.+E..A%	Sales Gr. GM Gr. Net In. Gr.	Net In. Gr. EPS Gr.	E..ARD Gr. EBIT Gr.	Op.CF Gr. GM Gr.	Sales Gr. Net In. Gr. E..ARD Gr.	Net In. Gr. Sales Gr. GM Gr.	Sales Gr. GM Gr. EPS Gr.	GM Gr. Sales Gr. EBIT Gr.	GM Gr. Sales Gr. E..ARD Gr.	E..ARD Gr. GM Gr. Sales Gr.	E..ARD Gr. Sales Gr. Net In. Gr.	Net In. Gr. E..ARD Gr. Sales Gr.
		20-0-0	11-3-0	12-5-2	9-5-4	15-3-0	7-4-0	6-6-0	4-4-4	4-3-3	7-5-3	7-4-3	10-5-5	8-6-3	14-3-3	5-5-4

7.2.18 Results for Security Software Companies

With 73 companies included in the cluster and over 350 k regressions with sufficient observations representing over 90% of the total potential in regressions, the security software cluster of companies is one of the best-covered segments in the study. The cluster also showed over 196 k regressions, with the expected positive correlation representing c. 50% of all potential regressions. Lastly, over 56 k regressions were statistically significant, resulting in excellent coverage of over 14% of the potential regressions. Table 7.42 presents the R-Squared values of the top 20 regressions each year, with values ranging from 57 to 92. Table 7.43 presents the analysis results with the top 10 regressions and the conclusions derived from the top 20 regressions.

Table 7.42 R^2 of top 20 regressions for security software companies

#	'07	'08	'09	'10	'11	'12	'13	'14	'15	'16	'17	'18	'19	'20	'21
1	92	89	81	81	89	92	89	78	85	83	75	80	74	74	84
2	89	89	79	80	88	91	86	78	82	82	75	76	72	72	80
3	87	87	78	79	88	91	86	75	81	81	72	74	70	70	76
4	86	87	78	78	87	90	83	75	81	81	71	74	70	70	75
5	86	86	78	77	86	89	83	71	81	81	71	74	69	69	71
6	85	86	78	76	86	89	82	70	80	81	67	73	69	69	65
7	84	86	78	76	85	88	82	70	79	80	67	71	69	69	63
8	84	86	78	75	84	88	81	70	78	80	67	70	68	68	63
9	83	86	77	74	84	87	81	69	76	80	66	69	67	68	63
10	83	85	77	73	83	87	81	69	76	79	66	68	67	68	61
11	83	85	77	72	83	86	80	69	76	79	66	68	67	67	61
12	82	84	77	72	82	86	80	69	76	79	66	67	67	67	60
13	82	83	77	72	82	86	79	69	75	79	66	67	66	65	60
14	81	82	77	72	81	86	79	68	74	79	65	67	66	65	59
15	81	82	76	71	80	85	79	68	74	78	65	66	65	65	59
16	81	82	76	70	80	85	78	68	74	78	65	66	64	64	59
17	80	82	76	70	80	85	78	67	73	78	64	66	63	64	59
18	80	81	76	70	80	85	78	67	72	77	64	65	63	64	58
19	79	81	74	70	79	84	78	67	72	77	64	65	63	63	58
20	79	80	74	70	79	84	78	67	72	77	64	64	63	63	57

Table 7.43 Results of top best-fitting regressions for security software companies

		2007	2008	2009	2010	2011	2012	2013	2014	2015	2016	2017	2018	2019	2020	2021
Multiples of top 10 regressions	1	EV/Asset FY+3	P/B FY+2	EV/EBITDA FY+3	EV/E..ARD FY+3	EV/Asset FY+2	EV/Asset FY+2	EV/Asset STM	EV/OP CF FY-1	EV/Sales FY-2	EV/E..ARD SLTM	EV/E..ARD FY-2	EV/E..ARD FY-2	EV/EBIT SLTM	EV/EBIT FY-2	EV/E..A-CX FY-2
	2	EV/Asset FY+2	P/B FY+2	P/Sales SLTM	EV/E..ARD STM	EV/Asset STM	EV/Asset NTM	EV/Asset STM	EV/OP CF SLTM	EV/E..ARD FY+2	EV/E..ARD FY0	EV/EBIT LTM	EV/E..ARD FY-2	EV/E..A-CX FY+1	EV/E..A-CX FY-2	P/FCF LTM
	3	EV/Asset FY+3	P/Sales FY+3	P/Sales FY0	EV/E..ARD SLTM	EV/Asset FY+3	EV/Asset FY+2	EV/Asset STM	EV/E..ARD FY+1	EV/E..ARD STM	EV/E..ARD SLTM	EV/E..A-CX FY+1	EV/E..ARD FY-2	EV/EBITDA FY+1	EV/E..A-CX FY0	P/FCF LTM
	4	EV/Asset FY+1	P/Sales FY+3	P/FCF FY-2	EV/E..ARD FY+2	EV/Asset NTM	EV/Asset FY+2	EV/E..ARD FY0	EV/EBIT SLTM	P/Sales FY-2	EV/E..ARD LTM	EV/E..A-CX LTM	EV/EBIT FY0	EV/EBIT FY0	EV/EBIT FY-2	EV/OP CF FY+1
	5	EV/Asset FY+3	P/Sales NTM	EV/Sales FY0	EV/E..ARD NTM	EV/Asset FY+3	EV/Asset NTM	EV/E..ARD LTM	EV/OP CF FY0	EV/E..ARD LTM	EV/E..ARD LTM	EV/E..A-CX NTM	EV/EBIT FY-2	EV/EBIT SLTM	EV/EBITDA LTM	EV/OP CF FY+1
	6	P/B FY+3	P/Sales FY0	EV/Sales SLTM	EV/E..ARD SLTM	EV/Asset FY+2	EV/Asset FY+2	EV/Asset STM	EV/OP CF FY0	EV/E..ARD FY+1	EV/OP CF FY0	EV/EBIT FY0	EV/E..ARD FY-2	EV/EBIT FY-1	EV/E..ARD LTM	EV/EBIT FY-1
	7	EV/Asset STM	P/B NTM	EV/Sales FY0	EV/E..ARD FY+3	EV/Asset STM	EV/Asset NTM	EV/EBITDA FY+3	EV/OP CF LTM	EV/E..ARD NTM	EV/E..ARD SLTM	P/E LTM	EV/EBIT SLTM	EV/EBITDA FY+1	P/FCF SLTM	P/E FY-1
	8	EV/Asset NTM	P/Sales FY+2	EV/Sales SLTM	EV/E..ARD FY+1	EV/Asset NTM	EV/Asset FY+1	EV/Asset FY+2	EV/E..ARD FY-2	EV/E..A-CX SLTM	EV/E..ARD SLTM	EV/E..ARD LTM	EV/E..ARD FY0	EV/EBIT FY-2	EV/E..ARD FY-2	EV/E..A-CX SLTM
	9	P/Sales STM	P/B NTM	EV/Sales SLTM	EV/E..ARD STM	EV/Asset FY+1	EV/Asset NTM	EV/Asset FY+2	EV/OP CF SLTM	EV/E..ARD FY+1	EV/E..ARD SLTM	EV/E..ARD FY-1	EV/EBIT SLTM	EV/E..ARD LTM	EV/E..A-CX LTM	EV/E..ARD LTM
	10	P/Sales LTM	P/B FY+2	EV/Sales FY0	EV/E..ARD FY+3	EV/EBITDA LTM	EV/Asset LTM	EV/E..ARD SLTM	EV/E..ARD NTM	EV/E..ARD FY0	EV/EBITDA FY+2	EV/E..ARD LTM	EV/E..ARD LTM	EV/E..A-CX FY+1	EV/EBITDA FY+1	EV/E..A-CX FY-2
	Σ 20	EV/Asset P/Sales P/B	P/Sales P/B EV/GM	EV/Sales P/Sales P/FCF	EV/E..ARD EV/Sales	EV/Asset EV/EBITDA	EV/Asset EV/E..ARD	EV/Asset EV/E..ARD P/B	EV/OP CF EV/E..ARD P/B	EV/E..ARD P/E P/Sales	EV/E..ARD EV/EBITDA EV/OP CF	EV/E..ARD EV/EBIT EV/E..A-CX	EV/E..ARD EV/EBIT P/FCF	EV/EBIT EV/E..A-CX EV/EBITDA	EV/E..A-CX EV/E..ARD EV/EBITDA	EV/E..A-CX P/FCF EV/OP CF
		9-7-2	11-8-1	12-5-1	15-5-0	17-3-0	19-1-0	12-5-1	9-7-1	11-3-1	17-2-1	10-3-3	10-6-2	8-4-3	6-5-4	5-4-4
Multiples of top 10 drivers	1	Sales Gr. FY+1	RoE FY+3	FCF Gr. FY-1	Sales Gr. LTM	GM Gr. STM	E..ARD Gr. STM	S.Gr.+E..A% FY+1	E..ARD Gr. FY+3	DPS Gr. STM	Sales Gr. STM	Sales Gr. FY0	GM Gr. STM	E..ARD Gr. STM	E..ARD Gr. FY0	E..ARD Gr. LTM
	2	Sales Gr. FY+1	RoE STM	FCF/Sales FY-2	Sales Gr. LTM	GM Gr. STM	E..ARD Gr. STM	S.Gr.+E..A% LTM	E..ARD Gr. NTM	Sales Gr. FY+1	E..ARD Gr. STM	E..ARD Gr. STM	GM Gr. FY+3	E..ARD Gr. STM	E..ARD Gr. LTM	DPS Gr. FY+2
	3	Sales Gr. FY+3	FCF/Sales FY-1	FCF/Sales FY-2	GM Gr. FY+2	GM Gr. STM	S.Gr.+E..A% FY+1	S.Gr.+E..A% FY+2	E..A-CX Gr. STM	Sales Gr. FY+1	Sales Gr. FY+2	E..ARD Gr. STM	Sales Gr. FY+3	E..ARD Gr. FY+3	E..ARD Gr. FY+2	DPS Gr. FY+3
	4	Sales Gr. FY+1	FCF/Sales SLTM	EBIT Gr. FY-1	Sales Gr. LTM	GM Gr. STM	E..ARD Gr. FY+2	E..ARD Gr. LTM	E..ARD Gr. FY+2	DPS Gr. STM	GM Gr. STM	E..ARD Gr. STM	E..ARD Gr. STM	E..ARD Gr. STM	E..ARD Gr. LTM	E..ARD Gr. FY+3
	5	Sales Gr. NTM	FCF/Sales SLTM	Op.CF/Sal. NTM	Sales Gr. LTM	GM Gr. FY+3	E..ARD Gr. FY+2	E..ARD Gr. LTM	E..ARD Gr. FY+3	Sales Gr. FY+1	Sales Gr. STM	E..ARD Gr. STM	Sales Gr. FY+3	E..ARD Gr. FY+3	E..ARD Gr. STM	E..ARD Gr. STM
	6	Sales Gr. FY+1	FCF/Sales SLTM	Op.CF/Sal. NTM	GM Gr. LTM	GM Gr. FY+3	GM Gr. STM	E..ARD Gr. STM	E..ARD Gr. STM	Sales Gr. FY+1	E..ARD Gr. FY+2	Sales Gr. LTM	Sales Gr. STM	E..ARD Gr. STM	E..ARD Gr. STM	E..ARD Gr. STM
	7	Sales Gr. FY+1	RoE FY+3	Op.CF/Sal. STM	Sales Gr. FY+1	GM Gr. FY+3	S.Gr.+E..A% FY+1	E..ARD Gr. LTM	E..ARD Gr. NTM	Sales Gr. FY+1	GM Gr. FY+2	E..ARD Gr. STM	E..ARD Gr. FY+3	E..ARD Gr. STM	Net In. Gr. FY 1	E..ARD Gr. STM
	8	Sales Gr. FY+1	FCF/Sales SLTM	Op.CF/Sal. STM	Sales Gr. LTM	GM Gr. FY+3	GM Gr. FY+2	E..ARD Gr. STM	GM Gr. LTM	DPS Gr. STM	Sales Gr. FY0	Sales Gr. FY0	GM Gr. STM	E..ARD Gr. LTM	GM Gr. STM	E..ARD Gr. STM
	9	FCF/Sales FY+3	RoE STM	Op.CF/Sal. FY+2	Sales Gr. FY+1	GM Gr. STM	GM Gr. STM	S.Gr.+E..A% FY+2	E..ARD Gr. STM	GM Gr. STM	GM Gr. STM	Sales Gr. FY0	E..ARD Gr. STM	Sales Gr. FY+3	E..ARD Gr. FY+3	GM Gr. STM
	10	FCF/Sales FY+3	RoE FY+2	Op.CF/Sal. FY+2	GM Gr. LTM	DPS Gr. FY+1	GM Gr. FY+2	GM Gr. LTM	Net In. Gr. STM	Sales Gr. FY+1	E..ARD Gr. FY+2	Sales Gr. LTM	Sales Gr. FY-1	E..ARD Gr. FY+3	E..ARD Gr. STM	E..ARD Gr. FY0
	Σ 20	Sales Gr. FCF/Sales	FCF/Sales RoE GM Gr.	Op.CF/Sal. FCF/Sales EBIT Gr.	Sales Gr. FCF/Sales GM Gr.	GM Gr. EBIT Gr. DPS Gr.	S.Gr.+E..A% GM Gr. E..ARD Gr.	E..ARD Gr. S.Gr.+E..A% GM Gr.	E..ARD Gr. Net In. Gr. Sales Gr.	Sales Gr. E..ARD Gr. GM Gr.	Sales Gr. E..ARD Gr. GM Gr.	Sales Gr. E..ARD Gr. EBIT Gr.	Sales Gr. E..ARD Gr. GM Gr.	E..ARD Gr. Sales Gr. EBITDA Gr.	E..ARD Gr. GM Gr. Sales Gr.	E..ARD Gr. DPS Gr. GM Gr.
		11-9-0	12-6-2	12-5-2	11-5-4	10-7-3	8-6-6	10-7-2	11-3-1	7-6-4	10-6-4	12-7-1	8-7-5	16-2-1	16-2-1	10-4-2

Evaluating the results concerning the multiples, a certain evaluation from Sales multiples to profitability multiples can be observed with some year EV/Assets coming out at the top. Looking at the P&L multiples, it can be observed that the first three years clearly show Sales multiples as being the most relevant, while in the following years, a clear switch towards EBITDA and similar multiples can be observed. This evolution is to be expected with a maturing industry. Considering that some of these companies have been in business since the beginning of the internet, such a transaction could have also happened in the past. Some of the reasons for the transition happening so late can be the increased focus on cyber-security over the past 15 years, the transition towards more recurring business models focusing on monthly fees as opposed to the sale of appliances, and the increased number of solutions and modules such companies sell. An additional interesting finding is the emergence of the EBITDA-CAPEX multiple as the main driver because companies in this segment often are CAPEX heavy (especially concerning their own developments). This finding suggests that investors look at profitability before such investments.

Drivers of the valuation multiples in the security software sector also show a certain evolution from Sales growth drivers to margin drivers in the year 2012 and 2013, back to Sales growth until 2013 with some small interruptions in the direction of the rule of 40 and EBITDA growth. The last three consistently show EBITDARD Growth as the key driver, followed by other growth measures each year.

It is fairly safe to conclude that companies in the security software cluster trade on an EV/EBITDA-CAPEX bases driven by EBITDARD growth. Both variables highlight that while profitability is important, investors are happy to exclude the CAPEX and R&D costs as part of the valuation. These conclusions can also be used as managerial and strategic recommendations for management teams and stakeholders in this industry.

7.2.19 Results for Social Network Companies

The social network cluster analysis yields less optimal results. Despite the business model existing since almost the beginning of the internet, as discussed at the beginning of the study, it is an industry that is often characterized by a winner takes it all model. This fact is reflected in the low number of players. This study identified only 15 comparable companies, which despite existing for some time, allow only for an analysis starting in 2015. The 15 companies generated 54 k regressions with sufficient observations, yielding nearly 37 k regressions with the necessary positive slope. Lastly, the study was surprising, with few statistically significant regressions. Only 5,084 regressions were statistically significant and could be used for the analysis. Table 7.44 presents the R-Squared values of the top 20 regressions in each year, while Table 7.45 presents the top 10 regressions and the summary of the results as derived from the top 20 regressions. The R-squared values are less good for some of the years, however, they are less optimal for the first two years of the study.

Table 7.44 R^2 of top 20 regressions for social network companies

#	'15	'16	'17	'18	'19	'20	'21
1	58	65	84	84	80	84	85
2	56	64	81	83	79	81	84
3	55	63	80	82	78	81	84
4	51	62	80	82	78	80	83
5	50	60	78	77	78	80	82
6	49	59	77	74	78	80	82
7	48	59	77	74	78	80	81
8	48	58	77	73	77	79	81
9	48	57	77	72	77	79	80
10	46	57	76	72	77	79	80
11	46	56	76	71	77	78	79

(continued)

Table 7.44 (continued)

#	'15	'16	'17	'18	'19	'20	'21
12	45	55	76	71	76	78	79
13	44	55	75	71	76	78	79
14	44	55	74	71	75	78	79
15	44	54	74	71	75	77	79
16	43	54	74	69	75	77	78
17	42	53	74	69	75	77	78
18	41	53	74	69	74	77	78
19	40	53	74	69	74	76	78
20	40	52	74	69	74	76	77

The summary multiples show a mix of bases changing from year to year without a clear development pattern. The first year shows P/Sales at the top, with the second year presenting Price to Earning as the winning multiple, while the 3rd year shows EV/Gross Margin. The 4th and 6th years return to Sales multiples, while the 5th presents an EBITDA multiple and the last year a Price to Book value multiple.

Reviewing the drivers, a pattern around growth can be recognized, with the rule of 40 being most relevant in half of the years and other growth multiples being relevant in the rest of the year. The last year presents RoE as the top driver.

Based on the analysis and the discussion, it is difficult to make a resilient recommendation as there is no clear development trend. It is just as difficult to recommend anything for the management teams or stakeholders looking to optimize valuation in this segment.

Table 7.45 Results of top best-fitting regressions for social network companies

		2015	2016	2017	2018	2019	2020	2021
Multiples of top 20 regressions	1	P/Sales LTM	P/E FY+1	P/B FY0	P/B FY-1	EV/EBITDA FY+2	EV/EBITDA FY+2	EV/EBITDA FY+1
	2	P/Sales LTM	P/E FY+1	EV/GM FY0	P/Sales FY-2	EV/EBITDA FY+2	P/B FY-2	P/B LTM
	3	P/E NTM	P/E FY+1	EV/GM FY0	P/Sales FY-2	EV/EBITDA FY+2	P/B FY-1	P/B LTM
	4	P/Sales LTM	P/E FY+1	EV/GM FY+1	P/Sales FY-2	P/B LTM	EV/Sales FY-2	EV/EBITDA NTM
	5	P/Sales LTM	P/Sales SLTM	EV/GM FY+1	P/Sales FY-2	EV/EBITDA STM	EV/EBITDA FY+2	P/B FY+1
	6	P/Sales FY+1	P/E LTM	EV/GM FY0	P/Sales FY-1	EV/EBITDA FY+2	EV/GM FY-2	P/B FY+1
	7	P/Sales LTM	P/E LTM	EV/GM FY0	P/Sales FY-2	EV/EBITDA STM	EV/Sales FY-1	EV/EBITDA FY+2
	8	P/Sales FY+1	P/E FY+1	EV/GM FY0	P/Sales FY-1	EV/EBITDA FY+2	EV/EBITDA FY+2	P/B NTM
	9	P/E NTM	P/Sales SLTM	EV/Sales SLTM	P/Sales FY-2	EV/EBITDA FY+2	EV/EBITDA FY+2	P/B FY+2
	10	P/E NTM	P/B FY+1	EV/GM FY0	P/Sales FY-1	P/B FY+1	EV/Sales FY-2	P/B NTM
	11	P/E FY+2	P/E LTM	P/B LTM	P/B SLTM	EV/EBITDA STM	EV/EBITDA FY+2	P/B STM
	12	P/B FY+1	P/E NTM	EV/GM NTM	P/Sales SLTM	EV/EBITDA FY+2	EV/EBITDA FY+2	P/B FY+3
	13	P/B FY+1	P/E LTM	EV/GM FY0	P/Sales FY-2	EV/EBITDA STM	EV/Sales FY-1	P/B FY+2
	14	P/Sales LTM	EV/E..A-CX FY+1	P/E LTM	EV/Sales SLTM	EV/EBITDA STM	EV/Sales SLTM	EV/EBITDA STM
	15	P/Sales FY+1	EV/EBIT FY+1	EV/GM LTM	EV/Sales FY-1	P/B FY0	P/B SLTM	P/B SLTM
	16	P/Sales FY+1	EV/EBIT FY+1	EV/GM LTM	EV/Sales SLTM	EV/EBITDA STM	EV/GM FY-2	P/B STM
	17	P/B FY+1	EV/EBIT FY+1	EV/Sales FY0	P/Sales FY-2	EV/EBITDA STM	EV/GM FY-1	P/B SLTM
	18	P/B NTM	P/FCF NTM	EV/GM FY+2	EV/Sales SLTM	EV/GM FY-2	EV/Sales FY0	P/B FY+3
	19	P/B FY+2	EV/E..A-CX FY+1	P/B FY+1	EV/Sales FY-1	P/B LTM	EV/EBITDA STM	EV/EBITDA LTM
	20	P/E NTM	P/FCF FY+2	EV/EBIT FY+3	EV/GM FY-1	EV/EBITDA FY+2	EV/Sales SLTM	P/B FY0
	Σ 20	P/Sales P/E P/B	P/E EV/EBIT	EV/GM P/B	P/Sales EV/Sales	EV/EBITDA P/B	EV/Sales EV/EBITDA P/B	P/B EV/EBITDA
		10-5-5	10-3-0	13-3-0	12-5-0	15-4-0	7-7-3	15-5-0
Multiples of top 20 drivers	1	S.Gr.+E..A% STM	EPS Gr. STM	RoE FY+3	RoE FY+3	E..A-CX Gr. NTM	E..A-CX Gr. STM	E..A-CX Gr. NTM
	2	S.Gr.+E..A% FY+3	EBITDA Gr. STM	GM Gr. NTM	S.Gr.+E..A% FY+3	EPS Gr. FY+3	RoE FY+3	RoE FY+3
	3	Sales Gr. FY+3	EBITDA Gr. FY+3	GM Gr. FY+1	S.Gr.+E..A% NTM	Op.CF Gr. STM	RoE FY+3	RoE STM
	4	Sales Gr. STM	EPS Gr. FY+3	S.Gr.+E..A% FY+2	S.Gr.+E..A% FY+2	RoE STM	S.Gr.+E..A% FY+3	E..A-CX Gr. NTM
	5	Sales Gr. FY+3	S.Gr.+E..A% FY+2	S.Gr.+E..A% NTM	EBITDA Mar. FY+3	E..A-CX Gr. NTM	E..A-CX Gr. FY+3	RoE FY+3
	6	S.Gr.+E..A% STM	EBITDA Gr. FY+3	Sales Gr. NTM	S.Gr.+E..A% NTM	E..A-CX Gr. FY+3	S.Gr.+E..A% FY+2	RoE STM
	7	S.Gr.+E..A% FY+2	EPS Gr. FY+3	Sales Gr. FY+1	EBITDA Mar. STM	EPS Gr. FY+3	S.Gr.+E..A% FY+3	E..A-CX Gr. NTM
	8	S.Gr.+E..A% FY+3	E..A-CX Gr. STM	S.Gr.+E..A% FY+1	S.Gr.+E..A% FY+2	FCF Gr. FY+3	EPS Gr. FY+3	RoE FY+3
	9	EPS Gr. FY+3	S.Gr.+E..A% NTM	S.Gr.+E..A% FY+2	S.Gr.+E..A% STM	E..A-CX Gr. STM	Op.CF Gr. STM	RoE FY+3
	10	Sales Gr. STM	RoE FY+3	S.Gr.+E..A% NTM	S.Gr.+E..A% FY+3	RoE STM	S.Gr.+E..A% STM	RoE STM
	11	Sales Gr. FY+3	EPS Gr. STM	RoE FY+3	RoE FY+3	Op.CF Gr. STM	EBITDA Gr. STM	RoE FY+3
	12	Asset Tur. FY+3	Net In. Gr. STM	S.Gr.+E..A% FY+2	S.Gr.+E..A% FY+3	Op.CF Gr. FY+3	Op.CF Gr. FY+3	RoE FY+3
	13	RoE FY+3	EBITDA Gr. STM	Sales Gr. FY+2	EBITDA Mar. FY+2	E..A-CX Gr. FY+3	S.Gr.+E..A% STM	RoE STM
	14	Sales Gr. FY+2	EPS Gr. STM	EPS Gr. FY+3	S.Gr.+E..A% FY+3	FCF Gr. FY+3	S.Gr.+E..A% FY+3	E..A-CX Gr. NTM
	15	Sales Gr. FY+3	EBITDA Gr. FY+3	GM Gr. NTM	S.Gr.+E..A% NTM	RoE FY+3	RoE FY+3	RoE STM
	16	Sales Gr. STM	EBITDA Gr. STM	S.Gr.+E..A% NTM	S.Gr.+E..A% FY+2	Op.CF Gr. FY+3	S.Gr.+E..A% NTM	RoE STM
	17	Asset Tur. STM	Op.CF Gr. FY+2	S.Gr.+E..A% FY+2	EBITDA Mar. NTM	E..A-CX Gr. STM	S.Gr.+E..A% FY+2	RoE FY+3
	18	Asset Tur. FY+3	E..A-CX Gr. FY+3	S.Gr.+E..A% FY+2	S.Gr.+E..A% NTM	S.Gr.+E..A% LTM	S.Gr.+E..A% FY+3	RoE STM
	19	Asset Tur. FY+3	EPS Gr. FY+3	RoE FY+3	S.Gr.+E..A% FY+2	RoE FY+3	E..A-CX Gr. STM	E..A-CX Gr. NTM
	20	EBITDA Gr. FY+3	E..A-CX Gr. FY+3	Net In. Gr. NTM	S.Gr.+E..A% LTM	EBITDA Gr. STM	S.Gr.+E..A% STM	RoE STM
	Σ 20	Sales Gr. S.Gr.+E..A%	EPS Gr. EBITDA Gr.	S.Gr.+E..A% Sales Gr.	S.Gr.+E..A% EBITDA Mar.	E..A-CX Gr. RoE Op.CF Gr.	S.Gr.+E..A%	RoE E..A-CX Gr.
		8-5-0	6-6-0	9-3-0	14-4-0	6-4-4	10-0-0	15-5-0

7.2.20 Results for Travel Companies

The travel industry cluster consisted of 21 companies that were public for a period enabling an analysis starting with 2014. The dataset showed nearly 125 k regressions with sufficient observations (at a threshold of 10 observations per regression), from which nearly 82 k had the required positive correlation between base and driver. About every 4th regression was then statistically significant, yielding over 19 k usable regressions. Table 7.46 presents the R-Squared values of the results containing all variables. The values are well over 75. The second analysis, excluding balance sheet variables, showed lower values, however, also above 70. Table 7.47 presents the results from the analysis containing all regressions, while Table 7.48 shows the analysis results excluding balance sheet variables. Before diving into the interpretation, it is worth noting that the travel industry was one of the most affected by the COVID-19 crisis, and this fact will mostly impact the results for 2020 and 2021. Furthermore, the analysis, including all variables, shows a strong dependence on book value multiples for the last 3 years, which despite being relevant in the light of COVID-19, it does not help with management recommendations. Consequently, two analyses were performed.

Table 7.46 R^2 of top 20 regressions for travel companies

#	'14	'15	'16	'17	'18	'19	'20	'21
1	90	87	90	89	90	89	93	88
2	90	87	88	89	90	88	92	86
3	87	84	88	88	89	88	90	85
4	87	84	87	88	89	87	90	85
5	87	83	87	87	87	87	89	83
6	87	83	86	86	87	86	88	83
7	86	82	86	85	86	86	88	82
8	86	82	84	85	86	86	88	81
9	86	82	84	85	86	86	88	81
10	86	82	83	84	86	85	88	80
11	85	82	82	84	86	85	86	80
12	85	82	82	84	86	85	86	79
13	85	82	80	84	85	85	85	79

(continued)

Table 7.46 (continued)

#	'14	'15	'16	'17	'18	'19	'20	'21
14	85	82	80	84	85	85	84	78
15	84	82	79	83	85	85	84	78
16	84	81	79	83	85	85	84	78
17	84	81	78	83	85	85	83	77
18	84	81	78	83	84	85	83	76
19	83	81	78	83	84	85	83	76
20	83	81	78	83	84	85	83	76

Evaluating the multiples, it can be seen that the period 2014–2017 was entirely based on EV/EBITDA and Price to Earning multiples. This factor is not surprising for an industry as mature as the online travel industry. Starting with 2018 (well before COVID-19), it can be seen that Price to Book is taking over as the leading base, with either EV/EBITDA or a Sales multiple being the second multiple. 2021 even shows Price to Earnings as the second multiple. Overlapping the results with the results excluding balance sheet multiples, it can be observed that 2018 has an EBITDA multiple as the lead in the second analysis, while 2019 shows Price to Sales as the leading base. The COVID-19 years show by a margin the EV to Gross Margin multiple as being the most relevant. This finding is not surprising as some travel companies can recognize some of the sales volume (e.g., the entire price) as revenues instead of just the commissions, and hence the Gross Margin is the most comparable "top line."

Analyzing the drivers, it can be observed that the rule of 40 was, together with EBITDA-CAPEX growth, were the main drivers in the pre-COVID-19 years. While the analysis containing all drivers shows a mix of RoE and RoA for the last 4 years, the analysis excluding balance sheet variables shows various margin drivers in the COVID-19 years (EBITDA, EBIT Margin, and Operative Cash Flow margin).

Despite these clear trends of EBITDA multiples before COVID-19 and the EV to Gross Margin multiples during the COVID-19 years and relatable driver development, it is impossible to extrapolate the current bases and drivers of valuation for companies in this sector in the post-COVID-19 world. 2022 was an extraordinarily good year for companies in this segment, so deriving a conclusion of use to management can only be done after a thorough revelation.

Table 7.47 Results of top best-fitting regressions for travel companies

Multiples of top 20 regressions	2014	2015	2016	2017	2018	2019	2020	2021
1	P/E STM	EV/EBITDA FY-1	P/E FY+2	EV/OP CF STM	EV/Sales FY-2	P/B LTM	P/B FY0	P/B FY-1
2	P/E STM	P/E STM	P/E NTM	EV/OP CF FY+3	EV/EBITDA FY-2	P/B FY+1	P/B SLTM	EV/EBIT FY-1
3	P/E STM	P/E FY-1	EV/EBITDA FY-2	EV/EBITDA NTM	EV/EBITDA FY-2	P/B NTM	P/B LTM	P/B FY-2
4	P/E FY+3	EV/EBITDA SLTM	EV/E..A-CX FY-2	EV/EBITDA FY+2	P/B STM	P/B FY+2	P/B FY0	P/B FY-1
5	P/E FY+3	P/E FY+2	EV/EBITDA SLTM	P/E LTM	P/B SLTM	P/B FY+1	P/B SLTM	P/B FY-1
6	EV/EBITDA STM	P/E FY+2	EV/EBITDA FY-1	EV/EBITDA FY-2	P/B LTM	P/B FY+1	P/B SLTM	P/B FY-2
7	EV/EBITDA STM	P/E FY+2	P/FCF LTM	P/E LTM	P/B FY+1	P/Sales SLTM	P/B FY-1	P/B FY-2
8	EV/EBITDA FY0	EV/E..A-CX FY-1	EV/EBIT FY-2	P/FCF FY0	P/B LTM	P/B FY0	P/B FY0	P/E FY+2
9	EV/EBITDA FY+3	EV/EBITDA FY0	P/E NTM	EV/OP CF NTM	P/B FY+1	P/Sales NTM	EV/Sales LTM	P/E FY0
10	P/E FY0	EV/EBITDA FY-1	EV/E..A-CX FY-1	EV/EBITDA FY-1	EV/EBITDA FY-2	P/B LTM	P/B FY-1	P/B FY-2
11	EV/EBITDA FY0	EV/EBITDA FY-1	EV/EBITDA FY-2	EV/EBITDA FY-2	P/B SLTM	P/B LTM	P/B LTM	EV/EBITDA FY-2
12	EV/EBITDA FY+3	EV/EBITDA SLTM	P/E FY+2	EV/EBITDA FY-2	P/B FY+3	P/B NTM	P/B LTM	P/B SLTM
13	EV/EBITDA STM	P/E STM	EV/E..A-CX FY-2	EV/OP CF STM	P/B SLTM	P/Sales STM	P/B LTM	EV/EBITDA FY-1
14	EV/EBITDA FY+3	P/E STM	P/B SLTM	EV/EBITDA FY-2	EV/EBITDA LTM	P/Sales FY0	EV/Sales FY+1	P/B FY-1
15	EV/EBITDA STM	P/E FY+2	EV/EBITDA STM	EV/OP CF FY+2	EV/EBITDA FY-1	P/B NTM	EV/Sales LTM	EV/GM FY+3
16	EV/EBITDA STM	EV/EBITDA FY0	P/Sales FY-1	P/FCF SLTM	P/B SLTM	P/B FY+1	P/B FY+1	P/B SLTM
17	P/E STM	P/E STM	EV/EBITDA FY-1	EV/EBITDA FY-1	EV/EBITDA FY-1	P/Sales NTM	EV/Asset FY+1	EV/GM FY-2
18	EV/EBITDA STM	EV/E..A-CX FY-1	EV/E..A-CX FY-1	EV/OP CF LTM	P/B SLTM	P/Sales FY+1	EV/Asset FY+1	EV/GM FY-2
19	EV/EBITDA FY+3	P/E FY+2	EV/OP CF FY+1	P/E LTM	EV/EBITDA FY-1	P/B LTM	P/B FY-2	EV/Sales FY+1
20	EV/EBITDA FY+3	P/B FY-1	P/B FY+3	EV/OP CF LTM	P/B SLTM	P/B FY+2	EV/Sales FY-1	P/E STM
Σ 20	EV/EBITDA P/E	P/E EV/EBITDA	EV/EBITDA P/E EV/E..A-CX	EV/EBITDA EV/OP CF	P/B EV/EBITDA	P/B P/Sales	P/B EV/Sales	P/B P/E
	13-7-0	10-7-0	6-4-4	8-7-0	12-7-0	14-6-0	14-4-0	10-3-0

Multiples of top 20 drivers	2014	2015	2016	2017	2018	2019	2020	2021
1	EBITDA Gr. FY+3	S.Gr.+E..A% FY+2	E..A-CX Gr. FY+3	GM Gr. NTM	S.Gr.+E..A% FY0	RoA FY0	RoA SLTM	RoA FY+3
2	EBITDA Gr. STM	EBITDA Gr. NTM	E..A-CX Gr. FY+3	GM Gr. NTM	S.Gr.+E..A% LTM	RoA FY0	RoA SLTM	GM Gr. FY+1
3	E..A-CX Gr. FY+3	Sales Gr. FY+2	E..A-CX Gr. FY-1	FCF/Sales FY-1	S.Gr.+E..A% FY+1	RoA FY0	RoA SLTM	RoA FY+3
4	EBITDA Gr. FY+3	S.Gr.+E..A% FY+2	E..A-CX Gr. FY-1	FCF/Sales FY-1	RoE FY+3	RoA FY0	RoA FY0	RoA FY-1
5	EBITDA Gr. STM	E..A-CX Gr. FY+2	RoA FY-1	EBITDA Gr. FY+3	RoE FY+3	RoE STM	RoA FY0	RoA STM
6	EBITDA Gr. FY+3	E..A-CX Gr. FY+3	E..A-CX Gr. FY-1	S.Gr.+E..A% FY+1	RoE STM	RoE FY+3	RoA FY-1	RoA FY-2
7	EBITDA Gr. STM	EBITDA Gr. NTM	Sales Gr. FY0	E..A-CX Gr. FY+3	RoE FY+3	S.Gr.+E..A% NTM	RoA FY-1	RoA FY-1
8	S.Gr.+E..A% FY+2	Op.CF/Sal. LTM	E..A-CX Gr. FY-1	S.Gr.+E..A% LTM	RoE FY+3	RoA FY0	RoA FY-1	E..A-CX Gr. FY+3
9	EBITDA Gr. FY+3	FCF/Sales LTM	E..A-CX Gr. STM	GM Gr. NTM	RoE STM	S.Gr.+E..A% STM	RoA FY-1	GM Gr. FY+3
10	Sales Gr. FY+2	FCF/Sales LTM	E..A-CX Gr. FY-1	S.Gr.+E..A% FY+1	S.Gr.+E..A% FY0	RoE STM	RoA SLTM	RoA STM
11	S.Gr.+E..A% NTM	S.Gr.+E..A% STM	S.Gr.+E..A% NTM	S.Gr.+E..A% NTM	RoE STM	RoA SLTM	RoA FY0	EBIT Gr. FY-1
12	EBITDA Gr. STM	FCF/Sales LTM	E..A-CX Gr. STM	S.Gr.+E..A% LTM	RoE FY+3	RoE FY+3	RoA FY-1	RoA FY+3
13	EBITDA Gr. FY+2	EBIT Gr. FY+2	S.Gr.+E..A% NTM	GM Gr. FY+1	RoE LTM	S.Gr.+E..A% STM	RoE STM	GM Gr. FY+3
14	EBITDA Gr. FY+2	EBIT Gr. STM	RoE FY+3	Sales Gr. NTM	FCF/Sales FY-2	S.Gr.+E..A% NTM	RoA FY-1	RoA FY-2
15	E..A-CX Gr. FY+3	EBITDA Gr. FY+1	RoA FY-1	GM Gr. NTM	Sales Gr. FY+3	RoE STM	RoA SLTM	FCF Gr. FY+2
16	EBIT Gr. FY+3	FCF/Sales FY+1	GM Gr. FY+2	S.Gr.+E..A% FY+1	RoE FY+2	RoE FY+2	RoA SLTM	RoA FY-1
17	EBITDA Gr. FY+2	E..A-CX Gr. FY+3	Op.CF/Sal. FY0	S.Gr.+E..A% LTM	Sales Gr. FY+2	S.Gr.+E..A% FY+3	RoA SLTM	EBITDA Mar. FY+3
18	EBITDA Gr. NTM	Op.CF/Sal. FY+1	S.Gr.+E..A% NTM	Sales Gr. FY+2	RoE FY+1	S.Gr.+E..A% STM	RoA FY-1	EBITDA Mar. FY-1
19	E..A-CX Gr. FY+3	E..A-CX Gr. STM	EBITDA Mar. FY-1	EBITDA Gr. STM	S.Gr.+E..A% LTM	RoE FY+3	RoA FY-1	Op.CF/Sal. FY-2
20	EBIT Gr. FY+3	S.Gr.+E..A% FY+2	RoE STM	Sales Gr. STM	RoE NTM	RoE FY+3	RoA FY-1	E..A-CX Gr. STM
Σ 20	EBITDA Gr. E..A-CX Gr.	E..A-CX Gr. S.Gr.+E..A% FCF/Sales	E..A-CX Gr. S.Gr.+E..A%	S.Gr.+E..A% GM Gr.	RoE S.Gr.+E..A%	RoE S.Gr.+E..A%	RoA	RoA
	12-3-0	4-4-4	9-3-0	7-5-0	12-5-0	8-6-0	19-0-0	10-0-0

Table 7.48 Results of top best-fitting regressions for travel companies (excl. BS variables)

Multiples of top 20 regressions

	2014	2015	2016	2017	2018	2019	2020	2021
1	P/E STM	EV/EBITDA FY-1	P/E FY+2	EV/OP CF STM	EV/Sales FY-2	P/Sales SLTM	EV/OP CF LTM	EV/EBIT FY-1
2	P/E STM	P/E STM	P/E NTM	EV/OP CF FY+3	EV/EBITDA FY-2	P/Sales NTM	EV/GM SLTM	P/E FY+2
3	P/E STM	P/E FY-1	EV/EBITDA FY-2	EV/EBITDA NTM	EV/EBITDA FY-2	P/Sales STM	EV/EBITDA STM	P/E FY0
4	P/E FY+3	EV/EBITDA SLTM	EV/E..A-CX FY-2	EV/EBITDA FY+2	EV/EBITDA FY-2	P/Sales FY0	EV/GM SLTM	EV/EBITDA FY-2
5	P/E FY+3	P/E FY+2	EV/EBITDA FY-1	P/E LTM	EV/EBITDA LTM	P/Sales NTM	EV/GM SLTM	EV/EBITDA FY-1
6	EV/EBITDA STM	P/E FY+2	P/FCF LTM	EV/EBITDA FY-2	EV/EBITDA FY-1	P/Sales FY+1	EV/GM FY-1	EV/GM FY+3
7	EV/EBITDA STM	P/E FY+2	EV/EBIT FY-2	P/E LTM	EV/EBITDA FY-1	P/Sales FY+1	EV/EBITDA FY-2	EV/GM FY-2
8	EV/EBITDA FY0	EV/E..A-CX FY-1	P/E NTM	P/FCF FY0	EV/EBITDA FY-1	P/Sales STM	EV/GM SLTM	EV/GM FY-2
9	EV/EBITDA FY+3	EV/EBITDA FY0	EV/E..A-CX FY-1	EV/OP CF NTM	P/FCF FY-1	P/Sales FY-1	EV/GM FY-1	EV/Sales FY+1
10	P/E FY0	EV/EBITDA FY-1	EV/EBITDA FY-2	EV/EBITDA FY-1	P/Sales FY-2	EV/GM FY0	P/FCF SLTM	P/E STM
11	EV/EBITDA FY0	EV/EBITDA FY-1	P/E FY+2	EV/EBITDA FY-2	EV/EBITDA FY-2	P/Sales LTM	P/E FY-2	P/Sales FY+3
12	EV/EBITDA FY+3	EV/EBITDA SLTM	EV/E..A-CX FY-2	EV/EBITDA FY-2	EV/EBITDA FY-2	P/Sales LTM	EV/E..A-CX FY-2	P/Sales FY+3
13	EV/EBITDA STM	P/E STM	P/Sales FY-1	EV/OP CF STM	EV/EBITDA FY+1	EV/Sales SLTM	EV/GM SLTM	EV/GM NTM
14	EV/EBITDA FY+3	P/E STM	EV/EBITDA FY-1	EV/EBITDA FY-2	EV/EBITDA NTM	P/Sales FY+2	EV/GM SLTM	P/Sales STM
15	EV/EBITDA STM	P/E FY+2	EV/E..A-CX FY-1	EV/OP CF FY+2	EV/EBITDA FY-2	P/Sales FY+3	P/FCF FY-1	P/Sales STM
16	EV/EBITDA STM	EV/EBITDA FY0	EV/OP CF FY+1	P/FCF SLTM	P/FCF FY-1	EV/EBITDA FY-2	EV/GM SLTM	P/Sales FY+1
17	P/E STM	P/E STM	EV/EBIT FY-1	EV/EBITDA FY-1	EV/EBITDA FY-1	P/Sales FY+2	EV/GM SLTM	EV/GM FY+2
18	EV/EBITDA STM	EV/E..A-CX FY-1	EV/OP CF LTM	EV/OP CF LTM	EV/EBITDA FY-2	EV/GM LTM	EV/EBITDA FY-1	P/E FY+2
19	EV/EBITDA FY+3	P/E FY+2	EV/EBITDA FY-2	P/E LTM	P/FCF FY-1	P/E FY+1	EV/EBITDA STM	EV/GM FY-2
20	EV/EBITDA FY+3	P/E FY+2	P/Sales FY-1	EV/OP CF LTM	EV/EBITDA FY-1	EV/EBITDA FY+3	P/Sales LTM	EV/GM FY+1
Σ 20	EV/EBITDA P/E	P/E EV/EBITDA	EV/EBITDA P/E EV/E..A-CX	EV/EBITDA EV/OP CF	EV/EBITDA P/FCF	P/Sales	EV/GM EV/EBITDA	EV/GM P/Sales
	13-7-0	11-7-0	5-4-4	8-7-0	15-3-0	14-0-0	10-4-0	7-5-0

Multiples of top 20 drivers

	2014	2015	2016	2017	2018	2019	2020	2021
1	EBITDA Gr. FY+3	S.Gr.+E..A% FY+2	E..A-CX Gr. FY+3	GM Gr. NTM	S.Gr.+E..A% FY0	S.Gr.+E..A% NTM	Net In. Gr. FY+2	GM Gr. FY+1
2	EBITDA Gr. STM	EBITDA Gr. NTM	E..A-CX Gr. FY+3	GM Gr. NTM	S.Gr.+E..A% LTM	S.Gr.+E..A% STM	EBIT Mar. FY0	E..A-CX Gr. FY+3
3	E..A-CX Gr. FY+3	Sales Gr. FY+2	E..A-CX Gr. FY-1	FCF/Sales FY-1	S.Gr.+E..A% FY+1	S.Gr.+E..A% STM	EBITDA Gr. FY+3	GM Gr. FY+3
4	EBITDA Gr. FY+3	S.Gr.+E..A% FY+2	E..A-CX Gr. FY-1	FCF/Sales FY-1	S.Gr.+E..A% FY0	S.Gr.+E..A% NTM	EBITDA Mar. SLTM	EBIT Gr. FY-1
5	EBITDA Gr. STM	E..A-CX Gr. FY+2	E..A-CX Gr. FY-1	EBITDA Gr. FY+3	FCF/Sales FY-2	S.Gr.+E..A% FY+3	EBITDA Mar. FY0	GM Gr. FY+3
6	EBITDA Gr. FY+3	E..A-CX Gr. FY+3	Sales Gr. FY0	S.Gr.+E..A% FY+1	Sales Gr. FY+3	S.Gr.+E..A% STM	EBIT Mar. FY0	FCF Gr. FY+2
7	EBITDA Gr. STM	EBITDA Gr. NTM	E..A-CX Gr. FY-1	E..A-CX Gr. FY+3	Sales Gr. FY+2	S.Gr.+E..A% FY+3	EBITDA Gr. FY0	EBITDA Mar. FY+3
8	S.Gr.+E..A% FY+2	Op.CF/Sal. LTM	E..A-CX Gr. STM	S.Gr.+E..A% LTM	S.Gr.+E..A% LTM	S.Gr.+E..A% FY+3	EBIT Mar. SLTM	EBITDA Mar. FY-1
9	EBITDA Gr. FY+3	FCF/Sales LTM	E..A-CX Gr. FY-1	GM Gr. NTM	S.Gr.+E..A% FY+3	S.Gr.+E..A% NTM	EBIT Mar. SLTM	Op.CF/Sal. FY-2
10	Sales Gr. FY+2	FCF/Sales LTM	S.Gr.+E..A% NTM	S.Gr.+E..A% FY+1	S.Gr.+E..A% FY0	S.Gr.+E..A% FY+2	E..A-CX Gr. NTM	E..A-CX Gr. STM
11	S.Gr.+E..A% NTM	S.Gr.+E..A% STM	E..A-CX Gr. STM	S.Gr.+E..A% NTM	Sales Gr. NTM	S.Gr.+E..A% STM	EBITDA Gr. FY0	EBITDA Mar. FY+3
12	EBITDA Gr. STM	FCF/Sales LTM	S.Gr.+E..A% NTM	S.Gr.+E..A% LTM	Sales Gr. FY+2	S.Gr.+E..A% FY+3	EBITDA Gr. FY0	E..A-CX M. FY+3
13	EBITDA Gr. FY+2	EBIT Gr. FY+2	GM Gr. FY+2	GM Gr. FY+1	FCF/Sales FY-2	S.Gr.+E..A% NTM	EBITDA Mar. STM	FCF Gr. FY+2
14	EBITDA Gr. FY+2	EBIT Gr. STM	Op.CF/Sal. FY0	Sales Gr. NTM	FCF/Sales FY-2	S.Gr.+E..A% STM	EBITDA Mar. FY+3	EBITDA Mar. FY+3
15	E..A-CX Gr. FY+3	EBITDA Gr. FY+1	S.Gr.+E..A% NTM	GM Gr. NTM	S.Gr.+E..A% NTM	S.Gr.+E..A% STM	E..A-CX Gr. NTM	E..A-CX M. FY+3
16	EBIT Gr. FY+3	FCF/Sales FY+1	EBITDA Mar. FY-1	S.Gr.+E..A% FY+1	S.Gr.+E..A% FY+2	EBITDA Gr. STM	EBITDA Mar. FY+2	Op.CF/Sal. FY-2
17	EBITDA Gr. FY+2	E..A-CX Gr. FY+3	E..A-CX Gr. FY-1	S.Gr.+E..A% LTM	S.Gr.+E..A% FY+1	S.Gr.+E..A% FY+3	S.Gr.+E..A% FY 1	FCF Gr. FY+2
18	EBITDA Gr. NTM	Op.CF/Sal. FY+1	EBIT Mar. SLTM	Sales Gr. FY+2	S.Gr.+E..A% FY+2	S.Gr.+E..A% FY+2	E..A-CX Gr. LTM	EBITDA Gr. FY+3
19	E..A-CX Gr. FY+3	E..A-CX Gr. STM	Net Mar. FY+2	EBITDA Gr. STM	S.Gr.+E..A% STM	E..A-CX Gr. STM	Sales Gr. FY+1	EBIT Mar. FY+3
20	EBIT Gr. FY+3	EBITDA Gr. STM	GM Gr. STM	Sales Gr. STM	S.Gr.+E..A% FY0	EBITDA Gr. FY+3	EBIT Mar. FY+3	Op.CF/Sal. FY-2
Σ 20	EBITDA Gr.	E..A-CX Gr. FCF/Sales EBITDA Gr.	E..A-CX Gr. S.Gr.+E..A%	S.Gr.+E..A% GM Gr.	S.Gr.+E..A%	S.Gr.+E..A%	EBITDA Mar. EBIT Mar. EBITDA Gr.	EBITDA Mar. Op.CF/Sal. GM Gr.
	12-0-0	4-4-4	10-3-0	7-5-0	13-0-0	17-0-0	5-5-4	4-3-3

7.2.21 Results for Vertical Software Companies

In addition to being the last industry to be discussed in detail, the vertical software cluster is one of the segments best covered from a data perspective. It includes 133 companies from around the world. Such a wide peer group would also enable a geographic split for researchers seeking further segmentation. It presented nearly 356 k regressions with sufficient observations representing 92% of the maximum possible. From these regressions, 243 k also have the required positive correlation, and over 1/3 of the remaining regressions turned out to be statistically significant, resulting in over 86 k regressions to be included in the analysis of the results. Table 7.49 presents the R-Squared values of the top 20 regressions, while Table 7.50 presents the full analysis, including the top 10 regressions and the summary based on the top 20 regressions. R-Squared values are very good, considering the size of the segment. While the R-Squared values are decreasing with time, this phenomenon is to be expected with an increasing number of publicly listed companies.

Table 7.49 R^2 of top 20 regressions for vertical software companies

#	'07	'08	'09	'10	'11	'12	'13	'14	'15	'16	'17	'18	'19	'20	'21
1	85	91	85	84	80	76	65	66	70	70	68	65	73	68	46
2	84	90	85	83	80	74	64	64	66	67	66	63	65	64	45
3	84	89	84	83	79	74	62	61	65	67	65	61	56	64	45
4	84	88	82	83	79	72	62	61	65	66	64	61	55	57	45
5	84	87	82	83	79	71	61	61	64	66	62	60	52	55	43
6	84	87	82	82	78	71	60	60	64	65	60	57	51	55	41
7	84	87	81	82	78	71	60	60	63	64	60	56	51	54	40
8	84	86	80	81	78	70	59	60	62	64	60	55	49	54	39
9	83	86	80	81	77	70	59	59	62	62	60	53	49	53	38
10	83	86	80	80	77	69	58	59	61	60	60	53	49	53	38
11	83	86	80	79	76	69	58	59	61	60	60	52	48	50	37
12	83	85	80	79	76	69	58	58	61	60	60	51	48	50	37
13	83	84	80	79	76	69	58	57	60	59	58	51	48	49	36

(continued)

Table 7.49 (continued)

#	'07	'08	'09	'10	'11	'12	'13	'14	'15	'16	'17	'18	'19	'20	'21
14	83	84	79	79	75	68	58	56	60	58	58	50	48	46	36
15	83	84	79	79	75	67	58	55	59	57	58	49	48	46	36
16	82	84	79	79	75	67	58	55	59	57	57	49	47	46	35
17	82	84	79	79	74	66	57	54	59	57	57	49	47	45	34
18	82	84	78	78	74	64	57	54	57	57	57	49	47	45	34
19	82	83	78	78	74	64	57	54	57	57	57	49	47	44	33
20	82	83	78	78	74	64	57	53	57	57	57	48	46	44	33

Evaluating the bases, one of the most "clean cuts" between sales and profitability bases can be observed in 2012. Practically, every multiple before 2012 was Sales based (excluding 2008, with Gross Margin being at the top, however, this segment generally does not have significant COGS), while virtually every multiple afterward was EBITDA or EBITDARD based.

The drivers show a less clear picture, with a good combination of both growth and margin drivers. The first 4 years show margin multiples coming first, while 2011 presents the rule of 40 as the main driver. Starting with 2012, either EBITDARD or Sales growth was the leading driver, with some exceptions in 2017, when dividends per share took the first position, 2018, when the rule of 40 came out at the top, and 2020 when EBITDARD margin was the best driver.

The results for the vertical software segment confirm the expectations. There was a clear transition from Sales multiples to profitability multiples while the drivers remained growth-focused. For management teams and stakeholders looking for recommendations, it can be said that EV/EBITDARD is the main valuation base, while Sales and Gross Margin growth are the main drivers.

Table 7.50 Results of top best-fitting regressions for vertical software companies

		2007	2008	2009	2010	2011	2012	2013	2014	2015	2016	2017	2018	2019	2020	2021
Multiples of top 10 regressions	1	P/Sales FY+1	EV/GM FY+3	P/Sales STM	EV/Sales STM	EV/Sales LTM	EV/E..ARD FY+2	EV/Sales SLTM	EV/E..ARD FY+2	P/E FY-2	EV/E..ARD FY0	EV/E..ARD FY0	EV/E..ARD FY-1	EV/E..ARD SLTM	EV/EBIT FY-2	EV/E..ARD LTM
	2	P/Sales LTM	EV/GM FY+3	P/Sales FY+1	EV/Sales FY+2	P/Sales SLTM	EV/E..ARD FY+2	P/Sales SLTM	EV/E..ARD NTM	EV/EBITDA LTM	P/E FY+1	EV/E..ARD FY0	EV/E..ARD SLTM	EV/E..ARD FY0	EV/EBIT FY-2	EV/E..ARD FY+1
	3	P/Sales LTM	EV/GM FY+3	EV/Sales FY+1	EV/Sales NTM	P/Sales FY-1	EV/E..ARD FY+2	EV/E..ARD FY-2	EV/EBITDA FY+1	EV/OP CF SLTM	P/E LTM	EV/E..ARD FY0	EV/E..ARD FY-1	EV/OP CF FY-1	P/FCF FY-1	EV/E..ARD FY+1
	4	P/Sales FY+1	EV/GM FY+3	P/Sales FY+2	EV/Sales STM	EV/Sales FY+1	EV/E..ARD STM	EV/EBIT FY-2	EV/GM FY-2	EV/E..ARD FY+3	EV/E..ARD FY0	EV/E..ARD FY0	EV/E..ARD FY-1	EV/E..ARD LTM	EV/E..A-CX FY-2	EV/E..ARD LTM
	5	P/Sales LTM	EV/GM FY+3	EV/Sales STM	EV/EBITDA FY+3	EV/Sales FY0	EV/E..ARD FY+2	EV/Sales FY0	EV/EBITDA LTM	EV/EBIT SLTM	EV/E..ARD FY0	EV/E..A-CX FY0	EV/E..ARD FY0	EV/E..ARD FY0	P/FCF FY-2	EV/E..ARD FY+1
	6	P/Sales FY+2	EV/GM FY+3	P/Sales NTM	EV/Sales FY+2	EV/EBITDA STM	EV/E..ARD FY+2	P/Sales FY0	EV/Sales FY-1	EV/OP CF FY-1	EV/E..ARD FY0	EV/E..ARD FY-1	EV/E..ARD LTM	EV/E..ARD SLTM	P/FCF FY-2	EV/Asset FY-2
	7	P/B FY0	EV/GM FY+3	P/Sales LTM	EV/Sales NTM	EV/Sales SLTM	EV/E..ARD STM	EV/E..ARD FY-2	EV/EBITDA LTM	EV/E..A-CX LTM	EV/E..ARD FY0	EV/E..ARD FY-1	EV/E..ARD FY-1	EV/E..ARD FY+3	P/FCF FY-2	EV/E..ARD LTM
	8	P/Sales FY+1	EV/GM FY+2	EV/Sales FY+1	EV/Sales LTM	P/Sales SLTM	EV/E..ARD FY+2	EV/E..ARD STM	EV/E..ARD FY+3	EV/E..ARD FY0	EV/E..ARD SLTM	EV/E..ARD FY-1	EV/E..A-CX FY0	EV/OP CF SLTM	P/FCF FY-2	EV/EBIT FY-2
	9	P/Sales FY+3	EV/GM FY+3	EV/Sales LTM	EV/Sales FY+1	EV/Sales FY-1	EV/E..ARD FY+2	EV/Sales LTM	EV/E..ARD FY-2	EV/E..ARD LTM	P/E FY+1	EV/E..ARD FY-1	EV/E..ARD LTM	EV/OP CF FY-2	P/FCF FY-2	EV/E..ARD FY+1
	10	P/Sales LTM	EV/GM FY+3	P/Sales FY+1	EV/E..ARD STM	EV/Sales NTM	P/B FY-2	EV/Sales SLTM	P/FCF SLTM	EV/E..ARD FY0	EV/E..ARD SLTM	EV/E..ARD FY-2	EV/Sales FY-1	EV/E..ARD SLTM	P/FCF FY-2	EV/E..ARD FY+1
	Σ 20	P/Sales	EV/GM	P/Sales EV/Sales	EV/Sales P/Sales	EV/Sales P/Sales	EV/E..ARD P/B	EV/Sales P/Sales EV/E..ARD	EV/E..ARD EV/EBITDA	EV/E..ARD EV/OP CF	EV/E..ARD P/E	EV/E..ARD	EV/E..ARD EV/Sales	EV/E..ARD EV/OP CF	P/FCF EV/E..ARD EV/EBIT	EV/E..ARD
		19-0-0	19-0-0	10-9-0	10-5-0	11-8-0	13-7-0	8-6-5	8-4-0	6-4-0	12-4-0	14-0-0	10-5-0	10-3-0	10-5-4	14-0-0
Multiples of top 10 drivers	1	Op.CF/Sal. STM	E..A-CX M. FY+2	E..A-CX M. SLTM	E..A-CX M. SLTM	S.Gr.+E..A% STM	E..ARD Gr. STM	E..ARD Gr. LTM	E..ARD Gr. FY0	E..ARD Gr. FY-1	Sales Gr. FY+2	DPS Gr. FY+1	Sales Gr. STM	DPS Gr. FY-1	E..ARD Gr. LTM	Sales Gr. STM
	2	Op.CF/Sal. STM	E..A-CX M. STM	E..A-CX M. SLTM	E..A-CX M. SLTM	S.Gr.+E..A% STM	E..ARD Gr. LTM	E..ARD Gr. LTM	E..ARD Gr. FY0	E..ARD Gr. NTM	E..ARD Gr. STM	GM Gr. STM	DPS Gr. LTM	DPS Gr. FY-1	E..ARD Gr. FY0	Sales Gr. STM
	3	S.Gr.+E..A% FY+3	E..A-CX M. LTM	E..A-CX M. SLTM	E..A-CX M. SLTM	S.Gr.+E..A% STM	E..ARD Gr. FY+2	Sales Gr. LTM	Sales Gr. STM	E..ARD Gr. NTM	E..ARD Gr. STM	DPS Gr. NTM	GM Gr. STM	E..ARD Gr. LTM	E..ARD Gr. LTM	GM Gr. STM
	4	Op.CF/Sal. FY+2	EBIT Mar. FY+2	E..A-CX M. SLTM	EBITDA Mar. SLTM	S.Gr.+E..A% STM	E..ARD Gr. STM	E..ARD Gr. LTM	S.Gr.+E..A% STM	Sales Gr. LTM	GM Gr. FY+2	Sales Gr. STM	DPS Gr. LTM	Sales Gr. STM	E..ARD Gr. FY0	GM Gr. STM
	5	Op.CF/Sal. FY+2	E..A-CX M. NTM	E..A-CX M. SLTM	E..ARD Gr. FY+3	S.Gr.+E..A% STM	EBITDA Gr. STM	E..ARD Gr. LTM	Sales Gr. FY+3	E..ARD Gr. FY+1	GM Gr. NTM	GM Gr. STM	DPS Gr. LTM	Sales Gr. STM	E..ARD Mar. FY+1	Sales Gr. FY+2
	6	Op.CF/Sal. STM	EBIT Mar. STM	E..A-CX M. SLTM	EBITDA Mar. SLTM	E..ARD Gr. FY+3	EBITDA Gr. FY+3	E..ARD Gr. LTM	Sales Gr. LTM	E..ARD Gr. FY+1	Sales Gr. NTM	EBITDA Gr. FY0	DPS Gr. LTM	Sales Gr. NTM	E..ARD Mar. NTM	Sales Gr. STM
	7	RoE FY+1	EBIT Mar. FY+3	E..A-CX M. SLTM	EBITDA Mar. SLTM	S.Gr.+E..A% STM	E..ARD Gr. FY+2	Sales Gr. NTM	Sales Gr. STM	E..ARD Gr. NTM	Sales Gr. STM	DPS Gr. FY+1	Sales Gr. FY+3	DPS Gr. FY-1	E..ARD Mar. FY+2	Sales Gr. FY+2
	8	Op.CF/Sal. NTM	E..A-CX M. FY+1	EBITDA Mar. FY-1	E..A-CX M. SLTM	S.Gr.+E..A% FY+3	E..ARD Gr. NTM	EBITDA Gr. NTM	E..ARD Gr. FY0	Sales Gr. FY+1	Sales Gr. FY+2	DPS Gr. NTM	E..ARD Gr. STM	E..ARD Gr. LTM	E..ARD Mar. STM	E..ARD Gr. FY-1
	9	Op.CF/Sal. STM	EBITDA Mar. FY+2	E..A-CX M. SLTM	E..A-CX M. SLTM	S.Gr.+E..A% STM	E..ARD Gr. FY+1	E..ARD Gr. LTM	Sales Gr. STM	Sales Gr. NTM	E..ARD Gr. FY+3	DPS Gr. LTM	DPS Gr. FY0	E..ARD Mar. SLTM	E..ARD Mar. FY+3	GM Gr. FY+3
	10	S.Gr.+E..A% STM	EBIT Mar. NTM	E..A-CX M. FY-1	E..ARD Gr. FY+3	S.Gr.+E..A% STM	RoE STM	E..ARD Gr. FY+1	E..ARD Gr. FY+2	GM Gr. FY+1	GM Gr. NTM	Sales Gr. STM	S.Gr.+E..A% FY0	Sales Gr. FY+2	E..ARD Mar. LTM	Sales Gr. FY+3
	Σ 20	Op.CF/Sal. S.Gr.+E..A%	E..A-CX M. EBIT Mar.	E..A-CX M. EBITDA Mar.	E..A-CX M. EBITDA Mar.	S.Gr.+E..A%	E..ARD Gr. EBITDA Gr.	E..ARD Gr. Sales Gr.	Sales Gr. E..ARD Gr.	E..ARD Gr. Sales Gr.	Sales Gr. E..ARD Gr.	DPS Gr. Sales Gr.	S.Gr.+E..A% DPS Gr.	Sales Gr. S.Gr.+E..A% E..ARD Mar.	E..ARD Mar. E..ARD Gr. Sales Gr.	Sales Gr. GM Gr.
		15-4-0	12-4-0	14-4-0	8-7-0	19-0-0	13-4-0	13-3-0	8-7-0	11-3-0	9-5-0	6-5-0	7-6-0	6-4-4	7-7-5	12-6-0

7.3 Conclusions of the Inferential Statistics

This chapter will discuss each hypothesis individually and summarize the results to enable the testing and discussion of each hypothesis.

7.3.1 Hypothesis 1: Clustering Increases Explanatory Power

Testing the first hypothesis required centralizing the R-Squared values of the regressions used to derive the conclusions of each industry. Table 7.51 presents each analysis's average R-Squared values of the top 20 regressions.

Table 7.51 Average R-Squared values of top 20 regressions for each cluster

Year	07	08	09	10	11	12	13	14	15	16	17	18	19	20	21
All combined	64	58	77	57	52	47	50	46	39	44	39	34	33	29	25
Analytics Soft.	n/a	n/a	n/a	n/a	n/a	n/a	83	88	90	85	90	80	75	74	68
Classifieds	n/a	n/a	n/a	85	87	89	86	73	72	79	75	76	85	83	81
Content Mone. F.	n/a	n/a	n/a	n/a	n/a	n/a	n/a	83	82	78	81	88	84	73	87
Content Mone.	n/a	n/a	n/a	n/a	n/a	62	63	76	88	91	87	74	73	69	76
Content Mone.*	n/a	n/a	n/a	n/a	n/a	62	63	74	83	88	87	68	68	63	68
Customer Acq.	n/a	n/a	n/a	n/a	n/a	n/a	80	84	94	86	85	84	84	79	69
Data Center	n/a	n/a	n/a	78	81	90	91	90	85	81	82	81	80	82	82
Divers./Portals	n/a	n/a	n/a	n/a	92	87	90	87	86	91	85	87	91	92	81
Divers./Portals*	n/a	n/a	n/a	n/a	92	87	90	86	86	91	85	86	88	84	75
eCommerce	85	89	85	83	83	81	85	85	79	82	79	80	79	70	71
Gambling	93	95	96	92	88	91	89	83	78	79	78	76	74	79	78
Gambling*	93	95	96	92	87	90	88	83	77	72	71	74	73	77	78
Gaming	n/a	n/a	85	89	80	76	77	72	80	78	71	72	76	71	70
Gaming*	n/a	n/a	82	82	77	76	73	72	80	75	71	68	71	60	59
Horizontal Soft.	76	87	88	82	84	74	78	77	64	67	67	57	53	50	51
Marketing	73	82	81	82	82	77	80	84	75	77	71	69	65	66	62
Marketplace	n/a	n/a	n/a	n/a	n/a	76	87	84	73	79	82	75	73	82	72

(continued)

Table 7.51 (continued)

Year	07	08	09	10	11	12	13	14	15	16	17	18	19	20	21
Online B2C Se.	n/a	n/a	n/a	n/a	n/a	60	67	87	81	83	80	76	81	78	85
Payment	82	89	90	92	89	89	82	84	87	71	75	84	72	71	76
Payment*	81	89	88	90	89	87	79	80	84	67	70	71	63	60	69
Platform Soft.	79	86	79	90	97	95	93	90	89	84	89	89	87	81	74
Security Soft.	83	84	77	74	83	87	81	70	77	80	67	69	67	67	65
Social Networks	n/a	n/a	n/a	n/a	n/a	n/a	n/a	n/a	47	57	77	74	77	79	80
Travel	n/a	n/a	n/a	n/a	n/a	n/a	n/a	86	82	83	85	86	86	87	80
Travel*	n/a	n/a	n/a	n/a	n/a	n/a	n/a	86	82	82	85	84	84	79	76
Vertical Soft.	83	86	81	80	77	69	59	58	62	61	60	54	51	52	39
Minimum	**73**	**82**	**77**	**74**	**77**	**60**	**59**	**58**	**47**	**57**	**60**	**54**	**51**	**50**	**39**

* analyses excluding balance sheet variables

The first line, "All combined," presents the values of the analysis containing all companies in one cluster, while the rest of the table presents the average for each analysis. It should be noted that industries requiring two analyses are shown twice to capture the analysis results, including all multiples and the analysis excluding balance sheet multiples. The last line shows the minimum value from the cluster-level analysis, which can be seen to be, at most, equal to the values shown in the first line.

Consequently, hypothesis 1 can be confirmed. Segmenting companies into groups of companies with a comparable business model can significantly increase the explanatory power of such analyses.

7.3.2 Hypothesis 2: Bases Transition from Sales Multiples to Profitability Multiples

Testing the second analysis requires centralizing and summarizing the results concerning the multiples from all industries and clusters. Table 7.52 summarizes each industry's conclusions in a simplified manner by showing the type of multiple that was most often encountered in the first 20 regressions of each cluster. Instead of showing each multiple as the detailed analysis does, it only shows "Sales" for Sales Multiples, GM for Gross Margin Multiples, "Profit." for Profitability Multiples such as EV/EBITDA, and "Book" for Book Value Multiples.

Table 7.52 Leading base/ multiple for each analyzed industry/cluster

Year	07	08	09	10	11	12	13	14	15	16	17	18	19	20	21
All	Sales	Sales	Sales	GM	Sales	Profit.	Profit.	Profit.	Profit.	Profit.	Profit.	Profit.	Profit.	Profit.	Sales
Analytics Soft.							Sales	Sales	Profit.	Profit.	GM	Sales	GM	Sales	Sales
Classifieds				Sales	Profit.	Book	Sales	Profit.	Profit.	Profit.	Sales	Book	Sales	Sales	Sales
Content Mone. F.								Profit.	Profit.	Sales	Sales	Book	Sales	Sales	Sales
Content Mone.*						Sales	Sales	Sales	GM	Sales	Sales	Sales	GM	GM	GM
Customer Acq.							Profit.	GM	GM	Sales	Profit.	Profit.	Profit.	Sales	Profit.
Data Center				Sales	Profit.	Sales	Sales	Sales	Sales	GM	Sales	Sales	Sales	Sales	Sales
Divers./Portals*					Profit.	Sales	Sales	Sales	Sales	Sales	Sales	Sales	Sales	Sales	Sales
eCommerce	Sales	Book	Sales	Sales	Sales	Sales	Sales	Sales	Sales	Sales	Profit.	Sales	Sales	Sales	Sales
Gambling*	Sales	Sales	Sales	Sales	GM	Sales	Sales	Sales	Sales	Sales	Profit.	Profit.	GM	GM	Sales
Gaming*			Sales	Sales	Sales	Profit.	Profit.	Sales	Sales	Profit.	GM	GM	GM	Sales	Sales
Horizontal Soft.	Sales	Sales	Sales	GM	Profit.	GM	Profit.	Book	Profit.	Profit.	Profit.	Profit.	Profit.	Profit.	Profit.
Marketing	Book	Sales	Sales	GM	Book	Profit.	Profit.	Profit.	Sales	Profit.	Profit.	Book	Profit.	Profit.	Profit.
Marketplace						Sales	Sales	Sales	Sales	Profit.	Profit.	Profit.	Book	Profit.	Profit.
Online B2C Se.						Sales	Sales	Sales	Sales	Sales	Sales	Profit.	Book	Book	Book
Payment*	Sales	Sales	Sales	Profit.	Sales	Sales	Sales	Sales	Sales	Profit.	Profit.	Sales	Sales	Sales	Profit.
Platform Soft.	Sales	Profit.	Profit.	Profit.	Profit.	Sales	Sales	Book	Book	Book	Profit.	Profit.	Profit.	Profit.	Profit.
Security Soft.	Book	Sales	Sales	Profit.	Book	Book	Book	Profit.	Profit.	Profit.	Profit.	Profit.	Profit.	Profit.	Profit.
Social Networks									Sales	Profit.	GM	Sales	Profit.	Profit.	Book
Travel*								Profit.	Profit.	Profit.	Profit.	Profit.	Sales	GM	GM
Vertical Soft.	Sales	GM	Sales	Sales	Sales	Profit.	Sales	Profit.	Profit.	Profit.	Profit.	Profit.	Profit.	Profit.	Profit.
% Sales	100	71	89	55	40	69	75	59	53	37	30	41	39	47	44
% Gross Margin	0	14	0	18	10	8	0	6	11	5	15	6	22	16	11
% Profitability	0	14	11	27	50	23	25	35	37	58	55	53	39	37	44

Summarizing the results by type is required as many multiples can represent the same dimension conceptually. To exemplify, while P/Sales and EV/Sales are two separate multiples calculated in different manners, they essentially represent from a base perspective the same type of base: Revenue-based Multiples. Similarly, despite including multiples types of EBITDAs and Cash Flow Multiples, which are useful for readers looking to optimize their own valuation, drawing a conclusion at such a detailed level does not help in analyzing the hypothesis from a conceptual perspective.

The results show clearly that most bases that evolve away from Sales Multiples become Profitability Multiples. While some industries show intermittent Profitability bases (e.g., Analytics Software, Classifieds, Customer Acquisition, and Gaming), the majority show a clear evolution (e.g., four separate software industries, marketing, marketplace, and Online B2C Services).

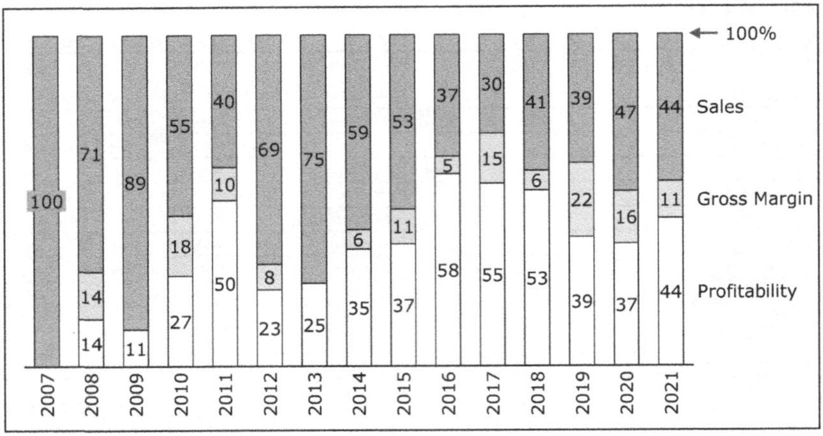

Fig. 7.3 Share of bases/ multiples by type for the period covered by the study

Figure 7.3 summarizes the bases by type based on the results presented in Table 7.52. The figure presents as a percentage the share of industries in which bases were "Sales," "Gross Margin," or "Profitability" Multiples. It can be seen clearly that the share of "Sales" decreased steadily over time from 100 to 30% in 2017 and 44% in the last year. It is interesting to see a slight return of Sales multiples in the last two years that were COVID-19 driven.

Based on the summaries, hypothesis 2 can be confirmed with valuation bases across various industries, part of the online-driven sector transitioning with time from Sales Multiples towards Profitability Multiples.

7.3.3 Hypothesis 3: Drivers Transition from Growth to Profitability

Evaluating the results to test the third hypothesis will be done similarly in the last sub-chapter. The drivers from all industries/clusters included in the study were summarized and classified into 6 groups representing similar concepts. Table 7.53 presents the summary with "Sal.Gr." representing Sales Growth, "GMGr." representing Gross Margin Growth, "Pr.Gr" meaning Profitability Growth, "R.o.40" indicating the Rule of 40 Driver, profitability margin as "Profit" and book value drivers with the annotation "Book."

An industry-level discussion is very difficult as the main drivers often switch between the 6 types. Furthermore, the drivers included are from a conceptual perspective, often close to one another. While Sales Growth and Profit Margin are at the opposite ends of meaning, Profitability Growth and the Rule of 40 represent drivers that are a mix of concepts implying both growth and margin.

Table 7.53 Leading drivers for each analyzed industry/cluster

Year	07	08	09	10	11	12	13	14	15	16	17	18	19	20	21
All	R.o.40	Profit.	Profit.	R.o.40	R.o.40	R.o.40	R.o.40	Sal.Gr.	Sal.Gr.	Sal.Gr.	R.o.40	Sal.Gr.	Sal.Gr.	Sal.Gr.	R.o.40
Analytics Soft.							Pr.Gr.	Sal.Gr.	Pr.Gr.	Sal.Gr.	R.o.40	GM Gr.	R.o.40	R.o.40	Pr.Gr.
Classifieds				Profit.	Pr.Gr.	Book	Profit.	Pr.Gr.	R.o.40	R.o.40	Profit.	Profit.	Profit.	Profit.	Profit.
Content Mone. F.								Sal.Gr.	Pr.Gr.	GM Gr.	Profit.	Book	Pr.Gr.	Pr.Gr.	Profit.
Content Mone.*						Pr.Gr.	Profit.	R.o.40	R.o.40	R.o.40	Profit.	R.o.40	Sal.Gr.	Profit.	R.o.40
Customer Acq.							R.o.40	R.o.40	Profit.	Profit.	Sal.Gr.	Sal.Gr.	Sal.Gr.	R.o.40	R.o.40
Data Center				Profit.	R.o.40	Profit.	Profit.	R.o.40	R.o.40	R.o.40	R.o.40	R.o.40	Profit.	Profit.	Profit.
Divers./Portals*					Pr.Gr.	Profit.	Sal.Gr.	Sal.Gr.	R.o.40	R.o.40	Profit.	Profit.	Profit.	R.o.40	Profit.
eCommerce	Pr.Gr.	R.o.40	R.o.40	R.o.40	R.o.40	R.o.40	Profit.	R.o.40	Profit.	Profit.	R.o.40	Profit.	R.o.40	R.o.40	Profit.
Gambling*	Profit.	Profit.	Profit.	Profit.	R.o.40	R.o.40	GM Gr.	Profit.	Sal.Gr.	Pr.Gr.	GM Gr.	Pr.Gr.	R.o.40	R.o.40	R.o.40
Gaming*			Pr.Gr.	R.o.40	Pr.Gr.	Pr.Gr.	Sal.Gr.	Profit.	Profit.	R.o.40	Pr.Gr.	Pr.Gr.	Pr.Gr.	Profit.	R.o.40
Horizontal Soft.	Profit.	Profit.	Profit.	R.o.40	Pr.Gr.	R.o.40	Pr.Gr.	Pr.Gr.	Pr.Gr.	Pr.Gr.	Pr.Gr.	Pr.Gr.	Pr.Gr.	Pr.Gr.	Pr.Gr.
Marketing	Profit.	Profit.	R.o.40	R.o.40	Pr.Gr.	Pr.Gr.	R.o.40	Sal.Gr.	Pr.Gr.	R.o.40	Pr.Gr.	R.o.40	Pr.Gr.	Sal.Gr.	GM Gr.
Marketplace						Profit.	Profit.	R.o.40	R.o.40	Pr.Gr.	R.o.40	Pr.Gr.	Pr.Gr.	Pr.Gr.	Pr.Gr.
Online B2C Se.						Sal.Gr.	Sal.Gr.	GM Gr.	R.o.40	Sal.Gr.	Sal.Gr.	Pr.Gr.	Pr.Gr.	Pr.Gr.	Pr.Gr.
Payment*	Profit.	Profit.	Pr.Gr.	Pr.Gr.	Profit.	R.o.40	R.o.40	R.o.40	Profit.	Pr.Gr.	Pr.Gr.	Pr.Gr.	Pr.Gr.	Sal.Gr.	Sal.Gr.
Platform Soft.	Sal.Gr.	Sal.Gr.	Sal.Gr.	Sal.Gr.	Pr.Gr.	Pr.Gr.	Pr.Gr.	Pr.Gr.	Pr.Gr.	Pr.Gr.	GM Gr.	GM Gr.	Pr.Gr.	Pr.Gr.	Pr.Gr.
Security Soft.	Sal.Gr.	Profit.	Profit.	Sal.Gr.	Profit.	Pr.Gr.	Profit.	Profit.	Pr.Gr.	Sal.Gr.	Sal.Gr.	Pr.Gr.	Profit.	Profit.	Profit.
Social Networks									Sal.Gr.	Pr.Gr.	R.o.40	R.o.40	Pr.Gr.	R.o.40	Book
Travel*								Pr.Gr.	Pr.Gr.	Pr.Gr.	R.o.40	R.o.40	R.o.40	Profit.	Profit.
Vertical Soft.	Profit.	Profit.	Profit.	Profit.	R.o.40	Pr.Gr.	Pr.Gr.	Sal.Gr.	Pr.Gr.	Sal.Gr.	Pr.Gr.	R.o.40	Sal.Gr.	Pr.Gr.	Sal.Gr.
% Sales Growth	25	13	11	18	0	7	18	26	10	20	15	5	15	10	11
% GM Growth	0	0	0	0	0	0	6	5	0	5	10	11	0	0	5
% Rule of 40	0	13	22	36	33	29	18	32	30	30	30	32	20	30	21
% Prof. Growth	13	0	22	9	50	43	24	21	40	35	25	37	45	30	26
% Profitability	63	75	44	36	17	21	35	16	20	10	20	16	20	30	37

Summarizing the data into a bar chart, adding up to 100%, as shown in Fig. 7.4, does not help identify trends. Another level of abstraction, as shown in Fig. 7.5, is required in order to draw conclusions. This presentation consolidates all mixed drivers independent of their form into a group entitled "Mix Growth and Profitability." While the hypothesis and reviewed literature suggested that drivers should transition from growth toward profitability, the summary shows that drivers transition away from simple drivers, such as top-line growth or profitability, towards mixed drivers incorporating both growth and margin components.

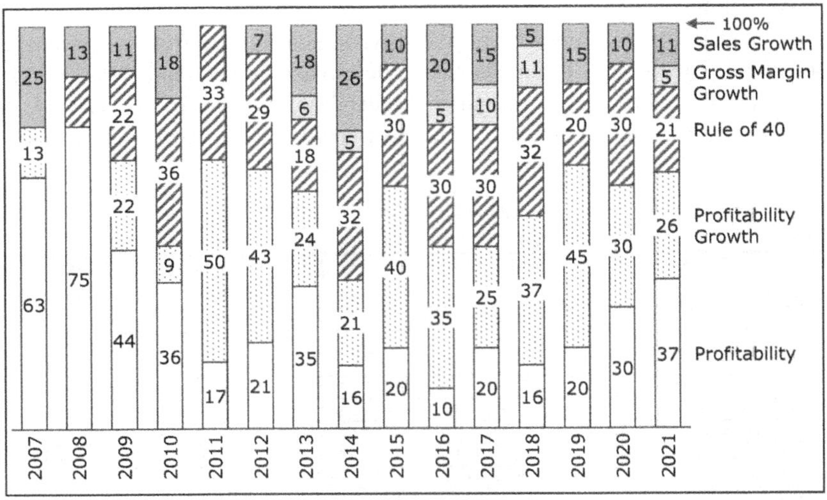

Fig. 7.4 Share of drivers by type for the period covered by the study

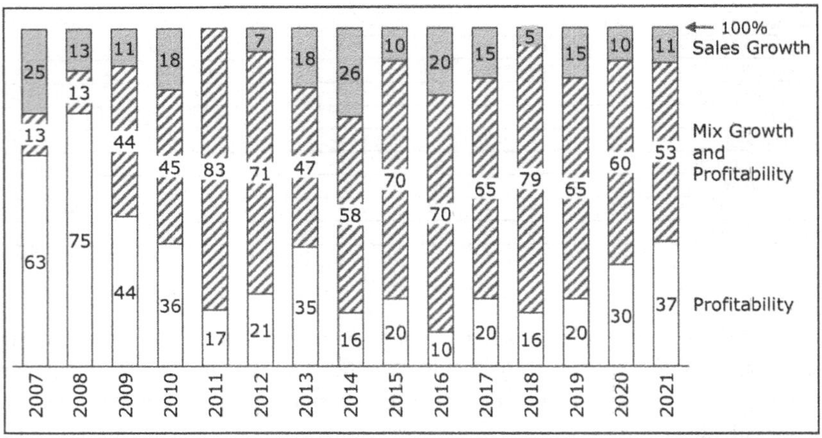

Fig. 7.5 Share of drivers consolidated into three types for the period covered by the study

Interpreting such a conclusion is challenging as multiple factors can cause it. First, it could mean that the internet-driven business models are in the middle of a longer transition phase that will eventually conclude in profitability drivers taking over (again), as seen in the last 2 years. Secondly, it could imply that investors started focusing on a new metric as a driver comprising a business's most important success factors: growth and margin. A clear-cut conclusion would require additional research and a new study design focusing only on this aspect.

Consequently, hypothesis 3 can not be confirmed, however, a variation thereof can be confirmed: valuation drivers transition from simple growth or margin drivers into mixed drivers comprising both aspects into one metric.

7.3.4 Hypothesis 4: Industry Metrics as Alternative to Time for Defining Points of Change

Having shown that valuation bases and drivers change over time, the next natural question is what makes bases and drivers change. As the base change is binary and transits from Sales to Profitability, evaluating various industry-level indicators as an alternative to time is possible. Gross Margin was excluded to allow for a more polarized analysis, however, including it does not change the conclusions significantly. This sub-chapter derives 11 separate industry-wide metrics and compares the average observations in periods where Sales was the leading multiple to the periods where Profitability was the leading base. While Table 7.55 shows the results, a detailed discussion is required.

Industry-wide indicators were calculated by averaging the Growth, LTM Margin, and NTM Margin of companies in a particular industry for each year in the study either cumulatively or as a simple average. The difference between a cumulative approach and the average approach is that large companies are heavily weighted as part of cumulative indicators, while a simple average will imply the same weight for all companies. To exemplify, calculating the cumulative average of the industry adds up revenues of all companies in the industry and calculates, based on this number, the growth for a particular year, while the simple average would take the growth rates of each individual company and average it out.

Indicators considered as an alternative:

- Average industry financials calculated as simple average (as shown in the upper part of Table 7.55 in the first four sub-tables): average actual LTM Sales Growth (shown as "Avg. Sales LTM Gr.") which calculates the growth between observed LTM Sales this year and last year; average NTM Sales Growth (shown as "Avg. Sales NTM Gr.") which calculates growth between LTM Sales and NTM Sales; average LTM Margin calculated relative to LTM Sales (shown as "Avg. LTM Margin"); and average NTM Margin calculated relative to NTM Sales (shown as "Avg. NTM Margin")

- Share of companies with negative EBITDA shown as "Share Neg. EBITDA": calculates the share of companies with a negative EBITDA by taking the count of such companies relative to the count of all companies in the study
- Long-term industry financials similar to the ones above, however, calculated using only the companies that showed observations since the beginning of the study (such approach takes out the additional dynamics caused by new peers joining the cluster): average NTM Sales Growth (shown as "LT Avg. Sal. NTM Gr.") which calculates growth between LTM Sales and NTM Sales; average LTM Margin calculated relative to LTM Sales (shown as "LT Avg. LTM Margin"); and average NTM Margin calculated relative to NTM Sales (shown as "LT Avg. NTM Margin")
- Cumulative industry financials are calculated based on the sum of financials: average NTM Sales Growth (shown as "Cumul. Sal. NTM Gr.") which calculates growth between LTM Sales and NTM Sales; average LTM Margin calculated relative to LTM Sales (shown as "Cumul. LTM Margin"); and average NTM Margin calculated relative to NTM Sales (shown as "Cumul. NTM Margin")

For the evaluation of the results, two final adjustments were made to the presentation: 1) The content monetization industry was taken out because the industry has not shown any years in which profitability was the main base/ multiple, and the travel industry was excluded from the averages due to extreme COVID-19 driven performance over the last years which skew the results, and 2) the industries where a clear transition from Sales to Profitability took place were marked with white (compared to gray for those that did not transition) to help differentiate between industries that occasionally showed Profitability as the main multiple and the ones that showed a clear transition. Table 7.54 summarizes the results presented in Table 7.55.

Table 7.54 Average of deltas (Profitability vs. Sales multiple periods) from Table 7.55

	Transitioned	
	No	Yes
Avg. Sales LTM Gr.	3%	3%
Avg. Sales NTM Gr.	2%	2%
Avg. LTM Margin	1%	−3%
Avg. NTM Margin	0%	−2%
Share Neg. EBITDA	2%	8%
LT Avg. Sal. NTM Gr.	0%	1%
LT Avg. LTM Margin	2%	0%
LT Avg. NTM Margin	1%	1%
Cumul. Sal. NTM Gr.	2%	3%
Cumul. LTM Margin	1%	0%
Cumul. NTM Margin	1%	0%

The results show little overall difference between the metrics observed during the Sales multiple-based valuation periods and the Profitability multiple-based valuation periods, with differences varying between 0 and 3% for both growth and EBITDA margins.

In terms of growth, the expectation was to see lower average growth for the Profitability based periods compared to Sales based periods. The positive figures that can be seen in Table 7.55 for growth-based indicators suggest that industries experience, on average higher growth during EBITDA-based periods, even though the difference is extremely low.

The terms of margin, the expectation was to see higher margins during periods with Profitability Bases, implying positive figures for such indicators in Table 7.55. The analysis shows, however, very low differences and sometimes negative differences. Similar unusual conclusions can be seen in the share of companies with negative EBITDA, which shows that the share increases once the base has transitioned to Profitability Multiples.

Table 7.55 Results testing alternative indicators to time as indicators for a base change

	Avg. Sales LTM Gr.			Avg. Sales NTM Gr.			Avg. LTM Margin			Avg. NTM Margin			Share Neg. EBITDA		
	Sales	Profit.	Δ	Sales	Profit.	Δ	Sales	Profit.	Δ	Sales	Profit.	Δ	Sales	Profit.	Δ
Analytics Soft.	14%	18%	4%	11%	6%	-4%	18%	17%	-1%	19%	14%	-5%	11%	18%	6%
Classifieds	13%	22%	9%	17%	21%	5%	25%	27%	2%	28%	28%	0%	15%	16%	1%
Content Mone. F.	17%	11%	-6%	3%	12%	8%	23%	23%	0%	24%	22%	-2%	5%	6%	1%
Customer Acq.	13%	15%	2%	13%	18%	5%	17%	18%	1%	20%	19%	0%	12%	8%	-4%
Data Center	15%	17%	2%	-1%	-8%	-7%	32%	28%	-4%	32%	29%	-3%	5%	14%	10%
Divers./Portals*	20%	30%	10%	13%	13%	0%	27%	40%	13%	28%	40%	12%	2%	0%	-2%
eCommerce	15%	20%	5%	8%	15%	7%	10%	9%	-1%	11%	9%	-1%	9%	19%	10%
Gambling*	15%	19%	4%	15%	12%	-2%	27%	27%	0%	29%	28%	-1%	7%	0%	-7%
Gaming*	16%	15%	-1%	16%	23%	7%	29%	26%	-3%	31%	28%	-3%	2%	4%	1%
Horizontal Soft.	8%	17%	9%	5%	13%	8%	16%	15%	-1%	19%	16%	-3%	8%	21%	13%
Marketing	9%	7%	-2%	9%	5%	-4%	12%	11%	-2%	14%	13%	-2%	9%	16%	7%
Marketplace	11%	18%	7%	13%	15%	1%	28%	17%	-11%	28%	18%	-10%	3%	25%	22%
Online B2C Se.	15%	18%	3%	27%	21%	-6%	12%	4%	-8%	13%	11%	-2%	20%	40%	20%
Payment*	12%	16%	4%	13%	18%	5%	24%	22%	-2%	26%	25%	-1%	9%	13%	4%
Platform Soft.	17%	16%	-1%	15%	15%	-1%	21%	20%	-2%	22%	22%	0%	23%	14%	-10%
Security Soft.	3%	12%	9%	0%	12%	12%	17%	15%	-2%	18%	17%	-1%	16%	20%	4%
Social Networks	18%	11%	-6%	6%	7%	1%	27%	25%	-1%	28%	26%	-2%	0%	5%	5%
Travel*	-18%	15%	33%	2%	17%	15%	10%	17%	7%	13%	20%	7%	24%	15%	-9%
Vertical Soft.	11%	12%	1%	9%	10%	1%	18%	18%	-1%	21%	19%	-1%	8%	12%	5%

	LT Avg. Sal. NTM Gr.			LT Avg. LTM Margin			LT Avg. NTM Margin			Cumul. Sal. NTM Gr.			Cumul. LTM Margin			Cumul. NTM Margin		
	Sales	Profit.	Δ	Sales	Profit.	Δ	Sales	Profit.	Δ	Sales	Profit.	Δ	Sales	Profit.	Δ	Sales	Profit.	Δ
Analytics Soft.	6%	7%	1%	24%	27%	3%	25%	27%	2%	7%	8%	1%	27%	27%	0%	28%	27%	0%
Classifieds	13%	13%	0%	42%	43%	1%	43%	44%	1%	16%	18%	2%	21%	21%	0%	22%	21%	0%
Content Mone. F.	2%	5%	3%	32%	32%	0%	32%	32%	0%	-1%	5%	6%	30%	28%	-1%	33%	30%	-3%
Customer Acq.	11%	9%	-2%	17%	23%	6%	21%	23%	3%	17%	19%	3%	13%	16%	3%	15%	18%	3%
Data Center	8%	13%	5%	34%	32%	-1%	34%	33%	-1%	12%	14%	2%	39%	40%	0%	41%	42%	1%
Divers./Portals*	18%	22%	4%	28%	39%	11%	28%	38%	11%	20%	26%	5%	39%	47%	8%	39%	46%	7%
eCommerce	12%	12%	0%	12%	13%	1%	12%	13%	1%	22%	24%	2%	8%	9%	1%	8%	10%	1%
Gambling*	20%	9%	-10%	25%	24%	-1%	28%	24%	-5%	7%	10%	3%	29%	30%	1%	30%	29%	-1%
Gaming*	21%	23%	2%	29%	27%	-1%	32%	30%	-3%	26%	21%	-5%	33%	30%	-3%	34%	32%	-3%
Horizontal Soft.	11%	11%	0%	18%	21%	3%	20%	22%	2%	8%	15%	6%	26%	25%	-1%	28%	25%	-3%
Marketing	10%	7%	-3%	15%	11%	-4%	17%	13%	-3%	7%	9%	2%	19%	18%	-1%	19%	18%	-1%
Marketplace	9%	9%	0%	22%	20%	-3%	23%	20%	-2%	18%	37%	19%	36%	27%	-9%	36%	24%	-12%
Online B2C Se.	24%	30%	6%	-5%	-11%	-6%	-1%	6%	7%	31%	26%	-5%	7%	10%	3%	10%	13%	3%
Payment*	9%	7%	-2%	27%	28%	2%	28%	29%	1%	16%	10%	-6%	29%	31%	1%	29%	31%	2%
Platform Soft.	11%	9%	-2%	33%	32%	-1%	33%	32%	-1%	9%	9%	0%	40%	41%	1%	40%	41%	1%
Security Soft.	9%	7%	-2%	20%	23%	3%	22%	24%	2%	6%	6%	0%	29%	31%	1%	29%	30%	1%
Social Networks	7%	6%	-1%	27%	23%	-4%	27%	25%	-2%	29%	23%	-5%	51%	50%	-1%	49%	48%	-1%
Travel*	1%	17%	16%	14%	20%	6%	17%	22%	5%	1%	15%	14%	21%	26%	6%	22%	27%	5%
Vertical Soft.	12%	8%	-4%	23%	24%	1%	24%	25%	1%	10%	11%	1%	20%	24%	3%	21%	25%	3%

While **Hypothesis 4 cannot be confirmed using this analysis,** selecting industry indicators does not imply that time is the only relevant factor concerning the point of change in Bases. While further and more comprehensive research is required, these results might also imply that the science and practice of valuation have not considered this factor in this form yet, similar to the way empirical research into the changes of bases and drivers is just commencing.

Conclusions: Original Contributions and Future Research

8

Being initiated by practice-rooted questions for which no empirically driven answers were available, the study embarks on a journey that proved much longer and more challenging than anticipated. The voyage comprised over 10% of all publicly listed companies, from which nearly half were considered individually and categorized into 21 clusters based on proprietary research. In addition to evaluating the proposed hypotheses and providing new findings, the study presents an extensive framework with significant potential for future research. The descriptive and inferential statistics components only scratch the surface of what is possible with this framework and dataset comprising nearly 100 million observations. The study goes as far as proposing and showing the relevance of a new valuation concept that accounts for and adjusts the valuation multiples and drivers used for relative valuation according to the development phase of an industry.

8.1 General Conclusions of the Ph.D. research

As the title states, the goal of the thesis is to link the "industry life-cycle" with the "business valuation" by using "internet-enabled" business models as the focus or case study. The intention is to observe the bases and drivers of relative valuation across the time period covered by the study, which corresponds with the time period in which internet-enabled businesses reached a certain level of maturity, and understand if the bases (multiples) and drivers (financial indicators) that explain the highest share of variation have changed. In the preparation of relative valuations, the literature and professional know-how suggest three generally valid concepts:

A. Trusculescu, *Business Valuation Across the Industry Life Cycle*,
https://doi.org/10.1007/978-3-658-49126-0_8

1. Comparability: companies included in a peer group (cluster) should have similar business models and financials;
2. Prices as multiples: the price of a company is to be calculated as EUR per unit of measurement (e.g., EV/ Revenue, EV/ EBITDA, Price per Earnings) using a similar analogy to the price per square meter; and
3. Multiples are "driven": by various financial metrics such as growth or margin, implying that a company with a higher growth rate or a higher margin should have a higher price per unit than one with lower growth or margin.

While this reasoning can be applied to virtually everything, businesses are complex entities with many financial variables that can be used to derive a valuation. Both the reference unit for the price and the indicators that increase or decrease the price per reference unit can be represented by virtually any financial metric. Furthermore, reference units and drivers can change over time depending on time, the life cycle of the company, or some industry financial metric.

This study implements the concept of "comparability" across all publicly listed companies with internet-enabled businesses to deriver 21 clusters that can be used independently of each other over the period of 15 years to observe the shift in reference units for multiples (bases) and drivers.

The study demonstrates for internet-enabled businesses the relevance of clustering and, for several industries part of the internet-enabled sector, the shift from Revenue Multiples to Profitability Multiples and from Profitability Drivers to Drivers combining Growth and Profitability. The study also tries to suggest metrics in addition to time that could cause an infliction point in Multiples and Drivers, however, it cannot identify evidence for the one factor that causes these changes. In addition to this limitation, it should be noted that the study focused on evaluating the key research questions, ignoring other research directions that can be explored using the same framework and data.

Further limitations of the study include the focus on public companies and the focus on the growth and early maturity phases of the industry life cycles. Both limitations are technical in nature and would require the redesign of the study. In most cases, private companies provide no financial information or forecasts, making the analysis at this level of detail impossible. Including initial phases of the industry life cycles would require including private companies as most companies in this phase are not publicly listed. Furthermore, including such companies would require the removal of the story vs. financials story component limitation, which would come with a significantly lower ability to provide accurate and precise answers. Including the last phase (the decline phase) of an industry life cycle would require the selection of new industries since internet-enabled business models are far away from this life stage.

The inclusion of publicly listed companies reduces the applicability to private situations to some extent, as the return expectations for public companies are often significantly lower than for private ones. The data availability of public companies makes, however, such studies possible. A similar study only including private companies would be incredibly difficult to implement due to data availability and other limitations. Lastly, it should be noted that there are methods to adjust valuation multiples of public companies for private situations making the findings relevant.

Despite the limitations, demonstrating shifts in Multiples and Drivers could represent the stepping stone for future research and potentially a new element in the corporate valuation toolbox.

8.2 Original Contributions

The study contributes to the scientific literature and professional know-how in multiple ways and closes serval research and knowledge gaps:

1. Extends the time period covered by existing literature on the Dot-Com bubble or similar studies performed at single points in time to cover the period 2007–2021;
2. Delivers one for the first investigations covering a long period of time (15 years) with each year compared to one another as opposed to single points in time or short periods of time;
3. Covers most relevant internet-enabled industries as part of 21 clusters as opposed to focusing on a single industry or a small number of industries and delivers industry-level conclusions;
4. Providers an empirically determined link between the coming of age of internet-enabled industries and related shifts in the Valuation Multiples and Drivers potentially representing a new element in corporate valuation; and
5. Derives a framework that could be used to study additional elements of importance in corporate valuation.

Contributions 1, 2, 3, and 4 represent direct contributions to the finance and internet-associated literature in the field and fill the described research and knowledge gaps described in the previous chapters. In particular, the study complements and extends the work of Schreiner, Harbott, Liu, Nissim and Thomas, as well as demonstrates and complements the work on the company and industry life cycles of Professor Damodaran.

Contributions 4 and 5 represent contributions to the field of theoretical research (creative and conceptual developments) by providing methods and frameworks aimed at similar research studies in the future, while contributions 3, 4, and 5 represent contributions to the field of applicative research (praxiological implications of the research findings) by providing tangible results and industry-level conclusions of high relevance for management teams and shareholder in each industry.

Based on the discussion in Sect. 2.3, there is a high likelihood that contributions to the fields of theoretical and applicative research will be highly relevant to future industries and technologies. Most technologies in sight have strong internet-based connectivity components that use the current known revenue types, implying that the results and findings can be applied by using extrapolation based on the industry life cycles.

8.3 Future Research

The extensive nature of the implemented study attempted to cover all relevant directions in terms of companies (all identified companies that could be relevant were considered without exceptions), financial indicators (all relevant indicators with sufficient data were included), types of variables (regular profit and loss statement and cash flow multiples were included in along book value multiples, and both growth and margin drivers were included along innovative multiples such as the Rule of 40) and timeframes (all feasible timeframes were included concerning both historical financials and forecasts). The vast framework could enable testing additional hypotheses, with some mentioned in this chapter.

Future research directions can be grouped into three categories based on the viability of the existing framework and data set:

Research questions that can be tested using the existing framework and data set:

- Adjust current assumptions: while the study makes, in addition to the limitations, very few assumptions, changing these could result in new results. The most important assumption relates to the ranges in which the multiples and drivers as considered relevant for a financials-based valuation. While these assumptions were well documented in the study and derived from both literature and practical applications, there might be other ways of deriving the ranges of relevance.

- Breakdown results to understand the importance of historical vs. forecast financials: the study focuses on the type of multiples and drivers and does not differentiate between historical and forward-looking variables. The results of each industry can be broken down further to understand, on the one side, the relevance of historical vs. forward-looking financials and, on the other side, the relevant periods (number of years backward or in the future).
- Breakdown results to understand the importance of geography: similarly to the previous research direction, the study does not account for differences in geographies and focuses on understanding shifts in multiples and drivers for 21 segments/industries. Some clusters have sufficient constituents to enable a comparison of geographies. Studies focusing on one particular industry could tackle this topic.

Research questions that can be tested using a marginally adjusted framework and data set:

- Testing ability to forecast business plans: Including a wide range of variables segmented by industry would, over a period of 15 years, enable the evaluation of the ability of brokers and analysts to forecast business performance. Such a study would complement and potentially challenge the findings of Bradley et al. as part of a study conducted by McKinsey (Bradley et al., 2018).

Research questions that would require new frameworks and/or data sets:

- Testing findings on new economic segments: while the study focuses on internet-enabled business models as these were recognized as part of the natural experiment the internet has presented, the same study can be performed on other sectors requiring, however, all stages to be repeated using the same framework. The segmentation stage, which groups companies into clusters, is critically important for good results.
- Apply other statistical models and frameworks: Given the broad scope of the data model and large data set, researchers could explore new statistical models and frameworks. It is worth noting that financial variables differing only by timeframe are highly correlated most of the time, while variables of similar

types are also highly correlated. Studies trying to apply other models or frameworks should account for this. Lastly, implementing time-series-type models is difficult when attempting to isolate years or periods.

- New variables: while this study sought to be as inclusive as possible regarding the variable types and financial variables included, including new variable types is possible. Other studies have also included operative variables such as the number of views or the number of users, however, it was impossible to procure such data for the entirety of the period covered by the study. Other variables or types of variables not considered could also be relevant.
- Identify new variables defining infliction points: as the current study focused on including industry variables as predictors of infliction points in valuation bases and drivers, other variables or forms of suggested variables could also come into question. Understanding better what causes shifts and changes in the valuation bases and drivers would be interesting.
- Studies focusing on private markets: While private markets are very untransparent, with little financial information available, it would be highly interesting to try replicating the present study on such circumstances. An entirely new framework and methodology would have to be developed to replicate the testing of the hypotheses on such markets.

The present study represents only the groundwork of what is possible to be researched and understood at the intersection between valuation and industry life cycles, an area of valuation less covered by researchers in the field. Suggestions and offers for collaboration are highly welcomed to help develop an understanding of this thrilling new area of valuation.

8.4 Praxiological Implications of the Ph.D. Thesis: Implications for Managers and Shareholders

Having initiated the study with questions from managers and shareholders, it is only fair to end it with the praxiological implications and recommendations for value-maximizing strategies. The study adds to the list of matters that founders, managers, and shareholders need to watch out for the valuation bases and the valuation drivers.

The findings show that the derivation of precise valuation multiples and drivers depends on the precise clustering of business models implying that a good understanding of the business models and revenue models of similar companies and competitors can help triangulate their own valuation.

Concerning the multiples (valuation bases), the study demonstrates, using several industries as case studies, that once an industry reaches a certain level of maturity, its valuation multiples shift from being top-line-based to being profitability-based. While the intention was to pinpoint the switch and relate it to a variable or equation to accurately predict future shifts, the variables used for the prediction were not more useful than time. While this finding implies that valuation has a certain "art" component, what is certain is that once an industry achieves profitability on average, after a certain amount of time (not immediately), the valuation base shifts towards profitability. Beyond the obvious conclusion that profitability is expected from a player if the industry is already profitable, it also shows that a growth strategy focusing on achieving profitability at some point in the future is not necessarily value-generating and that the strategy should be geared towards profitability if an exit is in sight.

Regarding drivers, the shift is also clear from profitability or growth alone towards combined drivers like the Rule of 40. This finding does not help solve the old growth vs. margin dilemma, however, it highlights the importance of profitable growth and positive unit economics for businesses where initial investment does not boost long-term profitability (e.g., SaaS with high initial investment).

While the conclusions are generalized, the industry-level conclusions in Sect. 7.2 should be consulted to determine a value-maximizing strategy.

References Thesis

Abbate, J. (2000). Inventing the Internet. MIT Press.

Aggarwal, A., & Bahl, N. (2021). Start-ups and Early Stage Companies—A Valuation insight—KPMG [Consulting report]. KPMG. https://assets.kpmg/content/dam/kpmg/kw/pdf/insights/2021/05/valuation-startup-web.pdf

Almeida, F., Duarte Santos, J., & Augusto Monteiro, J. (2020). The Challenges and Opportunities in the Digitalization of Companies in a Post-COVID-19 World. IEEE Engineering Management Review, 48(3), 97–103. https://doi.org/10.1109/EMR.2020.3013206

Amankwah-Amoah, J., Khan, Z., Wood, G., & Knight, G. (2021). COVID-19 and digitalization: The great acceleration. Journal of Business Research, 136, 602–611. https://doi.org/10.1016/j.jbusres.2021.08.011

Amazon.com Inc. (2022). Amazon.com Inc.—Annual Report 2021 [Annual Report]. https://d18rn0p25nwr6d.cloudfront.net/CIK-0001018724/f965e5c3-fded-45d3-bbdb-f750f156dcc9.pdf

Andreessen, M., & Bina, E. (2022, December 25). Mosaic Web Browser History—NCSA. LivingInternet. https://www.livinginternet.com/w/wi_mosaic.htm

Arand, D., Kerl, A., & Walter, A. (2015). When Do Sell-side Analyst Reports Really Matter? Shareholder Protection, Institutional Investors and the Informativeness of Equity Research. European Financial Management, 21(3), 524–555. https://doi.org/10.1111/j.1468-036X.2013.12028.x

Aste, T., Tasca, P., & Di Matteo, T. (2017). Blockchain Technologies: The Foreseeable Impact on Society and Industry. Computer, 50(9), 18–28. https://doi.org/10.1109/MC.2017.3571064

Attaran, M. (2021). The impact of 5G on the evolution of intelligent automation and industry digitization. Journal of Ambient Intelligence and Humanized Computing. https://doi.org/10.1007/s12652-020-02521-x

Aw, E. C.-X., Kamal Basha, N., Ng, S. I., & Ho, J. A. (2021). Searching online and buying offline: Understanding the role of channel-, consumer-, and product-related factors in determining webrooming intention. Journal of Retailing and Consumer Services, 58, 102328. https://doi.org/10.1016/j.jretconser.2020.102328

Aydin, R. (2019, September 20). How 3 guys turned renting air mattresses in their apartment into a $31 billion company, Airbnb [News]. Business Insider. https://www.businessinsider.com/how-airbnb-was-founded-a-visual-history-2016-2

A. Trusculescu, *Business Valuation Across the Industry Life Cycle*,
https://doi.org/10.1007/978-3-658-49126-0

Aydın, Ö., & Karaarslan, E. (2022). OpenAI ChatGPT Generated Literature Review: Digital Twin in Healthcare (SSRN Scholarly Paper No. 4308687). https://doi.org/10.2139/ssrn.4308687

Barr, A. (2012, August 10). Groupon Goods takes off, but raises accounting questions. Reuters. https://www.reuters.com/article/us-groupon-goods/groupon-goods-takes-off-but-raises-accounting-questions-idUSBRE8790Q820120810

Berners-Lee, T. (1989). Information Management: A Proposal (TBL-900620). https://cds.cern.ch/record/369245/files/dd-89-001.pdf

Berthold, M. R., Cebron, N., Dill, F., Gabriel, T. R., Kötter, T., Meinl, T., Ohl, P., Sieb, C., Thiel, K., & Wiswedel, B. (2008). KNIME: The Konstanz Information Miner. In C. Preisach, H. Burkhardt, L. Schmidt-Thieme, & R. Decker (Eds.), Data Analysis, Machine Learning and Applications (pp. 319–326). Springer. https://doi.org/10.1007/978-3-540-78246-9_38

Boulton, T. (2013, September 6). Everything You Ever Wanted to Know About Craig From Craigslist. Gizmodo. https://gizmodo.com/everything-you-ever-wanted-to-know-about-craig-from-cra-1262446153

boyd, danah m., & Ellison, N. B. (2007). Social Network Sites: Definition, History, and Scholarship. Journal of Computer-Mediated Communication, 13(1), 210–230. https://doi.org/10.1111/j.1083-6101.2007.00393.x

Brackenborough, S., Mclean, T., & Oldroyd, D. (2001). The Emergence of Discounted Cash Flow Analysis In The Tyneside Coal Industry c.1700–1820. The British Accounting Review, 33(2), 137–155. https://doi.org/10.1006/bare.2001.0158

Bradley, C., Hirt, M., & Smit, S. (2018, February 13). Strategy to beat the odds | McKinsey [Blog]. McKinsey. https://www.mckinsey.com/capabilities/strategy-and-corporate-finance/our-insights/strategy-to-beat-the-odds

Branchereau, G. (2018, March 2). The story of Spotify: Sweden's controversial king of music streaming [News]. The Local Sweden. https://www.thelocal.se/20180302/the-story-of-spotify-swedens-controversial-king-of-music-streaming/

Browning, J. (2005, March 7). Memories of Nasdaq's High. Wall Street Journal. https://www.wsj.com/articles/SB110995029690370706

Burden, D., & Savin-Baden, M. (2019). Virtual Humans: Today and Tomorrow. CRC Press.

Business Standard. (2020, July 30). Mark Zuckerberg bought Instagram as it was a "threat" to Facebook [News]. Business Standard. https://www.business-standard.com/article/international/mark-zuckerberg-bought-instagram-as-it-was-a-threat-to-facebook-120073000324_1.html

Camero, A., & Alba, E. (2019). Smart City and information technology: A review. Cities, 93, 84–94. https://doi.org/10.1016/j.cities.2019.04.014

Cavallo, A. (2017). Are Online and Offline Prices Similar? Evidence from Large Multi-channel Retailers. American Economic Review, 107(1), 283–303. https://doi.org/10.1257/aer.20160542

Chang, M. (2020, August 30). A Student's Guide to Writing A Buy-Side Equity Research Report. Romero Mentoring. https://romeromentoring.com/a-students-guide-to-writing-a-buy-side-equity-research-report/

Chaudhary, D., Kumar, P., & Rawat, S. (2021). Software as a Service for Upcoming Industries. In A. E. Hassanien, S. Bhattacharyya, S. Chakrabati, A. Bhattacharya, & S. Dutta

(Eds.), Emerging Technologies in Data Mining and Information Security (pp. 683–692). Springer. https://doi.org/10.1007/978-981-15-9927-9_66
Chaum, D. L. (1982). Computer Systems Established, Maintained and Trusted by Mutually Suspicious Groups. University of California, Berkeley. https://nakamotoinstitute.org/static/docs/computer-systems-by-mutually-suspicious-groups.pdf
Chen, Y. (2017). Integrated and Intelligent Manufacturing: Perspectives and Enablers. Engineering, 3(5), 588–595. https://doi.org/10.1016/J.ENG.2017.04.009
Chohan, U. W. (2022). Web 3.0: The Future Architecture of the Internet? (SSRN Scholarly Paper No. 4037693). https://doi.org/10.2139/ssrn.4037693
Christopher Hooton. (2019, November 26). Measuring The U.S. Internet Sector: 2019 • Internet Association. Internet Association. https://internetassociation.org/publications/measuring-us-internet-sector-2019/
Clark, A. (2008, February 1). How Jerry's guide to the world wide web became Yahoo. The Guardian. https://www.theguardian.com/business/2008/feb/01/microsoft.technology
CNN Money. (2000, June 7). Microsoft case in a nutshell [News]. CNN. https://money.cnn.com/2000/06/07/technology/microsoft_chronology/
Comer, D. (1983). The computer science research network CSNET: A history and status report. Communications of the ACM, 26(10), 747–753. https://doi.org/10.1145/358413.358423
Connolly, D. j., Olsen, M. D., & Moore, R. G. (1998). The Internet as a Distribution Channel. Cornell Hotel and Restaurant Administration Quarterly, 39(4), 42–54. https://doi.org/10.1177/001088049803900408
Cook, J. (2015, January 23). Jack Ma: Here's How Alibaba Will Become Bigger Than Walmart. Business Insider. http://uk.businessinsider.com/jack-ma-heres-how-alibaba-will-become-bigger-than-walmart-2015-1
Craig, W. (2022, August 12). The History of the Internet in a Nutshell [Blog]. WebFX. https://www.webfx.com/blog/web-design/the-history-of-the-internet-in-a-nutshell/
Curtis, S. K., & Lehner, M. (2019). Defining the Sharing Economy for Sustainability. Sustainability, 11(3), Article 3. https://doi.org/10.3390/su11030567
Damodaran, A. (2009). Valuing Young, Start-Up and Growth Companies: Estimation Issues and Valuation Challenges (SSRN Scholarly Paper No. 1418687). https://doi.org/10.2139/ssrn.1418687
Damodaran, A. (2018a, March). The Corporate Life Cycle: Growing up is hard to do! [Lecture]. https://pages.stern.nyu.edu/~adamodar/pdfiles/country/corporatelifecycleLongX.pdf
Damodaran, A. (Director). (2018b, November 13). Aswath Damodaran—Laws of Valuation: Revealing the Myths and Misconceptions—Nordic Business Forum [Youtube]. https://www.youtube.com/watch?v=c20_S-QgvsA
Damodaran, A. (2021). Valuation Course Spring 2021—New York University. Valuation Course Spring 2021—Session17. https://pages.stern.nyu.edu/~adamodar/podcasts/valspr21/session17slides.pdf
Damodaran, A. (2022, December 10). Damodaran Online: Home Page for Aswath Damodaran—Bio and Mission [Educational]. Damodaran Online. https://pages.stern.nyu.edu/~adamodar/

De Chant, T. (2011, October 27). In depth on Groupon's accounting practices. Expertly Wrapped. https://expertlywrapped.wordpress.com/2011/10/27/in-depth-on-groupons-accounting-practices/

De La Merced, M. J., & Rusli, E. M. (2011, September 23). Accounting Change Cuts Groupon's Revenue. DealBook. https://dealbook.nytimes.com/2011/09/23/groupon-changes-its-revenue-accounting/

Dowling, M., & Lucey, B. (2023). ChatGPT for (Finance) research: The Bananarama Conjecture. Finance Research Letters, 103662. https://doi.org/10.1016/j.frl.2023.103662

Dutfield, S. & Laura Mears. (2022, March 31). World Wide Web: Definition, history and facts. Livescience.Com. https://www.livescience.com/world-wide-web

Emerson, S. L. (1983, October). Usenet—A Bulletin Board for Unix Users. Byte Magazine, 08(10), 219.

Ericsson. (2023, January 28). The Internet of Things (IoT) technology—Why IoT changes everything [Corporate]. Ericsson.Com. https://www.ericsson.com/en/internet-of-things

Evangelista, B. (2002, September 4). Napster runs out of lives—Judge rules against sale. SFGATE. https://www.sfgate.com/business/article/Napster-runs-out-of-lives-judge-rules-against-2774278.php

FactSet Research Systems. (2022). FactSet Software and Database [Windows 10]. https://www.factset.com/

Farber, D. (2014, January 9). When iPhone met world, 7 years ago today [News]. CNET. https://www.cnet.com/tech/tech-industry/when-iphone-met-world-7-years-ago-today/

Feld, B. (2015, February 3). The Rule of 40% For a Healthy SaaS Company [Blog]. Brad Feld. https://feld.com/archives/2015/02/rule-40-healthy-saas-company/

Feltham, G. A., & Ohlson, J. A. (1995). Valuation and Clean Surplus Accounting for Operating and Financial Activities*. Contemporary Accounting Research, 11(2), 689–731. https://doi.org/10.1111/j.1911-3846.1995.tb00462.x

Finley, K. (2018, October 31). After 10 Years, Bitcoin Has Changed Everything—And Nothing [News]. Wired. https://www.wired.com/story/after-10-years-bitcoin-changed-everything-nothing/

Fisher, I. (1930). The Theory of Interest—As Determined by Impatience to Spend Income and Opportunity to Invest It. Macmillan.

Ford, H., & Crowther, S. (2006). My Life and Work. Book Jungle.

Forward, A., & Lethbridge, T. C. (2008). A taxonomy of software types to facilitate search and evidence-based software engineering. Proceedings of the 2008 Conference of the Center for Advanced Studies on Collaborative Research: Meeting of Minds, 179–191. https://doi.org/10.1145/1463788.1463807

Fried, I. (2010, August 16). At 15, Microsoft's Internet Explorer at a crossroads [News]. CNET. https://www.cnet.com/culture/at-15-microsofts-internet-explorer-at-a-crossroads/

Fuller, A., Fan, Z., Day, C., & Barlow, C. (2020). Digital Twin: Enabling Technologies, Challenges and Open Research. IEEE Access, 8, 108952–108971. https://doi.org/10.1109/ACCESS.2020.2998358

Gama, A. P. M., Segura, L. C., & Filho, M. A. F. M. (2016). Equity Valuation and Negative Earnings: The Case of the dot.com Bubble (1st ed. 2017 edition). Springer.

Gangatharan, A. (2008). The problem of periodization in history. Proceedings of the Indian History Congress, 69, 862–871.

GCA Altium. (2018a). Software Sector Report—August 2018.

GCA Altium. (2018b). Semiconductor Sector Report—September 2018.

GCA Altium. (2018c). Digital, Media & Internet Monitor—October 2018.

Gibbs, S. (2016, March 7). How did email grow from messages between academics to a global epidemic? The Guardian. https://www.theguardian.com/technology/2016/mar/07/email-ray-tomlinson-history

Gillette, F. (2011, June 23). The Rise and Inglorious Fall of Myspace. Bloomberg.Com. https://www.bloomberg.com/news/articles/2011-06-22/the-rise-and-inglorious-fall-of-myspace

Gligorijevic, B. (2011). Online retailing versus traditional stores in the purchasing decision making process. In M. MacCarthy (Ed.), Marketing in the Age of Consumerism: Jekyll or Hyde? Proceedings of the 2011 Australian and New Zealand Marketing Academy Conference (pp. 1–8). School of Marketing, Faculty of Business and Law, Tourism and Leisure, Edith Cowan University. http://anzmac.org/conference/2011/

Google LLC. (2022, December 26). How we started and where we are today—Google [Corporate]. How We Started and Where We Are Today—Google. https://about.google/our-story/

Gozalo-Brizuela, R., & Garrido-Merchan, E. C. (2023). ChatGPT is not all you need. A State of the Art Review of large Generative AI models (arXiv:2301.04655). arXiv. https://doi.org/10.48550/arXiv.2301.04655

Grandoni, D. (2013, April 1). The Man Who Invented The World's First Search Engine (But Didn't Patent It). HuffPost UK. https://www.huffpost.com/entry/alan-emtage-search-engine_n_2994090

Green, W. A. (1992). Periodization in European and World History. Journal of World History, 3(1), 13–53.

Greenspan, A. (1996, December 5). The Challenge of Central Banking in a Democratic Society [Government]. Federal Reserve Board. https://www.federalreserve.gov/boarddocs/speeches/1996/19961205.htm

Groupon. (2018, March 17). Groupon: Deals and Coupons for Restaurants, Fitness, Travel, Shopping, Beauty, and more. Groupon. https://www.groupon.com/

Han, D.-I. D., Bergs, Y., & Moorhouse, N. (2022). Virtual reality consumer experience escapes: Preparing for the metaverse. Virtual Reality, 26(4), 1443–1458. https://doi.org/10.1007/s10055-022-00641-7

Harbott, A. (2012). What drives Internet company valuation?—A business model approach to Internet value drivers [MBA Thesis]. Cass Business School, City University London. http://www.harbott.com/2012/09/25/mba-thesis-what-drives-internet-company-valuation/

Harris, K. (2018, July 17). Professor Aswath Damodaran on Valuation. Forbes. https://www.forbes.com/sites/kevinharris/2018/07/17/professor-aswath-damodaran-on-valuation/

Hawlitschek, F., Notheisen, B., & Teubner, T. (2018). The limits of trust-free systems: A literature review on blockchain technology and trust in the sharing economy. Electronic Commerce Research and Applications, 29, 50–63. https://doi.org/10.1016/j.elerap.2018.03.005

Helft, M. (2007, January 16). Netflix to Deliver Movies to the PC [News]. The New York Times. https://www.nytimes.com/2007/01/16/technology/16netflix.html

Helft, M., & Richtel, M. (2006, October 10). Venture Firm Shares a YouTube Jackpot. The New York Times. https://www.nytimes.com/2006/10/10/technology/10payday.html

Higson, C., & Briginshaw, J. (2000). Valuing Internet Business. Business Strategy Review, 11, 10–20. https://doi.org/10.1111/1467-8616.00125

Hitchner, J. R. (2017). Financial Valuation: Applications and Models (4th edition). Wiley.

Höfer, C. N., & Karagiannis, G. (2011). Cloud computing services: Taxonomy and comparison. Journal of Internet Services and Applications, 2(2), Article 2. https://doi.org/10.1007/s13174-011-0027-x

Hoffman, H. (2007, October 29). Web TV: Hulu's private beta goes live [News]. CNET. https://www.cnet.com/culture/web-tv-hulus-private-beta-goes-live/

Holthausen, R. W., & Zmijewski, M. E. (2012). Valuation with Market Multiples: How to Avoid Pitfalls When Identifying and Using Comparable Companies1. Journal of Applied Corporate Finance, 24(3), 26–38. https://doi.org/10.1111/j.1745-6622.2012.00387.x

Hootsuite Inc. (2023, January 27). Digital 2022—Global Overview Report—The Essential Guide to The World's Connected Behaviours [Corporate]. Www.Hootsuite.Com. https://hootsuite.widen.net/s/gqprmtzq6g/digital-2022-global-overview-report

Horvath, B. (2018). The recognition of resource use through industrial development from a social perspective. Studia Mundi—Economica, 5. https://doi.org/10.18531/Studia.Mundi.2018.05.01.68-78

Hoseini, L. (2013). Advantages and Disadvantages of Adopting ERP Systems Served as SaaS from the Perspective of SaaS Users. http://urn.kb.se/resolve?urn=urn:nbn:se:kth:diva-128516

Hossain, M. (2020). Sharing economy: A comprehensive literature review. International Journal of Hospitality Management, 87, 102470. https://doi.org/10.1016/j.ijhm.2020.102470

Isaac, M. (2021, October 28). Facebook Renames Itself Meta. The New York Times. https://www.nytimes.com/2021/10/28/technology/facebook-meta-name-change.html

Jenner, M. (2018). Netflix and the Re-invention of Television. Springer International Publishing.

Jones, D., Snider, C., Nassehi, A., Yon, J., & Hicks, B. (2020). Characterising the Digital Twin: A systematic literature review. CIRP Journal of Manufacturing Science and Technology, 29, 36–52. https://doi.org/10.1016/j.cirpj.2020.02.002

Kawamoto, D. (2002, January 2). TheGlobe.com's IPO one for the books [News]. CNET. https://www.cnet.com/tech/services-and-software/theglobe-coms-ipo-one-for-the-books/

Kim, B.-K. (2005). Internationalizing the Internet: The Co-evolution of Influence and Technology. Edward Elgar Publishing.

Kim, E. (2015, September 19). CEO of $50 billion Salesforce shared his epic founding story to inspire a small business owner. Business Insider. https://www.businessinsider.com/salesforce-benioff-shares-founding-story-2015-9

Kincaid, J. (2009, October 14). Dropbox Acquires The Domain Everyone Thought It Had: Dropbox.com. TechCrunch. https://techcrunch.com/2009/10/13/dropbox-acquires-the-domain-everyone-thought-it-had-dropbox-com/

Kingsnorth, S. (2022). Digital Marketing Strategy: An Integrated Approach to Online Marketing (3rd ed.). Kogan Page.

Kinnunen, J. (2022). ERP as Software-as-a-Service: Factors Depicting Large Enterprises Cloud Adoption. In M. R. Khosravi, Q. He, & H. Dai (Eds.), Cloud Computing (pp. 123–142). Springer International Publishing. https://doi.org/10.1007/978-3-030-99191-3_10

Kirstein, P. T. (1999). Early experiences with the Arpanet and Internet in the United Kingdom. IEEE Annals of the History of Computing, 21(1), 38–44. https://doi.org/10.1109/85.759368

Koller, T., Goedhart, M., Wessels, D., & McKinsey & Company Inc. (2010). Valuation: Measuring and Managing the Value of Companies, 5th Edition (5th edition). Wiley.

Koller, T., Goedhart, M., Wessels, D., & McKinsey & Company Inc. (2020). Valuation: Measuring and Managing the Value of Companies, University Edition (7th edition). Wiley.

Kong, Y., Wang, Y., Hajli, S., & Featherman, M. (2020). In Sharing Economy We Trust: Examining the Effect of Social and Technical Enablers on Millennials' Trust in Sharing Commerce. Computers in Human Behavior, 108, 105993. https://doi.org/10.1016/j.chb.2019.04.017

Krieger, T. (1995, September 1). Love and Money. Wired. https://www.wired.com/1995/09/love-and-money/

Langley, D. J., van Doorn, J., Ng, I. C. L., Stieglitz, S., Lazovik, A., & Boonstra, A. (2021). The Internet of Everything: Smart things and their impact on business models. Journal of Business Research, 122, 853–863. https://doi.org/10.1016/j.jbusres.2019.12.035

Laudon, K., & Traver, C. (2019). E-Commerce 2019: Business, Technology and Society 15th Edition (15th edition). Pearson.

Laudon, K., & Traver, C. (2020). E-Commerce 2020–2021: Business, Technology and Society, 16th Edition (16th edition). Pearson.

Lee, L.-H., Braud, T., Zhou, P., Wang, L., Xu, D., Lin, Z., Kumar, A., Bermejo, C., & Hui, P. (2021). All One Needs to Know about Metaverse: A Complete Survey on Technological Singularity, Virtual Ecosystem, and Research Agenda (arXiv:2110.05352). arXiv. https://doi.org/10.48550/arXiv.2110.05352

Liao, H. (2010). SaaS business model for software enterprise. 2010 2nd IEEE International Conference on Information Management and Engineering, 604–607. https://doi.org/10.1109/ICIME.2010.5477915

Links, C. (2022, May 24). The Evolution of Wi-Fi networks: From IEEE 802.11 to Wi-Fi 6E. Wevolver. https://www.wevolver.com/article/the-evolution-of-wi-fi-networks-from-ieee-80211-to-wi-fi-6e

Liu, J., Nissim, D., & Thomas, J. (2002). Equity Valuation Using Multiples. Journal of Accounting Research, 40(1), 135–172. https://doi.org/10.1111/1475-679X.00042

Liu, M., Fang, S., Dong, H., & Xu, C. (2021). Review of digital twin about concepts, technologies, and industrial applications. Journal of Manufacturing Systems, 58, 346–361. https://doi.org/10.1016/j.jmsy.2020.06.017

Living Internet. (2022, December 11). ARPANET IMP, Interface Message Processor. Living-Internet. https://www.livinginternet.com/i/ii_imp.htm

Ljungqvist, A., & Wilhelm Jr., W. J. (2003). IPO Pricing in the Dot-com Bubble. The Journal of Finance, 58(2), 723–752. https://doi.org/10.1111/1540-6261.00543

Long, T. (2012, February 7). Feb. 7, 2000: Mafiaboy's Moment. Wired. https://www.wired.com/2012/02/feb-7-2000-mafiaboys-moment/

Masoud, M., Jaradat, Y., Manasrah, A., & Jannoud, I. (2019). Sensors of Smart Devices in the Internet of Everything (IoE) Era: Big Opportunities and Massive Doubts. Journal of Sensors, 2019, e6514520. https://doi.org/10.1155/2019/6514520

Matthew Glotzbach. (2009, July 7). Google Apps is out of beta (yes, really) [Blog]. Official Google Blog. https://googleblog.blogspot.com/2009/07/google-apps-is-out-of-beta-yes-really.html

McGirt, E. (2007, May 1). Facebook's Mark Zuckerberg: Hacker. Dropout. CEO. [News]. Fast Company. https://www.fastcompany.com/59441/facebooks-mark-zuckerberg-hacker-dropout-ceo

McHugh, J. (2003, January 1). Google vs. Evil. Wired. https://www.wired.com/2003/01/google-10/

Megan Garber. (2011, October 12). The contribution conundrum: Why did Wikipedia succeed while other encyclopedias failed? [News]. Nieman Lab. https://www.niemanlab.org/2011/10/the-contribution-conundrum-why-did-wikipedia-succeed-while-other-encyclopedias-failed/

Meikle, S. (1994). Aristotle on Money. Phronesis, 39(1), 26–44.

Merkley, K., Michaely, R., & Pacelli, J. (2017). Does the Scope of the Sell-Side Analyst Industry Matter? An Examination of Bias, Accuracy, and Information Content of Analyst Reports. The Journal of Finance, 72(3), 1285–1334. https://doi.org/10.1111/jofi.12485

Microsoft Corp. (1996, April 30). Microsoft Internet Explorer Web Browser Available on All Major Platforms, Offers Broadest International Support. Stories. https://news.microsoft.com/1996/04/30/microsoft-internet-explorer-web-browser-available-on-all-major-platforms-offers-broadest-international-support/

Min, H., Caltagirone, J., & Serpico, A. (2008). Life after a dot-com bubble. International Journal of Information Technology and Management, 7(1), 21–35. https://doi.org/10.1504/IJITM.2008.015887

Morris, J. J., & Alam, P. (2012). Value relevance and the dot-com bubble of the 1990s. The Quarterly Review of Economics and Finance, 52(2), 243–255. https://doi.org/10.1016/j.qref.2012.04.001

Muíneacháin, C. Ó. (2012, May 24). Thanks, Al Gore [Podcast #30]. https://technology.ie/thanks-al-gore-podcast-30/

NOAH Advisors. (2018, October). NOAH Advisors—Sector Multiples [Corporate]. NOAH Advisors. https://www.noah-advisors.com/about/

Nofer, M., Gomber, P., Hinz, O., & Schiereck, D. (2017). Blockchain. Business & Information Systems Engineering, 59(3), 183–187. https://doi.org/10.1007/s12599-017-0467-3

Nollinger, M. (1995, September 1). America, Online! Wired. https://www.wired.com/1995/09/aol-2/

Novak, M. C. (2019, April 4). A Brief History of Communication and Innovations that Changed the Game [Corporate]. G2 Learning Hub. https://learn.g2.com/history-of-communication

O'Brien, J. M. (2002, December 1). The Netflix Effect. Wired. https://www.wired.com/2002/12/netflix-6/

O'Connell, B. (2020, February 27). History of Salesforce: Timeline and Facts. TheStreet. https://www.thestreet.com/technology/history-of-salesforce

Ohlson, J. A. (1995). Earnings, Book Values, and Dividends in Equity Valuation*. Contemporary Accounting Research, 11(2), 661–687. https://doi.org/10.1111/J.1911-3846.1995.TB00461.X

Olson, P. (2014, October 6). Facebook Closes $19 Billion WhatsApp Deal [News]. Forbes. https://www.forbes.com/sites/parmyolson/2014/10/06/facebook-closes-19-billion-whatsapp-deal/

Ou, E. (2019, June 20). I Tried Using Facebook's Libra Blockchain. It Didn't Work. Bloomberg.Com. https://www.bloomberg.com/opinion/articles/2019-06-20/facebook-s-libra-cryptocurrency-isn-t-actually-supposed-to-work

Oxford, T. (2009, December 26). Getting connected: A history of modems [News]. TechRadar. https://www.techradar.com/news/internet/getting-connected-a-history-of-modems-657479

Pelkey, J. (2022, December 11). The Seminal Experiment: 1965 | History of Computer Communications [Books]. History of Computer Communications. https://historyofcomputercommunications.info/section/4.2/the-seminal-experiment-1965/

Pentland, A. "Sandy." (2019, July 18). Digital cash and privacy: What are the alternatives to Libra? MIT Media Lab. https://www.media.mit.edu/posts/digital-cash-and-privacy-what-are-the-alternatives-to-libra/

Perri, L. (2022, August 10). What's New in the 2022 Gartner Hype Cycle for Emerging Technologies [Reserach]. Gartner. https://www.gartner.com/en/articles/what-s-new-in-the-2022-gartner-hype-cycle-for-emerging-technologies

Peter Lynch. (2023, January 28). Who Invented EBITDA? [Blog]. A Simple Model. https://www.asimplemodel.com/insights/who-invented-ebitda

Peters, J. W. (2007, February 26). With Joost, founders of Skype and Kazaa are going by the book—Technology & Media—International Herald Tribune. The New York Times. https://www.nytimes.com/2007/02/26/technology/26iht-joost.4727176.html

Peyrott, S. (2017, January 16). A Brief History of JavaScript [Blog]. Auth0—Blog. https://auth0.com/blog/a-brief-history-of-javascript/

Pilipets, E. (2019). From Netflix Streaming to Netflix and Chill: The (Dis)Connected Body of Serial Binge-Viewer. Social Media + Society, 5(4), 2056305119883426. https://doi.org/10.1177/2056305119883426

Pitta, J. (1999, November 1). Requiem for a Bright Idea. Forbes. https://www.forbes.com/forbes/1999/1101/6411390a.html

Pollack, N. (2010, December 27). Spotify Is the Coolest Music Service You Can't Use. Wired, 19(1). https://www.wired.com/2010/12/mf-spotify/

Portes, A., N'Goala, G., & Cases, A.-S. (2020, June 2). Should digital marketing practices be more transparent? An empirical investigation on the roles of consumer digital literacy and privacy concerns in self-service technologies. 16th International Research Conference in Service Management. https://hal.science/hal-02502389

Price, R. W. (2011, May 31). What caused the Internet Bubble of 1999? [Non-profit]. Global Entrepreneurship Institute. https://news.gcase.org/2011/05/31/what-caused-the-internet-bubble-of-1999/

Raihanian Mashhadi, A., Vedantam, A., & Behdad, S. (2019). Investigation of consumer's acceptance of product-service-systems: A case study of cell phone leasing. Resources, Conservation and Recycling, 143, 36–44. https://doi.org/10.1016/j.resconrec.2018.12.006

Rajagopal, S., Venusamy, K., .S, S., Poongodi, J., Suriyan, K., & Alagarsamy, M. (2022). Machine to machine communication enabled internet of things: A review. International

Journal of Reconfigurable and Embedded Systems (IJRES), 11, 126. https://doi.org/10.11591/ijres.v11.i2.pp126-134

Rajgopal, S., Kotha, S., & Venkatachalam, M. (2000). The Relevance of Web Traffic for Stock Prices of Internet Firms (SSRN Scholarly Paper No. 207989). https://doi.org/10.2139/ssrn.207989

Reis, J. Z., Gonçalves, R. F., Silva, M. T. da, & Kazantsev, N. (2022). Business Models for the Internet of Services: State of the Art and Research Agenda. Future Internet, 14(3), Article 3. https://doi.org/10.3390/fi14030074

Reuter, J. (2019, August 13). A brief history of internet service providers. Viasat.Com. https://news.viasat.com/blog/satellite-internet/a-brief-history-of-internet-service-providers

Richtel, M. (1997, October 20). U.S. Says Microsoft Violated 1995 Court Order on Windows [News]. The New York Times. https://archive.nytimes.com/www.nytimes.com/library/cyber/week/102097microsoft.html

Ritchie, D. M. (1980). The evolution of the unix time-sharing system. In J. M. Tobias (Ed.), Language Design and Programming Methodology (Vol. 79, pp. 25–35). Springer Berlin Heidelberg. https://doi.org/10.1007/3-540-09745-7_2

Ritter, M., & Schanz, H. (2019). The sharing economy: A comprehensive business model framework. Journal of Cleaner Production, 213, 320–331. https://doi.org/10.1016/j.jclepro.2018.12.154

Ritter, T., & Pedersen, C. L. (2020). Digitization capability and the digitalization of business models in business-to-business firms: Past, present, and future. Industrial Marketing Management, 86, 180–190. https://doi.org/10.1016/j.indmarman.2019.11.019

Robachevsky, A. (2013, November 26). Happy 30th Birthday, DNS! Internet Society. https://www.internetsociety.org/blog/2013/11/happy-30th-birthday-dns/

Roche, P., & Tandon, S. (2021, August 3). SaaS and the Rule of 40: Keys to the critical value creation metric | McKinsey [Blog]. McKinsey. https://www.mckinsey.com/industries/technology-media-and-telecommunications/our-insights/saas-and-the-rule-of-40-keys-to-the-critical-value-creation-metric

Rosenbaum, J., Pearl, J., Harris, J., & Perella, J. R. (2013). Investment Banking: Valuation, Leveraged Buyouts, and Mergers and Acquisitions (2 edition). Wiley.

Rosenbaum, J., Pearl, J., Harris, J., & Perella, J. R. (2020). Investment Banking: Valuation, LBOs, M&A, and IPOs (3rd edition). Wiley.

Roser, M. (2013). Economic Growth. Our World in Data. https://ourworldindata.org/economic-growth

Roy, G., & Shrivastava, A. K. (2020). Future of gig economy: Opportunities and challenges. IMI Konnect, 9(1), 14–27.

Rusli, E. M. (2012, April 9). Facebook Buys Instagram for $1 Billion. DealBook. https://dealbook.nytimes.com/2012/04/09/facebook-buys-instagram-for-1-billion/

Sachdev, R. (2020). Towards Security and Privacy for Edge AI in IoT/IoE based Digital Marketing Environments. 2020 Fifth International Conference on Fog and Mobile Edge Computing (FMEC), 341–346. https://doi.org/10.1109/FMEC49853.2020.9144755

Sakovich, N. (2023, February 3). Internet of Everything (IoE) vs. Internet of Things (IoT) | SaM Solutions [Blog]. Sam-Solutions.Com. https://www.sam-solutions.com:443/blog/what-is-internet-of-everything-ioe/

Saltan, A., & Smolander, K. (2021). How SaaS Companies Price Their Products: Insights from an Industry Study. In E. Klotins & K. Wnuk (Eds.), Software Business (pp. 1–13). Springer International Publishing. https://doi.org/10.1007/978-3-030-67292-8_1

Samuel, A. (2017, February 21). Meet the Black Technologist Who Changed How Your Brain Works. JSTOR Daily. https://daily.jstor.org/alan-emtage-first-internet-search-engine/

Saura, J. R. (2021). Using Data Sciences in Digital Marketing: Framework, methods, and performance metrics. Journal of Innovation & Knowledge, 6(2), 92–102. https://doi.org/10.1016/j.jik.2020.08.001

Saura, J. R., Ribeiro-Soriano, D., & Palacios-Marqués, D. (2021). Setting B2B digital marketing in artificial intelligence-based CRMs: A review and directions for future research. Industrial Marketing Management, 98, 161–178. https://doi.org/10.1016/j.indmarman.2021.08.006

Scarpi, D., Pizzi, G., & Matta, S. (2022). Digital technologies and privacy: State of the art and research directions. Psychology & Marketing, 39(9), 1687–1697. https://doi.org/10.1002/mar.21692

Schoenherr, S. E. (2004, May 5). The Digital Revolution. The Digital Revolution. https://web.archive.org/web/20081007132355/http://history.sandiego.edu/gen/recording/digital.html

Schreiner, A. (2007). Equity valuation using multiples: An empirical investigation. In Equity Valuation Using Multiples: An Empirical Investigation (p. 170). https://doi.org/10.1007/978-3-8350-9531-1

Sebenius, J. K. (2002). Negotiating Lessons From the Browser Wars. MIT Sloan Management Review. https://sloanreview.mit.edu/article/ negotiating-lessons-from-the-browser-wars/

Segaller, S. (1998). Nerds 2.0.1: A Brief History of the Internet (1st edition). TV Books Inc.

Shacklett, M. E. (2021, July). TCP/IP: What is TCP/IP and How Does it Work? [News]. Networking. https://www.techtarget.com/searchnetworking/definition/TCP-IP

Shah, S. (2021, February 10). SpaceX opens Starlink satellite internet pre-orders to the public [News]. Engadget. https://www.engadget.com/spacex-starlink-internet-preorders-121427490.html

Sharma, A. (2022, January 2). Facebook's crypto project sold amid regulatory pressure. Deutsche Welle. https://www.dw.com/en/facebook-backed-cryptocurrency-sold-amid-regulatory-pressure/a-60616823

Sherman, A. T., Javani, F., Zhang, H., & Golaszewski, E. (2019). On the Origins and Variations of Blockchain Technologies. IEEE Security & Privacy, 17(1), 72–77. https://doi.org/10.1109/MSEC.2019.2893730

Shontell, A. (2011, June 29). FLASHBACK: This Is What The First-Ever Website Looked Like. Business Insider. https://www.businessinsider.com/flashback-this-is-what-the-first-website-ever-looked-like-2011-6

Simon Chan. (2016, November 11). Digital Transformation and The Third Industrial Revolution | LinkedIn. Digital Transformation and The Third Industrial Revolution. https://www.linkedin.com/pulse/digital-transformation-third-industrial-revolution-simon-chan/

Statista. (2022, July). Internet and social media users in the world 2022 [Statistics]. Statista. https://www.statista.com/statistics/617136/digital-population-worldwide/

Statista. (2022, October 26). Number of monthly active Facebook users worldwide as of 3rd quarter 2022 (in millions) [Statistics]. Statista. https://www.statista.com/statistics/264810/number-of-monthly-active-facebook-users-worldwide/

Stearns, P. N. (2020). The Industrial Revolution in World History (5th edition). Routledge.

Stephenson, N. (1992). Snow Crash. Bantam Books. https://www.biblio.com/book/snow-crash/d/1501008295

Tänavsuu, T. (2018, March 9). "How can they be so good?": The strange story of Skype. Ars Technica. https://arstechnica.com/information-technology/2018/09/skypes-secrets/

Täuscher, K. (2022). Business Models in the Digital Economy: An Empirical Study of Digital Marketplaces [Working Paper]. Fraunhofer Center for International Management and Knowledge Economy. https://www.imw.fraunhofer.de/content/dam/moez/de/documents/Working_Paper/Working_Paper_Digital_Marketplaces_final.pdf

Täuscher, K., & Laudien, S. M. (2018). Understanding platform business models: A mixed methods study of marketplaces. European Management Journal, 36(3), 319–329. https://doi.org/10.1016/j.emj.2017.06.005

Taylor, C. (2020, February 12). SQL Slammer Virus (Harbinger of things to come) [Training]. CyberHoot. https://cyberhoot.com/cybrary/sql-slammer-virus/

Terry, D. B., Painter, M., Riggle, D. W., & Zhou, S. (1984). The Berkeley Internet Name Domain Server (UCB/CSD-84-182). EECS Department, University of California, Berkeley. http://www2.eecs.berkeley.edu/Pubs/TechRpts/1984/5957.html

The FulfillmentLab Inc. (2021, April 16). A Brief History of Ecommerce (and a Look at the Future) [Corporate]. The FulfillmentLab. https://www.thefulfillmentlab.com/blog/history-of-ecommerce

Thomas, J. (2007, July 20). Project Gutenberg Digital Library Seeks To Spur Literacy [Information]. America.Gov. https://web.archive.org/web/20080314164013/http://www.america.gov/st/washfile-english/2007/July/20070720151131CJsamohT0.6146356.html

Thorp, H. H. (2023). ChatGPT is fun, but not an author. Science, 379(6630), 313–313. https://doi.org/10.1126/science.adg7879

Tobin, J. (2012). Great Projects: The Epic Story of the Building of America, from the Taming of the Mississippi to the Invention of the Internet. Simon and Schuster.

University of Groningen—Groningen Growth and Development Centre. (2018, January 25). Maddison Project Database 2018. University of Groningen. https://www.rug.nl/ggdc/historicaldevelopment/maddison/releases/maddison-project-database-2018

U.S. National Venture Capital Association. (2012, May 5). Recent Stats & Studies—VC Investments Q1 '12—MoneyTree—National Data [Industry Association]. U.S. National Venture Capital Association. https://web.archive.org/web/20120505074841/http://www.nvca.org/index.php?option=com_content&view=article&id=344&Itemid=103

Vaya, D., & Hadpawat, T. (2020). Internet of Everything (IoE): A New Era of IoT. In A. Kumar & S. Mozar (Eds.), ICCCE 2019 (pp. 1–6). Springer. https://doi.org/10.1007/978-981-13-8715-9_1

Vlad Costea. (2020, April 8). ICYMI: David Chaum's Vault System: The World's First Blockchain [News]. Decentralize.Today. https://dt.gl/david-chaums-vault-system-the-worlds-first-blockchain/

Walden, D. C. (2022, December 11). Dave Walden, Looking back at the ARPANET effort, 34 years later—Internet History [News]. LivingInternet. https://www.livinginternet.com/i/ii_imp_walden.htm

Wauters, R. (2009a, April 29). Kickstarter Launches Another Social Fundraising Platform. TechCrunch. https://techcrunch.com/2009/04/29/kickstarter-launches-another-social-fundraising-platform/

Wauters, R. (2009b, August 27). 25 Years Later, First Registered Domain Name Changes Hands. TechCrunch. https://techcrunch.com/2009/08/27/25-years-later-first-registered-domain-name-changes-hands/

Wheale, P. R., & Amin, L. H. (2003). Bursting the dot.com "Bubble": A Case Study in Investor Behaviour. Technology Analysis & Strategic Management, 15(1), 117–136. https://doi.org/10.1080/0953732032000046097

Whistler, S. (Director). (2022, November 9). Starlink: The Internet's Next Big Step? Megaprojects. https://www.youtube.com/watch?v=7BKThhfz__E

Williams, J. B. (1997). The Theory of Investment Value. Fraser Publishing Company.

Winegar, A. G., & Sunstein, C. R. (2019). How Much Is Data Privacy Worth? A Preliminary Investigation. Journal of Consumer Policy, 42(3), 425–440. https://doi.org/10.1007/s10603-019-09419-y

Wlömert, N., & Papies, D. (2016). On-demand streaming services and music industry revenues—Insights from Spotify's market entry. International Journal of Research in Marketing, 33(2), 314–327. https://doi.org/10.1016/j.ijresmar.2015.11.002

Xiao, Z., Shu, W., & Owusu, A. O. (2021). An analysis of product strategy in cloud transition considering SaaS customization. Information Systems and E-Business Management, 19(1), 281–311. https://doi.org/10.1007/s10257-020-00499-9

Xu, H., Luo, X. (Robert), Carroll, J. M., & Rosson, M. B. (2011). The personalization privacy paradox: An exploratory study of decision making process for location-aware marketing. Decision Support Systems, 51(1), 42–52. https://doi.org/10.1016/j.dss.2010.11.017

Yang, Z., Sun, J., Zhang, Y., & Wang, Y. (2015). Understanding SaaS adoption from the perspective of organizational users: A tripod readiness model. Computers in Human Behavior, 45, 254–264. https://doi.org/10.1016/j.chb.2014.12.022

Younkins, E. W. (2005, September 15). Aristotle and economics [Blog]. Quebecoislibre.Org. http://www.quebecoislibre.org/05/050915-11.htm

Zhang, Q., Cheng, L., & Boutaba, R. (2010). Cloud computing: State-of-the-art and research challenges. Journal of Internet Services and Applications, 1(1), Article 1. https://doi.org/10.1007/s13174-010-0007-6

Zhao, Y., von Delft, S., Morgan-Thomas, A., & Buck, T. (2020). The evolution of platform business models: Exploring competitive battles in the world of platforms. Long Range Planning, 53(4), 101892. https://doi.org/10.1016/j.lrp.2019.101892

Zheng, P., Wang, Z., Chen, C.-H., & Pheng Khoo, L. (2019). A survey of smart product-service systems: Key aspects, challenges and future perspectives. Advanced Engineering Informatics, 42, 100973. https://doi.org/10.1016/j.aei.2019.100973

Zimmermann, K. A., & Emspak, J. (2022, April 8). Internet History Timeline: ARPANET to the World Wide Web [Blog]. Livescience.Com. https://www.livescience.com/20727-internet-history.html

References Company Analysis[1]

1-800-FLOWERS.COM Inc. (2020, December 25). 1-800-FLOWERS.COM Inc.—About Us. About Us. https://www.1800flowersinc.com/about-us

1Spatial Plc. (2020). 1Spatial Plc—Annual Report 2020 (p. 5) [Annual Report]. https://1spatial.com/media/iijboyrv/annual-report-2020.pdf

2U Inc. (2020). 2U Inc.—Annual Report 2019 (p. 72) [Annual Report]. https://s26.q4cdn.com/441000616/files/doc_financials/2019/ar/2019-2U-Annual-Report.pdf

8x8 Inc. (2020). 8x8 Inc.—Annual Report 2019 (p. 0) [Annual Report]. https://s22.q4cdn.com/193857950/files/doc_financials/2020/ar/e84ea8e3-b147-4651-ba12-dbf8d823109f.pdf

888 Holdings Plc. (2020). 888 Holdings Plc—Annual Report 2019 [Annual Report]. Online gambling including casino, poker, bingo and B2B services under the Dragonfish brand

1000mercis SA (Numberly). (2020, December 25). Our products | Numberly. Our Products | Numberly. https://numberly.com/en/our-products/

A10 Networks Inc. (2020). A10 Networks Inc.—Annual Report 2019 [Annual Report]. http://d18rn0p25nwr6d.cloudfront.net/CIK-0001580808/6ef96e13-67b7-4983-abbb-caccdd8b24d6.pdf

Absolute Software Corporation. (2020). Absolute Software Corporation—Annual Report 2020 [Annual Report]. https://www.absolute.com/media/5644/2020-abt-aif.pdf

Accelya Solutions India Ltd. (2021, November 13). Accelya Solutions India Ltd.—Airline Passenger Solutions [Corporate]. Accelya. https://w3.accelya.com/airline-passenger-solutions/

Access Intelligence Plc. (2020). Access Intelligence Plc—Annual Report 2019 [Annual Report]. https://cdn2.hubspot.net/hubfs/458431/Access%20Intelligence%20Plc%20Annual%20Report%202020.pdf

ACI Worldwide Inc. (2021). ACI Worldwide, Inc.—ACI Worldwide Analyst Day [Company presentation]. https://investor.aciworldwide.com/static-files/c24bdf79-789d-4f9b-aa81-22c133f528f7

Acroud AB. (2021, December 11). Acroud AB—About us—Products [Corporate]. Acroud AB. https://www.acroud.com/en/about-us/

Actozsoft. (2020, December 25). Actozsoft | Introduction. Actozsoft | Introduction. http://www.actoz.com/aboutus/introduction/english

Actusnews Wire. (2020, December 4). DALET company press release from 04/12/2020—Long path partners acquires a majority stake in DALET's share capital [News]. Actusnews. https://www.actusnews.com/en/dalet/pr/2020/12/04/long-path-partners-acquires-a-majority-stake-in-dalet_s-share-capital

AcuityAds Holdings Inc. (2020, December 26). Illumin Advertising Automation Reimagined | AcuityAds Inc | Solutions. Illumin Advertising Automation Reimagined | AcuityAds Inc | Solutions. https://www.acuityads.com/

[1] Presents the sources used to analyze individual companies, most often annual reports, which are audited, and company websites, product descriptions, and other company publications.

ad pepper media International N.V. (2021). Ad pepper media International N.V.—Annual Report 2020 [Annual Report]. https://adpeppergroup.com/wp-content/uploads/2021/03/adp_geschaeftsbericht-2020_WEB_Verschluesselt.pdf

Admicom Oyj. (2021, December 11). Admicom Oyj—About the company [Corporate]. Admicom Oyj—About the Company. https://www.admicom.fi/sijoittajille/

Adobe Inc. (2020). Adobe Inc.—Annual Report 2019 [Annual Report]. https://www.adobe.com/content/dam/cc/en/investor-relations/pdfs/ADBE-10K-FY19-FINAL.pdf

AdUX SA. (2021, December 29). AdUX EN—Group [Corporate]. http://www.adux.com/en/

ADVFN Plc. (2020). ADVFN Plc—Annual Report 2020 [Annual Report]. https://advfnplc.com/company-reports

Adyen NV. (2022). Adyen NV—Annual Report 2021 [Annual Report]. http://www.adyen.com/investor-relations

Aeria Inc. (2019). Aeria Inc.—Annual Report 2019 [Annual Report]. https://www.aeria.jp/pdf/yChBrIB6Q

Aferian plc. (2021). Aferian plc—Annual Report 2020 [Annual Report]. https://aferian.com/wp-content/uploads/2021/02/Amino-Technologies-Final-Results-2020-v2.pdf

AfreecaTV Co. Ltd. (2020). AfreecaTV—Investor Relations [Report]. http://corp.afreecatv.com/ir.php?page=irbbsview&idx=105

AhnLab, Inc. (2021, November 9). Business | AhnLab. AhnLab. http://company.ahnlab.com/en/company/business.do

Ailleron SA. (2021, December 11). Ailleron SA—Business segments [Corporate]. http://ailleron.com/pl/inwestorzy/

AirTrip Corp. (2020). AirTrip Corp.—Consolidated Financial Results for the Fiscal Year Ended September 30th, 2020 (FY9/20) [IFRS] [Annual Report]. https://www.airtrip.co.jp/en/datas/financial/pdf/020201208173422_ujVOw.pdf

Akamai Technologies Inc. (2020). Akamai Technologies Inc.—Annual Report 2019 [Annual Report]. https://www.ir.akamai.com/static-files/569d1024-6d2c-4fdd-bfd5-9ae3d5c85eab

Alfa Financial Software Holdings Plc. (2021). Alfa Financial Software Holdings Plc—Annual Report 2020 [Annual Report]. http://s3-eu-west-1.amazonaws.com/cdn.alfasystems.com/articleDownloads/Alfa_Systems_AR20_web1.pdf?mtime=20210412203346

Alibaba Group Holding Ltd. (2020). Alibaba Group Holding Ltd.—Fiscal Year 2020 Annual Report [Annual Report]. https://doc.irasia.com/listco/hk/alibabagroup/annual/2020/ar2020.pdf

All About, Inc. (2020, December 26). All About, Inc 株式会社オールアバウト: Overview | LinkedIn. All About, Inc 株式会社オールアバウト: Overview | LinkedIn. https://www.linkedin.com/company/allabout/

Alley, A. (2020, March 17). INAP files for bankruptcy, along with US subsidiaries [News]. Datacenterdynamics. https://www.datacenterdynamics.com/en/news/inap-files-bankruptcy-along-us-subsidiaries/

Allot Ltd. (2021). Allot Ltd.—Annual Report 2020 [Annual Report]. https://investors.allot.com/static-files/452fac17-3bc5-4119-a1d9-80a3a2cd6c72

Allscripts Healthcare Solutions Inc. (2020). Allscripts Healthcare Solutions Inc.—Annual Report 2019 [Annual Report]. https://investor.allscripts.com/static-files/4048d81b-d0a5-48af-a229-3b460f5c4385

Alphabet Inc. (2020). Alphabet Inc.—Annual Report 2019 [Annual Report]. https://abc.xyz/investor/static/pdf/20200204_alphabet_10K.pdf?cache=cdd6dbf
Altair Engineering Inc. (2021). Altair Engineering Inc.—Annual Report 2020 [Annual Report]. https://investor.altair.com/static-files/b55ccf23-c976-4fe3-bdf7-6354007c6baf
Alteryx, Inc. (2021). Alteryx, Inc.—Annual Report 2020 [Annual Report]. https://d18rn0p25nwr6d.cloudfront.net/CIK-0001689923/caca5fe8-54c8-4dd3-a0da-470bb2a49352.pdf
Alticast Corp. (2021, November 9). Alticast Corp.—About Us / History—Alticast's Best moment [Company profile]. Alticast. http://www.alticast.com/about/about02.html
AltPlus Inc. (2021, November 13). Service | altplus. Company Presentation. http://en.altplus.co.jp/service
Amadeus IT Group SA. (2020). Amadeus IT Group SA—Annual Report 2019 [Annual Report]. https://corporate.amadeus.com/documents/en/resources/corporate-information/corporate-documents/global-reports/2019/amadeus-global-report-2019.pdf
Amazon.com Inc. (2020). Amazon.com Inc.—Annual Report 2019 [Annual Report]. https://s2.q4cdn.com/299287126/files/doc_financials/2020/ar/2019-Annual-Report.pdf
Amber Road Inc. (2019). Amber Road Inc.—Annual Report 2018 [Annual Report]. https://sec.report/Document/0001314223-19-000007/
American Software, Inc. (2021). American Software, Inc.—Annual Report 2021 [Annual Report]. https://www.amsoftware.com/wp-content/uploads/2021/07/AMSWA-2021.04.30-10K-final-1.pdf
and factory, inc. (2018, April 27). and factory, inc.—Services [And factory, inc.—Services]. And Factory. https://andfactory.co.jp/app/
ANGI Homeservices Inc. (2020). ANGI Homeservices Inc—Annual Report 2019 [Annual Report]. https://ir.angihomeservices.com/static-files/424ada97-4486-4920-9e77-35dab3a48603
Anhui Wantong Technology Co., Ltd. (2021, November 8). Anhui Wantong Technology Co., Ltd.—About us. Anhui Wantong Technology Co., Ltd.—About Us. http://www.wantong-tech.net/
ANSYS, Inc. (2021). ANSYS, Inc.—Annual Report 2020 [Annual Report]. https://d18rn0p25nwr6d.cloudfront.net/CIK-0001013462/371fb2f3-2f28-4c74-a938-f5059091e783.pdf
AO World Plc. (2020). AO World Plc—Annual Report and Accounts 2020 [Annual Report]. https://www.ao-world.com/wp-content/uploads/2020/07/AO-World-Annual-Report-July-2020.pdf
Apax Partners. (2019, May 8). Funds advised by Apax Partners complete the acquisition of Trade Me | Apax Partners [Corporate]. Apax. https://www.apax.com/news-views/funds-advised-by-apax-partners-complete-the-acquisition-of-trade-me/
Appen Ltd. (2021). Appen Ltd.—Annual Report 2020 [Annual Report]. https://resources.appen.com/wp-content/uploads/2021/02/Appen-2020-Annual-Report.pdf
AppFolio Inc. (2020). AppFolio Inc—Annual Report 2019 [Annual Report]. https://s22.q4cdn.com/854805360/files/doc_financials/AR/50b00cf4-43c8-4798-98ac-3fc2f615ea54.pdf
Appian Corporation. (2021). Appian Corporation—Annual Report 2020 [Annual Report]. https://investors.appian.com/node/10071/html
Apptio Inc. (2021, November 6). About Apptio Solutions—Apptio [About Apptio Solutions—Apptio]. https://www.apptio.com/company/

Aptitude Software Group plc. (2021). Aptitude Software Group plc—Annual Report 2020 [Annual Report]. https://www.aptitudesoftware.com/wp-content/uploads/Annual-Report-2020.pdf

Aristocrat Leisure Limited. (2020). Aristocrat Leisure Limited—Annual Report 2020 [Annual Report].

Arlo Technologies, Inc. (2021). Arlo Technologies, Inc.—Annual Report 2020 [Annual Report]. https://d18rn0p25nwr6d.cloudfront.net/CIK-0001736946/5c806284-582b-4b3f-9a01-df860366f070.pdf

Artificial Solutions International AB. (2021). Artificial Solutions International AB—Annual Report 2020 [Annual Report]. https://www.investors.artificial-solutions.com/wp-content/uploads/Annual_Report_2020_ENG_Final.pdf

Artilium plc. (2020). Artilium plc—Annual Report 2019 [Annual Report].

Asgent Inc. (2020, December 26). Asgent: Business Domain | Services. Asgent: Business Domain | Services. https://www.asgent.com/Service/service.html

Asiasoft Corp. Public Co. Ltd. (2021). Asiasoft Corp. Public Co. Ltd.—Annual Report 2020 [Annual Report]. https://as.listedcompany.com/misc/ar/20210323-as-ar2020-en.pdf

ASJ Inc. (2020). ASJ Inc.—Annual Report 2019 [Annual Report].

ASKUL Corporation. (2021). ASKUL Corporation—Company Profile [Company Profile]. https://www.askul.co.jp/kaisya/english/company/overview.html

ASOS plc. (2020). ASOS plc—Annual Report and Accounts 2019 [Annual Report]. https://www.asosplc.com/~/media/Files/A/Asos-V2/reports-and-presentations/annual-strategic-report-2019-24102019.pdf

Aspen Technology Inc. (2019). Aspen Technology Inc.—Annual Report 2019 [Annual Report]. http://ir.aspentech.com/static-files/10589d59-24e9-4854-a960-1c1a89a9f316

Aspire Global Plc. (2021). Aspire Global Plc—Annual Report 2020 [Annual Report]. https://www.aspireglobal.com/wp-content/uploads/2021/04/Aspire-Global_AR_2020-1.pdf

Asseco Poland S.A. (2021). Asseco Poland S.A.—Company Profile [Company Profile].

Ateam Inc. (2017, February 3). Ateam—Lifestyle Support [Company presentation]. Ateam Inc. https://www.a-tm.co.jp/en/service/lifestyle/

Atlassian Corp. Plc. (2020). Atlassian Corp. Plc—Annual Report 2020 [Annual Report]. https://s2.q4cdn.com/141359120/files/doc_financials/2020/TEAM-2020_Annual_Report.pdf

ATLED CORP. (2021, November 13). ATLED CORP.—Products [Corporate]. ATLED CORP. https://www.atled.jp/

ATTRAQT Group PLC. (2020). ATTRAQT Group PLC—REPORT & FINANCIAL STATEMENTS for Year ended 31st December 2019 [Annual Report]. https://www.attraqt.com/media/4514/attraqt-group-plc-annual-report-and-accounts-2019.pdf

Attunity Ltd. (2019, May 6). Qlik Completes Acquisition of Attunity. /PRNewswire/ -- Attunity Ltd. (NasdaqCM: ATTU), a Leading Provider of Data Integration and Big Data Management Software Solutions, Announced Today The... https://www.prnewswire.com/il/news-releases/qlik-completes-acquisition-of-attunity-300844088.html

Aucfan Co. Ltd. (2020). Aucfan Co. Ltd.—Annual Report 2019 [Annual Report].

Aucnet, Inc. (2021). Aucnet, Inc.—Annual Report 2020 [Annual Report]. http://ir.aucnet.co.jp/ja/index.html

Auto Trader Group PLC. (2020). Auto Trader Group PLC—Annual Report and Financial Statements 2020 [Annual Report]. https://plc.autotrader.co.uk/media/2013/auto-trader-annual-report-2020.pdf

Autohome Inc. (2019). Autohome Inc.—Annual Report 2019 [Annual Report]. http://ir.autohome.com.cn/index.php/static-files/b03348f8-57e5-4403-a3a3-bdaef4993a3d

Autolus Therapeutics Plc. (2021). Autolus Therapeutics Plc—Annual Report 2020 [Annual Report]. https://autolus.gcs-web.com/static-files/c9d91c83-28ef-4d17-bf90-cdbfabb9f3b9

Avalara Inc. (2021). Avalara Inc—Annual Report 2020 [Annual Report]. https://d18rn0p25nwr6d.cloudfront.net/CIK-0001348036/2ee046ce-7d0d-47c1-a5a2-679620cb6cd2.pdf

Avast Plc. (2021). Avast Plc—Annual Report 2020 [Annual Report]. https://investors.avast.com/media/1401/annual-report-2020.pdf

Avensia AB. (2020, December 27). Consumer experience & operational excellence | Avensia. Consumer Experience & Operational Excellence | Avensia. https://www.avensia.com/products/

Aware, Inc. (2021). Aware, Inc.—Annual Report 2020 [Annual Report]. https://aware.gcs-web.com/static-files/006a116f-ac6c-4fbd-98de-627a65ddfc1d

Axway Software SA. (2021). Axway Software SA—Investor Presentation [Investor Presentation]. https://investors.axway.com/en/calendar-publications/presentation

B+S Banksysteme AG. (2020, December 27). B+S Banksysteme AG—Produkte | Bankanwendungen. B+S Banksysteme AG. https://bs-ag.com/

B2W Companhia Digital. (2019). B2W Companhia Digital—Annual Report 2019 [Annual Report]. https://hotsites.b2wdigital.com/relatorioanual2019_en.pdf

Baidu Inc. (2019). Baidu Inc.—Annual Report 2019 [Annual Report]. https://ir.baidu.com/static-files/ee02be35-ab39-496b-9119-3f30a5e99e6f

Bandwidth Inc. (2021). Bandwidth Inc.—Annual Report 2020 [Annual Report]. https://investors.bandwidth.com/static-files/c5bc0fef-f7f4-4daf-bed5-bd8b328301fa

Bango plc. (2021). Bango plc—Annual Report 2020 [Annual Report]. https://797d0754.flowpaper.com/annualreport20/

Baozun Inc. (2019). Baozun Inc—Annual Report 2019 [Annual Report]. https://ir.baozun.com/static-files/94518753-5b3b-418d-9a16-374e8cfaf7da

Basware Oyj. (2021). Basware Oyj—Annual Report 2020 [Annual Report]. https://investors.basware.com/~/media/Files/B/Basware-IR-V3/documents/en/reports/2021/annual-report-2020.pdf

Beeks Financial Cloud Group Plc. (2020). Beeks Financial Cloud Group Plc—Annual Report 2020 [Annual Report]. https://beeksgroup.com/wp-content/uploads/2020/10/BKS-Annual-report-2020.pdf

Beijing Century Real Technology Co., Ltd. (2021, November 13). Railway Integrated Monitoring System-Century Real [Company presentation]. Railway Integrated Monitoring System-Century Real. https://www.c-real.com.cn/tieluzonghejiankongxitong.html

Beijing Join-Cheer Software Co., Ltd. (2021, November 8). Beijing Join-Cheer Software Co., Ltd.—Company Profile. Beijing Join-Cheer Software Co., Ltd.—Company Profile. https://www.jiuqi.com.cn/gsjj.jhtml

Beijing Shiji Information Technology Co., Ltd. (2021, November 8). About the Shiji Group. About the Shiji Group. https://www.shijigroup.com/about/overview

Beijing Sinnet Technology Co., Ltd. (2021). Beijing Sinnet Technology Co., Ltd.—Annual Report 2020 [Annual Report]. http://www.sinnet.com.cn/home/invest/level/32
Beijing Tongtech Co., Ltd. (2021, November 13). Home—Dongfangtong official website—Security+ [Company profile]. Tongtech. http://www.tongtech.com/
Benefitfocus Inc. (2020). Benefitfocus Inc.—Annual Report 2019 [Annual Report]. https://investor.benefitfocus.com/static-files/9bdebcc8-7c86-4b7d-aa60-b8f31f8a7848
Beta Systems Software AG. (2021, November 14). Welcome to Beta Systems—Solutions [Corporate]. Beta Systems Software. https://www.betasystems.com/en/
bet-at-home.com AG. (2019). Bet-at-home.com AG—Annual Report 2019 [Annual Report]. https://www.bet-at-home.ag/cms/file/219076/0000000000090daa/219076.pdf
Betsson AB. (2021). Betsson AB—Annual Report 2020 [Annual Report]. https://vp273.alertir.com/afw/files/press/betsson/202103312273-1.pdf
Better Collective A/S. (2021, November 14). Better Collective—Our Brands [Corporate]. Better Collective. https://bettercollective.com/brands/
BHG Group AB. (2021). BHG Group AB—Annual Report 2020 [Annual Report]. https://mb.cision.com/Main/16507/3321376/1398445.pdf
BIO-key International Inc. (2021). BIO-key International, Inc.—Annual Report 2020 [Annual Report]. http://irdirect.net/filings/viewer/index/1019034/000143774921007486/
Bitauto Holdings Ltd. (2019). Bitauto Holdings Ltd.—Annual Report 2019 [Annual Report]. https://ir.bitauto.com/static-files/ac018909-4298-4292-a0f8-17e9416ee33d
Bizconf Telecom Co. Ltd. (2021, November 13). Super Vision Cloud [Product page]. Super Vision Cloud. https://www.bizconf.cn/superCloud
Black Knight Inc. (2021). Black Knight, Inc.—Annual Report 2020 [Annual Report]. https://s28.q4cdn.com/666206574/files/doc_financials/2020/ar/BKI_AnnualReport_2020.pdf
Blackbaud Inc. (2020). Blackbaud Inc.—Annual Report 2019 [Annual Report]. https://investor.blackbaud.com/static-files/9cd70119-4e13-4d47-b068-3c228c580417
Blackbird PLC. (2021). Blackbird PLC—2020 Final results presentation [Company presentation]. https://www.blackbird.video/wp-content/uploads/2021/07/IR-Deck_19-March-2021.pdf
BlackLine, Inc. (2021). BlackLine, Inc.—Annual Report 2020 [Annual Report]. https://investors.blackline.com/static-files/0213ad43-8d06-4171-8f54-bf651c9dd6a0
Bloomberg.com. (2021, November 6). Sogou Inc—Company Profile and News. Bloomberg.Com. https://www.bloomberg.com/profile/company/SOGO:US
Blucora, Inc. (2021). Blucora, Inc.—Annual Report 2020 [Annual Report]. https://www.blucora.com/static-files/47ee5867-453f-4fc2-abf2-f6bff37f3cc0
Blue Apron Holdings, Inc. (2021). Blue Apron Holdings, Inc.—Annual Report 2020 [Annual Report]. https://otp.tools.investis.com/clients/us/blue_apron/SEC/sec-show.aspx?FilingId=14736181&Cik=0001701114&Type=PDF&hasPdf=1
Blue Prism Group Plc. (2021). Blue Prism Group Plc—Annual Report 2020 [Annual Report]. https://investors.blueprism.com/sites/blueprism-ir-v2/files/fy20-statement.pdf
BOKU, Inc. (2021). BOKU, Inc.—Annual Report 2020 [Annual Report]. https://wp-boku-2020.s3.eu-west-2.amazonaws.com/media/2021/03/18182030/Boku-Inc-Annual-Report-and-Accounts-2020-Final.pdf
boohoo group Plc. (2020). boohoo group Plc—Annual Report and Accounts 2020 [Annual Report and Accounts 2020]. https://www.boohooplc.com/sites/boohoo-corp/files/all-documents/result-centre/2020/boohoo-com-plc-annual-report-2020-hyperlink.pdf

Booking Holdings Inc. (2020). Booking Holdings Inc.—Annual Report 2019 [Annual Report]. https://ir.bookingholdings.com/static-files/92c3d5b6-8f42-4686-afc1-f6bd61b94e06

Boozt AB. (2021). Boozt AB—Annual Report 2020 [Annual Report]. https://static1.squarespace.com/static/5e9d5bc80667c66d431bfb23/t/602232ec8f15bb53394e87bc/1612854003635/Boozt+-+Q4+report+2020+English.pdf

Bottomline Technologies, Inc. (2021). Bottomline Technologies, Inc.—Annual Report 2021 [Annual Report]. https://d18rn0p25nwr6d.cloudfront.net/CIK-0001073349/96961fd3-d59b-4b04-8fbc-96d8c662589f.pdf

Box Inc. (2020). Box Inc.—2020 Proxy Statement and Annual Report [Annual Report]. https://s21.q4cdn.com/328470014/files/doc_financials/2020/ar/Box-2020-Proxy-and-10-K-Combo-Book.pdf

Boxlight Corporation. (2021). Boxlight Corporation—Annual Report 2020 [Annual Report]. https://d18rn0p25nwr6d.cloudfront.net/CIK-0001624512/9b167585-3eb8-48f8-9b07-06c4ad061bb2.html

Brendan Menapace. (2018, October 1). CafePress Acquired by Snapfish in $25 Million Deal. Promomarketing. https://magazine.promomarketing.com/article/cafepress-will-be-sold-after-troubled-2018/

Brendan Sinclair. (2013, October 4). Gamevil acquires Com2uS. GamesIndustry.Biz. https://www.gamesindustry.biz/articles/2013-10-04-gamevil-acquires-com2us

Bridgeline Digital Inc. (2020). Bridgeline Digital, Inc.—Annual Report 2020 [Annual Report]. https://dd7pmep5szm19.cloudfront.net/2491/0001437749-20-025835.pdf

Brightcom Group Limited. (2020). Brightcom Group Limited—Annual Report 2019–2020 [Annual Report]. https://www.brightcomgroup.com/wp-content/uploads/2021/03/AnnualReport2019-2020.pdf

Brightcove Inc. (2020). Brightcove Inc.—Annual Report 2019 [Annual Report]. https://investor.brightcove.com/static-files/81a6775e-e76f-40b3-a2ee-1d1b96dca898

BrightView Holdings, Inc. (2020). BrightView Holdings, Inc.—Annual Report 2020 [Annual Report]. https://s22.q4cdn.com/142468460/files/doc_financials/2020/ar/BV-final-annual-report.pdf

BroadBand Tower, Inc. (2020, December 27). Our Business | About BroadBand Tower. BroadBand Tower, Inc. https://www.bbtower.co.jp/en/corporate/field/

Broadridge Financial Solutions Inc. (2021). Broadridge Financial Solutions, Inc.—Annual Report 2021 [Annual Report]. https://d18rn0p25nwr6d.cloudfront.net/CIK-0001383312/594d5ca1-559a-43c2-9102-e8b6b5481e33.pdf

Business-Intelligence of Oriental Nations Corporation Ltd. (2021, November 13). Business-Intelligence of Oriental Nations Corporation Ltd.—Front Page [Company Profile]. Business-Intelligence of Oriental Nations Corporation Ltd.—Front Page. https://www.bonc.com.cn/

Businesswire. (2021, November 5). Thoma Bravo Completes Acquisition of QAD [News]. Businesswire. https://www.businesswire.com/news/home/20211105005529/en/Thoma-Bravo-Completes-Acquisition-of-QAD

Cadence Design Systems, Inc. (2021). Cadence Design Systems, Inc.—Annual Report 2021 [Annual Report]. https://d18rn0p25nwr6d.cloudfront.net/CIK-0000813672/85b1751e-a82b-4ce1-91e8-a2450c89450f.pdf

Caesars Entertainment Inc. (2021, April 22). Caesars Entertainment Announces Completion of William Hill PLC Acquisition [News]. PRnewswire. https://www.prnewswire.com/news-releases/caesars-entertainment-announces-completion-of-william-hill-plc-acquisition-301274863.html

Cafe24 Corp. (2021). Cafe24 Corp.—Annual Report 2020 [Annual Report]. https://www.cafe24corp.com/download.php?id=file_bbs&no=37

Cango, Inc. (Cayman island). (2020). Cango, Inc. (Cayman island)—Annual Report 2019 [Annual Report]. https://sec.report/Document/0001193125-20-120953/#tx61939_5

Carasent ASA. (2021). Carasent ASA—Annual Report 2020 [Annual Report]. https://carasent.com/wp-content/uploads/2021/03/2020-Carasent-Group-Annual-Report-210325-FINAL.pdf

Cardlytics, Inc. (2021). Cardlytics, Inc.—Annual Report 2020 [Annual Report]. https://cardlytics.gcs-web.com/news-releases/news-release-details/cardlytics-announces-fourth-quarter-and-fiscal-year-2020

CareCloud, Inc. (2021). CareCloud, Inc.—Annual Report 2020 [Annual Report]. http://irdirect.net/filings/viewer/index/1582982/000149315221004837/

CareerIndex, Inc. (2021, November 14). CareerIndex—Service (What we do) [Corporate]. CareerIndex—Service (What We Do). http://careerindex.co.jp/

CarGurus, Inc. (2021). CarGurus, Inc.—Annual Report 2020 [Annual Report]. https://investors.cargurus.com/static-files/44aa6947-d70d-45aa-a8d9-73629330cee4

CarParts.com Inc. (2020). CarParts.com Inc—Annual Report 2019 [Annual Report].

Carsales.Com Limited. (2019). Carsales.Com Limited—Annual Report 2019 [Annual Report]. http://shareholder.carsales.com.au/FormBuilder/_Resource/_module/NwbnH0pKFk-uPGxM7cmTrw/docs/reports/annual/Annual_Report_2019.pdf

Cars.com, Inc. (2021). Cars.com, Inc.—Annual Report 2020 [Annual Report]. https://s27.q4cdn.com/849924952/files/doc_financials/2020/ar/Cars-2020-Annual-Report-FINAL.pdf

Carvana Co. (2021). Carvana Co.—Annual Report 2020 [Annual Report]. https://otp.tools.investis.com/clients/us/carvana/SEC/sec-show.aspx?FilingId=14746586&Cik=0001690820&Type=PDF&hasPdf=1

Castlight Health Inc. (2020). Castlight Health Inc.—Annual Report 2019 [Annual Report]. http://d18rn0p25nwr6d.cloudfront.net/CIK-0001433714/a90bd163-4667-4fa0-a824-c3b0c8444cde.pdf

Catena Media plc. (2021). Catena Media plc—Annual Report 2020 [Annual Report]. https://www.catenamedia.com/wp-content/uploads/2021/03/Catena_Media_Annual_Report_2020_Final_LR.pdf

Ceridian HCM Holding, Inc. (2021). Ceridian HCM Holding, Inc.—Annual Report 2020 [Annual Report]. https://d18rn0p25nwr6d.cloudfront.net/CIK-0001725057/86f1d22f-b334-400c-a0e6-156cad944d02.pdf

Cerner Corporation. (2020). Cerner Corporation—Annual Report 2019 [Annual Report]. https://www.cerner.com/-/media/cerner-media-united-states/annualreports/2019-cerner-annual-report.pdf?la=en&vs=1

CEWE Stiftung & Co. KGaA. (2020, August). CEWE Stiftung & Co. KGaA—Company Presentation [Company Presentation]. https://ir.cewe.de/download/companies/cewe/CompanyPresentation/CEWE_Company_Presentation_August_2020.pdf

Changyou.com Limited. (2020, April 14). Changyou.com Announces Filing of Definitive Plan of Merger for Going-Private Transaction. https://www.prnewswire.com/news-releases/changyoucom-announces-filing-of-definitive-plan-of-merger-for-going-private-transaction-301040336.html

Channeladvisor Corporation. (2020, July 13). Solutions Overview | efficiently acquire more customers and increase sales. ChannelAdvisor. https://www.channeladvisor.com/solutions/

Check Point Software Technologies Ltd. (2019). Check Point Software Technologies Ltd.—Annual Report 2019 [Annual Report]. https://www.checkpoint.com/downloads/investor/2019-CHKP-form-20F.pdf

Chegg Inc. (2020). Chegg Inc.—Annual Report 2020 [Annual Report]. http://d18rn0p25nwr6d.cloudfront.net/CIK-0001364954/41dad8b4-f952-4c0b-bd3a-858345d3b1d9.pdf

Chengdu Westone Information Industry, Inc. (2021, November 8). Introduction-Westone Information Industry Inc. Introduction-Westone Information Industry Inc. http://en.westone.com.cn/about/173.html

Cimpress Plc. (2019). Cimpress Plc—Annual Report 2019 [Annual Report]. https://ir.cimpress.com/static-files/124480f3-91e7-4ad1-b07f-346ce89f520d

Citrix Systems Inc. (2020). Citrix Systems Inc.—Annual Report 2019 [Annual Report]. https://investors.citrix.com/~/media/Files/C/Citrix-IR/documents/annual-reports/2019/Final-19AR_20Proxy-Web.pdf

Clavister Holding AB. (2021). Clavister Holding AB—Annual Report 2020 [Annual Report]. https://www.clavister.com/wp-content/uploads/2021/05/Clavister-Arsredovisning-2020-English.pdf

Cliq Digital AG. (2020). Cliq Digital AG—Annual Report 2019 [Annual Report]. https://corp.at2010.net/files/April2020/bsi1VIwIK76cBY8dmuVb.pdf

Cloudera, Inc. (2021). Cloudera, Inc.—Annual Report 2021 [Annual Report]. https://d18rn0p25nwr6d.cloudfront.net/CIK-0001535379/6e6b8917-99d8-41dc-9c4d-6cc277ba87a0.pdf

CMC Markets Plc. (2020). CMC Markets Plc—Annual Report 2020 [Annual Report]. https://www.cmcmarketsplc.com/media/1418/cmc-markets-plc-annual-report-and-financial-statements-2020.pdf

Cogobuy Group. (2019). Cogobuy Group—Annual Report 2018 [Annual Report]. https://static.cogobuy.com/uploads/cogobuy/file/201904/26/cdc23d63f154e192646821e8f817f830.pdf

Comarch S.A. (2021). Comarch S.A.—Annual Report 2020 [Annual Report]. https://www.comarch.com/files-com/file_624/Raport_Roczny_2020_EN_v3.pdf

CommVault Systems Inc. (2020). CommVault Systems Inc.—Annual Report 2020 [Annual Report]. https://ir.commvault.com/static-files/e5802259-96b2-405b-a98d-878849331d6f

Computer Programs and Systems Inc. (2020). Computer Programs and Systems Inc.—Annual Report 2019 [Annual Report]. https://investors.cpsi.com/download/companies/270136a/Annual%20Reports/AR%202019%20CPSI.pdf

comScore Inc. (2022). comScore Inc.—Annual Report 2021 [Annual Report]. https://ir.comscore.com/static-files/9d2a1c14-4f73-48b7-a986-005c49a6478e

Constant Contact Inc. (2021, September 1). Constant Contact Closes Acquisition of SharpSpring [News]. PRnewswire. https://www.prnewswire.com/news-releases/constant-contact-closes-acquisition-of-sharpspring-301367629.html

Constellation Software Inc. (2022). Constellation Software Inc.—Annual Report 2021 [Annual Report]. https://www.csisoftware.com/docs/default-source/press-releases/csi-financial-statements-q421---final.pdf?sfvrsn=1e67f663_3/%20CSI-Financial-Statements-Q421---Final%20.pdf

Copart Inc. (2021). Copart Inc.—Annual Report 2021 [Annual Report]. https://dd7pmep5szm19.cloudfront.net/2480/0000900075-21-000022.pdf

CoreLogic Inc. (2021). CoreLogic Inc.—Annual Report 2020 [Annual Report]. https://sec.report/Document/0000036047-21-000018/

Corero Network Security plc. (2021). Corero Network Security plc—Annual Report 2020 [Annual Report]. https://www.corero.com/who-we-are/investor-relations/

CoreSite Realty Corporation. (2021). CoreSite Realty Corporation—Annual Report 2020 [Annual Report]. https://investors.coresite.com/static-files/3feb5867-10f6-47fc-8ad3-a76043273919

Cornerstone Ondemand Inc. (2021). Cornerstone Ondemand Inc.—Annual Report 2020 [Annual Report]. https://sec.report/Document/0001401680-21-000011/

CoStar Group Inc. (2021). CoStar Group Inc.—Annual Report 2020 [Annual Report]. https://sec.report/Document/0001057352-21-000032/

Coupa Software, Inc. (2021). Coupa Software, Inc.—Annual Report 2021 [Annual Report]. https://investors.coupa.com/static-files/f2a8df89-6d3a-484a-a6ca-9ef4569dbebc

Craneware plc. (2021). Craneware plc—Annual Report 2021 [Annual Report]. https://public.craneware.com/assets/public/documents/Investors/Craneware_2021_Annual_Financial_Report.pdf

Crescent NV. (2021). Crescent NV—Solutions [Annual Report]. Crescent. https://www.option.com/solutions/

Crexendo Inc. (2021). Crexendo Inc.—Annual Report 2020 [Annual Report]. https://sec.report/Document/0001654954-21-002518/

Criteo SA. (2021). Criteo SA—Annual Report 2020 [Annual Report]. https://criteo.investorroom.com/download/CRTO+%28Criteo+S.A.%29++%2810-K%29+2021-02-26.pdf_.pdf

Crunchbase. (2020, December 27). AXEL MARK INC.—Crunchbase Company Profile & Funding. Crunchbase. https://www.crunchbase.com/organization/axel-mark-inc-

CTS Eventim AG & Co. KGaA. (2022). CTS Eventim AG & Co. KGaA—Annual Report 2021 [Annual Report]. https://corporate.eventim.de/fileadmin/user_upload/eventim/04_investor_relations/hauptversammlung/2022/en/Annual_Report_2021.pdf

Cuscapi Bhd. (2021). Cuscapi Bhd.—Annual Report 2021 [Annual Report]. https://www.insage.com.my/ir/cmn/downloading.aspx?sFileName=21302000044872&sReportType=AR&sCompanyCode=CUSCAPI

cyan AG. (2021). Cyan AG—Annual Report 2020 [Annual Report]. https://ir.cyansecurity.com/wp-content/uploads/sites/2/2021/04/cyan_AG_2020_Annual-Report.pdf+

CyberArk Software Ltd. (2022). CyberArk Software Ltd.—Annual Report 2021 [Annual Report]. https://d18rn0p25nwr6d.cloudfront.net/CIK-0001598110/b8f54510-e27c-4359-88f7-b293ffe7b1b4.pdf

Cybozu Inc. (2021, December 5). Cybozu Inc.—Stremline Operations and Processes [Corporate]. Kintone. https://www.kintone.com/what-is-kintone/

CYREN Ltd. (2022). CYREN Ltd.—Annual Report 2021 [Annual Report]. https://ir.cyren.com/websites/cyren/English/3110/sec-filings.html?shortDesc=Annual%20Report&format=convpdf&secFilingId=be471c7c-8244-42c4-a1ac-c64319b2801c

CyrusOne Inc. (2022). CyrusOne Inc.—Annual Report 2021 [Annual Report]. https://sec.report/Document/0001553023-22-000009/

D4t4 Solutions plc. (2022). D4t4 Solutions plc—Annual Report 2022 [Annual Report]. https://25503654.fs1.hubspotusercontent-eu1.net/hubfs/25503654/Annual-Report-2022.pdf

Dalian Zeus Entertainment Co., Ltd. (2021, November 8). Company Profile—Tianshen Entertainment loves to create happiness [Company Profile]. http://www.tianshenyule.com/about.aspx

Danaher Corporation. (2021). Danaher Corporation—Annual Report 2020 [Annual Report]. http://investors.danaher.com/download/Danaher+2020+Annual+Report.pdf

Daniel Thomas. (2021, October 28). Facebook changes its name to Meta in major rebrand. BBC News. https://www.bbc.com/news/technology-59083601

Dassault Systèmes SE. (2019, October 29). Dassault Systèmes Completes Acquisition of Medidata Opening Up a New World of Virtual Twin Experiences for Healthcare. Dassault Systèmes. https://www.3ds.com/newsroom/press-releases/dassault-systemes-completes-acquisition-medidata-opening-new-world-virtual-twin-experiences-healthcare

Data Horizon Co., Ltd. (2021, November 13). Data Horizon—Service introduction [Company presentation]. Data Horizon. https://www.data-horizon.com/en/

Datalex Plc. (2022). Datalex Plc—Annual Report 2021 [Annual Report]. https://www.datalex.com/wp-content/uploads/2022/04/Datalex-Annual-Report-2021.pdf

Defactostandard, Ltd. (2021). Defactostandard, Ltd.—Annual Report 2019 [Annual Report]. http://www.defactostandard.co.jp/ir/

Delivery Hero SE. (2021). Delivery Hero SE—Annual Report 2020 [Annual Report]. Marketplace

Delticom AG. (2022). Delticom AG—Annual Report 2021 [Annual Report]. https://pubcontent.delti.com/wp-content/uploads/2022/03/Delticom_AnnualReport_2021.pdf

DEMAE-CAN CO.LTD. (2022). Demae-can Business [Company presentation]. Demae-Can Business. https://corporate.demae-can.com/en/business/demaecan.html

DeNA Co. Ltd. (2022, September 13). DeNA Co. Ltd.—Company—Overview [Company presentation]. https://dena.com/intl/company/overview.html

Descartes Systems Group Inc. (2021). Descartes Systems Group Inc.—Annual Report 2021 [Annual Report]. https://www.descartes.com/content/media/documents/2020-05/fy2020_q4-AR.pdf

DesignOne Japan Inc. (2022, September 18). Company Info | DesignOne Japan, Inc. [Company profile]. Company Info | DesignOne Japan, Inc. https://www.designone.jp/en/

Despegar.com, Corp. (2021). Despegar.com, Corp.—Annual Report 2020 [Annual Report]. https://d18rn0p25nwr6d.cloudfront.net/CIK-0001703141/7d3f8809-6b1a-47e4-a9b0-d51c1ab9020d.pdf

Destiny Media Technologies Inc. (2021, November 28). Destiny Media Technologies | Investor Relations [Corporate]. https://investors.dsny.com/

DHI Group Inc. (2022). DHI Group Inc.—Annual Report 2021 [Annual Report]. https://sec.report/Document/0001393883-22-000025/

Digimarc Corporation. (2021). Digimarc Corporation—Annual Report 2020 [Annual Report]. https://www.sec.gov/ix?doc=/Archives/edgar/data/1438231/000156459021009019/dmrc-10k_20201231.htm

Digispice Technologies Ltd. (2021, December 5). DiGiSPICE—About us [Corporate]. DiGiSPICE—About Us. https://www.digispice.com/about.php

Digital Arts Inc. (2022, September 18). Our Business|About Digital Arts|Digital Arts [Company profile]. Our Business|About Digital Arts|Digital Arts. https://www.daj.jp/en/about/business/

Digital Garage Inc. (2022, September 18). Digital Garage | Business Introduction [Company profile]. Digital Garage | CONTEXT COMPANY. https://www.garage.co.jp/en/business/

Digital Realty Trust Inc. (2021). Digital Realty Trust Inc.—Annual Report 2020 [Annual Report]. https://sec.report/Document/0001558370-21-002191/

Digital Turbine Inc. (2022). Digital Turbine Inc.—Annual Report 2022 [Annual Report]. https://ir.digitalturbine.com/sec-filings/all-sec-filings/content/0001628280-22-016294/0001628280-22-016294.pdf

DocuSign, Inc. (2021). DocuSign, Inc.—Annual Report 2021 [Annual Report]. https://d18rn0p25nwr6d.cloudfront.net/CIK-0001261333/961d5ad0-fa5b-4c07-911f-7d3b81253049.pdf

Domain Holdings Australia Ltd. (2021). Domain Holdings Australia Ltd.—Annual Report 2021 [Annual Report]. https://shareholders.domain.com.au/FormBuilder/_Resource/_module/T9NtqvJX0UGSmtpsWXgLcA/file/2021-Annual-Report.pdf

Domo, Inc. (2021). Domo, Inc.—Annual Report 2021 [Annual Report]. https://s26.q4cdn.com/900411403/files/doc_financials/annual/10K-2020-Q4.pdf

dormakaba Holding AG. (2020). Dormakaba Holding AG—Annual Report 2021 [Annual Report]. https://report.dormakaba.com/2019_20/app/uploads/Annual-Report-2019-_-2020_en.pdf

dotDigital Group plc. (2021). dotDigital Group plc—Annual Report 2021 [Annual Report]. https://www.dotdigitalgroup.com/wp-content/uploads/2021/11/Dotdigital-Annual-Report-2021-1-Final.pdf

Dragonfish. (2020, December 25). Dragonfish—The B2B division of 888 that helps gaming companies deliver online results. Dragonfish—the B2B Division of 888 That Helps Gaming Companies Deliver Online Results. http://www.dragonfishtech.com/

Dropbox, Inc. (2021). Dropbox, Inc.—Annual Report 2020 [Annual Report]. https://dropbox.gcs-web.com/static-files/ad964ecc-1f04-444b-ba51-8c0d9425422f

Duluth Holdings Inc. (2021). Duluth Holdings, Inc.—Annual Report 2021 [Annual Report]. https://ir.duluthtrading.com/static-files/de4b597d-be8f-4e46-9d1b-e1374c4e5bbd

Duos Technologies Group Inc. (2021). Duos Technologies Group Inc—Annual Report 2020 [Annual Report]. https://ir.duostechnologies.com/sec-filings/annual-reports/content/0001553350-21-000232/0001553350-21-000232.pdf

eBay Inc. (2022). eBay Inc.—Annual Report 2021 [Annual Report]. https://d18rn0p25nwr6d.cloudfront.net/CIK-0001065088/9acde302-6685-4208-934b-33b9eeb5e25d.pdf

Ebiquity Plc. (2022). Ebiquity Plc—Annual Report 2021 [Annual Report]. https://www.ebiquity.com/media/188450/web_01_ebq_ar21.pdf

Ebix, Inc. (2021). Ebix, Inc.—Annual Report 2020 [Annual Report]. https://www.ebix.com/investors/pdf/Ebix-Q410k-2020.pdf

ECHO Marketing, Inc. (2021, November 10). Echo Marketing—Data driven, No.1 Performance marketing group [Company Profile]. echomarketing. http://echomarketing.co.kr/en/about

Efecte Oyj. (2021). Efecte Oyj—Investor presentation—Efecte 2020 results webcast [Company presentation]. https://investors.efecte.com/sites/default/files/Efecte%20-%20Earnings%20Call%202020%20updated.pdf

eGain Corporation. (2022). eGain Corporation—Annual Report 2021 [Annual Report]. https://sec.report/Document/0001558370-22-014362/

Ellie Mae Inc. (2019). Ellie Mae Inc.—Annual Report 2019 [Annual Report]. https://sec.report/Document/0001122388-19-000013/#s3CCCD1A7F53B28BCD5C6F48D13352BDA

ELMO Software Ltd. (2021). ELMO Software Ltd.—Annual Report 2021 [Annual Report]. https://investors.elmosoftware.com.au/DownloadFile.axd?file=/Report/ComNews/20210831/02415081.pdf

EMIS Group plc. (2021). EMIS Group plc—Annual Report 2020 [Annual Report]. http://www.emisgroupplc.com/investors/

Endava Plc. (2021). Endava Plc—Annual Report 2021 [Annual Report]. https://s22.q4cdn.com/220269410/files/doc_downloads/2021/Endava-20-F-FY21_Edgar-formatting-corrected.pdf

Endurance International Group Holdings Inc. (2020). Endurance International Group Holdings Inc.—Annual Report 2019 [Annual Report]. https://sec.report/Document/0001628280-20-001590/

Enghouse Systems Limited. (2021). Enghouse Systems Limited—Corporate Presentation [Company presentation]. https://www.enghouse.com/wp-content/uploads/2021/10/20211011-Enghouse-Corporate-Presentation-Q3-FY-21.pdf

Entain PLC. (2022). Entain PLC—Annual Report 2022 [Annual Report]. https://entaingroup.com/wp-content/uploads/2022/03/2021-Annual-Report.pdf

Envestnet Inc. (2022). Envestnet Inc.—Annual Report 2021 [Annual Report]. https://investor.envestnet.com/sec-filings/annual-reports/content/0001628280-22-003985/0001628280-22-003985.pdf

EOH Holdings Limited. (2021, November 20). IOCO—part of EOH Holdings [Corporate]. EOH. https://www.eoh.co.za/our-group/ioco-tech/

Eole, Inc. (2021, November 10). Corporate Services | Eole [Company Profile]. Eole. https://www.eole.co.jp/business/

EQ Inc. (2021). EQ Inc.—Annual Report 2020 [Annual Report]. https://assets.ctfassets.net/nph7if1oawhd/4MdUTAvSBhOEReWsSeBKzi/95526da214693f58910bf726196444fe/Financial_Statements_-English.pdf

EQS Group AG. (2021). EQS Group AG—Annual Report 2020 [Annual Report]. http://irpages2.equitystory.com/download/companies/equitystory/Annual%20Reports/DE0005494165-JA-2020-EQ-E-00.pdf

Equinix Inc. (2022). Equinix Inc.—Annual Report 2021 [Annual Report]. https://sec.report/Document/0001628280-22-003171/

Ericsson. (2021, November 22). Ericsson to acquire Vonage [Company news]. Ericsson. https://www.ericsson.com/en/press-releases/2021/11/ericsson-to-acquire-vonage-for-usd-6.2-billion-to-spearhead-the-creation-of-a-global-network-and-communication-platform-for-open-innovation

EROAD Limited. (2021). EROAD Limited—Annual Report 2021 [Annual Report]. https://www.eroadglobal.com/assets/Uploads/Global/Investor-documents/EROAD-AnnualReport-FY21-28May-Digital.pdf

E-Seikatsu Co. Ltd. (2021). E-Seikatsu Co., Ltd.—FY2021 Full-term Results Presentation Material [Results presentation]. http://www.e-seikatsu.info/IR/

Esker SA. (2021). Esker SA—2021 HY Investor presentation [Investor presentation]. https://www.esker.fr/sites/default/files/content/esk_inv_sept_2021_0.pdf

ESW Capital LLC. (2019, January 15). SLI Systems Acquired by ESW Capital [News]. PRnewswire. https://www.prnewswire.com/news-releases/sli-systems-acquired-by-esw-capital-300778581.html

E*TRADE Financial Corporation. (2020). E*TRADE Financial Corporation—Annual Report 2019 [Annual Report]. https://app.quotemedia.com/data/downloadFiling?webmasterId=103216&ref=114809404&type=HTML&symbol=ETFC&companyName=E*TRADE+Financial+Corporation&formType=10-K&formDescription=Annual+report+pursuant+to+Section+13+or+15%28d%29&dateFiled=2020-02-19&CK=1015780

Etsy Inc. (2022). Etsy Inc.—Annual Report 2021 [Annual Report]. https://d18rn0p25nwr6d.cloudfront.net/CIK-0001370637/619701ee-f7dc-4baa-9463-4374cfcef85e.pdf

Euronet Worldwide, Inc. (2021). Euronet Worldwide, Inc.—Annual Report 2020 [Annual Report]. https://ir.euronetworldwide.com/static-files/bda713b7-b725-4b74-9f3a-e7de2b1c1006

Eventbrite, Inc. (2021). Eventbrite, Inc.—Annual Report 2020 [Annual Report]. http://investor.eventbrite.com/overview/default.aspx

Everbridge Inc. (2022). Everbridge Inc.—Annual Report 2021 [Annual Report]. https://ir.everbridge.com/static-files/2b98ebf9-fcca-447a-b5a1-de563b403aee

EverQuote, Inc. (2021). EverQuote, Inc.—Annual Report 2020 [Annual Report]. https://d18rn0p25nwr6d.cloudfront.net/CIK-0001640428/31c1b0bc-63b1-4e67-be28-d314b63cdeb9.pdf

EVERTEC Inc. (2021). EVERTEC, Inc.—Annual Report 2020 [Annual Report]. https://s1.q4cdn.com/250184606/files/doc_financials/2020/ar/Annual-Repor-final-doc.pdf

Evolution AB. (2021). Evolution AB—Annual Report 2020 [Annual Report]. https://evolution-com-media.s3.eu-central-1.amazonaws.com/s3fs-public/1393581.pdf

Expedia Group Inc. (2022). Expedia Group Inc.—Annual Report 2021 [Annual Report]. https://d18rn0p25nwr6d.cloudfront.net/CIK-0001324424/936c054e-9c59-465f-a87e-c9144fb28bb1.pdf

Expert.ai S.p.A. (2021). Expert.ai S.p.A.—Annual Report 2020 [Annual Report]. https://www.expert.ai/wp-content/uploads/2020/09/BILANCIO-EXPERT20_en.pdf?

Extreme Networks, Inc. (2021). Extreme Networks, Inc.—Annual Report 2021 [Annual Report]. https://investor.extremenetworks.com/static-files/f19c85c5-cd99-4082-a753-2bc502697808

F5 Networks Inc. (2021). F5 Networks Inc.—Annual Report 2021 [Annual Report]. https://sec.report/Document/0001048695-21-000044/

FactSet Research Systems. (2021). FactSet Software and Database [Windows 10]. https://www.factset.com/

FactSet Research Systems Inc. (2021). FactSet Research Systems Inc.—Annual Report 2021 [Annual Report]. https://investor.factset.com/static-files/e758d2d8-ba1c-4894-924b-b18cbafb44ce

Fair Isaac Corporation. (2021). Fair Isaac Corporation—Annual Report 2021 [Annual Report]. https://fico.gcs-web.com/static-files/d5e7d807-3d5b-46a4-8e80-a7f4261fc37c

FalconStor Software, Inc. (2021). FalconStor Software, Inc.—Annual Report 2020 [Annual Report]. https://www.sec.gov/ix?doc=/Archives/edgar/data/922521/000162828021004460/falc-20201231.htm

Fang Holdings Limited. (2022, September 25). Investor Relations | Fang Holdings Limited | Corporate Profile [Company Profile]. Investor Relations | Fang Holdings Limited | Corporate Profile. https://ir.fang.com/investor-overview/

Farfetch Limited. (2021). Farfetch Limited—Annual Report 2020 [Annual Report]. https://d18rn0p25nwr6d.cloudfront.net/CIK-0001740915/97d5f8f5-4561-4732-b15d-bab28655dfc4.pdf

FASOO Co., Ltd. (2021, November 10). FASOO Co., Ltd.—Company Information [Company profile]. Fasoo. https://en.fasoo.com/company/

FFRI Security, Inc. (2021, November 13). FFRI Security, Inc.—FFRI yarai | FFRI Security, Inc—Product [Corporate]. FFRI Security, Inc.—FFRI Yarai | FFRI Security, Inc—Product. https://www.ffri.jp/en/index.htm?utm_source=website&utm_medium=redirect&utm_campaign=product

Fidelity National Information Services Inc. (2019, July 31). FIS Closes Acquisition of Worldpay, Enhancing its Global Technology Leadership Serving Merchants, Banks and Capital Markets—Press Releases | FIS [Company news]. FIS Global. https://www.fisglobal.com/en/about-us/media-room/press-release/2019/fis-closes-acquisition-of-worldpay-enhancing-its-global-technology-leadership

Fidelity National Information Services, Inc. (2021). Fidelity National Information Services, Inc.—Annual Report 2020 [Annual Report]. https://www.investor.fisglobal.com/static-files/1a114067-03fc-4a6d-9231-c9868323b8f6

Financial Times. (2020, December 27). Beenos Inc, 3328:TYO profile—FT.com. Beenos Inc, 3328:TYO Profile—FT.Com. https://markets.ft.com/data/equities/tearsheet/profile?s=3328:TYO

First Data Corporation. (2019). First Data Corporation—Annual Report 2019 [Annual Report]. https://sec.report/Document/0000883980-19-000009/

Fiserv, Inc. (2021). Fiserv, Inc.—Annual Report 2020 [Annual Report]. https://investors.fiserv.com/static-files/29cf5bb5-583e-417f-a267-7fcac3d7fa53

Five9 Inc. (2022). Five9 Inc.—Annual Report 2021 [Annual Report]. https://investors.five9.com/static-files/4dc14d56-36aa-4c50-9273-8680757127a8

Flexion Mobile Plc. (2021). Flexion Mobile Plc—Annual Report 2021 [Annual Report]. https://flexionmobile.com/content/uploads/2021/06/Flexion-Mobile-Plc-Annual-Report-31-Mar-2021.pdf

Flowscape Technology AB. (2021, December 12). Flowscape Technology AB—Investor Relationships—About Flowscape [Corporate]. Flowscape Technology—Investor Relationships—About Flowscape. https://flowscapesolutions.com/investor-relationships

Fluent, Inc. (2021). Fluent, Inc.—Annual Report 2020 [Annual Report]. https://investors.fluentco.com/sec-filings/sec-filing/10-k/0001437749-21-006165

Flutter Entertainment Plc. (2022). Flutter Entertainment Plc—Annual Report 2021 [Annual Report]. https://www.flutter.com/media/dvvn0ith/flutter-entertainment-plc-annual-report-2021.pdf

Focus Technology Co. Ltd. (2022, September 25). Focus Technology Co. Ltd.—About the company [Company profile]. Focus Technology Co. Ltd.—About the Company. https://www.focuschina.com/en/company.html

ForeScout Technologies, Inc. (2020). ForeScout Technologies, Inc.—Annual Report 2019 [Annual Report]. http://investors.forescout.com/static-files/8e104d7b-b60d-4d8c-a54b-da1c660ccbd4

FormPipe Software AB. (2021). FormPipe Software AB—Annual Report 2020 [Annual Report]. https://www.formpipe.com/globalassets/investor-relations/finansiella-rapporter/2021/formpipe-annual-report-2020.pdf

Fortinet Inc. (2022). Fortinet Inc.—Annual Report 2021 [Annual Report]. https://investor.fortinet.com/static-files/9fcde4ec-a3f0-4e19-bb7a-bbcb346903bc

Forward, A., & Lethbridge, T. C. (2008). A taxonomy of software types to facilitate search and evidence-based software engineering. Proceedings of the 2008 Conference of the Center for Advanced Studies on Collaborative Research: Meeting of Minds, 179–191. https://doi.org/10.1145/1463788.1463807

Frontier Digital Ventures Ltd. (2021). Frontier Digital Ventures Ltd.—Annual Report 2020 [Annual Report]. https://frontierdv.com/wp-content/uploads/2021/04/ye-2020pdf.pdf

F-Secure Oyj. (2022). F-Secure Oyj—Annual Report 2021 [Annual Report]. https://www.f-secure.com/content/dam/f-secure/en/investors/materials/annual-reports/2021/annual-report-2021.pdf

Funding Circle Holdings Plc. (2021). Funding Circle Holdings Plc—Annual Report 2020 [Annual Report]. https://fch-12917-s3.s3.eu-west-2.amazonaws.com/live/1016/2816/1085/Funding_Circle_Holdings_plc_Annual_Report_and_Accounts_2020.pdf

Funko, Inc. (2021). Funko, Inc.—Annual Report 2020 [Annual Report]. https://d18rn0p25nwr6d.cloudfront.net/CIK-0001704711/5974e25b-409e-4532-9338-b5880b6c15e8.pdf

Future plc. (2021, February 22). Future plc acquires GoCo Group plc [Company profile]. Future PLC. https://www.futureplc.com/blog/future-plc-acquires-goco-group-plc/

Fyber N.V. (2021). Fyber N.V.—Annual Report 2020 [Annual Report]. http://investors.fyber.com/assets/media/fyber-nv-annual-report-2020-sec.pdf

G5 Entertainment AB. (2022). G5 Entertainment AB—Annual Report 2021 [Annual Report]. https://corporate.g5e.com/sites/default/files/reports_files/2022-02/wkr0006.pdf

Gaia Inc. (2022). Gaia Inc.—Annual Report 2021 [Annual Report]. https://ir.gaia.com/sec-filings/all-sec-filings/content/0001564590-22-007683/0001564590-22-007683.pdf

Gaiax Co.Ltd. (2021, September 24). Gaiax Co.Ltd.—Business / Investment Portfolio. https://www.gaiax.co.jp/business-model/portfolio/

Gaming Innovation Group. (2021). Gaming Innovation Group, Inc.—Annual Report 2020 [Annual Report]. https://www.gig.com/wp-content/uploads/2021/04/GiG_AnnualReport_2020.pdf

GAN plc. (2022). GAN plc—Annual Report 2021 [Annual Report]. https://sec.report/Document/0001493152-22-010132/#ae_002

Geniee, Inc. (2021, November 14). SERVICES | Geniee,Inc. [Corporate]. Geniee. https://en.geniee.co.jp/services/

Gfinity PLC. (2021). Gfinity PLC—Full Year Results 2021 Presentation [Annual Report]. https://www.gfinityplc.com/wp-content/uploads/2021/11/Gfinity-Full-Year-Results-Presentation-2021.pdf

Gigas Hosting SA. (2021, November 12). Who we are—Gigas [Company Profile]. Who We Are—Gigas. https://gigas.com/en/empresa.html

GK Software SE. (2021). GK Software SE—Annual Report 2020 [Annual Report]. https://investor.gk-software.com/en/publications/financial-reports?task=download&cid=809

Global Industrial Company. (2021). Global Industrial Company—Annual Report 2020 [Annual Report]. https://d18rn0p25nwr6d.cloudfront.net/CIK-0000945114/69839b4d-8be6-4a02-9c37-aa97072bc85c.pdf

Global Payments Inc. (2022). Global Payments Inc.—Annual Report 2022 [Annual Report]. https://d18rn0p25nwr6d.cloudfront.net/CIK-0001123360/33ba5ce5-e783-46d2-914c-037bf6911f49.pdf

GlobalData Plc. (2022). GlobalData Plc—Annual Report 2021 [Annual Report]. https://www.globaldata.com/wp-content/uploads/2022/03/GlobalData-Annual-Report-2021_FINAL.pdf

Glodon Company Limited. (2021). Glodon Company Limited—Annual Report 2020 [Annual Report]. https://glodon-en2021.oss-ap-southeast-1.aliyuncs.com/uploads/public/611/091/7e5/6110917e586d9699218764.pdf

GoDaddy Inc. (2022). GoDaddy Inc.—Annual Report 2021 [Annual Report]. https://s23.q4cdn.com/406380394/files/doc_financials/annual/GDDY-Annual-Report-(4.22.2022).pdf

GREE Inc. (2022, September 25). GREE, Inc.—Business Overview [Company presentation]. GREE, Inc. Corporate Website. https://corp.gree.net/jp/en/business/

Groupon Inc. (2022). Groupon Inc.—Annual Report 2021 [Annual Report]. https://d18rn0p25nwr6d.cloudfront.net/CIK-0001490281/e9173d0f-0e1d-4a38-a14a-69d186eff40c.pdf

Grubhub Inc. (2021, June 15). Just Eat Takeaway.com completes acquisition of Grubhub [News]. PRnewswire. https://www.prnewswire.com/news-releases/just-eat-takeawaycom-completes-acquisition-of-grubhub-301312124.html

Gruppo MutuiOnline S.p.A. (2022). Gruppo MutuiOnline S.p.A.—Annual Report 2021 [Annual Report]. https://www.gruppomol.it/pdf/Annual%20report%20IFRS%202021_DEF.pdf

Guangdong Advertising Group Co., Ltd. (2021, November 8). About Shengguang_ Shengguang Group. About Shengguang_ Shengguang Group. http://www.gimc.cn/about.html?nowSelect=GIMC%E7%AE%80%E4%BB%8B

Guidewire Software Inc. (2022). Guidewire Software Inc.—Annual Report 2021 [Annual Report]. https://sec.report/Document/0001528396-22-000106/

Gunosy Inc. (2022, October 4). Service | Optimally deliver information to people around the world | Gunosy Inc. [Company Profile]. Gunosy Inc. https://gunosy.co.jp/en/service/

Hamee Corp. (2021). Hamee Corp.—Quarterly Report Q3 2021 [Quarterly Report]. http://hamee.co.jp/ir/

Hancom MDS Inc. (2021, November 9). Hancom MDS Inc.—Overview / History [Company profile]. Hancom MDS Inc. http://eng.mdstec.com/sub/index.asp?idx=010101

Harte-Hanks Inc. (2021). Harte-Hanks, Inc.—Annual Report 2020 [Annual Report]. https://app.quotemedia.com/data/downloadFiling?webmasterId=96484&ref=115743200&type=PDF&formType=10-K&formDescription=Annual+report+pursuant+to+Section+13+or+15%28d%29&dateFiled=2021-03-24&cik=45919&CK=45919

HealthStream Inc. (2021). HealthStream Inc.—Annual Report 2021 [Annual Report]. https://ir.healthstream.com/static-files/0d602852-f681-4742-81e9-b6f74e24e8ea

Hello Group Inc. (2021). Hello Group Inc.—Annual Report 2020 [Annual Report]. https://ir.hellogroup.com/static-files/346fbd29-6958-4f2e-b031-c08b5bc8edf0

HelloFresh SE. (2021). HelloFresh SE—Annual Report 2020 [Annual Report]. https://ir.hellofreshgroup.com/download/companies/hellofresh/Annual%20Reports/DE000A161408-JA-2020-EQ-E-00.pdf

HEROZ Inc. (2021). HEROZ, Inc.—Presentation Material for FY04/2022 Q1 Financial Results [Company presentation]. https://heroz.co.jp/ir-files/en/20210910/Presentation_Material_for_FY04-2022_Q1.pdf

Hightech Payment Systems SA. (2021). Hightech Payment Systems SA—Annual Report 2020 [Annual Report]. https://www.hps-worldwide.com/sites/default/files/investor/Annual%20Financial%20Report%202020.pdf

Hinchliffe, T. (2018, May 10). Japanese Company Acquires Spanish-born Mitula for €118M. Novobrief. https://novobrief.com/japanese-company-acquires-mitula/6560/

Hirsch, L. (2019, June 3). Flower delivery company FTD files for bankruptcy [News]. CNBC. https://www.cnbc.com/2019/06/03/flower-delivery-company-ftd-files-for-bankruptcy.html

HiTechPros SA. (2021, November 12). ALHIT.PA—Hitechpros SA Profile | Reuters. ALHIT.PA—Hitechpros SA Profile | Reuters. https://www.reuters.comundefined

Hobonichi Co., Ltd. (2021). Hobonichi Co., Ltd.—Annual Report 2021 [Annual Report].

HolidayCheck Group AG. (2021). HolidayCheck Group AG—Annual Report 2020 [Annual Report]. https://www.holidaycheckgroup.com/wp-content/uploads/2021/04/Annual-Report-2020-of-HolidayCheck-Group-AG-persuant-to-IFRS.pdf

home24 SE. (2021). Home24 SE—Annual Report 2020 [Annual Report]. https://www.home24.com/download/companies/homevierundzwanzig/Annual%20Reports/DE000A14KEB5-JA-2020-EQ-E-00.pdf

Hostelworld Group Plc. (2022). Hostelworld Group Plc—Annual Report 2021 [Annual Report]. https://www.hostelworldgroup.com/~/media/Files/H/Hostelworld-v2/reports-and-presentations/hostelworld-annual-report-2021.pdf

Hotto Link, Inc. (2021, November 13). Hotto Link Inc.—About us [Corporate]. Hotto Link Inc. https://www.hottolink.co.jp/english/

Howard, T. (2018, May 11). Zoopla parent ZPG agrees £2.2bn takeover by US private equity firm Silver Lake [News]. Proactiveinvestors NA. https://www.proactiveinvestors.com/companies/news/196814/zoopla-parent-zpg-agrees-22bn-takeover-by-us-private-equity-firm-silver-lake-196814.html

HubSpot Inc. (2022). HubSpot Inc.—Annual Report 2021 [Annual Report]. https://f.hubspotusercontent00.net/hubfs/53/wt-ir-files/PDF/15569834.pdf

HUYA, Inc. (2021, April 27). HUYA, Inc.—Company Profile [Annual Report]. Company Profile. http://ir.huya.com/index.php?s=64

Hypoport SE. (2022). Hypoport SE—Annual Report 2021 [Annual Report]. https://www.hypoport.com/hypoport/uploads/2022/01/2021-Q4-Annual-report-English.pdf

i3 Verticals Inc. (2021). i3 Verticals, Inc.—Annual Report 2021 [Annual Report]. https://investors.i3verticals.com/static-files/37136cde-e2f9-4d68-b742-36e897787120Nov 22, 2021

IAC. (2020, February 11). IAC Announces Close of $500 Million Care.com Acquisition. IAC Announces Close of $500 Million Care.Com Acquisition. https://www.prnewswire.com/news-releases/iac-announces-close-of-500-million-carecom-acquisition-301002873.html

IAC/InterActiveCorp. (2022). IAC/InterActiveCorp.—Annual Report 2021 [Annual Report]. https://ir.iac.com/static-files/c88e8391-55fb-4203-bc04-63ae039ad30d

iClick Interactive Asia Group Ltd. (2021). iClick Interactive Asia Group Ltd.—Annual Report 2020 [Annual Report]. https://app.quotemedia.com/data/downloadFiling?webmasterId=101533&ref=115803074&type=PDF&symbol=ICLK&companyName=iClick+Interactive+Asia+Group+Limited&formType=20-F&dateFiled=2021-04-21&CK=1697818

Ideagen PLC. (2021). Ideagen PLC—Annual Report 2021 [Annual Report]. https://investors.ideagen.com/media/lx3dadty/ideagen-annual-report-2021_v6.pdf

IFCA MSC Bhd. (2021). IFCA MSC Bhd.—Annual Report 2020 [Annual Report]. https://www.insage.com.my/ir/cmn/downloading.aspx?sFileName=21118000041614&sReportType=AR&sCompanyCode=IFCAMSC

iflytek Co., Ltd. (2021, November 8). About Us—IFLYTEK. About Us—IFLYTEK. https://www.iflytek.com/en/about-us.html

IG Group Holdings plc. (2022). IG Group Holdings plc—Annual Report 2022 [Annual Report]. https://www.iggroup.com/sites/ig-group/files/2022-08/ig-group-ar-2022.pdf

IGG Inc. (2022). IGG Inc.—Annual Report 2021 [Annual Report]. http://iis.quamnet.com/media/IRAnnouncement/799/EN_US/10220138-0.PDF

IHS Markit Ltd. (2022). IHS Markit Ltd.—Annual Report 2021 [Annual Report]. https://sec.report/Document/0001598014-22-000011/

i-mobile Co. Ltd. (2021, December 5). i-mobile | The Largest Advertising Platform in Japan—What i-mobile does [Corporate]. I-Mobile. http://www2.i-mobile.co.jp/en/index.aspx#scroll_position_aboutus

Imperva Inc. (2018). Imperva Inc.—Annual Report 2017 [Annual Report]. https://sec.report/Document/0001564590-18-003043/

Imperva Inc. (2019, January 10). Thoma Bravo Completes Imperva Acquisition [Company news]. Company. https://www.imperva.com/company/press_releases/thoma-bravo-completes-imperva-acquisition/

Infibeam Avenues Ltd. (2022). Infibeam Avenues Ltd.—Annual Report 2022 [Annual Report]. https://www.ia.ooo/wp-content/uploads/2022/08/Annual-Report-FY-2021-22.pdf

Info Edge India Ltd. (2022). Info Edge India Ltd.—Annual Report 2022 [Annual Report]. http://www.infoedge.in/pdfs/InfoEdge_Annual_Report_2022_Aug_2.pdf

Infocom Corporation. (2021, November 13). BUSINESS | Infocom Corporation. Infocom. https://www.infocom.co.jp/en/business.html

Infomedia Ltd. (2021). Infomedia Ltd—Annual Report 2021 [Annual Report]. https://www.infomedia.com.au/files/investors/FY21-AnnualReport.pdf

Innelec Multimedia SA. (2021, November 6). Innelec Multimedia SA—Company presentation [Company presentation]. Company Presentation. https://corporate.innelec.com/the-company/?lang=en

Inovalon Holdings Inc. (2021). Inovalon Holdings Inc.—Annual Report 2020 [Annual Report]. https://sec.report/Document/0001619954-21-000042/

Instem plc. (2021). Instem plc—Annual Report 2020 [Annual Report]. https://investors.instem.com/docs/2020-Instem-Annual-Report.pdf

Instructure Holdings Inc. (2021, July 21). Instructure Announces Pricing of Initial Public Offering [Company news]. Instructure Announces Pricing of Initial Public Offering. https://ir.instructure.com/news/news-details/2021/Instructure-Announces-Pricing-of-Initial-Public-Offering/default.aspx

Integrated Electronic Systems Lab Co. , Ltd. (2021, November 8). Home-Jicheng Electronics Co., Ltd.—About us. Home-Jicheng Electronics Co., Ltd.—About Us. https://www.ieslab.com.cn/

Integrated Research Limited. (2021). Integrated Research Limited—Annual Report 2021 [Annual Report]. https://www.ir.com/hubfs/01.%20Global/Annual%20Report%20to%20Shareholders%20FY20.pdf

Intelligent Systems Corporation. (2021). Intelligent Systems Corporation—Annual Report 2020 [Annual Report]. https://sec.report/Document/0001437749-21-004982/

Intelligent Wave Inc. (2021, November 13). Intelligent Wave Inc.—Service/Products [Corporate]. Intelligent Wave Inc. https://www.iwi.co.jp/service-products/

Internap Corporation. (2020). Internap Corporation—Annual Report 2019 [Annual Report]. https://sec.report/Document/0001628280-20-007086/

International Game Technology PLC. (2022). International Game Technology PLC—Annual Report 2021 [Annual Report]. https://d18rn0p25nwr6d.cloudfront.net/CIK-0001619762/7531bad3-af1e-432c-83a6-30987592d6b9.pdf

InterServ International, Inc. (2021). InterServ International, Inc.—Annual Report 2019 [Annual Report]. InterServ International, Inc.—Annual Report 2020

Intershop Communications AG. (n.d.). Intershop Communications AG—Annual Report 2021 [Annual Report]. Retrieved October 16, 2022, from https://www.intershop.com/files/Intershop-2020/materials_pdfs/Investors/en/financial-reports/2021/Intershop_AnnualReport-2021.pdf

Inuvo Inc. (2022). Inuvo Inc.—Annual Report 2021 [Annual Report]. https://investor.inuvo.com/sec-filings/all-sec-filings/content/0000829323-22-000015/0000829323-22-000015.pdf

Invibes Advertising NV. (2021, December 11). Invibes Advertising: Entdecken Sie die Stärken der in-feed Werbung [Corporate]. Invibes Advertising. https://www.invibes.com/de/de/

IQGeo Group PLC. (2021). IQGeo Group PLC—Annual Report 2020 [Annual Report]. https://f.hubspotusercontent00.net/hubfs/5217051/IQGeo_annual_report_2020.pdf

iQIYI, Inc. (2021). iQIYI, Inc.—Annual Report 2020 [Annual Report]. https://ir.iqiyi.com/static-files/f3e1dd2b-7a71-427c-8e71-dee3e44ea4a7

IRESS Limited. (2021). IRESS Limited—Annual Report 2020 [Annual Report]. https://www.iress.com/media/documents/Iress_2020_Annual_Report.pdf

iSelect Ltd. (2022). iSelect Ltd.—Annual Report 2022 [Annual Report]. https://www.iselect.com.au/content/uploads/2022/08/2022-Annual-Report.pdf

Issuer Direct Corporation. (2021). Issuer Direct Corporation—Annual Report 2020 [Annual Report]. http://quotes.quotemedia.com/data/downloadFiling?webmasterId=96484&ref=115699506&type=PDF&symbol=ISDR&companyName=Issuer+Direct+Corporation&formType=10-K&formDescription=Annual+report+pursuant+to+Section+13+or+15%28d%29&dateFiled=2021-03-04&CK=843006

Iteris Inc. (2021). Iteris, Inc.—Annual Report 2021 [Annual Report]. http://iterisinc.gcs-web.com/static-files/04c1c762-8842-430b-b6c0-b9fafb7f3759

ItoKuro Inc. (2021, November 7). ItoKuro, Inc.—Business Content [Business overview]. Business Content. http://www.itokuro.jp/ir/

ITT, Inc. (2021). ITT, Inc.—Annual Report 2020 [Annual Report]. https://ittcorp.gcs-web.com/node/26701/html

Jack Henry & Associates, Inc. (2021). Jack Henry & Associates, Inc.—Annual Report 2021 [Annual Report]. https://ir.jackhenry.com/static-files/94d6ce46-aa06-4bf7-8442-cb4f3ddfa075

Journeo plc. (2020). Journeo plc—Annual Report 2020 [Annual Report]. https://journeo.com/wp-content/uploads/2021/06/annual-report-2020.pdf

Juniper Networks, Inc. (2021). Juniper Networks, Inc.—Annual Report 2020 [Annual Report]. https://d18rn0p25nwr6d.cloudfront.net/CIK-0001043604/45d9bf71-b419-4121-a76e-72dc28839aa6.pdf

Just Eat Takeaway.com N.V. (2022). Just Eat Takeaway.com N.V.—Annual Report 2021 [Annual Report]. https://s3.eu-central-1.amazonaws.com/takeaway-corporatewebsite-dev/JET-JV2021-080322.pdf

Kamakura Shinsho, Ltd. (2021, November 7). Kamakura Shinsho, Ltd.—Company Profile [Company Profile]. Kamakura Shinsho, Ltd.—Company Profile. https://www.kamakura-net.co.jp/company/profile/

Kapsch TrafficCom AG. (2021). Kapsch TrafficCom AG—Annual Report 2021 [Annual Report]. https://www.kapsch.net/_Resources/Persistent/989ffa517c8364e3ca9b9fcb81d3d09198d8bf9a/KTC_Group_Report_2020-21.pdf

Kerlink SA. (2022). Kerlink SA—Annual Report 2021 [Annual Report]. https://www.kerlink.fr/wp-content/uploads/2022/04/Rapport-annuel-2021_EN.pdf

Keyware Solutions Inc. (2021, November 13). Business Field | Solutions | Keyware Solutions [Corporate]. Keyware Solutions Inc. https://www.keyware.co.jp/english/solutions/business_field.html

Kidoz, Inc. (2021). Kidoz, Inc.—Annual Report 2020 [Annual Report]. https://investor.kidoz.net/wp-content/uploads/2021/03/Kidoz-Inc-10K-2020-final.pdf

Kinaxis Inc. (2021). Kinaxis, Inc.—Annual Report 2020 [Annual Report]. http://s25.q4cdn.com/729569956/files/doc_financials/2020/ar/2020-AnnualReport-DIGITAL-FINAL.pdf

Kindred Group plc. (2022). Kindred Group plc—Capital Markers Days Presentation 2022 [Capital Markets Day Presentation]. http://www.kindredgroup.com/investors/

Kingnet Network Co., Ltd. (2021, November 9). Kingnet Network Co., Ltd.—Company Profile [Company profile]. Kingnet Network Co., Ltd.—Company Profile. https://www.kingnet.com/about/company

Koal Software Co. Ltd. (2021, December 5). Koal Software—Solutions [Corporate]. http://www.koal.com/solutions

Kogan.com Ltd. (2022). Kogan.com Ltd.—Annual Report 2022 [Annual Report]. https://www.kogancorporate.com/resources/pdf/library/2022%20Annual%20Report.pdf

KRM22 Plc. (2021). KRM22 Plc—Annual Report 2020 [Annual Report]. https://global-uploads.webflow.com/5ebbff2a0d9b49ff5e20dc90/6053580144f581f3a93fba71_KRM22%20FY20%20Annual%20Report.pdf

Lands' End Inc. (2022). Lands' End Inc.—Annual Report 2021 [Annual Report]. https://investors.landsend.com/static-files/cf508958-da0c-401c-954b-94b539b0229b

lastminute.com N.V. (2022). Lastminute.com N.V.—Annual Report 2021 [Annual Report]. https://res.cloudinary.com/lastminute-contenthub/image/upload/v1648059953/DAM/Artwork/lastminute.com/reports_presentations/2021/annual_report_2021.pdf

Leaf Group Ltd. (2021). Leaf Group Ltd.—Annual Report 2020 [Annual Report]. https://sec.report/Document/0001558370-21-001844/

Leaf Group Ltd. (2021, May 4). Leaf Group to be Acquired by Graham Holdings Company for $8.50 Per Share in All-Cash Transaction Valued at $323 Million. GlobeNewswire News Room. https://www.globenewswire.com/en/news-release/2021/04/05/2204205/0/en/Leaf-Group-to-be-Acquired-by-Graham-Holdings-Company-for-8-50-Per-Share-in-All-Cash-Transaction-Valued-at-323-Million.html

Learning Technologies Group Plc. (2021). Learning Technologies Group Plc—Annual Report 2020 [Annual Report]. https://www.ltgplc.com/wp-content/uploads/2021/04/LTG_Annual_Report_2020_Digital-1.pdf

LendingTree, Inc. (2021). LendingTree, Inc.—Annual Report 2020 [Annual Report]. https://investors.lendingtree.com/static-files/5f2c8da4-ae56-4e94-bfd0-f42044466fc1

LeoVegas AB. (2021). LeoVegas AB—Annual Report 2020 [Annual Report]. https://leovegasgroup.com/media/1601/leovegas-annual-report-2020.pdf

LightInTheBox Holding Co. Ltd. (2022). LightInTheBox Holding Co. Ltd.—Annual Report 2021 [Annual Report]. http://ir.lightinthebox.com/static-files/06373f3e-ff75-4b44-9300-a4448cd379ad

Limelight Networks Inc. (2022). Limelight Networks Inc.—Annual Report 2021 [Annual Report]. https://sec.report/Document/0001391127-22-000025/

Linedata Services SA. (2021). Linedata Services SA—Annual Report 2020 [Annual Report]. https://www.linedata.com/sites/default/files/2021-06/LDS%20-%20Consolidated%20Financial%20Statements%202020.12.pdf

Liquidity Services Inc. (2021). Liquidity Services Inc.—Annual Report 2021 [Annual Report]. https://investors.liquidityservices.com/static-files/193a3d9a-8284-4a07-8396-da8c0fdc9785

LIVECHAT Software S.A. (2021, November 20). LIVECHAT Software S.A.—Company Profile [Corporate]. LiveChat Investor Relations. https://investor.livechatinc.com/company-profile/

LiveHire Ltd. (2021). LiveHire Ltd.—Annual Report 2021 [Annual Report]. https://cdn-api.markitdigital.com/apiman-gateway/ASX/asx-research/1.0/file/2924-02414111-3A574326?access_token=83ff96335c2d45a094df02a206a39ff4

LivePerson Inc. (2022). LivePerson Inc.—Annual Report 2021 [Annual Report]. https://ir.liveperson.com/static-files/307c8d73-3903-4967-b17c-72ad5bea53c8

LiveRamp Holdings Inc. (2021). LiveRamp Holdings, Inc.—Annual Report 2021 [Annual Report]. https://d18rn0p25nwr6d.cloudfront.net/CIK-0000733269/26152526-66b7-433f-b0d1-226a79907644.pdf

LiveTiles Limited. (2021). LiveTiles Limited—Annual Report 2021 [Annual Report]. https://livetilesglobal.com/wp-content/uploads/2020/10/LiveTiles-2020-Annual-Report.pdf

LOCONDO, Inc. (2021). LOCONDO, Inc.—Company Introduction [Company Introduction]. https://www.locondo.co.jp/wp-content/themes/locondo.co.jp/common/download/COMPANY_Presentation%20(2021.8).pdf

LogMeIn Inc. (2020). LogMeIn Inc.—Annual Report 2019 [Annual Report]. https://sec.report/Document/0001564590-20-004769/

Logo Yazilim Sanayi ve Ticaret A.S. (2021, November 20). Logo Yazilim Sanayi ve Ticaret A.S.—Products [Corporate]. Logo Yazılım | Kurumsal İş Yazılımları | 444 56 46. https://www.logo.com.tr/

Lotto24 AG. (2021). Lotto24 AG—Annual Report 2020 [Annual Report]. https://www.lotto24-ag.de/download/companies/lotto24/Annual%20Reports/DE000LTT2470-JA-2020-PN-EQ-E-00.pdf

Lunden, I. (2020, April 23). JustEat Takeaway $7.6B merger approved, pair pick up $756M in new funding | TechCrunch [News]. Techcrunch. https://techcrunch.com/2020/04/23/justeat-takeaway-7-6b-merger-approved-pair-pick-up-756m-in-new-funding/

M2M Group SA. (2021, November 20). M2M Group SA—Solutions [Corporate]. M2M Group. https://www.m2mgroup.com/en/epayments-egov-solutions/

Macau Legend Development Ltd. (2021, November 10). Macau Legend Development Ltd—Corporate Profile [Corporate Profile]. Macau Legend Development Ltd. http://www.macaulegend.com/html/about_profile.php

Magic Software Enterprises Ltd. (2021). Magic Software Enterprises Ltd.—Annual Report 2020 [Annual Report]. https://www.magicsoftware.com/wp-content/uploads/2021/05/Magic_20F_2020-2.pdf

MakeMyTrip Ltd. (2022). MakeMyTrip Ltd.—Annual Report 2022 [Annual Report]. https://d18rn0p25nwr6d.cloudfront.net/CIK-0001495153/537fe409-663d-49a3-9451-4b2b055180b1.pdf

Mandiant Inc. (2022, September 12). Google Completes Acquisition of Mandiant [Company news]. Mandiant. https://www.mandiant.com/company/press-releases/google-completes-mandiant-acquisition

Manhattan Associates, Inc. (2021). Manhattan Associates, Inc.—Annual Report 2020 [Annual Report]. https://ir.manh.com/static-files/22e39bc1-41e9-45a5-ab71-e85898ef1908

Marchex Inc. (2022). Marchex Inc.—Annual Report 2022 [Annual Report]. https://investors.marchex.com/static-files/135a4ba4-5210-43be-a55b-1935fd674f62

Marin Software Inc. (n.d.). Marin Software Inc.—Annual Report 2021 [Annual Report]. Retrieved July 8, 2022, from https://d18rn0p25nwr6d.cloudfront.net/CIK-0001389002/7851ece4-79a3-459b-a599-1bb9c4090f18.pdf

Materialise NV. (2021). Materialise NV—Annual Report 2020 [Annual Report]. https://investors.materialise.com/static-files/f6b9dc72-5e60-4e86-9a13-81cf82001772

mCloud Technologies Corp. (2020). MCloud Technologies Corp—Annual Report 2019 [Annual Report]. https://s21.q4cdn.com/959970859/files/doc_financials/2019/ar/GetFile.pdf

mdf commerce inc. (2022). mdf commerce inc—Annual Report 2022 [Annual Report]. https://www.mdfcommerce.com/pdf/investors/financial-reports/2022/quarterly/en/q4_fs_en.pdf

Media and Games Invest SE. (n.d.). Media and Games Invest SE—Annual Report 2020 [Annual Report]. Retrieved August 19, 2021, from https://mgi.group/wp-content/uploads/2021/04/MGI-FY2020_Financial-Statements.pdf

Medidata Solutions Inc. (2019). Medidata Solutions Inc.—Annual Report 2018 [Annual Report].

Meet Group Inc. (2020a). Meet Group Inc—Annual Report 2019 [Annual Report]. https://sec.report/Document/0001078099-20-000011/

Meet Group Inc. (2020b, September 4). The Meet Group Announces Closing of Acquisition by eharmony Parent Company Parship Group [Company news]. https://www.businesswire.com/news/home/20200904005336/en/The-Meet-Group-Announces-Closing-of-Acquisition-by-eharmony-Parent-Company-Parship-Group

Megaport Ltd. (2021). Megaport Ltd.—Global Update—FY21 full year results [Annual Report]. https://yourir.info/resources/93d58eb1689d3802/announcements/mp1.asx/2A1314730/MP1_FY21_Full_Year_Results_and_Global_Update.pdf

Meitu, I. (2021). Meitu, Inc—Annual Report 2020 [Annual Report]. https://corp-static.meitu.com/corp-new/1616662711.4429/ew_01357ann-25032021.pdf

MercadoLibre Inc. (2022). MercadoLibre Inc.—Annual Report 2021 [Annual Report]. https://investor.mercadolibre.com/static-files/5d0af003-73a2-4e5e-898c-95957b644583

Meta Platforms Inc. (2022). Meta Platforms Inc.—Annual Report 2021 [Annual Report]. https://d18rn0p25nwr6d.cloudfront.net/CIK-0001326801/14039b47-2e2f-4054-9dc5-71bcc7cf01ce.pdf

Metaps, Inc. (2021, November 13). Metaps Inc.—Service [Corporate]. Metaps. https://metaps.com/wp-content/themes/metaps_v2

Micro Focus International plc. (2022). Micro Focus International plc—Annual Report 2021 [Annual Report]. https://www.microfocus.com/media/investors-report/annual-report-and-accounts-2021-report.pdf

MicroStrategy Incorporated. (2022). MicroStrategy Incorporated—Annual Report 2021 [Annual Report]. https://www.microstrategy.com/content/dam/website-assets/collateral/financial-documents/financial-document-archive/2021-annual-report.pdf

Mimecast Limited. (2021). Mimecast Limited—Annual Report 2021 [Annual Report]. https://investors.mimecast.com/static-files/eaff762e-91c3-4704-adcf-471434dc1367

Mimecast Limited. (2022, May 19). Permira Completes Acquisition of Mimecast | Mimecast [Corporate]. https://investors.mimecast.com/news-releases/news-release-details/permira-completes-acquisition-mimecast

MINDBODY, Inc. (2018, December 24). MINDBODY Enters into Definitive Agreement to be Acquired by Vista Equity Partners for $1.9 Billion. Mindbody. https://company.mindbodyonline.com/press/mindbody-enters-into-definitive-agreement-to-be-acquired-by-vista-equity-partners-for-19

Mitek Systems, Inc. (2020). Mitek Systems, Inc.—Annual Report 2020 [Annual Report]. https://investors.miteksystems.com/static-files/64205259-3d63-4a45-bda4-852d655108da

MiX Telematics Limited. (2021). MiX Telematics Limited—Annual Report 2021 [Annual Report]. https://d18rn0p25nwr6d.cloudfront.net/CIK-0001576914/34b8d71c-79d8-4d96-a3ff-8705ebe037c5.pdf

MobileIron Inc. (2020). MobileIron Inc.—Annual Report 2019 [Annual Report]. https://sec.report/Document/0001558370-20-002145/

Mobivity Holdings Corp. (2021). Mobivity Holdings Corp.—Annual Report 2020 [Annual Report]. https://sec.report/Document/0001562762-21-000136/

Moneysupermarket.com Group plc. (2022). Moneysupermarket.com Group plc—Annual Report 2021 [Annual Report]. https://corporate.moneysupermarket.com/~/media/Files/M/Moneysupermarket-V3/documents/MSMG_AR21%20Web%20PDF%20030322.pdf

MongoDB, Inc. (2021). MongoDB, Inc.—Annual Report 2021 [Annual Report]. https://d18rn0p25nwr6d.cloudfront.net/CIK-0001441816/01f4de89-fbb5-4313-8c9d-a61af15139ec.pdf

MonotaRO Co. Ltd. (2022). MonotaRO Co. Ltd.—Presentation Material for FY2021 Results [Annual Report]. http://corp.monotaro.com/en/ir/index.html

Moody's Corporation. (2018, August 30). Moody's to Acquire Reis, a Leader in Commercial Real Estate Data. Moody's to Acquire Reis, a Leader in Commercial Real Estate Data. https://ir.moodys.com/news-and-financials/press-releases/press-release-details/2018/Moodys-to-Acquire-Reis-a-Leader-in-Commercial-Real-Estate-Data/default.aspx

Morningstar Inc. (2022). Morningstar Inc.—Annual Report 2021 [Annual Report]. https://s21.q4cdn.com/198919461/files/doc_downloads/2022/05/c632fa36-1e45-47b6-9a0a-8c5afcf2cd09.pdf

MTI Ltd. (2012, October 10). MTI Ltd.—Services [Company Profile]. MTI Ltd. https://www.mti.co.jp/eng/?page_id=264

Muirhead, C. (2021, April 8). Minds + Machines plans sale of assets to GoDaddy subsidiary [News]. Proactiveinvestors UK. https://www.proactiveinvestors.co.uk/companies/news/946002/minds--machines-plans-sale-of-assets-to-godaddy-subsidiary-946002.html

mVISE AG. (2021). MVISE AG—Annual Report 2020 [Annual Report]. https://mvise.de/wp-content/uploads/2021/06/mVISE-AG-Konzerngescha%CC%88ftsbericht-2020.pdf

MySale Group plc. (2021). MySale Group plc—Annual Report 2021 [Annual Report]. https://www.mysalegroup.com/resources/data/reports/2021/MySale_Group_Plc-Annual_report_and_financial_statements-30062021-FINAL_signed.docx.pdf

NanJi E-Commerce Co Ltd. (2021, November 8). NanJi E-Commerce Co Ltd—Company Profile [Company Profile]. NanJi E-Commerce Co Ltd—Company Profile. http://www.nanjids.com/Home/Introduce/introduce.html

NantHealth Inc. (2021). NantHealth, Inc.—Annual Report 2020 [Annual Report]. https://ir.nanthealth.com/websites/nanthealth/English/3110/us-sec-filing.html?shortDesc=Annual%20Report&format=convpdf&secFilingId=aa6676de-6e58-4ead-81f5-617669fbcf62

Nasmedia Co., Ltd. (2021, November 9). Nasmedia Co., Ltd.—About us—Introduction to Nasmedia. Nasmedia. http://mobile.nasmedia.co.kr/

NAVER Corp. (2022). NAVER Corp.—Annual Report 2020 [Annual Report]. https://www.navercorp.com/navercorp_/ir/annualReport/2022/2020AR_NAVER_ENG_220203.pdf

Navinfo Co., Ltd. (2021, November 8). About NavInfo Europe. Navinfo. https://www.navinfo.eu/about-us/

NCsoft Corporation. (2022). NCsoft Corporation—IR Presentation Aug 2022 [Investor Presentation]. http://global.ncsoft.com/global/ir/structure.aspx

Nedap N.V. (2021). Nedap N.V—Annual Report 2020 [Annual Report]. https://nedap.com/wp-content/uploads/2021/03/Nedap-Annual-Report-2020.pdf

Nelly Group AB. (2022). Nelly Group AB—Annual Report 2021 [Annual Report]. https://www.nellygroup.com/wp-content/uploads/2022/04/ar-2021-nelly-group-ab-eng-final.pdf

Net Element Inc. (2021, August 31). Net Element Shareholders Approve Merger with Mullen Automotive [Net Element Shareholders Approve Merger with Mullen Automotive]. GlobeNewswire News Room. https://www.globenewswire.com/en/news-release/2021/08/31/2289444/0/en/Net-Element-Shareholders-Approve-Merger-with-Mullen-Automotive.html

Net Element Inc. (2021). Net Element Inc.—Annual Report 2021 [Annual Report].
NetDragon Websoft Holdings Limited. (2022). NetDragon Websoft Holdings Limited—Annual Report 2021 [Annual Report]. http://www.hkexnews.hk/listedco/listconews/sehk/2022/0425/2022042500579.pdf
NetEase Inc. (2022). NetEase Inc.—Annual Report 2021 [Annual Report]. https://ir.netease.com/static-files/5e8f4599-c552-43e2-bf73-8e2cbb60bd16
NetEnt AB. (2020). NetEnt AB—Annual Report Presentation 2019 [Annual Report Presentation]. https://www.netent.com/en/wp-content/uploads/sites/2/2020/02/netent-q4-ye-2019-presentation.pdf
NetScout Systems Inc. (2022). NetScout Systems Inc.—Annual Report 2022 [Annual Report]. https://www.netscout.com/shared/annual-report-2022/assets/pdfs/NetScout2022Form10-K.pdf
NetSol Technologies, Inc. (2011, March 15). NetSol Technologies Announces Launch of LeasePak-SaaS [Corporate]. NETSOL Technologies, Inc. https://ir.netsoltech.com/press-releases/detail/2264/netsol-technologies-announces-launch-of-leasepak-saas
New Relic Inc. (2022). New Relic Inc.—Annual Report 2021 [Annual Report]. https://d18rn0p25nwr6d.cloudfront.net/CIK-0001448056/b863b386-e75f-48a0-ab10-d79c75e79b0f.pdf
New Work SE. (2022). New Work SE—Annual Report 2021 [Annual Report]. https://www.new-work.se/NWSE/Investor-Relations/Geschaeftsberichte/en/NEW_WORK_AR_2021.pdf
Newgen Software Technologies Limited. (2021). Newgen Software Technologies Limited—Annual Report 2021 [Annual Report]. https://newgensoft.com/wp-content/uploads/2021/06/Annual-Report-2020-21.pdf
Nexgram Holdings Berhad. (2020). Nexgram Holdings Berhad—Annual Report 2020 [Annual Report]. https://nexgram.co/investor-relations/
NEXON Co. Ltd. (2022). NEXON Co. Ltd.—Annual Report 2021 [Annual Report]. https://pdf.irpocket.com/C3659/JZk2/J7ou/vinP.pdf
Nexon GT Co. Ltd. (2021, November 9). Nexon GT Co., Ltd.—Company development [Annual Report]. http://www.nexon-gt.com/#sub24
Nextdc Limited. (2022). Nextdc Limited—Annual Report 2022 [Annual Report]. https://www.nextdc.com/storage/app/media/3268_Next%20DC_AR%20FY22_FA_web.pdf
NextGen Healthcare, Inc. (2021). NextGen Healthcare, Inc.—Annual Report 2021 [Annual Report]. https://investor.nextgen.com/static-files/3f2b592b-5a1b-41a5-a48c-8fb3eaae463a
NIC Inc. (2021). NIC Inc.—Annual Report 2020 [Annual Report]. https://sec.report/Document/0001065332-21-000005/
NICE Ltd. (2021). NICE Ltd—Annual Report 2020 [Annual Report]. https://www.nice.com/Documents/SEC/20_f_sec_2020.pdf
Ningbo Ligong Environment and Energy Technology Co., Ltd. (2021, November 8). Ningbo Ligong Environment and Energy Technology Co., Ltd.—Company Profile [Company Profile]. Ningbo Ligong Environment and Energy Technology Co., Ltd.—Company Profile. http://www.lgom.com.cn/cn/about/
Northern Data AG. (2021). Northern Data AG—Annual Report 2020 [Annual Report]. https://ir.northerndata.de/homepage/attachment/2021_11_09_northern_data_geschaeftsbericht_2020_english_pre_version_screen/

NortonLifeLock Inc. (2022). NortonLifeLock Inc.—Annual Report 2021 [Annual Report]. https://d18rn0p25nwr6d.cloudfront.net/CIK-0000849399/29acdb10-c856-4503-a024-2a82aa359dde.pdf

Nuance Communications Inc. (2021). Nuance Communications, Inc.—Annual Report 2021 [Annual Report]. https://app.quotemedia.com/data/downloadFiling?webmasterId=101533&ref=116267931&type=PDF&symbol=NUAN&companyName=Nuance+Communications+Inc.&formType=10-K&dateFiled=2021-11-18&CK=1002517

Nucleus Financial Group Plc. (2021). Nucleus Financial Group Plc—Annual Report 2020 [Annual Report]. https://nucleusfinancial.com/sites/default/files/2021-04/0415.04_NFG_AnnualReports_2020.pdf

Nutanix Inc. (2022). Nutanix Inc.—Annual Report 2022 [Annual Report]. https://d18rn0p25nwr6d.cloudfront.net/CIK-0001618732/bc06b303-3ba4-4cc0-ad81-8fe0ae02c00a.pdf

Nuvei. (2019, January 8). Nuvei completes acquisition of SafeCharge for US $889 million, strengthening its global payment technology and reach [News]. GlobeNewswire News Room. https://www.globenewswire.com/en/news-release/2019/08/01/1895465/0/en/Nuvei-completes-acquisition-of-SafeCharge-for-US-889-million-strengthening-its-global-payment-technology-and-reach.html

Ocado Group PLC. (2022). Ocado Group PLC—Annual Report 2021 [Annual Report]. https://ocadogroup.com/media/qwlchfvz/ocado-group-annual-report-2021-full.pdf

Oisix ra daichi Inc. (2022, October 23). Oisix ra daichi Inc—Services [Company profile]. The Official Website of Oisix Ra Daichi Inc. https://www.oisixradaichi.co.jp

Okta, Inc. (2021). Okta, Inc.—Annual Report 2021 [Annual Report]. https://investor.okta.com/static-files/f369b7c6-f290-4d9a-9987-9c6ec61e881e

Omnicell, Inc. (2021). Omnicell, Inc.—Annual Report 2020 [Annual Report]. https://d18rn0p25nwr6d.cloudfront.net/CIK-0000926326/e627a61c-d34e-4a1e-90bb-49671f5f40a7.pdf

OneSpan Inc. (2021). OneSpan Inc.—Annual Report 2020 [Annual Report]. https://d18rn0p25nwr6d.cloudfront.net/CIK-0001044777/4f64e5c6-3be4-415f-bb1a-05d0cbd6da2c.pdf

OnTheMarket Plc. (2021). OnTheMarket Plc—Annual Report 2021 [Annual Report]. https://plc.onthemarket.com/wp-content/uploads/OnTheMarket_15085033.pdf

Open Text Corporation. (2021a). Open Text Corporation—Annual Report 2021 [Annual Report]. https://s23.q4cdn.com/197378439/files/doc_financials/2021/ar/OpenText-2021-Annual-Report.pdf

Open Text Corporation. (2021b, December 23). OpenText Buys Zix Corporation [Corporate]. Open Text Corporation. https://investors.opentext.com/press-releases/press-releases-details/2021/OpenText-Buys-Zix-Corporation/default.aspx

OpenDoor Inc. (2022, October 23). OpenDoor Inc. Business Description [Company Profile]. OpenDoor. https://www.opendoor.co.jp/en/business/index.html

OpenText. (2019, December 24). OpenText Buys Carbonite, Inc. OpenText. https://www.opentext.com/about/press-releases?id=D28DD45DE6F549608DA28FFC1C30DA68

Opera Ltd. (2021). Opera Ltd.—Annual Report 2020 [Annual Report]. https://investor.opera.com/node/8271/html

Oponeo.pl S.A. (2022). Oponeo.pl S.A.—Annual Report 2021 [Annual Report]. https://www.ir.oponeo.pl/en/investor-relations/reports/2813/annual-report-of-the-group-oponeopl-2021.html

OPTiM Corp. (2021, November 13). OPTiM Corp.—Services [Corporate]. OPTiM. https://www.optim.com/services

OptimizeRx Corporation. (2021). OptimizeRx Corporation—Annual Report 2020 [Annual Report]. https://investors.optimizerx.com/static-files/57e54526-0fa1-4597-9b18-3c4925247125

Otello Corporation ASA. (2022). Otello Corporation ASA—Annual Report 2021 [Annual Report]. https://otello.cdn.prismic.io/otello/47bdbc2b-5757-4336-824c-9ca203f676b2_Otello+Corporation+Annual+Report+2021.pdf

Overstock.com Inc. (2022). Overstock.com Inc.—Annual Report 2021 [Annual Report]. https://investors.overstock.com/static-files/6e421f2d-a7ea-4074-87b8-499bc7cb038e

Palo Alto Networks Inc. (2022). Palo Alto Networks Inc.—Annual Report 2021 [Annual Report]. https://investors.paloaltonetworks.com/static-files/c55c861e-a045-490b-bb28-f65989e43fa5

Pandora Media Inc. (2018). Pandora Media Inc.—Annual Report 2017 [Annual Report]. https://sec.report/Document/0001230276-18-000019/

Paradox Interactive AB. (2021). Paradox Interactive AB—Annual Report 2020 [Annual Report]. https://www.paradoxinteractive.com/investors/financial-reports/paradox-interactive-ab-publ-publishes-annual-report-for-2020

Park City Group Inc. (2022). Park City Group Inc.—Annual Report 2022 [Annual Report]. https://dd7pmep5szm19.cloudfront.net/2213/0001851734-22-000574.pdf

Paychex Inc. (2021). Paychex, Inc.—Annual Report 2021 [Annual Report]. https://investor.paychex.com/sec-filings/annual-reports/content/0000723531-21-000035/0000723531-21-000035.pdf

Paycom Software Inc. (2022). Paycom Software Inc.—Annual Report 2021 [Annual Report]. https://d18rn0p25nwr6d.cloudfront.net/CIK-0001590955/57e31113-f25c-48cb-9760-f2b69717fdc4.pdf

Paylocity Holding Corp. (2022). Paylocity Holding Corp.—Annual Report 2022 [Annual Report]. https://investors.paylocity.com/static-files/8c60dc4a-e1f8-42ca-b300-8dc7c063141c

PDF Solutions, Inc. (2021). PDF Solutions, Inc.—Annual Report 2020 [Annual Report]. https://ir.pdf.com/static-files/6e404f0d-a33f-4b75-9e17-45fd00edc8e0

Pegasystems Inc. (2021). Pegasystems Inc.—Annual Report 2020 [Annual Report]. https://pega.ir.edgar-online.com/efxapi/EFX_dll/EDGARpro.dll?FetchFilingCONVPDF1?SessionID=gRtwkSQ3yj_XGaC&ID=14719461

Penn National Gaming Inc. (2021, October 19). Penn National Gaming Completes Acquisition of Score Media and Gaming Inc. [News]. Businesswire. https://www.businesswire.com/news/home/20211019005903/en/Penn-National-Gaming-Completes-Acquisition-of-Score-Media-and-Gaming-Inc.

Perfect World Co., Ltd. (2021, November 9). Perfect World—Introduction to Perfect World. Perfect World. https://www.pwrd.com/cn/intro.html

Perion Network Ltd. (2022). Pet [Annual Report]. https://perionnetworkltd.gcs-web.com/static-files/6a656b2a-77fe-46a0-9f5b-8e77c32e60d5

PetMed Express Inc. (2022). PetMed Express Inc.—Annual Report 2021 [Annual Report]. https://dd7pmep5szm19.cloudfront.net/2517/0001437749-22-013417.pdf

Pinduoduo, Inc. (2021). Pinduoduo, Inc.—Annual Report 2020 [Annual Report]. https://investor.pinduoduo.com/static-files/c743159b-84f0-45fe-b244-788a7d1b4e7f

PITECO SpA. (2021). PITECO SpA—Annual Report 2020 [Annual Report]. https://www.pitecolab.it/wp-content/uploads/2021/05/Relazione-finanziaria-anno-2020-completa-ENGLISH.pdf

Playtech plc. (2022). Playtech plc—Annual Report 2021 [Annual Report]. https://ar21.playtech.com/

Pluralsight, Inc. (2021). Pluralsight, Inc.—Annual Report 2020 [Annual Report].

Plus500 Ltd. (2022). Plus500 Ltd.—Annual Report 2021 [Annual Report]. https://cdn.plus500.com/media/Investors/Reports/Plus500_Annual_Report_21.pdf

Praemium Ltd. (2011). Praemium Ltd—Annual Report 2021 [Annual Report]. https://www.praemium.com/media/4058/praemium-annual-report-2020.pdf

Priority Technology Holdings Inc. (2021). Priority Technology Holdings, Inc.—Annual Report 2020 [Annual Report]. https://ir.prth.com/all-sec-filings/content/0001653558-21-000040/0001653558-21-000040.pdf

Proactis SA. (2021, July 28). Pollen Street and DBAY complete acquisition of Proactis [Company news]. Proactis. https://www.proactis.com/uk/company/news/2021/july/pollen-street-dbay-complete-acquisition-proactis/

Professional Diversity Network, Inc. (2021). Professional Diversity Network, Inc.—Annual Report 2020 [Annual Report]. https://investor.prodivnet.com/annual-reports/content/0001493152-21-008401/0001493152-21-008401.pdf

Prologue SA. (2021). Prologue SA—Annual Report 2020 [Annual Report]. http://www.prologue.fr/pages/espace-actionnaires/

ProntoForms Corporation. (2021, November 12). Mobile Form Automation Solution | Paperless. ProntoForms. https://www.prontoforms.com/product/paperless-mobile-forms-overview

Proofpoint Inc. (2021). Proofpoint Inc.—Annual Report 2020 [Annual Report]. https://d18rn0p25nwr6d.cloudfront.net/CIK-0001212458/957ca607-1822-45d6-ab62-b7aeb5d3626b.pdf

Prophecy International Holdings Ltd. (2021). Prophecy International Holdings Ltd—Annual Report 2021 [Annual Report]. https://www.prophecyinternational.com/wp-content/uploads/Annual-Report-2021_PRO.pdf

PROS Holdings, Inc. (2021). PROS Holdings, Inc.—Annual Report 2020 [Annual Report]. https://d18rn0p25nwr6d.cloudfront.net/CIK-0001392972/185556f2-56d9-4671-aadb-343c9c864029.pdf

PTC Inc. (2020). PTC Inc.—Annual Report 2020 [Annual Report]. https://d18rn0p25nwr6d.cloudfront.net/CIK-0000857005/76379d41-cde3-4312-b33e-753cc5201a72.pdf

Pushpay Holdings Ltd. (2021). Pushpay Holdings Ltd—Annual Report 2021 [Annual Report]. http://nzx-prod-s7fsd7f98s.s3-website-ap-southeast-2.amazonaws.com/attachments/PPH/372046/345812.pdf

Q2 Holdings Inc. (2022). Q2 Holdings Inc.—Annual Report 2021 [Annual Report]. http://d18rn0p25nwr6d.cloudfront.net/CIK-0001410384/18b0fd8f-89fe-49ba-a6b8-e6c9037407ac.pdf

Qeeka Home (Cayman) Inc. (2021, November 10). Qeeka Home (Cayman) Inc.—Company Profile and Business [Company Profile]. Qeeka Home (Cayman) Inc. https://www.qeeka.com/en/business.html

QTS Realty Trust Inc. (2021, June 7). QTS Realty Trust to Be Acquired by Blackstone Funds in $10 Billion Transaction [News]. Prnewswire. https://www.prnewswire.com/news-releases/qts-realty-trust-to-be-acquired-by-blackstone-funds-in-10-billion-transaction-301306691.html

Qualys Inc. (2022). Qualys Inc.—Annual Report 2021 [Annual Report]. https://investor.qualys.com/static-files/44d1bbc9-1f2e-47bf-b439-822c9e127bf8
QuinStreet Inc. (2022). QuinStreet Inc.—Annual Report 2022 [Annual Report]. https://investor.quinstreet.com/static-files/05234a9a-8d21-4d6b-9632-3b96e3b7dbce
Quorum Information Technologies Inc. (2021). Quorum Information Technologies Inc.—Annual Report 2020 [Annual Report]. https://quoruminformationsystems.com/3d-flip-book/2020-annual-statement/
Quotient Technology Incorporated. (2022). Quotient Technology Incorporated—Annual Report 2021 [Annual Report]. https://d18rn0p25nwr6d.cloudfront.net/CIK-0001115128/877fc01e-6df5-48cf-ba50-1c8972cab57a.pdf
Qutoutiao, Inc. (2021). Qutoutiao, Inc.—Annual Report 2020 [Annual Report]. https://ir.qutoutiao.net/static-files/0d709f02-1d30-40ec-a1b0-1d3b6b917f15
Rachel Arndt. (2018, November 12). Athenahealth sold to Veritas Capital for $5.7 billion. Modern Healthcare. https://www.modernhealthcare.com/article/20181112/NEWS/181119999/athenahealth-sold-to-veritas-capital-for-5-7-billion
Radware Ltd. (2021). Radware Ltd.—Annual Report 2020 [Annual Report]. https://www.sec.gov/ix?doc=/Archives/edgar/data/1094366/000117891321001391/rdwr20f2020.htm
Rakuten Group, Inc. (2021). Rakuten Group, Inc.—Annual Report Presentation 2020 [Annual Report Presentation]. http://global.rakuten.com/corp/investors/documents/annual.html
Ramco Systems Limited. (2021, November 13). Global HR Software | ERP Software | Aviation Software—Ramco Systems [Corporate]. Ramco. https://www.ramco.com
Rank Group Plc. (2021). Rank Group Plc—Annual Report 2021 [Annual Report]. https://www.rank.com/content/dam/rank-group/corporate/documents/Results_Reports_Presentations/2021/Rank_Annual_Report_and_Financial_Statements_2021.pdf.downloadasset.pdf
Rapid7 Inc. (2022). Rapid7 Inc.—Annual Report 2021 [Annual Report]. https://d18rn0p25nwr6d.cloudfront.net/CIK-0001560327/c1113bca-0efe-456b-a979-375fde037a63.pdf
REA Group Ltd. (2022). REA Group Ltd—Annual Report 2022 [Annual Report]. https://onlinereports.irmau.com/2022/REA/
Real Matters, Inc. (2021). Real Matters, Inc.—Annual Report 2020 [Annual Report]. https://s26.q4cdn.com/837377722/files/doc_financials/2020/ar/Real-Matters-2020-Annual-Report.pdf
RealPage Inc. (2021, April 22). Thoma Bravo Completes Acquisition of RealPage [Company news]. RealPage Blog. https://www.realpage.com/news/thoma-bravo-completes-acquisition-of-realpage/
Recruit Holdings Co. Ltd. (2022). Recruit Holdings Co. Ltd.—Annual Report 2022 [Annual Report]. https://recruit-holdings.com/files/ir/library/upload/report_20221018revision_202203Q4_ar_en.pdf
Redfin Corporation. (2021). Redfin Corporation—Annual Report 2020 [Annual Report]. https://investors.redfin.com/node/11236/html
Renren Inc. (2021). Renren Inc.—Annual Report 2020 [Annual Report]. https://ir.renren-inc.com/static-files/a8136e76-2134-427d-8f98-e89613689f01
RhythmOne plc. (2017, September 5). RhythmOne plc to Acquire YuMe, Inc., Creating One of the Largest Independent Digital Video Advertising Marketplaces [News]. Businesswire. https://www.businesswire.com/news/home/20170904005417/en/RhythmOne-plc-to-Acquire-YuMe-Inc.-Creating-One-of-the-Largest-Independent-Digital-Video-Advertising-Marketplaces

RIB Software SE. (2021, November 20). RIB Software SE—Solutions [Corporate]. RIB Software. https://www.rib-software.com/en/solutions

Ribbon Communications Inc. (2020, March 3). Ribbon Communications Inc. Completes Merger with ECI Telecom Group Ltd. [Company news]. Ribbon Communications. https://ribboncommunications.com/company/media-center/press-releases/ribbon-communications-inc-completes-merger-eci-telecom-group-ltd

Rightmove plc. (2022). Rightmove plc—Annual Report 2021 [Annual Report]. https://plc.rightmove.co.uk/sites/rightmove/files/rightmove/investors/Rightmove_AR21_web.pdf

RingCentral Inc. (2022). RingCentral Inc.—Annual Report 2021 [Annual Report]. https://s24.q4cdn.com/639777509/files/doc_financials/2021/ar/d70a5012-30de-4271-a8f2-778056fd68b5-(1).pdf

RMA Global Ltd. (2020). RMA Global Ltd.—Annual Report 2020 [Annual Report]. https://lib.umso.co/lib_wTCvemxDCqXFUoGW/icsimjye69y91jl5.pdf

Rocket Internet SE. (2020, October 27). Rocket Internet SE: Delisting of shares of Rocket Internet SE from Frankfurt Stock Exchange effective end of October 30, 2020 [Company news]. Rocket Internet. https://www.rocket-internet.com/news/rocket-internet-se-delisting-of-shares-of-rocket-internet-se-from-frankfurt-stock-exchange-effective-end-of-october-30-2020

Roku, Inc. (2021). Roku, Inc.—Annual Report 2020 [Annual Report]. https://d18rn0p25nwr6d.cloudfront.net/CIK-0001428439/a80a3256-5d65-4070-92b1-cbf422b85d7e.pdf

Roper Technologies, Inc. (2021). Roper Technologies, Inc.—Annual Report 2020 [Annual Report]. https://d18rn0p25nwr6d.cloudfront.net/CIK-0000882835/4f6e9076-3103-4122-84ba-e54d1146b892.pdf

Rovio Entertainment Oyj. (2021). Rovio Entertainment Oyj—Annual Report 2020 [Annual Report]. https://investors.rovio.com/system/files/2021-03/Rovio_Annual_Report_2020%20%281%29.pdf

Rubicon Project. (2020, April 1). Rubicon Project and Telaria Complete Merger Following Stockholder Approvals [News]. Businesswire. https://www.businesswire.com/news/home/20200401005185/en/Rubicon-Project-and-Telaria-Complete-Merger-Following-Stockholder-Approvals

RumbleOn Inc. (2021). RumbleOn, Inc.—Annual Report 2020 [Annual Report]. https://dd7pmep5szm19.cloudfront.net/2473/0001654954-21-003633.pdf

Sabre Corp. (2022). Sabre Corp.—Annual Report 2021 [Annual Report]. https://investors.sabre.com/static-files/55f4846c-929f-4ff8-8fce-cec2b4cfd35f

Sage Group plc. (2020). Sage Group plc—Annual Report 2020 [Annual Report]. https://www.sage.com/investors/-/media/files/investors/documents/pdf/annual%20report/annual%20report%202020.pdf?la=en-gb

SailPoint Technologies Holdings, Inc. (2021). SailPoint Technologies Holdings, Inc.—Annual Report 2020 [Annual Report]. https://otp.tools.investis.com/clients/us/sailpoint_technologies/SEC/sec-outline.aspx?FilingId=14746269&Cik=0001627857&PaperOnly=0&HasOriginal=1

Saison Information Systems Co., Ltd. (2021, November 12). Our Businesses | Company Information | SAISON INFORMATION SYSTEMS [Company Profile]. Saison Information Systems. https://home.saison.co.jp/english/company/businesses.html

Sangameswaran, S. (2019, May 31). UK's Rank agrees to buy smaller gaming firm Stride in online push. Reuters. https://www.reuters.com/article/us-stride-gaming-m-a-rank-group-gb-idUSKCN1T11AG

Sapiens International Corporation NV. (2021). Sapiens International Corporation NV—Annual Report 2020 [Annual Report]. https://www.sapiens.com/investor-relations/

Scala Inc. (2022). Scala Inc.—Annual Report 2022 [Annual Report]. https://scalagrp.jp/pdf/en/ir/library/gyoseki/20220815_tanshin2206-4Q.pdf

Schiff, A. (2019, February 4). Taptica To Acquire Ad Tech Roll-Up RhythmOne For $176M [News]. AdExchanger. https://www.adexchanger.com/ad-exchange-news/taptica-to-acquire-ad-tech-roll-up-rhythmone-for-176m/

Scientific Games Corporation. (2021). Scientific Games Corporation—Annual Report 2020 [Annual Report]. https://scientificgames.gcs-web.com/static-files/86b32a0f-d309-4109-b968-97f257254aa2

Scout24 SE. (2021). Scout24 SE—Annual Report 2021 [Annual Report]. https://www.scout24.com/media/scout24/Investor_Relations/Berichte_und_Praesentationen/2021_EN/Scout24_Annual_Report_Group_Financial_Report_2021.pdf

Sea Ltd. (Singapore). (2021). Sea Ltd. (Singapore)—Annual Report 2020 [Annual Report]. https://cdn.sea.com/webmain/static/resource/seagroup/pressrelease/2021-04-17%20Sea%20Limited%20Files%20Annual%20Report%20on%20Form%2020-F/2021-04-16%20-%20Form%2020-F.pdf

Seal, T. (2019, October 2). Stars Group acquired by Paddy Power owner in US$6B deal—BNN Bloomberg [News]. BNN. https://www.bnnbloomberg.ca/stars-group-acquired-by-paddy-power-owner-in-us-6b-deal-1.1325248

secunet Security Networks AG. (2021, November 20). Leading IT security company in Germany | secunet AG—About us [Corporate]. Secunet. https://www.secunet.com/en/about-us/unternehmen

SecureKloud Technologies Limited. (2021). SecureKloud Technologies Limited—Annual Report 2021 [Annual Report]. https://www.securekloud.com/investor/annual-report/2020-2021/Annual-Report-2021.pdf

SecureWorks Corp. (2022). SecureWorks Corp.—Annual Report 2021 [Annual Report]. https://d18rn0p25nwr6d.cloudfront.net/CIK-0001468666/1e85a8f0-7b08-48eb-93d8-4668aa766b99.pdf

Seek Limited. (2022). Seek Limited—Annual Report 2022 [Annual Report]. https://wcsecure.weblink.com.au/pdf/SEK/02583802.pdf

Senetas Corporation Limited. (2020). Senetas Corporation Limited—Annual Report 2021 [Annual Report]. https://go.senetas.com/Senetas-2020-Annual-Report.pdf?_ga=2.244281985.587816520.1637435787-1900989786.1637435787

Sensyne Health Plc. (2021). Sensyne Health Plc—Annual Report 2021 [Annual Report]. https://assets.website-files.com/5cf7cc8a7a78cdaa7f8ad26e/615c7e2b4c8f97558a3cbe24_Sensyne%20AR21%20Interactive.pdf

ServiceSource International, Inc. (2021). ServiceSource International, Inc.—Annual Report 2020 [Annual Report]. https://ir.servicesource.com/static-files/3610cec6-f3c3-4621-ba6e-01ade562a5df

Serviceware SE. (2021). Serviceware SE—Annual Report 2020 [Annual Report]. https://serviceware-se.com/fileadmin/user_upload/investor-relations/serviceware-2020-q4-annual-report.pdf

SHARINGTECHNOLOGY. INC. (2021, November 6). SHARINGTECHNOLOGY. INC—Business and Services [Profile]. Business and Services. https://www.sharing-tech.co.jp/en/service/

Shennan Jinke Co., Ltd. (2021, November 8). Shennan Jinke Co., Ltd.—About us. Shennan Jinke Co., Ltd.—About Us. https://www.sunafin.com/about.php?id=2#main

Shenzhen Das Intellitech Co., Ltd. (2021, November 8). Shenzhen Das Intellitech Co., Ltd.—Business Profile. Shenzhen Das Intellitech Co., Ltd.—Business Profile. http://www.chn-das.com/en/AboutDashin/index.aspx

Shijiazhuang Changshan Beiming Technology Co., Ltd. (2021, November 8). Shijiazhuang Changshan Beiming Technology Co., Ltd.—About Us. Https://Www.Changshanfabric.Com/. https://changshanfabric.com:443/about-us/

Shop Apotheke Europe NV. (2022). Shop Apotheke Europe NV—Annual Report 2021 [Annual Report]. https://corporate.shop-apotheke-europe.com/uploads/ar-shop-apotheke-europe.pdf?_cchid=edf4d4a7c41617cc54ad4526206d676e

Shopify Inc. (2022). Shopify Inc.—Annual Report 2021 [Annual Report]. https://d18rn0p25nwr6d.cloudfront.net/CIK-0001594805/99a0d08d-4015-4a0a-a8fb-fe6ec66553c4.pdf

ShotSpotter, Inc. (2021). ShotSpotter, Inc.—Annual Report 2020 [Annual Report]. https://ir.shotspotter.com/annual-reports/content/0001564590-21-016134/ssti-10k_20201231.htm?TB_iframe=true&height=auto&width=auto&preload=false

Shutterfly Inc. (2019). Shutterfly Inc.—Annual Report 2018 [Annual Report]. https://sec.report/Document/0001125920-19-000008/

Shutterstock Inc. (2022). Shutterstock Inc.—Annual Report 2021 [Annual Report]. https://investor.shutterstock.com/static-files/b85c978f-2085-4e3e-bc06-5dcdd69eb4f9

Silicom Ltd. (2021). Silicom Ltd.—Investor Presentation [Investor Presentation]. https://www.silicom-usa.com/download/?action=https://www.silicom-usa.com/wp-content/uploads/2021/10/SilicomQ321.pdf

Silverlake Axis Ltd. (2021). Silverlake Axis Ltd.—Annual Report 2021 [Annual Report]. https://www.silverlakeaxis.com/img/pdf/SLAxis_AR2021.pdf

SimCorp A/S. (2021). SimCorp A/S—Annual Report 2020 [Annual Report]. http://www.simcorp.com/en/about/investor

Simei Media Co., Ltd. (2021, November 9). Sime Media Co., Ltd.—Company Profile. Sime Media Co., Ltd.—Company Profile. http://www.simei.cc/About

SINA Corp. (2020). SINA Corp.—Annual Report 2019 [Annual Report]. https://sec.report/Document/0001104659-20-052758/#ITEM4INFORMATIONONTHECOMPANY_117273

Sinodata Co., Ltd. (2021, November 9). Sinodata Co., Ltd.—Beijing Zhongke Jincai Technology Co., Ltd.—About us. Sinodata Co., Ltd.—Beijing Zhongke Jincai Technology Co., Ltd.—About Us. http://www.sinodata.net.cn/index.php?c=category&catid=1

SIOS Corp. (2021, November 13). SIOS Corp—What we do—High Availability for Critical Applications Your Business Depends On [Corporate Profile]. SIOS. https://us.sios.com/what-we-do/

Sirius XM Holdings Inc. (2018, September 24). SiriusXM to Acquire Pandora, Creating World's Largest Audio Entertainment Company [News]. Prnewswire. https://www.prnewswire.com/news-releases/siriusxm-to-acquire-pandora-creating-worlds-largest-audio-entertainment-company-300717442.html

SITO Mobile Ltd. (2020, October 8). Bankruptcy | SITO Mobile, Ltd. (SITO) [Investor Relations]. https://ir.sitomobile.com/bankruptcy/
SK Inc. (2021, November 9). SK Inc.—Industries. SK. https://eng.sk.com/industries
Smartsheet, Inc. (2021). Smartsheet, Inc.—Annual Report 2021 [Annual Report]. https://d18rn0p25nwr6d.cloudfront.net/CIK-0001366561/23ae9abb-bf40-48ea-bf71-b3b339cbd548.pdf
Smartspace Software Plc. (2021). Smartspace Software Plc—Annual Report 2021 [Annual Report]. https://www.smartspaceplc.com/hubfs/Smart%20Space%20-%20assets/investor%20relations%20docs/SmartSpace%20Annual%20Report%202021_web.pdf?hsLang=en
SMN Corporation. (2021, December 5). SMN Corporation—Products & Services [Corporate]. So-net Media Networks Corp. http://www.so-netmedia.jp/en/
Snap, Inc. (2021). Snap, Inc.—Annual Report 2020 [Annual Report]. https://investor.snap.com/financials/Annual-Report/default.aspx
Sonic Foundry Inc. (2021). Sonic Foundry Inc.—Annual Report 2021 [Annual Report]. https://sec.report/Document/0001437749-21-028230/
Sonos, Inc. (2020). Sonos, Inc.—Annual Report 2020 [Annual Report]. https://d18rn0p25nwr6d.cloudfront.net/CIK-0001314727/260b4476-595e-4e96-847b-ba8d2369a2fd.pdf
Sopheon plc. (2021). Sopheon plc—Annual Report 2020 [Annual Report]. https://sopheon-wpengine.netdna-ssl.com/wp-content/uploads/Sopheon-AR-2020-FINAL.pdf
Spark Networks SE. (2021). Spark Networks SE—Annual Report 2020 [Annual Report]. https://www.spark.net/static-files/221a03e8-2717-44e4-8ab2-601dc6f5969b
Speqta AB. (2021, November 28). Speqta AB—Our business model [Corporate]. Speqta. https://speqta.com/en/about/business-model
Splunk Inc. (2022). Splunk Inc.—Annual Report 2021 [Annual Report]. https://investors.splunk.com/static-files/1ca05ffd-4eef-44a9-8ada-b70cdf82c596
Sportech PLC. (2022). Sportech PLC—Annual Report 2021 [Annual Report]. https://www.sportechplc.com/wp-content/uploads/2022/05/Sportech-Annual-Report-2021-FINAL.pdf
Spotify Technology SA. (2021). Spotify Technology SA—Annual Report 2020 [Annual Report]. https://d18rn0p25nwr6d.cloudfront.net/CIK-0001639920/4e770a8c-ee99-49a8-9f9e-dcc191807b56.pdf
SPS Commerce Inc. (2022). SPS Commerce Inc.—Annual Report 2021 [Annual Report]. https://investors.spscommerce.com/static-files/7efe845c-a138-43f2-a252-ffc85e00e7b1
Square Inc. (2022). Square Inc.—Annual Report 2021 [Annual Report]. https://d18rn0p25nwr6d.cloudfront.net/CIK-0001512673/13386837-50ba-466f-b8ff-81824f066c1e.pdf
SRAX Inc. (2021). SRAX, Inc.—Annual Report 2020 [Annual Report]. https://sec.report/Document/0001493152-21-007542/
SRP Groupe SA. (2022). SRP Groupe SA—Annual Results 2021 [Earnings presentation]. https://www.showroomprivegroup.com/wp-content/uploads/2022/03/2022.03.10-EN-Press-Release_VFinal.pdf
SS&C Technologies Holdings Inc. (2022). SS&C Technologies Holdings Inc.—Annual Report 2021 [Annual Report]. https://d18rn0p25nwr6d.cloudfront.net/CIK-0001402436/8a1bb3e7-949e-4f69-8e71-0e8591eda676.pdf

SSH Communications Security Oyj. (2022). SSH Communications Security Oyj—Annual Report 2021 [Annual Report]. https://www.ssh.com/hubfs/SSH%20Annual%20Report%202021.pdf
Starbreeze AB. (2021). Starbreeze AB—Annual Report 2020 [Annual Report]. https://www.starbreeze.com/sbz-media/2021/04/Annual-Report-2020-Starbreeze-AB-3.pdf
Stitch Fix, Inc. (2021). Stitch Fix, Inc.—Annual Report 2021 [Annual Report]. https://investors.stitchfix.com/static-files/cbeb4e32-669b-4833-99bb-2bdb72f377c5
Streamline Health Solutions Inc. (2021). Streamline Health Solutions, Inc.—Annual Report 2021 [Annual Report]. https://investor.streamlinehealth.net/static-files/7ed4e795-43f3-4f61-a1da-9b2605db8e84
Stride Inc. (2022). Stride Inc.—Annual Report 2022 [Annual Report]. https://d18rn0p25nwr6d.cloudfront.net/CIK-0001157408/99bed441-ea63-4159-b655-a88ad262bdbe.pdf
Switch, Inc. (2021). Switch, Inc.—Annual Report 2020 [Annual Report]. http://investors.switch.com
Synacor Inc. (2021, February 11). Synacor Agrees to be Acquired by Centre Lane Partners [News]. Businesswire. https://www.businesswire.com/news/home/20210211005336/en/Synacor-Agrees-to-be-Acquired-by-Centre-Lane-Partners
Synchronoss Technologies Inc. (2022). Synchronoss Technologies Inc.—Annual Report 2021 [Annual Report]. https://synchronosstechnologiesinc.gcs-web.com/static-files/f5837c26-49ac-4db3-9669-2e50f32d89fd
Synopsys, Inc. (2020). Synopsys, Inc.—Annual Report 2020 [Annual Report]. https://www.sec.gov/ix?doc=/Archives/edgar/data/883241/000088324120000015/snps10312010-k.htm
SYS Holdings Co. Ltd. (2021). SYS Holdings Co. Ltd.—Company Profile [Company Profile]. https://www.syshd.co.jp/jp/company/profile.html
SysGroup plc. (2022). SysGroup plc—Annual Report 2022 [Annual Report]. https://www.sysgroup.com/images/uploads/SysGroup-Annual-Report-2022-Digital-FINAL.pdf
SYZYGY AG. (2022). SYZYGY AG—Annual Report 2021 [Annual Report]. https://www.syzygy-group.net/app/uploads//syzygy-group-annual-report-2021.pdf
Tableau Software Inc. (2019, August 1). Salesforce Completes Acquisition of Tableau [Corporate]. Tableau. https://www.tableau.com/about/press-releases/2019/salesforce-completes-acquisition-tableau
Tabula Rasa Healthcare, Inc. (2021). Tabula Rasa Healthcare, Inc.—Annual Report 2020 [Annual Report]. https://ir.tabularasahealthcare.com/static-files/5336701e-56ea-4aef-ba7d-3b843af5b81a
Talend SA. (2021, March 10). Talend to be Acquired by Thoma Bravo in a $2.4 Billion Transaction [Corporate]. Talend—A Leader in Data Integration & Data Integrity. https://www.talend.com/about-us/press-releases/talend-to-be-acquired-by-thoma-bravo-in-a-2-4-billion-transaction/
Tandem Group plc. (2021). Tandem Group plc—Annual Report 2020 [Annual Report]. https://tandemgroupplc.co.uk/wp-content/uploads/2021/04/Tandem-AR-2020-web-ready.pdf
Team17 Group PLC. (2021). Team17 Group PLC—Annual Report 2020 [Annual Report]. https://www.team17group.com/wp-content/uploads/2021/05/35524-Team17-AR20_WEB_Hires.pdf

Technology One Limited. (2020). Technology One Limited—Annual Report 2020 [Annual Report]. https://www.technologyonecorp.com/__data/assets/pdf_file/0016/143224/FY20-Annual-Report.pdf

TechTarget Inc. (2022). TechTarget Inc.—Annual Report 2021 [Annual Report]. https://d18rn0p25nwr6d.cloudfront.net/CIK-0001293282/5a616608-9f8e-498e-8f9b-f319b0f8bf75.pdf

TECSYS Inc. (2021). TECSYS Inc.—Annual Report 2021 [Annual Report]. https://www.tecsys.com/wp-content/uploads/2021/08/Tecsys_AnnualReport_EN_FY21.pdf

Teladoc Health Inc. (2022). Teladoc Health Inc.—Annual Report 2021 [Annual Report]. https://d18rn0p25nwr6d.cloudfront.net/CIK-0001477449/e84a58ca-096c-4dc4-8b37-1aa630f83328.pdf

Ten Square Games SA. (2021). Ten Square Games SA—Annual Report 2020 [Annual Report]. https://tensquaregames.com/wp-content/uploads/2021/03/TSG-RaportRoczny2020-ENG-SSF.pdf

Tenable Holdings, Inc. (2021). Tenable Holdings, Inc.—Annual Report 2020 [Annual Report]. https://investors.tenable.com/static-files/aa0b2fc4-d811-47df-a95b-17722a05dbe2

Teradata Corporation. (2022). Teradata Corporation—Annual Report 2021 [Annual Report]. https://d18rn0p25nwr6d.cloudfront.net/CIK-0000816761/970475ef-a056-4de5-ab75-3c5d7e0ecfd0.pdf

TF1 Group. (2018, April 27). The TF1 Group finalises the acquisition of the aufeminin Group from Axel Springer. https://groupe-tf1.fr/en/press-release/group-activity-development-acquisitions-sales-diversification/tf1-group-finalises-acquisition-aufeminin-group-axel-springer

The Charles Schwab Corporation. (2020, October 6). Schwab Completes Acquisition of TD Ameritrade [Corporate]. Businesswire. https://www.businesswire.com/news/home/20201006005590/en/Schwab-Completes-Acquisition-of-TD-Ameritrade

The Wall Street Journal. (2021, November 7). 6111.TW | Softstar Entertainment Inc. Company Profile & Executives—WSJ [News]. 6111.TW | Softstar Entertainment Inc. Company Profile & Executives—WSJ. https://www.wsj.com/market-data/quotes/TW/6111/company-people

TheMaven Inc. (2019, August 8). Maven Closes Acquisition of TheStreet, New Jim Cramer Deal Announced [News]. Businesswire. https://www.businesswire.com/news/home/20190808005215/en/Maven-Closes-Acquisition-of-TheStreet-New-Jim-Cramer-Deal-Announced

Thinkware Systems Corporation. (2021, November 9). About THINKWARE | THINKWARE [Company profile]. https://www.thinkware.com/Company/About

Thoma Bravo. (2020, March 24). Thoma Bravo Completes Acquisition of Instructure [Company news]. Thoma Bravo Completes Acquisition of Instructure. https://www.thomabravo.com/press-releases/thoma-bravo-completes-acquisition-of-instructure

Thoma Bravo. (2021, October 5). Thoma Bravo Completes Acquisition of Stamps.com [Company news]. Thoma Bravo. https://www.thomabravo.com/press-releases/thoma-bravo-completes-acquisition-of-stamps.com

Thomson Reuters Corporation. (2022). Reuters | Markets | Companies [News]. Reuters | Markets | Companies. https://www.reuters.com/markets/companies

Tian Ge Interactive Holdings Ltd. (2021). Tian Ge Interactive Holdings Ltd—Annual Report 2020 [Annual Report]. http://www.tiange.com/Upload/PDF/2021/Annual%20Report%202020.pdf

TIE Kinetix N.V. (2021). TIE Kinetix N.V.—Annual Report 2021 [Annual Report]. https://go.tiekinetix.com/annual-report-tiekinetix-nv-fy2021

Time Out Group PLC. (2019). Time Out Group PLC—Annual Report 2019 [Annual Report]. https://assets.timeout.com/application/pdf/0210bb44a07a49d9104ba6eb151f6d69/time_out_annual_report_2019.pdf

Trade Desk, Inc. (2021). Trade Desk, Inc.—Annual Report 2020 [Annual Report]. https://investors.thetradedesk.com/static-files/c2a95bea-47e8-4049-8850-676907a62d81

TradeDoubler AB. (2022). TradeDoubler AB—Annual Report 2021 [Annual Report]. https://www.tradedoubler.com/en//download/107091/

transcosmos Inc. (2021, November 12). Global Digital Transformation Partner transcosmos [Company Profile]. Global Digital Transformation Partner Transcosmos. https://www.trans-cosmos.co.jp/english/

Travelport Worldwide Limited. (2018, December 10). Travelport Worldwide Limited announces agreement to be acquired by affiliates of Siris Capital Group, LLC and Evergreen Coast Capital Corp. In all-cash transaction valued at approximately $4.4 billion [News]. PRnewswire. https://www.prnewswire.com/news-releases/travelport-worldwide-limited-announces-agreement-to-be-acquired-by-affiliates-of-siris-capital-group-llc-and-evergreen-coast-capital-corp-in-all-cash-transaction-valued-at-approximately-4-4-billion-300762487.html

Travelzoo. (2022). Travelzoo—Annual Report 2021 [Annual Report]. https://d18rn0p25nwr6d.cloudfront.net/CIK-0001133311/96f03ddf-c13d-40c4-baa3-73649e012389.pdf

Tremor International Ltd. (2022). Tremor International Ltd.—Annual Report 2021 [Annual Report]. https://investors.tremorinternational.com/static-files/41713a52-7733-41c7-b2ed-76409e0f4fff

Tribal Group plc. (2021). Tribal Group plc—Annual Report 2020 [Annual Report]. https://f.hubspotusercontent00.net/hubfs/2007157/Corporate/Tribal%20Annual%20Report%202020%20FINAL.pdf

TripAdvisor Inc. (2022). TripAdvisor Inc.—Annual Report 2021 [Annual Report]. https://ir.tripadvisor.com/static-files/3e32bcb6-bb03-47ea-bd68-e7a3e82c2d30

Trip.com Group Ltd. (2022). Trip.com Group Ltd.—Annual Report 2021 [Annual Report]. https://investors.trip.com/static-files/797136c4-ede8-45e3-8eaa-59ed1676bb81

trivago N.V. (2022). Trivago N.V.—Annual Report 2021 [Annual Report]. https://ir.trivago.com/static-files/dea2fe12-d0a6-45da-9b95-cb4d9bf57e53

TrueCar Inc. (2022). TrueCar Inc.—Annual Report 2021 [Annual Report].

Tucows Inc. (2022). Tucows Inc.—Annual Report 2021 [Annual Report]. https://tucows.com/wp-content/uploads/2022/03/2021-Q4-TCX-results-10K.pdf

Twilio Inc. (2022). Twilio Inc.—Annual Report 2021 [Annual Report]. https://d18rn0p25nwr6d.cloudfront.net/CIK-0001447669/359369d3-684d-4d07-9353-47cde561ce62.pdf

Twitter Inc. (2022). Twitter Inc.—Annual Report 2021 [Annual Report]. https://d18rn0p25nwr6d.cloudfront.net/CIK-0001418091/947c0c34-ca90-4099-b328-a6062adf110f.pdf

Tyler, J. (2021, August 17). Zooplus agrees to $3.5 billion private equity takeover | Pet Food Processing [News]. PETfoodprocessing. https://www.petfoodprocessing.net/articles/15003-zooplus-agrees-to-35-billion-private-equity-takeover

Tyler Technologies, Inc. (2021). Tyler Technologies, Inc.—Annual Report 2020 [Annual Report]. https://s3.amazonaws.com/sec.irpass.cc/499/0000860731-21-000014.pdf
Tyler Technologies Inc. (2021, April 21). Tyler Technologies Completes Acquisition of NIC [News]. Businesswire. https://www.businesswire.com/news/home/20210421005658/en/Tyler-Technologies-Completes-Acquisition-of-NIC
TZ Limited. (2021). TZ Limited—Investor Presentation [Investor Presentation]. https://tz.investorportal.com.au/
ULS Technology Plc. (2022). ULS Technology Plc—Annual Report 2022 [Annual Report].
Ultimate Software. (2019, May 3). Ultimate Software Completes Agreement to be Acquired by an Investor Group Led by Hellman & Friedman to Operate as a Privately Held Company [News]. Businesswire. https://www.businesswire.com/news/home/20190503005310/en/Ultimate-Software-Completes-Agreement-to-be-Acquired-by-an-Investor-Group-Led-by-Hellman-Friedman-to-Operate-as-a-Privately-Held-Company
Upland Software, Inc. (2021). Upland Software, Inc.—Annual Report 2020 [Annual Report]. https://d18rn0p25nwr6d.cloudfront.net/CIK-0001505155/4d582e79-035f-49d9-a68e-2ea8391c2a5a.pdf
USU Software AG. (2021). USU Software AG—Annual Report 2020 [Annual Report]. file:///C:/Users/adelin.trusculescu/Downloads/company_report_2020_en.pdf
Uxin Ltd. (2021). Uxin Ltd.—Annual Report 2021 [Annual Report]. https://ir.xin.com/static-files/dc548517-76df-474f-9c37-03e3366aa6d3
Uzabase, Inc. (2021). Uzabase, Inc.—Annual Report 2020 [Annual Report]. http://www.uzabase.com/ir/
Varonis Systems, Inc. (2021). Varonis Systems, Inc.—Annual Report 2020 [Annual Report]. https://d18rn0p25nwr6d.cloudfront.net/CIK-0001361113/8ff2f66e-ff09-495d-9444-4c392e571d99.pdf
Veeva Systems Inc. (2022). Veeva Systems Inc—Annual Report 2021 [Annual Report]. https://d18rn0p25nwr6d.cloudfront.net/CIK-0001393052/92ec0b47-e982-4287-a692-27d0d04fc445.pdf
Venustech Group, Inc. (2021, November 9). About Venustech | Company Introduction-Venustech. Company Introduction-Venustech. https://www.venustech.com.cn/new_type/gsjs/
Verint Systems Inc. (2022). Verint Systems Inc.—Annual Report 2021 [Annual Report]. https://verintsystems.gcs-web.com/static-files/ad85d749-a931-4aaf-bcca-a15fee6bfc17
VeriSign Inc. (2022). VeriSign Inc.—Annual Report 2021 [Annual Report]. https://investor.verisign.com/static-files/67f7b4c8-2f2d-48e7-898b-436a059fc34a
Veritone, Inc. (2021). Veritone, Inc.—Annual Report 2020 [Annual Report]. https://d18rn0p25nwr6d.cloudfront.net/CIK-0001615165/b994faa8-7fd6-4035-a5d1-ff13d605a6f8.pdf
Verkkokauppa.com Oyj. (2021). Verkkokauppa.com Oyj—Annual Report 2020 [Annual Report]. https://cdn-a.verkkokauppa.com/files/603f3/cf744/428a7/4d43a/82a9.pdf
Vipshop Holdings Ltd. (2022). Vipshop Holdings Ltd—Annual Report 2021 [Annual Report]. https://ir.vip.com/static-files/8c467b7c-ca1b-4498-b28f-732e1b262ad2
VIQ Solutions Inc. (2021). VIQ Solutions Inc.—Annual Report 2020 [Annual Report]. https://viqsolutions.com/financial-statements/2020/VQS-FY2020-%20Audited-FS.pdf
Vista Group International Ltd. (2021). Vista Group International Ltd—Annual Report 2020 [Annual Report]. https://www.vistagroup.co.nz/downloads/VGL_Annual_Report_2020.pdf

Vitec Software Group AB. (2021). Vitec Software Group AB—Annual Report 2020 [Annual Report]. https://www.vitecsoftware.com/globalassets/a-vitec-software-group/investor-relations/reports/vitec_annual_report_2020.pdf

Vixtel Technologies Holdings Ltd. (2021, November 10). Vixtel Technologies Holdings Ltd.—About Vixtel—Overview [Company profile]. Vixtel. https://www.vixtel.com/about/

VMware Inc. (2022). VMware Inc.—Annual Report 2021 [Annual Report]. https://ir-api.eqs.com/storage/ir/5e7064/sec-filings/a2cc9d22-7367-4548-a985-cf96d6feae60/Annual-Report.pdf

VNET Group, Inc. (2021). VNET Group, Inc.—Annual Report 2020 [Annual Report]. http://ir.21vianet.com/static-files/bc5df3db-d350-4b77-8360-984ba6c537f1

Vobile Group Ltd. (2021). Vobile Group Ltd.—Annual Report 2020 [Annual Report]. https://www.vobilegroup.com/downloads/annual-report-2020-en/

Vocera Communications, Inc. (2021). Vocera Communications, Inc.—Annual Report 2020 [Annual Report]. https://d18rn0p25nwr6d.cloudfront.net/CIK-0001129260/4e0e8015-4f7c-4fd1-a5c4-4c30943e084d.pdf

Waitr Holdings Inc. (2021). Waitr Holdings, Inc.—Annual Report 2020 [Annual Report]. https://investors.waitrapp.com/static-files/6d65617a-b230-4eba-aefc-0a74652301db

Wallix Group SA. (2021, December 11). Wallix Group SA—Product [Corporate Profile]. Wallix Group. http://www.wallix-bourse.com/informations-financieres/informations-reglementees.html

WANdisco Plc. (2021). WANdisco Plc—Annual Report 2020 [Annual Report]. https://www.wandisco.com/storage/app/media/investors/WANdiscoPlcAnnualReportAndAccounts2020.pdf

Wayfair Inc. (2022). Wayfair Inc.—Annual Report 2021 [Annual Report]. https://d18rn0p25nwr6d.cloudfront.net/CIK-0001616707/294b4ecb-7b3d-4720-98c5-f9192a9559a6.pdf

Web.com Group Inc. (2018, June 21). Web.com Announces Agreement to be Acquired by an Affiliate of Siris Capital Group, LLC for $25.00 per share in All Cash Deal Valued at Approximately $2 Billion [Company news]. Siris. https://www.siris.com/news/web-com-announces-agreement-to-be-acquired-by-an-affiliate-of-siris-capital-group-llc-for-25-00-per-share-in-all-cash-deal-valued-at-approximately-2-billion

Webjet Limited. (2022). Webjet Limited—Annual Report 2022 [Annual Report]. https://cmsmedia.webjetlimited.com/webjetltd-uploads/2022/05/WL_FY22_Annual_Report_MAY2022.pdf

Wedia SA. (2021, November 14). Wedia SA—Marketing solution [Corporate]. Wedia. https://www.wedia-group.com/marketing-solution/

Weibo Corp. (2022). Weibo Corp.—Annual Report 2021 [Annual Report]. http://ir.weibo.com/static-files/d9a801ff-b3f1-4369-8a9b-48dbe0949f5d

Whittaker, Z. (2020, December 1). Ivanti has acquired security firms MobileIron and Pulse Secure. TechCrunch. https://techcrunch.com/2020/12/01/ivanti-has-acquired-security-firms-mobileiron-and-pulse-secure/

WidePoint Corporation. (2021). WidePoint Corporation—Annual Report 2020 [Annual Report]. https://www.sec.gov/Archives/edgar/data/1034760/000165495421003119/wyy_10k.htm

WIIT SpA. (2021). WIIT SpA—Annual Report 2020 [Annual Report]. https://www.wiit.cloud/mr_upload/2021/09/WIIT-GRUOP-REPORT-YEAR-2020.pdf

windeln.de SE. (2022). Windeln.de SE—Annual Report 2021 [Annual Report]. https://corporate.windeln.de/wp-content/uploads/2022/05/Jahresabschluss-2021-FINAL-komprimiert_NEU.pdf

Winning Health Technology Group Co.,Ltd. (2021, November 13). Group Introduction-Weining [Company Profile]. Winning Health Technology Group Co.,Ltd. http://www.winning.com.cn/introduction.html

Wirtualna Polska Holding SA. (2022, November 5). Wirtualna Polska Holding SA—Who we are [Company Profile]. Https://Onas.Wp.Pl. https://onas.wp.pl

Wisetech Global Ltd. (2021). Wisetech Global Ltd.—Annual Report 2021 [Annual Report]. https://www.wisetechglobal.com/media/4gqjezke/wisetech-global-annual-report-2021.pdf

Wix.com Ltd. (2022). Wix.com Ltd.—Annual Report 2021 [Annual Report]. https://www.sec.gov/Archives/edgar/data/1576789/000117891322001359/zk2227541.htm

Workday Inc. (2022). Workday Inc.—Annual Report 2021 [Annual Report]. https://app.quotemedia.com/data/downloadFiling?webmasterId=101533&ref=116503169&type=PDF&symbol=WDAY&companyName=Workday+Inc.&formType=10-K&dateFiled=2022-02-28&CK=1327811

Workiva Inc. (2022). Workiva Inc.—Annual Report 2021 [Annual Report]. https://s21.q4cdn.com/997645077/files/doc_financials/2021/ar/2021_10_K_and_AR-(1).pdf

Wuhu Sanqi Interactive Entertainment Network Technology Group Co., Ltd. (2021, November 9). Company Profile-Sanqi Mutual Entertainment Official Website_Sanqi Mutual Entertainment, Play Heart Creates the World. https://www.37wan.net/introduction.html

Xero Limited. (2022). Xero Limited—Annual Report 2022 [Annual Report]. https://www.xero.com/content/dam/xero/pdfs/investors-financial-information/fy22-xero-limited-annual-report.pdf

XMReality AB. (2021, November 24). XMReality Remote Guidance—Our product [Corporate]. XMReality. https://xmreality.com/our-product/

XO Group Inc. (2018, September 25). XO Group Inc. To Become Privately Held Company and Merge With WeddingWire, Accelerating Growth Within Global Wedding Industry [News]. PRnewswire. https://www.prnewswire.com/news-releases/xo-group-inc-to-become-privately-held-company-and-merge-with-weddingwire-accelerating-growth-within-global-wedding-industry-300718397.html

Xref Ltd. (2021). Xref Ltd—Annual Report 2021 [Annual Report]. https://global-uploads.webflow.com/5e25051eb2b645149a115f3f/612ed652092752220558 6860_Xref-Annual-report-2021_FINAL%20(1).pdf

Yelp Inc. (2022). Yelp Inc—Annual Report 2021 [Annual Report]. https://d18rn0p25nwr6d.cloudfront.net/CIK-0001345016/6cfb0115-fe02-447b-a835-35393b9e7286.pdf

Yext, Inc. (2021). Yext, Inc.—Annual Report 2021 [Annual Report]. https://d18rn0p25nwr6d.cloudfront.net/CIK-0001614178/70c6c6bd-2a49-46f6-b5c0-a80917d73804.html

YOC AG. (2021). YOC AG—Annual Report 2020 [Annual Report]. https://yoc.com/wp-content/uploads/2021/05/yoc-EN-Geschaftsbericht-2020-pw.pdf

YRGLM Inc. (2021, November 13). YRGLM Inc. -Impact on the world-—Product [Corporate]. YRGLM Inc. http://www.yrglm.co.jp/en/

Yuke's Co., Ltd. (2021). Yuke's Co., Ltd.—Annual Report 2021 [Annual Report]. http://www.yukes.co.jp/company/finance/

Zalando SE. (2022). Zalando SE—Annual Report 2021 [Annual Report]. https://corporate.zalando.com/sites/default/files/media-download/Annual-Report_ZalandoSE_21_EN_220228_s.pdf

ZEAL Network SE. (2021). ZEAL Network SE—Annual Report 2020 [Annual Report]. https://www.zealnetwork.de/media/document/6e54efb2-8fad-43c0-bbeb-60a6ad78ea66/assets/ZEAL_E_AR2020_210409_sec.pdf

Zendesk Inc. (2022). Zendesk Inc.—Annual Report 2021 [Annual Report]. https://d18rn0p25nwr6d.cloudfront.net/CIK-0001463172/5703bb14-8b4a-411a-aac8-43177f0959f2.pdf

Zhao, M. (2018, May 17). Yoox Net-A-Porter to delist from Milan exchange [News]. S&P Global. https://www.spglobal.com/marketintelligence/en/news-insights/trending/9ovQmqCG4xoD_Qwg74EVJQ2

Zhejiang Century Huatong Group Co., Ltd. (2021, November 9). Century Huatong—Group Introduction. Century Huatong Official Website. https://www.sjhuatong.com/index.php/cn/?f=about

Ziff Davis Inc. (2022). Ziff Davis Inc.—Annual Report 2021 [Annual Report]. https://d18rn0p25nwr6d.cloudfront.net/CIK-0001084048/a86ff218-7bc3-4ddf-8f9a-30c227501025.pdf

ZIGExN Co. Ltd. (2021, March 15). ZIGExN Co. Ltd.—Our Services [Corporate]. 株式会社じげん || ZIGExN Co., Ltd. https://zigexn.co.jp/service/

Zillow Group Inc. (2021). Zillow Group, Inc.—Annual Report 2020 [Annual Report]. https://d18rn0p25nwr6d.cloudfront.net/CIK-0001617640/615b8971-4066-4a86-9fdb-30a7bfe0377c.pdf

Zscaler, Inc. (2021). Zscaler, Inc.—Annual Report 2021 [Annual Report]. https://ir.zscaler.com/sec-filings/sec-filing/10-k/0001713683-21-000175

Zuora, Inc. (2021). Zuora, Inc.—Annual Report 2021 [Annual Report]. https://d18rn0p25nwr6d.cloudfront.net/CIK-0001423774/fcff1601-8b39-4d7f-b48b-ab3a2e9f555b.pdf

Zur Rose Group AG. (2021). Zur Rose Group AG—Company presentation [Company presentation]. https://www.zurrosegroup.com/download/companies/zurroseag/Companypresentation/20211031_Zur_Rose_Group_AG_company_presentation.pdf

ZUU Co. Ltd. (2021, December 5). ZUU Online—Services [Corporate]. ZUU Online—Services. https://zuu.co.jp/service/

The manufacturer's authorised representative in the EU is Springer Nature Customer Service Centre GmbH, Europaplatz 3, 69115 Heidelberg, Germany. If you have any concerns regarding our products, please contact ProductSafety@springernature.com

Printed and bound by CPI Group (UK) Ltd, Croydon, CR0 4YY

30/09/2026

02225494-0010